ANDREW STONE
PIERA CHEN
CHUNG WAH CHOW

HONG KONG
& MACAU

C I T Y   G U I D E

INTRODUCING HONG KONG

Savour the delights of dim sum at Lin Heung Tea House (p178)

On first acquaintance, Hong Kong can overwhelm. Navigate its teeming, tightly packed sidewalks and you're met at every turn with neon signage, steam-filled canteens, molasses-slow traffic and a Babel of chatter.

Once this first sensory wave has rolled over you, though, take a deep breath and start swimming with the current, because you'll find Hong Kong is a place to delight in. Utterly safe and fantastically well organised, it offers small moments of perfection. You may find them on a plastic stool enjoying a bargain bowl of beef brisket soup or simply gazing at the thrilling harbour vistas. You'll find them taking afternoon tea in the cool of a five-star hotel lobby or enjoying beers in balmy, open-air party zones.

Hong Kong can nudge you out of your comfort zone but usually rewards you for it, so try the stinky beancurd, sample the shredded jellyfish, brave the hordes at the city-centre horse races, and join in the dawn t'ai chi. Escape the city limits and other experiences await – watching the sun rise from a remote mountain peak, hiking surf-beaten beaches or exploring deserted islands.

If it's pampering you're after, money can buy the ultimate luxuries in a city well used to serving its tiny, moneyed elite. Yet Hong Kong is also a city of simple pleasures. Most often it's the least pricey experiences – a $2 tram or ferry ride, a whiff of incense curling from temple rafters, savouring fishing-village sundowners and seafood – that are the stuff of priceless memories.

CITY LIFE

As usual in this city of trade and high finance, of runaway boom and spectacular bust, the big story is money. Dependent on the flow of containers through its massive port, and global money through its banks, Hong Kong underwent a profound shock when the world's financial system rocked its foundations. Hong Kong punters seesawed between despair and euphoria as the stock and property markets slumped and then rallied on the back of massive economic stimulus from China.

But the talk soon turned to recovery and to speculation about what a massive Chinese-government spending splurge might do for Hong Kong's stock exchange. Hong Kong's citizens also wondered what difference future infrastructure projects, such as the massive 30km Macau–Hong Kong bridge link, might make. The seemingly endless proposals for other such ambitious schemes, like the Guangzhou express train, also provoked complaints that tracts of the New Territories would be torn up to make way for it.

Preserving what remains of Hong Kong's heritage has become a hot topic in a city that never seemed to care about the old being torn down to make way for the new. Recently, the government, taken aback by the anger over the recent destruction of the much-loved Central Star Ferry pier, agreed to preserve parts of the striking Wan Chai Market building.

Discontent over the yawning wealth gap in Hong Kong is another surprise trend. While Hong Kong's public-housing dwellers suffered an uncertain year, the super rich seemed to be doing fine. In fact, public expressions of discontent grew in online chat rooms about absurd displays of wealth. A trivial detail revealed in court during the latest episode in the saga of the late billionaire Nina Wang was somehow the most significant. During a hearing over her contested will, her feng shui master revealed the duo had burned bank notes together more or less for fun.

If Hong Kong's rich seemed to be taking leave of reality, its government at least could claim to be maintaining its economic grip. According to the Economic Freedom of the World Annual Report, 2008 marked Hong Kong's 12th year as the world's most free economy.

But the scorecard was not perfect. US media watchdog Freedom House downgraded Hong Kong's press-freedom ranking from 'free' to 'partly free', in its Freedom of the Press report, reflecting concerns that the mainland was pressuring local media groups to stifle debate on sensitive topics.

While Hong Kong is far from being a true democracy, it continues to grant its citizens the extensive freedoms of commerce, expression, worship and association promised in 1997's handover agreement. The growing number of mainland petitioners travelling to Hong Kong in 2009 to publicise grievances about corruption, repression or hardship (too often routinely ignored and even punished over the border) underscored the city's considerable freedoms.

Revel in Lan Kwai Fong (p206), a pulsating centre of nightlife in Hong Kong

HIGHLIGHTS

HONG KONG ISLAND

The territory's financial, social and political heart occupies Hong Kong Island's iconic north shore, where towering skyscrapers climb from the busy harbour up steep, jungle-clad hills. Escape by hitting the greener, quieter south side of the island.

① Victoria Harbour
Float on one of the world's busiest and most exotic harbours (p298)

② The Peak
Ride the hair-raising Peak Tram for unbeatable harbour and city views (p89)

③ Ocean Park
Thrill rides, rare pandas, aquariums and cable-car rides with a view (p93)

④ Wet Markets
Fresh produce, exotic ingredients and some gore at the city's wet markets (p176)

⑤ Happy Valley
Listen to thundering hoofs and cheering crowds right in the city centre (p90)

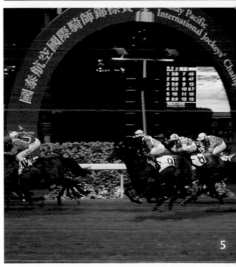

Teeming Kowloon (facing Hong Kong Island across the harbour) is home to traditional neighbourhoods, old-fashioned shops, lively markets, modern malls and many of Hong Kong's finest museums, galleries and arts venues.

1 Sik Sik Yuen Wong Tai Sin Temple
Divine the future alongside worshippers at the city's most interesting temple (p114)

2 Temple Street Night Market
Stock up on memorabilia beneath the glare of bare bulbs (p109)

3 Star Ferry
An unforgettable ride from Kowloon to Central (p275)

4 High Tea at the Peninsula
Dainty nibbles and fine tea, while soothed by a string quartet (p102)

5 Tsim Sha Tsui East Promenade
Spectacular harbour and skyline vistas day and night (p106)

6 Former Marine Police Headquarters
Explore this handsome architectural fragment of colonial Hong Kong (p102)

❶ Sai Kung Peninsula
Remote beaches, empty trails, amazing views and great seafood await (p129)

❷ Tsuen Wan
Fascinating temples, including those at the Yuen Yuen Institute, and important heritage sites nestle beneath the tallest mountain (p116)

❸ Hong Kong Wetland Park
Watch kingfishers dive in silence in this serene haven (p119)

NEW TERRITORIES

Hong Kong's lungs and its green playground, the mountain trails and nature reserves of the New Territories are ideal places to escape the crowds. Crumbling walled villages, massive temple complexes and a few good museums are other key attractions.

OUTLYING ISLANDS

Intimate little peeps at traditional village life, great seafood, brooding misty mountains and peaceful Buddhist temples are just some of the delights on the Outlying Islands, which offer an easy escape from high-rise modernity.

❶ Tian Tan Buddha
Vegetarian food, a giant bronze Buddha and great views via a cable car (p138)

❷ Lamma
Cross leafy Lamma's wooded hills for seafood and hidden coves (p134)

❸ Hiking on Lantau
Lose the crowds along Lantau's remote, rugged trails (p227)

MACAU

In a few short years this former Portuguese colony has been transformed from a peaceful backwater into a glitzy gambler's paradise – China's Las Vegas. If you're not here to try your luck, the historic delights and wonderful Macanese food are its most powerful drawcards.

3 1833 05470 3373

❶ Ruins of the Church of St Paul
The fine carvings on this church are captivating historical fragments (p317)

❷ Grand Lisboa Casino
This spectacular folly is the last word in over-the-top glitz (p342)

❸ Coloane Village
Sample Macau's quieter side, and explore the vivid Chapel of St Francis Xavier (p331)

❹ Monte Fort
The old cannons command fine views from this atmospheric fortress, which now houses a fascinating museum (p319)

❺ Portuguese food, Taipa Island
Hands down the best selection of Portuguese and Macanese food in Macau, including delicious egg-custard tarts (p338)

❻ Taipa House Museum
Inside this historic building, experience life in Macau as it used to be (p327)

❶ Shamian Island
Lose the crowds on this leafy, water-lapped island (p265)

❷ Shopping in Shenzhen
Cheap tailors, warehouses full of fabric, and art masterpieces for a song (p257)

EXCURSIONS

While you're in the region, it's worth trying to make some time for bustling Shenzhen, Hong Kong's brash border neighbour; Zhuhai, Macau's sleepy cousin; and Guangzhou, the Pearl River's largest, most captivating and historic city.

CONTENTS

INTRODUCING HONG KONG	2

HIGHLIGHTS	4

THE AUTHORS	14

GETTING STARTED	15
When to Go	15
Costs & Money	17
Internet Resources	18
(Un)sustainable Hong Kong	18

BACKGROUND	20
History	20
Arts	31
Architecture	37
Economy	39
Environment & Planning	40
Government & Politics	43
Media	43
Fashion	44

MEET THE LOCALS	45

NEIGHBOURHOODS & ISLANDS	53
Itinerary Builder	56
Hong Kong Island	61
Kowloon	98
New Territories	116
Outlying Islands	134

SHOPPING	153
Hong Kong Island	157
Kowloon	167

EATING	171
Hong Kong Island	176
Kowloon	191
New Territories	198
Outlying Islands	201

ENTERTAINMENT	205
Drinking	207
Nightlife	216
The Arts	219

SPORTS & ACTIVITIES	221
Health & Fitness	222
Activities	223
Spectator Sports	229

SLEEPING	231
Hong Kong Island	235
Kowloon	241
New Territories	248
Outlying Islands	249

DAY TRIPS & EXCURSIONS	251
Shenzhen	252
Zhuhai	259
Guangzhou	263

TRANSPORT	271

DIRECTORY	288

MACAU	305
Background	306
Neighbourhoods	312
Shopping	333
Eating	334
Entertainment	341
Sports & Activities	345
Sleeping	347
Transport	350
Directory	352

LANGUAGE	356

BEHIND THE SCENES	365

INDEX	374

MAP LEGEND	388

THE AUTHORS

Andrew Stone

Andrew lived in Hong Kong for a magical year and a half in 2000 and 2001 writing as a freelancer about Hong Kong and the wider region. He made his home on sleepy Lamma Island and has returned every year since to research magazine articles and guidebooks, including the previous edition of this guide and the 2nd edition of Lonely Planet's *Hong Kong Encounter*. Andrew updated the Neighbourhoods & Islands, Shopping, Entertainment, Directory and Transport chapters.

ANDREW'S TOP HONG KONG DAY

The day begins with laps of the Four Seasons pool (p240) – well, I can dream, can't I? Then it's time to thumb this guide and glance at the table on p56 for a reminder of the best of Hong Kong, and for coauthor Piera's top food picks (I like to think at least two meals ahead).

Then it's a toss-up between a dim sum breakfast amid the cheerful clatter of City Hall Maxim's Palace (p178) or a juice from Mix (p207) to go. I go for the dim sum, of course.

I board the Peak Tram for the cool breezes and stirring views of the Peak (p89), before stepping out on to thick jungle on the walk through Pok Fu Lam Country Park.

Whistling for a cab, I pop into Ocean Park (p93) to see how its pandas are getting along, before taking a bus back to the city. I nose around Sheung Wan's dried seafood and herbalist shops (p83), and grab a cheap bowl of noodles after working up an appetite wandering back to Central via Graham St Market (p65).

Evening is falling, so I hop on the Star Ferry (p275) to Tsim Sha Tsui for a waterside sundowner at Deck 'n Beer (p215), sticking around long enough for the evening lightshow (p106).

Time to get serious about food now, and I opt for Hang Zhou (p179) back over the water in Wan Chai. After braving the stinky beancurd, it's time to party. After a drink at Pawn (p212), it's time to hit Lan Kwai Fong (p216) and start a bar crawl west towards Soho, and then bed.

Piera Chen

Born and raised in Hong Kong, Piera studied English at Pomona College and works as a writer and editor in her hometown. She thoroughly enjoyed exploring the various manifestations of Hong Kong's eclectic culture for this, her first Lonely Planet commission. She wrote the Background, Eating and Sleeping chapters, and the Ann Hui and Kenny Chan interviews in the Meet the Locals chapter.

Chung Wah Chow

Chung Wah, a Hong Kong native and freelance writer, wrote the Macau and Day Trips & Excursions chapters. She has travelled extensively in China and elsewhere and coauthored Lonely Planet's *China* guide. Chung Wah loves visiting Macau to explore Macanese culture and cuisine. She is also an amateur dim sum connoisseur.

Hong Kong is such a modern, well-run city that you won't need to do much practical pre-trip planning. You could pretty much rock up with a passport, a toothbrush and a credit card and get stuff done.

The transport infrastructure is excellent and runs like clockwork, it's an incredibly safe city, English is widely spoken and the signage is mostly in English too. This is also a city with a strong service ethic, so you name it – buying clothes or toiletries, withdrawing cash, getting internet access, doing your laundry – and it will be done swiftly and with a smile.

This leaves you to spend most of your pre-trip efforts on the fun things, such as checking out if any festivals are going on in town, booking ahead for the most popular restaurants, checking the local listings and deciding where to base yourself.

Perhaps the only practical thing worth spending a bit of planning time on is your accommodation (p232). Hotels are not cheap and at busy times, such as during exhibition season, rooms can fill up and rates soar. Doing your homework can make a real difference to your wallet and your comfort.

WHEN TO GO

Hong Kong's subtropical climate can make it a punishingly hot and humid destination during the summer months. June to mid-September when humidity soars is the hottest time. Summer is also typhoon season, when tropical storms sweep rain and high winds off the South China Sea.

Even in late spring and early autumn, wandering Hong Kong's streets can be warm work. The best time to go climate-wise is in early spring (March and April) or late autumn (October and November), when the days are generally warm, fresh and (wind direction and mainland smoke stacks permitting) the air often clearer.

Things can cool down a good deal in winter, when it can often be overcast (as opposed to merely smoggy) and temperatures may even feel chilly enough to don warmer layers.

FESTIVALS & EVENTS

No matter what the time of year, you're almost certain to find some colourful festival or event occurring in Hong Kong. For the most part exact dates vary from year to year, so if you want to time your visit to coincide with a particular event, check the website of the Hong Kong Tourism Board (www.discoverhongkong.com). For tourist high and low seasons in Hong Kong, see p232.

Many Chinese red-letter days, both public holidays and privately observed affairs, go back hundreds, even thousands, of years and the true origins of some are often lost in the mists

of time. Most – but not all – are celebrated in both Hong Kong and Macau. For festivals and events specific to Macau, see p353. For dates of Hong Kong's public holidays, see p293.

January

CHINESE NEW YEAR
Southern China's most important public holiday takes place in late January/early February and is welcomed by a huge international parade at Tamar (now the PLA Central Barracks) site along the waterfront between Central and Wan Chai.

HONG KONG CITY FRINGE FESTIVAL
www.hkfringe.com.hk
The Fringe Club (p220) sponsors three weeks of eclectic performances both local and international between late January and early February.

February

HONG KONG ARTS FESTIVAL
www.hk.artsfestival.org
Hong Kong's most important cultural event is a month-long extravaganza of music, performing arts and exhibitions by hundreds of local and international artists.

HONG KONG MARATHON
www.hkmarathon.com
This major sporting event dating back to 1997 also includes a half-marathon and 10km race and attracts 30,000 participants.

SPRING LANTERN FESTIVAL
www.discoverhongkong.com/eng/events/chinese
-festivals.html
A colourful lantern festival on the 15th day
of the first moon (mid- to late February)
marks the end of the New Year period and
the day for lovers.

March
HONG KONG ARTWALK
www.hongkongartwalk.com
Some 40 galleries in Central, Soho and
Sheung Wan throw open their doors on a
weekday (usually Wednesday) from 6pm to
midnight to expose their art, offer viewers
snacks and drinks supplied by the areas'
restaurants and raise money for charity.

HONG KONG RUGBY WORLD CUP SEVENS
www.hksevens.com.hk
Hong Kong's premier sporting event, this
seven-a-side tournament is held over three
days at Hong Kong Stadium and attracts
teams and spectators from all over the
world.

April
HONG KONG INTERNATIONAL FILM FESTIVAL
www.hkiff.org.hk
This is a two-week extravaganza with
screenings of more than 240 films from
around the world.

BIRTHDAY OF TIN HAU
www.discoverhongkong.com/eng/events/chinese
-festivals.html
A festival in late April/early May in honour
of the patroness of fisherfolk and one of
the territory's most popular goddesses; in
Macau it is known as the A-Ma Festival.

CHEUNG CHAU BUN FESTIVAL
www.cheungchau.org
Taking place around late April/early May,
this is an unusual festival that is observed
uniquely on Cheung Chau (see p145).

KUNG HEI FAT CHOI (& HAPPY NEW YEAR, TOO)!
The Lunar New Year is the most important holiday of the Chinese year. Expect colourful decorations but not much
public merrymaking. For the most part, this is a family festival, though there is a parade on the first day, a fantastic
fireworks display over Victoria Harbour on the second evening, and one of the largest horse races is held at Sha Tin
on the third day.

Chinese New Year, which mainlanders call the Spring Festival, begins on the first new moon after the sun enters
Aquarius (ie sometime between 21 January and 19 February) and ends, at least officially, 15 days later. In Hong Kong
it is a three-day public holiday.

The build-up to the holiday – the end of the month known as the 'Bitter Moon', since it's the coldest part of the year
in Hong Kong – is very busy, as family members clean house, get haircuts and cook, all of which are prohibited during
the holiday. Debts and feuds are settled, and employees get a one-month New Year bonus. You'll see many symbols in
Hong Kong at this time of year, and they all have special meaning for people here. Chinese use a lot of indirect language,
and 'punning' is very important in the use of symbols. A picture of a boy holding a *gàm-yéw* (goldfish) and a *hòw-fàa*
(lotus flower) is wishing you 'abundant gold and harmony', since that's what the words can also mean when said in a
different tone. Symbols of *fùk* (bats) are everywhere, since the word also means 'good luck'. The peach and plum blos-
soms decorating restaurants and public spaces symbolise both the arrival of spring and 'immortality', while the golden
fruit of the kumquat tree is associated with good fortune. The red and gold banners you'll see in doorways are wishing
all and sundry 'prosperity', 'peace' or just 'spring'.

Punning also carries over into foods eaten during the Lunar New Year holidays. *Faat-choy* (sea moss) and *hò-sí* (dried
oysters) is a popular dish, as the names of the key ingredients can also mean 'prosperity' and 'good business'. Lots of fish,
gài (chicken), which also means 'luck', and *hàa* (prawns, or 'laughter') are served, as are noodles for longevity.

Of course, much of the symbolism and well-wishing has to do with wealth and prosperity. Indeed, '*gùng-háy
faatchòy*', the most common New Year greeting in southern China, literally means 'respectful wishes, get rich'. The
lài-sí packet is a small red and gold envelope in which new bills (usually $10 or $20) are enclosed
and given as gifts by married people to children and singles.

The first day of Chinese New Year will fall on 14 February in 2010, 3 February in 2011 and 23 January in 2012.

If you're planning to travel around this period, it pays to plan ahead, as huge numbers of people move around and
trains and planes can get booked solid.

May

BIRTHDAY OF LORD BUDDHA
www.discoverhongkong.com/eng/events/chinese
-festivals.html
A public holiday during which Buddha's statue is taken from monasteries and temples and ceremoniously bathed in scented water.

LE FRENCH MAY
www.lefrenchmay.com
A month of Gallic-inspired culture, food and (bien sûr) wine.

June

DRAGON BOAT FESTIVAL
www.discoverhongkong.com/eng/events/chinese
-festivals.html
This festival, also known as Tuen Ng (Double Fifth) as it falls on the fifth day of the fifth moon, commemorates the death of the 3rd-century BC poet-statesman who hurled himself into a river to protest against a corrupt government. Dragon-boat races are held throughout the territory and in Macau, but the most famous are at Stanley.

July

HONG KONG FASHION WEEK FOR SPRING/SUMMER
http://hkfashionweekss.tdctrade.com
This is the spring/summer section of the biannual Hong Kong Fashion Week.

August

HUNGRY GHOST FESTIVAL
www.discoverhongkong.com/eng/events/chinese
-festivals.html
Celebrated on the first day of the seventh moon (sometime between August and September), when the gates of hell are opened and 'hungry ghosts' (restless spirits) are freed for two weeks to walk the earth. On the 14th day, paper 'hell' money and votives in the shape of cars, houses and clothing are burned for the ghosts and food is offered.

September

MID-AUTUMN FESTIVAL
www.discoverhongkong.com/eng/events/chinese
-festivals.html
A colourful festival held on the 15th night of the eighth moon (sometime in September or October). It marks an uprising against the Mongols in the 14th century, when plans for a revolution were passed around in little round 'moon' cakes, which are still eaten on this day.

October

CHEUNG YEUNG
www.discoverhongkong.com/eng/events/chinese
-festivals.html
Celebrated on the ninth day of the ninth month (mid- to late October), this festival is based on a Han dynasty story in which an oracle advised a man to take his family to a high place to escape a plague. Many people still head for the hills on this day and also visit the graves of ancestors.

November

HONG KONG INTERNATIONAL CRICKET SIXES
www.hksixes.com
This two-day tournament pits Hong Kong's top cricketers against select teams from the eight test-playing nations.

December

HONG KONG WINTERFEST
www.discoverhongkong.com/winterfest
See the lights on the Statue Sq Christmas tree turn on and take in the baubles, fake snow and carol singers on open-topped antique trams.

COSTS & MONEY

Hong Kong is a relatively pricey destination. Accommodation is the biggest expense, followed by drinking in Hong Kong's bars. On a very tight budget you could survive on, say, $350 a day, but it would require a good deal of self-discipline. Better to budget something along the lines of $700 if you want to stay in the better class of guesthouse or a cheaper midrange hotel and do more than just eat bowls of noodles. If you want to sample the finer hotels and restaurants, you'll be paying the equivalent of most leading world cities. The real bargain compared to the likes of London and even New York is the incredibly cheap taxi fares; in fact, transport generally is

HOW MUCH?

Bowl of wonton noodles $15 to $35

Cup of coffee from $25

Fresh juice $12 to $22

Litre of bottled water $10 to $14

Pint of beer around $45 (from $25 at happy hour)

Wi-fi access free in malls and some hotels

Laundry (5kg) $50 to $60

Souvenir T-shirt $40 to $100

MTR fare (Central to Tsim Sha Tsui) $8.50; $7.90 with Octopus card

Peak Tram one way/return $22/33

Star Ferry fare (Central to Tsim Sha Tsui) 1st/2nd class $2.30/1.80

excellent value. For practical details on ATMs and foreign currency, see p297.

INTERNET RESOURCES

The Lonely Planet website, www.lonelyplanet .com, lists many useful Hong Kong links. Other helpful sites:

Asiaxpat (www.asiaxpat.com) A lifestyle site – restaurants, nightlife, trends – that includes advertorials.

bc magazine (www.bcmagazine.net) Nightlife and entertainment from one of Hong Kong's top nightlife freebies.

Blog Hong Kong (www.expat-blog.com/en/directory/asia /china/hong-kong) A useful collection of HK blogs, from Sex and the City–type expat scribes through to satirical ranters and foodie obsessives.

Discover Hong Kong (www.discoverhongkong.com) A good general resource if you're seeking inspiration with lots of pictures.

Gay Hong Kong (www.gayhk.com) The nightlife scene in Hong Kong for visitors and locals alike.

Google Maps, Hong Kong (maps.google.com.hk) Fast-loading maps with geo-tagged listings.

HK Clubbing (www.hkclubbing.com)

Hong Kong Journal (www.hkjournal.org) Insightful, in-depth features on the city.

Hong Kong Leisure and Cultural Services Department (www.lcsd.gov.hk)

Hong Kong Observatory (www.weather.gov.hk)

Hong Kong Tourism Board (www.discoverhongkong.com)

Hong Kong Yellow Pages (www.yp.com.hk)

South China Morning Post (www.scmp.com.hk)

Time Out Hong Kong (www.timeout.com.hk) Authoritative cultural and entertainment listings.

(UN)SUSTAINABLE HONG KONG

Oh dear. You're in the wrong city in the wrong country. Conspicuous consumption is the main pastime in Hong Kong's malls, which along with everything else are powered by the dirtiest fuel of all (coal). Hong Kong's token wind turbines merely underline its non-efforts in sustainable energy generation. Let's face it, even though it has great wilderness areas (see p41) Hong Kong isn't exactly a model ecocity and the options to use sustainable services are very limited.

Energy-efficient systems, such as geothermal and air source heat pumps and renewable generation through solar power, are barely gaining traction and buildings could be a lot greener.

Perhaps the only environmental upside to console yourself with is that a highly concentrated city like Hong Kong (and it most certainly is that) is sensationally energy efficient compared to cities with suburban sprawl and therefore higher vehicle use.

ADVANCE PLANNING

Three weeks before you go, check out some key Hong Kong websites and get to know what's going on – both in the headlines and after hours – by reading the local online media (p298), as well as local blogs (above). Check to see if your visit coincides with any major holidays or festivals (p15). Make sure your passport and other documents are in order.

One week before you go, book tickets for any major concerts or shows that might interest you at places such as the Hong Kong Cultural Centre (p99) or the Fringe Studio & Theatre (p220). Book a table at Lung King Heen (p177). Remember to book the cat sitter.

The day before you go, reconfirm your flight, check Hong Kong websites for any last-minute changes, weather updates (especially in the typhoon season; see p289) or cancellations at entertainment venues, and buy some Hong Kong dollars.

Hong Kong's efforts to offer recycling facilities are improving, but slowly. One of the few things you can do to help make a difference when eating out is to order only nonendangered species of fish, and from sustainable fisheries, by consulting the Hong Kong World Wide Fund for Nature Fish Identification Guide (www .wwf.org.hk/eng/conservation). The downside is that having long since exhausted its own inshore fish stocks, much of the fish consumed in Hong Kong is jetted in from other Asian fish markets.

HISTORY

The name Hong Kong came from the Cantonese *hèung-gáwng* ('fragrant harbour' or 'incense harbour'), which was inspired by the scent of sandalwood incense piled at what is now Aberdeen, on the western edge of the island. In the very long scale of history, Hong Kong as we know it today has existed for a mere blink of an eye. But there was a lot going on in the region before that wintry morning in 1841 when a contingent of British marines clambered ashore and planted the Union flag on the western part of Hong Kong Island, claiming it for the British Crown.

EARLY INHABITANTS

Hong Kong has supported human life since at least the Middle Neolithic Period (c 4000–2500 BC). Artefacts uncovered at almost 100 archaeological sites in the territory – most of them along the winding shoreline, including a rich burial ground discovered on the island of Ma Wan in 1997 and three hoards on the west coast of the Tuen Mun peninsula – suggest that the inhabitants of these settlements shared similar cultural characteristics to the people who lived in the Pearl River Delta. The remnants of Bronze Age habitations (c 1500–220 BC) unearthed on Lamma and Lantau Islands and at about 20 other sites – as well as the eight geometric rock carvings that can still be viewed at various locations along Hong Kong's coastline – also indicate that these early peoples practised some form of folk religion involving animal worship.

Other finds indicate Hong Kong's Stone Age inhabitants enjoyed a relatively nutritious diet of iron-rich vegetables, small mammals, shellfish and fish harvested far offshore. Early Chinese historical records refer to the diverse maritime peoples in China's southeastern coastal area as the 'Hundred Yue' tribes. Some of the prehistoric inhabitants of Hong Kong might have belonged to these tribes.

THE FIVE GREAT CLANS

Hong Kong, along with the Yue tribes in Guangdong, was incorporated into the Chinese empire during the Qin dynasty (c 221–207 BC). Archaeological finds from the following centuries showed that Hong Kong came under the influence of Han culture as more Han settlers migrated to the region. The discovery of coins and pottery from the Eastern Han dynasty (AD 25–220) on Lantau and Kau Sai Chau Islands and at several important digs, including a tomb at Lei Cheng Uk (p113) in central Kowloon and So Kwun Wat southeast of Tuen Mun, attests to this.

The first of Hong Kong's mighty 'Five Clans' – Han Chinese, whose descendants hold political and economic clout to this day – began settling the area around the 11th century. The first and most powerful of the arrivals was the Tang, who initially settled around Kam Tin (*tìn* means 'field'). The once-moated hamlet of Kat Hing Wai (*wài* means 'protective wall'; p121), which is probably the most visited of the remaining traditional walled villages in the New Territories, formed part of this cluster.

4000–1500 BC	214 BC	11th–15th centuries
Small groups of Neolithic hunter-gatherers and fisherfolk settle in coastal areas; a handful of tantalising archaeological finds – tools, pottery and other artefacts – are the only remnants left by these nomads.	Chinese emperor Qin Shi Huang conquers Nan Yue (present-day Guanxi, Guangdong and Fujian) after a long period of warring states. The inhabitants of Hong Kong come under greater cultural influence from the north.	Hong Kong's Five Clans – the Tang, the Hau, the Pang, the Liu and the Man – settle in what is now the New Territories and build walled villages in the fertile plains and valleys.

The Tang was followed by the Hau and the Pang, who spread around present-day Sheung Shui and Fanling. These three clans were followed by the Liu in the 14th century and the Man a century later.

The Cantonese-speaking newcomers called themselves *bún-dày* (Punti), meaning 'indigenous' or 'local' – something they clearly were not. They looked down on the original inhabitants, the Tanka, many of whom had been shunted off the land and had moved onto the sea to live on boats.

AN IMPERIAL OUTPOST

Clinging to the southern edge of the Chinese province of Canton (now Guangdong), the peninsula and islands that became the territory of Hong Kong counted only as a remote pocket in a neglected corner of the Chinese empire.

Hong Kong's first recorded encounter with imperial China in the 13th century was as brief as it was tragic. In 1276 the boy emperor, Duan Zong, was forced to flee to Guangdong as the Mongols swept aside the remaining army of the Song dynasty (AD 960–1279). Duan Zong and his younger brother, Bing, sought temporary refuge in Hong Kong. Duan Zong died a few months later. After Mongol ships defeated the tattered remnants of the imperial fleet in a battle on the Pearl River, a loyal Song official jumped into the sea carrying Bing, in an act of martyrdom, putting an end to the Song dynasty.

The Punti flourished until the struggle that saw the moribund Ming dynasty (1368–1644) overthrown. The victorious Qing (1644–1911), angered by the resistance put up by southerners loyal to the *ancien régime*, ordered in the 1660s a forced evacuation inland of all the inhabitants of China's southeastern coastal area, including Hong Kong.

These turbulent times saw the birth of the Triads (p29). Originally founded as patriotic secret societies dedicated to overthrowing the Qing dynasty and restoring the Ming, they would degenerate over the centuries into Hong Kong's own version of the Mafia. Today's Triads still recite an oath of allegiance to the Ming, but their loyalty is to the dollar rather than the vanquished Son of Heaven.

More than four generations passed before the population was able to recover to its mid-17th-century level, boosted in part by the influx of the Hakka (Cantonese for 'guest people'), who moved here in the 18th century and up to the mid-19th century. A few vestiges of their language, songs, folklore and cooking survive, most visibly in the wide-brimmed, black-fringed bamboo hats sported by Hakka women in the New Territories.

ARRIVAL OF THE OUTER BARBARIANS

For centuries, the Pearl River estuary had been an important trading artery centred on the port of Canton (now Guangzhou). Some of the first foreign traders or 'outer barbarians' were Arab traders who entered – and sacked – the settlement as early as the 8th century AD. Guangzhou was 2500km south of Peking, and the Cantonese view that the 'mountains are high and the emperor is far away' was not disputed in the imperial capital. The Ming emperors regarded their subjects to the south as no less than witches and sorcerers, their language unintelligible and their culinary predilections downright disgusting. It was therefore fitting that the Cantonese should trade with the 'outer barbarians'.

Regular trade between China and Europe began in 1557 when Portuguese navigators set up a base in Macau, 65km west of Hong Kong. Dutch traders came in the wake of the Portuguese,

1513	1557	1644
In an attempt to find a sea-trading route to China, Jorge Alvares, a Portuguese explorer, is the first European to visit the region, landing on Lintin Island, just to the west of Hong Kong Island.	Portuguese navigators set up a base in Macau, and are followed by Dutch and then French traders. Regular trade begins between China and Europe.	The Ming dynasty (1368–1644) is overthrown by the Qing dynasty, which reigns until 1911.

followed by the French. British ships appeared as early as 1683 from the East India Company concessions along the coast of India, and by 1711 the company had established offices and warehouses in Guangzhou to trade for tea, silk and porcelain.

OPIUM & WAR

China did not reciprocate Europe's voracious demand for its products, for the most part shunning foreign manufactured goods. The foreigners' ensuing trade deficit was soon reversed, however, after the British discovered a commodity that the Chinese did want: opium.

The British, with a virtually inexhaustible supply of the drug from the poppy fields of India, developed the trade aggressively. Alarmed by the spread of addiction and the silver draining from the country to pay for opium, the Qing emperor issued an edict in 1799 banning the trade of opium in China.

The ban had little effect and the lucrative trade continued. In late 1838 Emperor Dao Guang (r 1820–50) appointed Lin Zexu, governor of Hunan and Hubei and a mandarin of great integrity, to stamp out the opium trade. Upon arrival in Guangzhou, Lin surrounded the British factories in Guangzhou and cut off their food supplies, forcing them to turn over more than 20,000 chests of the drug.

The British chief superintendent of trade, Captain Charles Elliot, suspended all trade with China while he awaited instructions from London. The foreign secretary, Lord Palmerston, goaded by prominent Scottish merchants William Jardine and James Matheson, ordered an expeditionary force of 4000 men under Rear Admiral George Elliot (a cousin of Charles) to extract reparations and secure favourable trade arrangements from the Chinese government.

What would become known as the First Opium War (or First Anglo-Chinese War) began in June 1840. British forces besieged Guangzhou before sailing north and occupying or blockading a number of ports along the coast. In August, British forces reached the city of Tianjin, less than 160km away from Beijing. The emperor was forced to send his envoy (and Lin's successor) Qi Shan to negotiate with the Elliots. In exchange for the British withdrawal from northern China, Qi agreed to the Convention of Chuenpi (now Chuanbi), which ceded Hong Kong Island to Britain.

Though neither side, in fact, accepted the terms of the convention, a couple of subsequent events decided Hong Kong's fate. In January 1841 a naval landing party hoisted the British flag at Possession Point (now Possession St) on Hong Kong Island. The following month Captain Elliot attacked the Bogue Fort in Humen, took control of the Pearl River and laid siege to Guangzhou, withdrawing only after having extracted concessions from merchants there. Six months later a powerful British force led by Elliot's successor, Sir Henry Pottinger, sailed north and seized Amoy (Xiamen), Ningpo (Ningbo), Shanghai and other ports. With the strategic city of Nanking (Nanjing) under immediate threat, the Chinese were forced to accept Britain's terms.

The Treaty of Nanking abolished the monopoly system of trade, opened five 'treaty ports' to British residents and foreign trade, exempted British nationals from all Chinese laws and ceded the island of Hong Kong to the British 'in perpetuity'.

BRITISH HONG KONG

'Albert is so amused at my having got the island of Hong Kong', wrote Queen Victoria to King Leopold of Belgium in 1841. At the time, Hong Kong was little more than a backwater of about

1683	1757	1773
Ships from the British East India Company begin to arrive, and by 1711 the company has established offices and warehouses in Guangzhou to trade for tea, silk and porcelain.	An imperial edict limits Europeans to trade only via the cohong (local merchants' guild) in Guangzhou; growing discontent with the trading system sets the stage for the First Opium War in 1840.	Smuggle of opium to China skyrockets after the British East India Company monopolises production and export of Indian opium; addiction sweeps China like wildfire.

20 villages and hamlets. It did offer one distinct advantage for the British trading fleet, however: a deep, well-sheltered harbour strategically located in the Far East.

Hong Kong formally became a British possession on 26 June 1843, and its first governor, Sir Henry Pottinger, took charge. A primitive, chaotic and lawless settlement soon sprang up.

GROWING PAINS

What would later be called the Second Opium War (or Second Anglo-Chinese War) broke out in October 1856. The first stage of the war was brought to an end two years later by the Treaty of Tientsin (now Tianjin), which gave foreigners the right to diplomatic representation in Beijing.

Despite warnings from the Chinese, the British tried to capitalise on this agreement in 1859 by sending a flotilla carrying the first British envoy and minister plenipotentiary up the Pei Ho River to Beijing. The Chinese fired on the armada, which sustained heavy losses. Using this as a pretext, a combined British and French force invaded China and marched on Beijing. The victorious British forced the Chinese to the Convention of Peking in 1860, which ratified the Treaty of Tientsin and ceded the Kowloon Peninsula and Stonecutters Island to Britain. Britain was now in complete control of Victoria Harbour and its approaches.

Hong Kong's population had leapt from 33,000 in 1850 to 240,000 in 1896, and the British army felt it needed to command the mountains of the New Territories to protect the growing colony. When the Qing dynasty was at its nadir, the British government petitioned China to extend the colony into the New Territories. The June 1898 Convention of Peking handed Britain a larger-than-expected slice of territory that included 235 islands and ran north to the Shumchun (Shenzhen) River, increasing the colony's size by 90%.

A SLEEPY BACKWATER

While Hong Kong's major trading houses, including Jardine Matheson and Swire, prospered from their trade with China, the colony hardly thrived in its first few decades. Fever, bubonic plague and typhoons threatened life and property, and at first the colony attracted a fair number of criminals and vice merchants. Opium dens, gambling clubs and brothels proliferated; just a year after Britain took possession, an estimated 450 prostitutes worked out of two dozen brothels, including a fair number of foreign prostitutes clustered in Lyndhurst Tce.

Gradually, however, Hong Kong began to shape itself into a more substantial community. Gas and electrical power companies sprang up; ferries, trams, the Kowloon-Canton Railway and the newfangled High Level Tramway (later known as the Peak Tram) provided a decent transport network; and land was reclaimed. Nonetheless, from the late 19th century right up to WWII, Hong Kong lived in the shadow of the treaty port of Shanghai, which had become Asia's premier trade and financial centre – not to mention its style capital.

The colony's population continued to grow thanks to waves of immigrants fleeing the Chinese Revolution of 1911, which ousted the decaying Qing dynasty and ushered in several decades of strife, rampaging warlords and famine. The civil war in China kept refugee numbers high, but the stream became a flood after Japan invaded China in 1937.

Hong Kong's status as a British colony would offer the refugees only a temporary haven. The day after Japan attacked the US naval base at Pearl Harbor on 7 December 1941, its military machine swept down from Guangzhou and into Hong Kong.

1799	1841	1842
Alarmed by the spread of addiction and the silver draining from the country to pay for opium, the Qing emperor issues an edict banning the trade of opium in China.	British marines plant the Union flag on the western part of Hong Kong Island, claiming the land for the British Crown.	China cedes Hong Kong Island to Great Britain; in a letter to Captain Elliot, Lord Palmerston calls Hong Kong 'a barren island with hardly a house upon it' '[It] will never be a mart for trade...'

Conditions under Japanese rule were harsh, with indiscriminate massacres of mostly Chinese civilians; Western civilians were incarcerated at Stanley Prison on Hong Kong Island. Many Hong Kong Chinese fled to Macau, administered by neutral Portugal.

THE ROAD TO BOOMTOWN

After Japan's withdrawal from Hong Kong, and subsequent surrender in August 1945, the colony looked set to resume its hibernation. But events both at home and on the mainland forced the colony in a new direction.

Soon after the surrender of Japan, a civil war broke out in China between the Communists and the Nationalists. When the Communists came to power in 1949, many people were sure that Hong Kong would be overrun. But though the Chinese government continued to denounce the 'unequal treaties', it recognised Hong Kong's importance to the national economy.

The turmoil on the mainland unleashed a torrent of refugees – both rich and poor – into Hong Kong. The refugees brought along capital and cheap labour vital to Hong Kong's economic takeoff. On a paltry, war-torn foundation, local and foreign businesses built a huge manufacturing (notably textiles and garments) and financial services centre that transformed Hong Kong into one of the world's great economic miracles.

However, trouble flared up in the 1950s and '60s due to political and social discontent. Riots broke out in 1957 after local officials took down the Nationalist flag in a squatter area. In 1966 a one-man hunger strike against the price rise of ferry tickets soon escalated into days of widespread urban unrest in Kowloon.

In 1967, at the height of the so-called Cultural Revolution, when the ultraleftist Red Guards were in de facto control in China, Hong Kong's stability again looked precarious. The pro-communist groups in Hong Kong turned a labour dispute into an all-out 'anti-colonial movement'. Demonstrations, strikes and riots rocked the colony, and the violence soon mushroomed into bombings and arson attacks.

Hong Kong's economy was paralysed for months. The riot came to an end in December 1967, when Chinese Premier Zhou Enlai ordered the pro-communist groups to stop.

A SOCIETY IN TRANSITION

After 'a testing time for the people of Hong Kong', as the *Hong Kong Yearbook* summed it up at the end of 1967, the colonial government initiated a series of reforms to alleviate social discontent and to foster a sense of belonging to Hong Kong. In the next decade the government introduced more labour laws, and invested heavily in public housing, medical service, education and recreational activities for youth. In the early 1970s, the construction of the first three 'New Towns' – Sha Tin, Tsuen Wan and Tuen Mun – commenced, marking the start of a massive and unprecedented public-housing programme that would, and still does, house millions of Hong Kong people.

Although Hong Kong's stock market collapsed in 1973, its economy resumed its upward trend later in the decade. At the same time many of Hong Kong's neighbours began to mimic the colony's success. Just as their cheap labour was threatening to undermine the competitive edge of Hong Kong manufacturers, China began to emerge from its self-imposed isolation.

The 'Open Door' policy of Deng Xiaoping, who took control of China in the confusion after Mao Zedong's death in 1976, revived Hong Kong's role as the gateway to the mainland and it

1856	1894	1895
Chinese soldiers board the British merchant schooner *Arrow* to search for pirates, sparking the Second Opium War; French troops support the British in this war, while Russia and the US lend naval support.	Bubonic plague breaks out for the first time in Hong Kong, killing 2500 of mainly local Chinese and leading to a mass exodus from the territory; trade suffers badly as ships avoid the plague-infested port.	Sun Yat-sen, a newly qualified Chinese doctor from Guangzhou, uses Hong Kong as a base to drive an insurrection in southern China; it fails and the British ban Sun from the territory.

boomed. By the end of the 1980s, Hong Kong was one of the richest places in Asia, second only to Japan in terms of GDP per capita.

THE 1997 QUESTION

Few people gave much thought to Hong Kong's future until 1979, when the governor of Hong Kong, Murray MacLehose, raised the issue with Deng Xiaoping on his first official visit to Beijing. Britain was legally bound to hand back only the New Territories – not Hong Kong Island and Kowloon, which had been ceded to it forever. However, the fact that nearly half of Hong Kong's population lived in the New Territories by that time made it an untenable division.

It was Deng Xiaoping who decided that the time was ripe to recover Hong Kong, forcing the British to the negotiating table. The inevitable conclusion laid to rest the political jitters and commercial concerns that had in 1983 seen the Hong Kong dollar collapse – and subsequently be pegged to the US dollar. But there was considerable resentment that the fate of 5.5 million people had been decided without their input and that Whitehall had not provided Hong Kong people with full British passports and the right of abode in the UK.

Despite soothing words from the Chinese, British and Hong Kong governments, over the next 13 years the population of Hong Kong suffered considerable anxiety at the possible political and economic consequences of the handover. In the anxious years leading up to the handover, tens of thousands of Hong Kong citizens emigrated to Canada, the US, Australia, the UK and New Zealand.

ONE COUNTRY, TWO SYSTEMS

Under the agreement signed by China and Britain in December 1984, which is enshrined in a document known as *The Sino-British Joint Declaration on the Question of Hong Kong*, the 'British-administered territory' of Hong Kong would disappear and be reborn as a Special Administrative Region (SAR) of China. This meant the Hong Kong SAR would be permitted to continue with its current capitalist system, while across the border China's version of socialism would continue. The Chinese catchphrase for this was 'One Country, Two Systems'.

In 1988 the details of this rather unorthodox system of government were spelled out in *The Basic Law for Hong Kong*, the SAR's future constitution. The Basic Law, ratified by the National People's Congress (NPC) in Beijing in 1990, preserved Hong Kong's English common-law judicial system and guaranteed the right of property and ownership. It also included the right to strike and the rights of assembly, free speech, association, travel and movement, and religious belief. The SAR would enjoy a high degree of autonomy with the exception of foreign affairs and matters of defence.

As guarantees of individual freedoms and respect for human rights are written into China's own constitution, few Hong Kong Chinese held much faith in the Basic Law. Although Hong Kong under the British had never been more than a benignly ruled oligarchy, Whitehall had nevertheless promised to introduce democratic reforms prior to the handover. But it soon became apparent that British and Chinese definitions of democracy differed considerably. Beijing made it abundantly clear that it would not allow Hong Kong to establish its own democratically elected government. The chief executive was to be chosen by a Beijing-appointed panel of delegates; the people of Hong Kong would elect some Legislative Council (LegCo) members.

1898	1911	1937
China hands the New Territories to Britain; instead of annexing the 'New Territories', the British agree to sign a 99-year lease, beginning on 1 July 1898 and ending at midnight on 30 June 1997.	With waves of immigrants fleeing the Chinese Revolution on the mainland, the colony's population continues to grow.	Pouncing on a country weakened by a bloody civil war, Japan invades China; as many as 750,000 mainland Chinese seek shelter in Hong Kong over the next three years, fleeing the invaders.

TIANANMEN & ITS AFTERMATH

The concern of many Hong Kong people over their future turned to out-and-out fear on 4 June 1989, when Chinese troops massacred pro-democracy demonstrators in Beijing's Tiananmen Square. The events horrified Hong Kong people, many of whom had donated funds and goods to the demonstrators. As the Chinese authorities spread out to hunt down activists, an underground smuggling operation, code-named Yellow Bird, was set up in Hong Kong to spirit them to safety overseas.

The massacre was a watershed for Hong Kong. Sino-British relations deteriorated, the stock market fell 22% in one day and a great deal of capital left the territory for destinations overseas.

The Hong Kong government sought to rebuild confidence by announcing plans for a new airport and shipping port; with an estimated price tag of $200 billion (though $160 billion was actually spent), this was the world's most expensive infrastructure project of the day. But China had already signalled its intentions loudly and clearly.

Hong Kong–based Chinese officials who had spoken out against the Tiananmen killings were yanked from their posts or sought asylum in the US and Europe.

Local Hong Kong people with money and skills made a mad dash to emigrate to any country that would take them. During the worst period more than 1000 people were leaving each week, especially for Canada and Australia.

Tiananmen had strengthened the resolve of those people who either could not or would not leave, giving rise to the territory's first official political parties. In a bid to restore credibility, the government introduced a Bill of Rights in 1990 and the following year bestowed on Hong Kong citizens the right to choose 18 of the 60 members of the LegCo, which until then had been essentially a rubber-stamp body chosen by the government and special-interest groups.

Hong Kong is the only place under Chinese rule that still mourns those killed in 1989. Every year on 4 June, tens of thousands of people gather at Victoria Park to attend a candlelight vigil held in commemoration of those who lost their lives.

DEMOCRACY & THE LAST GOVERNOR

Hong Kong was never as politically apathetic as was generally thought in the 1970s and '80s. The word 'party' may have been anathema to the refugees who had fled from the Communists or Nationalists in the 1930s and '40s, but it wasn't necessarily anathema to their sons and daughters.

Born and bred in the territory, these first-generation Hong Kong youths were entering universities and colleges by the 1970s and becoming politically active. Like student activists everywhere, they were passionate and idealistic, agitating successfully for Chinese to be recognised as an official language alongside English. They opposed colonialism, expressed pride in their Chinese heritage and railed against the benign dictatorship of the Hong Kong colonial government. But their numbers were split between those who supported China – and the Chinese Communist Party – at all costs and those who had reservations or even mistrusted it.

The first to consider themselves 'Hong Kong people' rather than refugees from China, this generation formed the pressure groups that emerged in the 1980s to debate Hong Kong's future. By the end of the decade they were coalescing into nascent political parties and preparing for the 1991 LegCo elections.

One of the first parties to emerge was the United Democrats of Hong Kong, led by outspoken democrats Martin Lee and Szeto Wah. The pair, initially courted by China for

1941	1962	1967
After just over two weeks of fierce but futile resistance, British forces surrender to Japanese forces on Christmas Day; the population in Hong Kong is more than halved during almost four years of Japanese occupation.	The great famine caused by the Great Leap Forward in China drives 70,000 people to flee into Hong Kong in less than three months.	Riots and bombings by pro-communist groups rock Hong Kong; armed Chinese militia cross the border, killing five policemen and penetrating 3km into the New Territories before pulling back.

top picks

HISTORY BOOKS

- *Hong Kong: Epilogue to an Empire* (1997) by Jan Morris – this anecdotal history of the territory shortly before the handover moves between past and present as it explains what made Hong Kong so unique among the colonies of the British Empire. A dated but highly recommended read.
- *Hong Kong: Somewhere Between Heaven and Earth* (1996) by Barbara-Sue White – this anthology of writings from letters, diaries, novels, poems, short stories and biographies offers snapshots of Hong Kong's past and its spirit through the eyes of elites and common folks.
- *A Modern History of Hong Kong* (2007) by Steve Tsang – this well-researched and highly readable book by a prominent Hong Kong historian covers the birth of colonial Hong Kong to its end. It gives a balanced portrayal of the roles played by the British colonisers and local Chinese communities in the making of Hong Kong.
- *Old Hong Kong* (1999) by Formasia – this fascinating large-format pictorial of old photographs comes in three volumes: Volume I covers the period from 1860 to 1900; Volume II from 1901 to 1945; and Volume III from 1950 to 1997.

their anti-colonial positions and appointed to the committee that drafted the Basic Law, subsequently infuriated Beijing by publicly burning copies of the proto-constitution in protest over the Tiananmen massacre. Predictably, China denounced them as subversives.

Chris Patten, Hong Kong's 28th – and last – British governor arrived in 1992, pledging to sceptical citizens that democracy would get back on track. China reacted badly, first levelling daily verbal attacks at the governor, then threatening the post-1997 careers of any pro-democracy politicians or officials. When these tactics failed, China targeted Hong Kong's economy. Talks on certain business contracts and infrastructure projects straddling 1997 suddenly came to a halt, including the new airport programme.

Sensing that it had alienated even its supporters in Hong Kong, China backed down and in 1994 gave its blessing to the new airport at Chek Lap Kok. It remained hostile to direct elections, however, and vowed to disband the democratically elected legislature after 1997. A Provisional Legislative Council was elected by a Beijing-appointed election committee in 1996. The rival chamber met over the border in Shenzhen, as it had no legal status in Hong Kong until the transfer of power. This provisional body served until June 1998, when a new Legislative Council was elected partially by the people of Hong Kong, partially by business constituencies and partially by power brokers in Beijing.

As for the executive branch of power, the election was organised by China in 1996 to select Hong Kong's first post-colonial leader. But Tung Chee Hwa (1937–), the Shanghai-born shipping magnate destined to become the SAR's first chief executive, won approval by retaining Patten's right-hand woman, Anson Chan, as his chief secretary and Donald Tsang as financial secretary.

China agreed to a low-key entry into Hong Kong, and People's Liberation Army (PLA) troops were trucked straight to their barracks in Stanley, Kowloon Tong and Bonham Rd in the Mid-Levels. On the night of 30 June 1997 the handover celebrations held in the purpose-built extension of the Hong Kong Convention & Exhibition Centre in Wan Chai were watched by millions of people around the world. Chris Patten shed a tear while Chinese President Jiang Zemin beamed and Prince Charles was outwardly stoic (but privately scathing,

1971	1976	1982
A former child actor called Bruce Lee lands his first adult leading role in the kung fu film *The Big Boss*; it becomes a smash around the world.	The 'Open Door' policy of Deng Xiaoping, who took control of China after Mao Zedong's death, revives Hong Kong's role as the gateway to the mainland.	The prime minister of Britain, Margaret Thatcher, visits Beijing to begin talks on the future of Hong Kong; Hong Kong's future is sealed after two years of closed-door wrangling between the Chinese and British.

CHINA'S HONG KONG INVASION PLAN

The peaceful agreement that eventually settled the status of Hong Kong was by no means a foregone conclusion in the decades leading up to it. The key negotiators have since revealed just how touchy China felt about Hong Kong and how close it came to retaking the territory by force.

Margaret Thatcher, the British prime minister who negotiated the deal, said later that Deng Xiaoping, then China's leader, told her he 'could walk in and take the whole lot this afternoon'.

She replied that China would lose everything if it did. 'There is nothing I could do to stop you,' she said, 'but the eyes of the world would now know what China is like.'

Lu Ping, the top Chinese negotiator, recently confirmed that this was no bluff on Deng's part. Deng feared that announcing the date for the 1997 handover would provoke serious unrest in Hong Kong, and China would be compelled to invade as a result.

According to Lu, China had also been hours away from invading during 1967, at the height of the chaotic Cultural Revolution, when a radical faction of the People's Liberation Army (PLA) was poised to invade the British colony during pro-communist riots. The invasion was called off only by a late-night order from Premier Zhou Enlai to the local army commander, Huang Yongsheng, a radical Maoist who had been itching to invade.

describing the Chinese leaders in a diary leaked years later to the British tabloids as 'appalling old waxworks').

So the curtain fell on a century and a half of British rule, and the new chief executive Tung summed up Chinese feelings about the handover with the words: 'Now we are masters of our own house'.

HONG KONG POST-1997

Almost as soon as the euphoria of the 1997 handover faded, things started going badly in Hong Kong. The financial crisis that had rocked other parts of Asia began to be felt in Hong Kong at the end of 1997. A strain of deadly Avian Flu, which many people feared would become a worldwide epidemic, saw Hong Kong slaughter more than one million chickens.

The credibility of the SAR administration was severely damaged in 1999 when the government challenged a High Court ruling allowing residency rights for the China-born offspring of parents who became Hong Kong citizens after 1997. The ruling was based on certain clauses of the Basic Law – Hong Kong's mini-constitution – that made 1.6 million people from the mainland eligible for right of abode in the territory. The SAR administration appealed to the standing committee of the NPC, China's rubber-stamp parliament, to 'reinterpret' these clauses. The NPC complied, and ruled according to what the law drafters 'meant' but had somehow failed to write into law.

The mainland stands accused of interfering in Hong Kong's independence via what appears to be intrusion into the city's legal system, and the apparent withholding of universal suffrage from Hong Kong citizens.

Clearly the mainland government wields huge influence, both benign and malign, but in most cases still prefers to tread lightly, honouring the spirit of the handover agreement to a great extent. A measure of just how successful the handover has been came in a 2007 BBC interview with Margaret Thatcher. Marking the 10th anniversary of the handover of Hong

1989	1990	1997
More than one million Hong Kong people march in support of the pro-democracy movement in Beijing; Chinese tanks and troops mow down protesting students in Tiananmen Square.	The government introduces a Bill of Rights and in 1991 bestows on Hong Kong citizens the right to choose 18 of the 60 members of the Legislative Council.	The rain falls, Chris Patten cries and Hong Kong returns to Chinese sovereignty; Avian Flu breaks out, killing six people and leading to the slaughter of more than one million birds in a bid to contain the outbreak.

THE TRIADS

Hong Kong's Triads, which continue to run the territory's drug, prostitution, people-smuggling, gambling and loan-sharking rackets despite the change of government, weren't always the gangster operations they are today.

They were founded as secret and patriotic societies that opposed the corrupt and brutal Qing (Manchu) dynasty and aided the revolution that brought down that dynasty in 1911. The fact that these organisations had adopted Kwan Tai (or Kwan Yu), the god of war and upholder of righteousness, integrity and loyalty, as their patron, lent them further respectability. Unfortunately, the Triads descended into crime and illicit activities during the civil war on the mainland, and came in droves to Hong Kong after the communists came to power in 1949. Today they are the Chinese equivalent of the Mafia.

The communists smashed the Triad-controlled drug racket in Shanghai after the 1949 revolution. The Triads have long memories and, before the handover, many Hong Kong–based hoods have moved their operations to ethnic-Chinese communities in countries such as Thailand, the Philippines, Australia, Canada and the US. Since 1997, however, many Triads have moved back into Hong Kong and have even expanded their operations onto the mainland, establishing links with corrupt officials.

The definitive work on the Triads is *Triad Societies in Hong Kong* by WP Morgan, a former subinspector in the Royal Hong Kong Police.

Kong from Britain to China, Thatcher, to her own surprise, deemed China's overall performance a success.

There's much debate about how much influence the mainland is bringing to bear overtly or covertly in Hong Kong. The fact remains, however, that true democracy still looks to be a long way off. Chinese people might now rule the roost, but more than a decade on from colonial days, the LegCo remains essentially toothless and ultimate power rests with the chief executive (and his masters), just as it did with the British governor.

THE CLAMOUR FOR DEMOCRACY

Tung Chee Hwa had, increasingly, come to be seen as Beijing's lackey, often dictatorial and aloof but strangely weak and indecisive in times of crisis. Despite his poor standing in the polls, Tung was returned for a second five-year term in March 2002.

Controversy continued to dog his time in office, however, most notably in March 2003, with the government's failure to contain the Severe Acute Respiratory Syndrome (SARS) epidemic at an early stage, provoking a torrent of blame. The outbreak killed 299 people, infected 1755 and all but closed Hong Kong down for weeks.

In July 2003 the government came under fire yet again over a deeply unpopular piece of new legislation when it tried to turn Article 23 of the Basic Law into legislation. The bill dealt with acts 'endangering public security', such as treason, subversion and sedition, raising fears that Hong Kong's press freedom and civil liberties would be undermined. In the face of massive public protests – of 500,000 people or more – the government shelved the bill indefinitely.

In March 2005 Tung announced his resignation as chief executive. His replacement was the bow-tie-wearing chief secretary Sir Donald Tsang, who straddled both Hong Kong's regimes as financial secretary from 1995 to 2001.

Compared to Tung, Tsang was a welcome replacement for many. On good terms with the Beijing powerbrokers, he also sustained very high public approval ratings beyond the usual

2001	2003	2006
Tung Chee Hwa follows the lead of his Beijing political masters in labelling the Falun Gong a 'vicious cult' and limits the group's activities in Hong Kong.	The Closer Economic Partnership Agreement signed with the mainland government provides favourable business opportunities to Hong Kong's investors and industries.	A flood of pregnant mainland Chinese women entering Hong Kong to give birth and claim citizenship strains Hong Kong's maternity resources, spurring a ban on heavily pregnant women entering the territory.

DOS & DON'TS

There aren't many unusual rules of etiquette to follow in Hong Kong; in general, common sense will take you as far as you'll need to go. But on matters of identity, appearance, gift-giving and the big neighbour to the north, local people might see things a little differently than you do. For pointers on how to conduct yourself at the table, see p175.

- Clothing – beyond the besuited realm of business, smart casual dress is acceptable even at swish restaurants, but save your bikini for the beach and keep your thongs/flip-flops in the hotel.
- Colours – these are often symbolic to the Chinese. Red symbolises good luck and wealth (though writing in red can convey anger or unfriendliness). White symbolises death, so think twice before giving white flowers.
- Face – think status and respect (both receiving and showing): keep your cool, be polite and order a glass of vintage champagne at the Pen or Mandarin. That'll show 'em.
- Gifts – if you want to give flowers, chocolates or wine as a gift to someone, they may appear reluctant for fear of seeming greedy, but insist and they'll give in. Don't be surprised if they don't open a gift-wrapped present in front of you, though; to do so would be impolite. Cash is the preferred wedding gift and is given in the form of *lai-si* (p16).
- Name cards – Hong Kong is name-card crazy and in business circles they are a must. People simply won't take you seriously unless you have one (be sure to offer it with both hands). Bilingual cards can usually be printed within 24 hours; try printers along Man Wa Lane in Sheung Wan or ask your hotel to direct you. Expect to pay about $200 for 100 cards.

political honeymoon period. In 2007 Tsang stood again for election, and was elected with ease. He was the first chief executive not to stand unopposed. His rival, pro-democracy activist Alan Leong, came a distant second. However, Tsang soon suffered an erosion of public confidence when he was seen to renege on a series of promises, including delaying a highly anticipated consultation on reforming the electoral process for the chief executive and legislature to make the 2012 polls more democratic. Tsang's explanation was that the current financial crisis meant democratic reforms should take a lower priority. This was seen by democratic lawmakers as a cover-up for incompetence and dishonesty.

A 'CHINESE' CITY?

Visitors returning to Hong Kong since July 1997 would see and feel little material difference walking around the city today. Perhaps the most striking thing for returning visitors from the West is the influx of a new breed of visitor: mainland Chinese, who now make up more than half the territory's visitor numbers. On the other hand, some 218,000 Hong Kong residents are working in mainland China. For better or worse, Hong Kong and mainland China are increasingly integrated.

In the summer of 2008 Hong Kong became one of the six co-hosting cities of the Beijing Olympics. Amid the Olympics euphoria, it was clear that the international spotlight belonged to Beijing, and the equestrian events held in Hong Kong were the least popular sport in the city. However, Hong Kong was the only Chinese city where visible protests were allowed during the torch relay.

In many ways Hong Kong has benefited from closer ties with the mainland. The growth in Hong Kong's tourism would have been impossible without the influx of mainland tourists, and the Closer Economic Partnership Agreement signed with the mainland government in 2003 provided favourable business opportunities to Hong Kong's investors and industries.

But closer ties with the mainland have often been met with uneasy feelings. In September 2008 melamine-tainted milk products imported from the mainland were found in Hong Kong.

2007	2009	2009
A green paper examining the possible introduction of greater representation to create a more democratic system is released; democracy campaigners accuse the government of dragging out any move towards universal suffrage.	Hong Kong's population exceeds seven million and the unemployment rate grows to almost 5% in the face of the world's worst economic crisis since the Great Depression.	Some 150,000 people, according to the organisers, attend the 20th anniversary of the candlelight vigil held in Victoria Park to mark the 4 June 1989 crackdown on pro-democracy demonstrators in Beijing.

This scandal once again reminded Hong Kong people that there are good reasons why Hong Kong should never become a Chinese city, at least not now. But might history one day identify an equal and opposite reaction going on, too? Hong Kong's dazzling success and core values arguably exert 'soft' power that influences thinking on the mainland. It might be hard to measure, but in the enclave that sheltered and inspired the fathers of powerful mainland movements (Sun Yat-sen and Zhou Enlai), it should not be dismissed.

Yearnings for democracy and the economy aside, more than 10 years on from the handover, most Hong Kong people are proud to say they are citizens of the SAR as well, crucially, as subjects of China, however confusing and problematic that dual identity might sometimes seem.

ARTS

Hong Kong's arts scene is more vibrant than its reputation suggests. There are musical ensembles of all persuasions, an assortment of theatre groups, Chinese and modern dance troupes, and numerous art organisations. A number of new venues have emerged in recent years. Government funds allow organisers to bring in top international performers, and the number of international arts festivals hosted here seems to grow each year. Chinese opera performances can be seen in both formal settings and on the street.

That said, the government could do a lot more to nurture local art, in particular: Chinese opera, which Hong Kong – thanks to historical and cultural reasons – is better positioned than anywhere else to develop; and local literature, which has been marginalised by a cultural policy favouring performance arts, especially those with a higher entertainment value.

CINEMA

Once the 'Hollywood of the Far East', Hong Kong was for decades the third-largest motion-picture industry in the world (after Mumbai and Hollywood) and the second-largest exporter. Now it produces only a few dozen films each year, down from well over 200 in the early '90s, and up to half of all local films go directly to video format. Yet Hong Kong film continues to play an important role on the world stage as it searches for a new identity in the Greater China market.

Martial Arts

Hong Kong cinema became known to the West when a former child actor appeared as a sinewy hero in a kung fu film. But before Bruce Lee unleashed his high-pitched war cry in *The Big Boss* (1971), the kung fu genre was alive and kicking. The *Wong Fei-hung* series, featuring the adventures of a folk hero, has been named by the *Guinness Book of Records* as the longest-running cinema serial dedicated to one man, with roughly a hundred episodes made from 1949 to 1970 alone. The works of the signature directors of the period – Chang Cheh, whose macho aesthetics seduced Quentin Tarantino, and King Hu, who favoured a more refined style of combat – continue to influence films today. The '70s also saw the start of another trend spearheaded by actor-director-screenwriter Michael Hui, who produced comedies satirising the realities and dreams of Hong Kong people. *Games Gamblers Play* (1974) was the highest grossing film of its time, even surpassing those of Bruce Lee.

The decade after Lee's death saw the leap to stardom of two martial artists: Jackie Chan and Jet Li. Chan's blend of slapstick and action, as seen in *Snake in the Eagle's Shadow* (1978), a collaboration with action choreographer Yuen Wo-ping (who choreographed the action on *Crouching Tiger, Hidden Dragon* and *The Matrix*), became an instant hit. He later added stunts to the formula, resulting in the hits *Police Story* and the *Rush Hour* series. Li garnered international acclaim when he teamed up with director Tsui Hark in *Once Upon a Time in China* (1991). Despite his reputation for tampering with a print hours before its premiere, Tsui introduced sophisticated visuals and rhythmic editing into the martial arts genre, most notably in Hong Kong's first special effects extravaganza, *Zu: Warriors from the Magic Mountain* (1983). As a producer, he helped to create John Woo's gangster classic *A Better Tomorrow* (1986).

New Wave

Tsui Hark belonged to the New Wave, a group of filmmakers of the late '70s and '80s who grew up in Hong Kong, and were trained at film schools overseas as well as in local TV. Their works had a more contemporary sensibility, unlike those of their émigré predecessors, and were more artistically adventurous. Ann Hui (p52), Asia's top female director, is a New Waver who has won awards both locally and overseas. *Song of the Exile* (1990), a tale about the marriage between a Japanese woman and a Chinese man just after the Sino-Japanese War, won Best Film at both the Asian Pacific Film Festival and the Rimini Film Festival in Italy.

International Acclaim

The '90s saw Hong Kong gaining unprecedented respect on the global film-festival circuit. Besides Ann Hui, Wong Kar-wai received Best Director at the Cannes Film Festival for *Happy Together* in 1997. Auteur of the cult favourite *Chungking Express* (1994), Wong is famous almost as much for his elliptical mood pieces as for his disregard of shooting deadlines. In the same year, Fruit Chan bagged the Special Jury Prize at the Locarno International Film Festival with *Made in Hong Kong*, an edgy number shot on film stock Chan had scraped together while working on other projects. Over in the pulp scene, actor-comedian Stephen Chow attracted a sizeable fan following among Western viewers shortly after he plonked himself into the director's chair. In *Shaolin Soccer* (2001) and *Kungfu Hustle* (2004), Hong Kong's two highest-grossing films to date, his signature humour is given a surreal twist by digital technology.

Tough Times

Due to changes in the market, the Hong Kong film industry sank into a gloom in the mid-'90s from which it has not recovered. The return to China also presented problems related to censorship or, more often, self-censorship. But there have been sunny patches, too. *Infernal Affairs* (2002), directed by Andrew Lau and Alan Mak, made such an impact on its release that it was heralded as a box-office miracle, though it suffered some loss in translation in Martin Scorsese's remake, *The Departed*.

Election (2005) and *Election 2* (2006), by master of Hong Kong noir Johnnie To, also enjoyed immense critical and box-office success. To, who incorporates an experimental style into the commercial form of the action film, is the only filmmaker who consistently thrills both critics and mainstream audiences.

Film Festivals & Awards

The Hong Kong International Film Festival, now in its third decade, is the best in Asia – it boasts a laudable if precarious balance of art-house choices and titles offering red-carpet opportunities. Every March and April, film buffs from all over Asia, in particular mainland China, join local viewers for a 20-day spectacle. The Hong Kong Film Awards, held at the same time, is also among the most respected in this part of the world. The Hong Kong Film Archive (p91) is a treasure trove of Hong Kong films and resources on them. If you are

top picks

HONG KONG FILMS

- *The One-Armed Swordsman* (1967) – directed by Chang Cheh, this is the first of a new style of martial-arts films featuring male heroes and serious bloodletting.
- *Days of Being Wild* (1990) – set in the '60s, this star-studded piece directed by Wong Kar-wai is steered along by the characters' accounts of seemingly mundane events.
- *Once Upon a Time in China* (1991) – the first of Tsui Hark's five-part epic follows hero Wong Fei-hung (Jet Li) as he battles government officials, gangsters and foreign entrepreneurs to protect his martial-arts school in 19th-century China.
- *Summer Snow* (1995) – directed by Ann Hui (p52), this touching story revolves around a working mother trying to cope with a father-in-law suffering from Alzheimer's disease. It was the winner of the Silver Bear at the Berlin International Film Festival.
- *The Mission* (1999) – directed by Johnnie To, this film about a quirky bunch of bodyguards hired to protect a Triad boss showcases To's innovative approach to the action genre.
- *My Life as Mcdull* (2001) – a heart-warming and sometimes poignant animated film about a pig character. Winner of the Grand Prix at the Annecy International Animated Film Festival in France.
- *The Warlords* (2007) – directed by Peter Chan, this period war film about sworn brothers forced to betray one another by the realities of war shows it is possible to please both Hong Kong and mainland audiences.

interested in spotting Hong Kong locations on film, pick up a copy of the freebie *Hong Kong Movie Odyssey Guide* from the Hong Kong Tourist Board.

ART

Hong Kong is the third-largest art market in the world by auction turnover (after New York and London). Though this is largely due to the extended boom or, some would say, the over-heating of the Chinese art market, Hong Kong art has been nimbly riding the bull wave so far.

Contemporary Hong Kong art tends not to bother itself too much with grandiose narratives about nationhood and religion, preferring to take an introverted view of the world and expressing visions of Chineseness outside of the national frame.

Roots

The most distinct group of painters and sculptors to appear in Hong Kong were the proponents of the New Ink Painting movement who came to prominence in the late 1960s. Most were artists with strong links to China or its cultural heritage. The movement aimed at reconciling Chinese and Western ideas by steering traditional Chinese ink painting towards Abstract Expressionism. Lui Shou-kwan (1919–75), who came to Hong Kong in 1948, was the earliest and the best known of the New Ink Painting artists. Lui worked for the Yau Ma Tei ferry as a pier inspector and taught in his spare time. Speaking no English, his only experience of the West was through pictures and books he borrowed from the British Council library. Many of the artists who became associated with the movement were his students.

The only major artist to break free of the dominant style of the era was Luis Chan (1905–85). Born in Panama, Chan came to Hong Kong at the age of five, where he learnt to paint from art magazines and a correspondence course. Stylistically, Chan was a loner with no apparent allegiance to any painting tradition. He was also a genius who, particularly in his post-'60s works, transformed Hong Kong into a fantastical realm of dreams and hallucinations.

Avant-Garde

The 1980s and '90s saw the coming of age of artists born after WWII, many of whom had received their training abroad. Less burdened by the need to reconcile East and West, they devoted their efforts to defining avant-garde art, often through Western mediums. They were also politically engaged. Wong Yan-kwai, a painter educated in France, was arguably the most influential artist of that period and is still one of the most accomplished today. His powerful paintings in vibrant colours are uniquely free of any social or historical context. Wong's mural graces Club 71 (p209) in Central, where he is sometimes spotted playing the blues with his friends very late at night. London-trained Antonio Mak (1951–94) is Hong Kong's most famous contemporary sculptor and he's known for his figurative pieces in cast bronze.

Contemporary

Compared to their predecessors, Hong Kong's young artists – those born in the '70s and '80s – take a more internalised view of the world. Nonetheless, their works show eloquence in a host of mediums, from Wilson Shieh's cheeky urban paintings using Chinese *gongbi* (fine-brush) techniques to Jaffa Lam's sculpture installations.

The best place to view the works of modern Hong Kong painters is the Contemporary Hong Kong Art Gallery in the Hong Kong Museum of Art (p98) in Tsim Sha Tsui. Commercial galleries that specialise in local art are Grotto Fine Art and Hanart TZ Gallery (see the boxed text, p34).

Photography & Other Arts

Besides painters, Hong Kong is endowed with enough internationally competitive photographers to fill a photography museum. Working in black and white, documentary photographer Yau Leung (1941–97) captured some of the most stunning and iconic images of 1960s Hong Kong,

ART SPACES & GALLERIES

In addition to the commercial galleries below, nonprofit exhibition spaces include Para/Site Artspace (Map p80; ☎ 2517 4620; www.para-site.org.hk/pre.htm; 4 Po Yan St, Sheung Wan; ☷ noon-7pm Wed-Sun), the most consistent and promising of the local artists' cooperatives; Fotan Art Studios (Map pp58–9; www.fotanian.com), a labyrinth of artists' lofts in vacated factory buildings set against the rolling hills of Fo Tan; the nine-storey Jockey Club Creative Arts Centre (JCCAC; Map pp100–1; ☎ 2353 1311; www.hkbu.edu.hk/jccac; 30 Pak Tin St, Shek Kip Mei; ☷ 10am-10pm Mon-Sun), which was converted from an industrial building and houses artists' studios and workshops; and Cattle Depot Artist Village (Map pp100–1; ☎ 2104 3322, 2573 1869; 63 Ma Tau Kok Rd, To Kwa Wan; ☷ 2-8pm Tue-Sun), a one-time slaughterhouse that is home to a colony of local artists. The best time to visit Fotan Art Studios and the JCCAC is during their open studios (refer to their websites for the dates). You might also try the Hong Kong Visual Arts Centre (p73) in Hong Kong Park and the Hong Kong Arts Centre (p73) in Wan Chai.

None of the following galleries charge an admission fee.

- 10 Chancery Lane Gallery (Map p78; ☎ 2810 0065; www.10chancerylanegallery.com; Ground fl, 10 Chancery Lane, Central; ☷ 10am-6pm Mon-Sat) This gallery specialises in contemporary works by local, regional and international artists.
- Amelia Johnson Contemporary (Map p80; ☎ 2548 2286; www.ameliajohnsoncontemporary.com; Ground fl, 6-10 Sin Hing St, Central; ☷ 11am-7pm Tue-Sat) This gallery shows the works of emerging and established artists from Hong Kong and overseas in a range of media. It also runs an annual exhibition of works by promising young artists.
- Edge Gallery (Map p85; ☎ 2887 0313; www.edge-gallery.com; Ground fl, 60C Leighton Rd, Causeway Bay; ☷ 11am-8pm Tue-Fri, 2-8pm Sat) This up-and-coming gallery specialises in photography, painting and mixed media art from Hong Kong and the mainland.
- Grotto Fine Art (Map p78; ☎ 2121 2270; www.grottofineart.com; 2nd fl, 31C-D Wyndham St, Central; ☷ 11am-7pm Mon-Sat) This is the only gallery that represents exclusively Hong Kong artists. It features modern and contemporary works, from painting and sculpture to installation pieces.
- Hanart TZ Gallery (Map p67; ☎ 2526 9019; www.hanart.com; Room 202, 2nd fl, Henley Bldg, 5 Queen's Rd, Central; ☷ 10am-6.30pm Mon-Sat) Hanart is la crème de la crème of art galleries in Hong Kong and was instrumental in introducing contemporary Chinese art to the world.
- Osage Gallery (www.osagegallery.com); Kwun Tong (☎ 2793 4817; 5th fl, Kian Dai Industrial Bldg, 73-75 Hung To Rd; ☷ 10am-7pm Mon-Sun); Soho (Map p78; ☎ 2537 0688; 45 Caine Rd, Lower Ground Shop 1, cnr Old Bailey St; ☷ 10.30am-7.30pm Mon-Sat, noon-5pm Sun) With an 8000-sq-ft warehouse-style exhibition space in Kwun Tong and a smaller branch in Soho, this gallery specialises in Hong Kong, Chinese and Asian art.
- Schoeni Art Gallery (www.schoeni.com.hk; ☷ 10.30am-6.30pm Mon-Sat); Soho (Map p78; ☎ 2869 8802; 21-31 Old Bailey St); Central (Map p78; ☎ 2542 3143; 27 Hollywood Rd) This Swiss-owned gallery, the Central branch of which has been a feature on Hollywood Rd for almost a quarter of a century, specialises in neo-realist and postmodern mainland Chinese art.
- Sin Sin Fine Art (Map p88; ☎ 2858 5072; www.sinsin.com.hk; Ground fl, 1 Prince's Tce, Soho; ☷ 10.30am-7.30pm Tue-Sat, 2-7pm Sun) This eclectic gallery owned and run by a local fashion designer shows Hong Kong, mainland Chinese and Southeast Asian art.
- YY9 Gallery (Map pp62–3; ☎ 2574 3370; www.2bsquare.com; Ground fl, 83-85 Sing Woo Rd, Happy Valley; ☷ 10am-7pm Mon-Sat) Founded by a furnishing design consultant, this gallery shows local contemporary art in a range of media, from painting and photography to sculpture and ceramics.

while art photographer So Hing-keung (1959–) focuses on the shadows, figurative and literal, of the city, in creations known for their psychological depth. Some of the works of Hong Kong photographers can be seen in the Heritage Museum (p128).

Contemporary ceramics is another field in which Hong Kong artists enjoy an edge beyond the city's borders. Fiona Wong, one of the city's best-known ceramic artists, makes life-sized sculptural works of clothing, shoes and other familiar items.

The best sources for up-to-date information on contemporary Hong Kong and Asian art are the free monthly *Art Map* (www.artmap.com.hk), the Asia Art Archive (Map p80; ☎ 2815 1112; www.aaa. org.hk; 11th fl, Hollywood Centre, 233 Hollywood Rd, Sheung Wan; ☷ 10am-6pm Mon-Sat) and the Hong Kong International Association of Art Critics (www.aicahk.org), which has online reviews of exhibitions in the city.

MUSIC
Western
CLASSICAL
Western classical music is very popular in Hong Kong. The territory boasts the Hong Kong Philharmonic Orchestra, the Hong Kong Sinfonietta and the City Chamber Orchestra of Hong Kong. The city is a stop on the international classical music touring circuit, so opportunities to see big-name soloists and major orchestras abound throughout the year, especially during the Hong Kong Arts Festival (p15) in February/March. The Hong Kong International Piano Competition (http://chshk.brinkster.net) with its star-studded jury is held once every three years in October/November. The Academy for Performing Arts (www.hkapa.edu) has free concerts almost daily.

JAZZ
Jazz is hotting up in Hong Kong. The best time to experience world-class jazz in the city is during the Hong Kong International Jazz Festival (www.hkjazz.org) in November and the Hong Kong Arts Festival (p15) in February/March. Hong Kong also has a small but zealous circle of local musicians, including the 17-piece Saturday Night Jazz Orchestra (www.saturdaynight-jazz.com), which plays Big Band sounds every month, and Basic Notes (www.basicnotesbigband.com), formed by a group of jazz aficionados. Other names to watch out for include guitarist Eugene Pao, the first local jazz artist to sign with an international label, and pianist Ted Lo, who has played with Astrud Gilberto and Herbie Hancock.

Traditional Chinese
You won't hear much traditional Chinese music on the streets of Hong Kong, except perhaps the sound of the doleful *di-dáa,* a clarinet-like instrument played in funeral processions; the hollow-sounding *gú* (drums) and crashing *làw* (gongs) and *bạt* (cymbals) at lion dances; the *yi-wú,* a two-stringed fiddle favoured by beggars for its plaintive sound; or strains of Cantonese opera wafting from the radio of a minibus driver. You can sample this kind of music, albeit in a form adapted to a symphony orchestra model, at concerts given by the Hong Kong Chinese Orchestra (www.hkco.org). For more authentic fare, catch a Chinese opera or check out the Temple Street Night Market, where street performers deliver operatic excerpts.

Canto-Pop
Hong Kong's home-grown popular music scene is dominated by 'Canto-pop' – compositions that often blend Western rock, pop and R&B with Chinese melodies and lyrics. For a screaming, Day Gloed spectacle, attend a concert at the Hong Kong Coliseum in Hung Hom. Better still, try singing it at one of the territory's many karaoke bars. There are also acts making their marks from the edge of the mainstream, such as Chet Lam, an 'urban folk' singer-songwriter, and the Pancakes, a one-girl act who sings mostly in English.

THEATRE
Much, though not all, theatre in Hong Kong is Western in form, if not content. Traditional Chinese theatre can still be experienced, but Western theatre has been very influential. Most productions are staged in Cantonese, and a large number are new plays by Hong Kong writers. The fully professional Hong Kong Repertory Theatre (www.hkrep.com) and Chung Ying Theatre Company (www.chungying.com) put on Cantonese productions, very often with English titles. Theatre du Pif (www.thtduplf.com), formed by a professional Scottish-Chinese couple, puts on innovative works incorporating text, movement and visuals, in English and/or Cantonese. Theatre Action (http://theatreaction.blogspot.com) tackles literary drama texts from Jean Genet to Charlotte Perkins Gilman. Hong Kong Players (www.hongkongplayers.com), consisting of expatriate amateurs, mounts classical and modern productions in English. And Zuni Icosahedron (www.zuni.org.hk) creates conceptual multimedia works known for their experimental format.

Among the more popular venues are the Fringe Club theatres (p220) in Central. The Hong Kong Cultural Centre (p220), Hong Kong Academy for the Performing Arts (p219), Hong Kong City Hall (p219) and the Hong Kong Arts Centre (p219) all host foreign productions, ranging from large-scale Western musicals to minimalist Japanese theatre.

Chinese Opera

Chinese opera *(hei kuk)*, one of the three oldest dramatic art forms in the world, is a colourful, cacophonous spectacle featuring music, singing, martial arts, acrobatics and acting. It is a world away from its Western counterpart and admittedly can take some getting used to. Female characters, whether played by men or women, sing in falsetto. The instrumental accompaniment often takes the form of drumming, gonging and other nonmelodic punctuation. And the whole affair can last four to six hours. But the costumes are splendid and the plots are adapted from legends and historical tales with universal themes. If you happen to attend a performance by a leading Cantonese opera troupe such as Chor Fung Ming, you'll experience some of the best moments of Chinese opera.

Cantonese opera *(yuet-kɐk)* is a regional variety of Chinese opera that has evolved very well in Hong Kong, thanks to a different historical trajectory that has allowed it to retain its traditional features while incorporating influences from newer art forms such as cinema. Though born in Guangdong, it flourished in Hong Kong, particularly in the 1950s when opera virtuosi fleeing China composed and performed a spate of original works in the territory. But soon the limelight shifted to the sleek, leather-clad kid on the block – cinema, and things have been going downhill for Cantonese opera since. A shortage of performance venues is a problem. The privately owned Sunbeam Theatre (p220) in North Point is the last remaining Cantonese opera theatre in Hong Kong. Despite running three shows a day, it faces a closure crisis every few years when its lease expires, due to exorbitant land prices and government nonchalance.

The best way to experience Cantonese opera is by attending a 'performance for the gods' *(sun kung hei)* in a temporary theatre. During major Chinese festivals, such as the Lunar New Year, Mid-Autumn Festival and Tin Hau Festival, rural communities invite troupes to perform. The performances usually take place on a makeshift stage set up in a temple or a bamboo shed, and it is a jovial, laid-back event for the whole family that lasts several days.

For a more formal experience, try the Hong Kong Arts Festival (p15) in February/March. Ko Shan Theatre (www.lcsd.gov.hk/CE/CulturalService/KST) also has Cantonese opera offerings. But the most reliable venue for opera performances year-round is Sunbeam Theatre. At other times, you might stumble upon a performance at the Temple Street Night Market (p158) in Yau Ma Tei.

You can also check out the enlightening Cantonese-opera display at the Hong Kong Heritage Museum (p128), where the HKTB (p290) offers a Chinese-opera appreciation course every Saturday from 2.30pm to 3.45pm.

Other varieties of Chinese opera being performed in Hong Kong by local and/or visiting troupes include Peking opera, a highly refined form that uses almost no scenery but different kinds of traditional props; and Kun opera, the oldest form and one designated a Masterpiece of the Oral and Intangible Heritage of Humanity by Unesco.

LITERATURE

Hong Kong has long suffered from the misconception that it does not have a literature of its own, a situation not helped by the official lack of support for literary writing. But, in fact, the city has seen a thriving microclimate in the vast landscape of Chinese literature, where the same sun shining on other parts of China has spawned distinct smells, textures and voices.

From the 1920s to the '40s, Hong Kong was a haven for Chinese writers on the run. These émigrés continued their writing here, their influence lasting until the '70s when the first generation of writers born and/or raised locally came into their own. The relative creative freedom offered by the city has spawned works in a variety of genres and subjects, from prose poems to experimental novels, from swordplay romance to life as a make-up artist for the dead.

Hong Kong Collage: Contemporary Stories and Writing (ed Martha PY Cheung; 1998) is an important collection of fiction and essays by 15 contemporary local writers. *To Pierce the Material Screen: an Anthology of Twentieth Century Hong Kong Literature* (ed Eva Hung; *Renditions;* 2008) is a two-volume anthology featuring established figures, younger names and emerging voices, and spans 75 years. In *From the Bluest Part of the Harbour: Poems from Hong Kong* (ed Andrew Parkin; 1996), 12 modern poets reveal the emotions of Hong Kong people in the run-up to 1997. For critical articles on Hong Kong literature, check out the special Hong Kong issue (winter 2008) of the *Journal of Modern Literature in Chinese* (Lingnan University of Hong Kong).

The major literary festival in the city is the Hong Kong Literary Festival (June–July).

TRANSLATED HONG KONG FICTION

Many works by local Chinese writers have been translated into English, among other languages. Hong Kong's English bookstores carry some of them, but it's probably easier to buy or order directly from the publishers. Both the anthology mentioned in the introduction and many of the works listed below can be found in Renditions (☎ 2609 7399; www.renditions.org/renditions), a leading journal of Chinese literature in English published by the Chinese University of Hong Kong. The Hong Kong University Press (☎ 2550 2703; www.hkupress.org) also publishes works by local Chinese writers.

- *The Cockroach and Other Stories*, by Liu Yichang (*Renditions*; 1995) – Liu Yichang (1918–), Hong Kong's most respected senior writer, is believed to have written the first stream-of-consciousness novel in Chinese literature. 'The Cockroach' is a Kafkaesque exploration of psychology and philosophy. In 'Indecision', a woman is torn between staying in Hong Kong and returning to her mad husband in Shanghai.
- *Flying Carpet: A Tale of Fertillia*, by Xi Xi (Hong Kong University Press; 2000) – Xi Xi (1938–) is one of Hong Kong's most versatile and original fiction writers. This novel chronicles the rise and fall of one family and the development of a poor village into a modern metropolis, all told in the voice of a little girl who speaks with mythic insight.
- *A Girl Like Me and Other Stories*, by Xi Xi (ed Eva Hung; *Renditions*; 1996) – the narrator in the title story is a make-up artist for the dead, who feels doomed by her macabre job to a pale and loveless existence. The book also includes excerpts from *Elegy for a Breast,* the writer's personal account of her battle with cancer.
- *Islands and Continents: Short Stories*, by Leung Ping-kwan (ed John Minford; Hong Kong University Press; 2007) – anti-heroes enter the limelight against the background of Hong Kong history. In 'Postcolonial Affairs of Food and the Heart', a man devours the culinary and erotic delights of other cultures in a bid to find his identity. Leung (see the boxed text on p38) also published the bilingual *Travelling with a Bitter Melon: Selected Poems (1973–1998)*.
- *Love In a Fallen City. And Other Stories*, by Eileen Chang – Chang (1920–95) is considered by some to be the best modern Chinese writer. In the title story set during WWII, a divorcée pursues a liaison with a playboy from Shanghai to Hong Kong. Director Ann Hui (p52) made it into a film starring Chow Yun-fat. Chang also wrote *Lust, Caution*, a tale of love and espionage, which was adapted for film by Ang Lee.
- *My City: A Hong Kong Story*, by Xi Xi (*Renditions*; 1993) – this novel offers a personal vision of Hong Kong in the '60s and '70s through the lives of a telephone repairman, his family, friends and, come to think of it, pineapples and stationery. *Asia Weekly* ranked it one of the top 100 works of 20th-century Chinese fiction.
- *The Literary Review* 'Hong Kong Issue' (summer 2004) – featuring works by Liu Yichang, Xi Xi and Hong Kong poets, including Leung Ping-kwan.
- *Renditions* Nos 29 & 30 'Hong Kong' – a gem-studded anthology that includes 'Intersection', which inspired Wong Kar-wai's film *In the Mood for Love* (p32). Penned by Liu Yichang, it shows how the lives of two strangers crisscross in ways determined by the nature of the city. There are also stories by Ni Kuang, a prolific martial arts and sci-fi writer, who co-wrote screenplays with director Chang Cheh.
- *Renditions* No 45 'Eileen Chang' – a special issue on literary legend Eileen Chang, featuring fiction, drawings, photographs and critiques. In 'From the Ashes', Chang shrewdly relates life at the University of Hong Kong, where she was a student, in the wake of the Japanese attack.
- *Renditions* Nos 47 & 48 'Hong Kong Nineties' – a collection of '90s Hong Kong fiction. Two writers to watch are Wong Bik-wan (1961–) and Dung Kai-cheung (1969–). Wong, a flamenco dancer, writes with a violent passion. 'Plenty and Sorrow' is a tale about Shanghai, with a chunk of cannibalism thrown in. Dung recreates the legend of the Father of Chinese Agriculture in 'The Young Shen Nong'.

ARCHITECTURE

Welcome to the most dazzling skyline in the world. We defy you not to be awed as you stand for the first time at the harbour's edge in Tsim Sha Tsui and see Hong Kong Island's majestic panorama of skyscrapers marching up those steep jungle-clad hills.

This spectacle is thanks to the fact that in Hong Kong buildings are knocked down and replaced with taller, shinier versions almost while your back is turned. The scarcity of land, the pressures of a growing population and the rapacity of developers drive this relentless cycle of destruction and construction.

Over the years Hong Kong has played host to everything from Taoist temples and Qing dynasty forts to Victorian churches and Edwardian food markets, not that you'd know it walking down the average street. Commercial imperatives and the almost inexhaustible demand for social housing have resulted in these high-rise forests.

ART VERSES INVISIBILITY: LEUNG PING-KWAN

Why is food one of your favourite metaphors? (See 'Tea-Coffee', p174, and 'Basin Feast', p173.) When Hong Kong was returned to China in 1997, the West says, 'Poor you!', and China tells us, 'You should be happy!' But the reality is neither. Most of us aren't eager to embrace China's new nationalism, nor do they miss colonial days. But we carry on loving and eating. So instead of heroic tragedies, I write about the wear and tear of daily life, about history, about our emotional complexities through food and romance.

What are some of the features of Hong Kong literature? A mature urban sensibility. It was exploring the individual's psychology when mainland Chinese literature focused on collective values, experimenting with modernism when the latter was writing realist narratives about the building of a nation. Today the best mainland fiction is that depicting the lives of peasants – rural problems are the concern of contemporary China; but portrayals of urban life or foreign cultures tend to be melodramatic and clichéd. By contrast, Hong Kong literature talks about both with much greater sophistication.

Why is Hong Kong literature so 'invisible'? We don't have our own literary museum; our government does not promote literature through international cultural exchange. Our society and its representative media are commercially oriented and lack cultural vision. The Chinese government doesn't recognise Hong Kong literature because it's evolved for the most part under colonial rule, and words are ideology.

An interview with Hong Kong poet Leung Ping-kwan, aka 'Ya Si' (1948–).

Impressive though it might be on first acquaintance, there are downsides. The bulk of building here is of uninspired office and apartment blocks sprouting cheek by jowl in towns throughout the territory.

The government's risible record in preserving architecturally important buildings went almost entirely unregretted by the public at large until very recently. The destruction of the iconic Queen's Pier in Central marked a surprising reversal in public apathy. Heartfelt protests greeted the wrecking balls in late 2006, not that they did any good.

But things are looking slightly better. Anxious to make up for the Queen's Pier faux pas and to avoid another one, the government announced that the Wan Chai Market (p76) – a 70-year-old building in the Streamline Moderne architectural style and a conservation minefield – will be partially preserved. The Central District Police Station (p77) will also stay, but the debate now is whether the proposed design of a bamboo-scaffolding-like structure by the Swiss architect is 'preservation' or 'stereotyping', Suzie Wong–style.

In Kowloon the former Marine Police Headquarters in Tsim Sha Tsui has been turned into a hotel, but the original landscape has been razed completely by the developer. In an unprecedented move, the government launched a scheme (www.heritage.gov.hk) for the 'revitalisation' of historic monuments, which allows nonprofit organisations to pitch for the use of these buildings.

Despite the shortcomings of its new policy, the government seems at last to be heeding, albeit clumsily, the rising calls for heritage preservation.

TRADITIONAL CHINESE & COLONIAL ARCHITECTURE

About the only examples of precolonial Chinese architecture left in urban Hong Kong are Tin Hau temples that date back from the early to mid-19th century, including those at Tin Hau near Causeway Bay, Stanley, Aberdeen and Yau Ma Tei. Museums located in Chai Wan and Tsuen Wan have preserved a few Hakka village structures that predate the arrival of the British. For anything more substantial, however, you have to go to the New Territories or the Outlying Islands, where walled villages, fortresses and even a 15th-century pagoda can be seen.

Colonial architecture is also in short supply. Most of what is left is on Hong Kong Island, especially in Central, such as the Legislative Council building (formerly the Supreme Court; p68), built in 1912, and Government House (p67), residence of all British governors from 1855 to 1997. In Sheung Wan there is Western Market (1906; p82), and in the Mid-Levels the Edwardian-style Old Pathological Institute, now the Hong Kong Museum of Medical Sciences

(1905; p88). The Old Stanley Police Station (1859; p95) and nearby Murray House (1848; p95) are important colonial structures on the southern part of Hong Kong Island.

The interesting Hong Kong Antiquities & Monuments Office (Map p104; ☎ 2721 2326; www.amo.gov.hk; 136 Nathan Rd, Tsim Sha Tsui; ☼ 9am-5pm Mon-Sat), located in a British schoolhouse that dates from 1902, has information and exhibits on current preservation efforts.

CONTEMPORARY ARCHITECTURE

Hong Kong's verticality was born out of necessity – the scarcity of land and the sloping terrain have always put property at a premium in this densely populated place. Some buildings, such as Central Plaza (p73) and Two International Finance Centre (p69), have seized height at all costs; others are smaller but revel in elaborate detail, such as the Hongkong & Shanghai Bank building (p61). A privileged few, such as the Hong Kong Convention & Exhibition Centre (p73), have even made the audacious move to go horizontal.

Though the Hongkong & Shanghai Bank building and the Hong Kong International Airport in Chep Lap Kok (1998) – both by English architect Norman Foster, in Late Modern high-tech style – may be Hong Kong's best known modern architecture, there are quite a number of fine modernist buildings in the territory designed by old masters. The Lippo Centre (Map p72; 89 Queen's Way, Admiralty), which resembles koalas hugging a tree, is a pair of office towers built in 1987 by American Paul Rudolph.

The new Hong Kong Club building (Map p67; 1 Jackson Rd, Central), a reincarnation of Hong Kong's first gentlemen's club, was designed by Australian Harry Siedler in the '80s and features opposing concave and convex curves reminiscent of a swimming stingray. The deceptively modest-looking Mandarin Oriental (p240) was built in 1963 by John Howarth of Leigh & Orange Architects, a firm headquartered in Hong Kong.

For more on Hong Kong's contemporary architecture, pick up a copy of the illustrated pocket guide *Skylines Hong Kong*, by Peter Moss, or the more specialist *Hong Kong: A Guide to Recent Architecture*, by Andrew Yeoh and Juanita Cheung.

top picks

OLD AS NEW

- **Chi Lin Nunnery (p114)** Built to last a millennium, Hong Kong's only Buddhist nunnery is an immaculate replica of a Tang-dynasty monastery, a work of art in timber that embodies a flair and finesse rarely seen in faux-ancient architecture.
- **Crown Wine Cellars (p189)** This Unesco award–winning former ammo depot featuring underground wine cellars and a restaurant with bunkers was the last place in Hong Kong to surrender to the Japanese in WWII.
- **Maryknoll Convent School (Map pp100–1; ☎ 2336 0611; 130 Waterloo Rd, Kowloon Tong; MTR Kowloon Tong, 🚌 minibus 25)** A russet sprawl of cloistered courtyards and medieval towers, Hong Kong's most beautiful school was set up in 1937 to provide an inspired alternative to colonial-style education. Call about open days.
- **Shek Kip Mei Estate, Mei Ho House (Map pp100–1; Block 41, Shek Kip Mei Estate, Sham Shui Po; MTR Shek Kip Mei, exit A)** A future youth hostel, there's grace in the simplicity of this remaining block of Hong Kong's earliest public housing estate, built in 1953 for the victims of a squatter fire.
- **Nan Lian Garden (Map pp58–9; ☎ 3658 9311; www.nanliangarden.org)** This splendid Tang-style garden connected to Chi Lin Nunnery is adorned with a pagoda, tea pavilion (p198), koi pond, Buddhist pines, and sedimentary boulders resembling clouds.
- **Pawn (p180)** Four tenement houses and a century-old pawn shop make up this contemporary dining address in old Wan Chai.

ECONOMY

Soon after the handover, Hong Kong slumped into a recession as a result of the Asian financial crisis. The internet stock bubble provided a brief rebound, but when it burst the economy headed further south. More blows came in the form of 11 September 2001 and the deadly SARS epidemic. The economy finally bottomed out in mid-2003. But a little help from the Central Government, such as allowing individual tourists from the mainland to visit the city, soon had the economy back on its feet, and the stock market entered a four-year bull run until October 2007.

During the downturn, there was talk – ill-advised as it turned out – that Shanghai was the new Asian world city and Hong Kong was doomed to become a mere backwater. A mature economic hub, Hong Kong has the infrastructure and a clear rule of law, vital to business, that had taken decades to build. As China's epoch-making rise shifts into high gear, the city's expertise and infrastructure become vital to the development of Shanghai and Shenzhen as emerging financial centres. Most of the largest mainland enterprises are listed here, making Hong Kong the de facto financial centre of China.

For better or worse, Hong Kong's economic well-being is increasingly tied to the fortunes of China. Mainland tourists, having surged by half since the easing of travel restrictions, are now the largest source of tourism dollars. Local enterprises, from banks to retailers, are eager to tap the northern market for profit.

Hong Kong has the world's third-busiest port and the seventh-largest stock exchange, with a market capitalisation of $1.62 trillion. The value of initial public offerings handled here is second-highest in the world after London. And the city's economy is the most liberal in Asia, enjoying low taxes, a modern and efficient port and airport, excellent worldwide communications and strict anticorruption laws.

Critics would say that while Hong Kong's annual per capita GDP of US$29,134 (compared to China's $2982) makes it one of the richest cities in Asia, it is less impressive than it looks. The distribution of that wealth is far from even. Hong Kong has more billionaires than most countries, but many more people – in particular the losers of the knowledge economy and mainland migrants – struggle to meet fairly basic levels of subsistence.

In recent decades, Hong Kong has moved from labour- to capital-intensive industries – service industries employ about 85% of Hong Kong's workforce and make up more than 88% of its GDP. Telecommunications, banking, insurance, tourism and retail sales have pushed manufacturing into the background.

The change may have seen a dramatic increase in wages, but there has not been a comparable expansion of the welfare state, though welfare spending has shot up much faster than government spending since the 1990s. On the other hand, the government maintains a low tax regime, relying heavily on revenue from land sales and stamp duty on stock trading. Profit tax is only 16%. Generous personal tax allowances mean only a little more than 40% of the working population pays any salaries tax at all and a mere 0.3% pays the full 16%. The heaviest tax burden falls on the middle class, engendering much dissatisfaction.

ENVIRONMENT & PLANNING

THE LAND

Hong Kong measures 1104 sq km and is divided into four major areas: Hong Kong Island, Kowloon, the New Territories and the Outlying Islands.

Hong Kong Island covers 81 sq km, or just over 7% of the total land area. It lies on the southern side of Victoria Harbour, and contains Central, the main business district. Kowloon is a peninsula on the northern side of the harbour. The southern tip, an area called Tsim Sha Tsui (pronounced *jìm-sàa-jéui*), is a major tourist area. Kowloon only includes the land south of Boundary St, but land reclamation and encroachment into the New Territories gives it an area of about 48 sq km, or just over 4% of the total. The New Territories occupies 747 sq km, or more than 68% of Hong Kong's land area, and spreads out like a fan between Kowloon and the border with mainland China. What was once the territory's rural hinterland has become in large part a network of 'New Towns'. The Outlying Islands refers to the territory's 234 islands, but does not include Hong Kong Island or Stonecutters Island, which is off the western shore of the Kowloon peninsula and has been absorbed by land reclamation. Officially, the Outlying Islands are part of the New Territories and their 228 sq km make up just over 20% of Hong Kong's total land area.

Almost half the population lives in the New Territories, followed by Kowloon (30%), Hong Kong Island (19%) and the Outlying Islands (2%). A tiny percentage (about 3000 people) live at sea. The overall population density is 6400 people per sq km and the population may already have reached seven million.

GREEN HONG KONG

When you finally reach it, Hong Kong's countryside is very lush, and although only 12% of the land is forested, some 415 sq km (or 40% of the territory's total landmass) has been designated as protected country parks. These 23 parks – for the most part in the New Territories and Outlying Islands, but encompassing the slopes of Hong Kong Island too – comprise uplands, woodlands, coastlines, marshes and all of Hong Kong's 17 freshwater reservoirs. In addition, there are 15 'special areas' (eg Tai Po Kau Nature Reserve), as well as four protected marine parks and one marine reserve.

Hong Kong has an estimated 3100 species of indigenous and introduced plants, trees and flowers, including Hong Kong's own flower, the bauhinia *(Bauhinia blakeana)*. Hong Kong's beaches and coastal areas are also home to a wide variety of plant life, including creeping beach vitex *(Vitex trifolia)*, rattlebox *(Croatalaria retusa)*, beach naupaka *(Scaevola sericea)* and screw pine *(Pandanus tectorius)*.

One of the largest natural habitats for wildlife in Hong Kong is the Mai Po Marsh (p120). There are also sanctuaries in the wetland areas of Tin Shui Wai (Hong Kong Wetland Park) and Kam Tin.

Wooded areas throughout the territory are habitats for warblers, flycatchers, robins, bulbuls and tits. Occasionally you'll see sulphur-crested cockatoos, even on Hong Kong Island, and flocks of domestic budgerigars (parakeets) – domestic pets that have managed to fly the coop.

The areas around some of Hong Kong's reservoirs shelter a large number of aggressive long-tailed macaques and rhesus monkeys, both of which are non-native species. Common smaller mammals include woodland and house shrews and bats. Occasionally spotted are leopard cats, Chinese porcupines, masked palm civets, ferret badgers, wild boar and barking deer. An interesting (but rare) creature is the Chinese pangolin, a scaly mammal resembling an armadillo that rolls itself up into an impenetrable ball when threatened.

Frogs, lizards and snakes – including the red-necked keelback, which has not one but *two* sets of fangs – can be seen in the New Territories and the Outlying Islands. Hong Kong is also home to an incredible variety of insects. There are some 240 species of butterflies and moths alone, including the giant silkworm moth with a wingspan of over 20cm.

Hong Kong waters are rich in sea life, including sharks (three-quarters of Hong Kong's 40-odd gazetted beaches are equipped with shark nets) and dolphins, such as Chinese white dolphins (see the boxed text, p142) and finless porpoises. Endangered green turtles call on Sham Wan beach on Lamma to lay eggs (see the boxed text, p135), and there are some 90 species of stony coral. One of Hong Kong's few remaining colonies of horseshoe crab lives in Tung Chung Bay, where the first part of the proposed cross-delta bridge (p309) will be built.

POLLUTION

Given Hong Kong's affluence, the city could be much cleaner if its government chose to deal with the issues. But bureaucratic inertia and commercial interests have undermined efforts to improve Hong Kong's environment. Even a small measure such as taxing plastic bags entailed years of feasibility studies, consultation and policy debate, and it is yet to happen.

Plastic bags are only the tip of the iceberg in Hong Kong's waste crisis. Three large landfills in the New Territories now absorb all of Hong Kong's daily 16,500 tonnes of municipal waste

TRAVEL GREEN IN HONG KONG

If you have difficulty breathing on days when the official air pollution index is 'low', fear not. It's not your lungs that are clouding your judgement; it's the obsolete 20-year-old yardstick (www.epd-asg.gov.hk) used by the Hong Kong government to measure air pollution. For a clearer picture, you can consult Greenpeace's Real Air Pollution Index (www.greenpeace.org/china/en/hk-airpollution-map), which follows the WHO standard.

Hong Kong's seafood selections may be impressive, but in fact many are endangered or overfished. Check out WWF's Seafood Guide (www.wwf.org.hk/eng/conservation/seafood) for ecologically friendly choices.

You don't have to be a vegetarian or tree hugger to try Hong Kong's vegetarian eateries (www.ivu.org/hkvegan/gb/hkrest.html): many are as good as any other restaurants.

VERY SUPERSTITIOUS

While Hong Kong may appear as Western as a Big Mac on the surface, many old Chinese traditions persist. Whether people still believe in all of them or just go through the motions to please parents, neighbours or coworkers is hard to say. But Hong Kong Chinese are too astute to leave something as important as luck to chance.

For all its worldly ways, Hong Kong is a surprisingly religious place. The dominant religions are Buddhism and Taoism, entwined with elements of Confucianism, ancient animist beliefs and ancestor worship. The number of active Buddhists in Hong Kong is estimated at around 700,000.

Feng Shui

Literally 'wind water', feng shui ('geomancy' in English) aims to balance the elements of nature to create a harmonious environment. Practised since the 12th century, it still influences the design of buildings, highways, parks, tunnels and gravesites. To guard against evil spirits, who can move only in straight lines, doors are often positioned at an angle. For similar reasons, beds cannot face doorways. Ideally, homes and businesses should have a view of calm water (even a goldfish tank helps). Corporate heads shouldn't have offices that face westward, otherwise profits will go in the same direction as the setting sun.

Fortune-Telling

There are any number of props and implements that Chinese use to predict the future, but the most common method of divination in Hong Kong are the *chim* ('fortune sticks') found at Buddhist and Taoist temples. They must be shaken out of a box onto the ground and then read by a fortune-teller. Palm readers usually examine both the lines and features of the hand, and may also examine your facial features.

Numerology

In Cantonese the word for 'three' sounds similar to 'life', 'nine' like 'eternity', and the ever-popular number 'eight' like 'prosperity'. Lowest on the list is 'four', which shares the same pronunciation with the word for 'death'. As a result, the right number can make or break a business, and each year the government draws in millions of dollars for charity by auctioning off automobile licence plates that feature lucky numbers. The Bank of China Tower was officially opened on 8 August 1988 (8/8/88), a rare union of the prosperous numbers. August is always a busy month for weddings. On the other hand, much like the number 13 in the West, four is avoided in Hong Kong. Many buildings don't have a 4th floor or floors ending in four. Drivers don't favour the number on their license plates either.

Zodiac

As in the Western system of astrology, the Chinese zodiac has 12 signs, but their representations are all animals. Your sign is based on the year of your birth (according to the lunar calendar). Being born or married in a particular year is believed to determine one's fortune to some extent, so some parents plan for their children's sign. The year of the dragon sees the biggest jump in the birth rate, closely followed by the year of the tiger.

Signs are also believed to influence personality. Rats are loyal worriers; oxen make excellent spouses; you'll fear the wrath of tigers; rabbits are party animals; dragons dig a good adrenalin rush; snakes bewitch; horses have wanderlust; sheep are lazy artists; monkeys make play their business; roosters shop till they drop; dogs are loving and intelligent; and you can always count on pigs.

(though they will soon be full). As space for building large landfills is limited, the government introduced waste reduction schemes in 1998, but progress has been slow. Only 40% of household waste is recycled.

Hong Kong's most pressing environmental problem is air pollution, responsible for up to 2000 premature deaths a year. Not surprisingly, it has become a highly charged political and economic issue. Mounting public pressure has forced the government to take more decisive measures in recent years to control emissions from vehicles and power plants, the major source of air pollution. Government statistics show that the emission of most air pollutants has gone down, except sulphur dioxide, thanks to increased coal burning by power plants. That said, many travellers to Hong Kong might find it hard to breathe in congested areas such as Central, Causeway Bay and Mong Kok.

Hong Kong's famed harbour suffers from years of pollution by industry and sewage. In 2001 the government built a 23.6km underground tunnel to carry 75% of the sewage away from

Victoria Harbour. The scheme has improved the quality of the water in both the harbour and at Hong Kong's 41 gazetted beaches. In 2007, 25 beaches were rated 'good' in terms of water quality, compared to 10 in 1997. Water quality ratings of beaches can be found on the website of the Environmental Protection Department (www.epd.gov.hk).

The future of Hong Kong's environment will depend not only on the city's efforts, but also on whether pollution in the greater Pearl River Delta region will be tamed. Hong Kong relies on Guangdong for much of its drinking water and fresh food. The most polluted water in Hong Kong is found in Deep Bay, which is shared with nearby Shenzhen, and Hong Kong's air quality deteriorates drastically when winds bring pollution from the north. The governments of Hong Kong and Guangdong are working together to tackle regional pollution. Though progress has been slow, their success will bring a greener Hong Kong and Pearl River Delta.

GOVERNMENT & POLITICS

The government of the Hong Kong Special Administrative Region (SAR) is a complicated hybrid of a quasi-presidential system glued awkwardly onto a quasi-parliamentary model. It is not what could be called a democratic system, although it has democratic elements.

The executive branch of government is led by the chief executive, Donald Tsang, who was selected to replace business tycoon Tung Chee Hwa, following his resignation in March 2005. Uncontested, Tsang was elected by an 800-member election committee dominated by pro-Beijing forces in June and then voted in two years later in a contested election, when he comfortably beat pro-democracy legislator Alan Leong.

The chief executive selects members (currently numbering 30) of the Executive Council, which serves effectively as the cabinet and advises on policy matters. The top three policy secretaries are the chief secretary for administration, the financial secretary and the secretary for justice. Council members are usually civil servants or from the private sector.

The 60-seat Legislative Council (LegCo) is responsible for passing legislation. It also approves public expenditure and monitors the administration. Council members are elected for four-year terms.

On average, the pro-democracy bloc commands around 65% of the popular vote in direct elections. However, only half of the 60 LegCo seats are determined through direct election, with the other 30 chosen by narrowly defined, occupationally based 'functional constituencies'. With a few exceptions, 'corporate voting' is the rule, enfranchising only a few powerful and conservative members of each functional constituency.

The judiciary is headed by the chief justice and is, according to the Basic Law, independent of the executive and the legislative branches. The highest court in the land is the Court of Final Appeal, which has the power of final adjudication. The independence of the judiciary has been strictly retained since the handover.

The 18 District Councils are meant to give Hong Kong residents a degree of control in their local areas. These councils consist of elected representatives and appointed members. They have little power in territory-wide policy matters, though their members do try to gain political capital by speaking on them. All political parties make use of District Board elections to groom second-tier politicians.

The Basic Law stipulates that the chief executive and the LegCo will 'ultimately' be elected by universal suffrage, but provides no roadmap of when and how this will happen. Pro-democracy activists are urging that universal suffrage be realised as early as possible, but China's legislators announced in late 2007 that it will be implemented for elections for the chief executive in 2017 and for the LegCo in 2020. Though some have vowed to continue to fight, many in Hong Kong, out of pragmatism, have accepted the timetable.

MEDIA

A total of 44 daily (or almost daily) newspapers and upwards of 700 periodicals are published in the well-read territory of Hong Kong. The vast majority of the publications are in Chinese. *Ta Kung Pao*, *Wen Wei Pao* and *Hong Kong Commercial Daily* all toe the government line and are

CHINESE MEDICINE

Chinese herbal medicine remains very popular in Hong Kong and seems to work best for the relief of common colds, flu and chronic conditions that resist Western medicine, such as migraines, asthma and chronic backache. The pills on sale in herbal-medicine shops are generally broad-spectrum, while a prescription remedy will usually require that you take home bags full of specific herbs and cook them into a thick, bitter broth.

It is a widely held belief in China that overwork and sex wear down the body and that such 'exercise' will result in a short life. To counter the wear and tear, some Chinese practise *jeun-bó* (the consumption of tonic food and herbs). This can – but in Hong Kong does not usually – include, for example, drinking raw snake's blood or bear's bile, or eating deer antlers, all of which are claimed to improve vision, strength and sexual potency.

Like herbal medicine, Chinese acupuncture is used to treat long-term complaints rather than acute conditions and emergencies. The exact mechanism by which acupuncture works is not fully understood. The Chinese talk of energy channels or meridians, which connect the needle insertion point to the particular organ, gland or joint being treated. The acupuncture point is sometimes quite far from the area of the body being treated, and knowing just where to insert the needle is crucial. Acupuncturists have identified more than 2000 insertion points, but only about 150 are commonly used.

pro-Beijing. According to independent surveys, the most trusted newspapers are *Ming Pao*, Hong Kong's newspaper of record, and the business-orientated *Hong Kong Economic Journal.*

This is all relative, however; the press is not entirely free and journalists are inclined to self-censor. Media watchdog Reporters Without Borders placed Hong Kong 51st in its press freedom ranking for 2008, a slump from 18th place in 2002. Mainland Chinese influence, both overt and covert, has corroded press freedom, given the eagerness of many Hong Kong media owners to curry favour with the mainland. That said, the determination of journalists to uphold it should not be underestimated. For example, investigative reporting into the disproportionately high number of school children deaths in the May 2008 earthquakes in Sichuan revealed that many schools were built with substandard materials.

Two English-language dailies, the *South China Morning Post* and *The Standard,* compete for the expatriate and Westernised Chinese markets, though there is also an English-language version of *China Daily* on sale as well as other international dailies, including the *International Herald Tribune* and the *Financial Times*. For details, see p298. For information on Hong Kong radio, see p300, and see p301 for information on TV.

FASHION

Gone are the days when entire streets in Causeway Bay and Tsim Sha Tsui were studded with the boutiques of local fashion designers. Ever since the centre of garment manufacturing shifted to the mainland in the mid-1990s, the Hong Kong fashion industry has slipped out of its sequined party dress into something less comfortable. Many designers have turned their focus to overseas markets as well as the mainland market, where their sense of style is still in high demand for things chic, from cocktail dresses to the uniforms of the Chinese national team at the 2008 Beijing Olympics.

Nonetheless, some designers maintain a presence in Hong Kong. They include New York–based Vivienne Tam (p163), who trained in Hong Kong; celebrity couturier Barney Cheng, who sews luxurious gowns for the stars; Lulu Cheung (p160), with her subtle, nature-inspired pieces; Ruby Li, a talented designer known for her edgy and feminine creations, who has plans to develop her brand in London; Ranee Kok (p165), who turns to Chinese culture and art deco for her Ranee_K label; Cecilia Yau and her gowns; and Benjamin Lau, whose Madame Benjie line consists of structured pieces noted for their fine cutting. Blanc de Chine (p159) designs mostly tailored outfits that fuse Chinese aesthetics with Western influences. And the brother-and-sister duo behind Daydream Nation (available at Harvey Nicols, GOD and IT) concoct spunky pieces with a hint of theatricality.

Some of the more popular local brands are the IT group, with its www.izzue.com hip casual-wear line and its 5cm line of easy coordinates and trendy streetwear. Shanghai Tang (p161) has off-the-rack designs that turn cheongsams and Mandarin collar jackets on their heads. Initial's 11 stores sell Japan-influenced multifunctional urbanwear for the young.

See p156 in the Shopping chapter for a rundown on clothes shopping in Hong Kong.

MEET THE LOCALS

Getting to know a local in any city opens the place up in ways the unconnected visitor will never know. This applies doubly so for Hong Kong, whose depths aren't always easy to tap.

Language isn't the only barrier for non-Cantonese-speaking travellers without local friends. Outwardly, Hong Kong's citizens can seem a buttoned-up lot. Apart from the occasional spiky hairdo or very rare tattoo, the cult of individualism so ingrained in modern Western culture is much less visible in this externally more conformist and conservatively minded society.

An undemonstrative society it may be on the outside, but of course that just means there's more passion simmering away under the surface. Look closely for the subtle emotional undertow of one of Hong Kong's arthouse movies (p31) to get a sense of what we're talking about.

Just occasionally you'll see glimpses of this passion surface in Hong Kong's increasingly vibrant arts and music scene, in its rare but energetically staged public protests, in the intensity of a horse race or in the drama of the dragon-boating season.

In this chapter a fisherman, an artist, a firebrand politician, an arthouse filmmaker and the owner of a *dai pai dong* (traditional street stall or cafe) talk about their lives, and offer their insights and tips on how to get the most from a visit to Hong Kong.

Tea ceremony at Ngong Ping Village (p138) on Lantau

Name Mr Wai Tai So
Age 66
Occupation Proprietor of the Tak Yue *dai pai dong* at 18 St Francis St, Wan Chai
Residence Wan Chai

Top: historic Blue House (p76) in Wan Chai.
Bottom: seafood and meat for sale in a dai pai dong (p174).

What should we try on the menu? Try the tea, it's pretty special, and the coconut French toast.

How long has this place been open? My parents started the business in the 1950s when I was still at primary school.

What was life like back then? It was hard. The population of Hong Kong doubled almost overnight and there was not enough food. Because of the economic situation, families started running these businesses to feed their children, but only families with lots of children were allowed to apply to run *dai pai dongs*. I'm the youngest of 10 siblings.

What was Wan Chai like? It was a lot different in those days. You used to be able to see Lion Rock in the New Territories from here, and the Peak (p89). All the buildings were four storeys high or less. Everyone used to know each other and help each other out. Now, people are strangers. It used to be a poor area with a lot of drug addicts, but middle-class people are moving in now.

Top: a butcher weighs roast duck in a wet market (p176) in Central. Bottom: Wan Chai's modern skyline – Central Plaza (p73) with the Hong Kong Convention & Exhibition Centre (p73) in the foreground.

What do you do in your time off? I don't have that much leisure time. I might play mah-jong with my neighbours or read. I used to love going to the area around Hollywood Rd (p80); I used to pass it on my way to school.

Do you think there's a future in Hong Kong for your kind of old-style dai pai dong? Not really. There's no space for large refrigerators, which new rules demand. The government won't renew family licences. It would be very difficult to carry on if my mother passed away, as she is still the official licensee. In any case, my son isn't interested in carrying on the business. The hours are long. I'm 66 and I've been opening up at 6am and locking up at 10pm six days a week for the last 30 years. The government doesn't seem to care about the old buildings or the other things that make Hong Kong special, but it's beyond our control.

Name Carrie Chau, artist and creator of the WunYing Collection
Age 30
Occupation Graphic Designer
Residence New Territories

Top: 'Tai-chi — Single Whip Dip' sculpture by Ju Ming in Exchange Square (p66) in Central.
Bottom: Hong Kong Museum of Art (p98) in Tsim Sha Tsui.

Tell us about the WunYing Collection? WunYing is my Chinese name and it's my brand. You'll find my art on posters, postcards, matchboxes, books, coasters, T-shirts, tote bags, purses, key rings, notebooks, dolls and figurines. The Homeless store (p165) in Central sells some of it.

Why did you become an artist? It's always been my childhood dream. My aim is to make art everyone can enjoy and appreciate.

Your graphic design is very distinctive and other-worldly. What inspires your art? It could be simple things in my every-day life or nature, animals, my dreams, my gran's clothes or the wings of a fly. Anything can give me inspiration.

What's it like being an artist in Hong Kong? Support from the government is limited. Luckily, businesses are willing to hire creative people for all kinds of projects. Without that it would be impossible to survive as an artist in Hong Kong.

How would you describe your art? I'd say it's pretty contra-dictory! It's possible to experience ugliness in beauty, dimness in colour and sadness from happiness. I feel a bit like an alien, an outsider looking in.

Where would you send a visitor to Hong Kong? Apart from my gallery, I'd send them to Kadoorie Farm & Botanic Garden (p119). You would not recognise it as a place in Hong Kong. I love the work of Ju Ming, check out his sculpture in Exchange Square (p66).

Name The Honourable Leng Kwok Hung (aka Long Hair)
Age 53
Occupation Legislative Council member and political activist
Residence Kowloon Bay

Top: Club 71 (p209) in Soho. Middle: one of the many karaoke bars (p216) in Hong Kong. Bottom: the dome of the Legislative Council Building (p68) in Central.

You've gone from being a radical activist and protester to being a member of the Legislative Council (LegCo). Have you been able to change the system from within? LegCo is a rubber stamp and the system doesn't work. It's like a gentlemen's club. It has no real power. All I can do is show what a sham it is and keep pressing the government for a referendum on universal suffrage. I can also fight for people's labour rights, their social security, and getting the rich to pay more of their wealth back to society.

Where do your radical politics come from in conservatively minded Hong Kong? I read a lot when I was young and became a Trotskyite. The riots in Hong Kong in 1967 during the Cultural Revolution were also a big event for me.

Will Hong Kong ever be a true democracy? I can't see it. The mainland government will always have its way. People said China would open up after the Olympic Games, but I think it's going backwards.

You're never seen without your Che Guevara T-shirt. Why Che? He was a man with great dignity and high ideals and was prepared to give up things most of us will not.

Where do you go to relax in Hong Kong? I don't get much free time, but I sometimes make it down to Club 71 (p209) or maybe find a karaoke bar (p216).

49

Name Kenny Chan
Age 43
Occupation Seafood retail
Residence Ap Lei Chau

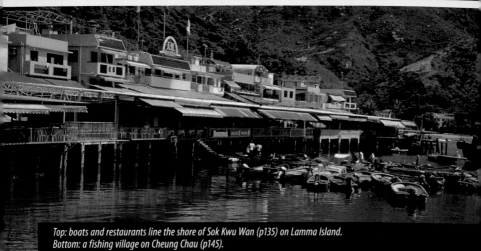

Top: boats and restaurants line the shore of Sok Kwu Wan (p135) on Lamma Island.
Bottom: a fishing village on Cheung Chau (p145).

What's a perfect day out for you? A day at sea. When I dated my wife, I took her fishing. We spent our honeymoon competing in a dragon-boat race in Thailand. We have dragon-boat practice in the typhoon shelter almost every night. On holidays, we go fishing with our daughter. You get the idea.

Where should visitors go in Hong Kong? Lamma Island (p134) for sightseeing. Ap Lei Chau for cheap seafood – buy it at the wet market below the Ap Lei Chau Market Cooked Food Centre (p190), then pay the stalls at the centre to cook it for you.

Were you a fisherman? I was in my teens. My parents were fishermen. The supermarkets have forced fishermen and fishmongers out of business.

What do you like about Hong Kong? We don't have earthquakes and bombings. We have the most dragon-boat teams in the world, and the most races – at least once a month all year round. But unlike in mainland China, none of us are paid. We're doing it because we love it!

Catch of the day at the wet market on Graham St (p176) in Central

Name Ann Hui
Age 63
Occupation Film director
Residence Hong Kong Island East

Top: locals exercising in Victoria Park (p86) in Causeway Bay. Middle: a movie monument on the Tsim Sha Tsui East Promenade (p106). Bottom: celebrity handprints on the Avenue of the Stars (p106), Tsim Sha Tsui East Promenade.

If you had a day all to yourself, what would you do? Swim at Victoria Park (p86), lunch at a *cha chaan teng* (tea cafe; p174) or McDonald's, then read at Victoria Park, and dinner at June Japanese Restaurant (p188).

What do or don't you like about Hong Kong? Like: you can be anywhere in 30 minutes. It's lively. It's receptive. Dislike: we measure everything with money.

What should visitors watch more of? Independent films. They tell you things about Hong Kong, sometimes by what they don't say. Stay away from TV dramas. Hong Kong is a lot more sophisticated than what they show you!

What do the developments in Hong Kong cinema mean for you? Big-budget, joint Hong Kong–mainland productions are the trend. If I want to continue directing feature films, I'll need to consider censorship issues and whether I'll fit in with that kind of filmmaking culture – I'm impatient and don't like being told what to do. But having always been at the margins of the mainstream, I've no qualms about directing indies or television.

Where would you want to live in your next life? Mexico, where leisure time is spent as reverently as work hours.

top picks

- Tsim Sha Tsui East Promenade (p106)
- The Peak (p89)
- The Star Ferry (p103 and p275)
- Cheung Chau (p145)
- Hiking on Lantau (p137 and p227)
- A seafood ramble on Lamma (p134)
- Tian Tan Buddha (p138)
- Ocean Park (p93)
- Sik Sik Yuen Wong Tai Sin Temple (p114)
- Hong Kong Wetland Park (p119)

What's your recommendation? www.lonelyplanet.com/hong-kong

There's much more to Hong Kong than its oft-photographed heart of glass and concrete. Much of the land area beyond its high-rise urban core comprises a striking and rugged mosaic of islands, craggy shores, mountains and jungle.

While the urban areas may be teeming with buildings and people, they are also pretty compact, hugging the coastal strips and valley bottoms. Without the suburban sprawl found in many Western cities, there's a surprising and often delightful proximity between high-density living and wild, open spaces in Hong Kong.

'there's a surprising and often delightful proximity between high-density living and wild, open spaces in Hong Kong'

In practical terms it's useful to think of Hong Kong as being divided into four main areas: Hong Kong Island, Kowloon, the New Territories and the Outlying Islands.

The beating commercial and social heart of Hong Kong lies in the first two of these areas: the skyscraper-clad northern edge of Hong Kong Island and the busy commercial and residential district of Kowloon, which face each other across Victoria Harbour. The land beyond this urban hub – most of it in the New Territories and the Outlying Islands – is far more sparsely populated and offers space, greenery and wilderness in abundance

This chapter begins in Central on the northern side of Hong Kong Island. As its name implies, this district is where much of what happens (or is decided) in Hong Kong takes place. To the west and contiguous to Central is more traditional Sheung Wan, which just about manages to retain the feel of pre-war Hong Kong in parts. Rising above Central are the Mid-Levels residential area and the Peak, home to the rich, the famous and the Peak Tram. To the east of Central are: Admiralty, a cluster of office towers, hotels and shopping centres; Wan Chai, a popular dining, shopping and entertainment area; and Causeway Bay, the most popular shopping district on Hong Kong Island.

By contrast, Hong Kong Island's southern edge is much less built up, comprising small, popular seaside towns, including Stanley – with its fashionable restaurants, cafes and famous market – and Aberdeen, Hong Kong's original settlement, where you can ride in a sampan (motorised launch) around the harbour.

North of Hong Kong Island and across Victoria Harbour is Kowloon. Its epicentre is the shopping and entertainment district of Tsim Sha Tsui. To the east are Tsim Sha Tsui East and Hung Hom, awash with hotels and museums. North of Tsim Sha Tsui are the working-class areas of Yau Ma Tei – where you'll find pawnshops, outdoor markets, Chinese pharmacies, mah-jong parlours and other retailers – and Mong Kok, a somewhat seedy district of street markets and brothels. Beyond are the districts of so-called New Kowloon, containing everything from cheap computers to Hong Kong's largest temple complex, Sik Sik Yuen Wong Tai Sin.

The New Territories is a mixed bag of uniform and architecturally bland housing estates and some surprisingly unspoiled rural areas and country parks. The real drawcards are the more tranquil areas containing old walled villages, mountains, important wetlands, forested nature reserves, and the idyllic Sai Kung Peninsula. Studded around these areas lie hundreds of islands, which are mostly uninhabited but all part of Hong Kong. Among the so-called Outlying Islands accessible on a day trip from Hong Kong Island are Cheung Chau, with its traditional village and fishing fleet; Lamma, celebrated for its restaurants and easy country walks; Lantau, the largest island of all, with excellent beaches and country trails; and tiny, laid-back Peng Chau.

The Transport boxes in this chapter provide quick reference for Mass Transit Rail (MTR), Kowloon-Canton Railway (also MTR), Light Rail and bus stations, ferry piers and tram stops in each district. For more see the Transport chapter (p271), and for suggestions on the best maps and plans, see p296.

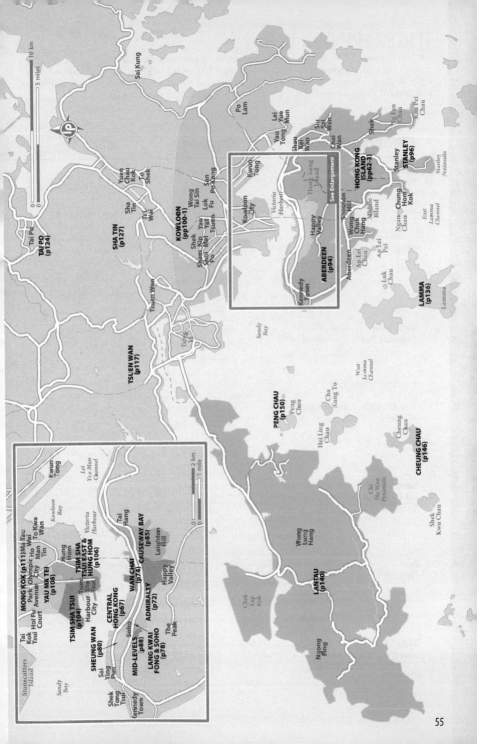

10 km
5 miles

Sai Kung

Po
Lam

Lei
Yue
Mun

Sheung
Wan

Tai Po
(p124)

Yuen
Chau
Kok
Tai
Shek

Sha
Tin

Tai
Wai

SHA TIN
(p127)

KOWLOON
(pp100-1)

Wong
Tai Sin

Yau
Yat
Tsuen

San
Po Kong

Lok
Fu

Sham
Shui
Po

Kip
Mei

Kwun
Tong

Kowloon
City

Victoria
Harbour

Hong Kong
Island

See Enlargement

HONG KONG
(pp62-3)

Siu
Sai
Wan

Chai
Wan

Shek

Stanley
STANLEY
(p96)

Stanley
Peninsula

Chung
Hom
Kok

Middle
Island

East
Lamma
Channel

Happy
Valley

ABERDEEN
(p94)

Shouson
Hill

Wong
Chuk
Hang

Aberdeen

Ap Lei
Chau

Ap Lei
Pai

Ngan
Chau

Luk
Chau

LAMMA
(p136)

Lamma

Kennedy
Town

Sandy
Bay

West
Lamma
Channel

PENG CHAU
(p150)

Peng
Chau

Cha
Kung To

Cheung
Chau

CHEUNG CHAU
(p146)

Hei Ling
Chau

Chi
Ma Wan
Peninsula

Shek
Kwu Chau

TSUEN WAN
(p117)

Tsing
Yi

Kwun
Tong

Lei
Yue Mun
Channel

Kowloon
Bay

Victoria
Harbour

Tai
Hang

Leighton
Hill

Happy
Valley

The
Peak

CAUSEWAY BAY
(p85)

WAN CHAI
(p74)

ADMIRALTY
(p72)

MONG KOK (p111)

Ma Tau
Wai

Ho Man
Tin

To Kwa
Wan

Olympic

Tai
Kok
Tsui

Hoi Fai
Court

Park
Avenue

YAU MA TEI
(p108)

Hung
Hom

TSIM SHA
TSUI EAST &
HUNG HOM (p106)

Tsim
Sha
Tsui

Harbour
City

TSIM SHA TSUI
(p104)

CENTRAL
HONG KONG
(p67)

SHEUNG WAN
(p80)

Soho

MID-LEVELS
(p88)

LANG KWAI
FONG & SOHO
(p78)

Sai
Ying
Pun

Shek
Tong
Tsui

Kennedy
Town

Stonecutters
Island

Sandy
Bay

Wong
Lung
Hang

LANTAU
(p140)

Chek
Lap
Kok

Ngong
Ping

2 km
1 mile

55

ITINERARY BUILDER

Most of the sights, activities and eating and drinking attractions in Kong Hong are concentrated into a fairly tight area comprising the northern edge of Hong Kong Island and the tip of Kowloon. Beyond these, things spread out into the larger and generally less built-up expanses of Hong Kong Island, the New Territories and the Outlying Islands.

AREA	ACTIVITIES	Outdoors	Shopping	Eating
Central & Lan Kwai Fong	Graham St Market (p65) Lan Kwai Fong & Soho (p77)	Landmark (p163) IFC Mall (p162)	Da Ping Huo (p182) L'Atelier de Joël Robuchon (p177) Lung King Heen (p177)
Sheung Wan	Man Wa Lane (p82) Possession St (p82) Western Market (p82)	Cat St (p82) Hollywood Rd (p80) Lock Cha Tea Shop (p165)	Gaia Ristorante (p184) Leung Hing Chiu Chow Seafood Restaurant (p185) Tim's Kitchen (p185)
Wan Chai & Causeway Bay	Happy Valley Racecourse (p90) Victoria Park (p86)	Times Sq (p167) Delay No Mall (p167) Coup de Foudre (p167)	Da Domenico (p186) Yin Yang (p179)
Tsim Sha Tsui	Kowloon Park (p102) Tsim Sha Tsui East Promenade (p106)	Harbour City (p169) Curio Alley (p169) Alan Chan Creations (p169) OM International (p169)	Spring Deer (p195) Hutong (p191) T'ang Court (p191) Mido Cafe (p196)
Mong Kok, Yau Ma Tei & New Kowloon	Kowloon Walled City Park (p113) Lei Yue Mun (p115)	Golden Computer Arcade (p170) Langham Place Mall (p170) Temple St Night Market (p109)	Dah Wing Wah (p200) Happy Seafood Restaurant (p199) Honeymoon Dessert (p200)
New Territories	Ng Tung Chai Waterfall & Kadoorie Farm & Botanic Garden (p119) Sai Kung Peninsula (p129) Tai Mo Shan (p118)	n/a	Nang Kee Goose Restaurant (p198) Hometown Teahouse (p203) Rainbow Seafood Restaurant (p202)
Outlying Islands	Cheung Chau walking tour (p148) Lantau Peak (p139) Lo So Shing Beach (p136)	n/a	Stoep Restaurant (p203)

HOW TO USE THIS TABLE

The table below allows you to plan a day's worth of activities in any area of the city. Simply select which area you wish to explore, and then mix and match from the corresponding listings to build your day. The first item in each cell represents a well-known highlight of the area, while the other items are more off-the-beaten-track gems.

Drinking & Nightlife	Sightseeing	Museums, Galleries, Monuments & Temples
Drop (p216) Philia (p209) Beijing Club (p216)	Hongkong & Shanghai Bank Building (p61) Hong Kong Zoological & Botanical Gardens (p65) Bank of China Buildings (p66)	Hanart TZ Gallery (p34) Statue Sq & Cenotaph (p64)
Lei Dou (p209) Barco (p208) Club 71 (p209)	Queen's Rd West Incense Shops (p81)	Man Mo Temple (p80) Dr Sun Yat Sen Museum (p88) Tai Ping Shan Temples (p82)
Champagne Bar (p211) Chinatown (p211) Pawn (p212)	Hong Kong Convention & Exhibition Centre (p73) Noonday Gun (p84) Golden Bauhinia (p73)	Hung Shing Temple (p73) Wan Chai Livelihood Museum (p76)
Deck 'n Beer (p215) Cloudnine (p218) Where (p215)	Former KCR Clock Tower (p99) Nathan Rd (p99) Peninsula Hong Kong (p102)	Hong Kong Museum of Art (p98) Hong Kong Museum of History (p107) Hong Kong Science Museum (p107)
n/a	Yuen Po St Bird Garden & Flower Market (p110) Chi Lin Nunnery (p114) Jade Market (p109)	Tin Hau Temple (p110) Sik Sik Yuen Wong Tai Sin Temple (p114)
Duke (p215) Poets (p215)	Sha Tin Racecourse (p128) Yuen Yuen Institute (p117) Hong Kong Wetland Park (p119)	Chinese University of Hong Kong Art Museum (p126) Hong Kong Heritage Museum (p128) Sam Tung Uk Museum (p118)
China Beach Club (p215) Island Society Bar (p215)	Ngong Ping (p138) Cheung Chau village (p148) Lamma Family Trail (p134)	Pak Tai Temple (p147)

HONG KONG SPECIAL ADMINISTRATIVE REGION (SAR)

10 km
5 miles

E F G H

Border
Crossing

Sha Tau Kok

Closed Area Boundary

Starling
Inlet

Kat O
Hoi

Crooked
Island

Tung
Ping Chau 30

Nam Chung
Reservoir

Luk
Keng

Yan
Chau
Tong

Crescent
Island

Tai Pang Wan
(Mirs Bay)

Hok Tau
Reservoir

Pat Sin Leng
Country Park

Bride's
Pool

Double
Island

Kat O &
Port Island
Country Parks

Port
Island

Chek Chau
Hau (Middle
Channel)

Fanling
Fanling

Hok Tau Wai

Hok Tau
Reservoir

Wong Leng
Shan
(639m)

Plover Cove
Country
Park

Hoi Ha
Wan Marine
Park

Tap Mun
Chau

9

11

KCR East

34 50 55
51

Plover
Cove
Reservoir

See Tap Mun Chau
Enlargement

River 14

Wilson Trail

Tai Po
Market

Tsung Tsai
Yuen

San Mun
Tsai

Tai Po

Tai Po
Kau

Ma Shi Chau
Protected
Area

Tolo
Channel

Lai Chi
Chong

Hoi Ha

Ko Lau Wan

18

Lead
Mine
Pass

Tai Po
Kau Nature
Reserve

Ma Liu
Shui

Ma On
Shan

Wu Kai
Sha

Nai
Chung

Sham
Chung

54

Sai Kung West
Country Park

Tai
Tan
Hoi Hap

53

Shing Mun
Country
Park

University

6
24 10

Ma On
Shan
(702m)

Sai Kung
Peninsula

Wong
Shek

Chek
Keng

Tai Long

Shing Mun
Reservoir

Racecourse

Fo Tan

Maclehose Trail

Pak
Tam Au

Ham
Tin

Tai
Long
Wan

Shing
Mun
Tunnel

Sha Tin

Ma On
Shan
Country
Park

Cham
Tau
Chau

Pak Tam
Chung

Sai Kung East
Country Park

Sai Wan

Tai Wo
Tunnel

Tai Wai

Sai
Kung

25

Kam Shan
Country
Park

Iate's
Cairn
Tunnel

Buffalo
Hill

Yim
Tin
Tsai

Pak
Sha
Chau

High Island
Reservoir

Hon Rock
Country
Park

Habi
Haven

Tai Tau
Chau

Lai Chi
Kok

Kowloon
Reservoir

Wong
Tai Sin

Diamond
Hill

Kowloon
Peak

Wilson Trail

37

Marina
Cove

Kiu Tsui
Chau

49

Trio
Beach

Port
Shelter

Kau Sai
Chau

Leung
Sheun
Wan

SOUTH
CHINA
SEA

Nam
Cheong

Kowloon
Tong

6

Tseung
Kwan O
Tunnel

Po
Lam

Tiu Chung
Chau

See
Chau

Wong
Nai
Chau

Kong
Tau Pai

Yau Ma Tei

Hung
Hom

Kwun
Tong

38

28

Po
Lam

Hang
Hau

Shelter
Island

Basalt
Island

Western
Harbour
Crossing

Tsim
Sha
Tsui

East Tsim Sha
Tsui MTR East
Rail MTR East
Terminal

Yau
Tong

High Junk
Peak
(344m)

Lang
Ha Wan

Clearwater Bay
Country Park

Bluff
Island

Cross
Harbour
Tunnel

Eastern
Harbour
Crossing

Shau
Kei
Wan

Lei Yue
Mun

Junk
Bay

Tai Au Mun

Victoria
Peak

Central

Wan
Chai

Causeway
Bay

Tseung Kwan O

Clearwater Bay

Tai Ha Shan
(273m)

Aberdeen
Tunnel

HONG KONG
ISLAND

29

46

Ap Lei
Chau

Aberdeen

Big
Wave
Bay

Joss
House
Bay

32

Tung
Lung Chau

Repulse
Bay

Stanley

Shek O

Mo Tat
Wan

Tai
Tam
Bay

Tung
O Wan

East Lamma Channel

Lo
Chau

Sung
Kong

Sham
Wan

39

Po
Toi

MAP INDEX

1 Hong Kong Island
p62–3

2 Kowloon p100–1

HONG KONG SPECIAL ADMINISTRATIVE REGION (SAR)

INFORMATION
Lo Wu HKTB Centre
羅湖旅客諮詢及服務中心 1 D2
Princess Margaret Hospital
瑪嘉烈醫院 2 E4
Tai Mo Shan Country Park
Visitor Centre
大帽山郊野公園遊客中心 3 D3

SIGHTS   (pp53-152)
Amah Rock 望夫石 4 E4
Chi Lin Nunnery 志蓮淨苑 5 E4
Chinese University of Hong
Kong 香港中文大學 6 F3
Chinese University of Hong
Kong Art Museum
香港中文大學文物館 .... (see 6)
Ching Chung Temple 青松觀 7 B3
Clearwater Bay First & Second
Beaches 清水灣一灘及二灘 8 F5
Fanling Market 粉嶺街市 9 E2
Fotan Art Studios 10 E3
Fung Ying Sin Temple
蓬瀛仙館 11 E2
Hebe Haven Yacht Club
白沙灣遊艇會 .... (see 47)
Kadoorie Farm & Botanic
Garden 嘉道理農場暨植物園 ..12 D3
Kat Hing Wai 吉慶圍 13 D3
Lam Tsuen Wishing Tree
林村許願樹 14 E2
Lantau Link Visitors Centre
青嶼幹線訪客中心 15 D4
Lions Nature Education Centre
獅子會自然教育中心 16 F3
Miu Fat Monastery 妙法寺 17 C3
Nan Lian Garden .... (see 5)
Ng Tung Chai Waterfall
梧桐寨瀑布 18 E3

Noah's Ark 19 D4
Ping Kong 20 D2
Ping Shan Heritage Trail
屏山文物徑 21 C3
Plover Cove Country Park
Visitor Centre
船灣郊野公園遊客中心 22 F2
Sai Kung Country Park Visitor
Centre
西貢郊野公園遊客中心 23 G3
Sha Tin Racecourse 沙田賽馬場 .24 E3
Sheung Yiu Folk Museum
上窰民俗文物館 25 G3
Shui Tau Tsuen 水頭 26 D2
Sik Sik Yuen Wong Tai Sin
Temple 27 E4
Silverstrand Beach 銀線灣 28 F4
Tai Miu Temple 太廟 29 F5
Tin Hau Temple 天后廟 30 H1
Tin Hau Temple 天后廟 31 A2
Tung Lung Fort 東龍洲炮台 32 G5

EATING   (pp171-204)
Chez Les Copains 33 F4
Chi Lin Vegetarian (Long Men
Lou) 龍門樓-志蓮素齋 .... (see 5)
Chung Shing Thai Restaurant
忠誠泰座泰國菜 34 F2
Dah Wing Wah 大榮華酒樓 35 C3
Happy Seafood Restaurant
歡樂海鮮酒家 36 C2
Kam Kau Kee Seafood
Restaurant
金九記海鮮火鍋酒家 37 F4
Lardos Steak House 38 F4
Ming Kee Seafood Restaurant
明記海鮮酒家 39 F6
Nang Kee Goose Restaurant
能記 40 D3

New Hon Kee 新漢記 41 A2
Pat Heung Kwun Yum Temple
八鄉觀音古廟 42 D3
Sha Tin 18 沙田18 .... (see 56)
Song Cha Xie 松茶榭 .... (see 5)

ENTERTAINMENT 🎭   (pp205-20)
Kwai Tsing Theatre 葵青劇院 43 D4
Tuen Mun Town Hall
屯門大會堂 44 C3
Yuen Long Theatre 元朗劇院 45 C3

SPORTS & ACTIVITIES   (pp221-30)
Clearwater Bay Golf & Country
Club
清水灣高爾夫球鄉村俱樂部 ...46 G5
Hebe Haven Yacht Club
白沙灣遊艇會 47 F4
Hong Kong Golf Club
香港哥爾夫球會 (粉嶺) 48 D2
Jockey Club Kau Sai Chau
Public Golf Course
賽馬會滘西洲公眾高爾夫球場
 ....49 G4
Tai Mei Tuk Fish Farm
大美督魚場 50 F2
Tai Mei Tuk Water Sports
Centre 大美督水上活動中心 ...51 F2
Tuen Mun Public Riding
School 屯門公眾騎術學校 52 B3
Wong Shek Water Sports
Centre 黃石水上活動中心 53 G3
YSO War Games 54 G3

SLEEPING 🛏   (pp231-50)
Bradbury Jockey Club Youth
Hostel
大尾篤白普理園賽馬會旅舍 ...55 F2
Hyatt Regency Hong Kong 56 F3

Hong Kong Island (or, to be more precise, the north edge of it) is the bit you usually see in the photos on tourist brochures. They seldom do justice to the feeling of actually standing looking at this dazzlingly modern metropolis clinging to steep wooded hills, and listening to the bustle and buzz of life in one of the most mesmerising islands on earth.

Hong Kong's most important district is Central, a district replete with corporate headquarters and five-star hotels, where the movers and shakers go to politick or do deals, and where wealthier visitors come to shop, eat and party. Pretty much the whole of the northern coast, between Central and Causeway Bay, is where things happen, though. It is where you'll find the ex-governor's mansion, the stock exchange, the Legislative Council and High Court, the best malls, the original horse-racing track and a host of other places that define Hong Kong's character.

One of the best ways to see the northern side of the island is to jump on one of the green double-decker trams that trundle between Kennedy Town in the west and Shau Kei Wan in the east. The southern side of Hong Kong Island has a totally different character from that of the north. The coast is dotted with fine beaches – including those at Big Wave Bay, Deep Water Bay, Shek O, Stanley and Repulse Bay – where the water is clean enough to swim.

CENTRAL

Shopping p157; Eating p176; Drinking p207; The Arts p219; Sleeping p240

All visitors to Hong Kong inevitably pass through Central (Map p67) – sightseeing, shopping, taking care of errands – en route to the bars and restaurants of Lan Kwai Fong and Soho, or boarding or getting off the Airport Express.

As Hong Kong's business centre, Central is the location for some impressive architectural one-upmanship (p37). With a compelling mix of styles, its skyscrapers offer a skyline that's utterly unique. As well as strolling around them, it's well worth standing back and taking it all in from the other side of the harbour, especially at night when these buildings put on a light show. Central is not just about skyscrapers, though. Its historic civic buildings, churches, parks and gardens are also well worth exploring.

The district was originally named Victoria, after the British sovereign who had ascended the throne just two years before a naval landing party hoisted the British flag at Possession Point west of here in 1841. But as the 'capital' of the territory, it has been called Central at least since WWII.

Above Central the residential Mid-Levels cling to steep, jungle-clad hillsides; above soars Victoria Peak, home to the super-rich and a great place from which to look back down on Central.

Though very much open to debate, Central's limits are Garden Rd to the east, somewhere between the disused Central Market and Wing On Centre to the west, Caine Rd and the Hong Kong Zoological & Botanical Gardens to the south, and the harbour to the north.

Central's main thoroughfares going west to east are Connaught Rd Central, Des Voeux Rd Central and Queen's Rd Central. Important streets running (roughly) south (ie uphill) from the harbour are Garden Rd, Ice House St, Pedder St and Pottinger St.

The best way to view Central is from the Star Ferry as it crosses the harbour from Kowloon.

HSBC BUILDING Map p67

1 Queen's Rd, Central; MTR Central (exit K)
Make sure you have a close-up look at the stunning headquarters of what is now HSBC (formerly the Hongkong & Shanghai Bank) headquarters, designed by British architect Sir Norman Foster in 1985. The building is a masterpiece of precision, sophistication and innovation. And so it

JUST LION THERE

Say hello to Stephen and Stitt, the pair of handsome bronze lions guarding the southern side of the HSBC headquarters. Named after the general managers of the two main branches in Hong Kong and Shanghai when they were cast in the 1930s, they have been through the wars (well, just one actually). Bullet scars from WWII still pepper their noble rumps and for years a piece of unexploded ordnance was lodged inside one of them until removed by a bomb disposal team. Rub their mighty paws for luck.

A pair of lion statues outside a doorway is a common sight in Hong Kong. The larger and fiercer the better, they ward off evil sprits, which all makes for good feng shui (the art of creating good energies in a building or living space; see the boxed text, p42).

MAP INDEX

1. Aberdeen p94
2. Admiralty p72
3. Causeway Bay p85
4. Central Hong Kong p67
5. Lan Kwai Fong & Soho p78
6. Mid-Levels p88
7. Sheung Wan p80
8. Stanley p96
9. Wan Chai p74

lonelyplanet.com

NEIGHBOURHOODS & ISLANDS   HONG KONG ISLAND

HONG KONG ISLAND

INFORMATION

Map Publication Centre		
地圖銷售處	1	F2
Matilda International Hospital		
明德國際醫院	2	C3
Queen Mary Hospital 瑪麗醫院	3	B3

SIGHTS   (pp53-152)

Hong Kong Film Archive		
香港電影資料館	4	F2
Hong Kong Museum of Coastal		
Defence 香港海防博物館	5	G2
Hong Kong University 香港大學	6	B2
Kwun Yam Shrine 觀音廟	7	E4
Law Uk Folk Museum		
羅屋博物館	8	G3
Longevity Bridge 長壽橋	(see 7)	
Madame Tussauds	(see 11)	
Ocean Park	9	D4
Peak Galleria	10	C3
Peak Tower 凌霄閣	11	C3
Police Museum 警察博物館	12	D3
Repulse Bay 淺水灣	13	E4
Sam Ka Tsuen Typhoon Shelter		
三家村避風塘	14	G2
Shek O Golf & Country Club		
石澳高爾夫球會	(see 41)	
University Museum & Art		
Gallery 香港大學美術博物館	(see 6)	
YY9 Gallery	15	E3

SHOPPING   (pp153-70)

Cityplaza 太古城	16	F2

EATING   (pp171-204)

Bi Yi Restaurant 巴依餐廳	17	C2
Cafe Deco	(see 10)	
Chinese Cuisine Training		
Institute 中華廚藝學院	18	B3
Chun Yeung St 春秧街	19	E2
Cococabana	20	E4
Crown Wine Cellars	21	D4
Fung Shing Restaurant		
鳳城酒家	22	E2
Gi Kee Seafood Restaurant		
銖記海鮮飯店	23	E3
Golden Valley 駿景軒	24	E3
Home Management Centre		
香港家政中心	25	E2
Lung Mun Seafood Restaurant		
龍門海鮮酒家	26	G2
Lung Yue Restaurant		
龍如海鮮酒樓	(see 26)	
Mun Nam Restaurant		
閩南小食館	27	E2
Peak Lookout 太平山餐廳	28	C3
Queen's Cafe 皇后飯店	29	E2
Sam Ka Tsuen Seafood		
Precinct	(see 26)	
Sea King Garden Restaurant		
海皇園林酒家	(see 26)	
Shek O Chinese & Thai		
Seafood 石澳中泰酒家	30	H5
Sun Chiu Kee 新釗記	31	E2
Tung Po Seafood Restaurant		
東青小館	32	E2
Verandah 露台餐廳	(see 13)	

West Villa 西苑酒家	(see 16)	
Yakitoritei 燒鳥亭	33	E3

ENTERTAINMENT   (pp205-20)

East End Brewery	34	F2
Paradiso Lounge	35	H5
Sunbeam Theatre 新光戲院	36	E2

SPORTS & ACTIVITIES   (pp221-30)

Cityplaza Ice Palace		
太古城中心滑冰皇宮	(see 16)	
Deep Water Bay Golf Club		
深水灣高爾夫球會	37	E4
Hong Kong Cricket Club		
香港木球會	38	E3
Hong Kong Tennis Centre		
香港網球中心	39	E3
Pok Fu Lam Public Riding		
School		
薄扶林公眾騎術中心	40	B3
Shek O Golf & Country		
Club 石澳高爾夫球會	41	H4

SLEEPING   (pp231-50)

City Garden Hotel Hong		
Kong 城市花園酒店	42	E2
Courtyard By Marriott		
Hong Kong 香港萬怡酒店	43	B2
Hotel Jen 仁民飯店	44	B2
Jockey Club Mount Davis		
Hostel 摩星嶺青年旅舍	45	B2
Ramada Hong Kong Hotel		
香港華美達酒店	46	B2

should be. On completion in 1985 it was the world's most expensive building (it cost upward of US$1 billion). The building reflects architect Sir Norman's wish to create areas of public and private space and to break the mould of previous bank architecture. The ground floor is public space, which people can traverse without entering the building; from there, escalators rise to the main banking hall. The building is inviting to enter – it's not guarded or off limits. Hong Kong Chinese, irreverent as always, call the 52-storey glass and aluminium structure the 'Robot Building'.

It's worth taking the escalator (🕑 9am-4.30pm Mon-Fri, 9am-12.30pm Sat) to the 3rd floor to gaze at the cathedral-like atrium and the natural light filtering through its windows.

STATUE SQUARE Map p67
Edinburgh Pl; MTR Central (exit K)

Don't be fooled by the name: Statue Square isn't full of statues. In fact just one survives here. Instead of the usual gods, warrior heroes or royalty, it's of a chubby man in a suit with a cheerful smile. This is Sir Thomas Jackson, a successful Victorian chief manager of the Hongkong & Shanghai Bank.

The square derives its name from the various effigies of British royalty once on display here, until they were spirited away by the Japanese during the occupation. While it lacks statues, there's plenty else to see. In the northern part, reached via a pedestrian underpass, is the Cenotaph (1923), a memorial to Hong Kong residents killed during the two world wars. Due west is the venerable Mandarin Oriental (p240), which opened in 1963 and is consistently voted as one of the best hotels in the world. To the east the Hong Kong Club Building (1 Jackson Rd) houses a prestigious club of that name that was still not accepting Chinese members until well after WWII. The original club building, a magnificent four-storey colonial structure, was torn down in 1981 despite public outcry and was replaced with the modern bow-fronted monstrosity there now.

On the south side of Chater Rd, Statue Square is a pleasant collection of fountains and seating areas, somewhat marred by the tiling, which gives them the look of a 1980s municipal washroom. Statue Square is also the meeting place of choice for tens of thousands of Filipino migrant workers on the weekend, especially on Sundays when it becomes a cacophony of Tagalog, Visayan and Ilocano (see boxed text, below).

MARKETS Map p67
MTR Central (exit B)
On the lower reaches west of the 800m-long Central Escalator, which transports pedestrians through Central and Soho and as far as Conduit Rd in the Mid-Levels, you'll find narrow streets containing market stalls and open-air canteens centred on the Graham St Market (Map p78).

With luck the market will still be there by the time you read this as redevelopment threatens the market's future. If it is still there, it's a compelling place to go if you want to have a close look at the exotic produce that Hong Kong prides itself in selling and consuming. Preserved 'thousand-year' eggs and fresh tofu curd scooped still steaming from wooden tubs are just some of the items on display. The squeamish should stay away, though: fish are cut lengthwise with the heart left beating so that it continues to beat and pump blood around the body, keeping it fresh.

HONG KONG ZOOLOGICAL & BOTANICAL GARDENS Map p67
☎ 2530 0154; www.lcsd.gov.hk/parks/hkzbg/en/index.php; Albany Rd; admission free; ☿ terrace gardens 6am-10pm, zoo & aviaries 6am-7pm, greenhouses 9am-4.30pm; ☒ 3B, 12, 40M or 13M from Central

top picks

TEMPLES
- Sik Sik Yuen Wong Tai Sin Temple (p114)
- Man Mo Temple (p80)
- Yuen Yuen Institute (p117)
- Ngong Ping (p138)
- Chi Lin Nunnery (p114)

This is a pleasant and surprisingly expansive collection of fountains, sculptures and greenhouses, plus a playground, zoo and some fabulous aviaries. Along with exotic trees, plants and shrubs, some 160 species of bird reside here. The zoo is surprisingly comprehensive, with more than 70 mammals and 40 reptiles, and is also one of the world's leading centres for the captive breeding of endangered species (there are 16 different species of endangered animal being bred here).

Albany Rd divides the gardens, with the plants and aviaries in the area to the east, close to Garden Rd, and most of the animals to the west. The animal displays are mostly primates (lemurs, gibbons, macaques, orang-utans etc); other residents include a rather forlorn-looking jaguar and radiated tortoises.

The gardens are at the top (ie southern) end of Garden Rd. It's an easy walk from

MAID IN HONG KONG
A large number of households in Hong Kong have an *amah*: a maid who cooks, cleans, minds the children and/or feeds the dog, and who either lives in or comes over once or twice a week. In the old days *amahs* were usually Chinese spinsters who wore starched white tunics and black trousers, put their hair in a long plait and had a mouthful of gold fillings. Their employers became their families. Today, however, that kind of *amah* is virtually extinct, and the work is now done by foreigners – young women (and increasingly men) from the Philippines, Indonesia, Nepal, Thailand and Sri Lanka on two-year renewable 'foreign domestic helper' (FDH) work visas.

Filipinos are by far the largest group, accounting for some 65% of the territory's 240,000 foreign domestic workers. While the Indonesians descend on Victoria Park and the Nepalese prefer Tsim Sha Tsui on their one day off a week (usually Sunday), Filipino *amahs* take over the pavements and public squares of Central. They come in their thousands to share food, gossip, play cards, read the Bible and do one another's hair and nails. You can't miss them around Statue Sq, Exchange Sq and the plaza below the HSBC building.

Though it doesn't seem very attractive, for young Filipinos a contract to work in Hong Kong is a dream come true and an answer to the poverty of the Philippines. Even though the minimum monthly salary is only $3500, it's still more than twice what they would earn in Singapore or Malaysia. The work is also a chance to attain, eventually, a better standard of living back home. But such opportunity doesn't come without a price. According to Hong Kong-based Asian Migrant Centre (www.asian-migrants.org), as many as 25% of foreign domestic helpers in Hong Kong suffer physical and/or sexual abuse from their employers. An organisation called the Federation of Asian Domestic Workers' Unions in Hong Kong is fighting to establish basic rights, protection from abuse and extortion, and a minimum wage in Hong Kong for these workers.

TRANSPORT – CENTRAL

Airport Express Hong Kong station below IFC Mall connects by underground walkway with Central MTR on one side and on the other to the Central ferries pier.

Bus Buses from all over the island start and end their journeys at Central bus terminus below Exchange Sq.

Central Escalator This runs from the former Central Market to the Mid-Levels.

MTR Central station on the Island and Tsuen Wan lines is at the heart of the neighbourhood.

Outlying Islands Ferry Ferries go to Discovery Bay (from pier 3), Lamma (pier 4), Cheung Chau (pier 5) and Lantau and Peng Chau (pier 6).

Peak Tram This runs from its lower terminus (33 Garden Rd) to the Peak.

Star Ferry Ferries from Tsim Sha Tsui and Hung Hom in Kowloon arrive at the Central ferries pier.

Tram The line runs east and west along Des Voeux Rd Central.

Central, but you can also take bus 3B or 12 from the stop in front of Jardine House on Connaught Rd Central or buses 40M and 13M from the Central bus terminus below Exchange Sq. The bus takes you along Upper Albert Rd and Caine Rd on the northern boundary of the gardens. Get off in front of Caritas House (Map p88; 2 Caine Rd) and follow the path across the street and up the hill to the gardens.

BANK OF CHINA BUILDINGS Map p67
MTR Central
To the east of the HSBC building is the old Bank of China (BOC) building (1 Bank St, Central), built in 1950, which now houses the bank's Central branch and, on the top three (13th to 15th) floors, the exclusive China Club, which evokes the atmosphere of old Shanghai.

The BOC is now headquartered in the awesome Bank of China Tower (1 Garden Rd) to the southeast, designed by Chinese-born American architect IM Pei and completed in 1990. This 70-storey building is Hong Kong's third-tallest structure after Two International Finance Centre in Central and Central Plaza in Wan Chai. The asymmetry of the building is puzzling at first glance, but it's really a simple geometric exercise. Rising from the ground like a cube, it is successively reduced, quarter by quarter, until the south-facing side is left to rise upward on its own.

Many local Hong Kong Chinese see the building as a huge violation of the principles of feng shui. For example, the bank's four triangular prisms are negative symbols in the geomancer's rule book; being the opposite to circles, these triangles contra-

dict what circles suggest – money, prosperity and perfection. The public viewing gallery (8am-6pm Mon-Fri) on the 43rd floor offers panoramic views of Hong Kong.

EXCHANGE SQUARE Map p67
8 Connaught Pl; MTR Central (exit A)
West of Jardine House, this complex of three elevated office towers is home to the Hong Kong Stock Exchange and a number of businesses and offices. The main draw for visitors is the attractive and relatively peaceful open-air space, featuring fountains and sculptures including Henry Moore's *Single Oval,* bronzes by Dame Elizabeth Frink and Taiwanese artist Ju Ming's memorable t'ai chi sculpture. Access is via a network of overhead pedestrian walkways stretching west to Sheung Wan and linked to many of the buildings on the other side of Connaught Rd. The ground level of the 52-storey Towers I and II is given over to the Central bus and minibus terminus.

FORMER FRENCH MISSION BUILDING Map p67
1 Battery Path; MTR Central (exit K)
The Court of Final Appeal, the highest judicial body in Hong Kong, is now housed in the neoclassical former French Mission building, a charming structure built by an American trading firm in 1868. It served as the Russian consulate in Hong Kong until 1915 when the French Overseas Mission bought it and added a chapel and a dome. The building was the headquarters of the provisional colonial government after WWII. Tree-lined Battery Path links Ice House St with Garden Rd. Just before the mission building is pretty Cheung Kong Garden, which

developers were required to lay out when they built the 70-storey Cheung Kong Centre to the south.

GOVERNMENT HOUSE Map p67
☎ 2530 2003; Upper Albert Rd; MTR Central (exit G)

Parts of this erstwhile official residence of the governor of Hong Kong, opposite the northern end of the Zoological & Botanical Gardens, date back to 1855 when Governor Sir John Bowring was in residence. Other features, including the dominant central tower linking the two original buildings, were added in 1942 by the Japanese, who used it as military headquarters during the occupation of Hong Kong in WWII. Hong Kong's first chief executive, Tung Chee Hwa, refused to occupy Government House after taking up his position in 1997, claiming the feng shui wasn't satisfactory, and his successor, Donald Tsang, has followed suit.

Government House is open to the public three or four times a year, notably one Sunday in March, when the azaleas in the mansion gardens are in full bloom.

HONG KONG CITY HALL Map p67
☎ 2921 2840; 5 Edinburgh Pl; ⏱ 9am-11pm; MTR Central (exit J3)

Southwest of Star Ferry pier, the recently face-lifted City Hall was built in 1962 and is still a major cultural venue in Hong Kong, with concert and recital halls, a theatre and exhibition galleries. Within the so-called Lower Block, but entered to the east of City Hall's main entrance, the Hong Kong Planning &

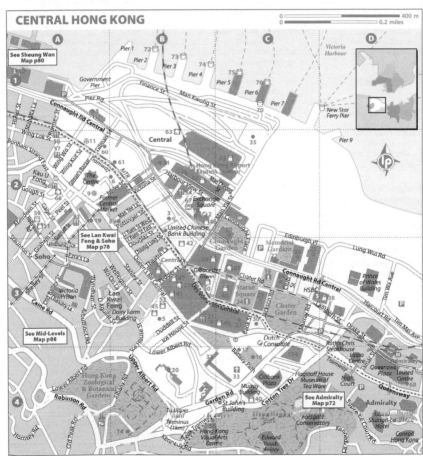

CENTRAL HONG KONG

NEIGHBOURHOODS & ISLANDS   HONG KONG ISLAND

CENTRAL HONG KONG

INFORMATION

American Chamber of
Commerce 美國商會 1 D3
Canadian Consulate
加拿大駐香港總領事館 2 B2
Chinese General Chamber of
Commerce
香港中華總商會 3 B2
Chinese Manufacturers'
Association of Hong Kong
香港中華廠商聯合會 ....(see 60)
City Hall Public Library
大會堂圖書館 ....(see 22)
Community Advice Bureau........... 4 A2
Drake International..................... 5 B3
Essential Chinese Language
Centre 主流漢語 6 B2
General Post Office
中央郵政局 7 C2
Hong Kong Labour
Department 勞工署 8 A1
IT. Fans 9 A2
Japanese Consulate
日本領事館 .... (see 2)
Macau Government Tourist
Office 澳門政府旅遊局 10 A1
PCCW i.Shop 11 A2
US Consulate
美國駐香港總領事館 12 B4

SIGHTS   (pp53-152)

Bank of China Tower
中國銀行大廈 13 C4
Botanical Gardens
Greenhouses
香港動植物公園溫室...............14 B4
Cenotaph 和平紀念碑 15 C3

Cheung Kong Garden...............16 C4
Court of Final Appeal
終審法院 17 C4
Exchange Square 18 B2
Former French Mission
Building
前法國傳道會大樓 ....(see 17)
Good Spring Co. 19 A2
Government House.....................20 B4
Hanart TZ Gallery 漢雅軒 21 B3
Hong Kong City Hall (High
Block) 香港大會堂高座 22 C3
Hong Kong City Hall (Low
Block) 香港大會堂低座 23 C3
Hong Kong Club Building
香港會所大廈 24 C3
Hong Kong Monetary
Authority Information
Centre
香港金融管理局諮詢中心... (see 35)
Hong Kong Planning &
Infrastructure Gallery
香港規劃及基建展覽館...........25 C3
Hong Kong Zoological &
Botanical Gardens 26 A4
HSBC 匯豐銀行大廈 27 C3
Jardine House 怡和大廈 28 C2
Legislative Council
Building 立法會大樓 29 C3
Old Bank of China
Building
舊中國銀行大廈 30 C3
One International Finance
Centre (One IFC)
國際金融中心一期 31 B2
SAR Government
Headquarters 政府總部 32 B4

St John's Cathedral
聖約翰座堂 33 C4
Statue Square 34 C3
Two International Finance
Centre (Two IFC)
國際金融中心二期...................35 C2
WWF For Nature Hong Kong
世界自然基金會香港辦事處... 36 B4

SHOPPING   (pp153-70)

Armani Fiori ....(see 39)
Blanc de Chine 37 B3
Bloomsbury Books 38 D3
Bookazine...............................(see 49)
Christie's................................(see 50)
Cigarro 39 B3
Cova ....(see 49)
Dymocks................................(see 31)
Fook Ming Tong Tea Shop
福茗堂 ....(see 44)
Government Publications
Office 政府刊物銷售處...........40 C4
Harvey Nichols........................(see 47)
HMV.......................................41 B3
Hong Kong Book Centre
香港圖書文具有限公司 42 B3
IFC Mall...................................43 C2
IFC Mall...................................44 B2
Joyce 45 B3
Kelly & Walsh...........................46 B2
Landmark 置地廣場 47 B3
Lane Crawford 連卡佛 ....(see 44)
Little Misses & Mini Masters.......(see 47)
Liuligongfang 琉璃工房 ....(see 41)
Lulu Cheung ....(see 47)
Mandarin Oriental Flower &
Gift Shop ....(see 65)

Infrastructure Exhibition Gallery (☎ 3102 1242; www
.infrastructure.gallery.gov.hk; 2 Murray Rd, Central; admission free; ⏰ 10am-6pm) may not sound like a
crowd-pleaser, but it will awaken the Mec-
cano builder in more than a few visitors.
The exhibition follows an 18.5m 'walk' past
recent, ongoing and future civil engineering, urban renewal and environment improvement projects, including the massive
land reclamation project underway outside
along the harbour side, which is leaving
City Hall marooned ever further inland.

JARDINE HOUSE Map p67

1 Connaught Pl; MTR Hong Kong (exit B2)
This 52-storey silver monolith punctured
with 1750 porthole-like windows was
Hong Kong's first true 'skyscraper' when it
opened as the Connaught Centre in 1973.
Inevitably the building has earned its own
irreverent nickname: the 'House of 1000
Arseholes'.

LEGISLATIVE COUNCIL BUILDING
Map p67

8 Jackson Rd; MTR Central (exit G)
The colonnaded and domed building on the
east side of Statue Square was once the old
Supreme Court. Built in 1912 of granite quar-
ried on Stonecutters Island, it has served as
the seat of the Legislative Council (LegCo)
since 1985. Standing atop the pediment is
a blindfolded statue of Themis, the Greek
goddess of justice and natural law. During
WWII it was a headquarters of the Gendar-
merie, the Japanese version of the Gestapo,
and many people were executed here. The
only time you'll see much going on is during
periodic protests (invariably well ordered
and controlled) when the council is sitting.

ST JOHN'S CATHEDRAL Map p67

☎ 2523 4157; www.stjohnscathedral.org.hk; 4-8
Garden Rd; admission free; ⏰ 7am-6pm; MTR
Central (exit J2)

CENTRAL HONG KONG

Miu Miu...(see 47)
Ocean Optical
海洋眼鏡有限公司 **48 C3**
Picture This...................................(see 49)
Prince's Building
太子大廈 **49 C3**
Shanghai Tang 上海灘 ....(see 37)
Sotheby ....(see 48)
Swank...**50 B3**
Three Sixty ....(see 47)
Toy Museum 玩具館 ....(see 49)
Vintage HK.....................................**51 A2**
Wah Tung China Arts
華通陶瓷藝術有限公司
....(see 51)
www.izzue.com **52 B3**

EATING 🍴   (pp171–204)
Amber ....(see 64)
Caprice ....(see 63)
City Hall Maxim's
Palace
大會堂美心皇宮 ....(see 23)
Crystal Jade
翡翠拉麵小籠包 ....(see 43)
Habibi **53 A2**
Habibi Cafe ....(see 53)
Hunan Garden 洞庭樓 **54 B2**
Inagiku 稻菊日本餐廳 ....(see 63)
Island Tang 港島廳 **55 B3**
L'Atelier de Joël
Robuchon..................................(see 47)
Lei Garden 利苑酒家 ....(see 43)
Lin Heung Tea House
蓮香茶樓 **56 A2**
Lung King Heen
龍景軒 ....(see 63)

Oliver's, the Delicatessen ....(see 49)
Pierre ....(see 65)
Prawn Noodle Shop
蝦麵店 **57 A2**
Pumpernickel 黑麥.......................**58 A2**
Sevva ....(see 49)
Three Sixty ....(see 47)
Zuma ....(see 47)

ENTERTAINMENT 🎭   (pp205–20)
Captain's Bar
匯豐銀行大廈 ....(see 65)
Club 71 七一吧 **59 A2**
Hong Kong City Hall (High
Block) 香港大會堂高座 ....(see 22)
Hong Kong City Hall (Low
Block) 香港大會堂低座 ....(see 23)
Mix ....(see 44)
MO Bar ....(see 47)
Oliver's, the Delicatessen ....(see 49)
Palace IFC Cinema ....(see 44)
Ponti Wine Cellars ....(see 50)
Red Bar ....(see 35)
Salon de Thé de Joël
Robuchon..................................(see 47)
Urbtix ....(see 22)

SPORTS & ACTIVITIES   (pp221–30)
Hong Kong Jockey Club
香港賽馬會 **60 A2**
Jubilee International Tour
Centre 銀禧國際旅遊 **61 B2**
Pure Fitness **62 B2**
Spa at the Four Seasons ....(see 63)

SLEEPING 🛏   (pp231–50)
Four Seasons 四季酒店 **63 B2**

Landmark Oriental **64 B3**
Mandarin Oriental
文華東方酒店 **65 C3**
Mingle Place at the Eden **66 A2**

TRANSPORT   (pp271–87)
Air New Zealand
新西蘭航空 ....(see 28)
British Airways 英國航空 ....(see 28)
Central Bus Terminus
(Exchange Sq)
中環巴士站 (交易廣場) **67 B2**
China Southern Airlines
南方航空/東方航空 **68 D4**
China Travel Service
中國旅行社 **69 B2**
HKKF Customer Service
Centre...(see 74)
New World First Ferry...................**70 C1**
Peak Tram Lower Terminus
山下纜車站 **71 C4**
Pier 2 (Ferries to Ma Wan)
二號碼頭 (往馬灣) **72 B1**
Pier 3 (Ferries to Discovery
Bay) 三號碼頭
(往愉景灣) **73 B1**
Pier 4 (Ferries to Lamma)
四號碼頭 (往南丫島) **74 B1**
Pier 5 (Ferries to Cheung
Chau) 五號碼頭
(往長洲) **75 C1**
Pier 6 (Ferries to Lantau &
Peng Chau) 六號碼頭
(往大嶼山及坪洲) **76 C1**
Qantas Airways 澳洲航空............(see 28)
Virgin Atlantic Airways
維珍航空.....................................(see 50)

Consecrated in 1849, this Anglican cathedral is one of the very few colonial structures still standing in Central. Criticised for blighting the colony's landscape when it was first erected, St John's is now lost in the forest of skyscrapers that make up Central. The tower was added in 1850 and the chancel extended in 1873.

Services have been held here continuously since the cathedral opened, except in 1944, when the Japanese Imperial Army used it as a social club. The cathedral suffered heavy damage during WWII and after the war the front doors were remade using timber salvaged from HMS *Tamar*, a British warship that used to guard the entrance to Victoria Harbour, and the beautiful stained-glass East Window was replaced. You walk on sacred ground in more ways than one at St John's: it is the only piece of freehold land in Hong Kong. There's usually a free organ concert at 1.15pm on Wednesdays. Enter from Battery Path. Around the corner

from the cathedral is the massive SAR Government Headquarters (18 Lower Albert Rd).

ONE & TWO INTERNATIONAL FINANCE CENTRE Map p67
MTR Hong Kong (exit F)
These two tapering, pearl-coloured colossi sit atop the International Finance Centre (IFC) Mall and Hong Kong station, terminus of the Airport Express and the Tung Chung lines. Both were partly designed by Cesar Pelli, the man responsible for Canary Wharf in London. One IFC (1 Harbour View St), which opened in 1999, is a 'mere' 39 levels tall. At 88 storeys, Two IFC (8 Finance St) was until recently Hong Kong's tallest (though not prettiest) building. Given the local penchant for bestowing nicknames on everything, Two IFC has been christened 'Sir YK Pao's Erection', a reference to the owner of the company that built the tower. The claimant to the title of Hong Kong's tallest building

now looms across the water in West Kowloon: the 118-floor, 484m (1590ft) International Commerce Centre (Map pp100–1).

You can't get to the top of Two IFC, but you can get pretty high up by visiting the Hong Kong Monetary Authority Information Centre (☎ 2878 1111; www.info.gov.hk/hkma/; 55th fl, Two IFC, 8 Finance St; admission free; ☒ 10am-6pm Mon-Fri, 10am-1pm Sat), which contains a research library and exhibition areas related to Hong Kong's currency, fiscal policy and banking history. There are guided tours at 2.30pm Monday to Friday, and 10.30am Saturday.

EXPLORING HONG KONG'S HEART
Walking Tour

1 Legislative Council Building Begin the walk at Statue Sq and take in the handsome outline of the neo-classical Legislative Council Building (p68), one of the few colonial-era survivors in the area and the seat of Hong Kong's modern legislature.

2 Bank of China Tower Begin walking southwest through Chater Garden park and cross over Garden Rd to the angular, modern lines of the Bank of China Tower (p66), with amazing views from the 43rd floor.

3 Flagstaff House Museum of Tea Ware Duck into Hong Kong Park for this free museum (opposite) displaying valuable pots, cups and other elegant tea ware. Sample some of China's finest teas down in the serene cafe.

4 St John's Cathedral From here take elevated walkways west over Cotton Tree Dr, through Citybank Plaza, over Garden Rd and through Cheung Kong Garden to the cathedral (p68), dating from 1849. It is a modest building to earn the title of cathedral, especially so set among the towering corporate cathedrals now surrounding it, but it is an important historic Hong Kong monument all the same.

5 HSBC building Follow Battery Path past the Former French Mission Building (p66) to Ice House St. Cross over and walk right (east) along Queen's Rd Central to the HSBC building (p61) and up the escalator, if it's open, to the large airy atrium. Walk through the ground-floor plaza to pat Stephen and Stitt (see the boxed text, p61), the two lions guarding the exit to Des Voeux Rd Central. The closest Central MTR

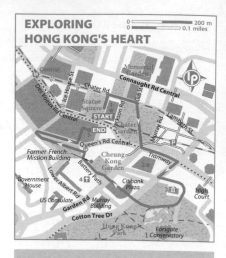

EXPLORING HONG KONG'S HEART

WALK FACTS
Start Statue Sq, Central
End Central MTR station (entrance/exit K)
Distance 1.5km
Time 45 minutes
Fuel stop Museum of Tea Ware Café

station entrance is then a short distance to the north along the pedestrian walkway between Statue Sq and Prince's Building.

ADMIRALTY & WAN CHAI
Shopping p163; Eating p178; Drinking p210; Nightlife p217; The Arts p219; Sleeping p235

To the east of Central is Admiralty (Map p72), which is very much a business district. It's an area the casual visitor might not even notice were it not for the dominating Pacific Place shopping centre (p164) and several modern buildings of note, including the blindingly gold Far East Finance Centre (Map p72; 16 Harcourt Rd), known locally as the 'Amah's Tooth' in reference to the traditional Chinese maids' preference for gold fillings and caps.

East of Admiralty is one of Hong Kong Island's most famous districts: Wan Chai (Map p74), or 'Little Bay'. Its three main roads are Jaffe, Lockhart and Hennessy Rds. The harbour is the limit to the north, and to the south it's (more or less) Queen's Rd East. Although Wan Chai had a reputation during the Vietnam War as an anything-goes red-light district, today it's a centre for shopping, business and more upmarket entertainment. If

MAXIMUM FUN, MINIMUM MONEY

Hong Kong is not a cheap place, but with a bit of planning you can spend a day in the city and spend very little money. Make it a Wednesday, which is 'admission free' day at six Hong Kong museums: Hong Kong Heritage Museum (p128), Hong Kong Museum of Art (p98), Hong Kong Museum of Coastal Defence (p91), Hong Kong Museum of History (p107), Hong Kong Science Museum (p107) and Hong Kong Space Museum (p103), excluding the Space Theatre.

Before you head out to some of these museums, why not try a free t'ai chi lesson (p227) in the morning courtesy of the Hong Kong Tourist Board.

Don't forget to catch up on your email using a free library internet terminal (p294) or using your own device and the free wifi (p294) in Hong Kong's shopping malls.

If you can't afford the entry to Ocean Park, take your own white-knuckle ride on the top deck of the bus to Shek O (p96) for some free and secluded beach action.

Make lunch your main meal of the day for the ideal combination of most calories, highest quality and lowest price. In the evening hit the bars in happy 'hour' for cheap drinks and in some cases free nibbles. Still hungry? Then get some $20 Tak Fat beef balls (p193) at this famous Tsim Sha Tsui *dai pai dong*, before putting your haggling face on and heading to the Temple Street Night Market (p109) for some shopping for inexpensive memorabilia, kitsch and crafts.

Other freebies and bargains:

- Bank of China (p66) Panoramic island views from the 43rd-floor public gallery.
- Star Ferry (p275) One of Hong Kong's must-do experiences, all for a bit of shrapnel.
- Chi Lin Nunnery (p114) Where peace and serenity doesn't cost a cent.
- Hong Kong Zoological & Botanical Gardens (p65) Free walks and gratis squawks.
- Kadoorie Farm & Botanic Garden (p119) Where the butterflies (and cows and dragonflies) are free.
- Tian Tan Buddha (p138) A cost-free superlative.
- Hong Kong Island tram (p284) A bargain ride across Hong Kong Island for a couple of dollars.

you want to see how far Wan Chai has come since then, check out the Hong Kong Convention & Exhibition Centre (p73). Don't just limit your explorations to this corner of 'new' Wan Chai, however. Sandwiched between Johnston Rd and Queen's Rd East (and also within the atmospheric area around Star St and St Francis St in Admiralty) are rows of narrow streets with all sorts of traditional shops, markets and workshops. Among these traditional commercial premises you'll also find a growing range of smart restaurants, cool bars and independent lifestyle retailers, making this Hong Kong's hippest up-and-coming neighbourhood.

HONG KONG PARK Map p72

☎ 2521 5041; www.lcsd.gov.hk/parks/hkp/en/index.php; 19 Cotton Tree Dr, Admiralty; admission free; ☼ park 6am-11pm, conservatory & aviary 9am-5pm; MTR Admiralty (exit C1), ⊞ 12A runs btwn Chater Rd in Central & Kennedy Rd, alight at the first stop on Cotton Tree Dr

Designed to look anything but natural, Hong Kong Park is one of the most unusual parks in the world, emphasising artificial creations such as its fountain plaza, conservatory, waterfall, indoor games hall, playground, t'ai chi garden, viewing tower, museum and arts centre. For all its artifice, the eight-hectare park is beautiful in its own weird way and, with a wall of skyscrapers

on one side and mountains on the other, makes for some dramatic photographs.

The best feature of the park is the delightful Edward Youde Aviary, named after a former Hong Kong governor (1982–86) and China scholar. Home to more than 600 birds representing some 90 different species, it's nothing like a conventional aviary and more like a bit of rainforest planted in the middle of the city. Visitors walk along a wooden bridge suspended some 10m above the ground and at eye level with tree branches, where most of the birds are to be found. The Forsgate Conservatory on the slope overlooking the park is the largest in Southeast Asia.

At the park's northernmost tip is the Flagstaff House Museum of Tea Ware (☎ 2869 0690; www.lcsd.gov.hk/ce/museum/arts/english/tea/Intro/eintro.html; 10 Cotton Tree Dr; admission free; ☼ 10am-5pm Wed-Mon). Built in 1846 as the home of the commander of the British forces, it is the oldest colonial building in Hong Kong still standing in its original spot. The museum, a branch of the Hong Kong Museum of Art (p98), houses a collection of antique Chinese tea ware: bowls, teaspoons, brewing trays, sniffing cups (used particularly for enjoying the fragrance of the finest oolong from Taiwan) and, of course, teapots made of porcelain or purple clay from Yixing. The ground-floor cafe is a great place to recharge over a pot of fine tea.

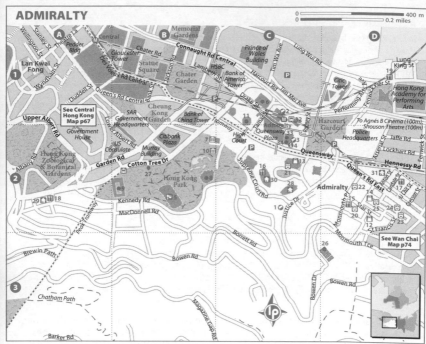

ADMIRALTY

ADMIRALTY

INFORMATION
British Consulate
英國領事館.............................. 1 C2
French Consulate
法國領事館.............................. 2 C1
German Consulate
德國領事館.............................. 3 C2
Hong Kong General
Chamber of Commerce
香港總商會.............................. 4 C2
Irish Consulate
愛爾蘭領事館.....................(see 30)

SIGHTS   (pp53–152)
Edward Youde Aviary
尤德觀鳥園.............................. 5 B2
Far East Finance Centre
遠東金融中心.......................... 6 C1
Flagstaff House Museum of
Tea Ware 茶具文物館.............. 7 B2
Forsgate Conservatory.............. 8 B2
Hong Kong Visual Arts
Centre 香港視覺藝術中心...... 9 B2
KS Lo Gallery 羅桂祥茶藝館....10 B2
Lippo Centre 力寶中心.............11 C1

SHOPPING   (pp153–70)
45R Jeans................................12 D2
Bookazine..........................(see 6)

Chinese Arts & Crafts 中藝..........(see 13)
City Chain 時間廊.................(see 13)
Hong Kong Records 香港唱片 ..(see 13)
Joyce....................................(see 13)
Kelly & Walsh......................(see 13)
Kent & Curwen...................(see 13)
Lane Crawford 連卡佛...........(see 13)
Liuligongfang 琉璃工房..........(see 13)
Pacific Custom Tailors ....(see 13)
Pacific Place 太古廣場........... 13 C2
Sonjia...................................14 D2
Vivienne Tam......................(see 13)
Wise Kids............................(see 13)

EATING   (pp171–204)
Café Too..........................(see 30)
Cine Città..............................15 D2
Great Food Hall...................(see 13)
Lock Cha Tea Shop 樂茶軒....(see 10)
Petrus 珀翠餐廳.....................16 C2
Prawn Noodle Shop 蝦麵店....17 D2
Pure Veggie House 心齋..........18 A2
Vero Lounge..........................19 D1
Yè Shanghai 夜上海...........(see 13)

ENTERTAINMENT   (pp205–20)
1/5.......................................20 D2
AMC Pacific Place..................21 C2
Classified..............................22 D2

Les Q....................................23 D2
Margaret River Wine Shop...........24 D2
Naturo+................................25 D2

SPORTS & ACTIVITIES   (pp221–30)
Bowen Road Sports Ground
寶雲道網球場........................26 D3
Hong Kong Squash Centre
香港壁球中心........................27 B2

SLEEPING   (pp231–50)
Conrad Hong Kong
香港港麗酒店........................28 C2
Garden View
女青年會園景軒......................29 A2
Island Shangri-La Hong Kong
港島香格里拉大酒店...............30 C2
Wesley Hong Kong 衛蘭軒......31 D2

TRANSPORT   (pp271–87)
Bus Station (Admiralty)
巴士站(金鐘).........................32 C1
China Eastern
南方航空/東方航空..............(see 4)
Licensing Division of the
Transport Department
運輸署牌照部........................33 C2
Singapore Airlines
新加坡航空............................34 C2

The KS Lo Gallery (☎ 2869 0690; 10 Cotton Tree Dr; admission free; ◷ 10am-5pm Wed-Mon), in a building southeast of the museum, contains rare Chinese ceramics and stone seals collected by the gallery's eponymous benefactor.

On the eastern edge of the park, the Hong Kong Visual Arts Centre (☎ 2521 3008; 7A Kennedy Rd; admission free; ◷ 10am-9pm Wed-Mon), housed in the Cassels Block of the former Victoria Barracks, supports local sculptors, printmakers and potters, and stages exhibitions.

Hong Kong Park is an easy walk from either Central or the Admiralty MTR station.

HONG KONG CONVENTION & EXHIBITION CENTRE Map p74

☎ 2582 8888; www.hkcec.com.hk; 1 Expo Dr, Wan Chai; 🚍 18

Due north of the Wan Chai MTR station, the Convention & Exhibition Centre, which was built in 1988 and extended onto an artificial island in the harbour for the hand-over in '97, has been compared with a bird's wing, a banana leaf and a lotus petal.

CENTRAL PLAZA Map p74

18 Harbour Rd, Wan Chai; 🚍 18

At just under 374m, Central Plaza, which was completed in 1992, is just 3m shorter than the newer Two IFC (p69). The glass skin of the tower has three different colours – gold, silver and terracotta – and the overall impression is rather garish. Central Plaza functions as one of the world's biggest clocks. There's method to the madness of the four lines of light shining through the glass pyramid at the top of the building between 6pm and midnight. The bottom level indicates the hour: red is 6pm, white 7pm, purple 8pm, yellow 9pm, pink 10pm and green 11pm. When all four lights are the same colour, it's right on the hour. When the top light is different from the bottom ones, it's 15 minutes past the hour. If the top two and bottom two are different, it's half-past the hour. If the top three match, it's 45 minutes past the hour. So what time is it now?

GOLDEN BAUHINIA Map p74

Golden Bauhinia Sq, 1 Expo Dr, Wan Chai; MTR Wan Chai (exit A5), 🚍 18

A 6m-tall statue (including pedestal) of Hong Kong's symbol, called the *Forever Blooming Bauhinia*, stands on the waterfront promenade just in front of the Hong Kong Convention & Exhibition Centre to mark the

TRANSPORT – ADMIRALTY

Bus Buses to and from destinations throughout Hong Kong Island operate from Admiralty bus station below Queensway Plaza and Admiralty MTR station.

MTR Admiralty station is on the Central and Tsuen Wan lines.

Tram Trams run east along Queensway, Johnston Rd and Hennessy Rd (Map p74) to Causeway Bay; and west to Central and Sheung Wan.

return of Hong Kong to Chinese sovereignty in 1997 and the establishment of the Hong Kong SAR. The flag-raising ceremony, held daily at 8am and conducted by the Hong Kong Police, has become a must-see for visiting tourist groups from the mainland. There's a pipe band on the 1st, 11th and 21st of each month at 7.45am.

HONG KONG ARTS CENTRE Map p74

☎ 2582 0200; www.hkac.org.hk; 2 Harbour Rd, Wan Chai; MTR Admiralty (exit E2)

Due east of the Academy for the Performing Arts is the Hong Kong Arts Centre. Along with theatres, including the important Agnès B Cinema (p219), you'll also find here the Pao Sui Loong & Pao Yue Kong Galleries (☎ 2824 53302582 0200; admission free; ◷ 10am-6pm, to 8pm during exhibitions). Extending over floors Nanshan four and five, there's room to host retrospectives and group shows in all visual media.

HONG KONG ACADEMY FOR THE PERFORMING ARTS Map p74

☎ 2584 8500; www.hkapa.edu; 1 Gloucester Rd, Wan Chai; MTR Admiralty (exit E2)

With its striking triangular atrium and an exterior Meccano-like frame, which is a work of art in itself, the academy building (1985) is a Wan Chai landmark and an important venue for music, dance and scholarship.

HUNG SHING TEMPLE Map p74

☎ 2527 0804; 129-131 Queen's Rd East, Wan Chai; ◷ 6am-6pm; 🚍 6 or 6A

Nestled in a nook on the southern side of Queen's Rd East, this narrow, dark and rather forbidding temple (also called Tai Wong Temple) is built atop huge boulders. It was erected in honour of a Tang-dynasty official who was known for his virtue (important) and ability to make predictions of great value to traders (ultra-important).

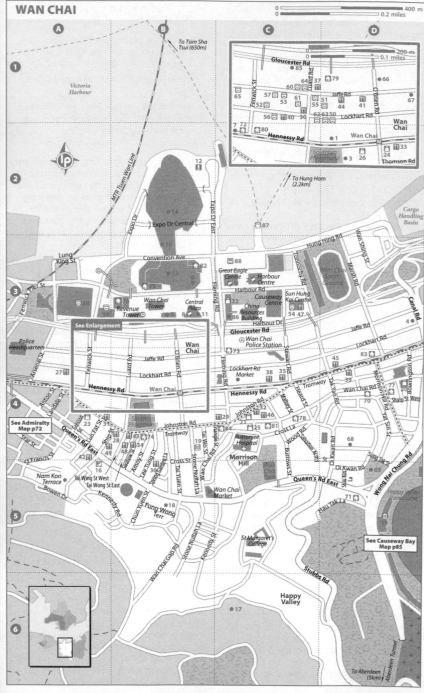

WAN CHAI

To Tsim Sha Tsui (650m)

Victoria Harbour

To Hung Ham (2.2km)

Cargo Handling Basin

MTR Tsuen Wan Line

Expo Dr

Expo Dr East

Lung King St

Fenwick Pier St

Expo Dr Central

Convention Ave

Wan Chai Tower

Central Plaza

Revenue Tower

Police Headquarters

See Enlargement

Wan Chai

Jaffe Rd

Lockhart Rd

Hennessy Rd

Wan Chai

Great Eagle Centre

Harbour Centre

Harbour Rd

Causeway Centre

China Resources Building

Harbour Dr

Sun Hung Kai Centre

Wan Chai Sports Ground

Gloucester Rd

Wan Chai Police Station

Fleming Rd

Lockhart Rd Market

Hennessy Rd

Jaffe Rd

Lockhart Rd

Tramway

Tonnochy Rd

Marsh Rd

Canal Rd

Wan Chai Rd

Morrison Hill Rd

Gresson St

Johnston Rd

Tramway

Ruttonjee Hospital

Morrison Hill

Queen's Rd East

St Francis St

Star St

Anton St

Landale St

Queen's Rd East

Tai Wing St West

Tai Wong St East

Swatow St

Amoy St

Lee Tung St

Spring Garden La

Cross St

Stone Nullah La

Tai Yuen St

Cross St

Wood Rd

Burrows St

Thomson Rd

Wan Chai

Nam Koo Terrace

Kennedy Rd

Bowen Dr

Wan Chai Market

St Margaret's College

Chun Yeung St

Fung Wang Terr

Wan Chai Gap Rd

Stone Nullah La

Kennedy St

Hau Tak La

Happy Valley

Stubbs Rd

See Causeway Bay Map p85

Wong Nai Chung Rd

Happy Valley Racecourse

Oi Kwan Rd

Shan Kwong Rd

Sung Tak La

See Admiralty Map p72

To Aberdeen (5km)

Aberdeen Tunnel

74

WAN CHAI

INFORMATION

Alliance Française
法國文化協會 1 D2
Australian Consulate
澳洲駐香港總領事館 2 C3
China Travel Service
中國旅行社 3 D2
Goethe-Institut 歌德學院 .... (see 59)
Hong Kong Federation of
Women
香港各界婦女聯合進會 4 D3
Hong Kong Immigration
Department 香港入境事務處 ... 5 B3
Hong Kong Trade
Development Council (Head
Office) 香港貿易發展局
(總辦事處) 6 B3
Joint Council for People with
Disabilities 香港復康聯會 7 C3
New Zealand Consulate
新西蘭駐香港總領事館 8 B3
South African Consulate
南非駐香港總領事館 9 C3
TDC Business InfoCentre
貿易發展局商貿資訊中心 10 B3

SIGHTS   (pp53-152)

Central Plaza 11 B3
Golden Bauhinia 金紫荊 12 B2
Hong Kong Academy for
Performing Arts
香港演藝學院 .... (see 58)
Hong Kong Arts Centre
香港藝術中心 .... (see 59)
Hong Kong Convention &
Exhibition Centre
香港會議展覽中心 13 B3
Hong Kong Convention &
Exhibition Centre (New
Wing) 香港會議展覽中心
(新翼) 14 B2
Hong Kong Racing Museum 15 D5
Hung Shing Temple 洪聖古廟 ... 16 A5
Lover's Rock 17 C6
Old Wan Chai Post Office 18 B5
Pao Sui Loong & Pao Yue Kong
Galleries
包兆龍& 包玉剛畫廊 .... (see 59)
Wan Chai Livelihood Museum ... 19 B4

SHOPPING   (pp153-70)

Bowrington Rd Market 20 D4
Bunn's Divers 賓氏潛水學院 ... 21 C4
Chinese Arts & Crafts 22 C3
Cosmos Books 天地圖書 23 A4
Design Gallery 設計廊 .... (see 13)
Joint Publishing 三聯書店 24 D2
Kung Fu Supplies
功夫用品公司 .... (see 21)

Sunmark Camping Equipment
晨峰露營用品 25 C4
Wan Chai Computer Centre
灣仔電腦城 26 D2

EATING 🍴   (pp161-94)

American Restaurant 27 A4
BO Innovation 廚魔 28 B4
Crystal Jade 翡翠拉麵小籠包 ... 29 C4
Flying Pan 30 C1
Fook Lam Moon 福臨門 31 A4
Grissini .... (see 75)
Hang Zhou Restaurant
杭州酒家 32 C4
Honolulu Coffee Shop
檀島咖啡餅店 33 D2
International Curry House
國際咖喱室 34 B4
Joy Hing Food Shop
再興燒臘飯店 35 C4
Kam Fung Cafe 金鳳茶餐廳 36 B5
Khana Khazana 37 C1
Kung Wo Tofu Factory
公和荳品 38 C4
Lei Garden 利苑酒家 39 D4
Liu Yuan Pavilion 留園雅敍 40 C1
Mang Ambo's Filipino
Restaurant 41 D1
Nino's Cozinha 42 A4
Pawn 43 B4
Sabah 44 D1
Saigon Pho 西貢越南湯河 45 D4
Tiffin Lounge .... (see 75)
Veggie Palace
貴德宮皇廷素宴 46 C4
Victoria City 海都海鮮酒家 47 C3
World Peace Cafe 天下太平 48 B4
Yin Yang 鴛鴦酒店 49 A4

ENTERTAINMENT 🎭   (pp205-20)

Agnés B Cinema .... (see 59)
Bar 109 .... 50 D1
Bridge 51 D1
Carnegie's 52 C1
Champagne Bar .... (see 75)
Chinatown 唐人街 53 C1
Cine-Art House 54 C3
Delaney's 55 C1
Devil's Advocate 56 C1
Dusk till Dawn 57 C1
Hong Kong Academy for
Performing Arts
香港演藝學院 58 A3
Hong Kong Arts Centre
香港藝術中心 59 A3
Hong Kong Convention &
Exhibition Centre (New
Wing) 香港會議 & 展覽中心
(新翼) .... (see 14)

Joe Banana's 60 C1
Mes Amis 61 C1
New Makati Pub & Disco 62 C1
Old China Hand 63 D1
Pawn .... (see 43)
Punchline Comedy Club .... (see 54)
Queen Elizabeth Stadium
伊利沙伯體育館 .... (see 69)
Skitz 64 C1
Urbtix .... (see 69)
Wanch 65 C1

SPORTS & ACTIVITIES   (pp221-30)

California Fitness 66 D1
Hong Kong Jockey Club 67 D1
Morrison Hill Public
Swimming Pool
摩利臣山公共游泳池 68 D4
Queen Elizabeth Stadium
伊利沙伯體育館 69 D5
Water Supplies Department ... (see 5)

SLEEPING 🛏   (pp231-50)

Charterhouse Hotel
利景酒店 70 D4
Cosmopolitan Hotel
香港麗都酒店 71 D5
Empire Hotel Hong Kong
香港皇悅酒店 72 C2
Fleming 芬名酒店 73 C4
Fraser Suites 74 B4
Grand Hyatt Hotel 君悅酒店 75 B3
Harbour View 香港灣景國際 ... 76 B3
Hotel Bonaparte 雅逸酒店 77 D4
JJ Hotel 君俊商務酒店 78 D1
Luk Kwok Hotel 79 D1
Metropark Hotel
灣仔維景酒店 80 C2
Mingle Place by the Park 81 C4
Renaissance Harbour View
Hotel 萬麗海景酒店 82 B3
Walden Hotel 華登酒店 83 C4
Ying King Apartment
英京迎賓館 84 C4

TRANSPORT   (pp271-87)

Buses to China .... (see 3)
China Travel Service
中國旅行社 .... (see 3)
Hong Kong Express
香港快遞 85 C1
Visa Office of the People's
Republic of China
中華人民共和國簽證辦事處 ... 86 C3
Wan Chai Ferry Pier
灣仔碼頭 87 C2
Wan Chai Ferry Pier Bus
Terminus
灣仔碼頭巴士總站 88 C3

OLD WAN CHAI POST OFFICE Map p74
Cnr Queen's Rd East & Wan Chai Gap Rd, Wan Chai; 🚌 **6 or 6A**

A short distance to the east of Wan Chai Market is this tiny but important colonial-style building erected in 1913 and now serving as a resource centre operated by the Environmental Protection Department (☎ 2893 2856; 🕙 10am-5pm Mon-Tue & Thu-Sat, 10am-1pm Wed, 1-5pm Sun).

WAN CHAI LIVELIHOOD MUSEUM
Map p74

☎ 2835 4376; http://cds.sev227.001at.com; 85 Stone Nullah Lane, Wan Chai; 🕙 11am-5pm; 🚌 6 or 6A
Established by local residents and cultural enthusiasts, this small museum in the historic Blue House (so known as it is a house and it's blue) celebrates local life over the decades in the tenement buildings around here, particularly the local handicrafts and small-scale factories once busy in the area (and in some cases still clinging on). There's also a small selection of local souvenirs.

LOVER'S ROCK Map p74
off Bowen Rd; 🚌 **green minibus 24A**

A kilometre or so northeast of the Police Museum is what the Chinese call Yan Yuen Sek, a phallus-shaped boulder on a bluff at the end of a track above Bowen Rd. This is a favourite pilgrimage site for childless women and those who think their lovers, husbands or sons could use the help of prayer and a joss stick or two. It's especially busy during the

Maidens' Festival, held on the seventh day of the seventh moon (mid-August). The easiest way to reach here is to take green minibus 24A from the Admiralty bus station. Get off at the terminus (Shiu Fai Tce) and walk up the path behind the housing complex.

OLD WAN CHAI'S FORGOTTEN STREETS
Walking Tour

1 Wanchai Livelihood Museum A short stroll from the main bus routes and Wan Chai MTR (exit A3), you'll start to get a feel for the neighbourhood as it was in the last century at this small museum (left).

2 Wan Chai Market The Streamline Moderne or Bauhaus-style exterior of this handsome and historic building is all that will remain (at least we hope it will remain…) of the market by the time you read this as a shopping centre goes up behind it. Once the hub of the neighbourhood, it was also used as a mortuary by Japanese forces in WWII.

WALK FACTS
Start Wan Chai Livelihood Museum
End Star St
Distance 1.2km
Time Two hours
Fuel stop Star Street

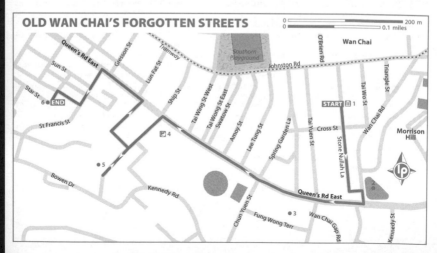

OLD WAN CHAI'S FORGOTTEN STREETS

3 Old Wan Chai Post Office This pocket-sized post office (opposite) is a charming and rare neighbourhood colonial relic.

4 Hung Shing Temple Peep inside this grand (if gloomy) temple (p73) to this civil-servant-turned-god, built in 1847.

5 55 Nam Koo Terrace Just west of the temple turn up the hill along Ship St and stand before 'the Ghost House', Hong Kong's most haunted house. Its history is a wretched one: it was used by Japanese soldiers as a brothel housing 'comfort women' in WWII. Now derelict, there are plans to turn this period building into a hotel.

6 Star St neighbourhood This is a quiet little corner of town that manages to contain the old, including a traditional, family-run *dai pai dong (daai pàai dawng)* on St Francis St (see the boxed text, p46) and the new, in the form of excellent little shops, cafes and bars. Admiralty MTR can be reached by an escalator and underground travelator entered at the bottom of Wing Fung St.

LAN KWAI FONG & SOHO

Eating p181; Drinking p208; Nightlife p216; The Arts p220
Lan Kwai Fong (Map p78), Hong Kong's party zone, has grown so fast that it is spilling out of its former boundaries – a narrow, L-shaped pedestrian street south of Queen's Rd Central and up hilly D'Aguilar St. These days the action now spills uphill along Wyndham St and up to Arbuthnot St. Popular with both Western expats and locals, in recent years it has become one of the first ports of call for mainland tour groups, although most often they're here to gawp – not to party. Lan Kwai Fong proper is a great place to head to if you want to sample the buzz of crowds of drinkers making merry en masse, especially at happy hour. If you're looking for a quiet beer or

something a tad more stylish and less beer-sodden, explore further west along Wyndham St or into Soho (from 'South Of HOllywood Rd'), which is *above* Hollywood Rd and another good hunting ground for great food and nightlife.

CENTRAL DISTRICT POLICE STATION
Map p78
10 Hollywood Rd; 🚌 26
For years a rather dismal air of abandonment has hung over this declared but boarded-up monument, which is a former police station and jail. By the time you read this, it's just possible that plans to repurpose and revamp the building as an art gallery, cinema, museum and boutique shopping mall will be taking physical shape. Defenders of Hong Kong's heritage buildings are hopeful the redevelopment plans, due for completion in 2012, will ensure the site avoids the fate of many other such sites – too often they are bulldozed to make space for a modern high-rise or suffer heavily commercialised reinterpretations, such as that visited on the handsome former Marine Police HQ in Tsim Sha Tsui (p102) – although not everyone is keen on the architect's initial concepts (see p37).

LI YUEN STREET EAST & WEST
Map p78
🕙 10am-7pm; MTR Central (exit C)
These two narrow and crowded alleyways linking Des Voeux Rd Central with Queen's Rd Central are called 'the lanes' by Hong Kong residents, and were traditionally the place to go for fabric and piece goods. Most vendors have now moved to Western Market (p82) in Sheung Wan, but while it's no great retail hunting ground you'll still find a mishmash of cheap clothing, handbags, backpacks and costume jewellery here.

LAN KWAI FONG & SOHO

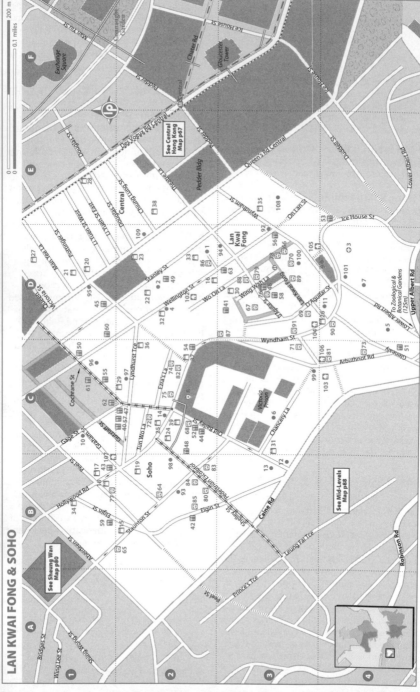

See Sheung Wan Map p80

See Central Hong Kong Map p67

See Mid-Levels Map p88

Lan Kwai Fong

Soho

Victoria Prison

To Zoological & Botanical Gardens (125m)

ICE HOUSE STREET & LOWER ALBERT RD Map p78

MTR Central (exit G)

This street has many interesting buildings. The attractive off-white stucco and red-brick structure at the top of the road is the Dairy Farm Building, built for the Dairy Farm Ice & Cold Storage Company in 1898 and renovated in 1913. Today it houses the Fringe Club (p220) and the illustrious Foreign Correspondents' Club of Hong Kong (☎ 2521 1511; www.fcchk.org). Towering above the Dairy

Farm Building on the opposite side of the road is the Bishop's House, built in 1851 and the official residence of the Anglican Bishop of Victoria.

From the Dairy Farm Building, Ice House St doglegs into Queen's Rd Central. Just before it turns north, a wide flight of stone steps leads down to Duddell St. The four wrought-iron China Gas lamps at the top and bottom of the steps were placed here in the 1870s and are listed monuments.

LAN KWAI FONG & SOHO

INFORMATION		
1010 CSL Outlet	1	D2
Color Six	2	D2
Hong Kong Central Hospital		
港中醫院	3	D4
Hong Kong Institute of		
Languages	4	D2
Martinizing	5	D4

SIGHTS	(pp53–152)	
10 Chancery Lane Gallery	6	C3
Bishop's House 主教公署	7	D4
Central District Police		
Station	8	C2
Dairy Farm Building	(see 9)	
Foreign Correspondents'		
Club of Hong Kong	(see 9)	
Fringe Club 藝穗會	9	D4
Graham St Market		
嘉咸街街市	10	C1
Grotto Fine Art 嘉圖	11	D4
Osage Gallery	12	B3
Schoeni Art Gallery	13	B3
Schoeni Art Gallery Branch	14	C2

SHOPPING	(pp153–70)	
Amours Antiques	15	B2
Anglo-Chinese Florist		
中西花店	16	D2
Arch Angel Antiques	17	B1
Arch Angel Fine Art	18	B1
Chine Gallery 華苑	19	B2
Chinese Arts & Crafts	20	D1
City Chain 時間廊	21	D1
Everbest Photo Supplies		
超然沖曬專門店	22	D2
H&M	23	D2
Hobbs & Bishops Fine Art	24	C2
Honeychurch Antiques	25	C2
Jilian, Lingerie On Wyndham	26	D4
Joint Publishing 三聯書店	27	D1
King Fook 景福珠寶	28	E1
Linva Tailor 年華時裝公司	29	C2
Mountain Folkcraft		
高山民藝	30	D3
Olympia Graeco-Egyptian		
Coffee 奧林比亞埃臣咖啡	31	C3
Pedder Red	32	D2
Photo Scientific 攝影科學	33	D2
Rock Candy	34	B1

Tai Sing Fine Antiques		
大成古玩有限公司	35	E3
Tai Yip Art Book Centre		
大業藝苑	36	C2
Teresa Coleman Fine Arts	37	C2
Tse Sui Luen 謝瑞麟珠寶	38	E2
Wattis Fine Art	39	C2

EATING	(pp171–204)	
Assaf	40	C2
Beyrouth Café Central	(see 40)	
Bon Appetit	41	D3
Cecconi's Italian	42	B2
Da Ping Huo 四川菜大平伙	43	B1
Flying Pan	44	C2
Honolulu Coffee Shop		
檀島咖啡餅店	45	D1
Koh-i-Noor 寶軒印度餐廳	46	D3
Lan Fong Yuen 蘭芳園	47	C2
Life Cafe	48	C2
Luk Yu Tea House 陸羽茶室	49	D2
Mak's Noodle 麥奀雲吞麵世家	50	C1
Mozart Stub'n	51	C4
O Sip Hah	52	C2
Olé Spanish Restaurant & Wine		
Bar	53	E4
Rughetta	54	C2
Ser Wong Fun 蛇王芬	55	C1
Sushi Kuu 壽司喰	56	D3
Tai Cheong Bakery 泰昌餅家	57	C2
Union J	58	D3
Vbest Tea House 緻好茶館	59	B1
Wang Fu 王府	60	D1
XTC	61	C1
Yellow Door Kitchen		
黃色門廚房	62	C1
Yung Kee Restaurant 鏞記	63	D3

ENTERTAINMENT	(pp205–20)	
Bar 1911	64	B2
Barco	65	B2
Beijing Club	66	D3
Bit Point	67	D3
Bohemian Lounge	68	C2
Cavern	69	D3
Club 97	70	D3
Dragon-I	71	C3
Drop	72	C2
DYMK	73	C4
Finds	(see 104)	

Fringe Gallery	(see 9)	
Fringe Studio Theatre		
香港藝穗會小劇場	(see 9)	
Gecko Lounge	74	C2
Homebase	75	C2
Insomnia	76	D3
Joyce Is Not Here	77	B1
La Dolce Vita	78	D3
Lei Dou	79	D3
Peak Cafe Bar 山頂餐廳	80	B2
Philia	81	C4
Propaganda	82	C2
Soho Wines & Spirits	83	B2
Solas	(see 71)	
Staunton's Wine Bar & Cafe	84	B2
Take Out Comedy Club	85	B2
Tastings	86	D2
Tivo	87	D3
Watson's Wine Cellar	88	D3
Whiskey Priest	89	D3
Works	90	D4
Yumla	(see 37)	
Yun Fu 雲府	91	D3

SPORTS & ACTIVITIES	(pp221–30)	
California Fitness	92	D3
DK Aromatherapy	93	D3
Elemis Day Spa	94	D3
Fightin' Fit	95	D1
Happy Foot Reflexology		
Centre 知足樂	96	C1
Healing Plants 草本堂	97	C2
Pure Fitness 萬玉堂	98	B2
Sideways Driving Club	99	C3
Yoga Central	100	D3
Yoga Fitness	101	D4

SLEEPING	(pp231–50)	
Hanlun Habitats (Main		
Office)	102	D2
Home2Home	103	C4
Hotel LKF 蘭桂芳酒店	104	D3
Ice House	105	D3
Ovolo	106	C4
Shama Main Office	107	B1

TRANSPORT	(pp271–87)	
Concorde Travel	108	E3
Natori Travel		
樂途旅遊有限公司	109	D2

SHEUNG WAN

Shopping p164; Eating p184; Drinking p210;
Sleeping p240, p237

Pockets of Sheung Wan (Map p80) still retain something of a feel of old Shanghai about them, although that is fast disappearing under the jackhammer, and many of the old 'ladder streets' (steep inclined streets with steps) that were once lined with stalls and street vendors have been cleared away to make room for more buildings or the MTR. Nevertheless this neighbourhood just west of Central is a great place to investigate on foot for its traditional shops and businesses.

Hollywood Rd, which got its name from all the holly bushes that once thrived here, is an interesting street to explore. The eastern end is lined with upmarket antique and carpet shops and trendy eateries. However, once you head west of Aberdeen St the scene changes: you'll soon be passing traditional wreath and coffin makers, as well as several funeral shops.

The limits of Sheung Wan are difficult to define, but basically the district stretches from the Sheung Wan MTR station in the east to King George V Memorial Park and Eastern St in the west. The harbour – or, rather, Connaught Rd West – is the northern border, while Hollywood Rd is the southern limit.

MAN MO TEMPLE Map p80
☎ 2540 0350; 124-126 Hollywood Rd; admission free; ◷ 8am-6pm; 🚌 26

You won't need a map to find the Man Mo Temple: just follow the smell of incense curling from giant cones suspended from the ceiling of this busy 18th-century tem-

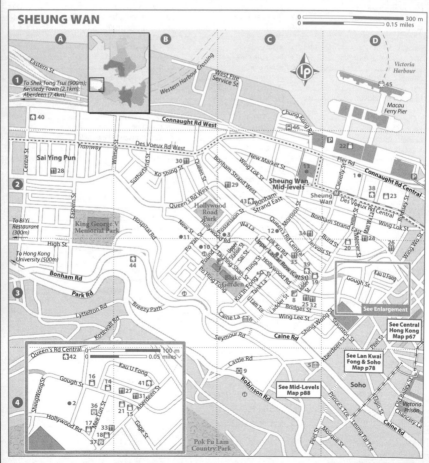

SHEUNG WAN

ple. One of the oldest and most famous in Hong Kong, Man Mo (literally 'civil' and 'martial') is dedicated to two deities. The civil deity is a Chinese statesman of the 3rd century BC called Man Cheung, who is worshipped as the god of literature and is represented holding a writing brush. The military deity is Kwan Yu (or Kwan Tai), a Han-dynasty soldier born in the 2nd century AD and now venerated as the red-cheeked god of war; he is holding a sword. Kwan Yu's popularity in Hong Kong probably has more to do with his additional status as the patron god of restaurants, pawnshops, the police force and secret societies such as the Triads (see the boxed text, p29).

Outside the main entrance are four gilt plaques on poles that are carried at procession time. Two plaques describe the gods being worshipped inside, while others request silence and respect within the temple grounds and warn menstruating women to keep out of the main hall. Inside the temple are two 19th-century sedan chairs shaped like houses, which are used to carry the two gods at festival time. The coils suspended from the roof are incense cones burned as offerings by worshippers. Off to the side are fortune-

TRANSPORT – SHEUNG WAN

Bus Buses 5 and 5A from Central call at 10 Des Voeux Rd, and bus 26 runs along Hollywood Rd between Sheung Wan and Central, Admiralty and Wan Chai.

Macau Ferry The terminal is at Shun Tak Centre.

MTR Sheung Wan station is on the Island line.

Tram These run along Des Voeux Rd Central and Des Voeux Rd West.

tellers ready and willing to tell you of your (undoubtedly excellent) fate.

QUEEN'S ROAD WEST INCENSE SHOPS Map p80

🚍 26

Head along Queen's Rd West, several hundred metres past the end of Hollywood Rd, and you'll find two or three shops selling incense and paper offerings. These are burned to propitiate the spirits of the dead. There's quite a choice of spirit-world comestibles to make a consumer heaven for the deceased, including complete mini-sets of kitchenware, fast-food meals, cars, gold and silver ingots, the popular

SHEUNG WAN

INFORMATION
Macau Government
Tourist Office Hong Kong
branch 1 D2

SIGHTS   (pp53–152)
Amelia Johnson
Contemporary.............................. 2 A4
Asia Art Archive................................ 3 C2
Cat Street Galleries 4 C3
Dr Sun Yat Sen Museum
孫中山紀念館 5 C4
Hong Kong Museum of
Medical Sciences
香港醫學博物館 6 C3
Kwun Yam Temple 觀音廟 7 C3
Man Mo Temple 文武廟 8 C3
Ohel Leah Synagogue
莉亞堂 9 C4
Pak Sing Ancestral Hall
百姓廟 10 B3
Para/Site Artspace
藝術空間 11 B2
Queen's Rd West Incense
Shops 12 C2
Western Market 西港城 13 C2

SHOPPING   (pp153–70)
Addiction 14 A4

Ecols 15 B4
Homeless 16 A4
Indosiam 17 A4
Karin Weber Gallery 18 A4
Lock Cha Tea Shop 樂茶軒 19 C3
Po Kee Fishing Tackle 寶記 20 D3
Ranee K..21 B4
Shun Tak Centre 信德中心 22 D2
Wing On 永安 23 D2

EATING   (pp171–204)
Bonheur 24 D2
Classified the Cheese Room 25 C3
Gaia Ristorante 26 D3
Honeymoon Dessert
滿記甜品 ....(see 13)
Kau Kee Restaurant
九記牛腩 27 B4
Kwun Kee Restaurant
坤記煲仔小菜.............................28 A2
Leung Hing Chiu Chow
Seafood Restaurant
兩興潮州海鮮飯店 29 C2
Lin Heung Kui 蓮香居 30 B2
Ngau Kee Food Cafe
牛記茶室 31 B4
Press Room..32 C3
Red Tavern 33 A4
Tims Kitchen 桃花源 34 C2

Yeoh's Bah Kut Teh
楊氏肉骨茶..................................35 C3

ENTERTAINMENT   (pp205–20)
Cage 36 A4
Sparkz ....(see 27)
Volume 37 A4

SLEEPING   (pp231–50)
Bauhinia Furnished Suites.............38 D2
Erba 39 C3
Island Pacific Hotel
港島太平洋酒店 40 A1
Lan Kwai Fong Hotel
蘭桂坊酒店 41 B4
Putman 42 A4
Sohotel 尚豪酒店 43 C2
YWCA Building 女青大廈 44 B3

TRANSPORT   (pp271–87)
Chu Kong Passenger
Transport...............................(see 22)
Macau Ferry Pier
港澳碼頭 45 D1
Macau Ferry Pier Bus
Terminus
港澳碼頭巴士站 46 C1
Shun Tak Centre
信德中心...............................(see 22)

A CHINESE CURE-ALL

So you're feeling a bit peaky. Below par. Liverish even. Why not see if a Chinese herbalist can pep you up? Might we suggest the Good Spring Co (Map p67; Cochrane St), directly beneath the Escalator?

First for the consultation: you will be asked a few questions, your pulse will be taken and then your tongue examined to reveal how balanced your humours are and whether you have too much heat or cold in your constitution.

According to the prognosis the tonic will very likely be a medicinal tea. This may be a simple herbal infusion or something containing more exotic ingredients. Some are helpfully described in the window, such as powdered deer's horn, monkey's visceral organs (the latter invaluable if you need to 'remove excessive sputum') and deer's tail (a marvel if you need to 'strengthen sinews' or 'treat the seminal emission').

Other ingredients might include desiccated deer's penis, dinosaur teeth or horse bezoars (gallstone-like balls formed in horses' stomachs, and the herbalist's poison antidote of choice).

Whatever the ingredients, the resulting brew is invariably dark brown, sour in smell and bitter to taste. Drink up now.

hell banknotes, and even computers and personal stereos. They are tempting to buy as souvenirs, but if you're superstitiously minded, remember that hanging onto these offerings rather than burning them is seen as bad luck here.

CAT ST Map p80

⊗ 9am-6pm; 🚍 26
Located southwest of Sheung Wan MTR station and just north of (and parallel to) Hollywood Rd is Upper Lascar Row, the official name of 'Cat St', which is a pedestrians-only lane lined with antique and curio shops and stalls selling found objects, cheap jewellery, ornaments, carvings and newly minted ancient coins. It's a fun place to trawl through for a trinket or two, but expect even the apparently recent memorabilia to be mass-produced fakes. There are proper shops on three floors of the Cat Street Galleries (Casey Bldg, 14/f 38 Lok Ku Rd; ⊗ 11am-7pm Mon-Sat), which is a small shopping centre that is entered from Upper Lascar Row.

WESTERN MARKET Map p80

☎ 6029 2675; 323 Des Voeux Rd Central & New Market St; ⊗ 9am-7pm; MTR Sheung Wan (exit B)
When the textile vendors were driven out of the lanes linking Queen's Rd Central and Des Voeux Rd Central in the early 1990s, they moved to this renovated old market (1906) with its distinctive four-corner towers. You'll find knickknacks, jewellery and toys on the ground floor, piece goods on the 1st floor and bolts of cloth on the floors above it. The top floor is a restaurant and wedding reception venue.

MAN WA LANE Map p80

MTR Sheung Wan (exit A1)
Just east of the Sheung Wan MTR station, this narrow alley is a good introduction to traditional Sheung Wan. Stalls here specialise in name chops: a stone (or wood or jade) seal that has a name carved in Chinese on the base. When dipped in pasty red Chinese ink, the name chop can be used as a stamp or even a 'signature'. The merchant will create a harmonious and auspicious Chinese name for you.

POSSESSION ST Map p80

🚍 26
A short distance west of Cat St, next to Hollywood Road Park and before Hollywood Rd meets Queen's Rd West, is Possession St. This is thought to be where Commodore Gordon Bremmer and a contingent of British marines planted the Union flag on 26 January 1841 and claimed Hong Kong Island for the Crown (though no plaque marks the spot). Queen's Rd runs in such a serpentine fashion as it heads eastward because it once formed the shoreline of Hong Kong Island's northern coast, and this part of it was called Possession Point.

TAI PING SHAN TEMPLES Map p80

🚍 26
Tai Ping Shan, a tiny neighbourhood in Sheung Wan and one of the first areas to be settled by Chinese after the founding of the colony, has several small temples clustered around where Tai Ping Shan St meets Pound Lane. Kwun Yam Temple (34 Tai Ping Shan St) honours the ever-popular goddess of mercy, Kun Iam – the Taoist equivalent of the Virgin Mary. Further to the north-

west, the recently renovated Pak Sing Ancestral Hall (42 Tai Ping Shan St) was originally a storeroom for bodies awaiting burial in China. It contains the ancestral tablets of around 3000 departed souls.

HONG KONG'S WHOLESALE DISTRICT

Walking Tour

1 Dried Seafood Shops Begin the tour at the Sutherland St stop of the Kennedy Town tram. Have a look at (and a sniff of) Des Voeux Rd West's many shops piled with all manner of desiccated sea life.

2 Herbalist Shops Walk south on Sutherland St to Ko Shing St, to browse the positively medieval-sounding goods on offer from the herbal-medicine traders.

3 Western Market At the end of Ko Shing St, re-enter Des Voeux Rd West and walk northeast. Continue along Connaught Rd West, where you'll find several floors of market stalls occupying the attractive colonial building housing the Western Market (opposite).

4 Birds' Nests, Ginseng & Funeral Offerings Shops At the corner of Morrison St, walk south past Wing Lok St and Bonham Strand, which are both lined with shops selling ginseng root and edible birds' nests. Then turn right onto Queen's Rd Central to the shops selling paper funeral offerings for the dead.

5 Leung Hing Chiu Chow Seafood Restaurant Hungry? Turn right onto Bonham Strand East then left onto Bonham Strand West for a quick Chiu Chow fix (p185).

6 Pak Sing Ancestral Hall & Kwun Yam Temple Back on Possession St, take a left into Hollywood Rd and then right to ascend Pound Lane to where it meets Tai Ping Shan St, where you'll spot two temples (opposite). Look

WALK FACTS

Start Kennedy Town tram (Sutherland St stop)
End Sheung Wan MTR station (entrance/exit B)
Distance 1.9km
Time One hour
Fuel stop Leung Hing Chiu Chow Seafood Restaurant

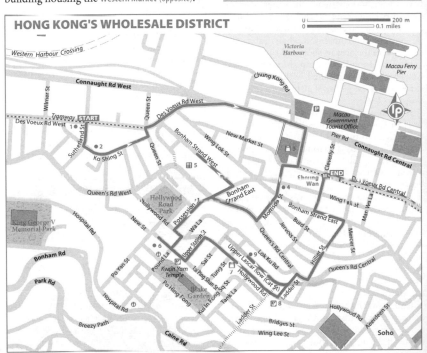

HONG KONG'S WHOLESALE DISTRICT

NEIGHBOURHOODS & ISLANDS HONG KONG ISLAND

to the right for Pak Sing Ancestral Hall and to the left for Kwun Yam Temple.

7 Hollywood Rd Turn left into Tai Ping Shan St, then left again to descend Upper Station St to the start of Hollywood Rd's antique shops (see p157). There's a vast choice of curios and rare, mostly Chinese, treasures.

8 Man Mo Temple Continuing east on Hollywood Rd brings you to the Man Mo Temple (p80), one of the oldest in the territory and dedicated to the civil and martial gods Man Cheung and Kwan Yu.

9 Cat St Market Take a short hop to the left down Ladder St to Upper Lascar Row, home of the Cat St Market (p82), which is well stocked with Chinese memorabilia and inexpensive curios and gift items. Ladder St brings you back to Queen's Rd Central. Cross the road and follow Hillier St to Bonham Strand. Due north is the Sheung Wan MTR station.

CAUSEWAY BAY

Shopping p166; Eating p186; Drinking p213; The Arts p219; Sleeping p239

If you want to experience the sheer mass of humanity Hong Kong is capable of containing on its narrow streets, visit Causeway Bay (Map p85) on a weekend lunchtime when multitudes descend on the area to shop and eat.

One of Hong Kong's top shopping areas, Causeway Bay is jammed with department stores, but it has plenty of attractions for non-shoppers too.

Known as Tung Lo Wan (Copper Gong Bay) in Cantonese, it was the site of a British settlement in the 1840s and was once an area of 'godowns' (a Hong Kong 'business' or pidgin English word for warehouses) and a well-protected harbour for fisherfolk and boatpeople.

The new Causeway Bay was built up from swamp and reclaimed land from the harbour. Jardine Matheson, one of Hong Kong's largest *háwng* (major trading houses or companies), set up shop here, which explains why many of the streets in the district bear its name: Jardine's Bazaar, Jardine's Crescent and Yee Wo St (the name for Jardine Matheson in Cantonese).

Causeway Bay is a relatively small but densely packed district. Canal Rd is its border to the west and Victoria Park is the eastern limit. From the harbour and the typhoon shelter it runs south to Leighton Rd. Tin Hau, the site of Hong Kong Island's most famous temple (erected in honour of the queen of heaven), is at the southeastern edge of Victoria Park.

NOONDAY GUN Map p85

221 Gloucester Rd; MTR Causeway Bay (exit D1)
Noel Coward made the so-called Noonday Gun famous with his satirical song 'Mad Dogs and Englishmen' (1924), about colonials who braved the fierce heat of the midday sun while the local people sensibly remained indoors: 'In Hong Kong/they strike a gong/And fire off a noonday gun/To reprimand each inmate/Who's in late.' Apparently when Coward was invited to pull the lanyard, he was late and it didn't go off until 12.03pm.

Built in 1901 by Hotchkiss of Portsmouth, this recoil-mounted 3lb cannon is one of the few vestiges of the colonial past in Causeway Bay and is its best-known landmark. The original six-pounder was lost during WWII; its replacement was deemed too noisy and was exchanged for the current gun in 1961. The gun stands in a small garden opposite the Excelsior Hotel on Gloucester Rd – the first plot of land to be sold by public auction in Hong Kong (1841) – and is fired at noon every day. Eight bells are then sounded, signalling the end of the forenoon watch. The gun also welcomes the New Year at midnight on 31 December.

Exactly how this tradition started remains a mystery. Some people say that Jardine Matheson fired the gun without permission to bid farewell to a departing managing director or to welcome one of its incoming ships. The authorities were so enraged by the company's insolence that, as

---

TRANSPORT – CAUSEWAY BAY

Bus From Admiralty and Central, buses 5, 5B and 26 stop along Yee Wo St.

Green Minibus Bus 40 from Stanley calls along Tang Lung St and Yee Woo St.

MTR Causeway Bay and Tin Hau stations are on the Central line.

Tram These run along Hennessy Rd and Yee Wo St to Central and Shau Kei Wan; along Percival St to Happy Valley; along Wong Nai Chung Rd to Causeway Bay, Central, Kennedy Town and Shau Kei Wan.

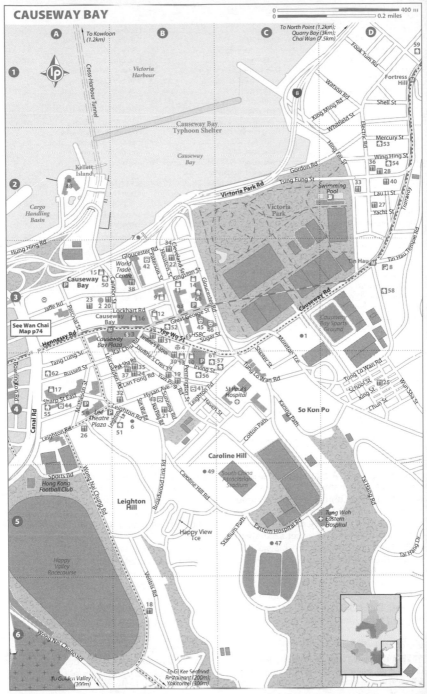

CAUSEWAY BAY

CAUSEWAY BAY

INFORMATION
Central Library 中央圖書館...........1 C3
Cyber Pro Internet......................2 A3
Hong Kong Island HKTB
   Centre
   港島旅客諮詢及服務中心 3 B3
PCCW i.Shop...............................4 B3
Towngas Cooking Centre
   煤氣烹飪中心..........................5 A4

SIGHTS   (pp53–152)
Edge Gallery................................6 B3
Noonday Gun 香港怡和午炮......7 B2
Royal Hong Kong Yacht Club
   香港遊艇會.........................(see 48)
Tin Hau Temple 天后廟 8 D3

SHOPPING   (pp153–70)
Coup de Foudre.....................(see 12)
Dada Cabaret Voltaire 9 B3
Delay No Mall............................10 B4
D-Mop......................................11 B3
HMV....................................(see 60)
In Square..............................(see 46)
Island Beverley 金百利商場....12 B3
Jardine's Bazaar 渣甸街...........13 B4
Kitty House Gift Shop...........(see 12)
Lane Crawford 連卡佛............(see 17)
LCX..14 B3
Mountaineering Services...........15 A3
Rainbow City.......................(see 12)
Sister..................................(see 12)
Sogo 崇光百貨.........................16 B3
Times Square 時代廣場...........17 A4
Walter Ma.............................(see 55)

EATING   (pp171–204)
Amigo......................................18 B6
Caroline Centre 嘉蘭中心........19 B4
Chang Won Korean
   Restaurant 莊園韓國料理.......20 A3

Citysuper.............................(see 17)
Crystal Jade
   翡翠拉麵小籠包.................(see 17)
Da Domenico 21 B4
Delicious Kitchen 美味廚 22 B3
Forum 富臨飯店....................23 A3
Golden Bull 金牛苑...............(see 17)
Goldfinch 金雀餐廳................24 B4
Honeymoon Dessert
   滿記甜品..........................(see 38)
Hong Kee Congee Shop
   康記粥店..............................25 D4
Hong Kong Old
   Restaurant 香港老飯店........(see 59)
Indonesian Restaurant
   1968 印尼餐廳1968...............26 A4
June Japanese Restaurant
   順壽司日本料理.....................27 D2
Kin's Kitchen 留家廚房 28 D2
Le Marron 29 B3
Mak's Noodle
   麥奀雲吞麵世家.....................30 B4
Man Fai 文輝 31 B3
Pak Lok Chiu Chow
   Restaurant
   百樂潮州酒樓.......................32 B4
Pumpernickel 黑麥...................33 D2
Pumpernickel 黑麥...................34 B3
Sushi Hiro 壽司廣...................35 B4
Sweet Auntie 甜姨姨...............36 D2
Tai Ping Koon 太平館...............37 B4
Tonkichi Tonkatsu
   丼吉日本吉列專門店餐廳.......38 B3
West Villa 西苑酒家 39 B4
Wu Kong Shanghai
   Restaurant 滬江大飯店 .....(see 17)
Yakitoritei 燒鳥亭.....................40 D2

ENTERTAINMENT   (pp205–20)
Brecht's Circle...........................41 B4

Dickens Bar.............................42 B3
East End Brewery & Inn
   Side Out..............................43 B4
Executive Bar...........................44 A4
Watson's Wine Cellar 酒窖.....45 B3
Windsor Cinema
   皇室戲院..............................46 B3

SPORTS & ACTIVITIES   (pp221–30)
Hong Kong Stadium.................47 C5
Royal Hong Kong Yacht
   Club 香港遊艇會...................48 A2
South China Athletic
   Association 南華體育會 49 B5

SLEEPING   (pp231–50)
Alisan Guest House
   阿里山賓館............................50 A3
Causeway Bay Guest
   House 華生旅舍.....................51 B4
Chung Kiu Inn 中僑賓館..........52 B3
Domus Mercury Serviced
   Apartments..........................53 D2
Empire Hotel 皇悅酒店............54 D2
Express by Holiday Inn
   香港銅鑼灣快捷假日酒店.......55 A4
Jia...56 B4
Lanson Place...........................57 C4
Metropark Hotel
   維景酒店..............................58 D3
Newton Hotel Hong Kong
   麗東酒店..............................59 D1
Park Lane Hong Kong
   柏寧酒店..............................60 B3
Regal Hongkong Hotel
   富豪香港酒店........................61 B4
Shama....................................62 A4

TRANSPORT   (pp271–87)
China Travel Service
   中國旅行社............................63 B3

punishment, Jardine's was ordered to fire the gun every day. A more prosaic explanation is that, as at many ports around the world (including London), a gun was fired at noon daily so that ships' clocks – crucial for establishing longitude and east-west distances at sea – could be set accurately.

The Noonday Gun is accessible via a tunnel through the basement car park in the World Trade Centre, just west of the Excelsior Hotel. From the taxi rank in front of the hotel, look west for the door marked 'Car Park Shroff, Marina Club & Noon Gun'. It's open from 7am to midnight daily.

VICTORIA PARK Map p85
☎ 2890 5824; www.lcsd.gov.hk/en/ls_park.php; Causeway Rd; free admission; MTR Causeway Bay & Tin Hau

At 17 hectares, Victoria Park is the biggest patch of public greenery on Hong Kong Island and is a popular place to escape to. The best time to stroll around is in the morning during the week, when it becomes a forest of people practising the slow-motion choreography of t'ai chi. At the weekend they are joined by Indonesian *amahs,* who prefer it to Central (see the boxed text, p65).

Between April and November you can take a dip in the swimming pool (☎ 2570 4682; adult/child 3-13 & senior over 60 $19/9; 6.30am-10pm with 1hr closure at noon & 5pm Apr-Oct, 6.30am-noon Nov). The park becomes a flower market a few days before the Chinese New Year and is the site of the Hong Kong Flower Show in March. It's also worth a visit during the Mid-Autumn Festival (p17), when people turn out en masse carrying lanterns.

CAUSEWAY BAY TYPHOON SHELTER

Map p85

off Hung Hing Rd, Causeway Bay

Not so long ago the waterfront in Causeway Bay used to be a mass of junks and sampans huddling in the typhoon shelter for protection, but these days it's nearly all yachts. The land jutting out to the west is Kellett Island, which has been a misnomer ever since a causeway connected it to the mainland in 1956, and further land reclamation turned it into a peninsula. It is home to the Royal Hong Kong Yacht Club (☎ 2832 2817), which retains its 'Royal' moniker in English only.

TIN HAU TEMPLE Map p85

☎ 2508 1234; 10 Tin Hau Temple Rd; ☻ 7am-5pm; MTR Tin Hau (exit B)

Southeast of Victoria Park, Hong Kong Island's most famous Tin Hau temple is relatively small and dwarfed by surrounding high-rises. Before reclamation, this temple dedicated to the patroness of seafarers stood on the waterfront. It has been a place of worship for three centuries, though the current structure is only about 200 years old. The temple bell dates from 1747, and the central shrine contains an effigy of Tin Hau with a blackened face.

WESTERN DISTRICTS

Sleeping p237

Beyond Sheung Wan the districts of Sai Ying Pun (Map p80) and Shek Tong Tsui (Map pp62–3) are often lumped together as 'Western' by English speakers. Kennedy Town is the working-class Chinese district at the end of the tramline.

While these districts are not perhaps among Hong Kong's must-see areas, they do contain pockets of interest and important historical links. Kennedy Town's maritime connections can still be felt the closer you get to the Praya (officially Kennedy Town New Praya), the name of which comes from the Portuguese *praia* meaning 'beach' or 'coast', which was commonly used in Hong Kong in the days when Portuguese merchants were a force to be reckoned with on the high seas.

The area wedged between the Mid-Levels and Sheung Wan doesn't have an official name as such, but is usually called Pok Fu Lam after the main thoroughfare running through it. It's a district of middle-class housing blocks, colleges and Hong Kong's most prestigious university.

TRANSPORT – WESTERN DISTRICTS

Bus Bus 3B from Jardine House in Central, buses 23, 40 and 40M from Admiralty, and bus 103 from Gloucester Rd in Causeway Bay all stop along Bonham Rd (Map p80).

HONG KONG UNIVERSITY Map pp62–3

☎ 2859 2111; www.hku.hk; Pok Fu Lam Rd; 🚌 23 & 40M from D'Aguilar St in Central

Established in 1911, HKU is the oldest and most prestigious of Hong Kong's eight universities. The Main Building, completed in the Edwardian style in 1912, is a declared monument. Several other early-20th-century buildings on the campus, including the Hung Hing Ying (1919) and Tang Chi Ngong Buildings (1929), are also protected.

The University Museum & Art Gallery (☎ 2241 5500; www.hku.hk/hkumag; Fung Ping Shan Bldg, 94 Bonham Rd; admission free; ☻ 9.30am-6pm Mon-Sat, 1.30-6pm Sun) houses collections of ceramics and bronzes spanning 5000 years, including some exquisite blue and white Ming porcelain. The bronzes are in three groups: Shang- and Zhou-dynasty ritual vessels; decorative mirrors from the Warring States period to the Tang, Song, Ming and Qing dynasties; and almost 1000 small Nestorian crosses from the Yuan dynasty, the largest such collection in the world. (The Nestorians formed a Christian sect that arose in Syria, were branded heretics and moved into China during the 13th and 14th centuries.) The museum is to the left of the university's Main Building and opposite the start of Hing Hon Rd.

THE MID-LEVELS

Eating p184; Sleeping p240

The Mid-Levels (Map p88) have relatively little to offer tourists in the way of sights, though there are a few gems, particularly houses of worship, hidden within the forest of marble-clad apartment blocks. Check out the Roman Catholic Cathedral of the Immaculate Conception (Map p88; ☎ 2522 8212; 16 Caine Rd), built in 1888 and financed largely by the Portuguese faithful from Macau; the Jamia Mosque (Map p88; ☎ 2523 7743; 30 Shelley St), erected in 1849 and also called the Lascar Mosque; and the Ohel Leah Synagogue (p88).

Another district with rather elastic boundaries, the Mid-Levels stretches roughly from

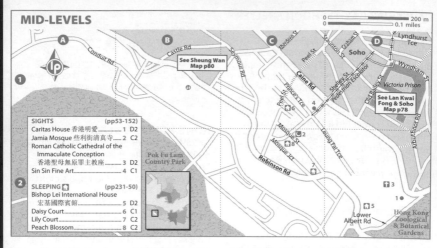

0 ____ 200 m
0 ____ 0.1 miles

Lyndhurst Tce

See Sheung Wan Map p80

Soho

Victoria Prison

See Lan Kwai Fong & Soho Map p78

Pok Fu Lam Country Park

Lower Albert Rd

Hong Kong Zoological & Botanical Gardens

SIGHTS	(pp53-152)
Caritas House 香港明愛 1	D2
Jamia Mosque 些利街清真寺 2	C2
Roman Catholic Cathedral of the Immaculate Conception 香港聖母無原罪主教座 3	D2
Sin Sin Fine Art 4	C1

SLEEPING	(pp231-50)
Bishop Lei International House 宏基國際賓館 5	D2
Daisy Court 6	C1
Lily Court 7	C2
Peach Blossom 8	C2

Hong Kong University and Pok Fu Lam in the west to Kennedy Rd in the east. Caine Rd is the northern boundary and the Peak the southern one. But the Mid-Levels are as much a state of mind as a physical area, and some people regard the middle-class residential areas further east to be the Mid-Levels as well.

DR SUN YAT SEN MUSEUM Map p80

☎ 2367 6373; http://hk.drsunyatsen.museum; 7 Castle Rd, Mid-Levels; adult/concession $10/5, free Wed; ✆ 10am-6pm Mon-Wed & Fri- Sat, 10am-7pm Sun; ⛟ 3B, alight at the Hong Kong Baptist Church on Caine Rd

Sun Yat-sen was an early 20th-century revolutionary, dedicated to overthrowing the Qing dynasty, and a key figure in modern Chinese history. He had many links with Hong Kong, not least of them being his education here and his formative experience of the colony's order and efficiency (standing in stark contrast to China at the time). Dr Sun's story is one of the more interesting chapters in China's history, to which the dull displays here do not really do justice. Audio guides cost $10.

HONG KONG MUSEUM OF MEDICAL SCIENCES Map p80

☎ 2549 5123; www.hkmms.org.hk; 2 Caine Lane; adult/concession $10/5; ✆ 10am-5pm Tue-Sat, 1-5pm Sun; ⛟ 3B alight at Ladder St bus stop on Caine Rd

This small museum houses medical implements and accoutrements (including an old dentistry chair, an autopsy table and herbal medicine vials and chests), and offers a rundown on how Hong Kong coped with the 1894 bubonic plague. The exhibits comparing Chinese and Western approaches to medicine are unusual and instructive, but the museum is less interesting for its exhibits than for its architecture: it's housed in what was once the Pathological Institute, a breezy Edwardian-style brick-and-tile structure built in 1905 and fronted by palms and bauhinia trees.

OHEL LEAH SYNAGOGUE Map p80

☎ 2589 2621, 2857 6095; 70 Robinson Rd; admission free; ✆ 10.30am-7pm Mon-Thu (by appointment only), service times 7am Mon-Fri, 6pm Mon-Thu; ⛟ 3B or 23

This renovated Moorish Romantic temple, completed in 1902 when that style of architecture was all the rage in Europe, is named after Leah Gubbay Sassoon, the matriarch of a wealthy (and philanthropic) Sephardic Jewish family that traces its roots back to

TRANSPORT – THE MID-LEVELS

Bus Bus 26 from Central calls along Hollywood Rd (Map p78); and bus 3B from Jardine House in Central and bus 23 from Admiralty stop at Robinson Rd (Map p67).

Central Escalator (Map p67) Use this for Caine Rd (museum) and Robinson Rd (synagogue).

Green Minibus Bus 8 or 22 from Central call at Caine Rd and Ladder St (Map p80).

the beginning of the colony. Be sure to bring some sort of ID if you plan to visit the sumptuous interior.

THE PEAK

Eating p187

On your first clear day in Hong Kong, make tracks for the cooler climes of the Peak (Map pp62–3), the highest point on the island. Not only does it offer some of the most spectacular views in the world, but it's also a good way to put Hong Kong and its layout into perspective. It's not a bad idea to repeat the trip up on a clear night; the views of illuminated Central below and Tsim Sha Tsui across the harbour in Kowloon are superb.

The Peak has been *the* place to live in Hong Kong ever since the British arrived. Taipans (company bosses) built summer houses here to escape the heat and humidity.

When people refer to the Peak, they generally mean the plateau (elevation 370m) with the seven-level Peak Tower, the huge titanium anvil rising above the Peak Tram terminus and containing themed venues, shops and restaurants; they don't mean the summit itself.

Half the fun of going up to the Peak is riding the Peak Tram (see p284). In 1885 everyone thought Phineas Kyrle and William Kerfoot Hughes were mad when they announced their intention to build a tramway to the top, but it opened three years later, silencing the scoffers and wiping out the sedan-chair trade in one fell swoop.

VICTORIA PEAK Map pp62–3

Some 500m to the northwest of the Peak Tram terminus, up steep Mt Austin Rd, Victoria Peak (552m) is the highest point on Hong Kong Island. The old governor's mountain lodge near the summit was burned to the ground by the Japanese during WWII, but the gardens remain and are open to the public.

You can walk around Victoria Peak without exhausting yourself. Harlech Rd on the south side and Lugard Rd on the northern slope together form a 3.5km loop that takes about an hour to walk. If you feel like a longer walk, you can continue for a further 2km along Peak Rd to Pok Fu Lam Reservoir Rd, which leaves Peak Rd near the car-park exit. This goes past the reservoir to the main Pok Fu Lam Rd, where you can get bus 7 to Aberdeen or back to Central.

TRANSPORT – THE PEAK

Bus Bus 15 from the Central bus terminus below Exchange Sq (Map p67) and bus 15B from Wan Chai and Causeway Bay (Map p74), via Police Museum, Caine Rd and Ladder St, both terminate at the bus station below the Peak Galleria.

Green Minibus Bus 1 from Edinburgh Pl (southeast of City Hall) in Central and bus 24A from Admiralty terminate at the Peak.

Peak Tram Join the tram at the lower terminus on Cotton Tree Dr (Map p67). The service disgorges passengers in Peak Tower (entrance level 4, exit level 3).

Another good walk leads down to Hong Kong University (p87). First walk to the west side of Victoria Peak by taking either Lugard or Harlech Rds. After reaching Hatton Rd, follow it down. The descent is steep, but the path is clear.

For information on the 50km-long Hong Kong Trail, which starts on the Peak, see p227.

PEAK GALLERIA Map pp62–3

118 Peak Rd; Peak Tram

Designed to withstand winds of up to 270km/h, theoretically more than the maximum velocity of a No 10 typhoon, this building is worth skipping unless you're after refreshments. You can reach the Peak Galleria's viewing deck, which is larger than the one in the Peak Tower, by taking the escalator to Level 3. Inside the centre you'll find a number of retail shops, from art galleries to duty-free stores. If you wish to eat, you'll find that prices are high and the quality low, as restaurants don't have to try too hard to find custom at this top visitor spot.

PEAK TOWER Map pp62–3

2849 0668; 128 Peak Rd; 10am-11pm Mon-Fri, 8am-11pm Sat, Sun & public holidays; Peak Tram

The anvil-shaped Peak Tower, with its attractions, shops and restaurants, is a good place to bring the kids and makes a good grandstand for many of the best views of the city and harbour. On Level 4 there's an outpost of Madame Tussauds (2849 6966; adult/child $150/80; 10am-10pm), with eerie (and often creepy) wax likenesses of international stars, as well as local celebrities such as Jackie Chan, Andy Lau, Michelle

Yeoh and Kelly Chen. There is an open-air viewing terrace with coin-operated binoculars on Level 5.

POLICE MUSEUM Map pp62-3

☎ 2849 7019; www.police.gov.hk/hkp-home/english/museum; 27 Coombe Rd; admission free; 2-5pm Tue, 9am-5pm Wed-Sun; 15 or 15B, alight at the stop btwn Stubbs Rd & Peak Rd

Housed in a former police station, this seldom-visited museum in neighbouring Wan Chai Gap, an attractive residential area en route to the Peak, deals with the history of the Hong Kong Police Force, which was formed in 1844. It's small and rather static, although the intriguing Triad Societies Gallery and the very well-supplied Narcotics Gallery are worthwhile.

HAPPY VALLEY

Eating p188

Happy Valley (Map p85) – called *Páau-máa-dáy* (Horse Running Place) in Cantonese – has been a popular residential area for expats since the early days of British settlement. However, having built their houses on what turned out to be swampland, early residents had to contend with severe bouts of malaria (the area was named with a grim sense of irony given the high mortality rate). There are some interesting cemeteries to the west and southwest of Wong Nai Chung Rd. They are divided into Protestant, Roman Catholic, Muslim, Parsee and Hindu sections, and date back to the founding of Hong Kong as a colony. The district's most important drawcard, however, is the Happy Valley Racecourse. Happy Valley is essentially the racetrack in the centre of circular Wong Nai Chung Rd and the residential areas to the east and south, where the main streets are Shan Kwong, Sing Woo and Blue Pool Rds.

HAPPY VALLEY RACECOURSE Map p85

☎ 2895 1523, 2966 8111; www.happyvalleyracecourse.com; 2 Sports Rd; admission $10; races usually held Sep-Jun on Wed & weekends (1st race 7.30pm); Happy Valley

Horse racing is the most popular live spectator sport in Hong Kong, not least because it offers one of the few legal ways to gamble in the city. An evening at the races here is also hugely atmospheric and is one of the quintessential Hong Kong things to do, if you happen to be around during one of the roughly fortnightly Wednesday evening races. The punters pack into the stands and trackside, and the atmosphere is electric.

The first horse races were held in 1846 at Happy Valley and became an annual event. Now meetings are held both here and at the newer and larger (but less atmospheric) Sha Tin Racecourse (p128) in the New Territories. For details on placing bets, see p230.

If you know nothing about horse racing but would like to attend, consider joining the Come Horseracing Tour available through Splendid Tours & Travel (p299) during the racing season. The tour includes admission to the Visitors' Box of the Hong Kong Jockey Club Members' Enclosures and a buffet lunch. Tours scheduled at night last about 5½ hours, while daytime tours are about seven hours long.

Though probably one for racing buffs only, you can also visit the Hong Kong Racing Museum (Map p74; ☎ 2966 8065; www.hkjc.com/english/museum/mu02_index.htm; 2nd fl, Happy Valley Stand, Wong Nai Chung Rd; admission free; 10am-5pm Tue-Sun, 10am-12.30pm on racing days), which has eight galleries and a cinema showcasing celebrated trainers, jockeys and horseflesh, and key races over the past 150 years. The most important event in the history of the Happy Valley Racecourse – individual winnings notwithstanding – was the huge fire in 1918 that killed hundreds of people. Many of the victims were buried in the cemeteries surrounding the track.

ISLAND EAST

Eating p188; Drinking p213; The Arts p219; Sleeping p240

Eastern (Map pp62–3) is a large, primarily residential district, with some of Hong Kong Island's largest housing estates (eg Tai Koo Shing in Quarry Bay). As elsewhere on the island, however, office towers stand cheek by jowl with residential areas. There are not as many restaurants and nightspots in this area to lure you onto the MTR's Central line, but there are a handful of top-class museums.

The Eastern District runs from Causeway Bay to Siu Sai Wan, at the eastern end of Hong Kong Island's north coast. Major settlements are North Point, Quarry Bay, Sai Wan Ho, Shau Kei Wan and Chai Wan.

North Point & Quarry Bay

North Point, settled largely by Shanghainese after WWII, is a somewhat down-at-heel district with a couple of interesting markets, and the Sunbeam Theatre (p220), one of the best places to see and hear Chinese opera. Tong Chong St opposite the Quarry Bay MTR station has had a facelift in recent years and is something of a restaurant and nightlife strip. The main attraction at Quarry Bay is Cityplaza (p167).

Sai Wan Ho

HONG KONG FILM ARCHIVE Map pp62-3
☎ 2739 2139, bookings 2734 9009, 2119 7383; www.filmarchive.gov.hk; 50 Lei King Rd; admission free; ☷ main foyer 10am-8pm Mon-Wed & Fri-Sun, box office noon-8pm daily, resource centre 10am-7pm Mon-Wed & Fri, 10am-5pm Sat, 1-5pm Sun; MTR Sai Wan Ho

The archive is well worth a visit, even if you know nothing about Hong Kong films and film-making. It preserves, catalogues and studies the fruit of the local film and TV industries – there are more than 6300 reels and tapes in the vaults – and related material such as magazines, posters, records and scripts; there's a small exhibition hall with themed exhibits (opening hours vary), including videos with subtitles, and a 127-seat

cinema (☎ 2119 7383) that shows Hong Kong and other films here throughout the year for $30 to $50. It's well worth checking out the program of temporary exhibitions online.

To reach the film archive from the Sai Wan Ho MTR station, follow exit A, walk north on Tai On St and west on Lei King Rd.

Shau Kei Wan

HONG KONG MUSEUM OF COASTAL DEFENCE Map pp62-3
☎ 2569 1500; http://hk.coastaldefence.museum; 175 Tung Hei Rd; adult/concession $10/5, admission free Wed; ☷ 10am-5pm Fri-Wed; MTR Shau Kei Wan

This museum doesn't exactly sound like a crowd pleaser, but its displays are as much about peace as war. It also occupies a knockout location in the Lei Yue Mun Fort (1887), which took quite a beating during WWII, and has sweeping views down to the Lei Yue Mun Channel and southeastern Kowloon.

Exhibitions in the old redoubt, which you reach by elevator from street level, cover Hong Kong's coastal defence over six

TRANSPORT – ISLAND EAST

MTR Take the Central line from Causeway Bay.

Tram A more atmospheric alternative to the MTR, it clatters sedately from Western Market (p82) in Sheung Wan to Shau Kei Wan.

North Point & Quarry Bay

Bus North Point: To get to the North Point Ferry bus terminus from Tsim Sha Shui take bus 110, which runs down Canton Rd. From the south of the island, bus 38 comes from Aberdeen bus terminus (by the promenade) or bus 77 from Aberdeen Main Rd, which runs along King's Rd in North Point. Bus 63 (or 65 on Sundays) comes from Stanley (the bus terminus is just up from the market). The only direct bus from Shek O is the 309 on Sundays, which runs along King's Rd in North Point.

Shau Kei Wan: To get to Shau Kai Wan bus terminus from Tsim Sha Shui take bus 110, which runs down Canton Rd. From the south of the island, take bus 77 from Aberdeen Main Rd. From Stanley bus 14 passes along Stanley Village Rd and takes you to Shau Kei Wan Rd close to the MTR station. From Shek O bus terminus take bus 9, which terminates at Shau Kei Wan MTR.

Ferry North Point: You can reach North Point by ferry from Kwun Tong, Hung Hom and Kowloon City.

Sai Wan Ho: Ferries from Kwun Tong and Sam Ka Tsuen (by Lei Yue Mun) on the mainland arrive here. There are also kaito services operating to Tung Lung Chau via Joss House Bay (although in significant numbers only on the weekend).

MTR By far the easiest way to reach this area is to use the Island line with stations at North Point, Quarry Bay, Tai Koo, Sai Wan Ho, Shau Kei Wan, Heng Fa Chuen and Chai Wan. North Point and Quarry Bay are also on Tseung Kwan O line.

Tram If you're coming from Central or Admiralty, North Point has a tram terminus, as does Shau Kei Wan, which is at the end of the line.

centuries, from the Ming and Qing dynasties, through the colonial years and Japanese invasion, to the resumption of Chinese sovereignty. There's a historical trail through the casemates, tunnels and observation posts almost down to the coast.

To reach the museum take the MTR to Shau Kei Wan station (exit B2). Then follow the museum signs on busy Tung Hei Rd for about 15 minutes. Bus 85, which is accessible via exit A3 and runs along Shau Kei Wan Rd between North Point and Siu Sai Wan, stops on Tung Hei Rd outside the museum.

Chai Wan

LAW UK FOLK MUSEUM Map pp62-3

☎ 2896 7006; www.lcsd.gov.hk/en/ce/museum /history/en/luf.php; 14 Kut Shing St; admission free; ⏲ 10am-6pm Mon-Wed & Fri-Sat, 1-6pm Sun; MTR Chai Wan

This small museum, a branch of the Hong Kong Museum of History, occupies two restored Hakka village houses that have stood in Chai Wan (Firewood Bay) – a district of nondescript office buildings, warehouses and workers' flats – for more than two centuries. The quiet courtyard and surrounding bamboo groves are peaceful and evocative, and the displays – furniture, household items and farming implements – simple but charming.

top picks

HONG KONG FOR CHILDREN

As well as Hong Kong's two theme parks, Ocean Park (opposite) and Disneyland (p144), Hong Kong offers plenty of amazement for kids as well as adults:

- Beaches (p223)
- Cityplaza Ice Palace skating rink (p228)
- Hong Kong Park (p71)
- Hong Kong Space Museum & Theatre (p103)
- Junk and sampan trips in Aberdeen Harbour (opposite)
- Noonday Gun (p84)
- Peak Tram (p284)
- Star Ferry (p275)
- Symphony of the Stars lightshow (p106)
- Tsim Sha Tsui East Promenade (p106)
- Zoological & Botanical Gardens (p65)

To reach the museum from the Chai Wan MTR station, follow exit B and walk for five minutes to the west.

ISLAND SOUTH

Eating p189; Drinking p213

The Southern District (Map pp62–3), which encompasses everything from Big Wave Bay and Shek O in the east to Aberdeen and Ap Lei Chau in the west, is full of attractions and wild spaces to escape into. This is Hong Kong Island's backyard playground – from the beaches of Repulse Bay and Deep Water Bay and the outdoor activities available at Shek O, to Stanley Market, the shoppers' paradise, and Ocean Park, the large amusement and theme park near Aberdeen.

Shek O lies halfway down a long peninsula in the southeast of Hong Kong Island; Stanley village is at the start of the next peninsula over, but you'll have to travel a bit further south to reach the best beach on Stanley peninsula. Further west along the southern coast is Repulse Bay, with its ever-heaving beach, Kwun Yam shrine, lucky bridge and posh shopping complex, and then Deep Water Bay, a much more serene beach and one of the best places in Hong Kong for wakeboarding (see p229).

Aberdeen is at the western edge of the southern coast. From here, buses return to the northern side of the island either through the Aberdeen Tunnel or Pok Fu Lam Rd along the west coast.

Buses, and to a lesser extent green minibuses, are the best form of transport for getting to and around the southern part of Hong Kong Island. Though some go via the Aberdeen Tunnel, many buses (eg bus 6 to Stanley and Repulse Bay) climb over the hills separating the north and south sides of the island. It's a scenic, winding ride; for the outbound trip, make sure you sit on the upper deck on the right-hand side.

Aberdeen

At first glance Aberdeen (Map p94) – or Heung Gong Tsai (Little Fragrant Harbour) in Cantonese – is not much to look at, but it's well worth a visit for the remnants of an almost bygone maritime era when thousands lived and worked on the junks and other traditional sailing craft moored in the harbour. Over the years the number of boats has dwindled as more and more of these boatpeople have moved into high-rises or abandoned fishing as a profession, but you can still see the odd family clinging onto their floating

TRANSPORT – ISLAND SOUTH

Bus Shek O: The easiest way to reach Shek O is to take bus 9 from Shau Kei Wan MTR station (exit A3). Bus 309 (Sunday and holidays only) runs here from Central, below Exchange Sq. If you're coming from Stanley, take bus 14 and change to bus 9 on Tai Tam Rd, at the junction with Shek O Rd.

Stanley: From Shau Kei Wan take bus 14 from Shau Kei Wan Rd, a short walk from the MTR station (exit A3). Buses 6, 6A, 6X, 66 and 260 all leave for here from Central, below Exchange Sq.

Aberdeen: From Aberdeen buses 73 and 973 run to Stanley, with both from Aberdeen Main Rd and the latter from the bus terminus by the promenade. Buses 73 and 973 also run here from Repulse Bay beach. From Tsim Sha Tsui take bus 973, which leaves from Concordia Plaza by the science museum. Green minibus 40 (24 hours) runs from Times Sq to Stanley via Tang Lung St and Yee Woo St in Causeway Bay.

Repulse Bay: From Central, below Exchange Sq, take bus 6, 6A, 6X, 66 or 260. From Stanley (the terminus is just up from the market) take bus 6, 6A, 6X, 66 or 260 (which go on to Central) or bus 73 or 973. To get here from Aberdeen take bus 73 or 973 – both stop on Aberdeen Main Rd and the latter at the bus terminus, too. From Tsim Sha Tsui take bus 973, which leaves from Concordia Plaza by the science museum.

Deep Water Bay: From Central, below Exchange Sq, take bus 6A, 6X or 260. From Stanley (the terminus is just up from the market) take bus 6A, 6X or 260 (which go on to Central) or bus 73 or 973. To get here from Aberdeen take bus 73 or 973 – both stop on Aberdeen Main Rd and the latter at the bus terminus, too. From Tsim Sha Tsui take bus 973, which leaves from Concordia Plaza by the science museum.

homes alongside fishermen working on their handsome seagoing boats. It's captivating to just soak up the minutiae of daily life on the harbour. It is also home to popular floating restaurants (p189) and to Ocean Park (below), Hong Kong's first, and still thriving, amusement park.

OCEAN PARK Map pp62-3

☎ 3923 2323; www.oceanpark.com.hk; Ocean Park Rd; adult/child 3-11yr $208/103; ☷ 10am-6pm; ☐ 6A, 6X, 70 & 75 from Central, 629 from Admiralty, 72, 72A & 92 from Causeway Bay or 973 from Tsim Sha Tsui

Despite the arrival of its shiny, new Disneyland competitor on Lantau (see p144), Ocean Park remains the best theme park in Hong Kong and continues to add rides, attractions, infrastructure, hotels and square footage. The investment in revamping its rides and attractions is already working. Visitor numbers have been soaring, thanks in part to the presence of four giant pandas and four very rare and very cute red pandas, all gifts from the mainland.

As well as excellent animal attractions and enclosures with some worthwhile educational content, the park also offers plenty of white-knuckle thrill rides, such as the celebrated roller coaster called the Dragon and the Abyss 'turbo drop'. In Marine Land you'll find sea lions and seals, daily dolphin and killer-whale shows, and aquariums. The

Atoll Reef is particularly impressive, with over 2000 fish representing 200 species in residence. Bird-watchers are also catered for with aviaries, a flamingo pond and the Amazing Birds Theatre, with regular aerial shows.

The park is divided into two main sections. The main entrance is on the Waterfront (lowland) side and is linked to the main section on the Summit (headland), where most of the attractions are found, by a scenic cable car. From some time in 2010 you'll also be able to take a marine-themed funicular train called the *Ocean Express*. The headland section affords beautiful views of the South China Sea. At the rear entrance, where a giant escalator will bring you down to Tai Shue Wan and Shum Wan Rd, is the Middle Kingdom, a sort of Chinese cultural village with temples, pagodas and traditional street scenes.

SAMPAN TOURS Map p94

Aberdeen Promenade

Sampan tours can easily be arranged along Aberdeen Promenade, which runs south and parallel to Aberdeen Praya Rd. You can have your choice of private operators, which generally mill around the eastern end of the promenade, or licensed operators registered with the HKTD, such as the Aberdeen Sampan Company (Map p94; ☎ 2873 0649; Aberdeen Praya Rd). The private sampans usually charge around $55 per person for a 30-minute ride (about $110 to Sok Kwu Wan and $130 to Yung Shue Wan on Lamma), though you should easily be able to bargain this down if there are several of you. Ferries to several spots on Lamma also operate from the promenade, as well as infrequent services to Stanley and Po Toi island (see the transport section for details, p276).

The promenade is easily accessed from Aberdeen bus terminus. To get to it just take the pedestrian subway under Aberdeen Praya Rd.

AP LEI CHAU Map p94
🚢 Ap Lei Chau

On the southern side of the harbour is Ap Lei Chau (Duck's Tongue Island), one of the most densely populated places in the world. It used to be a centre for building junks, but now it's covered with housing estates, including a huge one called South Horizons. There's not much to see there, but a walk across the bridge to the island affords good views. From Aberdeen Promenade you can get a boat across to Ap Lei Chau (adult/child under 12 $1.80/1). Ap Lei Chau is also a

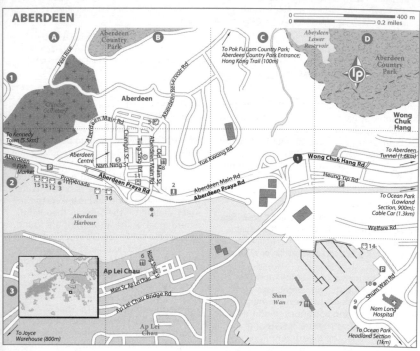

ABERDEEN

SIGHTS (pp53–152)
Aberdeen Sampan Company
香港仔三舨公司 1 A2
Hung Shing Shrine 洪聖古廟 2 B2
Private Sampans 3 A2
Private Sampans 4 B2
Tin Hau Temple 天后廟 5 B1

EATING 🍴 (pp171–204)
Ap Lei Chau Market Cooked
Food Centre 鴨利洲市政大廈 6 B3
Jumbo Kingdom Floating
Restaurant 珍寶海鮮舫 7 C3

Shan Loon Tse Kee Fish Ball
山窿謝記魚蛋 8 B2
Top Deck 珍之寶 ....(see 7)

SPORTS & ACTIVITIES (pp221–30)
Aberdeen Boat Club
香港仔遊艇會 9 D3
Aberdeen Marina Club
深灣遊艇俱樂部 10 D3

TRANSPORT (pp271–87)
Aberdeen Bus Terminus
香港仔巴士總站 11 B2

Boats to Ap Lei Chau
往鴨脷洲街渡 12 A2
Boats to Floating
Restaurants 往海鮮舫街渡 13 A2
Boats to Floating
Restaurants 往海鮮舫街渡 14 D3
Boats to Sok Kwu Wan & Mo
Tat Wan (Lamma) & Po Toi
往索罟灣、模達灣、蒲台島船
.... 15 A2
Boats to Yung Shue Wan
(Lamma) 往榕樹灣船隻 16 B2

destination for bargain hunters drawn to its discount outlet stores (see the boxed text, p155).

TEMPLES Map p94

Aberdeen Main Rd

If you've got time to spare, a short walk through Aberdeen will bring you to a renovated Tin Hau temple (182 Aberdeen Main Rd; 8am-5pm). Built in 1851, it's a sleepy spot but remains an active house of worship. Close to the harbour is a Hung Shing shrine (cnr Aberdeen Main Rd & Old Main St), a chaotic collection of altars and smoking, ovenlike incense pots. Both temples are a short walk from Aberdeen bus terminus.

Stanley

An easy bus or taxi ride 15km from Central, Stanley (Map p96) has an attractive market, beaches and good pubs and restaurants, which make it an appealing place to escape the concrete jungle. It had an indigenous population of about 2000 when the British took control of the territory in 1841, making it one of the largest settlements on the island at the time. A prison was built near the village in 1937 – just in time for the Japanese to intern the builders. Stanley Prison is a maximum security facility today. Hong Kong's contingent of British troops was housed in Stanley Fort at the southern end of the peninsula until 1995. It is now used by China's People's Liberation Army (PLA). There's a beach to the northeast of town that never gets as crowded as the one at Repulse Bay. The most important dragon-boat races are held at Stanley during the Dragon Boat Festival (Tuen Ng; p17) in early June.

STANLEY MARKET Map p96

Stanley Village Rd; 9am-6pm; 6, 6A, 6X or 260

No big bargains or big stings, just reasonably priced casual clothes (plenty of large sizes), bric-a-brac, toys and formulaic art, all in a nicely confusing maze of alleys running down to Stanley Bay. It's best to go during the week; on the weekend the market is bursting at the seams with tourists and locals alike.

MURRAY HOUSE Map p96

Stanley Bay; 6, 6A, 6X or 260

At the start of the Chung Hom Kok peninsula across the bay from Stanley Main St

top picks

MARKETS

- Graham St Market (p65)
- Temple St Night Market (p109)
- Yuen Po Flower Market (p110)
- Cat St (p82)
- Stanley (left)

(the waterfront promenade lined with bars and restaurants) stands this three-storey colonnaded affair. Built in 1848 as officers' quarters, it took pride of place in Central, on the spot where the Bank of China Tower now stands, for almost 150 years until 1982. It was re-erected here stone by stone and opened in 2001.

HONG KONG MARITIME MUSEUM

Map p96

2813 2322; www.hkmaritimemuseum.org; Ground fl, Murray House; adult/concession $20/10; 10am-6pm Tue-Sun; 6, 6A, 6X or 260

This small but interesting museum, occupying the ground floor of Murray House, consists of ancient and modern galleries charting the shipping history of Hong Kong. It's well worth a visit if you've already come to see Murray House. The modern gallery includes some fun interactive displays where you can test your skills at Morse code or even pilot a tanker through Hong Kong waters.

HONG KONG CORRECTIONAL SERVICES MUSEUM Map p96

2147 3199; www.csd.gov.hk/english/hkcsm /hkcsm.html; 45 Tung Tau Wan Rd; admission free; 10am-5pm Tue-Sun; 6, 6A, 6X or 260

Mock cells, gallows and flogging stands are the gruesome draws at this museum, about 500m southeast of Stanley Village Rd, which traces the history of jails, prisons and other forms of incarceration in Hong Kong.

OLD STANLEY POLICE STATION

Map p96

88 Stanley Village Rd; 6, 6A, 6X or 260

The most interesting building in the village itself is this two-storey structure that was built in 1859. It now contains a Wellcome supermarket.

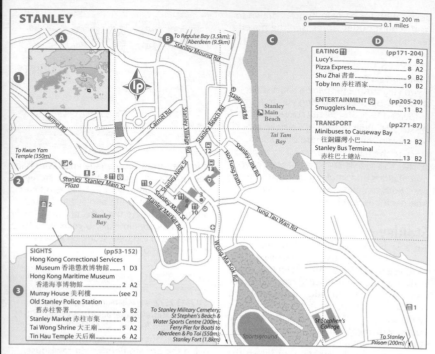

STANLEY

EATING 🍴 (pp171–204)
Lucy's...7 B2
Pizza Express...................................8 A2
Shu Zhai 書齋....................................9 B2
Toby Inn 赤柱酒家............................10 B2

ENTERTAINMENT 🎭 (pp205–20)
Smugglers Inn...................................11 B2

TRANSPORT (pp271–87)
Minibuses to Causeway Bay
往銅鑼灣小巴.................................12 B2
Stanley Bus Terminal
赤柱巴士總站.................................13 B2

SIGHTS (pp53–152)
Hong Kong Correctional Services
Museum 香港懲教物館........ 1 D3
Hong Kong Maritime Museum
香港海事博物館....................... 2 A2
Murray House 美利樓............... (see 2)
Old Stanley Police Station
舊赤柱警署................................ 3 B2
Stanley Market 赤柱市集......... 4 B2
Tai Wong Shrine 大王廟.......... 5 A2
Tin Hau Temple 天后廟........... 6 A2

NEIGHBOURHOODS & ISLANDS   HONG KONG ISLAND

ST STEPHEN'S BEACH & MILITARY CEMETERY Off Map p96
🚌 6A or 14

A great little tucked away spot, St Stephen's Beach, with a cafe, showers and changing rooms, is south of the village. In summer you can hire windsurfing boards and kayaks from the water-sports centre (see p229). To reach the beach, walk south along Wong Ma Kok Rd. Turn west (ie right) when you get to a small road (Wong Ma Kok Path) leading down to a jetty.

At the end of the road, turn south and walk past the boathouse to the beach. Bus 14 or 6A will take you close to the intersection with the small road.

Well worth a look is Stanley Military Cemetery for armed forces personnel and their families. The oldest graves date back to 1843 and are an intriguing document of the colonial era. The earlier graves show just how great a toll disease took on European settlers, while the number of graves from the early 1940s serves as a reminder of the many who died during the fight for Hong Kong and subsequent internment at the hands of occupying Japanese forces. The cemetery is just opposite the bus stop.

TEMPLES & SHRINES Map p96
🚌 6, 6A, 6X or 260

At the western end of Stanley Main St, past a tiny Tai Wong shrine and through the shopping complex called Stanley Plaza, is a Tin Hau temple (119 Stanley Main St; ⏰ 7am-6pm), built in 1767 and said to be the oldest building in Hong Kong. It has undergone a complete renovation since then, however, and is now a concrete pile (though the interior is traditional). A sign explains that the tiger skin hanging on the wall came from an animal that 'weighed 240 pounds, was 73 inches long, and three feet high [and] shot by an Indian policeman, Mr Rur Singh, in front of Stanley Police Station in the year 1942'.

Behind the Tin Hau temple is huge Ma Hang Estate. If you go across the front of the temple and follow the road, through the barriers and up the hill, you'll reach Kwun Yam Temple (⏰ 7am-6pm). The temple is on the left when you get to the roundabout at the top.

Shek O

Sometimes referred to as the 'last real village on Hong Kong Island', Shek O (Map pp62–3) has one of the best beaches on the island. Not as accessible as the beaches to the west (although it's only a 20-minute bus ride from Shau Kei Wan), the beaches here are usually less crowded.

Shek O has all sorts of activities to keep you amused plus some creditable dining and drinking options. Shek O beach has a large expanse of sand, shady trees to the rear, showers, changing facilities and lockers for rent. It's a good spot for swimming with several platforms offshore within a netted swimming area. In the village itself there's miniature golf (☎ 2809 4557; $13; ☯ 8am-6pmDec-Feb, 9am-5.30pm Mar-Nov) and from Dragon's Back, the 280m-high ridge to the west of the village, there's both paragliding and abseiling. Walking is possible around Shek O beach, though the terrain is steep and the underbrush quite thick in spots. You can also take advantage of several bicycle rental shops (bicycles from $15 a day), including Tung Lok Barbecue Store (☎ 2809 4692; ☯ Apr-Sep) in the centre of the village.

BIG WAVE BAY Map pp62-3
🚌 9 or 309 (Sun only)
This fine and often deserted beach is located 2km to the north of Shek O. To get to Big Wave Bay follow the road north out of town, travel past the 18-hole Shek O Golf & Country Club (☎ 2809 4458; Shek O Rd), then turn east at the roundabout and keep going until the road ends.

One of eight prehistoric rock carvings discovered in Hong Kong (see p20) is located on the headland above Big Wave Bay.

Repulse Bay

Repulse Bay (Map pp62-3) is the closest thing Hong Kong has to a posh beach suburb. It is home to some of Hong Kong's richest residents, and the hills around the beach are strewn with luxury apartment blocks. This includes the pink, blue and yellow wavy number with a giant square hole in the middle, a feature apparently added on the advice of a feng shui expert.

The long beach with tawny sand at Repulse Bay – Chin Shui Wan (Shallow Water Bay) in Cantonese – is the most popular on Hong Kong Island. Packed on the weekend and even

during the week in summer, it's a good place if you like people-watching. The beach has showers and changing rooms and shade trees at the roadside, but the water is pretty murky. Lifeguards keep extended hours here: from 9am to 6pm daily from March to November (8am to 7pm on Saturday and Sunday from June to August).

Middle Bay and South Bay, about 10 and 30 minutes to the south respectively, have beaches that are usually much less crowded.

KWUN YAM SHRINE Map pp62-3
Repulse Bay beach; 🚌 6, 6A, 6X or 260
Towards the southeast end of Repulse Bay beach is an unusual shrine to Kwun Yam. The surrounding area has an amazing assembly of deities and figures – goldfish, rams, the money god and other southern Chinese icons, as well as statues of the goddess of mercy and Tin Hau. Most of the statues were funded by local personalities and businesspeople during the 1970s. In front of the shrine to the left as you face the sea is Longevity Bridge; crossing it is supposed to add three days to your life.

REPULSE BAY Map pp62-3
109 Repulse Bay Rd; 🚌 6, 6A, 6X or 260
The Repulse Bay, a copy of the wonderful old colonial Repulse Bay Hotel, built in 1922 and bulldozed 60 years later, contains a small shopping mall and several food outlets, including the Verandah Restaurant (p191).

Deep Water Bay

A quiet little inlet with a beach flanked by shade trees, Deep Water Bay (Map pp62-3) is located a few kilometres northwest of Repulse Bay; lifeguards keep the same schedule as those at Repulse Bay beach, and in winter (ie December to February) they are on duty daily from 8am to 5pm. There are a few decent places to eat and have a drink, and some barbecue pits at the southern end of the beach. If you want a dip in the water, this spot is usually less crowded than Repulse Bay. Opposite the beach is the nine-hole Deep Water Bay Golf Club (p225). Deep Water Bay beach is a centre for wakeboarding (see p229).

Islandsiders might sniffily remark that the best experience you can have in Kowloon is to turn your back on it and look back towards Hong Kong Island's startling skyline. While there is a sense that Central's busy but scruffier neighbour is forever gazing enviously across the water at it (and, yes, those Island views are amazing), Kowloon has a great deal to offer.

This thriving, rumbustious area contains some of Hong Kong's best museums, sights, hotels and shopping. It is also where you start to leave behind sleek commercialism for a more absorbing and human-scale neighbourhood life of markets, temples, traditional shopping streets and crumbling tenement blocks.

top picks

KOWLOON

- Star Ferry (p275)
- Symphony of the Stars lightshow (p106)
- Former Maritime Police Headquarters (p102)
- Tsim Sha Tsui East Promenade (p106)
- Hong Kong Museum of Art (below)

Kowloon proper, the area ceded 'in perpetuity' to Britain by the Convention of Peking in 1860, extends north from the waterfront as far as Boundary St in Mong Kok. It covers about 12 sq km, but land reclamation and encroachment into the New Territories – the so-called New Kowloon – over the past 150-odd years has more than quadrupled its size.

Kowloon's most important area, Tsim Sha Tsui, has none of the slickness or sophistication of Hong Kong Island's Central, except within the confines of its top-end hotels. 'Tsimsy' is a riot of commerce and tourism.

While Kowloon's architecture has traditionally been less exciting than Hong Kong Island's, things are changing fast as the skyline creeps ever higher. The waterfront Hong Kong Cultural Centre in Tsim Sha Tsui was a stab at turning Hong Kong into something more than a territory obsessed with wealth (although the resultant building is hardly a triumph). The Peninsula Hotel is housed in one of Hong Kong's greatest colonial buildings and, at night, the promenade running east and northeast along Victoria Harbour from Star Ferry pier offers a technicolour backdrop of Central and Wan Chai.

There are some green spaces as well, including Kowloon Park with its aviary, pool and sculpture garden.

TSIM SHA TSUI

Shopping p167; Eating p191; Drinking p214; The Arts p220; Sleeping p241

Tsim Sha Tsui (Map p104; roughly pronounced 'j'ìm-s'àa-j'éui' and meaning 'Sharp Sandy Point') is Hong Kong's tourist ghetto. It is packed with hotels and inexpensive guesthouses, and the dining and drinking options are plentiful, if not as glittering as the ones across the water.

Tsim Sha Tsui is also a shopping destination. Clothing and shoe shops, restaurants, camera and electronics stores, and hotels are crammed into an area not much bigger than 1 sq km. Around Ashley, Hankow and Lock Rds is a warren of shops, restaurants and bars. Nightlife areas include Knutsford Tce and Minden Ave. Wandering these teeming, neon-blazing streets at night offers a unique buzz you just don't seem to get on Hong Kong Island.

The hotel and shopping district of Tsim Sha Tsui ('Tsimsy' or just 'TST' to locals) lies at the very tip of the Kowloon Peninsula to the south of Austin Rd. (The area between Austin and Jordan Rds is usually called Jordan by Hong Kong residents, but it can still be considered Tsim Sha Tsui here.) Chatham Rd South separates it from the hotels and shops of Tsim Sha Tsui East and the transport hub of Hung Hom.

Tsim Sha Tsui's western and southern boundaries – Victoria Harbour – are lined with top-end hotels, shopping centres as well as cultural venues.

HONG KONG MUSEUM OF ART
Map p104

☎ 2721 0116; www.lcsd.gov.hk/hkma; 10 Salisbury Rd; adult/concession $10/5, admission free Wed; ☻ 10am-6pm Fri-Wed, 10am-8pm Sat; 🚢 Star Ferry

Southeast of the Hong Kong Cultural Centre, the excellent Hong Kong Museum of Art is a must for lovers of the fine as well as the applied arts. It has seven galleries spread over six floors, exhibiting Chinese antiquities, Chinese fine art, historical pictures and contemporary Hong Kong art; it also hosts temporary international exhibitions.

The seventh gallery houses the Xubaizhi collection of painting and calligraphy. Highlights include some exquisite ceramics in the Chinese Antiques Gallery; the Historical Pictures Gallery, with its 18th- and 19th-century Western-style paintings of Macau, Hong Kong and Guangzhou; and the Gallery of Chinese Fine Art, which combines contemporary Chinese art and 20th-century collections of painting and calligraphy from Guangdong. Audio guides are available for $10, and there are free English-language tours at 11am Tuesday to Sunday.

When your feet get tired, take a seat in the hallway and enjoy the harbour views, or head for the Museum Café (☎ 2370 3860; 🕒 10am-9pm Fri-Wed). The Museum Bookshop (☎ 2732 2088; 🕒 10am-6.30pm Sun-Fri, 10am-8pm Sat) sells a wide range of books, prints and cards. Salisbury Gardens, which leads to the museum entrance, is lined with sculptures by contemporary Hong Kong sculptors. To reach the museum from the Tsim Sha Tsui MTR station, take exit E and walk south down Nathan Rd.

FORMER KCR CLOCK TOWER Map p104
Tsim Sha Tsui Public Pier; 🚢 **Star Ferry**
Immediately east of Star Ferry pier, this 44m-high clock tower (1915) was once part of the southern terminus of the Kowloon-

Canton Railway (KCR). Operations moved to the modern train station at Hung Hom to the northeast in late 1975. The station was demolished in 1978, though you can see a scale model of what it looked like at the Hong Kong Railway Museum (p123) in Tai Po in the New Territories.

HONG KONG CULTURAL CENTRE
Map p104
☎ 2734 2009; www.lcsd.gov.hk/CE/CulturalService/HKCC; 10 Salisbury Rd; 🕒 9am-11pm; 🚢 Star Ferry
On the one hand there are those who say that the virtually windowless, ski-jump-shaped Cultural Centre clad in pink ceramic tiles is an aesthetic horror. On the other hand…no, actually, come to think of it there is no other hand. By any measure it is an eyesore.

Despite being arguably the territory's most derided landmark, making woeful use of its spectacular location (and being compared with everything from a cheaply tiled public toilet to a roadside petrol station), inside it is a world-class venue containing a 2085-seat concert hall, a Grand Theatre that seats 1750, a studio theatre for up to 535, rehearsal studios and an impressive foyer. The concert hall even has a Rieger Orgelbau pipe organ (with 8000 pipes and 93 stops), one of the largest in the world.

On the building's south side is the beginning of a viewing platform from where you can admire Victoria Harbour and the skyline of Central and gain access to the Tsim Sha Tsui East Promenade and Avenue of the Stars (p106).

NATHAN ROAD Map p104
MTR Tsim Sha Tsui
Kowloon's 'Golden Mile' may sound romantic, but in truth its main thoroughfare (named after former Sir Matthew Nathan) is a bit of a traffic- and pedestrian-choked scrum of electronics shops and tenement blocks. It is nonetheless an iconic Hong Kong scene stacked with seedy guesthouses awkwardly rubbing shoulders with top-end hotels, touts selling 'copy' watches and tailors plying their trade on street corners. If that makes it sound edgy, in reality it is completely safe – which is just as well since you won't be able to

---

EIGHT PEAKS, NINE DRAGONS

The name 'Kowloon' is thought to have originated when the last emperor of the Song dynasty passed through the area during his flight from the Mongols in the late 13th century (see p21). He is said to have counted eight peaks on the peninsula and concluded that there must therefore be eight dragons there. But the young emperor was reminded that with him present, there were actually nine dragons. Kowloon is thus derived from the Cantonese words gáu, meaning 'nine', and *lùng*, meaning 'dragon'.

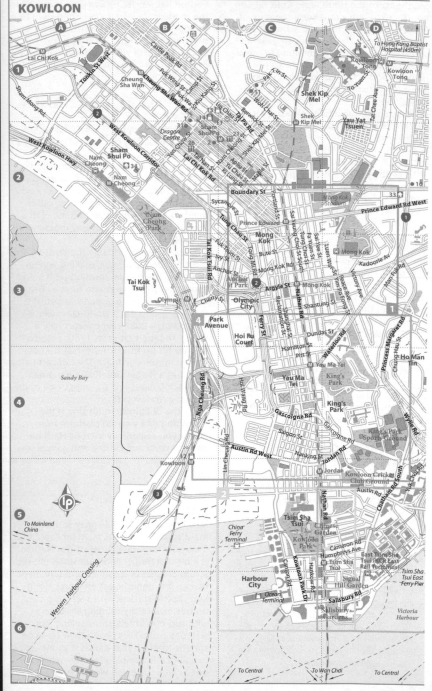

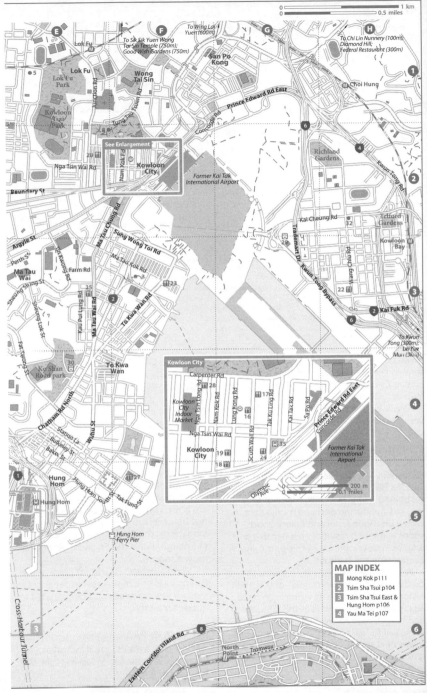

0 _____ 1 km
0 _____ 0.5 miles

To Sik Sik Yuen Wong
Tai Sin Temple (750m);
Good Wish Gardens (750m)

To Wing Lai
Yuen (600m)

To Chi Lin Nunnery (100m);
Diamond Hill;
Federal Restaurant (300m)

Lok Fu

Lok Fu
Park

Lok Fu

Wong
Tai Sin

San Po
Kong

Choi Hung

Kowloon Tsai
Park

Richland
Gardens

See Enlargement

Kowloon
City

Former Kai Tak
International Airport

Nga Tsin Wai Rd

Boundary St

Prince Edward Rd East

Concorde Rd

Kai Cheung Rd

Lefford
Gardens

Kowloon
Bay

Argyle St

Perth St

Ma Tau
Wai

Sung Wong Toi Rd

Ma Tau Kok Rd

Farm Rd

Ma Tau Chung Rd

Trademart Dr

Kwun Tong Bypass

Kwun Tong Rd

Kai Fuk Rd

To Kwa Wan Rd

Ko Shan
Road park

To Kwa
Wan

To Kwun
Tong (300m);
Lei Yue
Mun (3km)

Kowloon City

Carpenter Rd

Kowloon
City Indoor
Market

Kowloon
City

Nga Tsin Long Rd

Nam Kok Rd

Lung Kong Rd

Tak Ku Ling Rd

South Wall Rd

Kai Tak Rd

Sa Po Rd

Prince Edward Rd East

Concorde Rd

Former Kai Tak
International
Airport

Nga Tsin Wai Rd

Olympic Ave

200 m
0.1 miles

Chatham Rd North

Station La

Bulkeley St

Bailey St

Hung
Hom

Hung Hom

Hung Hom
Ferry Pier

Cross-Harbour Tunnel

Eastern Corridor Island Rd

North
Point

Tramway

MAP INDEX

1 Mong Kok p111
2 Tsim Sha Tsui p104
3 Tsim Sha Tsui East & Hung Hom p106
4 Yau Ma Tei p107

KOWLOON

INFORMATION
Country & Marine Parks
 Authority
 郊野公園及海岸公園管理局 1 B1

SIGHTS (pp53–152)
Apliu Street Market 鴨寮街 2 B2
Cattle Depot Artist Village
 牛棚藝術村 3 F3
City University of Hong Kong
 香港城市大學 4 D1
Festival Walk 又一城 ....(see 13)
Hong Kong Baptist University
 (Shaw Campus)
 香港浸會大學逸夫校園 5 E1
International Commerce
 Centre 6 B5
Jockey Club Creative Arts
 Center 賽馬會創意藝術中心 7 C1
Kowloon Walled City Park
 九龍寨城公園 8 E2
Lei Cheng Uk Han Tomb
 Museum 李鄭屋漢墓博物館 9 B1
Maryknoll Convent School
 瑪利諾修院學校 10 D2
Shek Kip Mei Estate Mei Ho
 House 石硤尾邨美荷樓 11 C1

SHOPPING (pp153–70)
Apliu Street Market 鴨寮街 .... (see 2)
Elements Shopping Mall 12 B4

Festival Walk 又一城 13 D1
Golden Computer Arcade
 黃金電腦商場 14 B1
Hong Kong Records
 香港唱片 ....(see 13)
New Capital Computer Plaza
 新高登電腦廣場 15 B1
Page One ....(see 13)

EATING (pp171–204)
Cheong Fat 昌發泰國粉麵屋 16 G4
Chong Fat Chiu Chow
 Restaurant 創發潮州飯店 17 G4
Hop Shing Chiu Chow
 Dessert 潮州合成甜品 18 G5
Islam Food 清真牛肉館 19 G4
King's Palace Congee &
 Noodle Bar 皇府 ....(see 13)
Kung Wo Tofu Factory
 公和豆品 20 E2
Kung Wo Tofu Factory
 公和豆品 21 C2
Mega Box 22 H3
Pak Kung Cafe 白宮冰室 23 F3
Queen's Cafe 皇后飯店 ....(see 13)
Ruamjai Thai Restaurant
 同心泰國菜館 24 G4
Sosam Tea House 蘇三茶室 25 E3
Taste ....(see 13)
Wah Nam Cafe Shop
 華南冰室 26 B2

Wing Lai Yuen (Yeung's
 Kitchen)
 詠藜園楊家菜 27 F5
Yee Heung Bean
 Products
 義香荳腐食品 28 F4

ENTERTAINMENT (pp205–20)
AMC Festival Walk
 又一城 AMC ....(see 13)
HITEC Rotunda
 國際展貿中心 29 G3
Ko Shan Theatre
 高山劇場 30 E4

SPORTS & ACTIVITIES (pp221–30)
Dragon Centre Sky Rink...............31 B2
Festival Walk Glacier
 又一城歡天雪地 ....(see 13)
Flight Experience ....(see 22)
Megalce ....(see 22)
Paintball Headquarters................32 H2

SLEEPING (pp231–50)
Caritas Lodge 明愛賓館 33 D2
Hong Kong Youth
 Hostels Association
 香港青年旅舍協會 34 B2

TRANSPORT (pp271–87)
Bus Stops 巴士站.........................35 G4

avoid criss-crossing it if you spend any time in the area. Anyone who chooses to stay at Chungking Mansions, Mirador Mansion or Golden Crown Guest House (see p241) will have this frenetic scene at their very doorstep.

FORMER MARINE POLICE HEADQUARTERS Map p104

Salisbury Rd, Tsim Sha Tsui; admission free; MTR Tsim Sha Tsui

Just being completed at the time of writing, this handsome declared monument with a boutique hotel and luxury goods shops is the end result of an extensive and lengthy redevelopment of this prime site overlooking the harbour.

While heritage lovers may baulk at the pretty nakedly commercial use of this 1884 historic building, at least visitors can once again get a close-up look at this site, which had been closed for years. The ship's mast was used to hoist typhoon signals while the tower next to it used to hoist and drop a globe on a pole to mark the time for ships in the harbour.

PENINSULA HONG KONG Map p104

☎ 2920 2888; www.peninsula.com; cnr Salisbury & Nathan Rds; MTR Tsim Sha Tsui

More than a Hong Kong landmark, the Peninsula, in the throne-like building opposite the Hong Kong Space Museum, is one of the world's great hotels (p241). Though it was being called 'the finest hotel east of Suez' just a few years after opening in 1928, the Peninsula was in fact one of several prestigious hostelries across Asia where everybody who was anybody stayed, lining up with (but not behind) the likes of the Raffles in Singapore, the Peace (then the Cathay) in Shanghai and the Strand in Rangoon (now Yangon).

Taking afternoon tea ($250; ⏰ 2-7pm) at the Peninsula is one of the best experiences in town – dress neatly and be prepared to queue for a table.

KOWLOON PARK Map p104

☎ 2724 3344; www.lcsd.gov.hk/en/parks/kp/en/index.php; 22 Austin Rd; ⏰ 5am-midnight; MTR Tsim Sha Tsui & Jordan

Built on the site of a barracks for Indian soldiers in the colonial army, Kowloon Park is an oasis of greenery and a refreshing escape from the hustle and bustle of Tsim Sha Tsui. Pathways and walls criss-cross the grass, birds hop around in cages, and towers and ancient banyan trees dot the landscape.

There's an aviary (6.30am-6.45pm Mar-Oct, 6.30am-5.45pm Nov-Feb) as well as a Chinese Garden and Sculpture Walk, featuring works by local artists. Kung Fu Corner, a display of traditional Chinese martial arts, takes place here from 2.30pm to 4.30pm on Sunday.

The renovated Kowloon Park Swimming Complex (2724 3577; adult/concession $19/9; 6.30am-10pm, 1hr close at noon & 5pm) comes complete with four pools and waterfalls. Visit on a weekday; on weekends there are so many bathers it's difficult to find the water.

HONG KONG SPACE MUSEUM & THEATRE Map p104

2721 0226; www.lcsd.gov.hk/CE/Museum /Space/e_dex.htm; 10 Salisbury Rd; adult/concession $10/5, admission free Wed; 1-9pm Mon & Wed-Fri, 10am-9pm Sat, Sun & public holidays; Star Ferry

Just east of the Hong Kong Cultural Centre, this golf-ball-shaped building consists of the Hall of Space Science, the Hall of Astronomy and the large Space Theatre, one of the largest planetariums in the world. Exhibits include a lump of moon rock, rocket-ship models and NASA's 1962 *Mercury* space capsule.

Closed at the time of research, the re-opened and refurbished museum may still not beat the nearby Science Museum (p107) for hands-on interest, but if it's raining a standby option is the attached Space Theatre, which screens 'sky shows' and Omnimax films on a massive screen. Lasting about 40 minutes, they are mostly in Cantonese, but translations by headphones are available.

The first show is at 1.30pm weekdays (12.20pm on Saturday and at 11.10am on Sunday) and the last at 8.30pm. Tickets are $32/16 for adults/concession ($24/12 in the front stalls); children under three are not allowed entry. Advance bookings can be made by phone up to an hour before show time.

KOWLOON MOSQUE & ISLAMIC CENTRE Map p104

2724 0095; 105 Nathan Rd; 5am-10pm; MTR Tsim Sha Tsui

North of the intersection of Nathan and Haiphong Rds, the Kowloon Mosque & Islamic Centre is the largest Islamic house of worship in Hong Kong. The present building, with its dome and carved marble, was completed in 1984 to serve the territory's 70,000-odd Muslims, more than half of whom are Chinese, and can accommodate 2000 worshippers. It occupies the site of a mosque built in 1896 for Muslim Indian troops.

Muslims are welcome to attend services here, but non-Muslims should ask permission to enter. Remember to remove your footwear.

OCEAN TERMINAL Map p104

2118 8666 24hr hotline; www.harbourcity.com .hk; Salisbury Rd; 10am-9pm; Star Ferry

Located to the north of the clock tower is Star House (3 Salisbury Rd), a frayed-looking retail and office complex. At its western end is the entrance to Ocean Terminal, the long building jutting into the harbour. It is part of the massive Harbour City shopping complex that stretches for half a kilometre north along Canton Rd and offers priceless views of Tsim Sha Tsui's western waterfront.

The stunning blue-and-white colonial structure located on the hill above where Canton and Salisbury Rds meet is the Former Marine Police Headquarters (opposite), which was built in 1884. Following a lengthy redevelopment of the site, there are new shops, cafes and restaurants,

TRANSPORT – TSIM SHA TSUI

Macau Ferries The China ferry terminal (Map p104) is on Canton Rd.

MTR Tsim Sha Tsui station (Map p104) on the Tsuen Wan line empties onto both sides of Nathan Rd. There's also a long tunnel linking it with Tsim Sha Tsui East MTR station (Map p106), the terminus of the MTR East Rail, although a couple of travelators make it less of a haul.

Star Ferry The pier (Map p104) is at western end of Salisbury Rd.

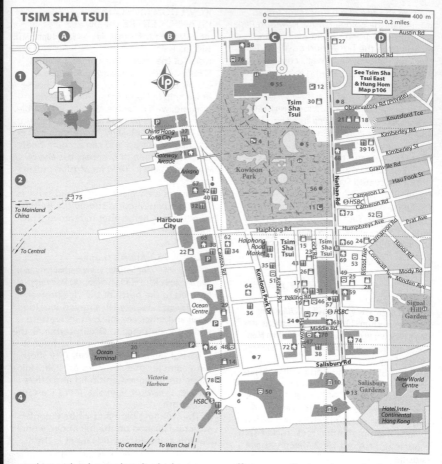

TSIM SHA TSUI

together with a luxury hotel, which should be in operation on the site by the time you read this.

TSIM SHA TSUI EAST & HUNG HOM

Eating p194; Drinking p214; Nightlife p218; Sleeping p244

The large triangular chunk of land east and northeast of Tsim Sha Tsui proper (Map p106), which was built entirely on reclaimed land, is a cluster of shopping centres, hotels and theatres. There are none of the old, crumbling buildings of 'real' Tsim Sha Tsui here – and, like most reclaimed areas, it has that soulless, artificial feel that will take decades to remove. But two of Hong Kong's most important museums are located here, and it

offers an excellent vantage point from which to admire the harbour and the Hong Kong Island skyline.

Among the features of Hung Hom, the contiguous district to the northeast, are the massive MTR East Rail station, on Wan Rd; the 12,500-seat Hong Kong Coliseum (☎ 2355 7234; 9 Cheong Wan Rd), which hosts concerts and sporting events; and the Hong Kong Polytechnic University (☎ 2766 5111; Hong Chong Rd), which is opposite the station.

Tsim Sha Tsui East is defined by Chatham Rd South to the west and Salisbury Rd to the south. The limit to the east is Hong Chong Rd, backed by the Hong Kong Coliseum and Hung Hom train station. To the north it ends at Austin Rd.

Hung Hom is further to the north and northeast and divided by the Hung Hom

TSIM SHA TSUI

INFORMATION
1010 CSL 1 B2
Kowloon HKTB Centre
　香港旅遊發展局 2 B4
Pacific Coffee Company ....(see 21)
Peninsula Academy ....(see 70)
Sincerity Travel/Hong Kong
　Student Travel 永安旅遊 ....(see 14)
Tsim Sha Tsui Post Office
　尖沙咀郵局 3 D3
Watertours ....(see 14)

SIGHTS   (pp53–152)
Aviary 百鳥苑 4 C2
Chinese Garden 5 D2
Former KCR Clock tower 6 C4
Former Marine Police
　Headquarters 前水警總部 7 C4
Hong Kong Antiquities &
　Monuments Office
　古物古蹟辦事處 8 D1
Hong Kong Cultural Centre
　香港文化中心 ....(see 50)
Hong Kong Dolphinwatch
　香港海豚觀察 ....(see 14)
Hong Kong Museum of Art
　香港藝術博物館 9 D4
Hong Kong Space Museum &
　Theatre 香港太空館 10 D4
Kowloon Mosque & Islamic
　Centre 九龍清真寺 11 C2
Kowloon Park Swimming
　Complex 九龍公園游泳池 12 C1
Museum Bookshop ....(see 9)
Museum Café ....(see 9)
Peninsula Hong Kong
　香港半島酒店 ....(see 70)
Sculpture Walk 雕塑廊 ....(see 56)
Sculptures 雕塑 13 D4

SHOPPING   (pp153–70)
Alan Chan Creations ....(see 70)
Chinese Arts & Crafts 中藝
　（香港）有限公司 14 C4
Curio Alley 15 C3
David Chan Photo Shop
　陳烘相機 16 D2
Giga Sports ....(see 20)
HMV 17 C3
King Fook 景福珠寶 18 D1
King Sing Jewellery
　景昇珠寶公司 ....(see 14)
KS Ahluwalia & Sons 19 C3
Lane Crawford 連卡佛 20 B4
Miramar Shopping Centre
　美麗華商場 21 D1
Muji ....(see 22)
Ocean Optical
　海洋眼鏡有限公司 22 B3
Ocean Sky Divers
　海天潛水訓練中心 23 C3
Om International 24 D3
Page One ....(see 29)

Premier Jewellery
　愛寶珠寶有限公司 25 D3
Sam's Tailor ....(see 69)
Star Computer City
　星光電腦城 ....(see 14)
Star House ....(see 14)
Swindon Books 辰衝 26 C3
Travelmax ....(see 20)
Tse Sui Luen 謝瑞麟珠寶 27 D1
Up Date Mall 28 D3
www.izzue.com 29 C3
Yue Hwa Chinese Products
　Emporium 裕華國貨 30 C1

EATING   (pp171–204)
Branto 印度素食餐廳 31 C3
Chungking Mansions
　重慶大廈 ....(see 59)
Citysuper 32 B2
Crystal Jade
　翡翠拉麵小籠包 33 B3
Din Tai Fung 鼎泰豐 34 C3
Gaylord Indian Restaurant
　爵樂印度餐廳 35 C3
Golden Bull 金牛苑 ....(see 20)
Hong Kong Old Restaurant
　香港老飯店 ....(see 21)
Hutong 胡同 ....(see 36)
Kung Tak Lam
　功德林上海素食 36 C3
Mak's Noodle
　麥奀雲吞麵世家 37 B2
Spring Moon 嘉麟樓 38 C4
Star Cafe 星座冰室 39 D2
Sweet Dynasty 糖朝 40 B2
Tak Fat Beef Ball
　德發牛肉丸 41 C3
T'ang Court 唐閣 ....(see 64)
Tonkichi Tonkatsu Seafood
　并吉日本吉列專門店餐廳 42 B2
Wellcome 惠康 43 C3
Wu Kong Shanghai
　Restaurant 滬江飯店 44 D3
XTC 45 B4
Yé Shanghai 夜上海 ....(see 66)

ENTERTAINMENT   (pp205–20)
Delaneys 46 C3
Felix 47 C3
Grand Ocean Cinema 48 C4
Hari's 夏利吧 49 D3
Hong Kong Cultural Centre
　香港文化中心 50 C4
Mes Amis 51 C3
New Wally Matt Lounge 52 D2
Spasso ....(see 22)
Tony's Bar 53 D3

SPORTS & ACTIVITIES   (pp221–30)
Hong Kong Jockey Club
　香港賽馬會 54 C3
Kowloon Park Sports Centre
　九龍公園體育館 55 C1
Kung Fu Corner 功夫閣 ....(see 56)

Sculpture Walk 雕塑廊 56 C2
Wing Chun Yip Man Martial
　Arts Athletic Association
　葉問國術總會 57 D3

SLEEPING   (pp231–50)
Beverly Guesthouse
　比華利賓館 ....(see 59)
BP International Hotel
　龍堡國際酒店 58 C1
Chungking House 鴻京酒店 ....(see 59)
Chungking Mansions 重慶大廈 ..59 D3
Cosmic Guest House 宇宙賓館 ..(see 69)
Dragon Inn 龍匯賓館 ....(see 59)
Four Seasons Guesthouse ....(see 59)
Garden Guest House ....(see 59)
Garden Hostel 花園旅館 ....(see 69)
Golden Crown Court 60 D3
Han Residence 61 D3
Holiday Guesthouse ....(see 59)
Hong Kong Hotels Association
　香港酒店業協會 62 C3
Kowloon Hotel Hong Kong
　九龍酒店 63 D3
Langham Hotel Hong Kong
　香港朗廷酒店 64 C3
Man Hing Lung Hotel
　萬興隆酒店 ....(see 69)
Marco Polo Gateway
　馬可孛羅港威酒店 65 B3
Marco Polo Hong Kong Hotel
　馬可孛羅香港酒店 66 B4
Marco Polo Prince
　馬可孛羅太子酒店 67 B2
Mei Lam Guest House
　美林賓館 ....(see 69)
Mira Hong Kong 68 D2
Mirador Mansion 美麗都大廈 69 D3
New Yan Yan Guesthouse
　新中華酒店 ....(see 59)
Park Guesthouse 百樂賓館 ....(see 59)
Peninsula Hong Kong
　香港半島酒店 70 C3
Royal Pacific Hotel & Towers
　皇家太平洋酒店 71 B2
Salisbury 香港基督教青年會 72 C4
Sealand House 海怡賓館 73 D2
Sheraton Hong Kong Hotel &
　Towers 香港喜來登酒店 74 D3
Tom's Guest House ....(see 59)
Traveller Services ....(see 21)
Travellers Hostel ....(see 59)
Yan Yan Guest House 欣欣賓館 ..(see 59)

TRANSPORT   (pp271–87)
China Ferry Terminal 中港碼頭 ..75 A2
Cross-Border Coach Terminus
　過境巴士站 76 C1
Eternal East Cross Border
　Coach (Buses to China)
　永東直巴 77 C3
Star Ferry Bus Terminal
　天星小輪巴士站 78 B4
Traveller Services ....(see 21)

Bypass into two parts: the station and coliseum on the west side and residential Hung Hom to the east.

TSIM SHA TSUI EAST PROMENADE
Map p106

📷 Star Ferry

One of the finest city skylines in the world has to be that of Hong Kong Island, and the promenade here is one of the best ways to get an uninterrupted view. It's a lovely place to stroll around during the day, but it really comes into its own in the evening, during the nightly Symphony of the Stars, a spectacular sound-and-light show involving 20 buildings on the Hong Kong Island skyline, which runs from 8pm to 8.20pm. The new Deck 'n Beer bar located here (p215) is

a great spot to have an alfresco, waterside drink (weather permitting).

Along the first part of the promenade is the Avenue of the Stars, which pays homage to the Hong Kong film industry and its stars, with handprints, sculptures and information boards, a brave but ultimately lacklustre effort to celebrate Hong Kong's film and TV industry.

The promenade officially starts at the New World Centre shopping centre and runs parallel to Salisbury Rd almost to the Hong Kong Coliseum and Hung Hom train station, but you can walk along the water all the way from Star Ferry pier in order to gain access to it. It gets especially crowded during the Chinese New Year fireworks displays in late January/early February and in June during the Dragon Boat Festival (p17).

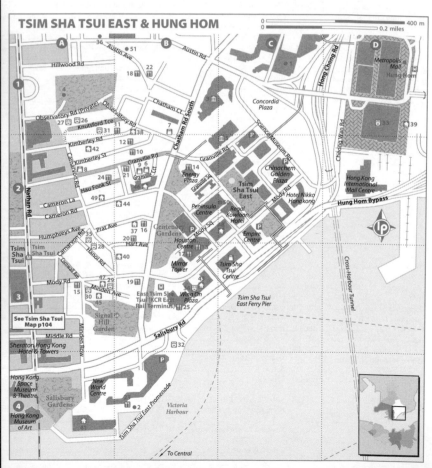

TSIM SHA TSUI EAST & HUNG HOM

HONG KONG MUSEUM OF HISTORY
Map p106

☎ 2724 9042; http://hk.history.museum; 100 Chatham Rd South; adult/concession $10/5, admission free Wed; ⏰ 10am-6pm Mon & Wed-Sat, 10am-7pm Sun & public holidays; MTR Tsim Sha Tsui (exit B2)

For a whistle-stop overview of the territory's archaeology, natural history, ethnography and local history, this museum is well worth a visit, not only to learn more about the subject but also to understand how Hong Kong presents its history to itself and the world.

'The Hong Kong Story' takes visitors on a fascinating walk through the territory's past via eight galleries, starting with the natural environment and prehistoric Hong Kong – about 6000 years ago, give or take a lunar year – and ending with the territory's return to China in 1997. You'll encounter replicas of village dwellings; traditional Chinese costumes and beds; a re-creation of an entire arcaded street in Central from 1881, including an old Chinese medicine shop; a tram from 1913; and film footage of WWII, including recent interviews with Chinese and foreigners taken prisoner by the Japanese.

TRANSPORT – TSIM SHA TSUI EAST & HUNG HOM

Ferry Star Ferries run from Central and Wan Chai to the Hung Hom ferry pier (Map p106).

MTR Take the Tsuen Wan line to Tsim Sha Tsui station (Map p104). East Tsim Sha Tsui and Hung Hong stations (Map p106) are on the MTR East Rail.

Free guided tours of the museum are available in English at 10.30am and 2.30pm on Saturday and Sunday.

HONG KONG SCIENCE MUSEUM
Map p106

☎ 2732 3232; http://hk.science.museum/eindex .php; 2 Science Museum Rd; adult/concession $25/12.50, admission free Wed; ⏰ 1-9pm Mon-Wed & Fri, 10am-9pm Sat, Sun & public holidays; MTR Tsim Sha Tsui (exit B2)

Illustrating the fundamental workings of technology, such as computers and telecommunications, and practical

TSIM SHA TSUI EAST & HUNG HOM

INFORMATION
Hong Kong Polytechnic
University.................................1 C1

SIGHTS (pp53-152)
Avenue of the Stars
星光大道.................................2 B4
Hong Kong Coliseum
紅磡體育館.........................(see 33)
Hong Kong Museum of
History 香港歷史博物館........3 B1
Hong Kong Observatory
香港天文台...............................4 A1
Hong Kong Polytechnic
University...............................(see 1)
Hong Kong Science Museum
香港科學館...............................5 C2

SHOPPING (pp153-70)
Beatniks....................................6 B2
Beverley Commercial Centre
百利商業中心.........................7 B1
Granville Rd 加連威老道.........8 A2
Rise Commercial Centre
利時商業大廈.........................9 B2

EATING (pp171-204)
Chang Won Korean
Restaurant 莊園韓國料理......10 B2
Fook Lam Moon 福臨門.........11 B1
Hansung Co 漢城美食............12 B2
Harbourside 港畔餐廳.......(see 41)
Hokahoka................................13 B3

Inagiku................................(see 40)
Ippei-An 麵屋一平安.............14 B2
Koh-i-Noor 寶軒印度餐廳.....15 A3
Kung Wo Tofu Factory
公和荳品...............................16 B2
Lei Garden 利苑酒家.............17 B3
Peking Dumpling Shop
北京水餃店...........................18 B1
Sabatini................................(see 48)
Spring Deer 鹿鳴春飯店........19 B3
Steak House.......................(see 41)
Swiss Chalet 瑞士餐廳..........20 B2
Tai Ping Koon 太平館............21 B2
Tin Heung Lau 天香樓...........22 B1
Towngas Cooking Centre
煤氣烹飪中心.......................23 B4
Wat Yat 唯一麵家.................24 A2
Woodlands 活蘭印度素食.....25 B3

ENTERTAINMENT (pp205-20)
Bahama Mama's.....................26 A1
Balalaika................................27 A1
Biergarten.............................28 A3
Chillax....................................29 A3
Cloudnine..............................30 A3
Dada.......................................31 A1
Deck 'N Beer..........................32 B3
Hong Kong Coliseum
紅磡體育館...........................33 D1
Lobby Lounge........................34 B3
Lobby Lounge....................(see 41)
Martini Bar.........................(see 48)
Where.....................................35 A2

SPORTS & ACTIVITIES (pp221-30)
Kowloon Cricket Club
九龍木球會...........................36 A1

SLEEPING (pp231-50)
Butterfly on Prat...................37 B2
Empire Kowloon
九龍皇悅酒店.......................38 B1
Harbour Plaza Metropolis.....39 D1
Hotel Panorama
麗景酒店...............................40 B3
InterContinental Hong
Kong 香港洲際酒店.............41 A4
Kimberley Hotel
君怡酒店...............................42 A2
Kowloon Shangri-La
九龍香格里拉大酒店............43 B3
Lee Garden Guest House
利園旅店...............................44 B2
Minden 棉登酒店..................45 A3
Park Hotel 百樂酒店.............46 B2
Phoenix Services Agency
峯寧旅運社.......................(see 51)
Pinnacle Apartment
豪居.......................................47 A3
Royal Garden 帝苑酒店.........48 C2
Star Guest House
星華旅運社...........................49 A2

TRANSPORT (pp271-87)
Avis..50 C2
Phoenix Services Agency
峯寧旅運社...........................51 B1

demonstrations of the laws of energy, physics and chemistry, the Hong Kong Science Museum is a great hands-on experience capable of entertaining adults as well as children. There are more than 500 displays.

HONG KONG OBSERVATORY Map p106
☎ 2926 8200; www.hko.gov.hk; 134A Nathan Rd; MTR Tsim Sha Tsui & Jordan

This historic monument, built in 1883, is sadly *not* open to the public. It continues to monitor Hong Kong's weather and sends out those frightening signals when a typhoon is heading for the territory (see boxed text, p289).

YAU MA TEI

Shopping p170; Eating p196; The Arts p220; Sleeping p246

Immediately to the north of Tsim Sha Tsui is Yau Ma Tei (Map p108), pronounced '*yàu-màa-dáy*' and meaning 'Place of Sesame Plants'. Today the only plants you'll find in this heavily urbanised neighbourhood are in the window boxes of *tàwng-láu*, the crumbling six-storey tenements that don't have lifts and more often than not have illegal huts on the

roof. The narrow streets full of shops and tenement buildings in Yau Ma Tei are much the same as those further south and north in Tsim Sha Tsui and Mong Kok, making this district practically indistinguishable from its neighbours.

Yau Ma Tei starts at Jordan Rd and reaches north to somewhere between Waterloo Rd and Argyle St. King's Park is its border to the east, while to the west it reaches Yau Ma Tei Typhoon Shelter in Victoria Harbour, the West Kowloon reclamation site, and the Kowloon station of the Tung Chung MTR and Airport Express lines.

Yau Ma Tei's narrow byways are good places to check out Hong Kong's more traditional urban society. It's especially rewarding to stroll along the streets running east to west between Kansu St and Jordan Rd, including Nanking St (mahjong shops and parlours), Ning Po St (paper kites and votives, such as houses, mobile phones and hell money to burn for the dead) and Saigon St (herbalist shops, kitchen suppliers, old-style tailors and pawnshops). On Shanghai St you'll find Chinese bridal and trousseau shops. See the walking tour p110 for a self-guided walk of this area.

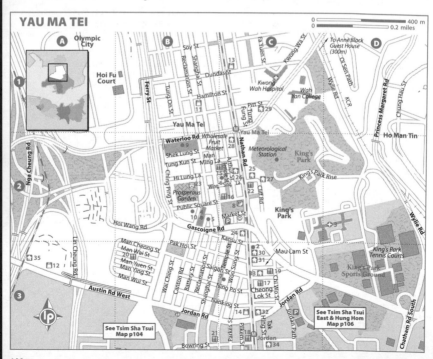

TEMPLE STREET NIGHT MARKET
Map p108

⏱ 2pm -11pm; MTR Yau Ma Tei (exit C)

The liveliest night market in Hong Kong, Temple St extends from Man Ming Lane in the north to Nanking St in the south and is cut in two by the Tin Hau temple complex. While you may find better bargains further north in New Kowloon, and certainly over the border in Shenzhen, it is still a good place to go for the bustling atmosphere and the smells and tastes on offer from the *dai pai dong* (open-air street stall) food.

People shop here for cheap clothes, watches, pirated CDs, fake labels, footwear, cookware and everyday items. Any marked prices should be considered suggestions – this is definitely a place to bargain.

You'll also find a surfeit of fortune-tellers, herbalists and, occasionally, some free, open-air Cantonese opera performances.

For street food, head for Woo Sung St, running parallel to the east, or to the section of Temple St north of the temple. You can get anything from a simple bowl of noodles to a full meal. There are also a few seafood and hotpot restaurants in the area.

The market officially opens in the afternoon, but most hawkers set up at about 6pm and start shutting up around 11pm.

TRANSPORT – YAU MA TEI

Bus Buses 2, 6, 6A and 9 run up Nathan Rd.

MTR Yau Ma Tei MTR station is on the Tsuen Wan and Kwun Tong lines, and Kowloon MTR is on the Tung Chung and Airport Express lines.

The market is at its best from about 7pm to 10pm, when it's clogged with stalls and people. If you want to carry on, visit the colourful wholesale fruit market (cnr Shek Lung St & Reclamation St; ⏱ midnight-dawn), which is always a hive of activity.

To reach Temple St market, take exit C2 from the Jordan MTR station and walk along Bowring St or exit C from the Yau Ma Tei MTR station and follow Man Ming Lane.

JADE MARKET Map p108

Battery St; ⏱ 10am-5pm; MTR Yau Ma Tei (exit C)

The Jade Market, near the Gascoigne Rd overpass just west of Nathan Rd and split into two parts by the loop formed by Battery St, has some 400 stalls selling all varieties and grades of jade from inside two covered markets. Unless you really know your nephrite from your jadeite, or your quality stone from your dyed tat, it's probably not wise to buy any expensive pieces

YAU MA TEI

INFORMATION
Kowloon Central Post
Office 九龍中央郵局 1 C2
Map Publication Centre
香港地圖銷售處 2 C3
Queen Elizabeth
Hospital
伊利沙伯醫院 3 D2

SIGHTS (pp53–152)
Jade Market 玉器市場 4 B2
Jade Market 玉器市場 5 B2
Temple Street Night
Market 廟街夜市 6 C2
Temple Street Night
Market 廟街夜市 7 C2
Tin Hau Temple 天后廟 8 C2
Wholesale Fruit Market
果欄 9 B2
Yau Ma Tei Police
Station 油麻地警署 10 C3

SHOPPING (pp153–70)
Chamonix Alpine
Equipment
沙木尼登山用品 11 B1
Elements 圓方 12 A3

Trendy Zone 潮流特區 13 C1
Yue Hwa Chinese
Products Emporium
裕華國貨 14 C3

EATING (pp171–204)
Hing Kee Restaurant
興記煲仔飯 15 C2
Lei Garden 利苑酒家 .... (see 12)
Mido Cafe 美都餐室 16 C2
Nathan Congee and
Noodle 彌敦粥麵家 17 C3
Pak Loh Chiu Chow
Restaurant
百樂潮州酒樓 .... (see 12)
Peking Restaurant
北京酒樓 18 C3
Tai Ping Koon 太平館餐廳 19 C3
Tim Kee French
Sandwiches
添記法式三文治 20 B3
Yeoh's Bah Kut Teh
楊氏肉骨茶 21 B3
Yokozuna 橫綱 22 C2

ENTERTAINMENT (pp205–20)
Broadway Cinematheque 23 B2

SLEEPING (pp231–50)
Alhambra Building
平安大樓 24 C2
Booth Lodge 卜維廉賓館 25 C2
Bridal Tea House Hotel
紅茶酒店 26 C2
Caritas Bianchi Lodge
明愛白英奇賓館 27 C2
Casa Hotel 28 C2
Cityview 29 C1
Eaton Hotel 逸東酒店 30 C3
Golden Island Guesthouse
金島賓館 .... (see 24)
Hakka's Guest House
嘉應賓館 .... (see 32)
Hong Kong Star
Guesthouse .... (see 24)
Nathan Hotel 彌敦酒店 31 C3
New Lucky House
華豐大廈 32 C3
Novotel 33 C3
Ocean Guest House
宏洋賓館 .... (see 32)
Rent-a-Room Hong Kong
訂房通 34 C3
W Hong Kong 35 A3
Ying Pin .... (see 32)

here, but there are plenty of cheap and cheerful trinkets on offer as well.

You can reach the market easily on foot from either the Jordan (exit A) or Yau Ma Tei (exit C) MTR stations. Bus 9 from the Star Ferry bus station will drop you off at the Kowloon Central Post Office at 405 Nathan Rd, which is just around the corner from the market.

TIN HAU TEMPLE Map p108

☎ 2508 1234; cnr Temple St & Public Square St; ⏰ 8am-5pm; MTR Yau Ma Tei (exit C)

A couple of blocks northeast of the Jade Market, this temple is dedicated to Tin Hau, the goddess of seafarers. The temple complex also houses an altar dedicated to Shing Wong, the god of the city, and to To Tei, the earth god. You'll find a row of fortune-tellers through the last doorway on the right from the main entrance facing Public Square St; signs indicate which ones speak English. An incense spiral that lasts 10 days will set you back a mere $130.

The Yau Ma Tei Police Station (Map p108; 627 Canton Rd), a short distance to the east along Public Square St, was built in 1922 and is a listed building.

MONG KOK

Shopping p170; Eating p196; Sleeping p247

A scrum of shoppers, stalls and cheap canteens, Mong Kok (Map p111; Prosperous Point) is one of Hong Kong's most congested working-class residential areas, as well as one of its busiest shopping districts.

This is where locals come to buy everyday items, such as jeans, tennis shoes, computer accessories and kitchen supplies. Take a look at Fife St, which has an amazing collection of stalls selling old vinyl, books, ceramics, machinery and music scores. Mong Kok is also a good place to buy backpacks, hiking boots and sporting goods (p170). Two blocks southeast of the Mong Kok MTR station (exit D3) is the Tung Choi St market (see the boxed text, p158), which runs from Argyle St in the north to Dundas St in the south.

The streets west of Nathan Rd reveal Hong Kong's seamier side; this is where you'll find some of the city's seediest brothels. Mostly run by Triads, these places are often veritable prisons for young women. The Hong Kong police routinely raid these places, but a look at the rows of pastel-coloured neon strip lights on so many blocks is an indication that

TRANSPORT – MONG KOK

MTR Mong Kok and Prince Edward MTR stations are on the Tsuen Wan and Kwun Tong lines. Mong Kok station is also on the MTR East Rail.

it's 'business as usual', despite the change in landlords.

Mong Kok starts somewhere between Waterloo Rd and Argyle St to the south and ends at Boundary St in the north – strictly speaking, anything beyond that is the New Territories. The limit to the east is Waterloo Rd as it heads northward to Kowloon Tong, and to the west the limit is the district of Tai Kok Tsui.

YUEN PO STREET BIRD GARDEN & FLOWER MARKET Map p111

☎ 2302 1762; Boundary St/Yuen Po St; ⏰ 7am-8pm; MTR Prince Edward (exit B1)

In this tiny but enchanting corner of Mong Kok, you should find a handful of old men out 'walking' their caged songbirds. Stick around long enough and you should see birds being fed squirming caterpillars with chopsticks. Birds are considered harbingers of good fortune, which is why you'll see some people carrying them to the racetrack.

There are also birds for sale from the stalls here, along with elaborate cages carved from teak and bamboo. Adjacent to the bird garden is the flower market on Flower Market Rd, which keeps theoretically the same hours but only gets busy after 10am, especially on Sunday.

To get to the bird garden and flower market, from the Prince Edward MTR station, come out of exit B1 and walk east along Prince Edward Rd West for about 10 minutes.

KOWLOON'S TEEMING MARKET STREETS

Walking Tour

1 Yuen Po Street Bird Garden & Flower Market A 10-minute walk away from Prince Edward MTR (exit A), Yuen Po Street Bird Garden is the gathering place for mostly old men who air their caged birds here and feed them grasshoppers with chop sticks. A little further along, Flower Market Rd (above) is lined with fragrant and exotic blooms and plants.

MONG KOK

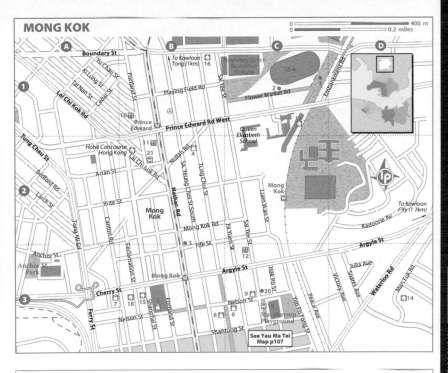

MONG KOK

INFORMATION

Hong Kong Trade &
Industry Department
工業貿易署 1 B2

SIGHTS   (pp53–152)
Flower Market 花墟 2 C1
Tung Choi St Market
女人街 .... (see 8)
Yuen Po St Bird Garden
園圃街雀鳥花園 3 C1

SHOPPING   (pp153–70)
KHS Bicycles 飛球單車行 4 B2
Langham Place Mall 朗豪坊 5 B3
Mong Kok Computer
Centre 旺角電腦中心 6 C3

Mong Kok Market 旺角街市 7 A3
Tung Choi St Market
女人街 8 B3
Wise Mount Sports
惠峰運動公司 9 C3

EATING   (pp171–204)
Fok Loi Kui Seafood
Restaurant
福來居海鮮飯店 10 B1
Fung Shing Restaurant
鳳城酒家 11 B2
Lei Garden 利苑酒家 12 C3

SPORTS & ACTIVITIES   (pp221–30)
Mong Kok Stadium
旺角大球場 13 C1

SLEEPING   (pp231–50)
Anne Black YWCA
女青柏顏露斯 14 D3
Langham Place Hotel
朗豪酒店 15 B3
Newton Hotel Kowloon
九龍麗東酒店 16 B1
Royal Plaza Hotel 帝京酒店 17 C1
Sunny Day Hotel 新天地酒店 18 B3

TRANSPORT   (pp271–87)
Buses to China
往中國大陸的士巴士 19 C3
China Travel Service
中國旅行社 20 C3
Trans-Island Chinalink (Buses
to China) 環島旅運有限公司 21 B2

2 Goldfish Market At the end of the street, take a left turn onto Sai Yee St, then right onto Prince Edward Rd West and then a left turn onto Tung Choi St: the first couple of blocks you'll see here are dominated by bicycle shops, but they then give way to a dozen or so shops trading in these extravagantly hued and weirdly shaped fish. You'll see an amazing variety, with the real rarities commanding high prices.

3 Tung Choi Street market Sharpen your elbows. This market (see boxed text, p158), also known as the Ladies' Market, is crammed with stalls and shoppers selling mostly inexpensive clothing. Refuel on Taiwanese at Tai Pak before continuing south.

4 Temple Street Night Market Beneath the bleaching glare of naked light bulbs, hundreds of stalls (p109) sell a vast array of booty

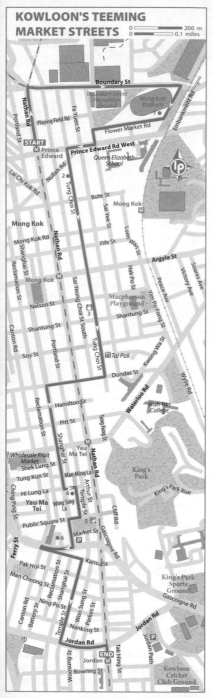

KOWLOON'S TEEMING MARKET STREETS

0   200 m
0   0.1 miles

WALK FACTS

Start Prince Edward MTR station (entrance/exit A)
End Jordan MTR station (entrance/exit A)
Distance 4.5km
Time Two hours
Fuel stop Tai Pak

from bric-a-brac to clothes, shoes, luggage and accessories. Turn right at Shanghai St, cut down Hi Lung Lane to Temple St and turn right. The market runs right down to Jordan Rd.

5 Tin Hau Temple Fragrant smoke curls from incense spirals at this atmospheric temple (p110) to the goddess of the sea. Fortune tellers nearby use everything from tarot cards, palmistry and even tame sparrows to deliver their predictions. Chinese opera singers sometimes also practice in the area.

6 Jade Market A great place to pick up an inexpensive trinket this large covered market (p109) contains dozens of stalls selling jade, the much-valued precious stone. At Jordan Rd turn east, then south into Nathan Rd to find Jordan MTR station.

NEW KOWLOON

Shopping p170; Eating p197; The Arts p220
New Kowloon (Map pp100–1) encompasses as many as 20 different neighbourhoods, but only half a dozen are of much interest to travellers. From west to east they are Sham Shui Po, Kowloon Tong, Kowloon City, Wong Tai Sin and Diamond Hill. The majority (and the places of interest described in this section) are within easy reach of an MTR station.

Sham Shui Po

A residential area of high-rises, Sham Shui Po (Map pp100–1) is famous for its market and computer emporiums (see p170). North of (and easily accessible from) the district is Lei Cheng Uk Han Tomb, an important archaeological find.

APLIU STREET MARKET Map pp100-1
Apliu St, btwn Nam Cheong St & Yen Chow St;
☼ **noon-midnight; MTR Sham Shui Po**
From the Sham Shui Po MTR station, take exit A1 and you'll soon fall right into this flea market, which makes a cheaper and

more interesting hunting ground than the Temple Street Night Market (p109) to the south. Everything from clothing to antique clocks and coins is on sale here, although the real speciality is secondhand electronic goods – radios, mobile phones, stereo systems, amplifiers and spare parts. The market spills over into Pei Ho St.

LEI CHENG UK HAN TOMB MUSEUM
Map pp100-1
☎ 2386 2863; www.lcsd.gov.hk/CE/Museum /History/en/lcuht.php; 41 Tonkin St; admission free; ☽ 10am-6pm Mon-Wed & Fri-Sat, 1-6pm Sun & public holidays; MTR Cheung Sha Wan (exit A3), 🚌 2 from the Star Ferry or 2A from Nathan Rd in Mong Kok, alight in front of the museum
First, a warning: this is a bit of a journey for what is an anticlimactic peek through perspex. Don't expect a terracotta army, but for those interested in the area's ancient history, this is a hugely significant burial vault dating from the Eastern Han dynasty (AD 25–220). It is one of Hong Kong's earliest surviving historical monuments and, believe it or not, was once on the coast.

The tomb consists of four barrel-vaulted brick chambers that take the form of a cross; they are set around a domed central chamber and many of the bricks contained moulded patterns of fish, dragons and the like. It's encased in a concrete shell for protection and visitors can only peep through a plastic window. The museum also contains a few pottery and bronze pieces taken from the tomb.

From Cheung Sha Wan MTR take exit A3 and walk northeast for 10 minutes along Tonkin St.

Kowloon Tong
As well as containing two of Hong Kong's most prestigious seats of learning – Hong Kong Baptist University (Map pp100-1; ☎ 3411 7400; Baptist University Rd, Kowloon), Hong Kong's most generously endowed seat of higher learning, and City University of Hong Kong (Map pp100-1; ☎ 2788 7654; Tat Chee Ave, Kowloon) – Kowloon Tong also has bridal shops with names like Cité du Louvre, where brides-to-be can buy their finery, have their photos done and even attend the ceremony itself. It is also a neighbourhood of knocking shops – 'no-tells', as one wag called them – with revolving beds, velvet-flock wallpaper and heart-shaped Jacuzzis.

They're very popular for 'matinees' and are rented by the hour.

FESTIVAL WALK Map pp100-1
☎ 2844 2223; 80-88 Tat Chee Ave; ☽ 11am-10pm; MTR Kowloon Tong
Kowloon Tong can claim Festival Walk, the territory's most luxurious shopping complex. In typical Hong Kong fashion, the centre boasts a fair few superlatives itself: Festival Walk has the largest cinema, bookshop and ice-skating rink (p228) in the territory. From the Kowloon Tong MTR station, take exit C2.

Kowloon City
Just west of what was once Kai Tak International Airport, the rather low-rent neighbourhood of Kowloon City (Map pp100–1) has two drawcards: a wonderful park that was once the infamous Kowloon Walled City, and a string of authentic and excellent-value Thai restaurants (p197). The old airport sits on a prime chunk of land, which is slowly being redeveloped.

KOWLOON WALLED CITY PARK
Map pp100-1
☎ 2716 9962, www.lcsd.gov.hk/parks/kwcp/en /index.php; Tung Tau Tsuen, Tung Tsing, cnr Carpenter Rd & Junction Rd; ☽ 6.30am-11pm; 🚌 1 from Star Ferry pier, alight opposite the park at Tung Tau Tsuen Rd
The walls that enclose this beautiful park were once the perimeter of a notorious village that technically remained part of China throughout British rule, as it was never included in the 1898 lease of the New Territories. The enclave was known for its vice, prostitution, gambling and

---

TRANSPORT – NEW KOWLOON

Bus Buses 5 and 26 leave from Tsim Sha Tsui to Ma Tau Chung Rd for Kowloon.

MTR The two MTR lines running up the spine of Kowloon are useful for getting around New Kowloon. Key stops on the Tsuen Wan line include Sham Shui Po and Cheung Sha Wan MTR stations; key stops on the Kwun Tong line include Kowloon Tong, Lok Fu, Wong Tai Sin and Diamond Hill MTR stations. The most important stop on the MTR East Rail line is Kowloon Tong station, which has an interchange with Kowloon Tong MTR station.

illegal dentists. In 1984 the Hong Kong government acquired the area, rehoused the residents elsewhere, built pavilions and ponds filled with turtles and goldfish and planted exquisite trees and shrubs, including a long hedge coaxed into the form of a dragon. The park opened in 1996. Close to the Carpenter Rd entrance of the park is the renovated Yamen building, once an almshouse. It contains displays on the history of the walled city, with a scale model of the village in the mid-19th century. At the park's north side are the remnants of the original South and East Gates.

Wong Tai Sin

The district of Wong Tai Sin to the north of Kowloon City is known for two things: its enormous and faceless housing estate and one of the most active and interesting temples in the territory.

SIK SIK YUEN WONG TAI SIN TEMPLE
Map pp58-9

☎ 2327 8141; Wong Tai Sin Rd; $2 donation requested; ☷ 7am-5.30pm; MTR Wong Tai Sin
An explosion of colourful pillars, roofs, lattice work, flowers and incense, this busy temple is a destination for all walks of Hong Kong society, from pensioners and businesspeople to parents and young professionals.

Some come simply to pray, others to divine the future with *chim* – bamboo 'fortune sticks' that are shaken out of a box on to the ground and then read by a fortune-teller (they're available free from the left of the main temple).

The complex, adjacent to the Wong Tai Sin housing estate, was built in 1973 and is dedicated to the god of that name, who began his life as a humble shepherd in Zhejiang province. When he was 15 an immortal taught Wong Tai Sin how to make a herbal potion that could cure all illnesses. He is thus worshipped both by the sick and those trying to avoid illness. He is also a favourite god of businesspeople. The image of the god in the main temple was brought to Hong Kong from Guangdong province in 1915 and was initially installed in a temple in Wan Chai, where it remained until being moved to the present site in 1921.

Behind the main temple and to the right are the Good Wish Gardens ($2 donation requested; ☷ 9am-4pm), replete with colourful pavilions

(the hexagonal Unicorn Hall, with carved doors and windows, is the most beautiful), zigzag bridges, waterfalls and carp ponds.

Below the main temple and to the left as you enter the complex is an arcade filled with dozens of booths operated by fortune-tellers, some of whom speak English. Expect a consultation to cost upwards of $100.

The busiest times at the temple are around Chinese New Year, Wong Tai Sin's birthday (23rd day of the eighth month – usually in September) and on weekends. Getting to the temple is easy. From the Wong Tai Sin MTR station, take exit B2 and then follow the signs or the crowds (or both).

Diamond Hill

Spread out below the peak of the same name, the residential district of Diamond Hill is due east of Wong Tai Sin and worth visiting solely for the nearby nunnery.

CHI LIN NUNNERY Map pp58-9

☎ 2354 1888; 5 Chi Lin Dr; admission free; ☷ nunnery 9am-5pm, garden 6.30am-7pm; MTR Diamond Hill
One of the most beautiful and arrestingly built environments in Hong Kong, this large Buddhist complex, originally dating from the 1930s, was rebuilt completely of wood (and not a single nail) in the style of the Tang dynasty in 1998. It is a serene place, with lotus ponds, immaculate bonsai tea plants and bougainvillea, and silent nuns delivering offerings of fruit and rice to Buddha and arhats (Buddhist disciples freed from the cycle of birth and death) or chanting behind intricately carved screens. The design (involving intricately interlocking sections of wood joined without a single nail) is intended to demonstrate the harmony of humans with nature. It's pretty convincing – until you look up at the looming neighbourhood high-rises behind the complex.

You enter the complex through the Sam Mun, a series of 'three gates' representing the Buddhist precepts of compassion, wisdom and 'skilful means'. The first courtyard, which contains the delightful Lotus Pond Garden, gives way to the Hall of Celestial Kings, with a large statue of the seated Buddha surrounded by the deities of the four cardinal points. Behind that is the main hall, containing a statue of the Sakyamuni Buddha flanked by two standing disciples and two seated bodhisattvas (Buddhist holy people). Below the complex is a cafe selling vegetarian snacks and dim sum for $14 to $25.

To reach the nunnery, take exit C2 of Diamond Hill MTR station, walk through the Hollywood Plaza shopping centre and turn east on to Fung Tak Rd. The nunnery is a five-minute walk away.

Lei Yue Mun

Southeast of the old Kai Tak airport is the residential neighbourhood of Kwun Tong (Map pp62–3), and a bit further southeast is the rapidly modernising fishing village of Lei Yue Mun (Map pp62–3). *Láy-yèw* means 'carp' and *mùn* is 'gate'; the 'carp gate' refers to the channel separating southeast Kowloon from Hong Kong Island, which is the narrowest entrance to Victoria Harbour. Across the water on the island and looming on the hillside is 19th-century Lei Yue Mun Fort, which now contains the Hong Kong Museum of Coastal Defence (p91).

SAM KA TSUEN SEAFOOD PRECINCT
Map pp62-3
MTR Yau Tong (Exit A2)
The 'village' of Lei Yue Mun is one of Hong Kong's prime seafood venues; around two-dozen fish restaurants (p198) line narrow, winding Lei Yue Mun Praya Rd overlooking the typhoon shelter. The area is a colourful and lively place to dine by the water at night and is always busy. To get here from the Yau Tong MTR station, use exit A2 and follow Cha Kwo Ling Rd and Shung Shun St south for 15 minutes or catch green minibus 24M from outside the station. Bus 14C links the Yau Tong Centre halfway down the hill with the Kwun Tong MTR station.

NEW TERRITORIES

By far Hong Kong's largest chunk of territory (747 sq km, or almost 68% of Hong Kong's land area), the New Territories (Map pp58–9) offers a great deal of cultural as well as natural interest. Ancient walled villages, wetlands teeming with aquatic and bird life, temple complexes and generous expanses of rugged, unspoiled country are just some of its attractions.

The eastern section, notably the Sai Kung Peninsula in the northeast and the area around Clearwater Bay further south, has some of Hong Kong's most beautiful scenery and hiking trails. Life in these more rural parts of Hong Kong is more redolent of times past – simpler, slower and often more friendly.

The New Territories was so named because the area was leased to Britain in 1898, almost half a century after Hong Kong Island and four decades after Kowloon were ceded to the crown. For many years the area was Hong Kong's rural hinterland; however, since WWII, when some 80% of the land was under cultivation, much of it has been urbanised. In the past two decades the speed at which this development has taken place has been nothing short of heart-stopping.

top picks

NEW TERRITORIES

- Sai Kung's beaches (p129)
- Hong Kong Wetland Park (p119)
- MacLehose Trail (p227)
- Tsuen Wan's monasteries and museums (left)
- Hong Kong Heritage Museum (p128)
- 10,000 Buddhas Monastery (p126)

Strictly speaking, everything north of Kowloon's Boundary St up to the border with mainland China is the New Territories. The northernmost part of the New Territories, within 1km of the Chinese frontier, is a 'closed border area' that is fenced and well marked with signs. It marks the boundary of the Hong Kong SAR with the Shenzhen Special Economic Zone (SEZ).

Almost four million people, up from less than half a million in 1970, call the New Territories home – about half the total population of Hong Kong. Most of them live in 'New Towns'. Since its inception in the 1950s, the New Towns program has consumed more than half of the Hong Kong government's budget, with much of the funding spent on land reclamation, sewage, roads and other infrastructure projects.

A glance at the MTR's network map shows how well connected much of it is by rail and the gaps are more than adequately filled by the extensive bus networks run for the most part by the Kowloon Motor Bus Co (KMB; ☎ 2745 4466; www.kmb.hk/english.php), alongside green minibuses, which run on just under 200 routes. For detailed bus route information check the KMB website. Getting around by taxi may not be quite the breeze it is in the urban centres, but it is still feasible: there are more than 2840 taxis cruising the streets and country roads of the New Territories. Ferries and *kaido* (small, open-sea ferries) serve the more remote areas and a few large communities on the coast.

TSUEN WAN

The Arts p220

Among the easiest destinations in the New Territories to reach, Tsuen Wan (Map p117), or 'Shallow Bay', is an industrial and residential New Town northwest of Kowloon, with some 290,000 inhabitants. It's nothing special to look at, but it does have a fine (though small) museum and some of the most colourful and active temple and monastic complexes in Hong Kong, including the serene Western Monastery (opposite) and the vivid Yuen Yuen Institute (opposite), stuffed with all manner of deities.

Chung On St, south of the Tsuen Wan MTR station, is famed for its jewellery and gold-smith shops. Tak Wah Park (☾ 6.30am-11pm) in the centre of town has ancient trees, footbridges over ponds and ornamental stone mountains. It's a peaceful place and an ideal spot to take a break from the hustle and bustle of the town around it.

The MTR station is on Sai Lau Kok Rd, with the Luk Yeung Galleria shopping centre above it. The main bus station is opposite the MTR on Castle Peak Rd (exit A2), but buses and green minibuses pick up and disgorge passengers throughout the New Town. Tsuen Wan is the last station on the Tsuen Wan MTR line. If you're really in a hurry to get there or back, change to the

Tung Chung MTR line at Lai King, which has fewer stops.

YUEN YUEN INSTITUTE Off Map p117
☎ 2492 2220; Lo Wai Rd; ⏱ 8.30am-5pm;
🚌 green minibus 81

Stuffed with vivid statuary of Confucian and Buddhist deities, the Yuen Yuen Institute, in the hills northeast of Tsuen Wan, is very much on the tourist trail but is well worth a visit nonetheless. The main building is a (vague) replica of the Temple of Heaven in Beijing. On the upper ground floor are three Taoist immortals seated in a quiet hall; walk down to the lower level to watch as crowds of the faithful pray and burn offerings to the 60 incarnations of Taoist saints lining the walls. This place is packed out at Chinese New Year. There are also

deities representing particular years and birth signs, to which worshippers pray and make offerings.

To reach both the Institute and the Western Monastery, take minibus 81 from Shiu Wo St, two blocks due south of Tsuen Wan MTR station (exit B1). Bus 43X from along Tai Ho Rd, further south of the MTR station (exit D), will drop you off on Sam Tung Uk Rd. The monastery is several hundred metres away and the institute is just up the hill. A taxi from the MTR station will cost around $35.

WESTERN MONASTERY Map p117
☎ 2411 5111; Lo Wai Rd; ⏱ 8.30am-5.30pm;
🚌 green minibus 81

A short distance down from the Yuen Yuen Institute, the Buddhist Western Monastery

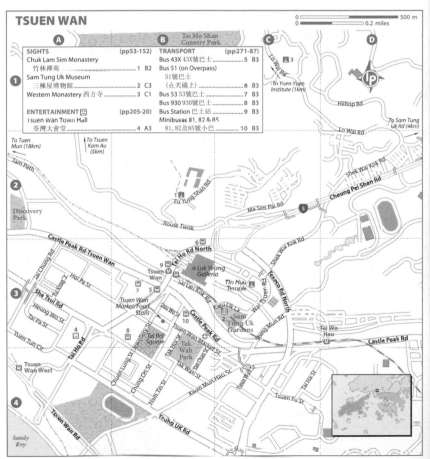

TRANSPORT – TSUEN WAN

Bus Many buses (but not all) from around the New Territories arrive at Tsuen Wan's central bus station, including bus 60M from Tuen Mun and 68M from Yuen Long. Bus 51 from Tai Mo Shan and Kam Tin stops along Tai Ho Rd.

MTR Tsuen Wan MTR station is on Tsuen Wan line. Tsuen Wan West station is on the West Rail line.

offers a sharp contrast to what's going on up the hill. This is a tranquil complex in which to pass the time, observing points of interest both architectural and spiritual. After being greeted by a bodhisattva statue in the entrance, the main building lies behind, styled as a classical Chinese palace. This comprises the Hall of Maitreya and the Great Buddha's Hall above it. Further behind is a another two-storey building where, depending on what time of day you visit, you may witness scores of monks chanting mantras. This building is topped by a spectacular nine-storey pagoda.

CHUK LAM SIM MONASTERY Map p117
☎ 2490 3392; Fu Yung Shan Rd; ⏰ 9am-4.30pm; 🚐 green minibus 85

In a lovely bucolic setting, Chuk Lam Sim Yuen (Bamboo Forest Monastery) is one of the most impressive temple complexes in Hong Kong. The temple was completed in 1932 when (legend has it) Tou Tei, the earth god, told an elderly monk to build it. Ascend the flight of steps to the first temple, walk to the back and enter the second. This second temple contains three of the largest golden Buddhas in the territory (though mere shadows of the big one on Lantau Island, p138). Flanking the trio on either side is an equally impressive line-up of 12 bodhisattvas, or Buddhists seeking enlightenment. The third temple contains another large image of Lord Gautama.

Chuk Lam Sim Monastery is northeast of Tsuen Wan MTR station. To reach it, take green minibus 85 from Shiu Wo St, which is two blocks due south of the MTR station (exit B1).

SAM TUNG UK MUSEUM Map p117
☎ 2411 2001; 2 Kwu Uk Lane; admission free; ⏰ 9am-5pm Wed-Mon; MTR Tsuen Wan

This imaginative and well-tended museum aims to portray traditional rural life as it was lived in this late-18th-century Hakka walled village, whose former residents, the Chan clan, were resettled in 1980. Within the complex a dozen three-beamed houses contain traditional Hakka furnishings, kitchenware, wedding items and agricultural implements, most of which came from two 17th-century Hakka villages in Bao'an county in Guangdong province. There are also special exhibits on such topics as rice farming in the New Territories. Behind the restored assembly and ancestral halls is the old village school, with interactive displays and videos on such topics as Hakka women, traditional crafts and traditional food.

At the Tsuen Wan MTR station, take exit E and walk five minutes southeast along Sai Lau Kok Rd to Kwu Uk Lane and the museum.

TAI MO SHAN

Hong Kong's tallest mountain is not Victoria Peak but Tai Mo Shan (Map pp58–9), the 'big misty mountain' that, at 957m, is nearly twice as high as that relative molehill (552m) on Hong Kong Island. Several hiking trails thread up and around it, but you'll need to bring your own food and water. The Countryside Series *North-East & Central New Territories* map is the one you want for this area (p296).

If you don't want to go it alone, contact any of the outfits listed on p226. The Tai Mo Shan Country Park Visitor Centre (Map pp58–9; ☎ 2498 9326; ⏰ 9.30am-4.30pm Sat, Sun & holidays) is located at the junction of Route Twisk (the name is derived from 'Tsuen Wan into Shek Kong') and Tai Mo Shan Rd, which is crossed by the MacLehose Trail.

To reach Tai Mo Shan from the Tsuen Wan MTR station, catch bus 51 on Tai Ho Rd North, alighting at the junction of Route Twisk and Tai Mo Shan Rd in Tsuen Kam Au. Follow Tai Mo Rd, which forms part of stage No 9 of the MacLehose Trail, east to the summit. On the right-hand side, about 45 minutes from the bus stop, a fork in the road

TRANSPORT – TAI MO SHAN

Bus Bus 64K links Tai Mo Shan with Yuen Long and Tai Po Market.

Green Minibus Bus 25K also runs between Tai Po Market and Tai Mo Shan.

leads south along a concrete path to the Sze Lok Yuen Hostel.

For information on accessing stages of the MacLehose Trail and the Wilson Trail near Tai Mo Shan, see p227.

NG TUNG CHAI WATERFALL & KADOORIE FARM & BOTANIC GARDEN Map pp58-9

☎ 2483 7200; www.kfbg.org.hk; Lam Kam Rd; admission free; ⏲ 9.30am-5pm; 🚌 64K

The scenic area around the Ng Tung Chai Waterfall is worth a detour. It is near the village of Ng Tung Chai, which is several kilometres north of Tai Mo Shan and just south of Lam Kam Rd. Reach the series of streams and waterfalls by taking the path leading to Ng Tung Chai and the Lam Kam Rd from the radio station on the summit of Tai Mo Shan.

Kadoorie Farm & Botanic Garden, southwest of Ng Tung Chai, is primarily a conservation and teaching centre, but the gardens are especially lovely, with many indigenous birds, animals, insects and plants in residence.

You can reach Kadoorie Farm most easily on bus 64K, which runs between Yuen Long MTR West Rail station and Tai Po Market MTR East station; get off on Lam Kam Rd near the sign for Ng Tung Chai village. If you walk from Tai Mo Shan to the village of Ng Tung Chai, you can catch green minibus 25K to Tai Po Market MTR East Rail station as well.

TUEN MUN

Eating p198; The Arts p220

The largest and most important New Town in the western New Territories, Tuen Mun (Map pp58–9) is not much of a destination in itself, but you may well transit through it as it is linked with other centres in Kowloon and the New Territories by the MTR West Rail. If you're travelling to Tuen Mun from Tsuen Wan or points in Kowloon or Hong Kong Island by bus, sit on the upper deck on the left side for spectacular views of the Tsing Ma Bridge, which links Kowloon with Lantau Island. In recent years a number of important archaeological discoveries have been made here, notably to the north and west of Tuen Mun town (see p20).

As always in New Towns, the centre of Tuen Mun is dominated by rather mundane commercial developments and shopping cen-

TRANSPORT – TUEN MUN

Bus An alternative route along the coast to Tuen Mun is to take bus 60M from Tsuen Wan MTR station (exit A3).

Ferry Services to Tuen Mun ferry pier arrive from Tung Chung, Sha Lo Wan and Tai O (all on Lantau). Ferries to the airport, Tung Chung and Tai O on Lantau depart from the pier to the southwest of the town centre.

Light Rail Tuen Mun is towards the southern end of the useful Light Rail network. Other major points include Tin Shui Wai, Yuen Long and Siu Hong. The station is linked to the MTR station.

MTR Tuen Mun is on the West Rail line.

tres. Most buses stop at the station just west of the town hall, where you'll also find the Town Centre station of the Light Rail.

HONG KONG WETLAND PARK
Map pp58-9

☎ 2708 8885; www.wetlandpark.com/en/index.asp; Wetland Park Rd, Tin Shui Wai; adult/child $30/15; ⏲ 10am-5pm; 🚆 line 705 or 706

The space and serenity of this 60-hectare ecological park make it a wonderful place to while away half a day. Its nature trails, bird hides and viewing platforms are windows on the wetland ecosystems and biodiversity of the northwest New Territories. The futuristic grass-covered headquarters houses interesting galleries (including one on tropical swamps), a film theatre, a large cafe and a viewing gallery. It's oddly pleasing to watch in silence as a kingfisher dives and then turn 180 degrees to be faced with a bank of high-rise apartment blocks. If you have binoculars then bring them; otherwise be prepared to wait to use the fixed points in the viewing galleries and hides.

To reach the Hong Kong Wetland Park, take the MTR West Rail to Tin Shui Wai and board Light Rail line 705 or 706, alighting at the Wetland Park stop. It can also be reached directly from Hong Kong Island, from the Admiralty MTR bus station on bus 967.

MIU FAT MONASTERY Map pp58-9

☎ 2461 8567; 18 Castle Peak Rd; ⏲ 9am-5pm; 🚆 line 751

Miu Fat Monastery in Lam Tei, due north of Tuen Mun town centre, is one of the best kept and most attractive Buddhist complexes in the territory. Guarding the entrance to the main temple are two stone lions and two stone elephants, and there are attractive gardens outside.

On the ground floor there's a golden likeness of Buddha in a glass case; on the 2nd floor are three larger statues of Lord Gautama. Don't miss the soaring new extension, a 42m tower with a top storey resembling a huge crystal lotus blossom that glows at night.

This is an active monastery that preserves more of a traditional character than many smaller temples; you'll see Buddhist nuns in droves wearing brown robes.

To get there take Light Rail line 751 from the Tuen Mun or Town Centre stops to Lam Tei station. The complex is on the opposite side of Castle Peak Rd; cross over the walkway and walk north 150m. Bus 63X, from the Mong Kok MTR station and the Star Ferry terminal in Tsim Sha Tsui, also stops in front of the monastery.

CHING CHUNG TEMPLE Map pp58-9
☎ 2370 8870; Tsing Lun Rd; ⏰ 7am-6pm; ⛟ line 505

Ching Chung Koon (Green Pine Temple) is a peaceful Taoist temple complex northwest of Tuen Mun town centre. The main temple – on the left at the far end of the complex past rows of bonsai trees, bamboo and ponds – is dedicated to Lu Sun Young, one of the eight immortals of Taoism who lived in the 8th century. Flanking a statue of him are two of his disciples. Outside the entrance to the main temple are pavilions containing a bell and a drum to call the faithful to pray or to rest. An annual Bonsai Festival is held here April.

Ching Chung Temple is directly opposite the Light Rail station of that name. To reach it from the Tuen Mun or Town Centre stations, catch line 505.

YUEN LONG
Eating p198; The Arts p220

There's nothing special at Yuen Long (Map pp58–9), a large town of more than 500,000 inhabitants, but it's an important transport hub and a gateway to the Mai Po Marsh (right). To the west of Yuen Long is the Ping Shan Heritage Trail, one of the best spots to spend a tranquil hour or two in the western New Territories.

MAI PO MARSH

This fragile ecosystem (Map pp58–9) abutting Deep Bay, south of the border with the mainland, simply teems with life. It is a protected network of mud flats, gày-wài (shallow shrimp ponds), reed beds and dwarf mangroves, offering a rich habitat of up to 340 species of migratory and resident birds, more than a third of them rarely seen elsewhere in the territory. The area attracts birds in every season but especially winter, when an average of 54,000 migratory waterfowl – including such endangered species as the Dalmatian pelican, black-faced spoonbill, spotted and imperial eagle and black vulture – pass through the marshes. In the centre is the Mai Po Nature Reserve, jointly managed by the World Wide Fund for Nature Hong Kong and the government's Agriculture, Fisheries & Conservation Department.

Despite its protected status, the marsh's future is precarious. The water quality in Deep Bay is among the worst in the Hong Kong coastal area. The Environmental Protection Department has found that levels of dissolved oxygen in the water have been declining since 1988. As a result, the numbers of crabs and mudskippers, on which the birds feed in winter, have declined. If the lower links of the food chain are imperilled, the birds that depend on Mai Po as a stopping ground during migration could disappear, taking with them endangered mammals such as the leopard cat and otter.

The culprit is the neighbouring city of Shenzhen in mainland China, which is pumping out a rapidly increasing amount of sewage, about half of which is untreated. Shenzhen is building more sewage-treatment facilities, but as the population of the city expands faster than its infrastructure, it's a race against time. Meanwhile, the only hope in the short term is that Hong Kong's increasingly wet summers will flush out and dilute many of the pollutants, helping to raise the number of crabs and mudskippers.

Mai Po Marsh comprises some 1500 hectares of wetlands. The part open to visitors, the Mai Po Nature Reserve, is in the centre. For more detailed information about this and other areas, contact the Hong Kong Bird Watching Society (www.hkbws.org.hk).

MAI PO NATURE RESERVE Map pp58-9
☎ 2471 3480; San Tin, Yuen Long; admission $120 (plus $200 deposit); ⏰ 9am-5pm; 🚌 76K from Fanling & Sheung Shui MTR East Rail stations or Yuen Long (On Tat Square station)

The 270-hectare nature reserve includes the Mai Po Visitor Centre (☎ 2471 8272) at the northeastern end, where you must register; the Mai Po Education Centre (☎ 2482 0369) to the south, with displays on the history and ecology of the wetland and Deep Bay; floating boardwalks and trails through the mangroves and mud flats; and a dozen hides (towers or huts from where you can watch birds up close without being observed). Disconcertingly, the cityscape of Shenzhen looms to the north.

Visitors are advised to bring binoculars (they may be available for rent at the visitor centre for $20) and cameras, and to wear comfortable walking shoes or boots but not bright clothing. It is best to visit at high tide (minimum 2m), when birds in their tens of thousands – mostly ducks, gulls, cormorants and kingfishers, but many rare species as well – flock to the area. Ring the weather hotline (☎ 187 8200) or the Hong Kong Observatory (☎ 2926 8200; www.hko.gov.hk/tide/etide main.htm) for tidal times.

Foreign visitors (but not Hong Kong residents) can visit the nature reserve unaccompanied, but numbers are limited so call well in advance to book a time. Pay the $100 entrance fee and $200 deposit at the visitor centre; the latter will be returned when you leave the reserve. For Hong Kong residents regular tours are run on weekends and public holidays. Again, these should be booked well in advance. If visiting on a weekend or holiday, call the Visitor Centre number above.

The World Wide Fund for Nature Hong Kong (WWFHK; Map p67; ☎ 2526 1011 24hr hotline; www .wwf.org.hk; 1 Tramway Path), adjacent to the entrance of the Peak Tram in Central, can arrange guided visits to the marsh; ring between 9am and 5pm on weekdays to book. Three-hour tours ($70) leave the visitor centre at 9am, 9.30am, 10am, 2pm, 2.30pm and 3pm on Saturday, Sunday and public holidays, but are conducted in English only when there are at least 10 visitors.

Bus 76K, which runs between Yuen Long and the Fanling and Sheung Shui MTR East Rail stations, will drop you off at Mai Po Lo Wai, a village along the main road just east of the marsh. The WWFHK car park is about a 20-minute walk from there. Red minibus 17 from San Fat St in Sheung Shui also goes

to Mai Po Lo Wai. Alternatively, a taxi from Sheung Shui will cost $60.

KAM TIN

The area around Kam Tin (Fertile Field; Map pp58–9) is where the Tangs, the first of Hong Kong's mighty Five Clans, settled in the 12th century AD and where they eventually built their walled villages (p20).

Walled villages, which usually had moats, are a reminder that Hong Kong's early settlers were constantly menaced by marauding pirates, bandits and imperial soldiers. They remain one of the most popular destinations for visitors to the New Territories.

Kam Tin contains two fortified villages: Kat Hing Wai and Shui Tau Tsuen. Most tourists go to Kat Hing Wai, as it is just off Kam Tin Rd, the main thoroughfare, and easily accessible. Shui Tau Tsuen is larger and less touristy, but don't expect to find remnants of ancient China. For details on Ping Kong, a seldom-visited walled village to the northeast, see p123.

KAT HING WAI Map pp58-9
🚌 64K

This tiny village is 500 years old and was walled in some time during the early Ming dynasty (1368–1644). It contains just one main street, off which a host of dark and narrow alleyways lead. There are quite a few new buildings and retiled older ones in the village. A small temple stands at the end of the street.

Visitors are asked to make a donation when they enter the village; put the money in the coin slot by the entrance. You can take photographs of the old Hakka women in their traditional black trousers, tunics and distinctive bamboo hats with black cloth fringes, but they'll expect you to pay (around $10).

Kat Hing is just south of Kam Tin Rd. If travelling from Yuen Long, get off at the first bus stop on Kam Tin Rd, cross the road and walk east for 10 minutes. Alternatively

---

TRANSPORT – KAM TIN

Bus Bus 64K stops along Kam Tin Rd on its way between Yuen Long and Tai Po Market MTR East Rail stations; bus 77K also goes to Yuen Long, Sheung Shui and Fanling.

take a taxi from Kam Sheung Rd MTR West station for less than $15.

SHUI TAU TSUEN Map pp58-9
🚌 64K

This 17th-century village, a 15-minute walk north of Kam Tin Rd, is famous for its prow-shaped roofs decorated with dragons and fish along the ridges. Tiny traditional houses huddle inside Shui Tau Tsuen's walls.

The Tang Kwong U Ancestral Hall (🕙 9am-1pm & 2-5pm Sat, Sun & public holidays) and the nearby Tang Ching Lok Ancestral Hall (🕙 9am-1pm & 2-5pm Wed, Sat & Sun) were built in the early 19th century for ancestor worship. The ancestors' names are listed on the altar in the inner hall and on the long boards down the side. The sculpted fish, on the roof of the entrance hall, symbolise luck; in Cantonese, the word for 'fish' (yéw) sounds similar to the word for 'plenty' or 'surplus'. Between these two buildings is the small Hung Shing Temple. South of them is Shui Tau Tsuen's most impressive sight, the renovated Yi Tai Study Hall (🕙 9am-1pm & 2-5pm Wed, Sat & Sun), built in the first half of the 19th century and named after the gods of literature and martial arts. The Tin Hau temple on the outskirts of the village to the north was built in 1722 and contains an iron bell weighing 106kg.

There's been a lot of building in and around Shui Tau Tsuen in recent years – the massive Tsing Long Hwy and the MTR West Rail extension straddle it to the west – and the old sits rather uncomfortably with the new. But the further north you walk beyond the village, the calmer and more tranquil it gets.

To reach Shui Tau Tsuen, which is signposted from Kam Tin Rd, walk north, go under the subway below the Kam Tin Bypass, pass Kam Tai Rd and cross over the river to Chi Ho Rd. Go over the small bridge spanning a stream, turn right and then left to enter the village from the east. The first thing you'll pass is the Yi Tai Study Hall.

FANLING & SHEUNG SHUI

A couple of lazy country villages (Map pp58–9) just a few years ago, Fanling and Sheung Shui now form one of the largest New Town conurbations in the New Territories, with more than 300,000 inhabitants. Get a feel for what they

were once like by walking around the Luen Wo Hu district at the northern end of Fanling. Major sights are thin on the ground here, but there's an important Taoist temple within easy walking distance and, a short bus ride away, a seldom-visited walled village and the Lung Yeuk Tau Heritage Trail. The posh 18-hole Hong Kong Golf Course (p225) at Fanling will be a draw for some.

Fanling and Sheung Shui are in the north-central New Territories, much closer to the mainland (5km) than they are to Tsim Sha Tsui (20km). They are linked by San Wan Rd, along which the bulk of buses and green minibuses serving the two New Towns travel.

FUNG YING SIN TEMPLE Map pp58-9
☎ 2669 9186; 66 Pak Wo Rd, Fanling; 🕙 8am-6pm; 🚇 Fanling

The main attraction in the area is this huge Taoist temple complex opposite the Fanling MTR East Rail station, and connected to it by an overhead walkway and subway. It has wonderful exterior murals of Taoist immortals and the Chinese zodiac, an orchard terrace, herbal clinic and a vegetarian restaurant (ground & 1st fl, Bldg A7; 🕙 10am-5pm). Most important are the dozen ancestral halls behind the main temple, where the ashes of the departed are deposited in what might be described as miniature tombs, complete with photographs.

MARKETS Map pp58-9
🕙 6am-8pm

These two lively markets frequented by Hakka people are worth a look, particularly early (ie before 10am). Sheung Shui market (Chi Cheong Rd) is 250m north of the Sheung Shui MTR East Rail station. To reach Fanling market

(Wo Mun St & Luen Un St) in the old district of Luen Wo Hui, walk north along Sha Tau Kok Rd for about 1.5km or catch bus 77K from the Fanling MTR East Rail station. This bus carries on to the market in Sheung Shui.

PING KONG Map pp58-9

🚌 77K

This sleepy walled village in the hills south of Sheung Shui is seldom visited by outsiders. Like other walled villages still inhabited in Hong Kong, it is a mix of old and new, and has a lovely little Tin Hau temple in the centre. You can also go exploring around the farming area behind the village compound.

To get to Ping Kong from Sheung Shui, catch green minibus 58K from the huge minibus station south of the Sheung Shui Landmark North shopping centre on San Wan Rd. The centre is a short walk northwest of Sheung Shui MTR East Rail station. Alternatively, bus 77K between Yuen Long and the Sheung Shui and Fanling MTR East Rail stations travels along Fan Kam Rd. Alight at the North District Hospital stop and walk southeast along Ping Kong Rd to the village.

A taxi from the Sheung Shui MTR East Rail station to Ping Kong will cost $23.

TAI PO

Eating p199

Another large residential and industrial New Town, Tai Po (Map p124) is the springboard for excursions into Plover Cove Country Park and Pat Sin Leng Country Park. Four Lanes Square, where four pedestrian streets converge in the centre of town, is a popular shopping area. The Old Tai Po District Office (Wan Tau Kok Lane) was built in 1907 and is one of the oldest examples of Western architecture in the New Territories.

Tai Po lies north and south of the Lam Tsuen River, at the westernmost point of Tolo Harbour, making it an excellent springboard for excursions into Plover Cove Country Park and Pat Sin Leng Country Park. It's an attractive market town and home to the Hong Kong Railway Museum (right).

Bicycles can be rented in season from several stalls around Tai Po Market MTR East Rail station, but try to arrive early – they often run out during the busiest times. A number of bicycle shops line Kwong Fuk Rd northwest of the MTR station.

One cycling route not to miss is the ride to Plover Cove Reservoir (p125) on the northeastern side of Tolo Harbour. Another is to the Chinese University of Hong Kong (p126) in Ma Liu Shui, on the southwestern side of the harbour. Allow half a day for either trip. There is also an inland route that goes to the university, but the coastal route linking the university with Tai Mei Tuk has the better views. Another option is to follow Ting Kok Rd east to the fishing village of San Mun Tsai (Map pp58–9).

HONG KONG RAILWAY MUSEUM
Map p124

☎ 2653 3455; 13 Shung Tak St; admission free; ⏰ 9am-5pm Wed-Mon; 🚉 Tai Wo

Housed in the former Tai Po Market train station, built in 1913 in traditional Chinese style, this museum is sure to appeal to train anoraks and young boys in particular. Exhibits, including a narrow-gauge steam locomotive dating back to 1911, detail the history of the development of rail transport in the territory. There is also much attention paid to the opening of the Kowloon–Canton Railway in 1910 and its original terminus in Tsim Sha Tsui, which moved to Hung Hong in 1975.

You can get to the museum most easily by alighting at Tai Wo MTR East Rail station, walking south through the Tai Wo Shopping Centre and housing estate, and crossing the Lam Tsuen River via Tai Wo Bridge (the small one with the Chinese roof) leading from Po Nga Rd. The museum is just southeast.

LAM TSUEN WISHING TREE Map pp58-9

Lam Kam Rd, Fong Ma Po; 🚌 64K

Until a short time ago Tai Po was the springboard for this large banyan tree, laden with coloured streamers of paper tied

---

TRANSPORT – TAI PO

Bus Bus 71K runs between the Tai Wo and Tai Po Market MTR East Rail stations.

Green Minibus For onward travel start at Tai Po Market MTR station or Heung Sze Wui St for bus 20K to San Mun Tsai; catch the bus at Tsing Yuen St for bus 25K to Ng Tung Chai (Tai Mo Shan).

MTR Take the MTR to Tai Po Market or Tai Wo East Rail stations.

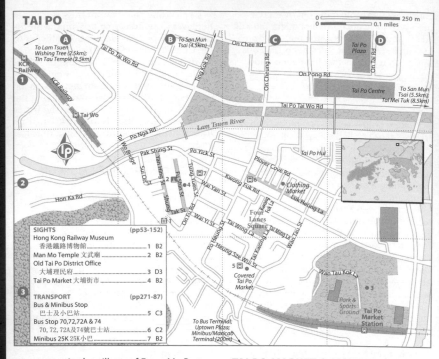

TAI PO

SIGHTS	(pp53-152)
Hong Kong Railway Museum 香港鐵路博物館	1 B2
Man Mo Temple 文武廟	2 B2
Old Tai Po District Office 大埔理民府	3 D3
Tai Po Market 大埔街市	4 B2

TRANSPORT	(pp271-87)
Bus & Minibus Stop 巴士及小巴站	5 C3
Bus Stop 70,72,72A & 74 70、72、72A及74號巴士站	6 C2
Minibus 25K 25K小巴	7 B2

to oranges, in the village of Fong Ma Po to the southwest. The idea was to write your wish on a piece of paper, tie it to the citrus fruit and then throw it as high as you could up into the tree. If your fruit lodged in the branches, you were in luck – and the higher it went, the more chance there was of your wish coming true. But things got, er, out of hand just once too often, and in 2005, a week after the end of Chinese New Year, a large branch of the tree came crashing to the ground, dashing most punters' wishes once and for all.

Focus switched to another tree nearby, which became the new arboreal oracle while the original was left to recover. However, this practice was soon stopped, too. In the name of conservation, wish makers can now only tie their wishing papers to Chinese-style wooden racks. You can still buy the wishing papers from vendors but you're unlikely to find any oranges for sale. At least there's a small Tin Hau temple nearby, replete with fortune-tellers, to compensate for your curtailed wish making.

To reach the tree catch bus 64K from the Tai Po Market MTR East Rail station and alight at Fong Ma Po.

TAI PO MARKET & MAN MO TEMPLE
Map p124
Fu Shin St; 6am-8pm; Tai Wo
Not to be confused with the MTR East Rail station of the same name, this street-long outdoor wet market is a stone's throw from the Hong Kong Railway Museum and is one of the busiest and most interesting markets in the New Territories. Towards the northern end of the same street, the double-hall Man Mo Temple (8am-6pm) is a centre of worship for the Tai Po area. It was founded in the late 19th century and, like the Man Mo Temple found in Sheung Wan (p80), it is dedicated to the gods of literature and of war.

PLOVER COVE
Sleeping p248
The area around Plover Cove Reservoir (Map pp58–9) is good hiking and cycling country, and well worth at least a full day's exploring. The village of Tai Mei Tuk, the springboard for most of the activities in the Plover Cove area, is about 6km northeast of Tai Po Market MTR East Rail station.

It may be worthwhile getting a copy of Universal Publications' *Tseung Kwan O, Sai Kung,*

Clearwater Bay or else the Countryside Series map *North-East & Central New Territories* (see p296).

Bicycles can be rented at Tai Mei Tuk at several locations, including Lung Kee Bikes (☎ 2662 5266; bicycle rental per day $20; ⏰ 9.30am-6pm). A bicycle track along the coast runs from Tai Mei Tuk to Chinese University at Ma Liu Shui. Ting Kok Rd in Lung Mei village is also where you'll find a row of popular restaurants (p199). Adjacent to the car park is the Tai Mei Tuk Fish Farm (p225), where you can try your luck angling for some freshwater fish.

The Plover Cove Country Park Visitor Centre (Map pp58–9; ☎ 2665 3413; ⏰ 9.30am-4pm Sat, Sun & public holidays), a short distance further east from the car park on Ting Kok Rd, is where the Pat Sin Leng Nature Trail (see below) to Bride's Pool starts.

PAT SIN LENG NATURE TRAIL Map pp58-9
🚌 75K

This excellent (and easy) 4.4km-long trail, which should take from two to 2½ hours, leads from the Plover Cove Country Park Visitor Centre at Tai Mei Tuk and heads northeast for 4km to Bride's Pool; there are signboards numbered 1 to 22, so there is little danger of getting lost. The elevation gain is only 300m, the scenery is excellent and the two waterfalls at Bride's Pool are delightful, but the place gets packed on the weekend. You can either return to Tai Mei Tuk via Bride's Pool Rd on foot or catch green minibus 20C, which stops at Tai Mei Tuk before carrying on to Tai Po Market MTR station. On Sunday and public holidays, bus 275R links Bride's Pool with Tai Po. If you carry on north from Bride's Pool to Luk Keng on Starling Inlet, you can catch green minibus 56K, which will take you to Fanling MTR station. Those looking for a more strenuous hike can join stage No 9 of the Wilson Trail (p227) at Tai Mei Tuk on the Plover Cove Reservoir and head west into the steep Pat Sin

Leng range of hills (named after the 'Eight Immortals' of Taoism) to Wong Leng Shan (639m). The trail then carries on westward to Hok Tau Reservoir and Hok Tau Wai (12km, four hours).

PLOVER COVE RESERVOIR Map pp58-9
🚌 75K

Plover Cove Reservoir was completed in 1968 and holds 230 million cubic metres of water; before then Hong Kong suffered from critical water shortages and rationing was not uncommon. Even after the reservoir opened, water sometimes had to be rationed; taps were turned on for only eight hours a day through the dry winter of 1980–81. The reservoir was built in a very unusual way. Rather than build a dam across a river, of which Hong Kong has very few, a barrier was erected across the mouth of a great bay. The sea water was siphoned out and fresh water – mostly piped in from the mainland – was pumped in.

TAI PO KAU

South of Tai Po is the small settlement of Tai Po Kau, to which most visitors wouldn't give a second thought were it not for the wonderful nature reserve here. Tai Po Kau Nature Reserve lies south of Tai Po, less than 1km inland from Tolo Harbour. The main entrance and the information centre are at the village of Tsung Tsai Yuen in the northernmost part of the reserve along Tai Po Rd.

TAI PO KAU NATURE RESERVE
Map pp58-9

Tai Po Rd; 🚌 70 or 72

The Tai Po Kau Nature Reserve is a thickly forested 460-hectare 'special area' and is Hong Kong's most extensive woodlands. It is home to many species of butterflies, amphibians, birds, dragonflies and trees, and is a superb place in which to enjoy a quiet walk. The reserve is crisscrossed with four main tracks ranging in length from 3km (red trail) to 10km (yellow trail), plus a short nature trail of less than 1km. If possible, avoid the reserve on Sunday and public holidays, when the crowds descend upon the place.

The reserve is supposed to emphasise conservation and education rather than recreation, and about 1km northwest of

TRANSPORT – PLOVER COVE

Bus Take bus 75K (and additionally 74K or 275R on Sundays and holidays) from Tai Po Market MTR East Rail station (Map p124) in Tai Po.

Green Minibus Bus 20C passes through Tai Po Market MTR station and Heung Sze Wui St (Map p124) in Tai Po on its way to Plover Cove.

TRANSPORT – TAI PO KAU

Bus Tai Po Kau Nature Reserve is well served by buses. Bus 70 passes through Jordan and Mong Kok on its way here. Bus 72 can be used to get here from nearby the Sha Tin and Tai Po Market MTR East Rail stations.

MTR A taxi from Tai Po Market MTR East Rail station will cost around $20, and from the University MTR East Rail station about $38.

the reserve entrance and down steep Hung Lam Drive is the Kerry Lake Egret Nature Park and the much-touted, over-priced Museum of Ethnology (☎ 2657 6657; www.taipokau.org; 2 Hung Lam Dr; adult/concession $18/12; ☺ 2pm-3pm & 5pm-6pm Sun & public holidays). In the same complex is the delightful, multicuisine Little Egret Restaurant (☎ 2657 6628; meals around $200).

UNIVERSITY

It's well worth making time to see the art museum at the Chinese University of Hong Kong (Map pp58–9; ☎ 2609 7000; www.cuhk.edu.hk/v6/en/), established in 1963, which is in Ma Liu Shui and served by University MTR East Rail station.

The University MTR East Rail station is southeast of the four campuses (Chung Chi Campus, New Asia Campus, Shaw Campus and United Campus). Ferries from Ma Liu Shui ferry pier, opposite the university on the eastern side of Tolo Hwy and about 500m northeast of University station, serve the Sai Kung Peninsula (p129) and Tap Mun Chau (p132) twice daily (p276). A taxi from the station to the pier will cost $14.

CHINESE UNIVERSITY OF HONG KONG ART MUSEUM Map pp58-9

☎ 2609 7416; www.cuhk.edu.hk/ics/amm; Sir Run Run Shaw Hall, Central Ave, admission free; ☺ 10am-5pm (closed public holidays); ⓡ University

The Chinese University of Hong Kong Art Museum is divided into two sections. The four-floor East Wing Galleries house a permanent collection of Chinese paintings, and calligraphy, but it is the ceramics, jade objets d'art and other decorative arts that are especially worth inspecting, including 2000-year-old bronze seals and a large collection of jade flower carvings. The West Wing Galleries stage five to six special exhibitions each year.

A shuttle bus from University station travels through the campus to the administration building at the top of the hill; for the museum, get off at the second stop. The bus runs every 20 to 30 minutes daily and is free except on Sunday ($5) from September to May. From June to August, it costs $1 Monday to Saturday and $5 on Sundays.

SHA TIN

Eating p199; The Arts p220; Sleeping p248

Although it is a large new town that has sprung from the blueprints of urban planners, Sha Tin (Sandy Field; Map p127; population 637,000) retains some traditional Chinese houses, giving parts of it a historical feel that's absent in most of the other New Towns. Built mostly on former mud flats, which produced some of the best rice in imperial China, it is now the place locals flock to on the weekends to place their bets at the nearby racecourse or to shop at Sha Tin's New Town Plaza (Map p127), one of the biggest shopping centres in the New Territories. For visitors, the drawcards are the temples and one of the best museums in Hong Kong.

Sha Tin lies in a narrow valley on both banks of a channel of the Shing Mun River. Fo Tan, where the racecourse is located, is to the northeast, and Tai Wei, where you'll find the Hong Kong Heritage Museum, is to the south. Though once separate villages, they are now extensions of the Sha Tin conurbation. Sha Tin MTR East Rail station is west of (and connected to) New Town Plaza in central Sha Tin. Buses arrive at and depart from the MTR East Rail station, the bus station below New Town Plaza and the one at City One Plaza on Ngan Shing St on the opposite side of the channel. You can rent bicycles from several kiosks in Sha Tin Park, south of New Town Plaza shopping centre.

10,000 BUDDHAS MONASTERY

Map pp58-9

☎ 2691 1067; admission free; ☺ 10am-5pm; ⓡ Sha Tin

Perched on Po Fook Hill about 500m northwest of Sha Tin MTR East Rail station, this quirky temple is worth the uphill hike to visit. Built in the 1950s, the complex actually contains more than 10,000 Buddhas. Some 12,800 miniature statues line the walls of the main temple and dozens of life-sized golden statues of Buddha's followers flank the steep steps leading to the monastery complex. There are several temples and pavilions split over two levels, as well as a nine-storey pagoda that can be climbed. For sustenance the complex also has a vegetarian restaurant (10.15am-4pm or 5pm). Be aware the temple may close if it's raining heavily.

To reach the monastery, take exit B at Sha Tin MTR station and walk down the ramp, passing a series of traditional houses at Pai Tau village on the left. Take the left onto Pai Tau St, and turn right onto Sheung

Wo Che St. At the end of this road, a series of signs in English will direct you to the left along a concrete path and through bamboo groves to the first of some 400 steps leading up to the monastery. An alternative route down is to take the path from the lower level. This will take you back down to the houses at Pai Tau Village by the rail station.

AMAH ROCK Map pp58-9
This boulder southwest of Sha Tin may look like just a rock, but it's an oddly

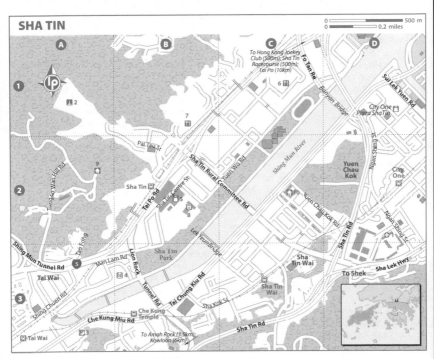

SHA TIN

SHA TIN

INFORMATION
Prince of Wales
Hospital
威爾斯親王醫院 1 D2

SIGHTS (pp53-152)
10,000 Buddhas
Monastery 萬佛寺 2 A1
Che Kung Temple
車公廟 3 A3
Hong Kong Heritage
Museum
香港文化博物館 4 B3

SHOPPING (pp153-70)
Shatin New Town Plaza
新城市廣場 5 B2

EATING (pp171-204)
Bay Phoon Town
周記避風塘 ....(see 5)
Cafe Merlion 魚尾獅餐廳 ....(see 5)
Chan Kun Kee 陳根記.................. 6 C1
Honeymoon Dessert
滿記甜品 ....(see 5)
Indonesian Restaurant
1968 印尼餐廳1968 ....(see 5)

Lung Wah Hotel 龍華酒店 7 B1
Shakey's Pizza Restaurant............(see 5)
Shanghai Xiao Nan Guo
小南國.....................................(see 5)

ENTERTAINMENT (pp205-20)
Sha Tin Town Hall
沙田大會堂 8 B2

SLEEPING (pp231-50)
Pilgrim's Hall...............................9 A2
Regal Riverside Hotel
麗豪酒店 10 C2

shaped one and, like many local landmarks in Hong Kong, it carries a legend. It seems that for many years a fisherman's wife would stand on this spot in the hills above Lion Rock Country Park, watching for her husband to return from the sea while carrying her baby on her back. One day he didn't come back – and she waited and waited. The gods apparently took pity on her and transported her to heaven on a lightning bolt, leaving her form in stone. The name of the rock in Cantonese is Mong Fu Shek, or 'Gazing Out for Husband Stone'. It's a popular place of pilgrimage for girls and young lovers during the Maidens' Festival on the seventh day of the seventh moon (mid-August).

As you take the MTR south from Sha Tin to Kowloon, Amah Rock is visible to the east (ie on the left-hand side) up on the hillside after Tai Wai MTR East Rail station, but before the train enters the tunnel.

CHE KUNG TEMPLE Map p127
☎ 2691 1733; Che Kung Miu Rd; admission free; ☻ 7am-6pm; ⊛ Che Kung Temple
This large Taoist temple complex, built in 1993, is on the opposite bank of the Shing Mun River channel in Tai Wai. It's dedicated to Che Kung, a Song-dynasty general credited with ridding Sha Tin of the plague; you'll see an enormous and quite powerful statue of the good general in the main temple to the left as you enter the complex. The main courtyard, flanked by eight statues of Taoist immortals, is always a hive of activity.

To reach the temple, take the MTR East Rail to Tai Wai station and change to the Ma On Shan Rail extension, alighting at Che Kung Temple station. The temple is just west of here.

TRANSPORT – SHA TIN

Bus Buses into and out of Sha Tin leave from/terminate at City One Plaza Sha Tin bus station. Bus 182 links Sha Tin with Wan Chai, Admiralty and Central. Bus 170 connects Sha Tin MTR East Rail bus station with Causeway Bay and Aberdeen. Bus 299 shuttles between Sha Tin and Sai Kung.

MTR Sha Tin, Tai Wai, Fo Tan and Racecourse stations are on the MTR East Rail line.

HONG KONG HERITAGE MUSEUM
Map p127
☎ 2180 8188; www.heritagemuseum.gov.hk; 1 Man Lam Rd; adult/concession $10/5, admission free Wed; ☻ 10am-6pm Mon & Wed-Sat, 10am-7pm Sun; ⊛ Sha Tin
Located southwest of Sha Tin town centre, this worthwhile museum is housed in a three-storey, purpose-built structure that is reminiscent of an ancestral hall. It has both rich permanent collections and innovative temporary exhibits in a dozen galleries.

The ground floor contains a book and gift shop, the wonderful Children's Discovery Gallery, with eight learning and play zones (including 'Life in a Village', 'Undersea Garden' and 'Mai Po Marsh') for kids aged four to 10, a Hong Kong Toy Story hands-on area for tots and an Orientation Theatre, with a 12-minute introductory video in English on the hour. There's also a lovely teahouse (☻ 10am-6pm).

Along with five thematic (ie temporary) galleries, the 1st floor contains the best of the museum's permanent collection: the New Territories Heritage Hall, with mock-ups of traditional shops, a Hakka fishing village and history of the New Towns; the Cantonese Opera Heritage Hall, where you can watch old operas on video with English subtitles, 'virtually' make yourself up as a Cantonese opera character on computer or just enjoy the costumes and sets; and the Chao Shao-an Gallery, devoted to the work of the eponymous water-colourist (1905–98) and founder of the Lingnan School of painting.

The 2nd floor contains another thematic gallery and the TT Tsui Gallery of Chinese Art, an Aladdin's cave of fine ceramics, pottery, bronze, jade and lacquerware, stone carvings and furniture. You may be interested in some of the gifts various Chinese provinces presented to China for the reunification, which are on display in the hallways.

To reach the Hong Kong Heritage Museum, take the MTR East Rail to Sha Tin station and walk south along Tai Po Rd. If coming from the Che Kung Temple, walk east along Che Kung Miu Rd, go under the subway and cross the footbridge over the channel. The museum is located 200m to the east.

SHA TIN RACECOURSE Map pp58-9
☎ 1817 hotline; www.sha-tin.com; Penfold Park; admission on race days public stands $10, members enclosures $100-150; ⊛ Racecourse or Fo Tan

Northeast of Sha Tin town centre is Hong Kong's second racecourse, which opened in 1978 and can accommodate up to 80,000 punters. In general, races are held on Saturday afternoon – and sometimes on Sunday and public holidays – from September to June; a list of race meetings is available from the HKTB or the racecourse website.

Bets are easily placed at one of the numerous computerised betting terminals run by the Hong Kong Jockey Club (p230). There is a worthwhile horseracing tour available for the interested but uninitiated through Splendid Tours & Travel (see p299).

The MTR Racecourse station, just west of the track, opens on race days only. Otherwise, get off at Fo Tan station and walk north along Lok King St and its extension, Lok Shun Path, for about 1.5km.

SAI KUNG PENINSULA

Eating p200; Drinking p215

The rugged and relatively remote Sai Kung Peninsula (Map pp58–9), in the northeastern New Territories, is the outdoor pursuits paradise of the New Territories; 60% of the peninsula is one huge 7500-hectare country park, divided into Sai Kung East and Sai Kung West. Though strictly speaking not on the peninsula, the 28,880-hectare Ma On Shan Country Park is contiguous with it and access is from Sai Kung Town.

The hiking is excellent in Sai Kung – the MacLehose Trail (p227) runs right across it – there's sailing galore and some of the best beaches in the territory are here. It is also a popular destination for groups who hire kaido, pack a picnic and drop anchor off one of its remote beaches.

The region is washed by Tolo Harbour to the north, Mirs Bay to the east and Port Shelter to the south. On the southern end of the peninsula is High Island Reservoir, once a sea channel and now Hong Kong's second-largest source of fresh water.

Two good websites devoted exclusively to the area are local listings site and guide www.exploresaikung.com and the district council's www.travelinsaikung.org.hk.

Sai Kung Town

Originally a fishing village, Sai Kung Town (Map p130) is now more of a leafy suburb for people working in Kowloon and on Hong Kong Island, but it still has some of the

TRANSPORT – SAI KUNG PENINSULA

Sai Kung Town

Bus From Sai Kung Town bus 299 heads to Sha Tin MTR East Rail, bus 92 runs to Diamond Hill and Choi Hung, bus 96R (Sunday and public holidays) heads to Wong Shek, Hebe Haven, and Choi Hung and Diamond Hill MTR stations, while bus 792M calls at Tseung Kwan O and Tiu Keng Leng MTR stations. Bus 94 goes to Wong Shek.

Green Minibus From Sai Kung Town, buses 1A, 1M and 1S (12.30am to 6.10am) go to Hebe Haven and Choi Hung MTR station.

Pak Tam Chung

Bus Take bus 94 from Sai Kung Town.

Hoi Ha

Green minibus Minibus 7 makes the run from Sai Kung Town daily, with the first departure at 8.45am and the last at 6.45pm. A taxi from there will cost around $100.

feeling of a port. Fishing boats put in an occasional appearance, and down on the waterfront there's a string of seafood restaurants that draw customers from all around the territory.

Sai Kung Town is an excellent base for hikes into the surrounding countryside. A kaido trip to one or more of the little offshore islands and their secluded beaches is also recommended (see the boxed text, p131). Windsurfing equipment can be hired from the Windsurfing Centre (☎ 2792 5605; ☼ from 9.30am-6pm Sat & Sun, call ahead weekdays) at Sha Ha (off Map p130), just north of Sai Kung Town. Bus 94, heading for the pier at Wong Shek and the springboard for Tap Mun Chau, will drop you off, or you could walk there from town in about 15 minutes.

Hebe Haven

The very small bay of Hebe Haven (Map pp58–9), which Cantonese speakers call Pak Sha Wan (White Sand Bay), is home to the Hebe Haven Yacht Club (☎ 2719 9682; www.hhyc.org.hk), which has a large fleet of yachts and other pleasure craft all but choking Marina Cove.

To swim at Trio beach, opposite the marina, catch a sampan from Hebe Haven to the long, narrow peninsula called Ma Lam Wat;

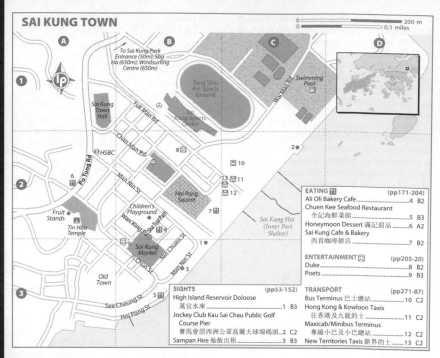

SAI KUNG TOWN

To Sai Kung Park Entrance (50m); Sha Ha (650m); Windsurfing Centre (650m)

Tang Shiu Kin Sports Ground

Swimming Pool

Sai Kung Town Hall

Sai Kung Sports Centre

HSBC

Sai Kung Hoi *(Inner Port Shelter)*

Hoi Pong Square

Children's Playground

Fruit Stands

Tin Hau Temple

Sai Kung Market

Old Town

See Cheung St

EATING (pp171-204)
Ali Oli Bakery Cafe 4 B2
Chuen Kee Seafood Restaurant
全記海鮮菜館 5 B3
Honeymoon Dessert 滿記甜品 6 A2
Sai Kung Cafe & Bakery
西貢咖啡餅店 7 B2

ENTERTAINMENT (pp205-20)
Duke 8 B2
Poets 9 B3

TRANSPORT (pp271-87)
Bus Terminus 巴士總站 10 C2
Hong Kong & Kowloon Taxis
往香港及九龍的士 11 C2
Maxicab/Minibus Terminus
專線小巴及小巴總站 12 C2
New Territories Taxis 新界的士 13 C2

SIGHTS (pp53-152)
High Island Reservoir Doloose
萬宜水庫 1 B3
Jockey Club Kau Sai Chau Public Golf Course Pier
賽馬會沼西洲公眾高爾夫球場碼頭 .. 2 C2
Sampan Hire 舢舨出租 3 B3

along the way you'll pass a small Tin Hau temple on a spit of land jutting out to the south. The beach is excellent and the sampan trip should only cost a few dollars. You can also walk to the peninsula from Sai Kung Town; it's about 4km.

LIONS NATURE EDUCATION CENTRE
Map pp58-9

☎ 2792 2234; Pak Kong; www.hknature.net/lnec /eng/; admission free; ⏱ 9.30am-5pm Wed-Mon; 🚌 92

Ideal for children, this 34-hectare attraction, located 2km northwest of Hebe Haven and just off Hiram's Hwy, is Hong Kong's first nature education centre and comprises everything from an arboretum, a medicinal plants garden and an insectarium to a mineral and rocks corner and a shell house. We love the Dragonfly Pond, which attracts up to a quarter of the more than 100 dragonfly species found in Hong Kong.

You can reach the centre on bus 92 from Diamond Hill MTR and Choi Hung, bus 96R on Sunday and holidays from Diamond Hill to Wong Shek Pier, and green minibus 1A from Choi Hung.

Pak Tam Chung

Pak Tam Chung (Map pp58–9) is the start of the MacLehose Trail (p227).

SAI KUNG COUNTRY PARK VISITOR CENTRE Map pp58-9

☎ 2792 7365; Tai Mong Tsai Rd; ⏱ 9.30am-4.30pm Wed-Mon; 🚌 94

While you're in Pak Tam Chung, visit the Sai Kung Country Park Visitor Centre, which is to the south of the village, just by the road from Sai Kung. It has excellent maps, photographs and displays of the area's geology, fauna and flora, as well as its traditional villages and Hoi Ha Wan Marine Park.

SHEUNG YIU FOLK MUSEUM
Map pp58-9

☎ 2792 6365; Pak Tam Chung Nature Trail; admission free; ⏱ 9am-4pm Wed-Mon; 🚌 94

This museum is a leisurely 20-minute walk from Pak Tam Chung south along the 1km-long Pak Tam Chung Nature Trail. The museum is part of a restored Hakka village typical of those found here in the 19th century. The village was founded about 150 years ago by the Wong clan, which built a kiln to make bricks. In the whitewashed dwellings, pigpens and cattle sheds – all surrounded by a high wall and watchtower to guard against raids by pirates – are farm implements, objects of daily use, furnishings and Hakka clothing.

Hoi Ha, Wong Shek, Chek Keng & Tai Long

There are several rewarding hikes at the northern end of the Sai Kung Peninsula starting in the little coves such as Hoi Ha, Wong Shek and Chek Keng, but note that the logistics of these hikes can be a bit tricky. Be sure to take along a copy of the *Sai Kung & Clearwater Bay*

Countryside Series map or Universal Publications' *Tseung Kwan O, Sai Kung, Clearwater Bay* (p296).

HOI HA WAN MARINE PARK Map pp58-9

☎ hotline 1823; Hoi Ha; 🚌 green minibus 7

A rewarding 6km walk in the area starts from the village of Hoi Ha (literally 'Under the Sea') on the coast of Hoi Ha Bay, now part of the Hoi Ha Wan Marine Park, a 260-hectare protected area blocked off by concrete booms from the Tolo Channel and closed to fishing vessels. It's one of the few places in Hong Kong waters where coral still grows in abundance and is a favourite with divers. You can visit anytime, but 1½-hour tours of the marine

---

ISLAND HOPPING IN SAI KUNG

Exploring the islands that dot the harbour is a delightful way to spend a few hours or even an entire day. Most *kaido* (small, open-sea ferries) leave from the piers on the waterfront, just in front of Hoi Pong Sq.

The easiest (and cheapest) way to go is to jump aboard a 'scheduled' *kaido* (ie one that goes according to demand and when full) bound for the small island of Yim Tin Tsai (return $35, 15 minutes, departs 10am and 11am, returns 2pm and 4pm Mon-Fri; an extra service on Saturday, Sunday and public holidays departs 9am and returns at noon).

On the way, the boat weaves through a number of small islands. The first island to the east of Sai Kung Town is Yeung Chau (Sheep Island). You'll be able to spot a horseshoe-shaped burial plot up on the slope; for reasons dictated by feng shui, the Chinese like to position graves with decent views of the sea. Southeast of Yeung Chau, Pak Sha Chau (White Sand Island) has a popular beach on its northern shore.

Just beyond Pak Sha Chau is the northern tip of the much larger Kiu Tsui Chau (Sharp Island), arguably the most popular island destination. Kiu Tsui Chau has several fine, sandy beaches: Kiu Tsui and, connected to it by a sand spit, Kiu Tau on the western shore; and Hap Mun on the island's southern tip. Both can be reached by *kaido* ($10) directly from Sai Kung Town.

Charming Yim Tin Tsai (Little Salt Field) is so-called because the original fisherfolk who lived here augmented their income by salt-panning. A few minutes' walk from the jetty up a small flight of steps to the left is St Joseph's Chapel, the focal point of the island. This is Yim Tin Tsai's only house of worship, which is most unusual in an area of Hong Kong where temples devoted to Tin Hau proliferate. Apparently the villagers, who all belong to the same clan, converted to Catholicism 150 years ago after St Peter appeared on the island to chase away pirates who had been harassing them. There's also a modest cafe open daily and plans for new facilities in the island, including a museum and hostel (see www.exploresaikung.com for further details).

Yim Tin Tsai is connected to the much larger island of Kau Sai Chau by a narrow spit of land that becomes submerged at high tide. Kau Sai Chau is the site of the 36-hole Jockey Club Kau Sai Chau Public Golf Course (Map p130; see also p225), a public links course that can be reached by the course's direct ferry from Sai Kung (adult/concession $50/30 return), which departs every 20 minutes daily from 6.40am to 9pm; the last boat back is at 10pm. Boats dock in Sai Kung Town at the long pier opposite the new Sai Kung Waterfront Park. The 19th-century Hung Shing Temple at the southern tip of Kau Sai Chau won a Unesco restoration award in 2000.

Beyond Kau Sai Chau is Leung Shuen Wan (High Island), a long trip from Sai Kung Town, and the High Island Reservoir, which was built in 1978 by damming what was once a large bay with dolooses (huge cement barriers shaped like jacks); sea water was then siphoned out and fresh water pumped in. You can see one example of a doloose (Map p130), weighing 25 tonnes, on display on the pier in Sai Kung Town.

If you want to be out on the water for a longer period or to have greater flexibility as to where you go, you can hire your own boat. *Kaido* owners can usually be found trawling for fares. Explain to the *kaido* owner where you want to go, how long you want to spend there and which way you wish to return. They don't speak much English, but if you point to the islands on Map pp58-9 in this book, they may get the picture. The usual price for this kind of trip is about $150 on weekdays, more on the weekend.

---

park are available in English at 10.30am and 2.15pm on Saturday, Sunday and public holidays. Be aware that you must register with the Agriculture, Fisheries & Conservation Department (AFCD; ☎ 1823) in advance, though.

TAP MUN CHAU
Eating p201

Tap Mun Chau (Map pp58–9), which translates as 'Grass Island', is very isolated and retains an old-world fishing village atmosphere. If you have the time (count on a full day and make sure you get your timing right), it's definitely worth the trip, and you will be rewarded with a feeling that's hard to come by in Hong Kong: isolation and a slightly otherworldly feel.

The sailing is particularly scenic from Wong Shek, as the boat cruises through the narrow Tai Tan Hoi Hap, which is more reminiscent of a fjord in Norway than a harbour in Hong Kong.

Delightfully sleepy Tap Mun Chau doesn't have accommodation, but you may get away with pitching a tent. There's only one restaurant on the island (p201), but there are shops selling snacks and drinks. The island is found off the northeast coast of the New Territories, where the Tolo Channel empties into Mirs Bay, which is Tai Pang Wan in Cantonese. Only Tung Ping Chau to the northeast in Mirs Bay is more remote.

As you approach the pier at Tap Mun village, you'll see fishing boats bobbing about in the small bay and, to the south, people working on fish-breeding rafts.

Tap Mun village is noted for its Tin Hau temple, which was built during the reign of Emperor Kang Xi of the Qing dynasty in the late 17th or early 18th century and is located northeast from where the boat docks. The Birthday of Tin Hau (p16) festival, celebrated in late April/early May, is big here, although most of the participants come from elsewhere in Hong Kong. Part of the temple is devoted to the god of war Kwan Tai (or Kwan Yu).

Other attractions here include seafood drying on racks in the sun, dragon boats bobbing in the harbour and, strangely, a herd of cows. It's an easy (and signposted) walk northward to Mau Ping Shan (125m), the island's highest point; a windy pebble beach on the southeastern shore; and an odd stone formation called

Balanced Rock, a couple of hundred metres south of the beach.

For ferry routes, schedules and fares for Tap Mun Chau, see p276.

TUNG PING CHAU

Kidney-shaped Tung Ping Chau (Map pp58–9), sitting in splendid isolation in Mirs Bay in the far northeast of the New Territories, is as remote as it gets in Hong Kong (making it a handy staging post in times past for gun and opium smugglers). The distance from Ma Liu Shui to the southwest, from where the ferry serving the island departs from, is around 25km.

It is part of Plover Cove Country Park (☎ 2665 3413; ⏰ 9.30am-4pm Sat, Sun & public holidays). The island, its rock pools and the waters around it – which teem with sea life (especially corals) – form Hong Kong's fourth marine park.

At one time the island, which is called Tung Ping Chau (East Peace Island) to distinguish it from Peng Chau (same pronunciation in Cantonese) near Lantau, supported a population of 3000, but now it is virtually deserted. The former village of Sha Tau is an eerie ghost town these days. There are a couple of tiny settlements on the northeastern side, including Sha Tau, where you'll find a food stall.

Tung Ping Chau is just 12km from the mainland's Daya Bay nuclear power station and has Hong Kong's only radiation shelter, at Tai Tong just north of the pier.

Tung Ping Chau's highest point is only about 40m, but it has unusual rock layers in its cliffs, which glitter after the rain. The island has some sandy beaches on its east coast that are good for swimming. The longest one, to the northeast, is Cheung Sha Wan. There is a small Tin Hau temple on the southwestern coast of the island, and some small caves dotting the cliffs. A good 6km walking trail encircles the whole island.

Tsui Wah Ferry Services runs ferries here on Saturdays, Sundays and public holidays. For ferry routes, schedules and fares for Tung Ping Chau, see p276.

CLEARWATER BAY PENINSULA

Clearwater Bay Peninsula (Map pp58–9) is a wonderfully untamed and roughly contoured backdrop to urban Hong Kong – at least that's the case on its eastern shore. It is wedged in by Junk Bay (Tseung Kwan O) to the west and Clearwater Bay (Tsing Sui Wan) sitting to the east; Joss House Bay (Tai Miu Wan) lies to the south.

Junk Bay is now the site of Tseung Kwan O, a New Town that was built on reclaimed land and has a growing population of more than 350,000 and a sixth MTR line, but the eastern coastline remains fairly unscarred and offers some exceptional walks, fine beaches and one of the most important temples dedicated to Tin Hau on the South China coast.

Clearwater Bay Peninsula is on the southeastern edge of the New Territories. The country park is divided into two parts: a long and narrow finger-shaped section stretching from Joss House Bay in the south almost to Port Shelter, and a half-moon-shaped section to the east between Lung Ha Wan and Clearwater Bay.

BEACHES Map pp58–9

Bus 91 passes Silverstrand beach (Ngan Sin Wan) north of Hang Hau before reaching Tai Au Mun; if you wish you can get off at Silverstrand and go for a dip. If you're heading for Lung Ha Wan, get off the bus at Tai Au Mun village and start walking. From Sai Kung, take bus 92 to where Hiram's Hwy and Clearwater Bay Rd meet and change there to bus 91.

From Tai Au Mun, Tai Au Mun Rd leads south to two fine, sandy beaches: Clearwater Bay First beach and, a bit further southwest,

Clearwater Bay Second beach. In summer, try to go during the week, as both beaches can get very crowded on the weekend.

CLEARWATER BAY COUNTRY PARK
Map pp58–9

The heart of the country park is Tai Au Mun, from where trails go in various directions, through the Clearwater Bay Country Park Visitor Centre (☎ 2719 0032; 9.30am-4.30pm Wed-Mon) to the southeast in Tai Hang Tun. Take Lung Ha Wan Rd north from Tai Au Mun to the beach at Lung Ha Wan (Lobster Bay) and return via the 2.3km Lung Ha Wan Country Trail.

TAI MIU TEMPLE Map pp58–9
☎ 2519 9155; 8am-5pm

Further south along Tai Au Mun Rd is this temple dedicated to Tin Hau. It is said to have been first built in the 13th century by two brothers from Fujian in gratitude to the goddess for having spared their lives during a storm at sea. It is particularly busy during the Tin Hau birthday festival (p16).

Just behind the temple is a Song-dynasty rock carving dating from 1274 and recording both the visit of a superintendent of the Salt Administration and the history of two temples in Joss House Bay. It is the oldest inscription extant in Hong Kong.

From Tai Miu, hikers can follow the 6.6km-long High Junk Peak Country Trail up to Tin Ha Shan (273m) and then continue on to High Junk Peak (Tiu Yu Yung; 344m) before heading eastward back to Tai Au Mun.

OUTLYING ISLANDS

Hong Kong's mosaic of islands number in the hundreds, although only a handful is inhabited. The largest 'Outlying Islands', which are usually sparsely populated, make handy boltholes for weekenders escaping the city or commuters who prefer a home close to space and greenery.

The attractions include country parks, with hundreds of kilometres of hiking trails, fresh(er) air and examples of some of the last remnants of traditional village life in Hong Kong. Explore them on a weekday and you're likely to have great expanses of these islands all to yourself.

Hong Kong's islands vary greatly in size, appearance and character. Many are little more than uninhabited rocks poking out of the South China Sea, while Lantau is almost twice the size of Hong Kong Island.

top picks

OUTLYING ISLANDS

- Tian Tan Buddha via cable car (p138)
- Cheung Chau's temples, harbour and street scenes (p145)
- Tai O's old-world atmosphere (p139)
- Lamma Family Trail (below)
- Pink dolphin-spotting (p142)

From the old-world streetscapes of Cheung Chau and Peng Chau to the monasteries of Lantau and the waterfront seafood restaurants of Lamma, Hong Kong's islands offer colour, variety and interest, along with a host of sights and activities. The islands are also an encyclopaedia of animal and plant life – a boon for nature lovers. What's more, some of Hong Kong's best beaches punctuate their rocky coasts.

Poisonous snakes are a rare but significant hazard to be aware of on Lamma and Lantau. See p293 for more details.

The islands listed here are all easily accessible from Hong Kong Island daily, and Cheung Chau and Lantau can be reached from Kowloon on the weekend as well. For details on routes, schedule and fares, see p276.

Because the tiny islands of Tap Mun Chau and Tung Ping Chau are best reached from the New Territories, they are covered on p132 and p132.

LAMMA

Eating p201; Drinking p215; Sleeping p249

With no roads or cars, leafy, low-rise Lamma (Map p136) makes a perfect place to find some space, peace and quiet. Gentle walks, lounging on the beach and browsing in the seafood restaurants and bars is the thing to do here (all the while studiously ignoring the socking great coal-powered fire station that looms behind a hill located near the main town of Yung Shue Wan). The territory's third-largest island after Lantau and Hong Kong Island, Lamma is home to an estimated 5000 fisherfolk, farmers and foreigners, and its hills are strewn with small homes and apartment blocks.

Perhaps the most interesting way for visitors to see a good portion of the island is to follow the 4km-long Family Trail that runs between Yung Shue Wan and Sok Kwu Wan. This takes a little over an hour, and you can return to Central by ferry from Sok Kwu Wan, Lamma's second village, which has alfresco seafood places that are a magnet for food lovers. Those with extra time should carry on to Tung O Wan, an idyllic bay some 30 minutes further south at the bottom of a steep hill, and perhaps return to Sok Kwu Wan via Mo Tat Wan.

Lamma is the closest inhabited island to Hong Kong Island; its northernmost tip is only 3km across the East Lamma Channel from Ap Lei Chau in Aberdeen. There are two main settlements on the island: Yung Shue Wan to the northwest and Sok Kwu Wan on the east coast of the island.

There's an HSBC branch (☎ 2233 3000; 19 Main St) and a post office (2 Main St) in Yung Shue Wan.

TRANSPORT – LAMMA

Ferry Ferries run from Yung Shue Wan pier to pier 4 of Central's Outlying Islands ferry terminal, Pak Kok Tsuen (Lamma) and Aberdeen; also from Sok Kwu Wan pier to pier 4 of Central's Outlying Islands ferry terminal, Man Tat Wan (Lamma) and Aberdeen.

YUNG SHUE WAN Map p136
🚢 Yung Shue Wan ferry

Though it's the larger of the island's two main villages, Yung Shue Wan (Banyan Tree Bay) remains a small place, with little more than a main street following the curve of the bay. Plastic was the big industry here at one time, but now restaurants, bars and other tourism-related businesses are the main employers. There is a small Tin Hau temple dating from the late 19th century at the southern end of Yung Shue Wan.

SOK KWU WAN Map p136
🚢 Sok Kwu Wan ferry

If you continue on the Family Trail you'll encounter a pavilion on a ridge, this time looking down onto Sok Kwu Wan (Picnic Bay), with its many fine restaurants, and fishing boats and rafts bobbing in the bay. Although still a small settlement, Sok Kwu Wan supports at least a dozen waterfront seafood restaurants that are popular with boaters. The small harbour at Sok Kwu Wan is filled with rafts from which cages are suspended and fish are farmed. If entering Sok Kwu Wan from the south (ie from the Family Trail linking it with Yung Shue Wan), you'll pass three so-called kamikaze caves: grottoes measuring 10m wide and 30m deep and built by the occupying Japanese forces to house motorboats wired with explosives to disrupt Allied shipping during WWII. They were never used. Further on and near the entrance to Sok Kwu Wan is a totally renovated Tin Hau temple dating back to 1826.

WIND TURBINE Map p136

Standing in elegant contrast to that CO_2-belching, coal-fired power station, Lamma's giant wind turbine, close to the top of the ridge just south east of Tai Peng village, makes a stirring sight (although in reality it is something of a white elephant generating far less power than was hoped for). There's a small information board on wind power and an electronic readout at its base showing the power output of the turbine, but there's not much else to do here but admire its feathered blades scything the breeze and to take in the dramatic backdrop of freighters setting sail far below, with Hong Kong Island looming in the background. To reach it follow the paths from Yung Shue Wan up to Tai Peng old village and turn right once you hit the concrete roadway linking the power station with Pak Kok.

HUNG SHING YEH BEACH Map p136
🚢 Yung Shue Wan ferry

About a 25-minute walk southeast from the Yung Shue Wan ferry pier, Hung Shing Yeh beach is the most popular beach on Lamma. Arrive early in the morning or on a weekday and you'll probably find it deserted, though you may find the view of the power station across the bay takes some getting used to. The beach is protected by a shark net and has toilets, showers and changing rooms. There are a few restaurants and drinks stands nearby – the latter open on the weekend only, except in summer – as well as the Concerto Inn (p202), a hotel that also serves so-so Western food.

LAMMA'S ENDANGERED TURTLES

Sham Wan has traditionally been the one beach in the whole of Hong Kong where endangered green turtles (Chelonia mydas), one of three species of sea turtle found in Hong Kong waters, still struggle onto the sand to lay their eggs from early June to the end of August.

Female green turtles, which can grow to a metre in length and weigh 140kg, take between 20 and 30 years to reach sexual maturity and always head back to the same beach where they were born to lay their eggs, which takes place every two to six years. Fearing that Sham Wan would catch the eye of housing-estate developers and that the turtles would swim away forever, the area was declared a Site of Special Scientific Interest and closed. It is patrolled by the Agriculture, Fisheries & Conservation Department (AFCD) from June to October. Some eight turtles are known to have nested here since 1997 and some are now being tracked by satellite.

As well as developers, a major hurdle faced by the long-suffering turtles is the appetite of Lamma locals for their eggs. In 1994 three turtles laid about 200 eggs, which were promptly harvested and consumed by villagers. Several years later villagers sold eggs to Japanese tourists for $100 each. There is now a $50,000 fine levied on anyone caught on the beach during the nesting season. Anyone taking, possessing or attempting to sell one of the eggs faces a fine of $100,000 and one year in prison.

Gwài-dáan, or 'turtle egg', by the way, is one of the rudest things you can call a Cantonese-speaking person.

LAMMA

LO SO SHING BEACH Map p136
🚤 Yung Shue Wan ferry

If you continue south from Hung Shing Yeh beach, the path climbs steeply until it reaches a Chinese-style pavilion located near the top of the hill. From this vantage point, it becomes obvious that the island is mostly hilly grassland and large boulders, though more and more trees are being planted.

You will pass a second pavilion that offers splendid views out to the sea; from here a path leads from the Family Trail down to Lo So Shing beach, the most beautiful on Lamma. The beach is not very big, but it has a nice cover of shade trees at the back that provide a break from the sun.

MO TAT WAN Map p136

The clean and relatively uncrowded beach at Mo Tat Wan is a mere 20-minute walk east of Sok Kwu Wan along a coastal path. Mo Tat Wan is OK for swimming, but has no lifeguards. You can also reach here by *kaido* from Aberdeen, which continues on to Sok Kwu Wan.

SHAM WAN Map p136

Sham Wan (Deep Bay) is another beautiful bay to the southwest that can be reached from Tung O Wan by clambering over the hills. A trail on the left about 200m up the hill from Tung O leads south to a small and sandy beach. Don't come here from June to October, when Hong Kong's endangered green turtles nest (see boxed text, p135).

LAMMA

INFORMATION
HSBC 匯豐銀行 1 D1
Post Office 郵局 2 D1

SIGHTS (pp53-152)
Tin Hau Temple 天后廟 3 A2
Tin Hau Temple 天后廟 4 B3
Wind Turbine 風車 5 B2

EATING 🍴 (pp171-204)
Bookworm Café 南島書蟲 6 D2
Concerto Inn 浪濤軒 ....(see 17)
Deli Lamma Café 7 D2
Han Lok Yuen 閒樂園酒家 8 B2

Kin Hing Tofu Dessert
建興阿婆豆腐花 9 B2
Lamcombe Seafood
Restaurant
南江海鮮酒樓 10 D2
Rainbow Seafood
Restaurant
天虹海鮮酒家 11 C3
Tai Yuen Restaurant
泰苑魚翅海鮮酒家 .... (see 11)
The Bay 星浪餐廳 12 C3

ENTERTAINMENT 🎭 (pp205-20)
Diesel's Bar 13 D2

Fountainhead Drinking Bar 14 D1
Island Society Bar 15 D1

SLEEPING 🛏 (pp231-50)
Bali Holiday Resort
優閒渡假屋 16 D1
Concerto Inn 浪濤軒 17 B2
Jackson Property Agency
輝煌地產代理公司 18 D1
Man Lai Wah Hotel
文麗華酒店 19 D1

TRANSPORT (pp271-87)
Ferry Terminal 20 C1

TUNG O WAN Map p136

While walking to Sok Kwu Wan from Yung Shue Wan or from Sok Kwu Wan itself, a detour to this small and secluded bay, with a long stretch of sandy beach, is highly recommended. Just before the Tin Hau temple at the entrance to Sok Kwu Wan, follow the signposted path to the right southward, up and over the hill to the tiny village of Tung O. The walk takes about 30 minutes over a rugged landscape, and the first half is a fairly strenuous climb up steps and along a path. Don't do this walk at night unless it's a full moon, as there are only a few street lights at the start in Sok Kwu Wan.

If coming from Mo Tat Wan, take the trail immediately to the west of the pavilion above the beach and follow the signposted path up the hill and through bamboo groves and fields. It takes about 25 minutes to reach the sleepy village of Yung Shue Ha on the fringes of the bay. All of the Chinese who live there are from the same clan and have the surname of Chow. A member of this clan, Chow Yun Fat, star of many a John Woo film, as well as *Crouching Tiger, Hidden Dragon*, was born and raised in Tung O.

The beach at Tung O Wan is a secluded and unspoiled stretch of sand, punctuated by chunks of driftwood and other flotsam.

LANTAU

Eating p202; Drinking p215; Sleeping p249

Hong Kong's largest island Lantau is home to some of the region's best and most remote beaches, plus traditional fishing villages, wilderness trails, glimpses of a Neolithic past, monasteries and monuments, including the giant Tian Tan Buddha. Part of its appeal is its generous dimensions, ruggedly beautiful terrain and small population.

Lantau (Cantonese for 'broken head'; Map p140) is also called Tai Yue Shan or 'Big Island Mountain' in Chinese – a name that refers both to its size and elevation. It is home to more than 200,000 people (and counting), yet at 144 sq km it is almost twice the size of Hong Kong Island. Its highest point, Lantau Peak (Fung Wong Shan; 934m), is almost double the height of Victoria Peak. More than half of the surface area – 78.5 sq km, in fact – is designated country park and there are several superb mountain trails, including the 70km Lantau Trail (p227), which passes over both Lantau Peak and Sunset Peak (869m).

Lantau is the last inhabited island west of Hong Kong Island; the next stops are Macau and the Zhuhai SEZ. Lantau has many small villages dotting the southern coast. From east to west the main ones are: Mui Wo, the 'capital' and the place where most of the ferries dock; Pui O and Tong Fuk along South Lantau Rd; and Tai O on the west coast. The largest settlement is the ever-growing New Town of Tung Chung on the north coast, which is accessible from Mui Wo by buses that climb steep Tung Chung Rd. Discovery Bay, a self-contained 'bedroom community' to the northeast, can be reached from Mui Wo by ferry. Not everyone on Lantau resides here of their own accord: the island is home to three prisons.

Rock carvings discovered at Shek Pik on the southwestern coast of Lantau suggest that the island was inhabited as early as the Bronze Age (3000 years ago), well before the arrival of the Han Chinese; a stone circle uncovered at Fan Lau may date from Neolithic times. The last Song-dynasty emperor passed through here in the 13th century while fleeing the Mongol invaders. He is believed to have held court in the Tung Chung Valley to the north, which takes its name from a local hero who gave up

SNAKES ALIVE

Take care when bushwalking, particularly on Lamma and Lantau Islands. Poisonous snakes, the most common being the bamboo pit viper, are a hazard, although they will not attack unless surprised or provoked. Go straight to a public hospital if bitten; private doctors do not stock antivenom. Other fauna to be aware of in the New Territories are wild boars, which can be hugely dangerous if they choose to attack. Steer well clear if you spot one and back off slowly if you've already got too close.

his life for the emperor. Tung Chung is still worshipped by the Hakka people of Lantau, who believe he can predict the future.

Like Cheung Chau, Lantau was once a base for pirates and smugglers, and a trading post for the British long before they showed any interest in Hong Kong Island.

There are some interesting traditional villages, such as Tai O on the west coast; several important religious sites, including the Po Lin Monastery and the adjacent Tian Tan Buddha, which is supposedly the largest outdoor Buddha statue in the world; and some excellent beaches, including Cheung Sha, the longest in Hong Kong.

Until the Lantau Link (the combined road and rail transport connection between Kowloon and Lantau) opened in 1997, the island was accessible only by ferry. Today you can reach the island from the rest of the territory by MTR, the Airport Express, a fleet of buses and by taxi.

HSBC (Map p143; ☎ 2984 1639; Mui Wo Ferry Pier Rd) has a branch in Mui Wo and there's an HSBC ATM (Tai O Market St) in Tai O, which you'll see as you cross the footbridge from the mainland to the island. The main post office (Map p143; Ngan Kwong Wan Rd) is a short distance west of the footbridge crossing the Silver River in Mui Wo.

They can also be hired from two bike kiosks (Map p143; ☎ 2984 7500, 2984 8232) near the Silvermine Beach Hotel in Mui Wo and from several in Pui O village.

NGONG PING PLATEAU Map p140

☎ 3666 0606; 11 Tat Tung Rd; 🚍 2 from Mui Wo, 21 from Tai O, 23 from Tung Chung or cable car
Perched 500m up in the western hills of Lantau is the Ngong Ping Plateau, a major drawcard for Hong Kong day-trippers and foreign visitors alike, especially since 1993,

when one of the world's largest statues of Buddha was unveiled here.

Po Lin Monastery (Precious Lotus; ☎ 2985 5248; www.plm.org.hk/blcs/en; ☿ 9am-6pm) is a huge Buddhist monastery and temple complex that was built in 1924. Today it seems more of a tourist honeypot than a religious retreat, attracting hundreds of thousands of visitors a year and still being expanded. Most of the buildings you'll see on arrival are new, with the older, simpler ones tucked away behind them. Bringing the masses in ever greater numbers to Po Lin is the 5.7km Ngong Ping 360 (www.np360.com.hk; adult/child/concession one way $63/30/49, return $96/48/74; ☿ 9am-6pm Mon-Fri, 10am-6.30pm Sat, Sun & special days), a cable car linking Ngong Ping with the centre of Tung Chung (downhill and to the north).

The ride is well worth taking, offering spectacular views over the airport as it transports you from the high-rise apartments of Tung Chung to the more rural landscapes of Lantau. The lower station is just opposite the Tung Chung MTR station. Less appealing is the upper station, which empties onto the 1.5-hectare Ngong Ping Village just west of the monastery complex. A blatant attempt to commercialise the whole experience, it includes several themed attractions, including two Disney-fied regurgitations of Buddhist stories: Walking with Buddha and the Monkey's Tale Theatre. They cost $36/18/28 each for adults/concession, but you won't miss much if you skip these rather sorry audiovisual 'experiences'. The journey takes 20 to 25 minutes, each glassed-in gondola carries 17 passengers and the system can move up to 3500 people per hour.

On a hill above the monastery sits the Tian Tan Buddha (☿ 10am-6pm), a seated representation of Lord Gautama some 23m high (or 26.4m with the lotus), or just under 34m if you include the podium. There are bigger Buddha statues elsewhere – notably the 71m-high Grand Buddha at Leshan in China's Sichuan province – but apparently these are not seated, outdoors or made of bronze. It weighs 202 tonnes, by the way. The large bell within the Buddha is controlled by computer and rings 108 times during the day to symbolise escape from what Buddhism terms the '108 troubles of mankind'.

The podium is composed of separate chambers on three different levels. On the first level are six statues of bodhisattvas, each of which weighs around two tonnes. On the second level is a small museum (☎ 2985 5248; ⊙ 10am-6pm) containing oil paintings and ceramic plaques of the Buddha's life and teachings. At busy times priority entry is given to those with meal tickets from the monastery's vegetarian restaurant, Po Lin Vegetarian Restaurant (p203).

It's well worth climbing the 260 steps for a closer look at the statue and surrounding views. The Buddha's Birthday (p17), a public holiday celebrated in late April or early May, is a lively time to visit, when thousands make the pilgrimage. Visitors are requested to observe some decorum in dress and behaviour. It is forbidden to bring meat or alcohol into the grounds.

A 2.5km concrete footpath to the left of the Buddha statue leads to the Lantau Tea Garden, the only one in Hong Kong. The tea bushes are pretty sparse and not worth a detour, but the garden is on the way to the Hongkong Bank Foundation SG Davis Hostel (p250) and Lantau Peak, and there are tea leaves for sale.

LANTAU PEAK Map p140
Known as Fung Wong Shan (Phoenix Mountain) in Cantonese, this 934m-high peak is the second-highest in Hong Kong after Tai Mo Shan (957m) in the New Territories. The view from the summit is absolutely stunning, and on a clear day it is possible to see Macau and Zhuhai some 65km to the west.

If you're hiking the length or the first several stages of the Lantau Trail (p227) to Ngong Ping, you'll cross the peak. If you want to just climb up from Ngong Ping, the easiest and most comfortable way to make the climb is to spend the night at the Hongkong Bank Foundation SG Davis Hostel (p250), get up at the crack of dawn and pick up the signposted trail at the hostel that runs southeast to the peak. Many climbers get up earlier to reach the summit for sunrise; take a torch and wear an extra layer of clothes, as it can get pretty chilly at the top in the early hours, even in summer.

Another signposted trail leading east from the hostel will take you along the northern slopes of Lantau Peak to Po Lam Monastery at Tei Tong Tsai and then south through a valley leading to Tung Chung, from where you can catch the MTR back to Kowloon or Hong Kong or bus 3M to Mui

Wo. This charming walk – if you ignore the airport to the north – also takes you past Lo Hon Monastery as well as Tung Chung Fort and Tung Chung Battery (p144).

LUNG TSAI NG GARDEN Map p140
🚌 1 from Mui Wo, 11 from Tung Chung, 21 from Ngong Ping
This magical garden southwest of Ngong Ping, with a lotus pond crossed by a rickety zigzag bridge, was built by a wealthy merchant in the 1930s in a small valley near where the village of Lung Tsai once stood. The site is rather derelict, but atmospheric nonetheless, and the gardens are in excellent condition. You can get here via a water catchment path and trail from the Tai O Rd, a continuation of South Lantau Rd just west of Keung Shan. Alight from the bus after the Kwun Yam temple on Tai O Rd, which is about 2km past the turn-off for the Tian Tan Buddha. You'll see a country park sign and the start of the water catchment.

TAI O Map p140
🚌 1 from Mui Wo, 11 from Tung Chung, 21 from Ngong Ping
A century ago this mostly Tanka village on the west coast of Lantau was an important trading and fishing port, exporting salt and fish to China. Today Tai O is in decline, except perhaps as a tourist destination offering an intriguing glimpse of the life of a traditional fishing village.

A few of the saltpans still exist, but most have been filled in to build high-rise housing. Older people still make their living from duck farming, fishing, making the village's celebrated shrimp paste and processing salt fish, which you'll see (and smell) everywhere. It remains a popular place for locals to buy seafood – both fresh and dried.

As recently as the 1980s Tai O also traded in IIs (illegal immigrants) brought from China under cover of darkness by 'snakeheads' (smugglers in human cargo) in long narrow boats, sending back contraband such as refrigerators, radios and TVs to the mainland.

Tai O is built partly on Lantau and partly on a tiny island about 15m from the shore. Until the mid-1990s the only way to cross was via a rope-tow ferry pulled by elderly Hakka women. That and the large number

LANTAU

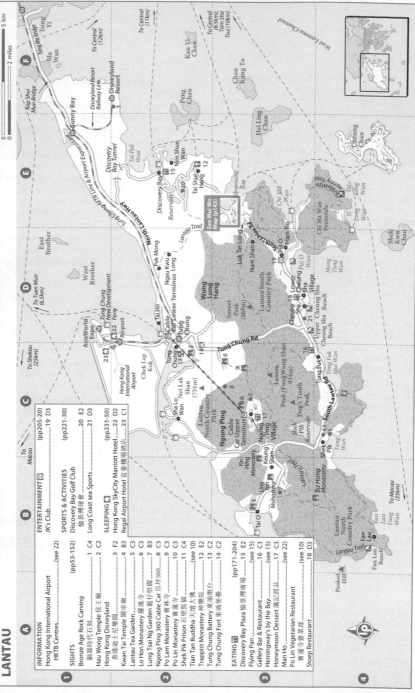

INFORMATION (pp53–152)
Hong Kong International Airport ....(see 22)
HKTB Centres...................................19 D3

SIGHTS (pp53–152)
Bronze Age Rock Carving 銅器時代石刻.........1 C4
Hau Wong Temple 侯王廟.......................2 C2
Hong Kong Disneyland
香港迪士尼樂園...............................3 F2
Kwan Tai Temple 關帝廟.......................4 B3
Lantau Tea Garden............................5 C3
Lo Hon Monastery 羅漢寺......................6 C3
Lung Tsai Ng Garden 龍仔悟園.................7 B3
Ngong Ping 360 Cable Car 昂坪360.............8 C3
Po Lam Monastery 寶林寺......................9 C3
Po Lin Monastery 寶蓮寺.....................10 C3
Shek Pik Prison 石壁監獄....................11 C4
Tian Tan Buddha 天壇大佛..................(see 10)
Trappist Monastery 神樂院...................12 E2
Tung Chung Battery 東涌炮台.................13 C2
Tung Chung Fort 東涌堡壘....................14 C2

EATING (pp171–204)
Discovery Bay Plaza 愉景灣廣場..............15 E2
Flying Pan...............................(see 15)
Gallery Bar & Restaurant...................16 E2
Hemingway's by the Bay...................(see 15)
Honeymoon Dessert 滿記甜品..................17 C3
Man Ho...................................(see 22)
Po Lin Vegetarian Restaurant
寶蓮寺素菜館.............................(see 10)
Stoep Restaurant...........................18 D3

ENTERTAINMENT (pp205–20)
JK's Club..................................19 D3

SPORTS & ACTIVITIES (pp221–30)
Discovery Bay Golf Club 愉景灣球會..........20 E2
Long Coast sea Sports......................21 D3

SLEEPING (pp231–50)
Hong Kong SkyCity Marriott Hotel...........22 D2
Regal Airport Hotel 富豪機場酒店............23 C1

TRANSPORT – LANTAU

Airport Express Takes you to Airport station at Chek Lap Kok.

Bus Mui Wo: Served by bus 1 from Tai O (from the bus terminus at the end of Tai O Rd), bus 2 from Ngong Ping and bus 3M from Tung Chung (main bus terminus by the MTR station).

Ngong Ping: Other than the cable car, the best way to get here is on bus 2 from Mui Wo (opposite the ferry pier) or bus 23 from Tung Chung (main bus terminus by the MTR station).

Tai O: Reached on bus 1 from Mui Wo (opposite the ferry pier), bus 11 from Tung Chung (main bus terminus by the MTR station) or bus 21 from Ngong Ping.

Tung Chung: Served by bus 3M from Mui Wo (opposite the ferry pier), bus 11 from Tai O (from the bus terminus at the end of Tai O Rd) and bus 23 from Ngong Ping.

All buses listed above run along some, or all of, South Lantau Rd, the junction with Tung Chung Rd being the point at which the bus will join or leave the route.

Ferry Mui Wo: Major services from Central leave from pier 6 at the Outlying Islands ferry terminal. Ferries also depart from Chi Ma Wan (also on Lantau), Cheung Chau and Peng Chau.

Chi Ma Wan: Served by the inter-island ferry from Mui Wo, Cheung Chau and Peng Chau.

Tai O: Reached by the service that operates from Tuen Mun in the New Territories via Sha Lo Wan and Tung Chung (both Lantau).

Tung Chung: Reached by a regular service from Tuen Mun. It's also served by the less-frequent service that comes from Tai O and Sha Lo Wan (both Lantau) before going on to Tuen Mun (or vice versa).

MTR Tung Chung station is at the end of the line of the same name.

Taxi Telephone the call service on ☎ 2984 1328 or 2984 1368. Sample fares to Ngong Ping and the Tian Tan Buddha from Mui Wo and Tung Chung/Tai O/Hong Kong International Airport are $125/45/145.

---

of sampans in the small harbour earned Tai O the nickname 'the Venice of Hong Kong'. Though the narrow iron Tai Chung footbridge now spans the canal, the rope-tow ferry is resurrected on some weekends and holidays: drop $1 in the box as you disembark. There are also brief river boat tours (☎ 9629 4581, 9645 6652; per 15/25min $10/20) departing from the footbridge.

Some of the tiny, traditional-style village houses still stand in the centre, including a handful of Tai O's famed stilt houses on the waterfront. There are a few houses that escaped a fire in 2000, plus a number of shanties, their corrugated-iron walls held in place by rope, and houseboats that haven't set sail for years.

The stilt houses and the local Kwan Tai temple dedicated to the god of war are on Kat Hing St. To reach them, cross the bridge from the mainland to the island, walk up Tai O Market St and go right at the Fook Moon Lam restaurant. There's a couple of other temples here, including an 18th-century one erected in honour of Hung Shing, patron of fisherfolk; it's on Shek Tsai Po St, about 600m west of the Fook Lam Moon restaurant.

SOUTH LANTAU RD Map p140

🚌 **1 from Mui Wo & Tai O, 2 from Ngong Ping, 3 from Tung Chung**

Just under 5km southwest of Mui Wo, Pui O is the first of several coastal villages along South Lantau Rd. Pui O has a decent beach, but as it's the closest one to Mui Wo it can get very crowded. The village has several restaurants, holiday flats galore and, in season, stalls renting bicycles.

Cheung Sha (Long Sand), at over 3km Hong Kong's longest beach, is divided into 'upper' and 'lower' sections; a trail over a hillock links the two. Upper Cheung Sha, with occasional good surf, is the prettier and longer stretch and boasts a modern complex with changing rooms, toilets, showers and a snack bar. Lower Cheung Sha village has a beachfront restaurant, Stoep Restaurant (p203). Long Coast Seasports (☎ 8104 6222; www.longcoast .hk; 29 Lower Cheung Sha Village; ☺ 10am-sunset Mon-Fri, 9am-sunset Sat & Sun) is a water-sports centre offering windsurfing, sea kayaking and wakeboarding. Prices vary widely, but basic windsurfing costs from $100/300/500 for an hour/half-day/day, while a single kayak rents for $60/180 for an hour/half-day. Beach umbrellas are also available from $50

THE PINK DOLPHINS OF THE PEARL RIVER

Between 100 and 200 misnamed Chinese white dolphins *(Sousa chinensis)* – they are actually bubble-gum pink – inhabit the coastal waters around Hong Kong, finding the brackish waters of the Pearl River estuary to be the perfect habitat. Unfortunately these glorious mammals, which are also called Indo-Pacific humpback dolphins, are being threatened by environmental pollution, and their numbers are dwindling.

The threat comes in many forms, but the most prevalent – and direct – dangers are sewage, chemicals, over-fishing and boat traffic. Some 200,000 cubic metres of untreated sewage are dumped into the western harbour every day, and high concentrations of chemicals such as DDT have been found in tissue samples taken from some of the dolphins. Several dolphins have been entangled in fishing nets, and despite the dolphins' skill at sensing and avoiding surface vessels, some have collided with boats. Pleasure boats buzzing around the Tai Po area are a particular menace.

The dolphins' habitat has also been diminished by the erosion of the natural coastline of Lantau Island and the destruction of many kilometres of natural coastline. The North Lantau Hwy consumed about 10km of the natural coastline. The Hong Kong Disneyland theme park required large amounts of reclamation in Penny's Bay.

Hong Kong Dolphinwatch (Map p104; ☎ 2984 1414; www.hkdolphinwatch.com; 15th fl, Middle Block, 1528A Star House, 3 Salisbury Rd, Tsim Sha Tsui) was founded in 1995 to raise awareness of these wonderful creatures and promote responsible ecotourism. It offers 2½-hour cruises (adult/student & senior/child under 12 $360/255/180) to see the pink dolphins in their natural habitat every Wednesday, Friday and Sunday year-round. Guides assemble in the lobby of the Kowloon Hotel Hong Kong (p244) in Tsim Sha Tsui at 9am for the bus to Tung Chung via the Tsing Ma Bridge, from where the boat departs; the tours return at 1pm. About 97% of the cruises result in the sighting of at least one dolphin; if none are spotted, passengers are offered a free trip.

a day. Some claim that the Venturi effect on the wind from Tung Chung makes this the best windsurfing in Hong Kong, especially from November to March.

The beach at Tong Fuk, the next village over from Cheung Sha, is not as nice, but the village has holiday flats, several shops and a popular roadside barbecue restaurant called Gallery (p203). To the northwest is the not-so-scenic sprawl of Ma Po Ping Prison.

West of Tong Fuk, South Lantau Rd begins to climb the hills inland before crossing an enormous dam holding back the Shek Pik Reservoir, completed in 1963, which provides Lantau, Cheung Chau and parts of Hong Kong Island with drinking water. Just below the dam is the granddaddy of Lantau's trio of jails, Shek Pik Prison. Below the dam to the south but before the prison is another Bronze Age rock carving, which is unusual in that it is so far from the coastline.

The trail along the water-catchment area east of Shek Pik Reservoir, with picnic tables and barbecue pits, offers some of the easiest and most peaceful walking on Lantau. From here you can also pick up the switchback trail to Dog's Tooth Peak (539m), from where another trail heads north to Lantau Peak.

CHI MA WAN Map p140

🚢 Inter-island service from Mui Wo & Cheung Chau
Chi Ma Wan, the large peninsula south of Mui Wo that can be reached via the inter-island ferry, is a relatively remote part of Lantau and an excellent area for hiking; just be sure to get a map (p296) as the trails are not always clearly defined or well marked.

The Chi Ma Wan ferry pier is on the northeast coast; the large complex just south of the pier is not a hostel but the Chi Ma Wan Correctional Institution. There's a decent beach to the south at Tai Long Wan.

FAN LAU Map p140

Fan Lau (Divided Flow), a small peninsula on the southwestern tip of Lantau, has a couple of good beaches and the remains of Fan Lau Fort, built in 1729 to protect the channel between Lantau and the Pearl River estuary from pirates. It remained in operation until the end of the 19th century and was restored in 1985. The sea views from here are sterling.

To the southeast of the fort is an ancient stone circle. The origins and age of the circle are uncertain, but it probably dates from the Neolithic or early Bronze Age and may have been used in rituals.

The only way to reach Fan Lau is on foot. To get here from Tai O, walk south from the bus station for 250m and pick up stage No 7 of the coastal Lantau Trail (p227), a distance of about 8km. The trail then carries on to the northeast and Shek Pik for another 12km, where you can catch bus 1 back to Mui Wo.

TRAPPIST MONASTERY Map p140
☎ 2987 6292; Tai Shui Hang; ⛴ kaido from Peng Chau

Northeast of Mui Wo and south of Discovery Bay at Tai Shui Hang is the Roman Catholic Lady of Joy Abbey – better known as the Trappist Monastery. The monastery is known throughout Hong Kong for its cream-rich milk, sold in half-pint bottles everywhere, but, alas, the cows have been moved to the New Territories and Trappist Dairy Milk now comes from over the border in China.

The Trappists, a branch of the Cistercian order, were founded by a converted courtier at La Trappe in France in 1662 and gained a reputation as being one of the most austere religious communities in the Roman Catholic Church. The Lantau congregation was established at Beijing in the 19th century. All of the monks here now are local Chinese.

Trappist monks take a vow of absolute silence, and there are signs reminding visitors to keep radios and music players turned off and to speak in low tones. Give the guys a break: they're up at 3.15am and in bed by 8pm.

You can reach the monastery on foot by following a well-marked coastal trail from the northern end of Tung Wan Tau Rd in Mui Wo, but it's much easier to get here by *kaido* from Peng Chau, Lantau's little island neighbour to the west. For details, see p276.

MUI WO Map p143
⛴ Lantau

Mui Wo (Plum Nest), Lantau's main settlement 'capital', is on Silvermine Bay, which is named for the silver mines that were once worked to the northwest along the Silver River. In fact, many foreign residents refer to Mui Wo as Silvermine Bay.

About a third of Lantau's population lives in the township of Mui Wo and its surrounding hamlets. There are several decent places to stay here and, though the options for eating and drinking are few, they are fine.

Silvermine Bay beach, to the northwest of Mui Wo, has been cleaned up and rebuilt in recent years and is now an attractive place, with scenic views and opportunities for walking in the hills above. There's a complex with toilets, showers and changing rooms open from April to October.

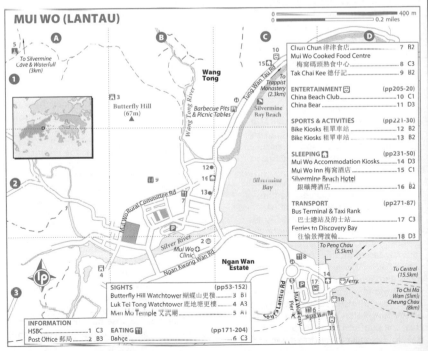

MUI WO (LANTAU)

Chun Chun 津津食店	7 B2
Mui Wo Cooked Food Centre	
梅窩碼頭熟食中心	8 C3
Tak Chai Kee 德仔記	9 B2

ENTERTAINMENT 🎭	(pp205-20)
China Beach Club	10 C1
China Bear	11 D3

SPORTS & ACTIVITIES	(pp221-30)
Bike Kiosks 租單車站	12 B2
Bike Kiosks 租單車站	13 B2

SLEEPING 🛏	(pp231-50)
Mui Wo Accommodation Kiosks	14 D3
Mui Wo Inn 梅窩酒店	15 C1
Silvermine Beach Hotel	
銀礦灣酒店	16 B2

TRANSPORT	(pp271-87)
Bus Terminal & Taxi Rank	
巴士總站及的士站	17 C3
Ferries to Discovery Bay	
往愉景灣渡輪	18 D3

SIGHTS	(pp53-152)
Butterfly Hill Watchtower 蝴蝶山更樓	3 B1
Luk Tei Tong Watchtower 鹿地塘更樓	4 A3
Man Mo Temple 文武廟	5 A1

INFORMATION	
HSBC	1 C3
Post Office 郵局	2 B3

| EATING 🍴 | (pp171-204) |
| Dahçe | 6 C3 |

143

If you have the time, consider hiking out to Silvermine Waterfall, the main feature of a picturesque garden near the old Silvermine Cave northwest of the town. The waterfall is quite a spectacle during the rainy season, when it swells and gushes; the cave was mined for silver in the latter half of the 19th century but has now been sealed off.

En route to the waterfall you'll pass the local Man Mo temple, originally built during the reign of Emperor Shen Zong (1573–1620) of the Ming dynasty and renovated a couple of times in the last century.

You can reach the temple, cave and waterfall by walking west along Mui Wo Rural Committee Rd and then following the marked path north. The 3km walk should take about an hour.

There are several old granite watchtowers in the area, including Luk Tei Tong Watchtower on the Silver River and Butterfly Hill Watchtower further north. They were built in the late 19th century as safe houses and as coastal defences against pirates.

HONG KONG DISNEYLAND Map p140

☎ 1830 830; http://park.hongkongdisneyland.com; adult/child 3-11/senior over 65 Mon-Fri $295/250/170, weekends & public holidays $350/250/170; MTR Disney Bay Resort

One of America's most famous cultural exports finally landed in Hong Kong in late 2005. It's divided into four main areas – Main Street USA, Fantasyland, Adventureland and Tomorrowland – but don't expect too much. This is a very small-scale Disney franchise (although there are plans to expand it) with a solitary real adrenaline-inducing roller coaster ride (Space Mountain), while the rest of the park is made up of tamer attractions and of course is rammed with outlets selling Disney merchandise and fast food.

There's plenty for younger children to enjoy, including the full complement of Disney characters patrolling the park and the odd show re-creating great Disney moments from films such as *Pirates of the Caribbean*, but take teenagers along and you may face a mutiny. The resurgent Ocean Park (p93) offers vastly more variety, thrills and amusement for all ages.

Disneyland is linked by rail with the MTR at the new futuristic Sunny Bay station on the Tung Chung line; passengers just cross the platform to board the dedicated train for Disneyland Resort station and the theme park. Journey times from Central/Kowloon/Tsing Yi stations are 10/21/24 minutes. Check the website for opening times, as they alter from month to month.

DISCOVERY BAY Map p140
🚇 Discovery Bay

Lying on the northeastern coast of Lantau, what locals have dubbed 'DB' is very much a world of its own (with not a little similarity to the cult '60s TV series *The Prisoner*). A dormitory community for professionals who commute to Central, Discovery Bay (Yue Ging Wan in Cantonese) has a fine stretch of sandy beach ringed by high-rises and more luxurious condominiums clinging to the headland to the north – but there is no pressing need to visit except to ogle at residents in their converted golf carts, which cost $200,000 a pop.

There is a handful of decent restaurants in Discovery Bay Plaza, just up from the ferry pier and the central plaza, and the 27-hole Discovery Bay Golf Club (see p225) perched in the hills to the southwest.

Buses make the run to and from Tung Chung and the airport at Chek Lap Kok via the Discovery Bay Tunnel and the North Lantau Hwy. A trail leading from the golf course will take you down to Silvermine Bay and the rest of Lantau in a couple of hours.

TUNG CHUNG Map p140
Tung Chung; 🚢 3M from Mui Wo, 11 from Tai O, 23 from Ngong Ping

Change has come to Tung Chung, on Lantau's northern coast, at a pace that can only happen in Hong Kong. This previously all-but-inaccessible farming region, with the small village of Tung Chung at its centre, has seen Chek Lap Kok, the mountain across Tung Chung Bay, flattened to build Hong Kong's international airport and a New Town rise up, served by the MTR.

As part of the territory's plans to solve its housing crisis, Tung Chung New Town has now become a 760-hectare residential estate. The expected population of Tung Chung and the neighbouring New Town of Tai Ho is 330,000 by 2012.

These developments and transport improvements have put an end to Tung Chung as a peaceful and secluded spot. But efforts have been made to protect Tung Chung Old Village. Buildings may rise no higher than three storeys and each floor can be no larger than

70 sq metres. In truth though there's not much 'old villlage' atmosphere left.

Annals record a settlement at Tung Chung as early as the Ming dynasty. There are several Buddhist establishments in the upper reaches of the valley, but the main attraction here is Tung Chung Fort (Tung Chung Rd; admission free; ☯ 10am-5pm Wed-Mon), which dates back to 1832, when Chinese troops were garrisoned on Lantau. The Japanese briefly occupied the fort during WWII. Measuring 70m by 80m and enclosed by granite-block walls, it retains six of its muzzle-loading cannons pointing out to sea.

About 1km to the north are the ruins of Tung Chung Battery, which is a much smaller fort built in 1817. All that remains is an L-shaped wall facing the sea, with a gun emplacement in the corner. The ruins were discovered only in 1980, having been hidden for about a century by scrub.

Facing Tung Chung Bay to the southwest in the village of Sha Tsui Tau is double-roofed Hau Wong Temple, founded at the end of the Song dynasty. The temple contains a bell dating from 1765 and inscribed by the Qing-dynasty emperor Qian Long.

CHEUNG CHAU

Eating p203; Sleeping p250

Once a refuge for pirates, Cheung Chau (Long Island; Map p146) occupies less than 2½ sq km of territory, its modest dimensions containing temples, beaches, fishing boats and mini chandleries, which make it a delightful destination for a day trip.

Fishing and aquaculture are important industries for a large number of the island's 30,000 inhabitants, a few of whom still live on junks and sampans anchored in the harbour. Bring your camera for some of the best shots of traditional maritime life on the South China coast.

Archaeological evidence, including a 3000-year-old rock carving uncovered just beyond the Warwick Hotel, suggests that Cheung Chau, like Lamma and Lantau, was inhabited at least as early as the Neolithic period. The island had a thriving fishing community at the time, and the early inhabitants – Hakka and Cantonese settlers – supplemented their income with smuggling and piracy.

Cheung Chau boasts several interesting temples, the most important being Pak Tai Temple, which hosts the annual Bun Festival: *the* red-letter day on Cheung Chau (see boxed text, below). The island has a few worthwhile beaches, and there are some relatively easy walks, including the one described on p148. When Canton (present-day Guangzhou) and Macau opened up to the West in the 16th century, Cheung Chau was a perfect base from which to prey on passing ships. The infamous and powerful 18th-century pirate Cheung Po Tsai is said to have had his base here, and you can still visit the cave where he supposedly stashed his booty at the southwestern tip of the island.

Cheung Chau village, where the ferry docks, is the only real settlement on the island. There is an HSBC (☎ 2981 1127; Lot 1116, Praya St) branch southeast of the cargo pier, and an ATM (19A Pak

CHEUNG CHAU'S BUN FESTIVAL

The annual Bun Festival (*Tàai-pìng chìng jiu* in Cantonese; www.cheungchau.org), which honours the god Pak Tai and is unique to the island, takes place over eight days in late April or early May, traditionally starting on the sixth day of the fourth moon. It is a Taoist festival, and there are four days of religious observances.

The festival is renowned for its bun towers: bamboo scaffolding up to 20m high that are covered with sacred rolls. If you visit Cheung Chau a week or so before the festival, you'll see the towers being built in front of Pak Tai Temple.

In the past, hundreds of people would scramble up the towers at midnight on the designated day to grab one of the buns for good luck. The higher the bun, the greater the luck, so everyone tried to reach the top. In 1978 a tower collapsed under the weight of the climbers, injuring two dozen people. Now everyone must remain on terra firma and the buns are handed out.

Sunday, the third day of the festival, features a procession of floats, stilt walkers and people dressed as characters from Chinese legends and opera. Most interesting are the colourfully dressed 'floating children' who are carried through the streets on long poles, cleverly wired to metal supports hidden under their clothing. The supports include footrests and a padded seat.

Offerings are made to the spirits of all the fish and livestock killed and consumed over the previous year. A priest reads out a decree calling on the villagers to abstain from killing any animals during the four day festival, and no meat is consumed.

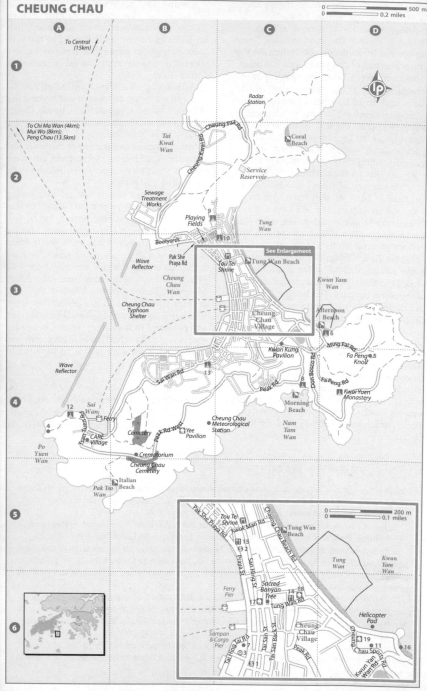

CHEUNG CHAU

To Central
(15km)

To Chi Ma Wan (4km);
Mui Wo (8km);
Peng Chau (13.5km)

Radar
Station

Tai
Kwai
Wan

Coral
Beach

Service
Reservoir

Sewage
Treatment
Works

Playing
Fields

Tung
Wan

Boatyards

Wave
Reflector

Pak She
Praya Rd

Cheung Pak Rd

Cheung Kwai Rd

Tou Tei
Shrine

Tung Wan Beach

See Enlargement

Kwun Yam
Wan

Cheung
Chau
Wan

Cheung Chau
Typhoon
Shelter

Cheung
Chau
Village

Afternoon
Beach

Ming Fat Rd

Wave
Reflector

Sai Wan Rd

Kwan Kung
Pavilion

Peak Rd

Don Bosco Rd

Fa Peng
Knoll

Fa Peng Rd

Kwai Yuen
Monastery

Sai
Wan

Ferry

Fa Tuen Rd

Peak Rd West

Cemetery

CARE
Village

Yee
Pavilion

Cheung Chau
Meteorological
Station

Morning
Beach

Nam
Tam
Wan

Po
Yuen
Wan

Crematorium

Cheung Chau
Cemetery

Pak Tso
Wan

Italian
Beach

Enlargement

Pak She Praya Rd

Tou Tei
Shrine

Kwiok Man Rd

Cheung Chau Beach Rd

Tung Wan
Beach

Praya St

San Hing St

Tung
Wan

Kwun
Yam
Wan

Ferry
Pier

Sacred
Banyan
Tree

Tung Wan Rd

Helicopter
Pad

Tai San St

Tai San Back St

Sampan
& Cargo
Pier

Tai Hing Tai Rd

Cheung
Chau
Village

Peak Rd

Cheung Chau Sports Rd

Kwun Yam Wan Rd

CHEUNG CHAU

INFORMATION
HSBC...1 C6
HSBC ATM 匯豐銀行提款機...........2 C5
Post Office 郵局...................................3 C6

SIGHTS   (pp53–152)
Cheung Po Tsai Cave 張保仔洞.....4 A4
Fa Peng Knoll..5 D4
Kwun Yam Temple 觀音廟...............6 D3
Market 街市...7 C6
Nam Tam Wan Tin Hau Temple
南氹灣天后廟.....................................8 C4

Pak She Tin Hau Temple
北社天后廟...9 B2
Pak Tai Temple 北帝廟...................10 C3
Rock Carving 長州石刻...................11 D6
Sai Wan Tin Hau Temple
西灣天后廟.......................................12 A4
Tai Shek Hau Tin Hau Temple
大石口天后廟.................................13 B4

EATING 🍴   (pp171–204)
Hometown Teahouse
故鄉茶寮...14 C6

New Baccarat 新金湖海鮮酒家..15 C5

SPORTS & ACTIVITIES   (pp221–30)
Cheng Chau Windsurfing
Watersports Centre
長洲滑浪風帆中心露天茶座...16 D6

SLEEPING 🛏   (pp231–50)
Cheung Chau Accommodation
Kiosks...17 C6
Cheung Chau B&B.............................18 C6
Warwick Hotel 華威酒店.............19 D6

She Praya Rd) north of the ferry pier. The post office (2A Tai Hing Tai Rd) is in the market complex. The market (⏱ 8.30am–5pm) is a hive of activity, with meat and fish being sold on the ground floor and a variety of other goods upstairs.

PAK TAI TEMPLE Map p146
☎ 2981 0663; Pak She Fourth Lane; ⏱ 7am–5pm; 🚇 Cheung Chau

This colourful and recently restored temple from 1783 is the oldest on the island and is the focus of the annual Cheung Chau Bun Festival (see the boxed text, p145) in late April or early May. It is dedicated to the Taoist deity Pak Tai, the 'Supreme Emperor of the Dark Heaven', military protector of the state, guardian of peace and order, and protector of fisherfolk. Legend tells that early settlers from Guangdong province brought an image of Pak Tai with them to Cheung Chau and, when the statue was carried through the village, Cheung Chau was spared the plague that had decimated the populations of nearby islands. A temple dedicated to the saviour was built six years later.

BEACHES Map p146
🚇 Cheung Chau

Tung Wan beach, Cheung Chau's longest and most popular beach (though not its prettiest), lies at the end of Tung Wan Rd, due east of the ferry pier. The best part of Tung Wan is the far southern end, which is a great area for windsurfing. Just south of Tung Wan beach, Kwun Yam Wan beach is known to English speakers as Afternoon Beach and is a great spot for windsurfing.

Windsurfing has always been an extremely popular pastime on Cheung Chau, and Hong Kong's only Olympic gold-medal winner to date, Lee Lai-shan, who took the top prize in windsurfing at the 1996 Olympics in Atlanta, grew up here. At the

northern end of Afternoon Beach, the Cheung Chau Windsurfing Water Sports Centre (☎ 2981 2772; www.ccwindc.com.hk; 1 Hak Pai Rd; ⏱ 10am–7pm) rents sailboards for between $90 and $150 per hour, as well as single/double kayaks for $60/130. There are also windsurfing courses available for $600/800 per day. The best time for windsurfing here is between October and December.

At the southeastern end of Afternoon Beach a footpath leads uphill past a Kwun Yam temple, which is dedicated to the goddess of mercy. Continue up the footpath and look for the sign to the Fa Peng Knoll. The concrete footpath takes you past quiet, tree-shrouded villas.

From the knoll you can walk down to signposted Don Bosco Rd; it leads due south to rocky Nam Tam Wan (also known as Morning Beach), where swimming is possible. If you ignore Don Bosco Rd and continue walking west, you'll come to the intersection of Peak and Kwun Yam Wan Rds. Kwun Yam Wan Rd and its extension, School Rd, will take you back to Cheung Chau village.

Peak Rd is the main route to the island's cemetery in the southwestern part of the island; you'll pass several pavilions along the way built for coffin bearers making the hilly climb. Once at the cemetery it's worth dropping down to Pak Tso Wan (Italian Beach), a sandy, isolated spot that is good

TRANSPORT – CHEUNG CHAU

Ferry Services from Central leave from pier 5 of the Outlying Islands ferry terminal. Ferries can also be taken from Mui Wo and Chi Ma Wan on Lantau and from Peng Chau. Additionally, regular kaido operate between Cheung Chau village (Sampan pier) and Sai Wan in the south of the island.

for swimming. At this point Peak Rd West becomes Tsan Tuen Rd, which continues north to Sai Wan.

CHEUNG CHAU VILLAGE Map p146
🚇 Cheung Chau

The island's main settlement lies along the narrow strip of land connecting the headlands to the north and the south. The waterfront is a bustling place and the maze of streets and alleyways that make up the village are filled with old Chinese-style houses and tumble-down shops selling everything from plastic buckets to hell money and other combustible grave offerings. The streets close to the waterfront are pungent with the smell of incense and fish hung out to dry in the sun.

SAMPAN RIDES Map p146
🚇 Cheung Chau

A great way to see the harbour and soak up the fishing village atmosphere is to charter a sampan for half an hour (expect to pay $60 to $100 depending on the day, the season and the demand). Most sampans congregate around the cargo pier, but virtually any small boat you see in the harbour can be hired as a water taxi. Just wave and two or three will come forward. Be sure to agree on the fare first.

CHEUNG PO TSAI CAVE Map p146
🚇 Cheung Chau

This 'cave' – in truth not much more than a hole in some rocks – on the southwestern peninsula of the island is said to have been the favourite hideout of the notorious pirate Cheung Po Tsai, who once commanded a flotilla of 600 junks and had a private army of 4000 men. He surrendered to the Qing government in 1810 and became an official himself, but his treasure is said to remain hidden here.

It's a 2km walk from Cheung Chau village along Sai Wan Rd, or take a *kaido* (adult/child from $3/2, dependent on passenger numbers) from the cargo ferry pier to the pier at Sai Wan. From here the walk is less than 200m (uphill).

TIN HAU TEMPLES Map p146
🚇 Cheung Chau

Cheung Chau has four temples dedicated to Tin Hau, the empress of heaven and patroness of seafarers. Pak She Tin Hau Temple

lies 100m northwest of the Pak Tai Temple. Nam Tam Wan Tin Hau temple is just north of Morning Beach; Tai Shek Hau Tin Hau temple is to the west on Sai Wan Rd. Sai Wan Tin Hau temple is west of Sai Wan (Western Bay), on the southwestern tip of the island. You can walk there or catch a *kaido* from the cargo pier.

ISLAND LIFE
Walking Tour

1 Cheung Chau Ferry Pier Head north along Praya St, where a row of mostly seafood restaurants face the harbour. Praya St becomes Pak She Praya Rd after the turn-off for Kwok Man Rd, and from here you can look out at the many junks and sampans moored in the harbour and typhoon shelter.

2 Pak Tai Temple At Pak She Fourth Lane, turn right and shortly you'll see the colourful temple (p147), built in 1783. The Pak She Tin Hau Temple is behind, about 100m to the northwest. The temple is within the grounds of the Chung Shak-Hei home for the aged.

3 Pak She St & San Hing St You'll pass traditional Chinese houses and several shops selling traditional Chinese medicine, incense and paper hell money to be burned in memory of the dead. Further south, and on the left at the intersection of Pak She St and Kwok Man Rd, is a small Tou Tei shrine, dedicated to the overworked earth god.

4 Hometown Teahouse Thirsty? Then why not stop at this teahouse (p203) for a refreshing drink by the amiable Japanese proprietors here.

5 Rock Carving Turn right and walk along Cheung Chau Beach Rd to a 3000-year-old rock carving of two identical geometric designs, just beyond the Warwick Hotel. Behind the hotel is Cheung Chau Sports Rd; walk up and when you see a pavilion, turn right onto Kwun Yam Wan Rd and from there onto Peak Rd, which takes you around to the other side of the pavilion.

6 Cheung Chau Meteorological Station Follow Peak Rd West about 500m past Kam Kong Primary School to the Meteorological Station, offering splendid views of the island and sea. A bit further south and through the trees

ISLAND LIFE

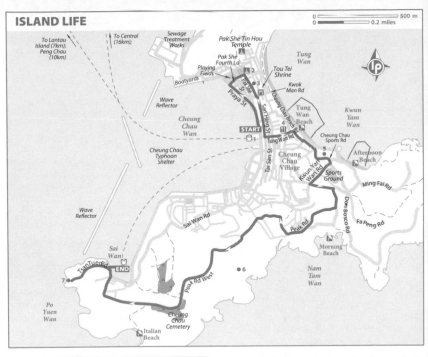

WALK FACTS

Start Cheung Chau ferry pier
End Sai Wan (then a *kaido* to Cheung Chau ferry pier)
Distance 4.5km
Time 2½ hours
Fuel stop Hometown Teahouse

to the left is Cheung Chau Cemetery, affording a quiet and solemn view out to sea. Stay left where the path splits in the cemetery.

7 Cheung Po Tsai Cave Follow the signs for Sai Wan and signs to the Cheung Po Tsai Cave (opposite), a place where pirates of old were supposed to have buried their booty. Return via the well-signposted *kaido* (adult/child $3/2) to Cheung Chau village. Alternatively, follow Sai Wan Rd around the bay and north back to the village (20 to 30 minutes).

PENG CHAU

Eating p204

Tiny Peng Chau (Map p150) is fairly flat and not especially beautiful, but it does have its charms.

The appeal of visiting Peng Chau lies in slackening your pace to match the island's, and soaking up the traditional sights and sounds, such as the clatter of mahjong tiles with the plaintive accompaniment of Cantonese opera leaking from old transistors.

It is perhaps the most traditionally Chinese of the Outlying Islands, with narrow alleyways, crowded housing, a covered wet market near the ferry pier, a couple of small but important temples, and interesting shops selling everything from Thai goods to New Age products. There are also a few closet-sized restaurants whose sea views have unfortunately been ruined by a massive concrete 'wave reflector' and promenade running along the shore south of the ferry pier.

Until recently the island's economy was supported by fishing and some cottage industries now all but dead (having moved to mainland China), though you will find a couple of porcelain and gift shops on Wing Hing and Wing On Sts. There's a branch of HSBC (☎ 2233 3000; 1 Wing Hing St; Mon, Wed & Fri) nearby. The post office is due west near the start of the promenade.

Looking not unlike a plumped-out horseshoe jettisoned from Lantau's northeast coast,

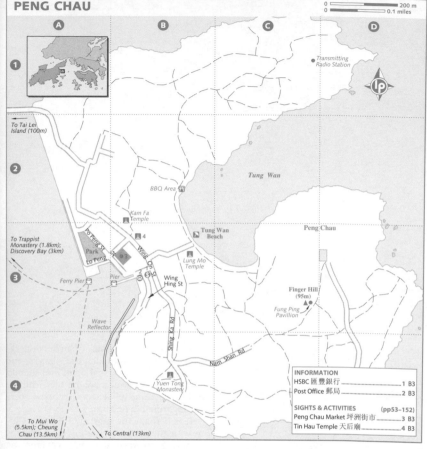

PENG CHAU

0 ————— 200 m
0 ————— 0.1 miles

Transmitting Radio Station

To Tai Lei Island (100m)

BBQ Area

Tung Wan

Kam Fa Temple

To Trappist Monastery (1.8km); Discovery Bay (3km)

Park to Peng

Tung Wan Beach

Peng Chau

Lung Mo Temple

Ferry Pier

Pier

Wing Hing St

Finger Hill (95m)

Fung Ping Pavillion

Wave Reflector

Shing Ka Rd

Nam Shan Rd

Yuen Tong Monastery

To Mui Wo (5.5km); Cheung Chau (13.5km)

To Central (13km)

INFORMATION
HSBC 匯豐銀行 1 B3
Post Office 郵局 2 B3

SIGHTS & ACTIVITIES (pp53–152)
Peng Chau Market 坪洲街市 3 B3
Tin Hau Temple 天后廟 4 B3

Peng Chau is just under 1 sq km in area. It is inhabited by around 7000 people, making it far more densely populated than its larger neighbour.

There are no cars on Peng Chau, and you can walk around it easily in an hour. Climbing the steps up to Finger Hill (95m), the island's highest point, and topped with the winged

Chinese-style Fung Ping Pavilion, offers some light exercise and excellent views. To get to it from the ferry pier, walk up Lo Peng St, turn right at the Tin Hau temple, containing a century-old 2.5m-long whale bone blackened by incense smoke, and walk south along Wing On St. This gives way to Shing Ka Rd, and Nam Shan Rd leads from here east up to Finger Hill. The water at otherwise-pleasant Tung Wan Beach, a five-minute walk from the ferry pier, is too dirty for swimming and is not served by lifeguards.

MA WAN

Ma Wan (Map p140) was once famous as the gateway to Kowloon, where foreign ships would drop anchor before entering Chinese waters. If you want to get away from it all Ma

NEIGHBOURHOODS & ISLANDS OUTLYING ISLANDS

Wan, a flat, rapidly developing island between the northeastern tip of Lantau and the New Territories, is hardly the place to go. It has a couple of temples devoted to Tin Hau, a long beach on the east coast at Tung Wan and a massive, high-end residential community called Park Island. Basically you're here to view some startling engineering feats (the Lantau Link) and perhaps to visit Ma Wan Park (☎ 3446 1163; www.mawanpark.com; ☉ 9am-5pm daily), an appealing park and open space that also serves as an education centre focusing on nature, energy use and the environment. You can't fail to notice Noah's Ark, a 'lifesize' version of the biblical craft with plastic versions of the world's animals strolling down the gangplank.

LANTAU LINK BRIDGES Map p140
The real reason to come to Ma Wan is to take in the enormity of Tsing Ma Bridge to the east and, to a lesser extent, Kap Shui Mun Bridge on the west. Together they form the rail and road link connecting Lantau with the New Territories via Tsing Yi Island. While catapulting Ma Wan headlong into the next century, the bridge has guaranteed an end to the island's solitude. Neighbouring Tsing Yi has a special viewing platform for those particularly interested in seeing the bridge up close (below).

NOAH'S ARK Map pp58–9
☎ 3411 8888; www.noahsark.com.hk; 33 Pak Yan Road, Ma Wan; admission adult/child $100/85; ☉ 10am-6pm; Central-Park Island ferry
Looking like it has beached beneath the Tsing Ma Bridge, this peculiar mini–theme park is loosely dedicated to the biblical story of Noah, and has plenty of fun interactive games and distractions for younger kids as well as plenty of refreshment options.

TSING YI
Tsing Yi (Map pp58–9), disfigured by oil depots and extended by land reclamation, serves as a stepping stone for the gigantic Tsing Ma Bridge, which is a 1377m suspension bridge. Don't even think about visiting the beaches here.

Tsing Yi is the large island to the east of Ma Wan on the MTR's Tung Chung and the Airport Express lines.

Airport Express Tsing Yi station has services from Hong Kong and Kowloon or the airport.

Green minibus For the Lantau Viewing Platform and Visitor Centre take minibus 308M from Tsing Yi MTR station (exit A1).

MTR Tsing Yi station is on the Tung Chung line.

LANTAU LINK VISITORS CENTRE
Map pp58–9
☎ 2495 5825, 2495 7583; admission free; ☉ 10am-5pm Mon-Fri, 10am-6.30pm Sat & Sun; MTR Tsing Yi, ☒ green minibus 308M
The Lantau Link Visitors Centre and its viewing platform (admission free; ☉ 7am-10.30pm Sun-Fri, 7am-1.30am Sat) is where you can take in the enormity of Tsing Yi Bridge and the Lantau Link, the combined road and rail transport connection between the New Territories and Lantau. The centre contains models, photographs and videos of the construction process – very much a crowd-pleaser for trainspotters and the hard-hat brigade.

The Lantau Link has since been overshadowed somewhat by the Stonecutter's Bridge, a graceful 1.5km span bridging the gap between the massive international container terminal in the New Territories and Tsing Yi Island.

The visitors centre for the Lantau Link is in the northwest corner of Tsing Yi Island just to the south of Ting Kau Bridge. To reach it, take the MTR to Tsing Yi station, use exit No A1 and board minibus 308M in Maritime Sq, which will drop you off at the centre's car park.

TUNG LUNG CHAU
Standing guard at the eastern entrance to Victoria Harbour is the island of Tung Lung Chau (Map pp58–9), or 'East Dragon Island', whose

Ferry Kaido run from Sai Wan Ho on Hong Kong Island via Joss House Bay on the Clearwater Bay Peninsula in the New Territories. There are single sailings on Tuesday and Thursday, with more regular services only on weekends and public holidays. A weekend and holiday service also operates from Sam Ka Tsuen near Yau Tong MTR.

position was once considered strategic enough for protection. According to the experts the island is Hong Kong's premier spot for rock climbing (see the boxed text, p224).

Tung Lung Chau lies to the south of the Clearwater Bay Peninsula across the narrow Fat Tong Mun channel. To the west is Shek O and Big Wave Bay on Hong Kong Island's east coast. In addition, the northwest tip of the island boasts an important rock carving of what is generally thought to be a dragon. It is quite possibly the oldest such carving in the territory and it is certainly the largest, measuring 2.4m by 1.8m. The ferry pier is close by.

TUNG LUNG FORT Map pp58-9
🏯 Tung Lung Chau

Tung Lung Fort, on the northeastern corner of the island, was built in the late 17th or early 18th century and was attacked a number of times by pirate bands before being abandoned in 1810. The fort once consisted of 15 guardhouses and was armed with eight cannons, but little of it remains today except for the outline of the exterior walls. There's an information centre (🕑 9am-4pm Wed-Mon) here.

PO TOI
Eating p204

A solid favourite of weekend holiday-makers with their own seagoing transport, Po Toi (Map pp58–9) is the largest of a group of four or five islands – one is little more than a huge rock – off the southeastern coast of Hong Kong Island. Hong Kong's territorial border lies just 2km to the south. Visitors frequent the seafood restaurants beyond the jetty at Tai Wan, the main settlement, in the island's southwest.

There's some decent walking on Po Toi, a tiny Tin Hau temple across the bay from the pier, and, on the southern coast, rock formations that (supposedly) look like a palm tree, a tortoise and a monk, and some mysterious rock carvings resembling stylised animals and fish. You can see everything here in an hour.

TRANSPORT – PO TOI

Ferry *Kaido* run to the ferry pier from Aberdeen and Stanley on Tuesdays, Thursdays, weekends and public holidays.

SHOPPING

top picks

- Arch Angel (p157)
- Chinese Arts & Crafts (p164)
- Coup de Foudre (p167)
- Delay No Mall (p166)
- Joyce (p160)
- Lulu Cheung (p160)
- Muji (p168)
- Shanghai Tang (p161)
- Wattis Fine Art (p158)

What's your recommendation? www.lonelyplanet.com/hong-kong

Everyone knows Hong Kong as a place of neon-lit retail pilgrimage. This city is positively stuffed with glitzy shopping malls, its giant temples to massive and conspicuous consumption.

Yet while any international brand worthy of its logo has at least one outlet here, Hong Kong's reputation as a bargain hunter's paradise is largely a thing of the past. While you can still find some bargains, these days you can get pretty much anything that's on sale here a few notches cheaper just over the border in China. Asia's world city charges world-city prices for most things, and it has to: have you seen the rent the landlords charge?

While you will find an embarrassment of top-end global brands here, local brands worth spending your money on are harder to find. The profusion of quirky, creative one-offs or unique local goods you might find in cities such as London, New York, Sydney or Copenhagen is lacking in Hong Kong. The overall impression after trawling the city's malls is of an overwhelming familiarity and homogeneity. You could be anywhere in the world really.

Of course, there are some honourable exceptions among a small band of local designers and some trailblazing retailers. So where should you look?

Cool independents are springing up in the narrow streets of Soho and to a lesser extent old Wan Chai, while the crowded minimalls of Causeway Bay offer some quintessentially Asian shopping experiences. A new breed of Chinese and Japanese mini department/lifestyle stores, such as Muji (p168) and Delay No Mall (p167), are also excellent places for value, design interest and style across a range of goods.

What's worth shopping for? Clothing (off the peg or tailored), shoes, jewellery, luggage and, to a lesser degree nowadays, cameras and electronic goods are the city's strong suits. Excellent art and antiques shops also abound.

There's more good news. Wherever you end up shopping, in general the shopping experience is made pretty easy. Service is attentive, opening hours are long, credit cards are widely accepted and the government will have a fight on its hands if it ever tries to revive shelved plans for a sales tax, so the marked price is the price you'll pay. Sales assistants in department or chain stores rarely have any leeway to give discounts, but you can try bargaining in owner-operated stores and certainly in markets.

OPENING HOURS

In the Central and Western Districts, daily shop hours are generally from 10am to 7.30pm, and in Causeway Bay and Wan Chai some open later (about 11am), but many will stay open until 9.30pm or 10pm. In Tsim Sha Tsui, Mong Kok and Yau Ma Tei, they close around 9pm, and in Tsim Sha Tsui East at 7.30pm. Some smaller shops close for major holidays – sometimes for up to a week – especially during Chinese New Year. Many also close on Sunday. We've included opening hours in reviews only where the hours differ dramatically from these standard times.

Winter sales are during the first three weeks in January; summer sales are in late June and early July.

BARGAINING

Bargaining is a way of life at retail outlets throughout Hong Kong, with the exception of department stores and clothing chain shops,

where the prices marked are the prices paid. Some visitors operate on the theory that you can get the goods for half the price originally quoted. Many Hong Kong residents believe that if you can bargain something down that low, then you shouldn't be buying from that shop anyway. If the business is that crooked – and many are, particularly in the Tsim Sha Tsui tourist ghetto – it will probably find other ways to cheat you (such as selling you electronic goods with missing components or no international warranty).

Price tags are supposed to be displayed on all goods. If you can't find a price tag, you've undoubtedly entered one of those business establishments with 'flexible' – ie rip-off – prices.

DUTY FREE

The only imported goods on which there is duty in Hong Kong are tobacco, perfumes, cosmetics, cars and certain petroleum products. In general, almost anything – from cameras and electronics to clothing and jewellery – will be cheaper when you buy it outside duty-free shops.

WARRANTIES & GUARANTEES

Every guarantee should carry a complete description of the item (including the model and serial numbers), as well as the date of purchase, the name and address of the shop it was purchased from, and the shop's official name chop (stamp).

Many imported items come with a warranty registration with the words 'Guarantee only valid in Hong Kong'. If it's a well-known brand, you can often return this card to the importer in Hong Kong to get a warranty card for your home country.

A common practice is to sell grey-market equipment (ie imported by somebody other than the official local agent). Such equipment may have no guarantee at all, or the guarantee may be valid only in the country of manufacture (which will probably be either China or Japan).

REFUNDS & EXCHANGES

Most shops are loath to give refunds, but they can usually be persuaded to exchange purchases that haven't been soiled or tampered with. Make sure you get a detailed receipt that enumerates the goods, as well as the amount and payment method.

There is really no reason to put a deposit on anything unless it is an article of clothing being made for you or you've ordered a new pair of glasses. Some shops might ask for a deposit if you're ordering an unusual item that's not normally stocked, but this isn't a common practice.

SHIPPING GOODS

Some shops will package and post goods for you, especially large items. It's a good idea to find out whether you will have to clear the goods at the country of destination. Make sure you keep all the receipts.

Smaller items can be shipped from the post office. United Parcel Service (UPS; ☎ 2735 3535) also offers services from Hong Kong to some 40 countries worldwide. It ships by air and accepts parcels weighing up to 70kg. DHL (☎ 2400 3388) is another option.

WHAT TO BUY
Antiques

Hong Kong has a rich and colourful array of Asian, especially Chinese, antiques on offer, but serious buyers will restrict themselves to the reputable antique shops and auction houses only; Hong Kong imports many forgeries and expert reproductions from China and Southeast Asia. Just remember that most of the really good pieces are sold through the auction houses such as Christie's (p158), especially at its auctions in spring and autumn.

Most of Hong Kong Island's antique shops are bunched along Wyndham St and Hollywood Rd in Central and Sheung Wan. The shops at the western end of Hollywood Rd tend to be cheaper and carry more dubious 'antiques' – tread carefully through this minefield of reproductions, books, magazines, Chinese propaganda posters, badges from the Cultural Revolution and so on.

For Chinese handicrafts and other goods (hand-carved wooden pieces, ceramics, paintings, cloisonné, silk garments), the main places to go are the large China-run emporiums

---

SHOPPING STRIPS

The main shopping areas are Central (p157) and Causeway Bay (p166) on Hong Kong Island and Tsim Sha Tsui (p167) in Kowloon. Nathan Rd in Tsim Sha Tsui is the main tourist strip. Central is good for clothing (from international high-end brands to the hautest of haute couture), as well as books, cameras and antiques. Causeway Bay has a lot of department stores and low-end clothing outlets, while old Wan Chai (p163) has a sprinkling of interesting clothing and interiors places.

Either side of the Kowloon peninsula you'll also find ever-increasing retail space, including at the Elements mall in West Kowloon and at Megabox (Map pp100–1; Wang Chui Rd, Kowloon) to the east near Kai Tak airport in Kowloon Bay.

Warehouse sales and factory extras can be found along Granville Rd (p168) in Tsim Sha Tsui, in Causeway Bay and on Ap Lei Chau (p94), the island opposite Aberdeen. Most of these deal in ready-to-wear garments, but there are a few that also sell carpets, shoes, leather goods, jewellery and imitation antiques. Often prices aren't that much less than in retail shops, and it's important to check purchases carefully, as refunds are rarely given, and many articles are factory seconds and imperfect.

scattered throughout the territory, such as Chinese Arts & Crafts (p164) and Yue Hwa Chinese Products Emporium (p170).

Clothing

The best places to find designer fashion and top-end boutiques are in the big shopping centres and malls, especially Landmark (p163) in Central, Pacific Place (p164) in Admiralty and Festival Walk (p170) in Kowloon Tong. The best hunting grounds for warehouse sales and factory extras are generally in Tsim Sha Tsui at the eastern end of Granville Rd (p168); check out Austin Ave and Chatham Rd South as well. On Hong Kong Island, Jardine's Bazaar (Map p85) in Causeway Bay has low-cost garments and there are several sample shops and places to pick up cheap jeans in Lee Garden Rd. The street markets on Temple St (p109) in Yau Ma Tei and Tung Choi St (p158) in Mong Kok have the cheapest clothes. You may also try Li Yuen St East and Li Yuen St West (p77), two narrow alleyways linking Des Voeux Rd

CLOTHING SIZES

Women's clothing

Aus/UK	8	10	12	14	16	18
Europe	36	38	40	42	44	46
Japan	5	7	9	11	13	15
USA	6	8	10	12	14	16

Women's shoes

Aus/USA	5	6	7	8	9	10
Europe	35	36	37	38	39	40
France only	35	36	38	39	40	42
Japan	22	23	24	25	26	27
UK	3½	4½	5½	6½	7½	8½

Men's clothing

Aus	92	96	100	104	108	112
Europe	46	48	50	52	54	56
Japan	S		M	M		L
UK/USA	35	36	37	38	39	40

Men's shirts (collar sizes)

Aus/Japan	38	39	40	41	42	43
Europe	38	39	40	41	42	43
UK/USA	15	15½	16	16½	17	17½

Men's shoes

Aus/UK	7	8	9	10	11	12
Europe	41	42	43	44½	46	47
Japan	26	27	27½	28	29	30
USA	7½	8½	9½	10½	11½	12½

Measurements approximate only; try before you buy

Central with Queen's Rd Central. They are a jumble of inexpensive clothing, handbags, backpacks and costume jewellery.

Although many people still frequent Hong Kong's tailors, getting a suit or dress made is no longer a great bargain. Remember that you usually get what you pay for. Most tailors will require a 50% nonrefundable deposit, and the more fittings you have, the better the result.

Computers

Hong Kong is a popular, competitively priced place to buy personal computers. Most people buy their computers in Kowloon, where there are loads of centres selling computers and related equipment. There's a much greater choice and prices are lower, but 'caveat emptor' is the phrase to bear in mind as you browse. Hong Kong Island does have a couple of reasonable computer arcades, including the Wan Chai Computer Centre (p164).

Gems & Jewellery

The Chinese attribute various magical qualities to jade, including the power to prevent ageing and accidents. The circular disc with a central hole worn around many Hong Kong necks represents heaven in Chinese mythology. The Jade Market (p109) in Yau Ma Tei is diverting, but unless you're knowledgeable about jade, limit yourself to modest purchases.

Hong Kong carries a great range of pearls, and opals are said to be good value. Retail prices for other precious stones are only marginally lower than elsewhere.

The more reputable jewellery-shop chains will issue a certificate that states exactly what you are buying and guarantees that the shop will buy it back at a fair market price.

The only carved ivory products being sold here *legally* are those that were manufactured before a 1989 ban came into effect or those made of marine ivory. Ivory retailers must have all sorts of documentation to prove where and when the goods were made.

Leather Goods & Luggage

Most of what gets sent to the Hong Kong market from China is export quality, but check carefully because there is still a lot of rubbish on sale. All the big brand names such as Louis Vuitton and Gucci are on display in Hong Kong department stores, and you'll also find some local vendors in the luggage

DEFENSIVE SHOPPING, BLOW BY BLOW

Hong Kong is *not* a nest of thieves just waiting to rip you off, but pitfalls can strike the uninitiated.

Whatever you are in the market for, always check prices in a few shops before buying. The most common way for shopkeepers in Hong Kong to cheat tourists is to simply overcharge. In the tourist shopping district of Tsim Sha Tsui, you'll rarely find price tags on anything. Checking prices in several shops therefore becomes essential. But Hong Kong merchants weren't born yesterday; they know tourists comparison-shop. So staff will often quote a reasonable or even low price on a big-ticket item, only to get the money back by overcharging on accessories.

Spotting overcharging is the easy part, though. Sneakier (but rarer) tricks involve merchants removing vital components that should have been included for free (and demanding more money when you return to the shop to get them). Another tactic is to replace some of the good components with cheap or imitation ones.

Watch out for counterfeit-brand goods. Fake labels on clothes are the most obvious example, but there are fake Rolex watches, fake Gucci leather bags, even fake electronic goods. Pirated CDs and DVDs are a positive steal (in more ways than one) but are of poor quality and rapidly deteriorate.

Hong Kong's customs agents have cracked down on the fake cameras and electronic goods, and the problem has been pretty much solved. However, counterfeit brand-name watches remain very common and are constantly being flogged by the irritating touts patrolling Nathan Rd. If you discover that you've been sold a fake brand-name watch by a shopkeeper when you thought you were buying the genuine article, call the police (☎ 2527 7177).

If you have any trouble with a dodgy merchant, call the HKTB's Quality Tourism Services (QTS; ☎ 2806 2823; www.qtshk.com) if the shop is a tourist-board member; the HKTB logo will be displayed on the front door or in some other prominent place. Otherwise, contact the Hong Kong Consumer Council (☎ 2929 2222; www.consumer.org.hk) for advice Monday to Friday between 9am and 5.45pm.

business. If you're just looking for a casual bag or daypack, check out Li Yuen St East and Li Yuen St West (p77) in Central or Stanley Market (p95).

Photographic Equipment

Never buy a camera without a price tag. This will basically preclude most of the shops in Tsim Sha Tsui. One of the best spots in Hong Kong for buying photographic equipment is Stanley St in Central, where competition is keen. Everything carries price tags, though some low-level bargaining may be possible. Tsim Sha Tsui has a couple of shops on Kimberley Rd dealing in used cameras and there are plenty of photo shops on Sai Yeung Choi St in Mong Kok.

Watches

Shops selling watches are ubiquitous in Hong Kong and you can find everything from a Rolex to Russian army timepieces and diving watches. Avoid the shops without price tags. The big department stores and City Chain (p163) are fine, but compare prices.

HONG KONG ISLAND

Central and Causeway Bay are the main shopping districts on Hong Kong Island, with Wan Chai lagging pretty far behind.

CENTRAL, LAN KWAI FONG & SOHO

Central has a mix of midrange to top-end shopping centres and street-front retail; it's popular with locals and tourists alike. This is a good place to look for cameras, books, antiques and designer threads. The Landmark shopping mall in Central has designer boutiques, shops selling crystal and so on. The IFC Mall is for high fashion.

ARCH ANGEL ANTIQUES
Map p78   Antiques
☎ 2851 6848; 53-55 Hollywood Rd; 🚌 26
Though the specialities are antique and ancient porcelain and tombware, Arch Angel packs a lot more into its three floors: it has everything from mah-jong sets and terracotta horses to palatial furniture. It also operates an art gallery, Arch Angel Fine Art (Map p78; ☎ 2854 4255; 38 Peel St) across the road, which deals in paintings by Vietnamese artists.

HOBBS & BISHOPS FINE ART
Map p78   Antiques
☎ 2537 9838; 28 Hollywood Rd; 🕙 10am-5.30pm Mon-Sat; 🚌 26
This shop smelling of beeswax specialises in lacquered Chinese wooden furniture from the 19th and early 20th centuries.

TO MARKET, TO MARKET…

For budget shopping, there's no better place to start than at one of Hong Kong's busy covered markets or street markets.

The biggest one in the territory is the Temple Street night market (p109) in Yau Ma Tei, which basically runs parallel to (and west of) Nathan Rd from Jordan Rd in the south to Man Ming Lane in the north and is divided by Tin Hau Temple. It is the place to go for cheap clothes, watches, pirated CDs and DVDs, fake labels, footwear, cookware and everyday items, as well as dai pai dong (*dgai pàai dawng;* open-air street stall) food. The best time to visit is between 7pm and 10pm.

The Tung Choi St market (Map p111; ☾ noon-11.30pm), two blocks east of Nathan Rd and the Mong Kok MTR station, mainly sells cheap clothing. It is sometimes called Ladies' Market to distinguish it from Men's St (the Temple Street night market) because the stalls in the latter once sold only menswear. Though there are still a lot of items on sale for women on Tung Choi St, vendors don't discriminate and anyone's money will do nowadays. Vendors start setting up their stalls as early as noon, but it's best to get here between 1pm and 6pm when there's much more on offer.

There are other bustling markets on Apliu St (Map pp100–1; ☾ noon-9pm) in Sham Shui Po, one block west of Sham Shui Po MTR station, and in the streets running off Tai Po's Four Lane Sq (Map p124) in the New Territories.

If you're looking strictly for clothing, try Jardine's Bazaar (Map p85) in Causeway Bay. A bit more upmarket and a tourist attraction in its own right is Stanley Market (p95), in the village of that name on the south coast of Hong Kong Island. Another market worth visiting is Western Market (p82) near the Macau ferry terminal in Sheung Wan.

Its taste leans towards the sleek and handsome rather than gilded and showy pieces.

HONEYCHURCH ANTIQUES
Map p78   Antiques
☎ 2543 2433; 29 Hollywood Rd; ☾ closed Sun; 🚌 26
This fine shop, run by an American couple for more than four decades, specialises in antique Chinese furniture, jewellery and antique English silver. There's a wide range of stock, with items from the early Chinese dynasties right up to the 20th century.

TAI SING FINE ANTIQUES
Map p78   Antiques
☎ 2525 9365; 12 Wyndham St; MTR Central
Tai Sing has been selling quality Chinese antiques for more than half a century, with a special focus on porcelain. Two of the shop's six floors are now devoted to European furniture, including a dandy assemblage of art deco pieces.

TERESA COLEMAN FINE ARTS
Map p78   Antiques
☎ 2526 2450; Ground fl, 79 Wyndham St; 🚌 26
This is the finest shop in Hong Kong for purchasing antique Chinese textiles, including rare *chi fu,* the formal court robes of valuable silk worn by the Chinese emperor, princes and imperial ministers. The shop also deals in Chinese export paintings from the 18th and 19th centuries and antique fans.

WATTIS FINE ART
Map p78   Antiques
☎ 2524 5302; www.wattis.com.hk; 2nd fl, 20 Hollywood Rd; ☾ closed Mon; 🚌 26
No place in Hong Kong has a better collection of antique maps for sale than Wattis Fine Art. The selection of old photographs of Hong Kong and Macau is also very impressive. You enter the shop from Old Bailey St.

CHINE GALLERY
Map p78   Antiques, Carpets
☎ 2543 0023; www.chinegallery.com; 42A Hollywood Rd; 🚌 26
The carefully restored furniture – the lacquered cabinets are fab – at this shop come from all over China, and hand-knotted rugs are sourced from remote regions such as Xinjiang, Ningxia, Gansu, Inner Mongolia and Tibet. It sells statues and collectibles, too.

AMOURS ANTIQUES
Map p78   Antiques, Clothing & Accessories
☎ 2803 7877; 45 Staunton St; ☾ 12.30-9.30pm Sun-Thu, 12.30-10.30pm Fri & Sat; 🚌 26
This wonderful shop stocks antique (well, old) rhinestone jewellery, frocks, and a darling clutch of beaded and tapestry bags dating from early last century. There are also vases, candle holders and Buddha figurines. Good gift-shopping territory.

CHRISTIE'S
Map p67   Auction House
☎ 2521 5396; Room 2203-2208, 22nd fl, Alexandra House, 16-20 Chater Rd; MTR Central (exit J2)
Christie's regular sales in ceramics, jade, jewellery, stamps, snuff bottles, art,

traditional and contemporary Chinese paintings and calligraphy. It holds its spring (May) and autumn (November) pre-auction previews in the Hong Kong Convention & Exhibition Centre (p73) in Wan Chai.

JOINT PUBLISHING Map p78 · Books
☎ 2868 6844; 9 Queen Victoria St; MTR Central (exit A)
This primarily Chinese-language bookshop has a good range of English-language books about China, and CDs and DVDs for studying the language. It's also strong on local maps and maps of China. Most English-language titles are on the mezzanine floor. There are 15 other JP outlets, many in MTR stations, including a branch in Wan Chai (Map p74; ☎ 2838 2081; 158 Hennessy Rd).

TAI YIP ART BOOK CENTRE Map p78 · Books
☎ 2524 5963; Room 101-102, 1st fl, Capitol Plaza, 2-10 Lyndhurst Tce; MTR Central (exit C)
Tai Yip has a terrific selection of books about anything that is Chinese and artsy: calligraphy, jade, bronze, costumes, architecture, symbolism. This is a good place to look deeper if you're planning on buying art in Hong Kong. There are outlets in

several of Hong Kong's museums, including the Hong Kong Museum of Art (p98).

GOVERNMENT PUBLICATIONS OFFICE Map p67 · Books, Maps
☎ 2537 1910; Room 402, 4th fl, Murray Bldg, 22 Garden Rd; ☺ closed Sun; 🚌 3B, 12 or 40M
All Hong Kong government publications, including hiking maps, are available here.

BLANC DE CHINE
Map p67 · Clothing & Accessories
☎ 2524 7875; Room 201 & 203A, 2nd fl, Pedder Bldg, 12 Pedder St; MTR Central (exit D1)
This sumptuous store specialises in traditional Chinese men's jackets, off the rack or made to measure. There's also a lovely selection of silk dresses for women. The satin bed linens are exquisite (as are the old ship's cabinets in which they are displayed).

H&M Map p78 · Clothing & Accessories
☎ 2110 9546; 68 Queen's Rd Central; MTR Central (exit D2)
This Swedish chain has finally brought its inexpensive, of-the-moment clothing to Hong Kong. The appeal of H&M is discount prices on lines that track high-end

A READER'S DIGEST

For antiquarian or Chinese-language booksellers see the main listings sections. There's an excellent choice in the city for English language books; here's a roundup.

Bloomsbury Books (Map p67; ☎ 2526 5387; Shop 102, 1/F Hutchison House, 10 Harcourt Rd; ☺ closed Sun; MTR Central, exit J3) Strong business, legal, literary and children's sections.

Bookazine (Map p67; ☎ 2522 1785; Shop 309-313A, 3rd fl, Prince's Bldg, 10 Chater Rd; MTR Central, exit G) Dependable range of books, magazines and stationery. Also a branch in Admiralty (Map p72; ☎ 2866 7522; Shop C, Upper Ground fl, Far East Finance Centre, 16 Harcourt Rd; MTR Admiralty, exit B).

Dymocks (Map p67; ☎ 2117 0360; Shop 2007-2011, 2nd fl, IFC Mall, 8 Finance St; MTR Central, exit A) Mainstream selection of books and magazines in several branches.

Hong Kong Book Centre (Map p67; ☎ 2522 7064; www.swindonbooks.com; Basement, On Lok Yuen Bldg, 25 Des Voeux Rd Central; MTR Central, exit B) Basement shop with a vast selection of books and magazines, particularly business titles.

Kelly & Walsh (Map p72; ☎ 2522 5743; Shop 236, 2nd fl, Pacific Place, 88 Queensway, Admiralty; MTR Admiralty, exit C1) A good selection of art, design and culinary books plus a handy kids' reading lounge. There's also a Central branch (Map p67; ☎ 2810 5128; Shop 305, 3rd fl, Exchange Square Tower I; MTR Central, exit A).

Page One (Map pp100–1; ☎ 2778 2808; Shop LG1 30, Lower Ground fl, Festival Walk, 80-88 Tat Chee Ave, Kowloon Tong; MTR Kowloon Tong, exit C2) Hong Kong's best selection of art and design magazines and books; it's also strong on photography, literature, film and children's books. There's also a smaller branch in Tsim Sha Tsui (Map p104; ☎ 2730 6080; Shop 3202, 3rd fl, Gateway Arcade, Harbour City, 25-27 Canton Rd; MTR Tsim Sha Tsui, exit A1).

Swindon Books (Map p104; ☎ 2366 8001; 13-15 Lock Rd; MTR Tsim Sha Tsui, exit C1) An excellent range and knowledgeable staff. Strong on local books and history in particular.

fashion trends closely, partly with the help of fashion collaborations with the likes of Madonna, Stella McCartney and Kylie Minogue.

JOYCE Map p67 Clothing & Accessories

☎ 2810 1120; Ground fl, New World Tower, 16 Queen's Rd Central; MTR Central (exit D1)
This multidesigner store is a good choice if you're short of time rather than money: Issey Miyake, Alexander McQueen, Marc Jacobs, Comme des Garçons, Chloé, Pucci, Yohji Yamamoto and several Hong Kong fashion names are just some of the designers whose wearable wares are on display. There's another branch of Joyce in Admiralty (Map p72; ☎ 2523 5944; Shop 334, 3rd fl, Pacific Place, 88 Queensway). For the same duds at half the price, visit Joyce Warehouse (☎ 2814 8313; 21st fl, Horizon Plaza Arcade, 2 Lee Wing St, Ap Lei Chau; ☺ closed Mon), opposite the Aberdeen waterfront.

JILIAN, LINGERIE ON WYNDHAM
Map p78 Clothing & Accessories

☎ 2826 9295; Ground fl, 31 Wyndham St; MTR Central (exit D2)
Swimwear and a vast range of French and Italian lingerie, from gossamer delicates small enough to swallow with a glass of water to rather outré corsetry with strings and stays and such. There's even a small range of men's designer smalls if you just can't put up with your man's industrial-sized underpants any longer. Labels stocked include Eres, Argentovivo, ID Sarrieri, Cadolle, Aubade, Bacirubati, Pin-up Stars, Jonquil, Revanche de la Femme, Rosa Cha and Grigioperla.

LINVA TAILOR Map p78 Clothing & Accessories

☎ 2544 2456; Ground fl, 38 Cochrane St; ☒ 26
This is the place to come to have your very own cheongsam (tight-fitting Chinese dress) tailored. Bring your own silk or choose from Miss Tong's selection. The proprietors are also happy to mail completed items, if you're pushed for time.

LULU CHEUNG Map p67 Clothing & Accessories

☎ 2537 7515; Shop B63, Basement, Landmark Bldg, 1 Pedder St; MTR Central (exit G)
Local designer Lulu makes sophisticated, understated women's casual wear and elegant evening gowns using natural fabrics – such as wool, cotton, silk and linen – in muted tones. Cheung often works with layers and textures using mesh or floral embroidery.

MIU MIU Map p67 Clothing & Accessories

☎ 2523 7833; Shop B24, Basement, Landmark Bldg, 1 Pedder St; MTR Central
Clean lines, the best fabrics and a lush colour palette define the high-end fashion from this Prada spin-off. Great (and pricey) shoes and handbags, too. A range of smaller accessories makes it a good place to hunt for presents.

THE WARDROBE OF SUZIE WONG

There's nothing quite like a cheongsam, the close-fitting sheath that is as Chinese as a bowl of won ton noodle soup. It lifts where it should and never pulls where it shouldn't. And those thigh-high side slits – well, they're enough to give any man apoplexy. It's sensuous but never lewd; it reveals without showing too much.

Reach into any Hong Kong Chinese woman's closet and you're bound to find at least one cheongsam (qípáo in Mandarin), the closest thing Hong Kong has to national dress. It's there for formal occasions like Chinese New Year gatherings, work (restaurant receptionists and nightclub hostesses wear them), school (cotton cheongsams are still the uniform at several colleges and secondary schools) or for the 'big day'. Modern Hong Kong brides may take their vows in white, but when they're slipping off for the honeymoon, they put on a red cheongsam.

It's difficult to imagine that this bedazzling dress started life as a man's garment. During the Qing dynasty, the Manchus ordered Han Chinese to emulate their way of dress – elite men wore a loose 'long robe' (chèung-pò) with a 'riding jacket' (mǎa-kwáa) while women wore trousers under a long garment. By the 1920s, modern women in Shanghai had taken to wearing the androgynous changpao, which released them from layers of confining clothing. From this outfit evolved the cheongsam.

The 'bourgeois' cheongsam dropped out of favour in China when the Communists came to power in 1949 and was banned outright during the Cultural Revolution, but the 1950s and '60s were the outfit's heyday. This was the era of Suzie Wong (the cheongsam is sometimes called a 'Suzie Wong dress') and, although hemlines rose and dropped, collars stiffened and more darts were added to give it a tighter fit, the cheongsam has remained essentially the same: elegant, sexy and very Chinese.

SHANGHAI TANG
Map p67   Clothing & Accessories

☎ 2525 7333; Basement & Ground fl, Pedder Bldg, 12 Pedder St; MTR Central (exit D1)

Updated versions of traditional Chinese garments including cheongsams and collarless jackets with a modern cut and edge featuring lots of lime and orange. It also stocks accessories and Chinese-styled gift items with a modern twist. Custom tailoring is available.

VINTAGE HK Map p67   Clothing & Accessories

☎ 2545 9932; 57-59 Hollywood Rd, Central; ☺ 10am-6pm; MTR Central (exit D2)

Definitely worth a look for its small, well-selected range of vintage wear, for which you need not do much rummaging.

HARVEY NICHOLS
Map p67   Department Store

☎ 3695 3389; www.harveynichols.com; Landmark Bldg, 1 Pedder St; MTR Central (exit G)

Britain's Harvey Nichols has brought its diverse, profuse and on-the-pulse range of couture and smart street fashions to Hong Kong, occupying four floors at the Landmark.

LANE CRAWFORD Map p67   Department Store

☎ 2118 3388; Level 3, IFC Mall, 8 Finance St; MTR Central (exit A)

This branch of Hong Kong's original Western-style department store, the territory's answer to Harrods in London, is the flagship now that the store located on Queen's Rd Central has closed. There are also branches in Admiralty (Map p72; ☎ 2118 3668; 1st & 2nd fls, Pacific Place, 88 Queensway), Causeway Bay (Map p85; ☎ 2118 3638; Ground & 1st fls, Times Sq, 1 Matheson St) and Tsim Sha Tsui (Map p104; ☎ 2118 3428; Ground & 1st fls, Ocean Terminal, Harbour City, Salisbury Rd).

SWANK Map p67   Department Store

☎ 2868 3804 (ladies), 2810 0769; Shop 202, 2nd fl, Alexandra House, 16-20 Chater Rd; MTR Central (exit H)

A long-standing fashion powerhouse, the Swank stocks a good range of established, mainly European labels, including Kenzo, Sonia Rykiel, Christian Lacroix and Givenchy, plus a smattering of up-and-coming talent from Hong Kong and the world's fashion centres.

OCEAN OPTICAL Map p67   Eyewear

☎ 2868 5670; Shop 5, Ground fl, Cascade, Standard Chartered Bank Bldg, 4-4A Des Voeux Rd Central; MTR Central (exit G)

Both frames and lenses can be cheaper (in some case, much cheaper) in Hong Kong than what you would pay at home, and we do not know of a better optician in Hong Kong than Ocean Optical. There's a branch in Tsim Sha Tsui (Map p104; ☎ 2735 0611; Shop 326, 3rd fl, Ocean Centre, Harbour City, 3-9 Canton Rd).

FOOK MING TONG TEA SHOP
Map p67   Food & Drink

☎ 2295 0368; Shop 3006, IFC Mall, 8 Finance St; MTR Central (exit A)

Tea-making accoutrements and carefully chosen teas of various ages and grades, from gunpowder to Nanyan Ti Guan Yin Crown Grade – costing anything from $10 to $9000 per 100g.

OLYMPIA GRAECO-EGYPTIAN
COFFEE Map p78   Food & Drink

☎ 2522 4653; Ground fl, 24 Old Bailey St; ☺ closed Sun; 🚌 26

This place has been around since, well, anyone can remember, and it still grinds the best beans in town.

THREE SIXTY Map p6/   Food & Drink

☎ 2111 4480; 3rd & 4th fls, Landmark Bldg, 1 Pedder St; MTR Central (exit G)

A fabulous addition to Hong Kong's food scene, Three Sixty sells a great range of organic and natural foods, as well as top-notch imports of hard-to-find ingredients from all over the world. The prices, of course, are high. There's also a terrific food court with cuisine from all over the world on the upper floor.

LIULIGONGFANG Map p67   Gifts & Souvenirs

☎ 2973 0820; Shop 20-22, Ground fl, Central Bldg, 1-3 Pedder St; MTR Central

Exquisite coloured-glass objects, both practical (vases, candle holders, jewellery) and ornamental (figurines, crystal Buddhas, breathtaking sculptures) from renowned Taiwanese glass sculptor Loretta Yang Hui-Shan are on display and for sale here. There's another branch in Admiralty (Map p72; ☎ 2918 9001; Shop 320, 3rd fl, Pacific Place, 88 Queensway).

MOUNTAIN FOLKCRAFT
Map p78   Gifts & Souvenirs

☎ 2523 2817; 12 Wo On Lane; ☿ closed Sun; MTR Central

This is one of the nicest shops in the city for folk craft. It's piled with bolts of batik and sarongs, clothing, wood carvings, lacquerware and papercuts made by ethnic minorities in China and other Asian countries. The shop attendants are friendly, and prices, while not cheap, are not outrageous either.

PICTURE THIS Map p67   Gifts & Souvenirs

☎ 2525 2820; Shop 212, Prince's Bldg, 10 Chater Rd, Central; MTR Central (exit H)

The vintage Hong Kong posters, photographs, reproductions and antique maps on sale here make great souvenirs or gifts, but they are on the pricey side.

WAH TUNG CHINA ARTS
Map p67   Gifts & Souvenirs

☎ 2543 2823; 59 Hollywood Rd; ☿ closed Sun; ⬤ 26

Wah Tung, the world's largest supplier of hand-decorated ceramics, has some 18,000 items on display at this showroom, just east of Pacific Place. You'll find everything from brightly painted vases and ginger jars to reproduction Tang-dynasty figurines.

KING FOOK Map p78   Jewellery

☎ 2822 8573; Ground fl, King Fook Bldg, 30-32 Des Voeux Rd Central; MTR Central (exit C)

King Fook, with a grandiose gilded entrance, stocks a large range of watches, top-end fountain pens and baubles. There's another branch in Tsim Sha Tsui (Map p104; ☎ 2313 2788; Shop G1, Miramar Shopping Centre, 118-130 Nathan Rd).

ROCK CANDY Map p78   Jewellery

☎ 2549 1018; 1 Elgin St, Soho; ⬤ 26

Made from black glass and with pin-prick lights illuminating display cases, this goth-glam jewellery shop (and its ubertrendy gewgaws) has to be seen to be believed.

TSE SUI LUEN Map p78   Jewellery

☎ 2921 8800; Ground fl, Commercial House, 35 Queen's Rd Central; MTR Central (exit D2)

This is the most sparkling of Tse Sui Luen's dozen or so outlets and is worth visiting for its sheer opulence or garishness – however

you see it. There's another branch in Tsim Sha Tsui (Map p104; ☎ 2926 3210; Shop A & B, Ground fl, 190 Nathan Rd).

HMV Map p67   Music

☎ 2739 0268; 1st fl, Central Bldg, 1-3 Pedder St; MTR Central (exit D1)

This Aladdin's cave of music not only has Hong Kong's largest choice of CDs, DVDs and cassettes but also a great range of music-related literature. There are branches in Causeway Bay (Map p85; ☎ 2504 3669; 1st fl, Style House, Park Lane Hotel, cnr Gloucester Rd & Great George St) and Tsim Sha Tsui (Map p104; ☎ 2302 0122; 2nd fl, HK Pacific Centre, 28 Hankow Rd).

EVERBEST PHOTO SUPPLIES
Map p78   Photographic Equipment

☎ 2522 1985; 28B Stanley St; MTR Central, exit D2

This extremely reliable shop is where many of Hong Kong's professional photographers buy their equipment. Same day or next-day China visas are an odd but useful sideline here.

PHOTO SCIENTIFIC
Map p78   Photographic Equipment

☎ 2525 0550; 6 Stanley St; ☿ 9am-7pm Mon-Sat; MTR Central (exit D2)

This is the favourite of Hong Kong's pro photographers. You'll almost certainly find equipment elsewhere for less, but Photo Scientific has a rock-solid reputation with labelled prices, no bargaining, no arguing and no cheating.

PEDDER RED Map p78   Shoes, Accessories

☎ 2118 3712; 64-66 Wellington St, Central; ☿ 10am-6.30pm; MTR Central (exit D1)

This is the flagship for a small local chain called On Pedder that specialises in its own and other (famous brand) shoes and accessories for women. Perhaps the best place for shoes in Hong Kong.

IFC MALL Map p67   Shopping Mall

☎ 2295 3308; www.ifc.com.hk; 8 Finance St; MTR Hong Kong, exit F

As if Central didn't have nearly enough luxury retail space already, this swanky shopping centre was built. It boasts 200 high-fashion boutiques linking the One and Two IFC towers and the Four Seasons Hotel. Outlets include Patrick Cox, Geiger, Longchamp, Kenzo, Vivienne Tam, Zegna…

we could go on. The Hong Kong Airport Express Station is downstairs.

LANDMARK Map p67   Shopping Mall
☎ 2525 4142; www.centralhk.com; 1 Pedder St; MTR Central, exit G

The most central of all shopping centres, the Landmark has high fashion and good eating in a pleasant, open space. It has become a home almost exclusively to the very high-end fashion brands and boutiques (Gucci, Louis Vuitton, TODs etc) and a handful of worthwhile refreshment stops.

PRINCE'S BUILDING Map p67   Shopping Mall
☎ 2504 0704; www.centralhk.com; 10 Chater Rd; MTR Central, exit K

You may find the layout of Prince's Building disorienting, but it's worth a look for its speciality fashion, toy and kitchenware shops. The selection is rather eclectic – from high-end boutiques such as Chanel and Cartier on the ground floor to booksellers, Mothercare, jewellers, stationers and luggage shops on the levels above. It's an especially good place to bring the kids, as almost the entire 3rd floor is given over to children's shops.

CITY CHAIN Map p78   Watches
☎ 2259 9020; Ground fl, Man Yee Bldg, 67 Queen's Rd Central; MTR Central (exit D2)

City Chain stocks every type of wristwatch imaginable – from the stylish and dressy to the funky and glitzy. It has some two-dozen outlets in Hong Kong, including one in Admiralty (Map p72; ☎ 2845 9403; Shop 112, 1st fl, Pacific Place, 88 Queensway).

ADMIRALTY & WAN CHAI

Admiralty, bordering Wan Chai, has one of Hong Kong Island's glitziest shopping malls, Pacific Place, just opposite Admiralty station, to which it is connected by elevated and underground walkways.

Wan Chai is a good spot for medium and low-priced clothing, sporting goods and footwear, but the area caters mainly for locals. The district has little glamour, but it is well worth hunting for bargains.

COSMOS BOOKS Map p74   Books
☎ 2866 1677; Basement & 1st fl, 30 Johnston Rd, Wan Chai; 🚌 6, 6A or 6X

This chain-store branch has a good selection of China-related books in the basement. Upstairs are English-language books (nonfiction is strong) plus one of Hong Kong's best stationery departments. Enter the Wan Chai store from Lun Fat St and the Tsimsy branch from Granville Rd.

SONJIA Map p72   Clothing, Homewares
☎ 2529 6223; 2 Sun St, Wan Chai; 🕑 9.30am-7.30pm Mon-Sat; MTR Admiralty (exit F)

Sumptuous, romantic womenswear creations from this Anglo-Korean Hong Kong designer in silk, velvet and fine cotton, much of it hand-finished with embroidery, plus vintage jewellery and a few international labels, such as Lagerfeld. The adjoining store stocks a select bunch of elegant homewares to suit every taste.

45R JEANS Map p72   Clothing & Accessories
☎ 2175 5545; 7 Star Street; MTR Admiralty (exit F)

Can jeans be desirable enough to be worth thousands of Hong Kong dollars? Only you can decide, but there's no doubt the finishing flourishes and high-end fabric and dyeing give them that 'one-off' look. They fit well, too.

KENT & CURWEN
Map p72   Clothing & Accessories
☎ 2840 0023; Shop 372, 3rd fl, Pacific Place, 88 Queensway, Admiralty; MTR Admiralty, exit F

Distinguished suits, dress shirts, ties, cufflinks and casual tops for the gentleman who'd rather look to the manor born than arriviste broker.

PACIFIC CUSTOM TAILORS
Map p72   Clothing & Accessories
☎ 2845 5377; Shop 110, 1st fl, Pacific Place, 88 Queensway, Admiralty; MTR Admiralty (exit C1)

This is one of our favourite bespoke tailors in Hong Kong. It'll make or copy anything; turnaround on most items is two or three days, including two fittings. Count on about $4000 for a suit.

VIVIENNE TAM Map p72   Clothing & Accessories
☎ 2918 0238; www.viviennetam.com; Shop 209, 2nd fl, Pacific Place, 88 Queensway, Admiralty; MTR Admiralty (exit F)

This enduring brand from New York–based designer Tam, who was trained in Hong Kong, sells eminently wearable, feminine but also streetwise women's foundation pieces, light gossamer dresses and slinky tops, plus a range of accessories.

WAN CHAI COMPUTER CENTRE
Map p74   Computers

1st fl, Southorn Centre, 130-138 Hennessy Rd, Wan Chai; ☒ closed Sun; MTR Wan Chai (exit B2)
This place, on the northern edge of Southorn Playground, is a cut above Hong Kong's computer emporiums. The prices on pretty much everything digital are generally keener than the local chain stores.

CHINESE ARTS & CRAFTS
Map p72   Department Store

☎ 2523 3933; Shop 220, Pacific Place, 88 Queensway, Admiralty; MTR Admiralty (exit F)
Mainland-owned CAC is probably the best place in Hong Kong to buy quality bric-a-brac and other Chinese trinkets; it's positively an Aladdin's cave of souvenirs. On Hong Kong Island there are also branches in Central (Map p78; ☎ 2901 0338; Ground fl, Asia Standard Tower, 59 Queen's Rd Central) and Tsim Sha Tsui (Map p104; ☎ 2735 4061; 1st fl, Star House, 3 Salisbury Rd), and there's also a huge one in Wan Chai (Map p74; ☎ 2827 6667; Lower Block, China Resources Bldg, 26 Harbour Rd).

DESIGN GALLERY Map p74   Gifts & Souvenirs
☎ 2584 4146; Level 1, Hong Kong Convention & Exhibition Centre, 1 Harbour Rd, Wan Chai; ☒ 18
Supported by the Hong Kong Trade Development Council, this shop showcases local design in the form of jewellery, toys, ornaments and gadgets. It's a chaotic but often rewarding gaggle of goodies. A great place to find present-buying inspiration. There's also a branch in the check-in hall at the airport (☎ 2261 2524; TE07, Level 7).

HONG KONG RECORDS
Map p72   Music

☎ 2845 7088; Shop 252, 2nd fl, Pacific Place, 88 Queensway, Admiralty; MTR Admiralty, exit F
This local outfit has a good selection of Cantonese and international sounds, including traditional Chinese, jazz, classical and contemporary music. There's also a good range of DVDs and VCDs of both Chinese films and Western movies with Chinese subtitles. There's also a Kowloon Tong branch (Map pp100–1; ☎ 2265 8299; Shop L1-02, Level 1, Festival Walk, 80-88 Tat Chee Ave).

SUNMARK CAMPING EQUIPMENT
Map p74   Outdoor Gear

☎ 2893 8553; 1st fl, 121 Wan Chai Rd, Wan Chai; ☒ noon-8pm Mon-Sat, 1.30-7.30pm Sun; ☒ 6, 6A or 6X
Head here for hiking and camping gear and waterproof clothing of all sorts. There's also a small selection of second-hand gear. Enter from Bullock Lane.

PACIFIC PLACE Map p72   Shopping Mall
☎ 2844 8988; www.pacificplace.com.hk; 88 Queensway, Admiralty; MTR Admiralty (exit F)
One of the city's best shopping malls, Pacific Place has, if anything, gone further upmarket recently. There are a couple of hundred outlets, dominated by higher-end men's and women's fashion (from the likes of Burberry, Chanel, Chloé, Loewe, Marc Jacobs and Versace) and accessories (Bottega Veneta, Coach, Fendi, Gucci etc). There's also a Lane Crawford department store.

BUNN'S DIVERS Map p74   Sporting Goods
☎ 3422 3322; Mezzanine, Chuen Fung House, 188-192 Johnston Rd, Wan Chai; MTR Wan Chai (exit A3)
Masks, snorkels, fins, regulators, tanks – Hong Kong's longest-established dive shop also runs dive tours and training courses.

KUNG FU SUPPLIES
Map p74   Sporting Goods

☎ 2891 1912; Room 6A, 6th fl, Chuen Fung House, 188-192 Johnston Rd, Wan Chai; ☒ 6, 6A or 6X
If you need to stock up on martial-arts accessories or just want to thumb through a decent collection of books, this is the place to go. The staff here is very helpful.

SHEUNG WAN

For antiques and curios, head for Hollywood Rd, which starts in Central and ends up in Sheung Wan, where there is a long string of shops selling Asian items. Some of the really good spots have genuine finds, but beware of what you buy. Western Market (p82) is a good spot for buying fabrics and curios. There are also a couple of big department stores in the area.

KARIN WEBER GALLERY
Map p80   Antiques, Fine Art

☎ 2544 5004; www.karinwebergallery.com; 20 Aberdeen St; ☒ 26

Karin Weber has an enjoyable mix of Chinese country antiques and contemporary Asian artworks. She also gives short lectures on antiques and the scene in Hong Kong, and is able to arrange antique-buying trips to Guangdong for serious buyers.

INDOSIAM Map p80   Books, Antiques
☎ 2854 2853; 1st fl, 89 Hollywood Rd; ☯ 2-7pm; 🚌 26

Hong Kong's first (and only) truly antiquarian bookshop deals in rare titles relating to Asian countries. It's particularly strong on Thailand, China and the former French colonies (ie Vietnam, Cambodia, Laos).

RANEE K Map p80   Clothing
☎ 2108 4068; 16 Gough St, Central; ☯ 10am-6.30pm; MTR Sheung Wan (exit A2)

Young local designer Ranee K is a rising star for her combinations of dramatic prints and textures, as well as for her deft adoption of cuts and styles from both East and West in her evening and ready-to-wear lines.

WING ON Map p80   Department Store
☎ 2852 1888; 211 Des Voeux Rd Central; MTR Sheung Wan, exit E3

'Forever Peaceful' is notable for being locally owned. It carries a range of goods but is especially well known for inexpensive electronics and household appliances.

LOCK CHA TEA SHOP
Map p80   Food & Drink
☎ 2805 1360; Ground fl, 290B Queen's Rd Central; 🚌 26

This favourite shop sells Chinese teas of infinite variety, as well as tea sets, wooden tea boxes and well-presented gift packs of various cuppas. A great bonus is that you can try before you buy. Enter the shop from Ladder St.

ADDICTION Map p80   Homewares
☎ 2581 2779; 15 Gough St, Central; ☯ 9.30am-6.30pm; MTR Sheung Wan (exit A2)

Ever more independent retailers are opening up in this corner of Soho, and this one sells quirky and endearing design interpretations of everything from lamps to cushions to T-shirts, most of them portable enough to consider buying and taking home.

top picks

MIGHTY MICROMALLS

Crammed into old buildings, above MTR stations, up escalators and in back lanes are Hong Kong's micromalls consisting of microshops, selling designer threads, a kaleidoscope of kooky accessories and a colourful closet of funky footwear. This is where Hong Kong's youngest mall-trawlers go for clothes and trinkets. The best shopping is done from 3pm to 10pm, when *all* the shops are open.

- Beverley Commercial Centre (Map p106; 87-105 Chatham Rd South, Tsim Sha Tsui; MTR East Tsim Sha Tsui, exit P3) Enter via the passage north of Observatory Rd
- Island Beverley (Map p85; 1 Great George St, Causeway Bay; MTR Causeway Bay, exit E)
- Rise Commercial Centre (Map p106; 5-11 Granville Circuit, Tsim Sha Tsui; MTR Tsim Sha Tsui, exit B2)
- Trendy Zone (Map p108; Chow Tai Fook Centre, 580A Nathan Rd, Mong Kok; MTR Mong Kok, exit D2)
- Up Date Mall (Map p104; 36-44 Nathan Rd, Tsim Sha Tsui; MTR Tsim Sha Tsui, exit A1)

ECOLS Map p80   Homewares, Gifts
☎ 3106 4918; 8 & 10 Gough St, Central; MTR Sheung Wan (exit A2)

Smart, creative interiors stuff including furniture, bowls, candles and bags, some of it small enough to pack as gift items and all of it made from recycled materials.

HOMELESS Map p80   Homewares, Gifts
☎ 2581 1880; 29 Gough St, Central; MTR Sheung Wan (exit A2)

This flagship of a small but growing contemporary interiors retail chain is packed full of good ideas and portable gifts to take home, from smart gadgets such as laser clocks to quirky practical and decorative mugs, chairs, and decorative items.

PO KEE FISHING TACKLE
Map p80   Sporting Goods
☎ 2543 7541; 6 Hillier St; ☯ closed Sun; MTR Sheung Wan (exit A2)

The guys at Po Kee have had the market cornered – hook, line and sinker – on fishing supplies since 1933, when it served Hong

Kong's commercial fishing fleet. Now it exclusively serves sports-fishing enthusiasts.

CAUSEWAY BAY

Causeway Bay has perhaps the largest weekend crowds and the broadest spectrum in terms of price. It is a crush of department stores and smaller outlets selling designer and street fashion, electronics, sporting goods and household items. A good up-and-coming neighbourhood for hip fashions is springing up along Paterson and Kingston Sts close to Victoria Park. Causeway Bay also has a few lively street markets. Jardine's Bazaar (actually a street) and the area behind it are home to stalls and shops peddling cheap clothing, luggage and footwear. The area is also home to the huge Times Square shopping mall.

D-MOP Map p85
Clothing & Accessories

☎ 2203 4130; Shop B, Ground fl, 8 Kingston St; MTR Causeway Bay (exit E)

This is the main outlet for one of Hong Kong's edgier designer lines. It specialises in slinky tops, some out-there one-offs, cool shoes and a handful of hip hipsters from international labels such as Tsubi.

DADA CABARET VOLTAIRE
Map p85   Clothing & Accessories

☎ 2890 1708; Shop F-13A, 1st fl, Fashion Island, 47 Paterson St; ⏱ 12.30-10pm; MTR Causeway Bay (exit E)

Selling bold urban clothing in primary colours also sported by the staff, this is just one of many fine shops in the Fashion Island micromall, where you'll also find branches of shoe god Patrick Cox, Armani Exchange and Gay Giano.

LCX Map p85
Clothing & Accessories

☎ 2890 5200; 9 Kingston St, Fashion Walk, Causeway Bay; ⏱ noon-10pm Mon-Fri, noon-10.30pm Sat & Sun; MTR Causeway Bay (exit E)

This fashion outlet is a good example of the new stores sending Causeway Bay upmarket. Inside the stylishly lit plate glass you'll find clothes from top urban labels, including Marc Jacobs, Calvin Klein, Paul & Joe and Sonia Rykiel, plus upmarket beauty lines.

SISTER Map p85
Clothing & Accessories

☎ 2504 1016; Shop 331, 3rd fl, Island Beverley, 1 Great George St; ⏱ 2-11pm; MTR Causeway Bay (exit E)

This 'trendy fashion store' sells young Hong Kong designer wear verging on the wacky, which is saying something given the competition in this mall.

WALTER MA Map p85
Clothing & Accessories

☎ 2838 7655; Ground fl, 33 Sharp St East; ⏱ noon-10pm Mon-Fri, noon-10.30pm Sat & Sun; MTR Causeway Bay (exit A)

Sophisticated but comfortable women's fashions from the daddy of Hong Kong's home-grown fashion industry. It ranges

---

GIVE GIFT, GAIN FACE

If you're invited around to dinner or have a reason for buying a gift for locals, a lukewarm bottle of cheap plonk or a bunch of limp carnations from the nearest convenience store just won't do. Gift giving is an important way to gain (or lose) face. Do yourself and your intended recipients a favour, avoid embarrassment by making an effort. And don't forget that white flowers are associated with death and funerals, so it's best to pick another colour.

Anglo-Chinese Florist (Map p78; ☎ 2921 2986; Ground fl, Winway Bldg, 50 Wellington St; MTR Central, exit D2) If you've been invited to someone's home and you wish to bring flowers – as is de rigueur here – stop by Anglo-Chinese. You'll also find some exquisite bonsai here.

Armani Fiori (Map p67; ☎ 2532 7766; Chater House, 11 Chater Rd; MTR Central, exit H) Chic modern flower arrangements and plant gifts. Minimalist look, maximum prices.

Cigarro (Map p67; ☎ 2810 1883; Shop 5, Ground fl, St George's Bldg, 2 Ice House St; MTR Central, exit G) There's nothing like a fat cigar to pay your respects to that alpha male who has everything. This smoke shop in Central comes to the rescue with Cuban, Dominican and Nicaraguan stogies, among others.

Cova (Map p67; ☎ 2869 8777; Shop 134-5, 1/fl Princes Bldg; MTR Central, exit H) Fine cakes and confectionery in opulent golden tins and wrappings.

Mandarin Oriental Flower Shop (Map p67; ☎ 2825 4019; Ground fl, Mandarin Oriental, 5 Connaught Rd Central; MTR Central, exit F) Exquisite flowers, of course.

from smart-casual office wear to more glamorous evening wear.

IN SQUARE Map p85 Computers
10th-11th fls, Windsor House, 311 Gloucester Rd; MTR Causeway Bay (exit D1)
This landmark building in Causeway Bay houses dozens of reliable computer shops, selling both hardware and software. There's also space to browse at leisure here, unlike the usual electronics warren.

DELAY NO MALL Map p85 Department Store
☎ 2577 6988; 68 Yee Wo St; ☯ noon-10pm; MTR Causeway Bay (exit F)
As much of an experience as a clothes shop, this supercool multifloor shop from the G.O.D. homewares chain is all about being on top of the latest trends, including retail ones. This magpie retail concept has a tattoo parlour, sleep-pod installation and a bar-café (a branch of the slick FINDS bar-restaurant from Lan Kwai Fong; see p209). You'll find fashion, jewellery, homewares and beauty products from a well-selected group of hip brands.

SOGO Map p85 Department Store
☎ 2833 8338; www.sogo.com.hk; 555 Hennessy Rd; MTR Causeway Bay (exit B)
This Japanese-owned store, in the hub of Causeway Bay, has 12 well-organised floors and more than 37,000 sq metres of retail space. The range is mind-boggling: over 20 brands of ties just for starters. Eclectic departments include the Barbie Counter and the Character's Shop.

MOUNTAINEERING SERVICES
Map p85 Outdoor Gear
☎ 2541 8876; Ground fl, 271 Gloucester Rd; MTR Causeway Bay (exit D1)
This excellent and centrally located shop sells climbing and hiking gear and pretty much everything you need for tackling Hong Kong's hills and country parks.

COUP DE FOUDRE Map p85 Shoes
☎ 3428 2655; 222 & 223 Island Beverley, 1 Great George St; MTR Causeway Bay (exit E)
If you can't find the shoe design you've had in your head, then come to this place, which will custom-make shoes to your designs and, it claims, have them ready for you within three days

CITYPLAZA Map pp62-3 Shopping Mall
☎ 2568 8665; www.cityplaza.com.hk; 18 Tai Koo Shing Rd, Tai Koo Shing, Quarry Bay; MTR Tai Koo (exit D2)
The largest shopping centre in eastern Hong Kong Island, with 180 shops (mainly fashion and electronics), Cityplaza is directly linked to the MTR. Being further from the main business district, it charges retailers lower rents, which can translate into lower prices for shoppers. There's a Wing On department store here, as well as an ice-skating rink.

RAINBOW CITY Map p85 Shopping Mall
☎ 2881 1423; 1st fl, Fashion Island, Great George St; MTR Causeway Bay (exit E)
Japanese cartoons and all manner of kitsch is splashed across the clothes and bags in vivid technicolour in this store aimed at local teens, tweens and 20-somethings.

TIMES SQUARE Map p85 Shopping Mall
☎ 2118 8900; www.timessquare.com.hk; 1 Matheson St; MTR Causeway Bay (exit A)
The 10 floors of retail organised by type are slightly less high end than in Central. Fashion brands and outlets include Lane Crawford, Anne Sui, Aquascutum, Birkenstock, Marks & Spencer, Vivienne Westwood and Vivienne Tam. There are plenty of electronics and homewares. There are restaurants on the 10th to 13th floors, and snack bars, cafés and a supermarket in the basement.

KOWLOON

Shopping in Kowloon is a bizarre mix of the down at heel and the glamorous, and an afternoon's stroll through its shopping quarters should yield quite a few surprises.

TSIM SHA TSUI, TSIM SHA TSUI EAST & HUNG HOM

Nathan Rd is the main tourist strip, a huge avenue with side streets full of camera, watch and electronics shops, and leather and silk emporiums. Although this is the part of town where you're most likely to become a victim of sharp practice, Tsim Sha Tsui is also home to a large number of above-board designer and signature shops. Some of these are found in Nathan Rd, but the bulk are in Harbour City, a labyrinthine shopping complex with a mall that stretches nearly 1km from the Star Ferry terminal north along Canton Rd. Many hotels in Tsim Sha Tsui have very upmarket boutique shopping arcades, most notably the Peninsula and the Hotel Inter-Continental.

BEATNIKS Map p106   Clothing & Accessories
☎ 2739 8494; Shop 1, Rise Commercial Bldg, Granville Circuit; MTR Tsim Sha Tsui (exit B1)
The selective stock ensures a visit to this vintage-clothing shop isn't like the jumble-sale rummage you get with many second-hand outlets. The focus here is on street styles and left-field cool, rather than on high fashion or couture.

GRANVILLE ROAD
Map p106   Clothing & Accessories
Granville Rd; MTR Tsim Sha Tsui (exit B2)
If you want to hunt for bargains and have the time and inclination to riffle through racks and piles of factory seconds, the dozen or so factory outlet stores along Granville Rd should reward you with items at a fraction of store prices. It's pot luck as to what labels you will find, although they tend to be familiar, slightly premium mainstream casual and leisure brands (both international and local). Hotspots include UNO OUN (29 Granville Rd), Sample Moon (30 Granville Rd) and the Baleno Outlet Store (24B Granville Rd).

MUJI Map p104   Clothing & Accessories, Homewares
☎ 3188 1818; L4 Ocean Centre, Harbour City, Tsim Sha Tsui; MTR Tsim Sha Tsui (exit L4)
This Japanese mini-department-store chain is somewhere between the amazingly diverse iterations you'll find in Japan and the slightly blander versions you'll find

in Europe. You name it – this place has a smart, inexpensive version of it whether it be smart and wearable his and hers fashion, stationery, accessories, snacks or household items.

SAM'S TAILOR Map p104   Clothing & Accessories
☎ 2367 9423; Shop K, Burlington Arcade, 92-94 Nathan Rd; ☺ 10am-7.30pm Mon-Sat, 10am-noon Sun; MTR Tsim Sha Tsui (exit B1)
It's not certain that Sam's is the best tailor in Hong Kong, but it's the most aggressively marketed and best known. Sam's has stitched up everyone – from royalty and rock stars to us.

WWW.IZZUE.COM
Map p104   Clothing & Accessories
☎ 2992 0612; Shop 2225, 2nd fl, Gateway Arcade, Harbour City, 25-27 Canton Rd; MTR Tsim Sha Tsui (exit E)
You'll find simple, energetic and comfortable styles in this chain of bright, modern boutiques. There are 15 outlets throughout the territory, including a branch in Central (Map p67; ☎ 2868 4066; Upper Ground fl, 10 Queen's Rd Central).

STAR COMPUTER CITY
Map p104   Computers
2nd fl, Star House, 3 Salisbury Rd; ⚓ Star Ferry
This is the largest complex of retail computer outlets in Tsim Sha Tsui, with some two-dozen shops selling PDAs, laptops, computer games, and all manner of cables and accessories. You could certainly do slightly better on price further north in Mong Kok,

JUST FOR KIDS
For hundreds of square feet and dozens of outlets dedicated solely to children, head to the ground floor of the Ocean Terminal (p103) at Harbour City in Tsim Sha Tsui, which is packed with children's clothes, shoe and toy shops. The following independents should also have something for most youngsters.

Kitty House Gift Shop (Map p85; ☎ 2890 6968; Shop 229, Island Beverley, 1 Great George St, Causeway Bay; MTR Causeway Bay, exit E) This is just one of the dozens of microstores crammed into Island Beverley selling Japanese cartoon ephemera such as Hello Kitty, the cat with no mouth. It's an abiding attraction for young locals. A good place for kitsch gifts and toys.

Little Misses & Mini Masters (Map p67; ☎ 2156 1118; Shop 307, 3rd fl, Prince's Bldg, 10 Chater Rd; MTR Central, exit G) Horrible name, but this expat-managed independent has some stylish clothing and a few upmarket toys.

Toy Museum (Map p67; ☎ 2869 9138; Shop 320, 3rd fl, Prince's Bldg, 10 Chater Rd; MTR Central, exit K) Top-of-the-line teddy bears, action men, Beanie Babies and Pokemon paraphernalia are crammed into a tight space here.

Wise Kids (Map p72; ☎ 2868 0133; Shop 134, 1st fl, Pacific Place, 88 Queensway, Admiralty; MTR Admiralty, exit F) Nothing to plug in, nothing with batteries: Wise Kids concentrates on engaging kids' creativity and craft skills.

but as well as being handier, these outlets are probably a bit more reliable.

ALAN CHAN CREATIONS
Map p104   Gifts & Souvenirs

☎ 2723 2722; www.alanchancreations.com; Shop 5A, Basement, Peninsula Hong Kong, Salisbury Rd; MTR East Tsim Sha Tsui (exit L4)

Alan Chan has designed everything – from airport logos to soy-sauce bottles – and now lends his name to stylish souvenirs, such as clothing and ceramic pieces. Some items he has a direct hand in; others he simply approves of. Cool, contemporary Chinese design that should inspire plenty of gift ideas.

CURIO ALLEY Map p104   Gifts & Souvenirs
🕙 10am-8pm; MTR Tsim Sha Tsui (exit C1)

This is a fun place to shop for name chops, soapstone carvings, fans and other Chinese bric-a-brac. It's found in an alleyway between Lock and Hankow Rds, just south of Haiphong Rd.

KING SING JEWELLERY Map p104   Jewellery
☎ 2735 7021; Shop 14, Ground fl, Star House, 3 Salisbury Rd; 🚢 Star Ferry

A long-standing jeweller with a wide selection of diamonds, pearls and gold items, many of them made by its own goldsmiths. The sales staff is pleasant and not pushy.

OM INTERNATIONAL Map p104   Jewellery
☎ 2366 3421; 1st fl, Friend's House, 6 Carnarvon Rd; 🕙 closed Sun; MTR Tsim Sha Tsui (exit B2)

This place has an excellent selection of saltwater and freshwater pearls, and some good deals. The staff is scrupulously honest, helpful and friendly.

PREMIER JEWELLERY
Map p104   Jewellery

☎ 2368 0003; Shop G14-15, Ground fl, Holiday Inn Golden Mile Shopping Mall, 50 Nathan Rd; MTR Tsim Sha Tsui (exit G)

This third-generation family firm is directed by a qualified gemmologist and is one of our favourite places to shop. The range isn't huge, but if you're looking for something particular, give Premier Jewellery a day's notice and a selection will be ready in time for your arrival. Staff can also help you design your own piece.

GIGA SPORTS Map p104   Outdoor Gear
☎ 2115 9930; Shop 244-247, 2nd fl, Ocean Terminal, Harbour City, Salisbury Rd; 🕙 10am-8pm; 🚢 Star Ferry

This vast sports superstore is Hong Kong's largest, with a wide range of sports equipment, backpacks, clothing and footwear.

TRAVELMAX Map p104   Outdoor Gear
☎ 3188 4271; Shop 270-273, 2nd fl, Ocean Terminal, Harbour City, Salisbury Rd; 🚢 Star Ferry

Travelmax sells both lightweight and cold-weather outdoor gear; kids' sizes are available. There's a good range of Eagle Creek travel products here, too.

DAVID CHAN PHOTO SHOP
Map p104   Photographic Equipment

☎ 2723 3886; Shop 15, Ground fl, Champagne Court, 16 Kimberley Rd; MTR Tsim Sha Tsui (exit B1)

If you've decided to give the digital age a miss altogether, or at least still use film cameras, this dealer is one of the most reliable in Hong Kong and sells both new and antique cameras.

HARBOUR CITY Map p104   Shopping Mall
☎ 2118 8666; www.harbourcity.com.hk; 3-9 Canton Rd; MTR Tsim Sha Tsui (exit C1)

This is an enormous place, with 700 shops, 50 food and beverage outlets, and five cinemas. Outlets are arrayed in four separate zones: for kids, sport, fashion, and cosmetics and beauty. There's also a large Lane Crawford department store. Every major brand is represented.

KS AHLUWALIA & SONS
Map p104   Sporting Goods

☎ 2368 8334; 8C Hankow Rd; MTR Tsim Sha Tsui (exit E)

Long established, this store is well stocked with golf gear, tennis racquets, cricket bats, shirts and balls. It's cash only, and no prices are marked, so haggle away.

OCEAN SKY DIVERS
Map p104   Sporting Goods

☎ 2366 3738; www.oceanskydiver.com; 1st fl, 17-19 Lock Rd; MTR Tsim Sha Tsui (exit C1)

Along with a full range of diving and snorkelling gear, this place is also worth consulting about dive courses and ideal dive sites all around the Hong Kong's coastline and islands.

YAU MA TEI & MONG KOK

To the north of Tsim Sha Tsui, Yau Ma Tei and Mong Kok cater mostly to local shoppers and offer good prices on clothing, sporting goods, camping gear, footwear, computers and other daily necessities. There's nothing very exotic available here, but for your everyday items they're popular spots, and it is fun to see how the local people shop and to check out what they are buying.

TRENDY ZONE Map p108   Clothing & Accessories
Chow Tai Fook Centre, 580A Nathan Rd; 1-10pm; MTR Mong Kok (exit E2)
A terribly uncool name, yes, but you'll find a couple of dozen quirky little fashion outlets crowded into this micromall selling new and vintage gear for guys and gals. It's very urban and aimed largely at a teen and 20-something clientele.

MONG KOK COMPUTER CENTRE
Map p111   Computers
8-8A Nelson St, Mong Kok; 1-10pm; MTR Mong Kok (exit E2)
This centre has three floors of computer shops. In general, it's geared more towards the resident Cantonese-speaking market than foreigners, but you can normally get better deals here than in Tsim Sha Tsui. Check out Winframe System (2300 1238; Shop 106-107) on the 1st floor.

YUE HWA CHINESE PRODUCTS EMPORIUM Map p108   Department Store
2384 0084; 301-309 Nathan Rd; MTR Yau Ma Tei (exit D)
This enormous place, with seven floors of ceramics, furniture, souvenirs and clothing, has absolutely everything the souvenir-hunting tourist could possibly want, as well as bolts of silk, herbs, clothes, porcelain, luggage, umbrellas and kitchenware. There's also a branch in Tsim Sha Tsui on Kowloon Park Dr (Map p104; 2317 5333; 1 Kowloon Park Dr) that's entered from Peking Rd.

CHAMONIX ALPINE EQUIPMENT
Map p108   Outdoor Gear
2770 6746; 1st fl, On Yip Bldg, 395 Shanghai St; MTR Yau Ma Tei (exit B2)
Far-flung but worth the trip, this Mong Kok shop, run by an avid mountaineer, has a wide range of camping, hiking and climbing equipment.

WISE MOUNT SPORTS
Map p111   Outdoor Gear
2787 3011; Ground fl, 75 Sai Yee St; 11.30am-10.30pm; MTR Mong Kok (exit E2)
This is a long-standing family-run shop with camping gear, swimming goggles, pocket knives, compasses, hard-wearing bags and even sports trophies for sale.

LANGHAM PLACE MALL
Map p111   Shopping Mall
3520 2800; 8 Argyle St; MTR Mong Kok (exit C3)
This 15-storey supermall has some 300 shops that stay open till as late as 11pm. The focal point of the mall is the high-tech Digital Sky, where special events take place.

KHS BICYCLES Map p111   Sporting Goods
2733 7777; 201 Tung Choi St; MTR Mong Kok (exit A2)
A well-stocked shop offering a range of bikes from urban runabouts to mountain bikes and a good supply of accessories.

NEW KOWLOON

Shopping venues in New Kowloon run the gamut from glittering shopping malls, such as Festival Walk in Kowloon Tong, to the cut-price computer centres of Sham Shui Po.

GOLDEN COMPUTER ARCADE
Map pp100-1   Computers
Basement & 1st fl, 146-152 Fuk Wa St, Sham Shui Po; Sham MTR Shui Po (exit B1)
This centre sells computers and components, as well as software, VCDs and DVDs, all at the lowest prices this side of Shenzhen.

NEW CAPITAL COMPUTER PLAZA
Map pp100-1   Computers
1st & 2nd fls, 85-89 Un Chau St, Sham Shui Po; MTR Sham Shui Po (exit B1)
This emporium of computer shops has a good range of stock and helpful staff who can produce enough English to close a sale.

FESTIVAL WALK Map pp100-1   Shopping Mall
2844 2222; www.festivalwalk.com.hk; 80-88 Tat Chee Ave, Kowloon Tong; 10am-midnight; MTR Kowloon Tong (exit C2)
Festival Walk is a huge and glittering shopping mall with Hong Kong's largest cinema and ice-skating rink. It has a good midrange selection of some 200 shops and around two-dozen restaurants as well.

top picks

- Da Domenico (p186)
- Dah Wing Wah (p200)
- Hang Zhou Restaurant (p179)
- L'Atelier de Joël Robuchon (p177)
- Mido Cafe (p196)
- Spring Deer (p195)
- T'ang Court   (p191)
- Tung Po Seafood Restaurant (p189)
- Woodlands (p195)
- Yin Yang (p179)

EATING

A chef from Hong Kong planted the city firmly in the world's culinary firmament by becoming the first ever Chinese chef to receive the top ranking of three stars from the début *Michelin Hong Kong and Macau* guide in 2009. The French bible of gastronomy also gave seven restaurants in the city two stars while fourteen received one star. Despite cries about why most of the inspectors were not local Chinese and the bias towards French restaurants, most Hong Kongers were at least a little pleased with the results.

It came as no surprise that the top honour went to the chef of Lung King Heen (p177), a restaurant specialising in Cantonese cooking. Hong Kong's Cantonese cuisine is the best in the world. It's a cuisine known for its obsession with fresh ingredients. Seafood restaurants display tanks full of finned and shelled creatures enjoying their final moments on *terra infirma*. Housewives complained about the 'fridge taste' of previously frozen chicken when Avian Flu forced them to forgo buying live chickens. Cantonese dishes are characterised by delicate and balanced flavours, obtained through restrained use of seasoning, and light-handed cooking techniques such as steaming and quick stir-frying.

In Hong Kong, Cantonese cuisine refers largely to the culinary styles of Guangdong (Canton) province, as well as Chiu Chow (Chaozhou) and Hakka cuisines. Chiu Chow cooking reflects a penchant for seafood and condiments. Deep-fried soft-boned fish comes with tangerine oil, and braised goose is accompanied by a vinegar and garlic dip. Hakka cuisine, known for its saltiness and use of preserved meat, was popular in Hong Kong in the 1960s and '70s. Salt-baked chicken and pork stewed with preserved vegetables fed many hungry families and workers from the city's construction sites.

Though originating in Guangzhou, Cantonese cuisine underwent significant development in Hong Kong. Dim sum, for example, has expanded to include mango pudding, egg tarts and other delicacies. Hong Kong's chefs also pride themselves on innovation. They will seize upon a new ingredient and find ways to use it. For example, asparagus is a vegetable little known in the rest of China, but Hong Kong chefs serve it every day, combining it with baby abalone and olive oil or with caviar and preserved eggs.

In the last half century, Hong Kong has developed into an epicentre of international trade. The lifestyle of its population has become cosmopolitan, and so have the things people eat. In Western dining, hotels play an important role. As it lacks an established culinary institute, Hong Kong has always relied on resource-rich hotel groups to bring in trained non-Chinese, although such dependence has decreased with the development of many stand-alone restaurants.

It is hard to have a conversation in Hong Kong without mentioning food. Many greet each other by asking, '*Láy sik-jó faan may?*' (Have you eaten yet?) Dim sum lunch on Sunday is a way of life for many families, and the thickness of the dumpling skin and the colour of the green vegetable are all part of the discussion. Office workers debate the choices of the *Michelin Hong Kong and Macau* guide, while armchair gourmands post hundreds, even thousands, of restaurant reviews on www.openrice.com, a foodies' website. Food is so much more than a necessity in Hong Kong. It's a tangible and tantalising piece of its culture, a means through which a people who have had little say in the larger matters of their home and future explore the world and express themselves.

HISTORY & CULTURE

The modern history of Hong Kong begins with the First Opium War (p22), but the roots of its cuisine go much further back. The local inhabitants who dwelled here ate what they could herd and grow or catch from the sea. Certain ancient food traditions from these peoples remain, most notably walled village cuisine (see the 'Dah Wing Wah' boxed text on p200), including the 'basin feast' (*poon choy*). The story has it that the last emperor of the southern Song dynasty (AD 1127–1279), fleeing from the Mongols, retreated to a walled village in Hong Kong with his entourage. The villagers, lacking decent crockery, piled all kinds of food into a large basin to serve the royal guests (see Basin Feast, opposite). *Poon choy* has become a dish for festive occasions in the New Territories ever since.

The British Crown Colony maintained its stability and prosperity for most of its 150 years. Many of the best mainland cooks, especially those from Guangzhou, eventually found refuge in Hong Kong. Given the colony's resources to play around with, they strived for the best and the most exotic, making Hong Kong the 'real' Guangzhou.

With the declaration of the People's Republic of China in 1949, floods of immigrants from Shanghai, Peking (Beijing) and Sichuan came looking for safety, jobs and a new life. Shanghainese cuisine with its preference for sweetness and wine became an instant favourite. The arrival of these immigrants turned Hong Kong into a melting pot of Chinese regional cuisines, and the rest, literally, is history.

DINING LOCAL
Dim Sum

Dim sum (*dím sàm*) are Cantonese tidbits consumed with tea for breakfast or lunch. The term literally means 'to touch the heart', and the act of eating dim sum is referred to as yum cha (*yám chàa*), meaning 'to drink tea'.

In the postwar period, yum cha was largely an activity of single males, who met over their breakfast tea to socialise or exchange tips about job-seeking. As these first-generation migrants settled down, yum cha became a family activity.

Each dish, often containing two to four morsels steamed in a bamboo basket, is meant to be shared. In old-style dim sum places, just stop the waiter and choose something from the cart. Modern venues give you an order slip, but it's almost always in Chinese only. However, as dim sum dishes are often readymade, the waiters should be able to show you samplings to choose from.

Soy Sauce Western

'Soy sauce Western' (*sí-yàu sai-chaan*) is a cuisine that emerged in the 1950s featuring Western dishes of eclectic origins prepared with a large dollop of wisdom from the Chinese kitchen. It's believed to have been popularised by Tai Ping Koon, a restaurant founded in Guangzhou in the Qing dynasty by the sous-chef of a foreign trading company. The first Hong Kong branch of the restaurant was opened in 1935.

Tai Ping Koon created a new cuisine by tweaking Western recipes, such as replacing dairy products with local seasoning to appease lacto-intolerant Chinese stomachs and putting rice on the menu. But the new invention soon met its nemesis. After the Bolshevik Revolution in 1917, tens of thousands of White Russians sought refuge in Shanghai, where they opened cafes specialising in what came to be known as Shanghainese–Russian food. And in 1949, it filtered into Hong Kong.

For a while, there were two competitive schools of Western-style cooking in the British colony: Cantonese and Shanghainese. Both offered affordable dining at a time when authentic Western eateries catered almost exclusively to expatriates. But soon they merged

---

BASIN FEAST

There should be roast rice-duck and pan-fried prawns on top
Order of the classes are clearly laid out in layers
But the poking chopsticks gradually reverse
the priced five-spice chicken and the lowly pigskin
The Sung army once sought shelter here after defeat
wolfed down the fishermen's reserves from big wooden basins
dining on the beach in crude circles, with no elegance of the past
Away from the capital, they tried wild flavours of the rural folks.

Unable to stay on top, they collapse with general consumption
No escape from touching bottom colours, whether you like it or not,
no way to block exchanges between humble mushrooms and rare squids
Reversed relationships taint each other and affect the purity on top
Nobody can stop the meat juice from trickling down, and let
the bottom most turnip absorb all the flavours in all its sweetness.

Leung Ping-kwan (translated by himself)

into each other, spawning soy sauce Western as we know it.

A meal cooked in this fashion typically begins with Russian borscht followed by a main of baked pork chop over fried rice, or beef Stroganoff with rice.

Over the years, soy sauce Western dishes have made their way onto the menus of *cha chaan tengs* (see Tea Cafes, below), cafeterias, even McDonald's. Queen's Cafe (p197) and Tai Ping Koon (p186) still make decent soy sauce Western dishes.

Tea Cafes

Tea cafes (*cha chaan tengs*) appeared in the 1940s as cheap and cheerful neighbourhood eateries serving Western-style beverages and snacks to those who couldn't afford Earl Grey and cucumber sandwiches. Since then, their menus have expanded to include popular Chinese and soy sauce Western dishes. Many tea cafes have their own bakeries creating Western pastries with Chinese characteristics. Some of the better known are the pineapple bun (*bo law bao*), which does not contain said fruit, the cocktail bun with coconut stuffing (*gai may bao*), the ubiquitous egg tart (*daan taht*) and its Macanese cousin, the Portuguese egg tart.

Cha chaan tengs are perhaps best known for their Hong Kong–style 'pantyhose' milk tea (*nai cha*) – a strong brew made from a blend of several types of black tea with crushed egg shells thrown in for silkiness. It's filtered through a fabric that hangs like a stocking, hence the name, and drunk with evaporated milk. 'Pantyhose' milk tea is sometimes mixed with three parts coffee to create the quintessential Hong Kong drink, tea-coffee or *yin yeung* (literally meaning 'mandarin duck', a symbol of matrimonial harmony; see left).

Cha chaan tengs often appear as settings in local films because they're the only places where you'd see lovers, Triads, students and retirees sharing a table. For a retro experience, go to Kam Fung Cafe (p181), Lan Fong Yuen (p184), Mido Cafe (p196), Pak Kung Cafe (p198), Star Cafe (p193) and Wah Nam Cafe Shop (p197). For the modern version, we recommend Honolulu Coffee Shop (p180) and Sun Chiu Kee (p189).

Dai Pai Dongs

If during your wanderings you see a makeshift food stall built into a rickety hut, with tables and stools spilling onto the sidewalk, you've sighted a *dai pai dong* (*dáai-pàai-dawng*), an open-air cooked-food stall. After WWII, the colonial government issued licences to the families of deceased and injured civil servants so that they could operate food stalls for a living. The licence was large, so locals referred to these places as 'big licence stall' or '*dai pai dong*'.

Dai pai dong can spring up anywhere – by the side of a slope, in an alley or under a tree, surviving on borrowed time, in borrowed spaces. However, these traditional places for under-the-stars dining are fast disappearing. The government has persuaded many stall holders to move into cooked-food centres and wet markets for easy management.

The culinary repertoire of *dai pai dong* varies from stall to stall. One operator can specialise in congee (rice porridge) while its neighbour whips up seafood dishes that give restaurants a run for their money. In places where there's a cluster of *dai pai dong*, you can order from different operators.

The following are recommended for the food and the atmosphere: Ap Lei Chau Market Cooked Food Centre (p190), Chan Kun Kee (p199), Gi Kee Seafood Restaurant (p188), Tak Chai Kee (p202), Tak Fat Beef Balls (p193) and Tung Po Seafood Restaurant (p189).

HOW HONG KONG PEOPLE EAT

Busy Hong Kongers take their breakfast and lunch at tea cafes and fast-food outlets three times a week on average. A full breakfast at these places consists of buttered toast, fried eggs and spam, instant noodles and a drink. Not surprisingly, this breakfast flopped an assessment of the nutritional values of common Hong Kong breakfasts by the Consumer

---

COFFEE, TEA OR TEA-COFFEE?

Tea fragrant and strong, made from five different blends, in cotton bags or legendary stockings – tender, all-encompassing, gathering – brewed in hot water and poured into a teapot, its taste varying subtly with the time in water steeped. Can that fine art be maintained? Pour the tea

into a cup of coffee, will the aroma of one interfere with, wash out the other? Or will the other keep its flavour: roadside foodstalls streetwise and worldly from its daily stoves mixed with a dash of daily gossips and good sense, hard-working, a little sloppy.... an indescribable taste.

Leung Ping-kwan
(translated by Martha Cheung)

Council. The winner was *jùk*, a rice porridge also known as congee, with dim sums of rolled rice sheets *(chéung fán)* and steamed dumplings with pork and shrimp *(siù máai)*.

Lunch for office workers can mean a bowl of wonton noodles, a plate of rice with Chinese barbecue, or something more elaborate. With the economic downturn, packed lunches, usually made up of leftovers from dinner, are in style again.

Afternoon tea is popular at the weekends. On weekdays, it is the privilege of labourers and ladies of leisure – the former because they need the energy, the latter because it's their first meal of the day. Workers are said to vanish, Cinderella fashion, at 3.15pm sharp everyday for egg tarts and milk tea. For *tai-tais* (married women, especially the leisured wives of businessmen), it could mean a traditional English affair or a bowl of fish-ball noodles consumed at the hairdresser's.

Dinner is the biggest meal of the day. If prepared at home, what's on the table depends on the traditions of the family. Dining out is extremely common, as the majority of people live within walking distance of eateries.

ETIQUETTE

Hong Kong people are casual about etiquette at the table. Before the SARS outbreak in 2003, most Hong Kongers would think nothing of sticking their chopsticks into a communal dish, which can raise sanitation issues. Now many ask for separate serving chopsticks or spoons with each dish if the restaurant does not already provide them.

At Chinese meals, all dishes are shared. Except for soup and staples, help yourself to no more than the equivalent of two mouthfuls at a time. If you can't manage chopsticks, don't be afraid to ask for a fork. All restaurants have them.

Your plate is the preferred spot for bones, but at budget places diners put them on the table beside their plate or bowl. If you find that disconcerting, place a Kleenex under or over your rejects.

Toothpicks are available at all eateries, even high-end Western restaurants. The right way to use them is to cover your mouth with one hand while using the toothpick with the other.

COOKING COURSES

Hong Kong is a good place to hone your skills in the art of Chinese cookery.

Chinese Cuisine Training Institute (Map pp62–3; ☎ 2538 2200; www.ccti.vtc.edu.hk; 7th fl, Pokfulam Training Centre Complex, 145 Pok Fu Lam Rd, Pok Fu Lam) Four-hour course for groups of at least 10 that surveys the full spectrum of Chinese cooking for $620 per head including lunch.

Home Management Centre (Map pp62–3; ☎ 2510 2828; www.hec.com.hk; 10th fl, Electric Centre, 28 City Garden Rd, North Point) Wednesday English-language class teaches three simple Chinese recipes in two hours for $85. On the website go to the Electric Living/Home Management Centre section.

Peninsula Academy (Map p104; ☎ 2920 2888; The Peninsula, Salisbury Rd, Tsim Sha Tsui) Every two months one of the chefs from the five-star hotel teaches a different cuisine for $1100 per head (including lunch).

Towngas Cooking Centre (Map p85; ☎ 2576 1535; www.towngascooking.com; Basement, Leighton Centre, 77 Leighton Rd, Causeway Bay) Classes in a range of Chinese cooking styles and other culinary subjects for $300 to $350. There's also a Tsim Sha Tsui branch (Map p106; ☎ 2367 2707; Shop L030, New World Centre, 18-24 Salisbury Rd).

PUBLICATIONS

The best sources for travellers looking for more restaurant recommendations than we are able to make here are the biannual *Good Eating* guide by the *South China Morning Post* (special@scmp.com), published in March and October, and the annual *HK Magazine Restaurant Guide* by HK Magazine (asiacity@asia-city.com.hk), published in February or March. Both offer reviews and listings of hundreds of eateries throughout the territory. *The Guide: Hong Kong's Restaurant Guide* from *bc magazine* (www.bcmagazine.net) has reviews of Hong Kong restaurants in all price categories.

The Hong Kong Tourism Board (HKTB; p302) distributes an annual booklet called *Best of the Best Culinary Guide,* featuring award-winning local dishes and where to find them. Lonely Planet's *World Food Hong Kong,* while not a restaurant guide per se, will take you on an in-depth culinary tour of the territory.

PRACTICALITIES
Opening Hours

Where possible we have given opening and closing (last order) times for all restaurants reviewed, though some may change over time. Most restaurants are closed for at least a couple of days during the Lunar New Year (p293).

How Much?

You can make a meal out of wonton noodles and some greens and it would cost you no more than $30, and fast-food chains such as Cafe de Coral (www.cafedecoralfastfood.com), Fairwood (www.fairwood.com.hk) and MX (www.maxims.com.hk /html/fastfood) would serve you a set meal (soup, main and coffee) for about $40. Otherwise, a proper sit-down lunch costs at least $80 and for dinner about $120 per head. Upscale restaurants will set you back at least $500 per person for dinner.

Booking Tables

Most restaurants midrange or above take reservations. At some with preset menus, prior booking is mandatory. Booking is also required for popular places that serve two or even three seatings a night.

Tipping

Tipping is not a must in Hong Kong restaurants, as waiters supposedly get full salaries and every bill includes a 10% service charge. But the service charge almost always goes into the owner's coffers so if you like the service, tip as you see fit. Most people leave behind the small change.

Smoking

All indoor spaces of eateries are now technically smoke-free. Nicotine addicts are seeking out restaurants with unsheltered outdoor spaces where the smoking ban does not apply. In districts such as Soho (p181), where restaurants tend to have open fronts, customers often step outside to get their fix.

Self-Catering

The two major supermarket chains here, Park'N'Shop and Wellcome, have megastores that offer groceries as well as takeaway cooked food. Their gourmet counterparts include Great

PRICE GUIDE

The price indicators below are based on Hong Kong dollars per person at a meal.

$$$$	Over $700
$$$	$400-700
$$	$200-399
$	Under $200

Food Hall (Map p72; ☎ 2918 9986; Basement, Two Pacific Place, Admiralty; ☾ 10am-10pm); Citysuper, with a handful of branches, including Causeway Bay (Map p85; ☎ 2506 2888; Basement 1, Times Sq, Causeway Bay; ☾ 10.30am-10pm); Oliver's, the Delicatessen (Map p67; ☎ 2810 7710; 2nd fl, Prince's Bldg, 10 Chater Rd; ☾ 8.30am-8pm) in Central; and Taste (Map pp100-1; Festival Walk, Kowloon Tong; ☾ 7am-midnight). Three Sixty (Map p67; ☎ 2111 4480; 3rd & 4th fl, Landmark Bldg, 1 Pedder St; ☾ 7am-9pm; MTR Central, exit C) offers expensive organic produce. Wet markets for fresh produce can be found all over town, including on Graham St (Map p67; ☐ 5B) in Central, Bowrington Rd (Map p85; MTR Causeway Bay, exit A), Chun Yeung St (Map pp62-3; MTR North Point, exit A2) and Canton Rd (Map p111; MTR Mong Kok, exit C3). They usually open at 6am and close around 7pm.

HONG KONG ISLAND

Catering facilities on Hong Kong Island run the gamut from Michelin-level restaurants to pavement cafes offering Asian fusion, to an embarrassment of ethnic cuisines – from Indian and Spanish to Shunde and Japanese.

CENTRAL

Central offers a diverse range of dining experiences covering everything from *cha chaan tengs* (tea cafes) and affordable ethnic food to Western restaurants that boast celebrity chefs.

AMBER Map p67   Modern European $$$$
☎ 2132 0066; www.mandarinoriental.com/landmark; 7th fl, Landmark Mandarin Oriental, 15 Queen's Rd Central; lunch from $500, weekend brunch $348; ☾ 6.30-10.30am, noon-2.30pm Mon-Fri, 11.30am-3pm Sat, 6.30-10.30pm Mon-Sat; MTR Central (exit G)
This restaurant, which boasts two Michelin stars, used to attract much expense-account dining. Now with fewer customers due to the recession, the dusk lighting from the hanging organ pipes looks almost sad. But the service is still flawless and the food, including the Dungeness crab (in five textures and at four temperatures), still of an exceptional standard.

CAPRICE Map p67   Modern French $$$$
☎ 3196 8888; www.fourseasons.com/hongkong; Four Seasons Hotel, 8 Finance St; set lunch from $380; ☾ noon-2.30pm, 6-10.30pm; MTR Hong Kong (exit E1)

In an age when celebrity chefs compete to design the most inscrutable menu, the one here (set dinner from $1280) is capriciously straightforward. Yet comprehensibility hasn't hurt our enjoyment of dishes such as beef flank with cauliflower gratin in red-wine sauce. The artisanal cheeses, delivered weekly from France, are arguably Hong Kong's best. Illuminated floors add a funky touch to the opulent decor.

INAGIKU Map p67   Japanese $$$$

☎ 2805 0600; www.fourseasons.com/hongkong; Level 4, Four Seasons Hong Kong, 8 Finance St; lunch from $200, dinner from $600; ◷ 11.30am-3pm, 6-11pm; MTR Central (exit A)

Inagiku is, in a word, perfection. It's one of the best (and priciest) Japanese restaurants in town, with tasteful interiors and harbour views to boot. The *kaiseki* (traditional many-course meal) showcases seasonal ingredients that are impeccably prepared and artfully presented. Fans claim the branch at the Royal Garden (Map p106; ☎ 2733 2933; 1st fl, Royal Garden Hotel, 69 Mody Rd; MTR Tsim Sha Tsui East, exit P2) is even better.

L'ATELIER DE JOËL ROBUCHON

Map p67   Modern French $$$$

☎ 2166 9000; www.joel-robuchon.com; Shop 401, Landmark, Queen's Rd Central; ◷ 7.30-10am, noon-2.30pm, 6.30-10.30pm, no breakfast Sat; MTR Central (exit G)

Indulge your taste for variety at the Chef of the Century's red-and-black workshop. Nestled in the bottomless bread basket is an assortment of three-bite wonders; the tapas ($250 to $400) are out of this world, especially the foie gras mini-burgers; and there's a 70-page wine list. Despite its two Michelin stars, L'Atelier insists this is not haute cuisine. It's not untrue – it serves breakfast ($280).

PIERRE Map p67   Modern French $$$$

☎ 2825 4001; www.mandarinoriental.com/hong kong; Mandarin Oriental, 5 Connaught Rd; lunch $360; ◷ noon-3pm Mon-Fri, 7-10.30pm Mon-Sat, closed Sun; MTR Central (exit F)

The godfather of fusion, Pierre Gagnaire, flaunts his revolutionary cuisine in the city that embodies the concept. The menu is an edgy and provocative affair; dessert might be a caramelised rocket salad – and it works. Dithering gourmands should try the tasting menu ($1488). The decor, with

portholes and chandelier, reminds one of a cruise liner, especially when the harbour view is added.

ISLAND TANG Map p67   Cantonese, Dim Sum $$$

☎ 2526 8798; www.islandtang.com; Shop 222, Galleria, 9 Queen's Rd Central; set lunch for 2 from $596; ◷ noon-10pm; MTR Central (exit D1)

With its stunning art deco interior à la 1930s Shanghai, Island Tang could easily have been the kind of restaurant where, as the Chinese say, one comes to 'eat the decor'. But, surprisingly, you'd come for the food too. The Cantonese selections range from fried milk to abalone, which means a meal can set you back $300 or $3000. Dim sum is available all day.

LUNG KING HEEN

Map p67   Cantonese, Dim Sum $$$

☎ 3196 8888; www.fourseasons.com/hongkong; Four Seasons Hotel, 8 Finance St; set lunch $400, set dinner $880; noon-2.30pm Mon-Sat, 11.30am-3pm Sun, 6-10.30pm Mon-Sun; MTR Central (exit A)

The world's only Chinese restaurant to receive three stars from the Michelin guide. The food is excellent though not peerless in Hong Kong. It's the view of the harbour and the service that make Lung King Heen truly unbeatable. Dim sum is impeccable; the signature steamed lobster and scallop dumplings sell out early.

SEVVA Map p67   International, Asian $$$

☎ 2537 1388; www.sevvahk.com; Penthouse, 25th fl, Princes Bldg, 10 Chater Rd; lunch/tea from $200; ◷ noon-midnight Mon-Thu, noon-2am Fri & Sat; MTR Central (exit F)

Owner and style guru Bonnie Gokson has her casual glamour stamped all over this restaurant, which features a climbing garden, contemporary European art and a chicly healthy menu. But the pièce de résistance is the wrap-around outdoor terrace commanding million-dollar views of Central that will surely get you high, even if the famed crunch cake doesn't.

ZUMA Map p67   Modern Japanese $$$

☎ 3657 6388; www.zumarestaurant.com; Levels 5 & 6, Landmark, 15 Queen's Rd Central; ◷ noon-3pm Mon-Sat, 11.30am-3pm Sun, 6-11pm Mon-Sun; MTR Central (exit G)

This uberchic import from London specialises in Japanese cuisine with a modern twist and has miles of space in which to serve it. There is a robata counter, a sushi bar and a terrace. The Sunday brunch ($428), with free-flowing sake and champagne for an extra $122, is very popular.

HABIBI Map p67 — Egyptian $$
☎ 2544 6198; www.habibi.com.hk; Shop B & D, Ground fl, 112-114 Wellington St; mains $145-200; ⏰ 11am-3pm Mon-Fri, 5pm-midnight Mon-Sat; 🚇 40M
Whether or not Habibi serves strictly authentic Egyptian food is a moot point – the halal food is very good and the setting is the Cairo of the 1930s – all mirrors, tassels, velvet cushions, ceiling fans and hookahs. Habibi's casual and takeaway section next door, Habibi Cafe (Map p67; ☎ 2544 3886; ⏰ 11am-11pm), is a lot cheaper, with meze from $25 to $40, meze platters $85 to $105, mains $60 to $110 and a weekday set lunch for $65.

HUNAN GARDEN Map p67 — Hunanese $$
☎ 2868 2880; 3rd fl, Forum, Exchange Sq, Connaught Rd, Central; set meals for 2 from $320; ⏰ 11.30am-3pm, 5.30-11.30pm; MTR Central (exit A)
One of very few Hunanese eateries in town, this relaxing restaurant serves decent Hunanese classics such as honey-glazed Hunan ham, and fish with toasted soy-bean sauce. Chinese music performance nightly (7pm to 9pm).

CITY HALL MAXIM'S PALACE
Map p67 — Cantonese, Dim Sum $
☎ 2521 1303; 3rd fl, Low Block, Hong Kong City Hall, 1 Edinburgh Pl; dim sum $25-50, compulsory tea fee per person $12; ⏰ 11am-4.30pm Mon-Sat, 9am-4.30pm Sun, 5.30-10.45pm Mon-Sun; 🚇 13
Noisy, gaudy and cheery, this is the kind of restaurant that formed the earliest memories of yum cha for many Hong Kongers. The dim sum (11am to 4pm Monday to Saturday, 9am to 4pm Sunday) comes in infinite varieties and is paraded on trolleys. A table by the window will let you watch land reclamation in progress where the old Queen's Pier used to be.

LIN HEUNG TEA HOUSE
Map p67 — Cantonese, Dim Sum $
☎ 2544 4556; 160-164 Wellington St; ⏰ 6am-11pm, dim sum to 3.30pm; MTR Sheung Wan (exit E2)
In the morning, this famous tea house is packed, just as it was in 1926, with older men reading newspapers. Dim sum

(from $12), served from trolleys, is quickly snapped up, so hover near the kitchen if you want more choices. The big bun and liver *siu mai* are coveted items, prized more for their nostalgic value than their taste. But the lotus-root patties and the braised stuffed duck ($150, advance booking required) live up to their reputation. Go west for the new branch, Lin Heung Kui (Map p80; ☎ 2156 9328; 1st fl-3rd fl, 40-50 Des Voeux Rd W; ⏰ 6am-3.30pm, 5.30-11pm; MTR Sheung Wan, exit B).

PRAWN NOODLE SHOP
Map p67 — Noodles, Malaysian $
☎ 3184 0505; Shop 201, 2nd fl, Grand Millennium Plaza, 181 Queen's Rd Central; bowl of noodles $35; ⏰ 11.30am-7.45pm Mon-Sat; MTR Sheung Wan (exit E2)
This neat place serves palatable Penang-style Malaysian *laksa* and prawn noodles that keep homesick Malaysian expats coming back. There's a branch in Wan Chai (Map p72; ☎ 2520 0268; Shop 4, Rialto Bldg, 2 Landale St; MTR Wan Chai, exit B2).

ADMIRALTY & WAN CHAI
Wan Chai, and to a lesser extent Admiralty, is a happy hunting ground for ethnic restaurants. Name your cuisine and then MTR, bus or tram it down to the Wanch. You're certain to find it here.

BO INNOVATION Map p74 — Chinese $$$$
☎ 2850 8371; www.boinnovation.com; 60 Johnston Rd; lunch from $178, dinner from $680; ⏰ noon-2.30pm Mon-Fri, 7-10pm Mon-Sat; MTR Wan Chai (exit B2)
Alvin Leong, the tattoo-sporting chef of this trendy spot with two Michelin stars, is the enfant terrible of Hong Kong's culinary scene. We were impressed by his takes on molecular gastronomy (Chinese sausage and rice ice-cream), and even more so by the fact that there were dishes we'd love to eat every day (noodles with *uni* and fish roe).

GRISSINI Map p74 — Italian $$$$
☎ 2588 1234; http://hongkong.grand.hyatt.com; Grand Hyatt Hong Kong, 1 Harbour Rd; lunch from $400, dinner from $700; ⏰ noon-2.30pm, 7-10.30pm Mon-Fri & Sun, 6.30-10.30pm Sat; MTR Wan Chai (exit A1)
Fluffy, chewy and addictive, the foot-long grissini (bread sticks) here are – appropriately – the best in town. But leave room

for the Milanese specialties, especially the pasta and risotto, and pair them with a bottle from the 1000-strong cellar. This stylish restaurant has floor-to-ceiling windows commanding views of the harbour. The Sunday brunch ($455), with its exquisite, strictly Italian offerings, is our favourite buffet in town.

PETRUS Map p72 — French $$$$

☎ 2820 8590; www.shangri-la.com; 56th fl, Island Shangri-La Hotel, Pacific Place, Supreme Court Rd; set lunch from $368, set dinner from $1380; ✆ 7-10am, noon-2.30pm, 6-10.30pm; MTR Admiralty (exit F)

With its head (and prices) in the clouds, Petrus was known as one of the finest Western restaurants in Asia, even before it plucked one star from the Michelin firmament. Here traditional French cuisine is served under crystal chandeliers, the views are riveting and the wine list will move connoisseurs to tears. Coat and tie required for men.

CAFÉ TOO Map p72 — Western $$$

☎ 2820 8571; www.shangri-la.com; Level 7, Island Shangri-La, Pacific Place, Supreme Court Rd; lunch buffet from $298, dinner buffet from $418; ✆ 6.30am-12.30am, buffet noon-2.30pm, 6.30-10pm; MTR Admiralty (exit C1)

If value and variety are what you're after, don't miss this upbeat and airy restaurant where the buffet is an extravagant performance showcasing fresh seafood, dim sum, noodles of all persuasions, curries and desserts.

CINE CITTÀ Map p72 — Italian $$$

☎ 2529 0199; www.elite-concepts.com; Ground fl, Starcrest Bldg, 9 Star St, Wan Chai; set lunch $138/168; ✆ noon-3pm Mon-Fri, 6pm-midnight Mon-Sun; MTR Admiralty (exit F)

The Michelin inspectors who recommended this sleek place probably enjoyed twirling their *taglioni* between real-life supermodels and blown-up stills of Fellini movies almost as much as they did the stellar Italian fare. The *bigoli* with duck ragout and *porcini* is absolutely divine; the friendly sommelier can help you pick a bottle from the famous wine list.

YIN YANG Map p74 — Chinese $$$

☎ 2866 0868; 18 Ship St; lunch $180-280, dinner $560-1000; ✆ noon-2.30pm, 7-10.30pm, dinner only Sat, closed Sun; MTR Wan Chai (exit B2)

Margaret Xu, the soft-spoken chef of Yin Yang, calls her cooking New Hong Kong. A former ad-agency owner who taught herself how to cook, Margaret grows organic vegetables and fruits in Yuen Long and uses ancient preparation methods, such as stone-grinding and roasting in terracotta ovens. Chinese cooking at its absolute, rarefied best this is not. But what Margaret sometimes lacks in technique, she compensates for with passion and originality. Nowhere is this more apparent than in her award-winning 'waterless' soup and in condiments such as the galangal dip with extra-virgin olive oil that lends wings to her famed roast chicken. Margaret also gives her own take on local classics such as baked pork chop over rice and mock shark's fin soup. Yin Yang is housed in a three-storey 1930s heritage building. Reservations essential.

HANG ZHOU RESTAURANT

Map p74 — Hangzhou, Shanghainese $$

☎ 2591 1898; 1st fl, Chinachem Johnston Plaza, 178-188 Johnston Rd; lunch from $100, dinner from 200; ✆ 11.30am-2.30pm, 5.30-10.30pm; MTR Wan Chai (exit A5)

Hangzhou cuisine is similar to its Shanghainese cousin, but generally lighter in taste. This modern establishment has clearly mastered the art of both. There's not a trace of grease on the deep-fried frog's legs ($98), and hardcore health nuts will be converted by the braised pork belly with steamed buns ($78). For a challenge, order the steamed stinky beancurd.

LIU YUAN PAVILION

Map p74 — Shanghainese $$

☎ 2804 2000; 3rd fl Broadway, 54-62 Lockhart Rd; meal from $150; ✆ noon-3pm, 6-11pm; MTR Wan Chai (exit C)

This pretty restaurant in yellows and light browns serves superb Shanghainese dishes, including crab stir-fried with egg yolk and sweet rice pudding with eight treasures. The cook can be a little heavy-handed with the salt.

LOCK CHA TEA SHOP

Map p72 — Tea, Vegetarian $$

☎ 2801 7177; www.lockcha.com; Ground fl, KS Lo Gallery, Hong Kong Park; dim sum from $12, tea from $20; ✆ 10am-10pm; MTR Admiralty (exit C1)

Set in the lush environs of Hong Kong Park, Lock Cha offers a dozen teas and many more varieties of vegetarian dim sum in a graceful setting. Chinese music performances and tea talks on Sunday (4pm to 6pm, $80 per person).

NINO'S COZINHA
Map p74 — Portuguese, Macanese $$
☎ 2866 1868; 31 Ship St; dinner $200-600; ☺ noon-3pm, 6-10.15pm; MTR Wan Chai (exit B2)
This gem hidden in a quiet corner off Queen's Rd East cooks up the best Portuguese fare in town. Classics such as the oxtail stew ($158) and baked duck rice ($110) evolved from heirloom recipes of the Portuguese-Chinese owners. Hearty fare cooked from the heart. Book early.

PAWN Map p74 — English $$
☎ 2866 3444; www.thepawn.com.hk; 62 Johnston Rd; set lunch from $150; ☺ 2nd fl noon-2.30pm, 6-11pm Mon-Sun, 1st fl 11am-midnight Mon-Sat, 11am-11pm Sun; MTR Wan Chai (exit A3)
In its previous incarnation, this handsome three-storey establishment was a row of tenement houses and the century-old Woo Cheong pawn shop. In the presence of history, not to mention the tasteful contemporary interiors designed by a local film director, diners tend to be lenient with the food, but we actually found the English fare quite decent, by any standard.

PURE VEGGIE HOUSE
Map p72 — Vegetarian, Chinese $$
☎ 2525 0556; 3rd fl, Coda Plaza, 51 Garden Rd; ☺ 11am-10pm; ☒ 12A from Admiralty MTR station
A cross between an ancient scholar's study and a rustic inn, this upscale Buddhist eatery serves excellent, MSG-free vegetarian food. It offers a 10-course meal for two ($400) and an all-you-can-eat dinner hotpot ($98).

VEGGIE PALACE
Map p74 — Vegetarian, Cantonese $$
☎ 2838 6505; Shop B, 1st fl, Ming Fung Bldg, 140 Wan Chai Rd; lunch $168, dinner $198; ☺ noon-3pm, 6-10pm; MTR Wan Chai (exit A3)
The 10-course meals that Buddhist owner and chef Mrs Fung whips up here are as fabulously funky as her well-coiffed, bespectacled self. With creations like sea coconut and papaya soup, mixed mushroom tart, seaweed and pomelo salad with peanut sauce, who needs meat? It's packed

at the weekends, so book a few days in advance. Extra helpings free.

VICTORIA CITY Map p74 — Cantonese $$
☎ 2827 9938; 2nd fl, Sun Hung Kai Centre, 30 Harbour Rd; lunch from $150, dinner per person from $250; ☺ 11am-10.30pm Mon-Sat, 10.30am-10.30pm Sun; MTR Wan Chai (exit A)
This banquet hall–style restaurant is a great option for sampling 'yellow oil' crabs or *wong yau hai* (female crabs with creamy yellowish fat permeating their body as a result of the sun's heat causing the fat in their livers to break down). From June to August, fans of the delicacy flock here for their fix (from $328 per crab). The restaurant's roasted beef brisket ($68) and rice rolls pan-fried with XO sauce (a spicy seafood-based condiment; $55) are vivid reminders that Victoria City was once one of the top Cantonese restaurants in Hong Kong.

AMERICAN RESTAURANT
Map p74 — Northern Chinese $
☎ 2527 7277; Ground fl, Golden Star Bldg, 20 Lockhart Rd, Wan Chai; meal under $150; ☺ 11am-11.30pm; MTR Wan Chai (exit C)
The friendly American (which chose its name to attract Yank sailors cruising the Wanch for sustenance while on R&R during the Vietnam War) has been serving decent Northern Chinese cuisine for well over half a century, including a rarely seen Northern delicacy – pig's throat stir-fried with parsley.

HONOLULU COFFEE SHOP
Map p74 — Tea Cafe $
☎ 2575 1823; Ground fl & Mezzanine fl, 176-178 Hennessy Rd; meal under $40; ☺ 6am-midnight; MTR Wan Chai (exit A4)
You'll forgive the nondescript decor of this *cha chaan teng* once you've sampled its highly inhalable egg-custard tarts. They come with a flaky crust and a rich, creamy centre. There's a branch in Central (Map p78; ☎ 2526 8063; 33 Stanley St; ☺ 7am-2am; MTR Central, exit B).

INTERNATIONAL CURRY HOUSE
Map p74 — Indian, Southeast Asian $
☎ 2529 0088; 26-30 Tai Wong St East; meal from $80; ☺ 11am-midnight Mon-Sat; MTR Wan Chai (exit A3)
For 30 years, curry junkies have been tripping out on curries in all colours of the

rainbow (red, green, yellow…) at this humble restaurant. Authentic, you ask? Well, when the oyster curry ($100) and the dry crab curry (from $200) are this mind-blowing, especially when eaten with *paratha*, authenticity should take a chill pill.

JOY HING FOOD SHOP
Map p74   Cantonese $
☎ 2519 6639; Block C, 265-267 Hennessy Rd; ◷ 10am-10.30pm Mon-Sat; MTR Wan Chai (exit A4)
This basic stall is your best bet for Cantonese barbecue – succulent slivers of pork, goose, chicken and liver over freshly steamed rice (from $22).

KAM FUNG CAFE Map p74   Tea Cafe $
☎ 2572 0526; 41 Spring Garden Lane; meal under $40; ◷ 7am-7pm; MTR Wan Chai (exit A3)
This *cha chaan teng* established in 1956 is famous for its iceless, ice-cold milk tea ($14), a shrewd invention that ensures the prized beverage doesn't diminish in taste over its lifetime. The chicken pie ($6.50) is lovely when fresh from the oven.

KHANA KHAZANA
Map p74   Indian, Vegetarian $
☎ 2520 5308; www.khanakhazana.hk; 1st fl, Dannies House, 20 Luard Rd; lunch buffet Mon-Fri $88, Sun $138; ◷ noon-3pm, 6-11.30pm Mon-Fri, noon-11.30pm Sat & Sun; MTR Wan Chai (exit A1)
Statues of Lord and Radha Krishna guard the entrance to this nifty restaurant serving upscale Indian vegetarian fare. We enjoyed the vegetarian tandooris ($58 to $78).

MANG AMBO'S FILIPINO RESTAURANT
Map p74   Filipino $
☎ 2143 6877; 120 Jaffe Rd, Wan Chai; ◷ 11am-10pm; MTR Wan Chai (exit A1)
Pinoy domestic workers, musicians and businessmen come to this hole-in-the-wall for its skewers, crispy pan-roasted pork and pork blood stew. A full meal will set you back a hefty $30.

SABAH Map p74   Malaysian $
☎ 2143 6626; Shops 4 & 5, 98-108 Jaffe Rd; set lunch $60; ◷ 7.30am-midnight; MTR Wan Chai (exit A1)
Sabah in the heart of Wan Chai serves Malaysian food tempered for the Hong Kong palate, though that doesn't seem to keep the peeps from the Consulate General of Malaysia

from coming. The pièce de résistance is the fluffy *roti canai* ($20), which is tossed, twirled and kneaded before your eyes.

SAIGON PHO Map p74   Vietnamese $
☎ 2833 6833; 319 Hennessy Rd; ◷ 11.30am-midnight; MTR Wan Chai (exit A4)
In terms of price performance, this modest eatery makes some of the best *pho* (bowl small/medium/large $32/$36/$42) in town, with tender beef in broth fragrant with herbs, and a bottomless side of chilli peppers the way we like it. The Vietnamese curries come with buttered baguette straight out of the oven.

WORLD PEACE CAFE
Map p74   Vegetarian, International $
☎ 2527 5870; www.worldpeacecafe.hk; 21-23 Tai Wong St East; set lunch from $68; ◷ noon-2.30pm Mon-Sat, 6.30-9pm Fri & Sat; MTR Wan Chai (exit B2)
This coolly eco- and vegan-friendly restaurant staffed by volunteer waiters is said to be inspired by Kadampa Buddhism. Consuming its organic dishes and fair-trade coffee while soaking up the positive vibes will leave you feeling cleansed in more ways than one.

LAN KWAI FONG & SOHO
Soho is awash in restaurants, and most of them are midrange or top-end. The area is accessible by the Central Escalators, or bus 26 can be caught from Caroline Centre (Map p85) in Causeway Bay or Pacific Place (Map p72) in Admiralty.

MOZART STUB'N Map p78   Austrian $$$
☎ 2522 1763; www.mozartstubn.com; 8 Glenealy; lunch from $380; ◷ noon-3pm, 6.30pm-midnight Mon-Sat; MTR Central (exit D2)
This classy Austrian (do *not* say German) establishment has been serving excellent food in a traditional setting for over 20 years. The dishes may sound Teutonic, but they are served in sensible portions. If you're in Lan Kwai Fong, go to the junction of Wyndham and Ice House Sts. Then walk up Glenealy towards the Hong Kong Zoological and Botanical Gardens.

CECCONI'S ITALIAN Map p78   Italian $$$
☎ 2147 5500; 43 Elgin St; set lunch from $98, set dinner from $398; ◷ noon-3pm, 6pm-midnight
If you want Italian food in stylish surrounds, Cecconi's fits the bill. But if you're intent on

VEGGIES BEWARE

There are probably more than 101 ways to accidentally eat meat in Hong Kong. Sensitivity towards vegetarians is generally not high. If you are a strict vegetarian, you may as well forget about dim sum. A plate of green is probably cooked in meat stock and served with oyster sauce. Superior broth, made with chicken and Chinese ham, is a prevalent ingredient, even in dishes where no meat is visible. In budget restaurants, chicken powder is used liberally. The safe bet for veggies wanting to go Chinese is either a vegetarian eatery or upscale Chinese establishments. Large monasteries, notably Chi Lin Nunnery (p198) and Po Lin Monastery (p203), often have vegetarian restaurants, though you will also find many in the city. For more options besides the ones recommended in this guide, visit www.ivu.org/hkvegan/gb/hkrest.html.

having a tête-à-tête over the roasted figs with goat's curd, you'll find the tables too close for comfort.

OLÉ SPANISH RESTAURANT & WINE BAR Map p78 Spanish $$$

☎ 2523 8624; 1st fl, Shun Ho Tower, 24-30 Ice House St; tapas $60-315; noon-3pm, 6.30pm-midnight Mon-Sat; MTR Central (exit D2)
Any Spaniard living in Hong Kong would point to this charismatic place as the best Spanish restaurant in town. Here the suckling pig ($255) is roasted to perfection. The *angulas* (baby eels) in hot garlicky oil ($575) conjure up memories of Spain. And where else would you see jaded gourmands weeping over a potato salad ($60)?

SUSHI KUU Map p78 Japanese $$$

☎ 2971 0180; 1st fl, Wellington Place, 2-8 Wellington St; noon-11pm Mon-Thu & Sun, noon-12.30am Fri & Sat; MTR Central (exit D2)
The fruits of the sea are sweet at this chill hangout, and the presentation is inviting. The lunch sets don't come cheap (from $200), but every bite is a treat, especially the sushi rice bowl.

ASSAF Map p78 Lebanese $$

☎ 2851 6550; Shop B, Ground fl, Lyndhurst Bldg, 37 Lyndhurst Tce; set lunch $88, set dinner veg/meat $195/175; ☺ noon-midnight Mon-Thu, noon-1am Fri & Sat; ☐ 40M
This cosy place specialises in meze and other tasty titbits, including baklava soaked in rose syrup ($60 for four pieces). The Assaf brothers also own the Beyrouth Cafe Central (Map p78; ☎ 2854 1872; 39 Lyndhurst Tce) next door, which does takeaway sandwiches, kebabs and so on from $50.

DA PING HUO Map p78 Sichuanese $$

☎ 2559 1317; Lower Ground fl, Hilltop Plaza, 49 Hollywood Rd; set dinner $280; ☺ 6.30pm-midnight Mon-Sat; ☐ 26

Da Ping Huo's industrial grey interior is accented with contemporary Chinese paintings by the Sichuanese owner Wang Hai. The palatable 14-course set dinner alternates between spicy and nonspicy selections. Dishes have become noticeably tamer in recent years, but the singing of the chef, Mrs Wang, is still fiery hot. Reservations essential.

KOH-I-NOOR Map p78 Indian $$

☎ 2877 9706; 1st fl, California Entertainment Bldg, 34-36 D'Aguilar St; ☺ 11.30am-2.30pm, 6-11pm Mon-Sat; MTR Central (exit D2)
Fine northern Indian cuisine with sophisticated presentation is what you get here. The most expensive dish is the leg of lamb ($330), which is great for sharing. The weekday vegetarian/meat lunch-time buffet is a steal at $60. There's a branch in Tsim Sha Tsui (Map p106; ☎ 2369 0783; 1st fl, 3-4 Peninsula Mansion, 16C Mody Rd; ☺ 11am-3pm, 6-11pm; MTR Tsim Sha Tsui, exit G).

LUK YU TEA HOUSE

Map p78 Cantonese, Dim Sum $$
☎ 2523 5464; 24-26 Stanley St; lunch from $150, dinner from $300; ☺ 7am-10pm; MTR Central (exit D2)
This elegant establishment, known for its delicious pig's lungs and almond soup ($140), is arguably the most famous teahouse in Hong Kong. With Eastern art deco interiors featuring ceiling fans and stained-glass windows, it could almost be the setting of a mystery novel. In fact, a property tycoon was shot and killed here by a hitman a few years ago. Dim sum is available till 5.30pm.

O SIP HAH Map p78 Thai Fusion $$

☎ 3622 3222; 12 Old Bailey St; set lunch from $78, set dinner from $169; ☺ noon-3pm, 6pm-midnight Mon-Fri, noon-midnight Sat & Sun; MTR Central (exit D2)

You'd never guess by the modern baroque setting that this tiny restaurant serves delectable Thai fusion dishes under its black chandeliers. The signature crab ($218) bursts with melty crab butter. Flavour heaven or cholesterol hell? Whatever the verdict, you'll love it, just like you'll love the grilled ribs ($258) and the fusion desserts.

RUGHETTA Map p78   Italian $$
☎ 2537 7922; basement, Carfield Commercial Bldg, 75-77 Wyndham St; set lunch from $105; ⏰ noon-2.30pm Mon-Sat, 6.30-10.30pm Mon Sun; ⓜ 26
This basement restaurant with a branch in New York City serves reliable 'Roman' (read earthy Italian) cuisine – though it might suffer after being discovered by the cheap lunch crowd.

UNION J Map p78   American $$
☎ 2537 2368; www.elite-concepts.com; 1st fl, California Tower, 30 D'Aguilar St; lunch from $98; ⏰ noon-3pm Mon-Fri, 6pm-midnight Mon-Sat; MTR Central (exit D2)
This new kid on the block has a 16-strong menu showcasing well-prepared 'New American' fare such as steak tartar with cherry-olive tapenade and puréed egg yolk ($148), and a cheesecake ($48) that arrives in a Chinese takeout box. They're best washed down with the awesome home-made sodas ($55).

YELLOW DOOR KITCHEN
Map p78   Sichuanese, Shanghainese $$
☎ 2858 6555; www.yellowdoorkitchen.com.hk; 6th fl, 37 Cochrane St; set lunch $72, set dinner $288; ⏰ noon-2.30pm Mon-Fri, 6.30-11pm Mon-Sat; MTR Central (exit D1)
This homely eatery that is recommended by the Michelin inspectors lets you enjoy variety even when you're dining solo. Dishes such as clams with spicy chilli sauce are served in taster-sized portions that add up to a lip-smacking whole. Gracing a wall is the calligraphic graffiti of Tsang Tsou Choi (1921–2007). Reservations a must here.

YUNG KEE RESTAURANT
Map p78   Cantonese, Dim Sum $$
☎ 2522 1624; www.yungkee.com.hk; 32-40 Wellington St; lunch $50-300, dinner from $200; ⏰ 11am-11.30pm; MTR Central (exit D2)

The roast goose (from $120) here has been the talk of the town since 1942, and it's not the only thing that justifies the Michelin star. According to an urban myth, a bowl of sweet red-bean soup here sells for $500 because it's made with century-old orange peel prized for its medicinal value. But while the owner does own some vintage peel, none of it is likely to pop up in your bowl ($22). Dim sum is available from 2pm to 5pm Monday to Saturday, and 11am to 5pm Sunday.

VBEST TEA HOUSE Map p78   Cantonese $
☎ 3104 0890; www.vbest.com.hk; 17 Elgin St; lunch from $80, dinner from $150; ⏰ noon-3pm, 6-11pm Mon-Sat
Tucked away on a steep street off Soho, this subdued family-run establishment serves MSG-free comfort food. The owners' children grew up on this, so you can't go too wrong. The prawns with rice vermicelli and the pork-and-chive wontons are divine.

FLYING PAN Map p78   American $
☎ 2140 6333; www.the-flying-pan.com; 9 Old Bailey St; breakfast sets $39-106; ⏰ 24hr
Fancy eggs Benedict, chocolate waffles, even a full English breakfast for dinner? No problem. Breakfast is served 24/7 in a 1950s-American-diner setting at the Flying Pan. There are branches in Wan Chai (Map p74; ☎ 2528 9997; 3rd fl, Empire Land Commercial Centre, 81-85 Lockhart Rd; MTR Wan Chai, exit C) and Discovery Bay (Map p140; ☎ 2987 7749; Shop G31, D Deck, Discovery Bay).

LIFE CAFE Map p78   Vegetarian, International $
☎ 2810 9777; www.lifecafe.com.hk; 10 Shelley St; ⏰ 9am-10pm
Life is a vegetarian's dream, serving organic vegan food and dishes free of gluten, wheat, onion and garlic. Delicious take-away salads from the deli counter cost $50 to $75, and the large one can feed a small family.

BON APPETIT Map p78   Vietnamese, Thai $
☎ 2525 3553; 14B Wing Wah Lane; ⏰ 10am-midnight Mon-Sat; MTR Central (exit D2)
Cheap but tasty dishes for those who prefer to blow their cash on drinks are available at this Vietnamese and Thai nook in Wing Wah Lane, the northern extension of Lan Kwai Fong. Filled baguettes, and rice and noodles are generally around $50.

SER WONG FUN Map p78 Cantonese $

☎ 2543 1032; 30 Cochrane St; 11am-10.30pm;
MTR Central (exit D1)
This snake speciality shop always looks a
little festive – it has red tablecloths and
it's packed. In the cooler months, diners
flock here for the snake soup ($65), which
is eaten with lemon leaves and fritters.
Non-snake eaters come for the duck's liver
sausage and chicken claypot rice ($32), and
a plethora of simple and tasty dishes.

TAI CHEONG BAKERY Map p78 Bakery $

☎ 2544 3475; 32 Lyndhurst Tce, Central;
7.30am-9pm Mon-Sat, 8.30am-9pm Sun;
40M
Tai Cheong was famous for its lighter-than-
air profiteroles (sa yung; $5 each) until
former governor Chris Patten was photographed wolfing down its egg-custard tarts
($5 each). Since then 'Fat Patten' egg tarts
have hogged the limelight.

LAN FONG YUEN Map p78 Tea Cafe $

☎ 2544 3895, 2854 0731; 2 Gage St; 7am-6pm
Mon-Sat; 5B
Don't be fooled by the rickety facade. It
hides an entire cha chaan tang. Lan Fong
Yuen (1952) is largely believed to be the
inventor of 'pantyhose' milk tea (p174). Over
a thousand cups of the silky brew ($13) are
sold per day. Watch staff work their magic
while you wait for a table. A cover charge
($20 per head) applies. The new branch
(☎ 2850 8683; 4A-6 Gage St; 8am-8pm), practically next door, is open on Sundays.

MAK'S NOODLE

Map p78 Noodles, Cantonese $
☎ 2854 3810; 77 Wellington St; noodles $28-40;
11am-8pm; 40M
At this legendary shop, noodles are made
the traditional way with a bamboo pole
and served perched on a spoon placed over
the bowl so they won't go soggy. The beef
brisket noodles are equally remarkable.
Branches: Causeway Bay (Map p85; ☎ 2895 5310; 44
Jardines Bazaar; 11am-midnight; MTR Causeway Bay,
exit F), Tsim Sha Tsui (Map p104; ☎ 2730 0710; Shop C03,
2nd fl, Gourmet Express, China Hong Kong City, 33 Canton
Rd; 7am-10pm; MTR Tsim Sha Tsui, exit A1).

WANG FU Map p78 Northern Chinese $

☎ 2121 8006; Shop A, Jade Centre, 98-102 Wellington St; 11am-10.30pm Mon-Sat; 40M

At this clean little stall, you'll see visitors
from Beijing demolishing plate after plate
of dumplings. There are nine delicious varieties ($30), including lamb and cumin, and
the popular egg and tomato (available after
6pm). The branch (☎ 2121 8089; 65 Wellington
St; closed Sat) across the street also serves
northern Chinese dishes.

SHEUNG WAN, THE MID-LEVELS & WESTERN DISTRICTS

West of Central, Sheung Wan and Western
Districts are known for their local Chinese, in
particular, Chiu Chow cuisine. Restaurants in
the Mid-Levels cater mostly to local residents
who don't feel like making the trek down to
Soho or Central.

GAIA RISTORANTE Map p80 Italian $$$

☎ 2167 8200; www.gaiaristorante.com; Ground
fl, Grand Millennium Plaza, 181 Queen's Rd Central;
lunch from $300, dinner from $400; noon-
2.45pm, 6.30-11pm; MTR Sheung Wan (exit E2)
Gaia was considered the best Italian restaurant in Hong Kong not so long ago.
Now the attention has shifted to Da Domenico
(p186). Such is the fickle nature of Hong
Kong foodies. Yet the standard at Gaia
remains high (as do the prices), and blue-
berries are used in unexpected ways.

RED TAVERN Map p80 European $$$

☎ 2559 0737; www.red-tavern.net; 17 Aberdeen St; lunch from $100, dinner from $380;
11.30am-3pm, 6.15-11.45pm Mon-Sat
The former chef of Pierrot at the Mandarin
Oriental is serving up set meals of fine
European fare for a third of the price and
a fraction of the stuffiness at this atmospheric little place. There's no corkage and
the range of stemware is impressive. Get
a table by the door for maximum ceiling
height.

BONHEUR Map p80 French $$

☎ 2544 6333; www.bonheur-restaurant.com; 6th
fl, Pemberton, 22-26 Bonham Strand East; set lunch
from $108, set dinner from $358; noon-2pm,
6.30-10.30pm Mon-Sat; MTR Sheung Wan (exit A2)
Bonheur is one of the few French eateries
in town where the nuanced lobster bisque
and the succulent pork loin won't burn
a hole in your pocket. If you're craving
contrast, take a seat by the windows that

overlook tenement buildings. Booking is mandatory.

BI YI RESTAURANT Map pp62-3 Xin Jiang $$

☎ 2484 9981; Ground fl, 43 Water Street, Sai Ying Pun; ⏰ noon-3pm Tue-Sun, 6-10pm Mon-Sun; dinner $100-150; MTR Central (exit B), green minibus 55

In a city where gamey tastes are often tamed to please sensitive Cantonese palates, Bi Yi is a lamb lovers' paradise. Here you can savour the meat in all its splendour – grilled, braised, fried or boiled with lashings of spices and herbs – in a rustic setting. Take green minibus 55 outside the United Chinese Bank Bldg on Des Voeux Rd Central and disembark at St Paul's College.

LEUNG HING CHIU CHOW SEAFOOD RESTAURANT Map p80 Chiu Chow $$

☎ 2850 6666; 32 Bonham Strand West; meals $80-500; ⏰ 11am-midnight; MTR Sheung Wan (exit A2)

At Leung Hing, you can indulge in hearty Chiu Chow staples such as scrambled eggs with baby oysters, pan-fried noodles with vinegar and sugar, and cold crab. It's crowded but clean, and no one will snub you for not ordering the shark's fin.

PRESS ROOM Map p80 European $$

☎ 2525 3444; www.thepressroom.com.hk; 108 Hollywood Rd; 3-course dinner from $250; ⏰ noon-11pm Mon-Fri, 10am-11pm Sat & Sun; 🚌 26

Occupying the former address of Hong Kong's longest-running newspaper, *Hua Qiao Daily*, this bistro serves decent food that, unfortunately, is accompanied by impersonal service and mediocre acoustics. We prefer its sibling next door, Classified the Cheese Room (Map p80; ☎ 2525 3454; www.classifiedfoodshops.com.hk; 108 Hollywood Rd; ⏰ noon-11pm Mon-Fri, 10am-11pm Sat & Sun), where you can sample over 20 kinds of fromage in a state-of-the-art ageing room (cheese platter from $150) before deciding which go best with your red.

TIM'S KITCHEN Map p80 Cantonese $$

☎ 2543 5919; 93 Jervois St; ⏰ noon-3pm, 6.30-10.30pm Mon-Sat; MTR Sheung Wan (exit A2)

This restaurant, with one Michelin star, was started by the former chef of a banking tycoon. Expect well-executed Cantonese dishes in unpretentious surrounds. Popular dishes, such as stir-fried prawn ($110), crab claw poached with wintermelon ($160) and

braised pomelo skin ($55), need to be pre-ordered. A minimum charge of $200 per person applies to lunch reservations.

KAU KEE RESTAURANT Map p80 Noodles $

☎ 2850 5967; 21 Gough St; noodles from $25; ⏰ 12.30-7.15pm, 8.30-11.30pm, Mon-Sat; MTR Sheung Wan (exit E2)

You can argue till the noodles go soggy about whether crowded Kau Kee has the best beef brisket in Hong Kong. Whatever the verdict, the meat – served with noodles in a beefy broth – is definitely hard to beat.

KWUN KEE RESTAURANT

Map p80 Cantonese $

☎ 2803 7209; Wo Yick Mansion, 263 Queen's Rd W, Sai Ying Pun; ⏰ 11.30am-2.30pm, 6-11.30pm Mon-Sat, 6-11.30pm Sun; 🚋 tram

Hong Kong's top brass make pilgrimages to this very local place for its claypot rice ($38 to $50, available only at dinner) – a meal-in-one in which rice and toppings such as Chinese sausage and chicken are cooked in claypots over charcoal stoves until the grains are infused with the juices of the meat and a layer of rice crackle is formed at the bottom of the pot.

NGAU KEE FOOD CAFE

Map p80 Cantonese $

☎ 2546 2584; 3 Gough St; ⏰ 11am-12.30am; MTR Sheung Wan (exit E2)

The beef brisket with turnip ($80) and the stuffed eggplant ($55) are famed at this crowded eatery. The boss, a skinny fellow with a perm, will be happy to recommend dishes when he's not doubling as the delivery boy.

YEOH'S BAH KUT TEH Map p80 Malaysian $

☎ 2543 2181; Shop G61-62, Midland Centre, 328 Queen's Rd Central; ⏰ 11.30am-10pm; MTR Sheung Wan (exit A2)

Bah Kut Teh is a soup dish made by boiling Chinese medicinal herbs and spices with pork ribs. Common in Singapore and Malaysia, it's eaten with chilli peppers over rice. In Hong Kong, Yeoh's version, served in a claypot with mushrooms and tofu puffs, is the closest you can get to the real thing (bowl small/medium/large $35/70/140). There's a branch in Jordan (Map p108; ☎ 2730 1821; 159 Woo Sung St; ⏰ 11.30am-11pm; MTR Jordan, exit C1).

CAUSEWAY BAY

Busy Causeway Bay is an eclectic amalgam of restaurants and cuisines, many upscale. It also has a lot of Japanese restaurants because of all the Japanese department stores headquartered here.

DA DOMENICO Map p85 Italian $$$$
☎ 2882 8013; 8 Hoi Ping Rd; meals from $500; ⏰ 12.15-1.30pm, 7-9.30pm Mon-Sat; MTR Causeway Bay (exit A)
Easily the best Italian restaurant in Hong Kong, this place serves excellent southern Italian cooking in an airy dining room. Ingredients including seafood are flown in weekly from Italy. No surprise the mozzarella deserves praise; the linguini with red shrimps and the grilled calamari (both $480) should be enshrined. The Roman chef-owner is a temperamental fellow, but who cares when he cooks this well? Dinner reservations essential.

FORUM Map p85 Cantonese, Dim Sum $$$$
☎ 2891 2555; 485 Lockhart Rd; ⏰ 11.30am-3pm, 6-11pm; MTR Causeway Bay (exit C)
The abalone dishes at this expensive eatery have fans from across the world. What restaurant owner Yeung Koon-Yat does with these molluscs has earned him membership of Le Club des Chefs des Chefs and the moniker 'King of Abalone'. If on a budget, you can make a meal of dim sum for under $200.

LE MARRON Map p85 French $$$
☎ 2881 6662; www.marron.com.hk; 12th fl, Ying Kong Mansion, 2-6 Yee Wo St; min charge $320; ⏰ 6pm-midnight; MTR Causeway Bay (exit D2)
This could have been Madame Bovary's boudoir-turned-brasserie had she come to Hong Kong. Gold-framed mirrors, lacy partitions, sunset lighting, a piano even – a cosy place, albeit a little cluttered. The food is good and portions are quite generous. But the noise – Madame would have thought that most unglamorous!

SUSHI HIRO Map p85 Japanese $$$
☎ 2822 8758; 10th fl, Henry House, 42 Yun Ping Rd; set lunch $90-290, set dinner options $370/500; ⏰ noon-2.30pm Mon-Sun, 6.30-11pm Mon-Sat, 6-10.30pm Sun; MTR Causeway Bay (exit F)
This glorified restaurant is one of the many authentic sushi bars tucked away in commercial buildings, much like the way it is in Tokyo. Like other sushi bars of this grade, it offers a seasonal choice of fish that changes on a weekly basis, and the chef will happily pick the best for you.

GOLDEN BULL Map p85 Vietnamese, Chinese $$
☎ 2506 1028; 1103 Food Forum, 11th fl, Times Sq, 1 Matheson St; set lunch options for 2 $178/208; ⏰ noon-3pm, 6-11pm; MTR Causeway Bay (exit A)
The crowds don't come for the portions (small) and the prices (high), but for the pleasant decor and the tasty Vietnamese and fusion food. The beef pho ($98) and spring rolls ($58) are excellently made, even if not 100% authentic.

INDONESIAN RESTAURANT 1968
Map p85 Indonesian $$
☎ 2577 9981; www.ir1968.com; 28 Leighton Rd; meals from $150; ⏰ noon-11pm; MTR Causeway Bay (exit A)
Despite the year of its establishment (1968), this restaurant is all teak chic and Bali cool. It's rumoured that the fine-looking brothers who're sometimes seen manning the restaurant have almost as much pull as the rendang and gado-gado. There's a branch in Sha Tin (Map p127; ☎ 2699 8777; Shop 701, New Town Plaza Phase 1, Sha Tin).

PAK LOK CHIU CHOW RESTAURANT
Map p85 Chiu Chow, Dim Sum $$
☎ 2576 8886; 23-25 Hysan Ave; meals from $120-500; ⏰ 11am-11pm; MTR Causeway Bay (exit F)
This old Chiu Chow restaurant still turns out reliable crab cakes and oyster omelettes, and you get unlimited refills of 'kung fu' tea – 'Iron Goddess' tea drunk the Chiu Chow way, using many tea leaves and a short infusion time. The cups are tiny, but downing too many of these will keep you up all night. There's a branch in Tsim Sha Tsui (Map p108; ☎ 3691 9168; Shop 1028D, L1/F, Elements, Kowloon Station Airport Express, 1 Austin Rd West; ⏰ 11am-4pm, 6-11pm Mon-Fri, 9am-4pm, 5.30-11pm Sat & Sun; MTR Kowloon, exit A1).

TAI PING KOON
Map p85 Soy Sauce Western, Chinese $$
☎ 2576 9161; www.taipingkoon.com; 6 Pak Sha Rd; meals from $150; ⏰ 11am-midnight; MTR Causeway Bay (exit F)
Soy sauce Western (p173) is believed to have been invented in the kitchen of the

first Tai Ping Koon, founded in 1860 in Guangzhou. Today tasty classics such as smoked pomfret and roast pigeon are still served in neat, if a little worn, surrounds by the waiters who have been around for decades. The restaurant is also famous for its soufflé, which is sized like a hen and comes in a casserole. There are branches in Yau Ma Tei (Map p108; ☎ 2384 3385; 19-21 Mau Lam St, Yau Ma Tei; MTR Jordan, exit B2) and Tsim Sha Tsui (Map p106; ☎ 2721 3559; 40 Granville Rd; MTR Tsim Sha Tsui, exit B1).

WEST VILLA Map p85   Cantonese, Dim Sum $$
☎ 2882 2110; Shops 101-102, 1st fl, Lee Gardens Two, 28 Yun Ping Rd; ☯ 11am-midnight Mon-Sat, 10am-midnight Sun; MTR Causeway Bay (exit E)
West Villa does the *char siu* (barbecued pork) job well – just slightly charred at the edges and with a golden lean-to-fat ratio. But *char siu* ($118) alone would not have earned this modern family-run operation a Bib Gourmand from the Michelin people. It also makes some of the best soy-sauce chicken in town ($150 for half) and a beautiful soup ($298, pre-ordering required) comprising chicken, conch meat, honeydew melon, and a dozen other ingredients its competitors would kill to know. There's a branch in Taikoo Shing (Map pp62–3; ☎ 2885 4478; Shop 208, 2nd fl, Cityplaza II, 18 Taikoo Shing Rd; MTR Tai Koo Shing, exit D2).

DELICIOUS KITCHEN
Map p85   Shanghainese $
☎ 2577 7720; 9-11B Cleveland St; ☯ 11am-11pm; MTR Causeway Bay (exit E)
The Shanghainese rice cooked with shredded Chinese cabbage is so good at this *cha chaan teng* that fashionistas are tripping over themselves to land a table here. It's best with the honey-glazed pork chop (from $43 including rice).

GOLDFINCH
Map p85   Soy Sauce Western, Chinese $
☎ 2577 7981; 13-15 Lan Fong Rd; ☯ 11am-12.30am; MTR Causeway Bay (exit A)
Tony Leung, Maggie Cheung and Faye Wong dined here in Wong Kar-wai's *In the Mood for Love* and *2046*. If that doesn't get you through the door, the decor, which has remained unchanged since the '60s, should. Food-wise, steer clear of the steaks and you'll be fine.

MAN FAI Map p85   Noodles $
☎ 2890 1278; 22-24 Jardine's Bazaar; ☯ 9am-2am; MTR Causeway Bay (exit F)
Any time of day you can see people squeezed together here at the few communal tables, slurping up noodles. It's not a heaven for hygienists, but it is for Chiu Chow squid-ball lovers. The signature balls, desired for their al dente texture, are served with a variety of noodles ($20) and with other ingredients such as beef balls and crispy fish skin (assorted $23).

PUMPERNICKEL CAFE
Map p85   Bakery, European $
☎ 2576 1302; Shop B, 13 Cleveland St, Fashion Walk; set lunch from $68; ☯ 11am-11pm; MTR Causeway Bay (exit E)
This laid-back cafe treats its bread with as much reverence as its salads and pastas, which makes it a refreshing choice for a light meal. Intellectual types like to fuel up here before attending the 4 June candlelight vigil at Victoria Park. There are branches in Tin Hau (Map p85; ☎ 2578 0854; 1A Lau Li St; ☯ 9.30am-11pm; MTR Tin Hau, exit A2) and Sheung Wan (Map p67; ☎ 2815 3711; Shop 4, Golden Centre, 188 Des Voeux Rd; ☯ 8am-7pm Mon-Fri, 10am-7pm Sat; MTR Sheung Wan, exit E2).

TONKICHI TONKATSU SEAFOOD
Map p85   Japanese $
☎ 2577 6617; 412, Podium 4, World Trade Centre, 280 Gloucester Rd; meals from $150; noon-3pm, 6-10.30pm; MTR Causeway Bay (exit D4)
The battered fried pork chop and oysters at this place measures up to the top shops in Tokyo, and it comes with the obligatory pestle and roasted sesame. There's a branch in Tsim Sha Tsui (Map p104; ☎ 2314 2998; Ground fl, 100 Canton Rd; MTR Tsim Sha Tsui, exit A1).

THE PEAK
You'd hardly venture all the way up Victoria Peak for a meal; food here takes its place in the queue behind the views and the attractions of the Peak Tower. But there are a few options from which to choose.

CAFE DECO Map pp62-3   International $$
☎ 2849 5111; www.cafedecogroup.com; Levels 1 & 2, Peak Galleria, 118 Peak Rd; set lunch $88; ☯ 11am-midnight Mon-Thu, 11am-1am Fri & Sat, 9.30am-midnight Sun; ⊕ Peak Tram
With its spectacular views and art deco–inspired furnishings, this restaurant need

not have made too much effort with the menu. Yet the bistro dishes, sushi and sashimi plates, and oyster bar are above average. Brunch ($328) is served from 9.30am to noon on Sunday.

PEAK LOOKOUT
Map pp62-3 International, Asian $$
☎ 2849 1000; www.thepeaklookout.com.hk; 121 Peak Rd; lunch from $200, dinner from $300; ⏱ 10.30am-11.30pm Mon-Thu, 10.30am-1am Fri, 8.30am-1am Sat, 8.30am-11.30pm Sun; 🚋 Peak Tram
Whether you like its colonial air or not, you'll admit that this 60-year-old establishment, with seating in a glassed-in veranda and on an outside terrace, has more character than all other Peak eateries combined. The food is excellent – especially the Indian and Western selections – as are the views.

HAPPY VALLEY
In general, the restaurants and cafes in Happy Valley cater to local residents, though a few are worth making the trip out for.

AMIGO Map p85 French, International $$$$
☎ 2577 2202; www.amigo.com.hk; Amigo Mansion, 79A Wong Nai Chung Rd; lunch from $300, dinner from $600; ⏱ noon-3pm, 6pm-midnight; 🚋 tram
Call us old-fashioned but this relic with a Spanish name and Gallic twists is a place full of memories. The waiters still wear black tie and white gloves, there are strolling musicians, and women are handed roses as they leave. The food is reliably good and you'll get a free cake if you go on your birthday.

GOLDEN VALLEY
Map pp62-3 Cantonese, Sichuanese $$
☎ 2961 3330; 1st fl, Emperor Hotel, 1A Wang Tak St; ⏱ 11am-11pm; 🚌 1 from Des Voeux Rd Central, or 🚋 tram
The Cantonese-Sichuanese restaurant at this hotel owned by controversial entertainment mogul Albert Yeung whips up the best spicy Sichuanese hotpot in town (soup base $120, dishes from $30). The standard of the dim sum is also high. Canto-pop fans may even catch a glimpse of Mr Yeung's protégés – we certainly did.

GI KEE SEAFOOD RESTAURANT
Map pp62-3 Dai Pai Dong, Cantonese $
☎ 2574 9937; Shop 4, 2nd fl, Wong Nai Chung Municipal Services Bldg, 2 Yuk Sau St; meals $50-200; ⏱ 5.30pm-12.30am; 🚌 1 from Des Voeux Rd Central, or 🚋 tram
Reserve a table or expect to queue for a plastic stool at this *dai pai dong* perched above a wet market. Chan Chung-fai, the man in the kitchen who turns out tantalising dishes such as chicken with fried garlic and shark's fin soup, is an award-winning Cordon Bleu chef with a huge fan following that includes the likes of Zhang Ziyi and Jacky Chan.

ISLAND EAST
North Point is home to a sizeable Fujian population and there are a few eateries specialising in dishes from this province. Quarry Bay has the largest collection of restaurants in the entire district, especially in and around Tong Chong St, but these places offer nothing special. Tai Hang, a quiet residential neighbourhood hidden behind Causeway Bay, is home to a handful of interesting eateries.

FUNG SHING RESTAURANT
Map pp62-3 Cantonese, Shunde $$
☎ 2578 4898; 62-28 Java Rd, North Point; ⏱ 9am-3pm, 6-11pm; MTR North Point (exit A2)
Dear old Fung Shing may try to hide its wrinkles, but the green-eyed, gilt phoenix reveals its age. It's a traditional Cantonese restaurant that specialises in the cuisine of the Shunde district, which was formerly known as 'Fung Shing' (Phoenix City). Naturally the must-tries here are Shunde classics, such as fried prawn on toast ($100 for 10 pieces), stir-fried milk ($80) and minced quail meat wrapped in lettuce ($98). There's another branch in Mong Kok (Map p111; ☎ 2381 5261; 1st-2nd fl, 749 Nathan Rd; MTR Prince Edward, exit C2).

JUNE JAPANESE RESTAURANT
Map p85 Japanese $$
☎ 2234 6691; 56 Electric Rd, Tin Hau; ⏱ noon-2.30pm Mon-Sun, 6-11pm Tue-Fri, 6-10pm Sat-Mon; MTR Tin Hau (exit A2)
This restaurant may not have an enormous repertoire, but the sushi and sashimi are very fresh. The menu at June also includes handmade *udon* and foie gras on rice ($100).

KIN'S KITCHEN Map p85 Cantonese $$

☎ 2571 0913; 9 Tsing Fung St, Tin Hau;
⏰ noon-3pm, 6-11pm; MTR Tin Hau (exit A2)
Opened by art critic–turned-gourmand
Lau Kin-wai, this understated restaurant
mentioned in the Michelin guide touts its
Cantonese classics with a modern spin. The
owner, looking quite the *bon vivant* with
silver hair and rosy cheeks, is sometimes
seen explaining dishes such as the delicious signature smoked chicken (half/whole
$268/134) to customers.

YAKITORITEI Map p85 Japanese $$

☎ 2566 9982; Tsing Fung Bldg, 10 Tsing Fung St,
Tin Hau; meals from $200; ⏰ 6pm-2.30am; MTR
Tin Hau (exit A2)
The speciality here is skewers, and they're
good. You can even watch your food being
cooked. Our favourites are eel, ox tongue
and chicken wings. Be prepared to dig
some way into your pockets – skewers and
beer complement each other all too well.
There's a branch in Happy Valley (Map pp62–3;
☎ 2838 5377; Shop C, 49-51, Shing Wo Rd; ⏰ 6.30pm-
2.30am; 🚌 1 from Des Voeux Rd Central, or 🚋 tram).

HONG KEE CONGEE SHOP

Map p85 Congee, Noodles $
☎ 2808 4518; 11 King St, Tai Hang; ⏰ 6am-
midnight; MTR Tin Hau (exit B)
Humble Hong Kee has been sitting quietly
in this corner of Tai Hang for 30 years. Each
day the grandpa repeats the ritual of rolling
steamed rice sheets to make *cheung fun*
(rice roll, $10), while his children prepare
the congee ($6 to $22) and noodles ($6),
and his grandsons entertain with their
antics.

MUN NAM RESTAURANT

Map pp62-3 Fujianese $
☎ 2807 2168; 25 Kam Ping St, North Point;
⏰ 7.30am-9.30pm; MTR North Point (exit B1)
This shabby Fujian place is famous for
its authentic Fujianese noodles, rice and
snacks. We dare you to try the jelly sand-
worm terrine ($12 for two pieces)!

SUN CHIU KEE

Map pp62-3 Tea Cafe, Cantonese $
☎ 2566 4361; 377 King's Rd, North Point; meal
under $55, ⏰ 7am-1am, MTR North Point (exit B3)
The best of the Sun Chiu Kee chain, Office
workers come to this *cha chaan teng* from

Central for its cheap, hearty grub, which
gives restaurant food a run for its money.

TUNG PO SEAFOOD RESTAURANT

Map pp62-3 Dai Pai Dong, Cantonese $
☎ 2880 9399; 2nd fl, Municipal Services Bldg,
99 Java Rd, North Point; meals $80-180;
⏰ 5.30pm-12.30am, reservations 2.30-5.30pm;
MTR North Point (exit A1)
Tung Po has revolutionised *dai pai dong*
and it's not hard to see why. Beer is served
in chilled blue-and-white porcelain bowls.
The staff strut around in rubber boots and
Madonna mics. Boss 'Ruby' taps into his
experience (in Western cuisine) and talent
(a nominee for Best Supporting Actor in the
Hong Kong Film Awards) to create Cantonese dishes at once unusual and unusually
good. Try the prawn sautéed with egg yolk,
squid-ink noodles, and fried rice wrapped
in lotus leaf.

ISLAND SOUTH

The restaurants in this district are as varied
as the settlements themselves. While the
choice is obviously limited in smaller places
such as Shek O and Repulse Bay, you'll still
manage to eat decent Thai at the former,
and enjoy one of the most delightful
venues on any coast at the latter. Stanley
boasts an embarrassment of choices, none
particularly outstanding, while Aberdeen
and Ap Lei Chau are home to a few hidden
gems if you dig beneath the kitsch.

Aberdeen

The lively harbour of Aberdeen is reachable
by bus 70 from Exchange Square (Map p67),
Central.

CROWN WINE CELLARS

Map pp62-3 European $$$
☎ 2580 6287; www.crownwinecellars.com; 18
Deep Water Bay Drive, Shouson Hill, ⏰ 6.30-11pm
Mon-Fri, 12.30pm-midnight Sat, 12.30-10.30pm
Sun; minibus 6
Wine lovers and fans of military history
should make a trip to this former ammo
depot constructed by the British military
just before WWII (p39). You can tour the site
and have a meal (dinner from $350) there
by subscribing to the one-time 'silver'
membership free of charge. Take minibus 5
on Lockhart Rd, right behind Sogo depart-
ment store in Causeway Bay. Minibuses

leave roughly every 10 minutes and make a stop at the top of Deep Water Bay Drive. If you don't feel like making the 5- to 10-minute trek down Deep Water Bay Drive, there are a few minibuses that take you to the doorstep of Crown Wine Cellars. On weekdays, they leave Causeway Bay on the hour until 3pm, and on Saturday, Sunday and public holidays they leave on the half-hour until 6.30pm. It's the only public vehicle that turns into Deep Water Bay Drive.

TOP DECK Map p94 International $$$

☎ 2552 3331; www.cafedecogroup.com; Top fl Jumbo Kingdom, Shum Wan Pier Dr, Wong Chuk Hang; ⏰ 6-11.30pm Tue-Thu, 6pm-1am Sat, 9am-11.30pm Sun & public holidays
Resort-style awnings meet a garish red-and-green Chinese pagoda on the rooftop of Jumbo Kingdom. The decor is trippy at Top Deck, but the harbour is drop-dead gorgeous and there's free-flowing champagne at the Sunday brunch ($350; ⏰ 11.30am to 4.30pm).

JUMBO KINGDOM FLOATING RESTAURANT Map p94 Cantonese $$

☎ 2553 9111; www.jumbo.com.hk; Shum Wan Pier Dr, Wong Chuk Hang; lunch $60-200; ⏰ 11am-11.30pm Mon-Sat, 7am-11.30pm Sun
The larger of two floating restaurants moored in Aberdeen Harbour, the Jumbo has interiors that look like Beijing's Imperial Palace crossbred with Macau's Casino Lisboa – a flamboyant spectacle so kitsch it's fun. The food is overpriced but fairly good. There's free transport for diners from the pier on Aberdeen Promenade.

SHAN LOON TSE KEE FISH BALL Map p94 Noodles $

☎ 2552 3809; 80-82 Old Main St; noodles per bowl $20-72; ⏰ 10am-6pm
This stall started from a nearby cave (shan loon) decades ago and it has since grown into a busy restaurant. The signature fish balls are al dente and they are great eaten with ho fan (flat rice noodles).

AP LEI CHAU MARKET COOKED FOOD CENTRE Map p94 Dai Pai Dong, Seafood $

1st fl, Ap Lei Chau Municipal Services Bldg, 8 Hung Shing St; minibus 36X from Lee Garden Rd, Causeway Bay, or from Aberdeen Promenade by sampan
Sharing a building with a market, six dai pai dong operators cook up a storm in

sleepy Ap Lei Chau. Pak Kee (☎ 2555 2984; ⏰ 6-11.30pm) and Chu Kee (☎ 2555 2052; ⏰ 6pm-midnight) both offer simple but tasty dishes in the $40 to $60 range, and affordable seafood selections. You can also buy seafood from the wet market downstairs and pay them to cook it for you the way you want. Every evening, fishermen and dragon boaters come here for the cheap beer (large bottle $12 to $22) and the food. If you don't mind plastic stools and alpha males trying to out-talk each other, this is the place to go for local flair. It's a stone's throw from the Hung Shing shrine (p95).

Stanley

Far-flung Stanley is reachable by bus 6, 6A, 6X or 260 from Exchange Square (Map p67), Central.

LUCY'S Map p96 International $$

☎ 2813 9055; 64 Stanley Main St; ⏰ noon-3pm, 7-10pm Mon-Fri, noon-4pm, 6.30-10pm Sat, noon-4pm, 6-9.30pm Sun
This cool oasis within Stanley Market has been around for much longer than most of its neighbours. The menu changes frequently as fresh produce and inspiration arrive. A set dinner of two/three courses for $250/290 is available from Sunday to Thursday only.

SHU ZHAI Map p96 Chinese $$

☎ 2813 0123; 80 Stanley Main St, Stanley; ⏰ noon-10pm Mon-Fri, 11am-10pm Sat & Sun
There's more gimmick than grace to this breezy restaurant that resembles an ancient repository for works of literature, but the hand-shredded fish ($100) and the dim sum ($25 to $35) are not bad. There is a door connecting the restaurant to a branch of Dymocks bookshops.

PIZZA EXPRESS Map p96 Pizza, International $

☎ 2813 7363; 90 Stanley Main St; meals $100-200; ⏰ 11.30am-11pm
Despite its pedestrian name, this pizza place offers more palatable fare and better service than many of its more exotic-sounding neighbours.

TOBY INN Map p96 Cantonese $

☎ 2813 2880; U1-U2, 126 Stanley Main St; meals $80-150; ⏰ 5.30am-10.30pm
This modest eatery is the neighbourhood restaurant of Stanley, with elderly people

dropping in for dim sum at the crack of dawn, dragon boaters stopping by for seafood after practice, and families coming in for simple dishes throughout the day.

Shek O

SHEK O CHINESE & THAI SEAFOOD

Map pp62-3   Thai, Cantonese $

☎ 2809 4426; 303 Shek O Village; lunch from $50, dinner from $80; ⏱ 11.30am-10pm; 🚌 9 from MTR Shau Kei Wan (exit A3)

This hybrid of a place is hardly authentic in either category, but the portions are generous, the staff are convivial and the cold Tsingtao beers just keep on flowing.

Repulse Bay & Deep Water Bay

These little beach resorts are reachable by bus 6, 6A, 6X or 260 from Exchange Square (Map p67), Central.

VERANDAH Map pp62-3   International $$$

☎ 2292 2822; www.therepulsebay.com; 1st fl, The Repulse Bay, 109 Repulse Bay Rd; ⏱ noon-2.30pm, 3-5.30pm (tea) & 7-11pm Tue-Sat, 11am-2.30pm (brunch), 3.30-5.30pm (tea) & 7-11pm Sun

The restored and refurbished Verandah is still hushed and formal, with heavy white tablecloths and demurely clinking cutlery, but the entrance hall is more spacious and the new marble staircase with wooden banisters will make professionals of the most inexperienced photographers. The Sunday brunch (adult/child $418/209) is famous (book ahead). The afternoon tea ($178 per person), including the champagne tea set ($218 per person), is the south side's best.

COCOCABANA Map pp62-3   Mediterranean $$

☎ 2812 2226; 2nd fl, Beach Bldg, Island Rd, Deep Water Bay; set lunch $278, set dinner $398; ⏱ 12.30-midnight, closed Mon lunch

Clichéd as it may sound, it's all location, location, location. The service is rather lax, but with the sound of the waves, dishes such as bouillabaisse and duck confit go down well.

KOWLOON

Kowloon doesn't have quite as many upmarket restaurants as Hong Kong Island does, but there's a riveting assortment of ethnic eateries

to fit all budgets in Tsim Sha Tsui. For hearty local fare, head for Yau Ma Tei or Mong Kok. Kowloon City is renowned for its excellent Thai and Chiu Chow eateries.

TSIM SHA TSUI

Tsim Sha Tsui, once the stronghold of Shanghainese migrants, has been home to Indians, Russians, Pakistanis, Japanese, Filipinos and Koreans. No surprise then that it claims the lion's share of ethnic restaurants in Kowloon. It's the destination for Shanghainese, Northern Chinese and Korean food.

HUTONG Map p104   Northern Chinese $$$

☎ 3428 8342; 28th fl, 1 Peking Rd; set dinner $880; ⏱ noon-3pm, 6-11pm; MTR Tsim Sha Tsui (exit C1)

Entering Hutong, which has one Michelin star, is like walking onto a Zhang Yimou film set. It's ancient China recreated for the modern Western imagination replete with red lanterns and Buddha's busts. Mind you, it's all quite stylish, the service is great, the views stunning and the food is actually quite impressive.

SPRING MOON

Map p104   Cantonese, Dim Sum $$$

☎ 2315 3160; www.peninsula.com; 1st fl, Peninsula Hong Kong, Salisbury Rd; set lunch $368, set dinner $928; ⏱ 11.30am-2.30pm Mon-Sat, 11am-2.30pm Sun, 6-10.30pm Mon-Sun; MTR Tsim Sha Tsui (exit E)

The Peninsula's flagship Chinese restaurant, Spring Moon is a graceful teahouse in 1920s art deco style, where you can savour excellent teas and dim sum (from $50, lunch only) while basking in friendly service and the croonings of 1930s songstresses.

T'ANG COURT

Map p104   Cantonese, Dim Sum $$$

☎ 2375 1133; http://hongkong.langhamhotels .com; Langham Hotel, 8 Peking Rd; ⏱ 11am-2.30pm Mon-Fri, noon-2.30pm Sat & Sun, 6-10.30pm Mon-Sun; MTR Tsim Sha Tsui (exit L4)

If the baked oysters with port ($220) and crispy eel with lemon and honey sauce ($190) make you wonder why T'ang Court has got only two Michelin stars, wait till you try the award-winning dishes. This suave establishment captures some of the finest moments of Cantonese cuisine.

YÈ SHANGHAI
Map p104   Shanghainese, Dim Sum $$$

☎ 2376 3322; www.elite-concepts.com; 6th fl, Marco Polo Hongkong Hotel, 3 Canton Rd; meals from $200; ☽ 11.30am-2.30pm, 6-10.30pm; MTR Tsim Sha Tsui (exit L4)
The Michelin inspectors liked this stylish restaurant with great views, but the dishes may have less oil and a higher price tag than a Shanghainese grandma thinks appropriate. Once she's tasted the minced pigeon with pine nuts and flaky pockets ($128), however, she may change her mind. There's an Admiralty branch (Map p72; ☎ 2918 9833; Shop 332, Level 3, Pacific Place, 88 Queensway; MTR Admiralty, exit F).

GAYLORD INDIAN RESTAURANT
Map p104   Indian $$

☎ 2376 1001; 1st fl, 23-25 Ashley Rd; lunch buffet Mon-Sat $98, dinner buffet Sun $168; ☽ noon-3pm, 6-10.30pm; MTR Tsim Sha Tsui (exit E)
Kowloon's classiest Indian restaurant has been entertaining a predominantly Indian clientele since 1972. Though pricier than similar places in town, the cosy alcoves, excellent northern Indian fare and live sitar music (from 7.30pm) compensate.

HONG KONG OLD RESTAURANT
Map p104   Shanghainese, Dim Sum $$

☎ 2722 1812; Shop F, 4th fl, Knutsford Steps, Miramar Shopping Centre, 132 Nathan Rd; dinner $120-300; ☽ 11am-3pm, 5.30-11pm; MTR Tsim Sha Tsui (exit B)
The walnuts with smoked eggs and the braised pork hock are so good at this restaurant even the cholesterol police would make an exception. Herbivores will drool over the 40 vegetarian offerings. There's a North Point branch (Map p85; ☎ 2508 1081; Basement, Newton Hotel Hong Kong, 218 Electric Rd; MTR Fortress Hill, exit A).

KUNG TAK LAM
Map p104   Shanghainese, Vegetarian $$

☎ 2312 7800; 7th fl, 1 Peking Rd; meals from $100; ☽ 11am-11pm; MTR Tsim Sha Tsui (exit C1)
Everyone loves the fried rice with seaweed and pine nuts at this relaxing Shanghainese vegetarian restaurant, and kidults will have a blast with the DIY cold noodles.

WU KONG SHANGHAI RESTAURANT
Map p104   Shanghainese, Dim Sum $$

☎ 2366 7244; www.wukong.com.hk; Basement, Alpha House, 27-33 Nathan Rd; dinner from $160; ☽ 11.30am-midnight; MTR Tsim Sha Tsui (exit E)

If you don't mind the staff looking daggers when you dawdle over your banana fritters, the specialities at this pleasant Shanghainese restaurant – cold pigeon in wine and Shanghainese *pot-au-feu* – are worth a trip across town. The four-course hairy crab meal (from $400, October to December) is also divine. There's a branch in Causeway Bay (Map p85; ☎ 2506 1018; 13th fl, Times Sq, 1 Matheson St; ☽ 5.45-10.45pm; MTR Causeway Bay, exit A).

BRANTO
Map p104   Vegetarian, Indian $

☎ 2366 8171; 1st fl, 9-11 Lock Rd; meals $50-110; ☽ 11am-3pm, 6-11pm; MTR Tsim Sha Tsui (exit E)
Branto offers basic vegetarian Indian food, basic service, basic surroundings and non-stop Indian music videos.

CHUNGKING MANSIONS
Map p104   Indian $

36-44 Nathan Rd; MTR Tsim Sha Tsui (exit D1)
Chungking Mansions, a building known for its backpacker hostels, is home to the largest concentration of cheap Indian and Pakistani eateries in Hong Kong. But considering that over 120 nationalities pass through its doors in a single year, Chungking's culinary repertoire is rather conservative. A good lunch at the places recommended below will start at about $60.

For people-watching and some friendly conversation, check out the joints on the ground and 1st floors, which are popular with traders and merchants in the building. Delhi Club (☎ 2368 1682; Flat C3, 3rd fl, C Block; ☽ noon-3.30pm, 6-11.30pm) serves decent Indian food, such as chicken tikka ($55) and chicken tandoori ($25) under funky blue lighting. To dine in relative quiet, head for Everest Club (☎ 2316 2718; Flat D6, 3rd fl, D Block; ☽ 11.30am-3pm, 6-11.30pm), where the food is decent but a little less colourful than the other offerings in the building. Pakistan Mess (☎ 2368 1564; Flat C2, 4th fl, C Block; ☽ 11.30am-11.30pm) does good northern Indian halal food. Meat curries start from $40 and veggie curries from $30.

Shama Restaurant (☎ 2724 8787; Flat 48, Ground fl; ☽ 11am-midnight) is a great spot for people-watching over a cold draft Carlsberg. Taj Mahal Club (☎ 2722 5454; Flat B4, 3rd fl, B Block; ☽ 11.30am-3pm, 6-11.30pm) whips up a mean rogan josh ($60). This place can also do you *raan mussalam* ($275), a leg of lamb cooked in the tandoor and feeding six to eight people, if given advance warning.

CRYSTAL JADE

Map p104   Shanghainese, Northern Chinese $

☎ 2622 2699; Shop 3328, 3rd fl, B Zone, Harbour City, 17 Canton Rd; ⏲ 11am-11pm Mon-Fri, 10.30am-11pm Sat & Sun; MTR Tsim Sha Tsui (exit A1)

People were queuing for a table at this place long before it received a mention in the Michelin guide, and rightly so: the dishes here are mouth-watering, especially the noodles ($32 to $45). There are branches all over town, including in Central (Map p67; ☎ 2295 3811; Shop 2018-2020, 2nd fl, Tower Two, IFC Mall, 1 Harbour View St; ⏲ 11am-11pm; MTR Hong Kong, exit E1), Causeway Bay (Map p85; ☎ 2506 0688; Basement B221A, Times Sq, 1 Matheson St; MTR Causeway Bay, exit A) and Wan Chai (Map p74; ☎ 2573 8844; Shop 301, Tai Yau Plaza, 181 Johnston Rd; ⏲ 11am-11pm; MTR Wan Chai, exit A5).

DIN TAI FUNG

Map p104   Shanghainese, Northern Chinese $

☎ 2730 6928; www.dintaifung.com.tw; Shop 130, 3rd fl, 30 Canton Rd; ⏲ 11.30am-10.30pm; MTR Tsim Sha Tsui (exit C1)

The juicy pork-filled siú lùng bàau ($48) at this famous Taiwanese chain are comparable to some of the best in Shanghai. Other classics, such as noodles with braised beef ($58) and taro buns, can be anyone's comfort food. There's always a line at the door.

STAR CAFE

Map p104   Tea Cafe $

☎ 2721 2908; 36-37 Champagne Ct, 16 Kimberley Rd; noodles $20-26; ⏲ 8am-9.30pm Mon-Sat; MTR Tsim Sha Tsui (exit B1)

This cafe opened in 1966 and little has changed. Designers and office workers come here for the ambience and the red-bean ice. Fans of old Cantonese movies should ask Mr Lam or his English-speaking grandson to show them the mirror given to Mr Lam's father by veteran Cantonese movie stars.

TAK FAT BEEF BALLS

Map p104   Dai Pai Dong, Noodles $

☎ 2376 1179; Haiphong Rd Temporary Market, Haiphong Rd; ⏲ 9am-8pm; MTR Tsim Sha Tsui (exit A1)

This famous dai pai dong is one of a handful operating in this 'temporary' market, which has been temping here for the last 30 years. Pick a seat in the sprawl and order the beef ball noodles ($20), which are famed for their bounce and their hint of dried orange peel.

SWEET DYNASTY

Map p104   Congee, Dessert $

☎ 2199 7799; 100 Canton Rd; ⏲ 8am-midnight Mon-Thu, 8am-11pm Fri, 7.30am-11pm Sat, 7.30am-midnight Sun; MTR Tsim Sha Tsui (exit A1)

From a dessert-and-congee shop, the Sweet Dynasty has evolved into a mini

---

SWEET HONG KONG

The Chinese are not traditionally known for their sweet tooth. Steamed cakes are eaten occasionally as dim sum, often with strong tea. Sweet soups, a southern speciality made by boiling pulses, seeds and root vegetables, are consumed as a late-night snack, for their taste and their positive effects on health. Traditional desserts do not contain dairy products, as many Chinese are lactose-intolerant. All this, however, has been changing as people adopt an increasingly Westernised way of life. Now teenagers call themselves 'chocoholics', and office workers talk about saving stomach space for cheesecake.

Sweets in Hong Kong run the gamut from dessert soups and Chinese pastries to Southeast Asian sago puddings and Western confectionery. For a sampler of Hong Kong–style sweets, your best bet is Honeymoon Dessert (p200) and Sweet Dynasty (above). Sweet Auntie (Map p85; ☎ 2508 6962; Shop A4, 96 Electric Rd; ⏲ 3pm-2am Mon-Sat, 7pm-2am Sun; MTR Tin Hau, exit A2) does wonderful things with tofu. Hop Shing Chiu Chow Dessert (Map pp100–1; ☎ 2383 3026; 9 Lung Kong Rd; ⏲ 12.30pm-1am; 🚌 5C from Tsim Sha Tsui Star Ferry) specialises in sweet soups with Chiu Chow touches. For well-made local pastries, head for Sai Kung Cafe and Bakery (p201) and Tai Cheong Bakery (p184).

XTC, with branches in Central (Map p78; ☎ 2541 0500; www.xtc.com.hk; 45 Cochrane St; ⏲ noon-midnight Mon-Thu & Sun, noon-2am Fri & Sat; MTR Central, exit D1) and Tsim Sha Tsui (Map p104; ☎ 2368 3602; KP-01, Star Ferry Terminal; ⏲ 11am-midnight Mon-Fri & Sun, 11am-1am Sat; 🚢 Star Ferry) and a handful of other places, makes the best gelato in town. Modern and airy Vero Lounge (Map p72; ☎ 2559 5882; 1st fl, Fenwick Pier, 1 Lung King St; ⏲ 9am-7pm Mon-Fri, 9am-6pm Sat, closed Sun; MTR Admiralty, exit E2) serves drinking chocolate ($35) and decadent desserts created with chocolate made in-house. Tiffin Lounge (Map p74; ☎ 2584 7822; www.hongkong grand.hyatt.com; Grand Hyatt Hong Kong, 1 Harbour Rd; per person $198; ⏲ 7-10.30pm; MTR Wan Chai, exit A1) at the Grand Hyatt has a sumptuous dessert buffet.

empire with locations in Shanghai, Taiwan and Japan, its extensive menu embracing all things casual and Cantonese. But its desserts (from $17 to $50) and congee are still the best. It's clean and modern, but gets crowded when busy.

TSIM SHA TSUI EAST & HUNG HOM

Tsim Sha Tsui East is livening up with the extension of KCR East Rail line, which is connected with the MTR and has an exit right outside Kowloon Shangri-La.

FOOK LAM MOON
Map p106   Cantonese, Dim Sum $$$$
☎ 2366 0286; www.fooklammoon-grp.com; Shop 8, 1st fl, 53-59 Kimberley Rd; ☷ 11.30am-3pm Mon-Sat, 11am-3pm Sun, 6-11pm Mon-Sun; MTR Tsim Sha Tsui (exit B1)

One of the top Cantonese restaurants in town, FLM is dubbed 'celeb canteen' by the local tabloids. But even if you're not a tycoon, FLM takes care of you from the minute you walk out of the lifts, with cheongsam-clad hostesses waiting to escort you to your table. The huge menu contains expensive items such as shark's fin and abalone, which would shoot your bill up to at least $1000 per head. Dim sum (from $50) is available till 3pm. The branch in Wan Chai (Map p74; ☎ 2866 0663; Shop 3, Newman House, 35-45 Johnston Rd; ☷ 11.30am-3pm, 6-10.30pm; MTR Wan Chai, exit B2) has a one-star Michelin rating.

TIN HEUNG LAU
Map p106   Hangzhou, Shanghainese $$$$
☎ 2366 2414; 18C Austin Ave; per person from $500; ☷ noon-2pm, 6-10pm; MTR Jordan (exit D)

Filmmaker Stephen Chow and former chief executive Tung Chee Hwa are regulars at this tired-looking establishment considered by some to be the best Hangzhou restaurant in China. It's famous for its crab dishes during hairy crab season (October to February), and the fragrance of its smoked yellow croaker (over $700) is the stuff of urban legend.

STEAK HOUSE
Map p106   Steakhouse, International $$$
☎ 2313 2323; http://hongkong-ic.dining.inter continental.com; InterContinental Hong Kong, 18 Salisbury Rd; steaks from $548; ☷ 6-11pm Mon-Sat, noon-2.30pm Sun

At this first-rate steakhouse, the imported beef exhilarates even without the trimmings (exotic salts and mustard blends, gourmet steak knives), and the salad bar ($300 per person) is a garden of delight. Harbourside (☎ 2313 2495; ☷ 6am-midnight) in the same hotel has great pizzas, Western and Asian dishes, and a Sunday champagne brunch (noon to 2.30pm) that's a favourite of the buffet brigade.

SABATINI ITALIAN Map p106   Italian $$$
☎ 2733 2000; www.rghk.com.hk; 3rd fl, Royal Garden Hotel, 69 Mody Rd; set lunch from $198; ☷ noon-2.30pm, 6-11pm; MTR East Tsim Sha Tsui (exit P2)

It's easy to overindulge at this warm, rustic restaurant – the hearty Roman fare is exceptional and the antipasto spread ($258) is a feast on its own.

CHANG WON KOREAN RESTAURANT
Map p106   Korean $$
☎ 2368 4606; 1G, Kimberly St; lunch from $60, dinner from $100; ☷ noon-4am; MTR Tsim Sha Tsui (exit B1)

One of the most authentic Korean restaurants in town, Chang Won makes delectable beef ribs, seafood pancakes and cold noodles, and the staff are generous with side dishes. But the toilet is not for the faint-hearted. Chang Won has a branch in Causeway Bay (Map p85; ☎ 2836 3877; 1-2/F, 500 Jaffe Rd; MTR Causeway Bay, exit C).

SWISS CHALET Map p106   Swiss, European $$
☎ 2191 9197; 12-14 Hart Ave; ☷ noon-midnight Mon-Sat, 6pm-midnight Sun; MTR Tsim Sha Tsui (exit N1)

Once inside this cosy restaurant with fake Swiss windows, you'll see half the customers happily swirling and dunking into pots of fondue. The speciality comes in 13 varieties ($188 to $280), including chocolate. There's also a range of great meat dishes, including deer carpaccio ($135).

HOKAHOKA Map p106   Japanese $$
☎ 2366 1784; 51-52 Houston Centre, 63 Mody Rd; set lunch from $58; ☷ noon-2.30pm, 6pm-midnight; MTR East Tsim Sha Tsui (exit P2)

At this authentic Japanese *izakaya* with *tatami* seating, do as the Japanese do: order the succulent grilled beef and wash it down with a pint or three of chilled Asahi ($38).

LEI GARDEN Map p106   Cantonese, Dim Sum $$

☎ 2722 1636; B2F, Houston Centre, 63 Mody Rd; dinner from $250; ☯ 11.30am-2.45pm Mon-Sat, 11am-2.45pm Sun, 6-10pm Mon-Sun; MTR East Tsim Sha Tsui (exit P2)

Military-like quality control (which obviously doesn't extend to the decor) has earned two of nine Lei Garden branches, including this one, a Michelin star. Don't miss its award-winning creation: sweet sago soup with mango and pomelo ($25 a bowl). There are branches in Central (Map p67; ☎ 2295 0238; Shop 3007-3011, 3rd fl, International Finance Centre; ☯ 11.30am-2.30pm, 6-10pm; MTR Hong Kong, exit E1), Wan Chai (Map p74; ☎ 2892 0333; 1st fl, CNT Tower, 338 Hennessy Rd; ☯ 11am-3pm, 6-10.30pm; MTR Causeway Bay, exit A), West Kowloon (Map p108; ☎ 2196 8133; Shop 2068-70, 2nd Level, Elements, 1 Austin Rd West; ☯ 11.30am-2.30pm Mon-Sat, 11am-2.45pm Sun, 6-10.30pm Mon-Sun; MTR Kowloon, exit A1), and Mong Kok (Map p111; ☎ 2392 5184; 121 Sai Yee St; ☯ 11.30am-2.30pm Mon-Sat, 11am-2.30pm Sun, 6-10.30pm Mon-Sun; MTR Mong Kok East, exit B).

SPRING DEER Map p106   Northern Chinese $$

☎ 2366 4012; 1st fl, 42 Mody Rd; dinner from $150; ☯ noon-2.30pm, 6-10.30pm; MTR Tsim Sha Tsui (exit M2)

Brisk, bright and busy, the Spring Deer is believed to be Hong Kong's most authentic northern Chinese restaurant. The roast mutton is the best south of Xinjiang, while the deep-fried bamboo shoots and preserved cabbage tossed with glazed walnuts is a scrumptious mouthful. Book up to 10 days in advance for a weekend dinner.

HANSUNG CO Map p104   Korean $

☎ 2367 5025; Shop 3, 10 Kimberley St; mains $50-70; ☯ noon-10pm; MTR Tsim Sha Tsui (exit B1)

Fans of Korean soaps love this stylish little shop for homemade fast food and a clean, contemporary feel absent from other eateries in the neighbourhood. There are about 30 dishes ($50 to $70) on the menu. The fried meat patty with green beans and the Korean rice cake are popular.

PEKING DUMPLING SHOP
Map p106   Northern Chinese $

☎ 2368 3028; Shop A2, 15B, Austin Rd; ☯ 11.30am-11.30pm; MTR Jordan (exit D)

This tiny shop whips up decent pastries and noodles (per serving $7 to $32) of the chewy northern variety. Get your carb fix in booths or, if the smell of grease gets to you, on the go.

WOODLANDS Map p106   Indian, Vegetarian $

☎ 2369 3718; Upper Ground fl, 16 & 17 Wing On Plaza, 62 Mody Rd; ☯ noon-3.30pm, 6.30-10.30pm; MTR East Tsim Sha Tsui (exit P1)

In its latest location above a department store, good old Woodlands continues to offer excellent-value Indian vegetarian food to compatriots and the odd local. Dithering gluttons should order the thali meals ($70 to $75), which arrive on a round metal plate with 10 tiny dishes, a dessert and bread.

IPPEI-AN Map p106   Japanese, Noodles $

☎ 2722 4826; http://ippeian.com; Shop B1, Energy Plaza, 92 Granville Rd; ☯ 11.30am-3pm, 6-11pm; MTR East Tsim Sha Tsui (exit P2)

If you didn't lose your way trying to find this secluded restaurant, you'll see Japanese expats happily slurping up noodles (per bowl $55 to $75) or winding down over ice-cold beer and manga comics. And you'll want to join them.

KUNG WO TOFU FACTORY
Map p106   Chinese, Tofu $

☎ 2632 4680; 27 Prat Ave; ☯ 8am-11pm Mon-Sat, noon-10pm Sun; MTR East Tsim Sha Tsui (exit P2)

At century-old Kung Wo, stone-milled tofu comes braised, fried, stuffed or in the company of fruits (tofu snacks from $12). For nostalgic ambience, visit the old shops in Sham Shui Po (Map pp100-1; ☎ 2386 6871; 118 Pei Ho St; ☯ 6am-9pm; MTR Sham Shui Po, exit B1) and Kowloon City (Map pp100-1; ☎ 2718 0976; 67 Fuk Lo Tsun Rd; ☯ 8am-8pm Mon-Fri, 8am-9pm Sat & Sun; 🚌 5C from Tsim Sha Tsui Star Ferry or 101 from Statue Sq, Central). There are new branches, including one in Wan Chai (Map p74; ☎ 2877 8389; 253-261 Hennessy Rd; ☯ 10am-8pm Mon-Sat, noon-7pm Sun; MTR Wan Chai, exit A4).

WAT YAT
Map p106   Shanghainese, Northern Chinese $

☎ 2311 1498; 5-6 Hau Fook St; ☯ 7-10.30am Mon-Thu & Sun, 7am-11pm, Fri & Sat; MTR Tsim Sha Tsui (exit B1)

The only place left in Tsim Sha Tsui where you can have a traditional Shanghainese breakfast of savoury soy milk and stuffed glutinous rice rolls. There's also a selection of northern-style pastries. Ask for an English menu (rice and noodles $20 to $33 per serving). Hau Fook St is a few blocks east of Nathan Rd in Tsim Sha Tsui. Walking north from the intersection of Carnarvon and Cameron Rds, it's the first lane on your right.

WING LAI YUEN (YEUNG'S KITCHEN)
Map pp100-1   Sichuanese, Shanghainese $
☎ 2320 6430; www.yp.com.mo/winglaiyuen; Shops 106-107, Site 8, Wonderful Worlds of Whampoa, 7 Tak On St, Hung Hom; ⏱ 6am-10.30pm; minibus 6 from MTR Hung Hom station
A household name for *daam daam min* (spicy Sichuanese noodles), Wing Lai Yuen was opened in 1947 in the squatter shacks of Diamond Hill where Nationalist soldiers from Chongqing used to live. According to rumour, it was martial-arts director Chang Che who gave Wing Lai Yuen its name. Now it has an English menu and a branch in Macau, but the excellent noodles ($18 per bowl) are still handmade.

YAU MA TEI & MONG KOK

Most eateries worth a visit in this part of Kowloon are classics that have survived cut-throat competition and urban development. Temple St, the area around the night market, is a traditional place for cheap eats and snacks. Anything upmarket will usually be inside a hotel of some sort.

FOK LOI KUI SEAFOOD RESTAURANT
Map p111   Dai Pai Dong, Seafood $
☎ 2394 4418; 4-6 & 17 Ki Lung St; dinner $120-300; ⏱ 6pm-2am; MTR Prince Edward (exit D)
Business is so good here that the owner has to rent extra space nearby to seat his customers. Still, come sundown, there'll be tables on the sidewalks and SUVs abandoned in the middle of the road by diners eager for the mouth-watering sautéed razor clams in black-bean sauce, the steamed scallops or the fried squid with salt and pepper. There's no menu. Just point and ask for the price. The owner, Mr 'Cowboy' Kee, speaks a little English.

PEKING RESTAURANT
Map p108   Northern Chinese $
☎ 2735 1316; 1st fl, 227 Nathan Rd; set dinner for 2 from $300; ⏱ 11am-2.30pm, 5.30-10.30pm; MTR Jordan (exit C1)
This restaurant is so China Town c 1970 that you'd expect Bruce Lee to show up

for dinner with his *nunchaku*. It may also feel a little cramped if you're chubbier than Bruce. But you won't mind because the roast duck is crispy and the waiters pleasant, even if a little too efficient.

HING KEE RESTAURANT
Map p108   Dai Pai Dong, Cantonese $
☎ 2384 3647; 19 Temple St, Yau Ma Tei; ⏱ 5.30pm-1am; MTR Yau Ma Tei (exit C)
Previously a roadside stall that started out by whipping up hearty claypot rice and oyster omelettes ($20) for night revellers and Triads, Hing Kee now serves the same under a roof but without the atmosphere.

MIDO CAFE Map p108   Tea cafe, Chinese $
☎ 2384 6402; 63 Temple St; meals $25-80; ⏱ 9am-10pm; MTR Yau Ma Tei (exit B2)
Established in 1950, Mido with its mosaic tiles and metal latticework stands astride a street corner that comes to life at sundown. Ascend to the spacious upper floor and take a seat next to a wall of iron-framed windows overlooking Tin Hau Temple (p87). The food is passable, but when you feel the breeze lapping at your hair, there's poetry in everything.

NATHAN CONGEE AND NOODLE
Map p108   Congee, Noodles $
☎ 2771 4285; 11 Saigon St, Jordan; ⏱ 7.30am-11.30pm; MTR Jordan (exit B2)
This honest, low-key eatery has been making great congee (from $25) and noodles (from $20) for the last half-century. Order a side of fritters (to be dunked into the congee and eaten slightly soggy), tackle a pyramidal Chinese rice dumpling, or conquer the blanched fish skin tossed with parsley, garlic, sesame oil and peanuts ($23).

TIM KEE FRENCH SANDWICHES
Map p108   Sandwiches $
☎ 2385 7939; 30A Man Yuen St, Jordan; baguettes regular/large $21/40; ⏱ 11am-midnight; MTR Jordan (exit A)
You'd love to sink your teeth into this shop's warm, crispy Franco-Vietnamese baguettes stuffed with meaty delights and pickled carrots – we did.

YOKOZUNA Map p108   Japanese, Noodles $
☎ 2783 0784; 466-472 Nathan Rd; ⏱ noon-11pm; MTR Yau Ma Tei (exit C)

Yokozuna has remained firmly planted in this corner of Yau Ma Tei for over two decades. The al dente noodles (from $42) come in a rich pork, soy sauce or miso broth with a variety of garnishes.

NEW KOWLOON

New Kowloon has an eclectic collection of eateries, most notably Thai and Chiu Chow restaurants in Kowloon City and seafood restaurants at Lei Yue Mun Village.

Sham Shui Po

WAH NAM CAFE SHOP

Map pp100-1   Tea Cafe $

☎ 2728 0182; 87 Kweilin St; ⏱ 6am-6pm; MTR Sham Shui Po (exit A2)

Mr Chow, the 80-year-old owner, who can be seen chatting with customers at this local joint, has a penchant for funky striped walls. The barbecued pork ($16) with egg over rice is a favourite of the geeks who hang out at Golden Computer Arcade (p170).

Kowloon Tong

To go to Festival Walk where the following two eateries are located, take the MTR to Kowloon Tong and exit C1 will take you to the mall.

KING'S PALACE CONGEE AND
NOODLE BAR Map pp100-1   Congee, Noodles $$

☎ 2265 7777; Shop 19, L1/F, Festival Walk, 80 Tat Chee Ave; ⏱ 11am-11pm

At King's Palace, you can feast like royalty on poor man's fare in modern surrounds. You can't go wrong ordering anything on the menu, but the famous 'God of Cookery' rice with barbecued pork and egg, supposedly inspired by a Stephen Chow film, is absolute food porn ($43).

QUEEN'S CAFE

Map pp100-1   Soy Sauce Western, Chinese $$

☎ 2265 8288; www.queenscafe.com; Shop 18, L1/F, Festival Walk, 80 Tat Chee Ave; set lunch $70, set dinner $125-290; ⏱ 11am-11pm

Queen's is a veteran of soy sauce Western cuisine (p173), which accounts for its subdued yet assured atmosphere and its hearty baked dishes. The first Queen's was opened in 1952 by a man who had apprenticed under White Russian chefs in Shanghai. There's another branch in North

Point (Map pp62–3; ☎ 2576 2658; Shop 022, Ground fl, Island Place, 500 King's Rd; ⏱ 11am-10.30pm; MTR North Point, exit B3).

Kowloon City

Restaurants in Kowloon City can be reached by taking minibus 25M from exit B2 of Kowloon Tong MTR station (Map pp100–1), bus 5C from the Star Ferry bus terminal (Map p104) or bus 101 from Statue Square (Map p6/), Central.

CHONG FAT CHIU CHOW RESTAURANT

Map pp100-1   Chiu Chow $$

☎ 2383 3114; 60-62 South Wall Rd; ⏱ 11.30am-midnight

Food critics adore this spritely old shop for its unusual Chiu Chow fare. You'll see plates laden with delicacies such as fried pomfret (from $100) and soups simmering in woks (from $40) in the open kitchen. Don't miss the sek-làu-gài (chicken wrapped in little egg-white sacs; $13 each), the cold 'pei pa' shrimp (from $100) and the sugar-coated taro ($5 per piece).

CHEONG FAT Map pp100-1   Thai, Noodles $

☎ 2382 5998; 27 South Wall Rd; ⏱ 11.30am-11.30pm

This humble joint is famous for its authentic Chiang Mai soup noodles (from $20), but don't get stuck on them noodles. The open kitchen has appetising cooked dishes on display, such as pork trotters with preserved vegetables. Place your order and jive to Thai music videos while you wait.

ISLAM FOOD Map pp100-1   Halal, Chinese $

☎ 2382 2822; Ground fl, 1 Lung Kong Rd, Kowloon City; ⏱ 11am-11pm

Take care when sinking your teeth into the signature beef pastry ($20 for two) because they'll squirt. Less spectacular though still good are the lamb dishes and dumplings. It's not the cleanest place, but fans don't seem to mind.

RUAMJAI THAI RESTAURANT

Map pp100-1   Thai, Noodles $

☎ 2383 6983; 5 Tak Ku Ling Rd; meals $30-120; ⏱ 11.30am-11.30pm

Thai diners here like to order meat wrapped in lettuce leaves and papaya salad with salted crab. You can't go wrong doing the same. It has a new branch (⏱ 2716 4588; 11-13 Tak Ku Ling Rd; ⏱ 11am-midnight) nearby.

YEE HEUNG BEAN PRODUCTS
Map pp100-1   Tofu, Chinese $

☎ 2382 5006; 74 Nga Tsin Long Rd; ⏱ 11am-8pm
Housewives, workers and schoolchildren
have been coming here for fried tofu ($10)
or sweet tofu pudding ($5) for over half a
century. These connoisseurs believe the
tofu here is dense and smooth, with nutty
notes.

To Kwa Wan
SOSAM TEA HOUSE
Map pp100-1   Chinese, Fusion $$

☎ 2714 3299; Shop 10, Mega Bldg, 1 Maidstone
Rd, To Kwa Wan; meals $50-200; ⏱ 12.30-10.30pm
Tue-Sun
At this artsy tea house, bowls hand-
painted with flowers sit atop placemats of
crocheted lace, and jars of lychee wine vie
for space with books on a wooden shelf
next to the open kitchen, where the owner
gives her take on familiar Chinese dishes.
Indochina dragonplum, an ancient fruit,
appears in a sauce for handmade shrimp
roe noodles, and it's delicious. To get here,
take minibus 27M from Mong Kok MTR
station (exit B2) and disembark at the final
stop.

PAK KUNG CAFE Map pp100-1   Tea Cafe $
☎ 2362 2276; 91 Ma Tau Kok Rd, To Kwa Wan;
meals under $40; ⏱ 5.30am-10.30pm; 🚌 5C from
Tsim Sha Tsui Star Ferry
The owners of this spacious *cha chaan teng*
have taken such care to preserve the 1960s
atmosphere that we spilled our tea when
we saw the ESPN Star Sports channel play-
ing on TV.

Diamond Hill
CHI LIN VEGETARIAN (LONG MEN LOU)
Map pp58-9   Vegetarian, Chinese $

☎ 3658 9388; Nan Lian Garden, 60 Fung Tak Rd;
lunch $85, dinner $110; ⏱ 11.30am-9pm; MTR
Diamond Hill (exit C2)
The location behind a waterfall and tasty
vegetarian food, including steamed rice
with mixed mushrooms, make dining here
a superb way to begin or end your visit to
Chi Lin Nunnery and Nan Lian Garden (see
the boxed text, p39). The elegant Song Cha Xie
(Pavilion of Pine and Tea; ☎ 3658 9390; tea leaves $120-
300; ⏱ noon-7.30pm) nearby specialises in the
art of Chinese tea drinking.

Lei Yue Mun
One of Hong Kong's most popular seafood
venues, the village of Lei Yue Mun has over
a dozen seafood restaurants and seafood
stalls lining a winding road overlooking the
typhoon shelter.

Once you've settled down in a restaurant, go
outside and pick your dinner from one of the
stalls with live seafood tanks, making sure you
know how much you're paying and for what.
The restaurant will take care of the rest.

The more popular restaurants include Lung
Mun Seafood Restaurant (Map pp62–3; ☎ 2717 9886; 20
Hoi Pong Rd C), Lung Yue Restaurant (Map pp62–3; ☎ 2348
6332; 41 Hoi Pong Rd C) and Sea King Garden Restaurant
(Map pp62–3; ☎ 2348 1408; 39 Hoi Pong Rd C). They
open from around noon to 11pm.

To get to Lei Yue Mun from Yau Tong MTR
station (Map pp62–3), use exit A2 and follow Cha
Kwo Ling Rd and Shung Shun St south for 15
minutes or catch green minibus 24M from
outside the station. Bus 14C links the Yau Tong
Centre halfway down the hill with the Kwun
Tong MTR station (Map pp62–3).

NEW TERRITORIES
With very few exceptions, the New Territories
is not an area offering a surfeit of culinary
surprises. The following recommendations
are basically to help you find sustenance along
the way.

TUEN MUN
You'll find plenty of Chinese restaurants and
noodle shops in Tuen Mun town centre, but
it's best to travel out a bit further for some-
thing unusual and delicious.

NANG KEE GOOSE RESTAURANT
Map pp58-9   Cantonese $

☎ 2491 0392; 13 Sham Hong Rd, Sun Tsuen, Sham
Tseng; roast goose per plate from $80; ⏱ 10.30am-
11pm; 🚌 234A or 234B from Tsuen Wan town centre
Sham Tseng has long been famous for roast
goose, and this 50-year-old place is the
most-visited restaurant in the area. Savour
the crispy skin and succulent meat with
some beer, and there can be no complaint.

YUEN LONG
This historical town – known traditionally
for three 'treasures': rice, grey mullet and
oysters (in Lau Fau Shan along the coast) –
has a handful of restaurants worth trekking

north for. See the Dah Wing Wah boxed text (p200) for walled-village cuisine.

HAPPY SEAFOOD RESTAURANT
Map pp58-9   Cantonese, Seafood $$
☎ 2472 3450; 12 Shan Ting St, Lau Fau Shan; meals $250-800; ☯ 11am-10pm; ⛟ K65 or minibus 34 from Yuen Long (East) bus terminus, south of Yuen Long Light Rail station

The innovative seafood dishes here are – would you believe? – the brainchild of a cocky 23-year-old who is the world's youngest chef to receive a Cordon Bleu medal. Talented Lau Ka-lun is said to have played truant from school at age 11 so he could cook in his mum's restaurant. Lau's signature fried rice with crab roe, scallops and ostrich meat ($88) is literally bursting with creativity. He also does wonders with oysters, a Lau Fau Shan speciality.

PAT HEUNG KWUN YUM TEMPLE
Map pp58-9   Chinese $
☎ 2477 5168, 9077 5393; 87 Pat Heung Upper Village; per basin for 10-12 $838, per basin for 2 $150; ☯ 11.30am-2pm; ⛟ 51 from Nina Tower, Tsuen Wan

The folks here claim their *poon choy* (or basin feast; see p173) recipe dates back to the end of the Southern Song dynasty (AD 1127–1279), when the defeated emperor fled from the Mongolians to what is the New Territories today. Apparently, the proof is in the duck, stewed the same way it was 800 years ago. Reservations a must.

TAI PO & AROUND
Tai Po town centre features decent street food and the many Chinese eateries serve up old-style Hakka dishes hard to come by in more Westernised parts of Hong Kong. Tai Mei Tuk, the springboard for the Plover Cove area 6km to the northeast, boasts a number of eateries along Ting Kok Rd, many of them Thai.

CHUNG SHING THAI RESTAURANT
Map pp58-9   Thai $
☎ 2664 5218; 69B-72, Tai Mei Tuk Village, Ting Kok Rd; ☯ 8am-midnight; 75K bus or minibus 20C from MTR Tai Po Market

This chaotic open-air restaurant holds the secret to making perfect grilled meats. The pork neck, beef cubes (both $58) and eel skewer ($60) are among the best in town. Most other dishes, though still decent, have been tweaked to suit local palates.

SHA TIN
The multilevel, three-phase shopping mall New Town Plaza (Map p127), connected to the Sha Tin KCR station, has more eateries than you can shake a chopstick at. Our favourites are all in Phase 1; they include Bay Phoon Town (Map p127; ☎ 2628 0218; Shop 710, New Town Plaza Phase 1; ☯ 11am-11.30pm), Shakey's Pizza Restaurant (Map p127; ☎ 2608 0889; Shop 121; ☯ 11.30am-10.30pm Mon-Fri, 11am-10.30pm Sat & Sun), Shanghai Xiao Nan Guo (Map p127; ☎ 2894 8899; Shop 709; ☯ 11.30am-3.30pm, 6-11.30pm), Cafe Merlion (Map p127; ☎ 2605 3636; Shop 127; ☯ noon-10.30pm) and Honeymoon Dessert (Map p127; ☎ 2602 6366; Shop 704A; ☯ 11.30am-11.30pm).

SHA TIN 18
Map pp58-9   Cantonese, Northern Chinese $$
☎ 3723 1234; www.hongkong.shatin.hyatt.com; Hyatt Regency Hong Kong, 18 Chak Cheung St; ☯ 11.30am-3pm, 5.30-10.30pm; MTR University East Rail

When done right, the Peking duck (whole $398, half $218, 24-hour advance booking required) here – with skin airy like a kiss – is excellent, but sometimes the birds aren't rescued from the heat in time, and they taste burnt. However, that is a kink this just-opened restaurant may be able to iron out, given time. The pot-stickers ($68), mustard greens ($70) and Chinese-themed desserts are quite delicious. Take a ringside seat at the show kitchen and see if you agree with us. The Hyatt Regency is a five-minute walk from University MTR station.

CHAN KUN KEE
Map p127   Dai Pai Dong, Cantonese $
☎ 2606 1390; 3-5 Dai Pai Dong, Wo Che Estate Market; ☯ 6pm-1am; ⛟ 85k from Sha Tin New Town Plaza

Located below a public housing estate, this 30-year-old *dai pai dong* has improvised a tin roof, ceiling fans and a TV, so its customers can bask in homely luxury while they dine. The hand shredded chicken ($52) and steamed eel with black-bean sauce ($58) are perfect with beer.

LUNG WAH HOTEL RESTAURANT
Map p127   Cantonese $
☎ 2691 1828; www.lungwahhotel.hk; 22 Ha Wo Che; ☯ 11am-11pm; MTR Sha Tin (exit B), walk north for 10min along the railway line

This former holiday home was turned into a hotel in 1951, where Bruce Lee was

DAH WING WAH

The walled villages in the New Territories are traditionally homes to the Hakka, a roaming and hardworking people who moved to Hong Kong, among many other places, from the Central Plains of China. Their lifestyle spawned a unique cuisine featuring the liberal use of salt, preserved ingredients and fatty meat.

Established in 1950, Dah Wing Wah (Map pp58–9; 2nd fl, Koon Wong Mansion, 2-6 On Ning Rd; ☽ 6am-midnight; 🚌 968 or N968 from Tin Hau bus terminus) is the most famous restaurant in Hong Kong for walled-village dishes. Its head chef and managing partner, Hugo Leung Man-to, is famous for his efforts at enhancing and preserving traditional dishes. Hugo sources local ingredients from small farms and food producers whenever possible, and complements them with his insightful experience and innovations in cooking. He thinks shrimps in Hong Kong, mostly farmed in mainland China, taste bland, so he boosts them with Baxter's lobster bisque. His ideas work. People have been zooming into this far corner of town to line up for tables. Must-eats include lemon-steamed grey mullet, smoked oysters and Malay sponge cake. Hugo hosts TV food shows, designs gourmet tours and writes newspaper columns.

supposed to have stayed during the filming of *The Big Boss*. It's now a restaurant, frequented by nostalgic adults and history lovers. You'll find a small playground out front where peacocks are kept in cages, and an outdoor area where old men come to play mah-jong. Food-wise, stick with the roast pigeon ($68).

SAI KUNG

Sai Kung town is chock-a-block with eateries, but you'd make a special trip here only for a couple. It's reachable by bus 92 from Diamond Hill MTR bus terminus (exit C2). To get to Pak Sha Wan, take minibus 1A or 1M from Sai Kung Town.

CHEZ LES COPAINS Map pp58-9 French $$
☎ 2243 1918; www.chezlescopains.com; 117 Pak Sha Wan; ☽ 6-10.30pm Mon-Fri, 12.30pm-midnight Sat & Sun, closed Tue; set lunch $120-190, set dinner $390-490, tea $90
This friendly restaurant with warm-coloured walls is where bubbly Cordon Bleu chef Bonnie lives and feeds her customers, many of whom make a special trip from town just to savour her homemade goose liver terrine, duck leg confit and French *andouillette* (a rustic tripe sausage).

CHUEN KEE SEAFOOD RESTAURANT
Map p130 Cantonese, Seafood $$
☎ 2792 6938; 87-89 Man Nin St; set meals for 2 $348; ☽ 7am-11pm
This is the plush new branch of the Michelin-recommended Chuen Kee (Map p130; ☎ 2791 1195; 53 Hoi Pong St; ☽ 11am-11pm), the grand-daddy of Sai Kung seafood restaurants. The elaborate display of fish and crustaceans at

the door may make you cringe, but cringe will turn to crave once you've had a bite of the cooked versions.

KAM KAU KEE SEAFOOD RESTAURANT
Map pp58-9 Cantonese, Seafood $
☎ 2719 8432; 145 Pak Sha Wan; dishes $75-200; ☽ 11.30am-3pm, 5.30-11pm
Chef Kam shops every morning for ingredients to make dishes such as deep-fried soft-bone fish, typhoon shelter tofu and steamed chicken, to make sure that the hikers and divers who frequent his restaurant after a day out will be greeted with wholesome food and cheap beer ($10 per large bottle) in the least pretentious surroundings.

ALI OLI BAKERY CAFE
Map p130 European, Bakery $
☎ 2792 2655; www.alioli.com.hk; 11 Sha Tsui Path; ☽ 8am-7.30pm Mon-Fri, 8am-9pm Sat & Sun
No trip to Sai Kung is complete without stopping at this bakery, where you can gorge on wonderful European-style bread (from $4 to $30), pies and homemade preserves (from $35) while people-watching at one of the outdoor tables. Ali Oli also offers breakfasts (from $20) and set lunches (from $35).

HONEYMOON DESSERT
Map p130 Chinese Desserts $
☎ 2792 4991; www.honeymoon-dessert.com; 9, 10A, B&C Po Tung Rd; per person $30; ☽ 1pm-2.45am
This dessert shop specialising in Chinese desserts such as sweet walnut soup and durian pudding is so successful that it's got branches all over China and in Indonesia,

EATING NEW TERRITORIES

not to mention some 20 locations in Hong Kong, including Sheung Wan (Map p80; ☎ 2851 2606; Shop 4-8, Ground fl, Western Market, 323 Des Voeux Rd Central; ☺ noon-midnight; MTR Sheung Wan, exit C) and Causeway Bay (Map p85; ☎ 2881 8336; Shop 423, Podium 4, World Trade Centre, 280 Gloucester Rd; ☺ 1-11.30pm Sun-Thu, 1pm-midnight Fri & Sat; MTR Causeway Bay, exit A).

LARDOS STEAK HOUSE

Map pp58-9   Steakhouse $$

☎ 2719 8168; 4B Hang Hau Village, Tseung Kwan O; set lunch $65; ☺ noon-3pm, 6pm-10.30am Mon-Fri, noon-10.30pm Sat & Sun; MTR Hang Hau (exit B), minibus 11 to Hang Hou Village
If you're in Tseung Kwan O, this tiny steakhouse owned by a seasoned meat supplier is your best option for a meal. The succulent chunks of meat are attractively priced ($239 for a 16-oz T-bone steak).

SAI KUNG CAFE AND BAKERY

Map p130   Bakery $

☎ 2792 3861; 6-7 Hoi Pong Sq; ☺ 7am-10.30pm
The local alternative to Ali Oli above, this corner cafe sells sensational Hong Kong–style bread. When fresh from the oven, their pineapple buns ($6) are heavenly.

TAP MUN CHAU

You won't starve to death on remote Tap Mun, but you also won't have much choice in the way of venues. There's only one restaurant on this far-flung island, which technically belongs to the Tai Po District but is connected to Sai Kung by ferry.

NEW HON KEE

Map pp58-9   Cantonese, Seafood $

☎ 2328 2428; 4 Tap Mun Hoi Pong St; meals from $60; ☺ 11am-2pm Mon-Fri, 11am-4.30pm Sat & Sun; ⛴ Tap Mun ferry from Ma Liu Shui (MTR University)
This seafood restaurant, popular with islanders and visitors alike, is a short walk northeast of the ferry pier on the way to Tin Hau temple.

OUTLYING ISLANDS

Restaurants and other eateries vary widely from island to island. Some, like those on Lantau (and to a large extent Cheung Chau), are just convenient refuelling stations as you head for (or return from) your destination.

Others, such as the seafood restaurants in Lamma's Sok Kwu Wan (p202) or on Po Toi (p204), are destinations in their own right.

LAMMA

Lamma offers the greatest choice of restaurants and cuisines of any of the Outlying Islands. Most people head directly to Sok Kwu Wan for a fix of Cantonese seafood, but Yung Shue Wan, the most populated village, has a vast and eclectic range, and there are a couple of other venues elsewhere on the island that are worth the trip. The trail between Sok Kwu Wan and Yung Shue Wan, divided by a small hill, is popular among leisure hikers. The journey will take you through Hung Shing Yeh Beach.

Yung Shue Wan

Yung Shue Wan has a large choice of places for people to eat, mostly dispersed along its main (and only) street. To get here, take a ferry from Pier 4 in front of Exchange Square or from Aberdeen near the wholesale fish market.

BOOKWORM CAFÉ

Map p136   Cafe, Vegetarian $

☎ 2982 4838; www.bookwormcafe.com.hk; 79 Main St; ☺ 10am-9pm Mon-Fri, 9am-10pm Sat, 9am-9pm Sun; ⌨
This legendary place is not just a great vegetarian cafe-restaurant with fruit juices and organic wine ($35 per glass) but also a second-hand bookshop and an internet cafe.

DELI LAMMA CAFE

Map p136   Cafe $

☎ 2982 1583; 36 Main St; set lunch $70; ☺ 9am-2am
This relaxed cafe-restaurant serves everything, from continental fare to Indian and Mediterranean, with a fair few pasta dishes and pizzas. It has an excellent bar and views of the harbour.

LAMCOMBE SEAFOOD RESTAURANT

Map p136   Cantonese, Seafood $

☎ 2982 0881; 47 Main St; meals from $120; ☺ 11am-2.30pm, 5-10pm
Lamcombe has been serving up tasty fried squid and steamed scallops on the half-shell for over 10 years. Though slightly pricier than similar establishments nearby,

portions are big and the location is more rustic. Vegetarians will love the eggplant and tofu hotpot.

Hung Shing Yeh

This popular beach southeast of Yung Shue Wan, about 500m from the pier, has a waterfront hotel, Concerto Inn (Map p136; ☎ 2982 1668; 28 Hung Shing Yeh Beach; set dinner $88 ☯ 9-10.30am, noon-10pm), where you can have Western and Southeast Asian food on the terrace. You'll also find the famous Kin Hing Tofu Dessert (Map p136; Yung Shue Wan Back St; ☯ 10am-6pm Sat, Sun & public holidays) and pigeon restaurant Han Lok Yuen (Map p136; ☎ 2982 0608; 16-17 Hung Shing Yeh Wan; pigeon each $65; ☯ 11.30am-9pm).

Sok Kwu Wan

An evening meal at Sok Kwu Wan is an enjoyable way to end a trip to Lamma. The restaurants line the waterfront on either side of the ferry pier and will be chock-a-block on weekend nights with locals and expats who have arrived by ferry, on boats laid on by the restaurants themselves, on company junks or on private yachts. Most of the dozen or so restaurants offer the same relatively high-quality seafood at similar prices, but a few places stand out from the pack. There's a ferry service from Pier 4 in front of Exchange Square.

RAINBOW SEAFOOD RESTAURANT
Map p136   Chinese, Seafood $$
☎ 2982 8100; www.rainbowrest.com.hk; Shops 1A-1B, Ground fl, 23-25 First St; meals from $150; ☯ 10am-10.30pm
The Rainbow, with a waterfront location, specialises in seafood, especially steamed grouper, lobster and abalone. A plus is that when you book a table, you have the option of being transported by small ferry from Central Pier 9 and Tsim Sha Tsui Public Pier. Call or check the website for sailings.

TAI YUEN RESTAURANT
Map p136   Chinese, Seafood $
☎ 2982 8386, 2982 8391; 15 First St; ☯ 10am-11pm
This small, intimate place offers less frenetic, friendlier service than most of the other places in Sok Kwu Wan.

Mo Tat Wan

In this relatively remote corner of Lamma there's a slightly upmarket Western restaurant, the Bay (Map p136; ☎ 2982 8186; 7 Beach Front; mains $98-138; ☯ 11am-10pm; 🚢 from Aberdeen near the wholesale fish market).

LANTAU

The lion's share of Lantau's restaurants is in Mui Wo (Silvermine Bay), but you certainly won't starve in places further afield, such as the settlements along South Lantau Rd, on the Ngong Ping Plateau and in Tai O. Discovery Bay has its own line-up of eateries around Discovery Bay Plaza (Map p140).

Mui Wo

You'll find a slew of restaurants, noodle shops and bars to the southwest of the ferry pier. There are also some restaurants on the way to Silvermine Bay Beach and on the beach itself. There's a ferry service from Pier 6 in front of Exchange Square.

BAHÇE Map p143   Turkish $
☎ 2984 0222; Shop 19, Ground fl, Mui Wo Centre, 3 Ngan Wan Rd; kebabs from $90; ☯ 11am-10.30pm Mon-Fri, 9.30am-10.30pm Sat & Sun
'The Garden' might be a somewhat ambitious name for this small eatery, but it has all our Turkish favourites, including sigara böreği (filo parcels filled with cheese) and yaprak dolmasi (stuffed vine leaves).

CHUN CHUN Map p143   Chinese, Vietnamese $
☎ 294 7727; 35 Rural Committee Rd; meals under $40; ☯ 8.30am-5.30pm
Lantau residents have been coming for years to this modest joint for its excellent Vietnamese-style noodles flavoured with lemon grass. They're best consumed with ice-cold bottled Coke.

MUI WO COOKED FOOD CENTRE
Map p143   Chinese $
Just off the Mui Wo ferry pier to your right, there's a cooked food centre with a couple of stalls selling dim dum from 6am till late afternoon, where you need to get your own food from the kitchen counter. There are also a few seafood restaurants that open from afternoon till midnight with tables facing the sea.

TAK CHAI KEE Map p143   Dai Pai Dong, Seafood $
☎ 2984 1265; 1 Chung Hou Rd; ☯ 11am-10pm
At this family-run eatery, you can munch on fresh, affordable seafood (from $55)

while being entertained by the felines-in-residence.

Discovery Bay

The restaurants in the circular plaza opposite the ferry pier at Discovery Bay (Map p140) offer a wide variety of cuisines. There's a ferry service from Pier 3 in front of Exchange Square.

HEMINGWAY'S BY THE BAY
Map p140   Caribbean, Barbecue $$

☎ 2987 8855; www.hemingwaysdb.com; Shop G09, D Deck, Discovery Bay Plaza; ☾ 2pm-1am Mon-Fri, 10am-2am Sat & Sun; 🛳 Discovery Bay
It may not feel exactly like Havana here, but when the weather is clear, this beach-front restaurant makes for a great escape. You can even see the fireworks going off in Disneyland every evening from 8.30pm. Try the signature burger ($105) and the mojito ($72).

South Lantau Road

Cheung Sha and Tung Fuk, two of the villages along South Lantau Rd, Lantau's main east–west thoroughfare, have decent restaurants from which to choose.

GALLERY BAR & RESTAURANTS
Map p140   Barbecue $$

☎ 2980 2582; 26 Tong Fuk Village; ☾ 6-10.30pm Mon-Sat, noon-10.30pm Sun; 🚌 1, 2 or 3
This restaurant, on a terrace with an arbour overlooking South Lantau Rd, has great Mediterranean and Turkish dishes and a decent barbecue. Oven-baked thin-crust pizzas (from $85) are another must-try.

STOEP RESTAURANT
Map p140   Mediterranean, South African $$

☎ 2980 2699; 32 Lower Cheung Sha Village; ☾ 11am-10pm Tue-Sun; 🚌 1 or 2 from Mui Wo
This Mediterranean-style restaurant with a huge terrace that's located right on Lower Cheung Sha Beach has acceptable meat and fish dishes and a South African *braai* (barbecue; $90 to $150). Be sure to book on the weekend.

Ngong Ping

An artificial Chinese village has been built alongside Ngong Ping Skyrail, featuring a range of casual dining options that include noodle joints, fusion restaurants, Starbucks as well as a branch of Honeymoon Dessert (Map p140; see also p200). For some no-frills vegetarian treats, the Po Lin Monastery is only a short walk away.

PO LIN VEGETARIAN RESTAURANT
Map p140   Vegetarian $

☎ 2985 5248; Ngong Ping; set meals regular/ deluxe $60/100; ☾ 11.30am-4.30pm; 🚌 23 from Mui Wo
This famous monastery (p138) has a reputation for inexpensive but substantial vegetarian food. The restaurant is located in the covered arcade to the left of the main monastery building. Buy your ticket there or at the ticket office below the Tian Tan Buddha statue. Sittings take place every half-hour.

Tai O

Tai O, a village on the western coast, is famous for its excellent seafood restaurants, many of which display their names in Chinese only. Take bus 4 from Mui Wo.

CHEUNG CHAU

In Cheung Chau village, south of the cargo pier and at the start of Tai Hing Tai Rd, there are a number of food stalls with fish tanks where you can choose your finned or shelled creatures at more or less market prices and then pay the stallholders to cook them the way you like. Pak She Praya Rd, running northwest off Praya St, is loaded with seafood restaurants that face the typhoon shelter and its flotilla of junks and sampans. There's a ferry service from Pier 5 in front of Exchange Square.

HOMETOWN TEAHOUSE
Map p146   Cafe $

☎ 2981 5038; 12 Tung Wan Rd; ☾ 11.30am-9pm, closed days vary btwn 1 per week & 1 per fortnight
This idyllic place that is run by an amiable Japanese couple serves lunch and dinner, but the afternoon tea – sushi and red-bean pastries ($4) – is what you should come for.

NEW BACCARAT Map p146   Chinese, Seafood $
☎ 2981 0606; 9A Pak She Praya Rd; set meals from $138; ☾ 11am-10.30pm
This restaurant has been around for so long you have to believe it's doing

something right. Seafood-wise it serves everything from steamed fish to fried mantis shrimp.

WINDSURFING WATERSPORTS CENTRE & CAFE

Map p146   International $

☎ 2981 8316; www.ccwindc.com.hk; 1 Hak Pai Rd; ⏰ 10am-6pm

A favourite hangout of windsurfers and divers, this place is owned by Lai Gun, uncle of the champion windsurfer Lee Lai-shan who won Olympic gold for Hong Kong in Atlanta. On a balmy afternoon, this cafe is a great spot to relax over fries ($25), fish steak ($65) and a bottle of wine ($180).

PENG CHAU

There are a couple of local Chinese stores that serve up instant noodles and sandwiches near the waterfront. Take a ferry from Pier 6 in front of Exchange Square.

PO TOI

MING KEE SEAFOOD RESTAURANT

Map pp58-9   Chinese, Seafood $$

☎ 2849 7038; ⏰ 11am-11pm; 🚢 Po Toi ferry from Ma Liu Shui (University KCR)

This is one of a handful of restaurants in the main village of Po Toi Island, south of Hong Kong Island, and is by far the most popular with day-trippers. Make sure you book ahead on the weekend.

ENTERTAINMENT

top picks

- InterContinental Lobby Lounge (p214)
- Tastings (see the boxed text on p211)
- Drop (p216)
- Gecko Lounge (p210)
- Yumla (p217)
- Pawn (p212)

Hong Kong knows to party hard and does so visibly and noisily. The clubbing and bar scenes are as busy as ever and the creative destruction being visited on some venues by the economic turmoil has cleared space for some exciting new bars and nightspots.

It may be less voluble but the arts scene is also healthier than ever. Beyond the neon of the bars of Wan Chai or Central the increasingly busy cultural calendar includes drama, Cantonese opera, dance and live music.

Most weeks, half a dozen local arts companies perform anything from Cantonese opera to English-language versions of Chekhov plays. Locally cultivated drama and dance are among the most enjoyable in Asia, and the schedule of foreign performances is often stellar.

Nightlife Strips & Districts

If you want to cut down your options for a night out, narrow your search to Hong Kong Island's north shore along the area between Wan Chai in the east and Soho to the west.

This area has the lion's share of the territory's most popular pubs, bars and clubs, plus the cultural venues of Central and Wan Chai, so classical music concerts, theatre, opera and the like are within easy striking distance.

Much of Central's fun nightlife revolves around the now-legendary Lan Kwai Fong and the streets immediately above and to the west of it. During busy times it can be full to bursting. Lan Kwai Fong's clientele tends to be young, hip, cashed up and increasingly Chinese as well as expatriate. It's huge fun if you're in the mood for revelry, but it can be a bit of a circus and arguably the better bars these days are to be found elsewhere.

Geared more to dining than drinking, Soho is worth a look for more intimate venues; it's just a short journey away on foot or via the Central Escalator up the hill. The extent of the bar district is stretching ever further west towards Sheung Wan these days.

While Wan Chai remains a byword for sleaze (and a longstanding port of call for American sailors and GIs since the Vietnam War) it has cleaned its act up of late. Much of the western part of the district offers lively, respectable bars, although hostess bars still line Lockhart Rd. What might be dubbed old Wan Chai, further inland behind the tram tracks, is becoming another little epicentre of fine dining and sophisticated drinking (check out the Pawn, p212), making it an area well worth exploring.

Pickings get thinner the further east you go from here, but there are a few nightspots in Causeway Bay and Quarry Bay.

While Kowloon may play second fiddle to Hong Kong Island, if you head back from the bustle of Nathan Rd there are some great little bar areas, not least the karaoke bar scene around Minden Rd and a more touristy, but no less buzzy, food-and-drink ghetto along Knutsford Terrace in the north of Tsim Sha Tsui.

What's On

Several freebies offer up-to-date listings, including HK Magazine (www.asia-city.com), a comprehensive entertainment magazine that also has articles on current trends and reviews of restaurants and bars. It appears on Friday and can be picked up at restaurants, bars, shops and hotels throughout the territory.

Also worth checking out is bc magazine (www.bcmagazine.net), a fortnightly guide to Hong Kong's entertainment and partying scene. One of the most useful features in this highly visual and glossy publication is its complete listing of bars and clubs. It is also free and can usually be found alongside copies of HK Magazine.

Time Out (www.time-out.com.hk) magazine, meanwhile, offers more polished and extensive fortnightly coverage of the entertainment scene online and in print (HK$18).

The Hong Kong Arts Centre (www.hkac.org.hk) publishes Artslink, a monthly with listings of performances, exhibitions and art-house film screenings. Another invaluable source of information is the monthly Artmap (www.artmap.com.hk), a map with listings that's available free at venues throughout the territory.

Tickets & Reservations

Expect to pay around $70 for a seat up the back for the Hong Kong Philharmonic and from about $500 and up for a performance by big-name international acts or an international musical such as Chicago. Bookings for most cultural events can be made by telephone or the internet with Urbtix (☎ 2111 5999; http://urbtix.cityline .com.hk; ☯ 10am-8pm). There are Urbtix windows at the Hong Kong City Hall (Map p67; ☯ 10am-9.30pm) in Central, Queen Elizabeth Stadium (Map p74) in Wan Chi and the Hong Kong Cultural Centre (Map p104) in Tsim Sha Tsui. The Fringe Theatre and the Academy for Performing Arts use HK Ticketing (☎ 3128 8288; www.hkticketing.com).

You can also book tickets for many films and concerts and a great variety of cultural events over the phone or online through City-line (☎ 2317 6666; www.cityline.com.hk).

DRINKING

Drinking venues in Hong Kong run the gamut from British-style pubs to flashy style bars and tiny karaoke boltholes aimed at a young Cantonese clientele. Quite a few bars also serve food, blurring the line between drinking joint and restaurant. Much of Hong Kong's nightlife takes place in top-end hotels where inventive cocktails, skilled bar staff and some of the best views in town attract visitors and locals.

Depending on where you go, beer costs at least $45 a pint (though it's cheaper at happy hour). Overall, Central and Soho offer the best areas to explore for bars. The pubs in Wan Chai are cheaper and more relaxed, and those in Tsim Sha Tsui tend to attract more locals than visitors.

Opening Hours

Bars generally open at noon or 6pm and close anywhere between 2am and 6am. Wan Chai bars stay open the latest.

HAPPY HOUR

During certain hours of the day, most pubs, bars and even certain clubs give discounts on drinks (usually from a third to half off) or offer two-for-one deals. Happy hour is usually in the late afternoon or early evening – 4pm to 8pm, say – but the times vary widely from place to place. Depending on the season, the day of the week and the location, some pubs' happy hours run from noon until as late as 10pm, and some start up again after midnight.

HONG KONG ISLAND
Central

CAPTAIN'S BAR Map p67   Bar
☎ 2522 0111; Ground fl, Mandarin Oriental, 5 Connaught Rd Central; ☯ 11am-2am Mon-Sat, 11am-1am Sun; MTR Central (exit F)
This is a clubby, suited place that serves ice-cold draught beer in chilled silver mugs, as well as some of the best martinis in town. This is a good place to talk business, at least until the cover band strikes up at 9pm. Dress is smart casual (no shorts or sandals).

MO BAR Map p67   Bar
☎ 2132 0077; Landmark, 15 Queen's Rd, Central; ☯ 11am-2am Mon-Sat; MTR Central (exit D1)
If you want style and substance, the swish MO Bar, attached to the Mandarin's new swanky outpost, offers a luxurious, softly lit setting, great service and first-rate wines and cocktails.

BOOZE-FREE DRINKING HAVENS

If you're after non-alcoholic refreshment or you want to avoid the ambience of a bar, there are plenty of choices in the main urban areas, beyond the ubiquitous outlets of chain cafes. Here are some favourites:

Lobby Lounge (Map p106; ☎ 2733 8740; Kowloon Shangri-La Hotel, 64 Mody Rd, Tsim Sha Tsui East; ☯ 7am-midnight) Not strictly alcohol-free, but this spacious lobby's spectacular tapestries, comfy sofas and muted earth tones are the perfect place to enjoy a tea or booze-free cocktail to the soothing accompaniment of a string quartet.

Mix (Map p67; ☎ 2843 2128; 3/F Two Exchange Square; Central; MTR Central) Being healthy in Hong Kong has become just that bit easier thanks to the spread of these excellent fresh juice bars across town. They also offer free internet access.

Naturo + (Map p72; ☎ 2865 0388; 6 Sun St, Wan Chai; snacks from $35; ☯ 9am-6pm) If the weather's fine head to this leafy Wan Chai haven and take your tea, coffee and a select range of snacks, including wonderful Tibetan yak cheesecake, outside under the trees.

Salon de Thé de Joël Robuchon (Map p67; ☎ 2544 2237; Shop 315, Landmark 34F, Central; cakes from $35; ☯ 8am-8pm) If you want an inexpensive slice of this famed chef's high-end food, try the salted caramel tarts or other pastries served with fine teas in this annexe to the restaurant upstairs.

RED BAR Map p67   Bar
☎ 8129 8882; L4, Two IFC, 8 Finance St, Central;
🕑 noon-midnight Mon-Thu, noon-3am Fri & Sat,
noon-10pm Sun; MTR Hong Kong (exit F)
Red Bar's combination of alfresco drinking and harbour views is hard to beat on
Hong Kong Island. DJs playing funk and
jazz turn up the volume as the weekend
approaches.

Lan Kwai Fong & Soho

BAR 1911 Map p78   Bar
☎ 2810 6681; 27 Staunton St, Soho; 🕑 5pm-
midnight Mon-Sat, happy hour 5-9pm Mon-Sat; 🚌 26
This is a refined bar with fine details
(stained glass, burlwood bar, ceiling fan)
and a 1920s Chinese vibe. It's usually a tad
less crowded than nearby competitors,

which makes it a great haven from the
hubbub of the 'Fong.

BARCO Map p78   Bar
☎ 2857 4478; 42 Staunton St, Soho; 🕑 4pm-1am
Sun-Thu, 4pm-late Fri & Sat, happy hour 4-8pm;
MTR Central
One of our favourite Soho bars, Barco has
great staff, is small enough to never feel
empty, and attracts a cool mix of locals
and expats.

BIT POINT Map p78   Bar
☎ 2523 7436; Ground fl, 31 D'Aguilar St; 🕑 noon-
3am Mon-Fri, noon-4am Sat, 4pm-2am Sun, happy
hour 4-9pm; MTR Central (exit D2)
Owned by the same lot as Biergarten (p214),
Bit Point is essentially a German-style bar
where beer drinking is taken very seriously.

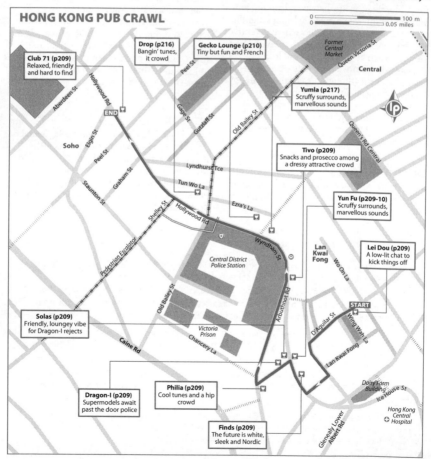

HONG KONG PUB CRAWL

Club 71 (p209)
Relaxed, friendly
and hard to find

Drop (p216)
Bangin' tunes,
it crowd

Gecko Lounge (p210)
Tiny but fun and French

Former
Central
Market

Central

Yumla (p217)
Scruffy surrounds,
marvellous sounds

Soho

Tivo (p209)
Snacks and prosecco among
a dressy attractive crowd

Yun Fu (p209-10)
Scruffy surrounds,
marvellous sounds

Lei Dou (p209)
A low-lit chat to
kick things off

Lan
Kwai
Fong

Central District
Police Station

START

Solas (p209)
Friendly, loungey vibe
for Dragon-I rejects

Victoria
Prison

Dragon-I (p209)
Supermodels await
past the door police

Philia (p209)
Cool tunes and a hip
crowd

Dairy Farm
Building

Hong Kong
Central
Hospital

Finds (p209)
The future is white,
sleek and Nordic

Most beers here are draught pilsners that you can get in a glass boot if you have a thirst big enough to kick. Bit Point also serves some pretty solid Teutonic fare.

CLUB 71 Map p67 Bar
☎ 2858 7071; Basement, 67 Hollywood Rd, Central; ⏰ 3pm-2am Mon-Sat, 6pm-1am Sun, happy hour 3-9pm; 🚌 26
This friendly place occupying a quiet, tucked-away alley north of Hollywood Rd is named after the huge protest march held on 1 July 2003. It's a quiet spot with a pleasant little terrace, ideal for some low-key beers among its left-field customers. Find it by taking a sharp right down a narrow alley off Hollywood Rd or via a small footpath running west off Peel St.

FINDS Map p78 Bar
☎ 2522 9318; www.finds.com.hk; 2nd fl, LKF Tower, 33 Wyndham St, Central; ⏰ noon-late Mon-Sat; MTR Central (exit D2)
Scandinavian food and drink is the theme at this elegant 'scapas' (Scandinavian tapas) bar commanding a prime spot above teeming Lan Kwai Fong. There's a fine range of Scandinavian spirits, including some fantastic Finnish Akavit-style firewater. There's a small balcony if it's a fine night.

LA DOLCE VITA Map p78 Bar
☎ 2186 1888; Cosmos Bldg, 9-11 Lan Kwai Fong Lane; ⏰ 11am-2am Mon-Thu, 11.30am-3am Fri, 2pm-3am Sat, 2pm-1am Sun, happy hour 5.30-8pm; MTR Central (exit D2)
This is a popular place for post-work brews, with room to prop on the heart-shaped bar or stand on the terrace and watch the preening mob crawl by.

LEI DOU Map p78 Bar
☎ 2525 6628; 20-22 D'Aguilar St, Lan Kwai Fong; ⏰ 5pm-2am, happy hour 6-8pm; MTR Central (exit D2)
A calm art-nouveau-styled oasis on the edge of the Lan Kwai Fong revelry, relaxed Lei Dou is ideal if you want to chat and sip rather than rage and swill. The mellow music is at conversational levels.

PEAK CAFE BAR Map p78 Bar
☎ 2140 6877; 9-13 Shelley St, Soho; ⏰ 11am-2am Mon-Sat, 11am-midnight Sun, happy hour 5-8pm; 🚌 13, 26, 40M

The fixtures and fittings of the much-missed Peak Cafe, from 1947, have moved down the hill to this comfy bar with super cocktails and excellent nosh. The only thing missing is the view.

PHILIA Map p78 Bar
☎ 2147 2389; 4-8 Arbuthnot Rd, Central; ⏰ 5pm-late Mon-Sat; MTR Central (exit D2)
A short escalator ride from the throngs along Wyndham St, intimate Philia caters to a hip crowd of 20-something music lovers. Depending on the night, the DJ will be playing rare hip hop, jazz, edgy house, electro or indie music you can dance to.

SOLAS Map p78 Bar
☎ 9154 4049; www.solas.com.hk; 60 Wyndham St, Central; ⏰ noon-2am Mon-Sat; MTR Central (exit D2)
Nearby Tivo (below) may have the edge for its drinks list and evening nibbles, but this relaxed, friendly place, with punchy cocktails and a DJ playing cool lounge sounds, isn't a bad plan B.

TIVO Map p78 Bar
☎ 2116 8055; www.aqua.com.hk; 43-55 Wyndham St, Central; ⏰ noon-2am Mon-Sat; MTR Central (exit D2)
One of the best of a lively little string of bars along lively Wyndham St, Tivo is a cut above the peanuts and beer standard of the 'Fong, just around the corner. Wine, *aperitivo* (Italian pre-dinner snacks) and an often glamorous crowd make a winning combination.

DRAGON-I Map p78 Bar, Club
☎ 3110 1222; www.dragon-i.com.hk; Upper Ground fl, the Centrium, 60 Wyndham St; ⏰ noon-midnight Mon-Sat, happy hour 3-9pm Mon-Sat (terrace); 🚌 26
This fabulous venue on the edge of Soho serves as club, indoor bar and restaurant, with a terrace over Wyndham St filled with caged songbirds. The door policy isn't usually as exclusive as it used to be, although it still doesn't hurt to be a rock star or starlet.

YUN FU Map p78 Bar, Restaurant
☎ 2116 8855; www.aqua.com.hk; Basement, 43-55 Wyndham St, Central; ⏰ noon-2am Mon-Sat; MTR Central (exit D2)
Look out for the Chinese characters before you reach Tivo and descend to this

tiny but delightful circular bar. The fantastical Imperial China theming is actually part of the pioneering restaurant of the same name, but even if you're not dining, it's well worth stopping for one of the fresh fruit cocktails and to soak up the sounds coming from the DJ's tiny cubby hole.

SOHO WINES & SPIRITS

Map p78   Food & Drink

☎ 2530 1182; 37 Staunton St; 🚌 26
Its name notwithstanding, this place's forte is its large selection of beer and spirits. If it's not here, it probably isn't made or consumed any longer. Its prices tend to be keen, thanks to the shop's hospitality-trade wholesaling business.

GECKO LOUNGE

Map p78   Lounge, Wine Bar

☎ 2537 4680; Lower Ground fl, 15-19 Hollywood Rd; 🕒 4pm-2am Mon-Thu, 4pm-4am Fri & Sat, happy hour 6-9pm; MTR Central (exit D1)
Entered from narrow Ezra's Lane off Co-chrane or Pottinger Sts, Gecko is an intimate lounge and wine bar run by a friendly French sommelier and wine importer with a penchant for absinthe. The well-hidden DJ mixes good sounds with kooky Parisian tunes, and there's usually live music on Tuesday and Wednesday. Great wine list, obviously.

WHISKEY PRIEST Map p78   Pub

☎ 2869 0099; Ground & 1st fl, 12 Lan Kwai Fong; 🕒 4pm-1am Tue-Thu, 4pm-3am Fri & Sat, noon-1am Sun, happy hour 4-10pm Mon-Sat, noon-1pm Sun; MTR Central (exit D2)
The first, and so far only, Irish pub (hence the 'e' in 'whiskey') to hit Lan Kwai Fong has Guinness, Kilkenny and Harp on tap, and 60 types of whiskey.

STAUNTON'S WINE BAR & CAFÉ

Map p78   Wine Bar

☎ 2973 6611; 10-12 Staunton St, Soho; 🕒 10am-2am Mon-Fri, 8am-2am Sat & Sun, happy hour 5-9pm; 🚌 26
Staunton's, on the corner of Shelley St, is swish, cool and on the ball with decent wine, a Central Escalator–cruising scene and a lovely terrace. If you're hungry, there's light fare downstairs and a fabulously remodelled international restaurant above.

Sheung Wan

SPARKZ Map p80   Bar

☎ 2127 7533; 18 Gough St, Central; 🕒 11am-late Mon-Sun; MTR Central (exit A), 🚌 26
Run by a former sommelier, Sparkz' back-lit bottles of wine lining the walls and the comfortable seating say it all – it's about wine, boasting 150 different varieties. It's a cosy place for a drink and a chat among a well-heeled professional crowd.

CAGE Map p80   Bar, Restaurant

☎ 2816 6739; 3 Mee Lun St, NoHo; 🕒 6pm-late Mon-Sat, happy hour 7-9pm Mon-Sat; 🚌 26
Escape the crowds at this endearingly decorated (including some antique bird cages) and intimate newcomer, which boasts two outdoor terraces overlooking quiet streets in a charming little corner of Sheung Wan.

Wan Chai

Wan Chai now has two nightlife areas worth exploring. The busier and more established occupies the western ends of Jaffe and Lock-hart Rds; the other is a small but burgeoning food-and-bar enclave springing up in 'old' Wanchai, further inland. Check out the bars and dining spots in and around the Ship St area – including the excellent the Pawn (p212) – close to the tram tracks, as well as the area around St Francis, Wing Fung and Star Sts further west towards Pacific Pl.

BAR 109 Map p74   Bar

☎ 2861 3336; 109 Lockhart Rd; 🕒 noon-3am, happy hour 3-9pm; MTR Wan Chai (exit C)
Tired of rubbing, er, shoulders with working girls in the Wanch? Well, even if not, the 109 will give you 110 reasons to flock here. It's a serious chill-out zone cobbled from a 1920s-vintage bakery and divided into three sections, including a bar, a covered 'outside' area and a 1st-floor balcony.

BRIDGE Map p74   Bar

☎ 2865 5586; Shops A-B, 1st fl, Beverly House, 93-107 Lockhart Rd, Wan Chai; 🕒 24hr, happy hour noon-10pm; MTR Wan Chai (exit C)
This large and airy bar, with great windows overlooking the frenzy of Lockhart Rd, is open 24 hours, serving cocktails to the denizens and the doomed of Wan Chai. It's less frenetic than most of its neighbours.

CHAMPAGNE BAR Map p74 — Bar

☎ 2588 1234 ext 7321; Ground fl, Grand Hyatt Hotel, 1 Harbour Rd, Wan Chai; ☽ 5pm-2am; MTR Wan Chai (exit A1)

Take your fizz in the sumptuous surrounds of the Grand Hyatt's Champagne Room, kitted out in art deco furnishings to evoke Paris of the 1920s. Live blues or jazz happens most evenings and the circular main bar is always busy.

CHINATOWN Map p74 — Bar

☎ 2861 3588; 78-82 Jaffe Rd, Wan Chai; ☽ noon-2.30am, happy hour noon-6pm; MTR Wan Chai (exit C)

The kitsch Chinese Brothel theming may sound a tad over the top, but fear not: this is nothing like one of the nearby go-go bars. The soft lighting and large red lanterns actually combine to make this one of the more relaxed Wan Chai watering holes. It's busy but seldom frantic, and the service from cheongsam-wearing waitresses is swift and friendly.

MES AMIS Map p74 — Bar

☎ 2527 6680; 81-85 Lockhart Rd, Wan Chai; ☽ noon-2am Sun-Thu, noon-6am Fri & Sat, happy hour 4-9pm; MTR Wan Chai (exit C)

This easy-going place is in the lap of girly club land. It has a good range of wines as well as a Mediterranean-style snacks list. There's a DJ from 11pm on Friday and Saturday. There's also another branch in

---

GRAPE EXPECTATIONS

Wealthier drinkers in Hong Kong have long been eager to splash out on fine wine, but more than ever wine has become the white-collar drink of choice here. Restaurants increasingly trade on their wine lists, hiring sommeliers in ever-greater numbers, while the number of wine shops has grown markedly in the last few years.

This is thanks, in part, to the government's decision to remove all taxes on wine imports, giving the city's wine industry something to cheer about. While some grumble that not all those savings seem to have been passed on to shoppers and drinkers, prices have been creeping down and there are excellent deals out there during happy hour in the bars, and lately also in the bottle shops, which have been forced to price more keenly thanks to a sluggish economy.

One of the most exciting new developments for wine lovers is the arrival of new bars offering tastings of premium wines using new 'enomatic' technology that permits them to open a bottle and preserve the contents indefinitely. It means that tasting a seriously rare (and expensive) wine is possible without completely bankrupting yourself. You create a tab by handing over your credit card in exchange for a smart card, which you use to operate the wine dispensing machines, which can deliver a few millilitres for an inexpensive taste or a full glass once you've made your choice.

Want to sample the finest wines known to humanity? Hong Kong is the place to do it.

Try…

Tastings (Map p78; ☎ 2523 6282; Basement, Yuen Yick Bldg, 27 & 29 Wellington St, Central; ☽ noon-late; MTR Central exit D2) Down a narrow side street just off Wellington St, Tastings offers about two dozen wines from its enomatic marvels, including some seriously high-end reds. Good service and advice are on hand.

Watson's Wine Cellar (Map p78; ☎ 2537 6998; Lower Ground fl, 1-13 D'Aguilar St; MTR Central, exit D2) More centred on sales than a place to socialise, Watson's enomatic machines enable you to try wine before you head into the attached shop to buy. Knowledgeable staff will assist in the shop, but leave you to get on with the machines and tastings in the cellar itself.

…Then Buy

Les Q (Map p72; ☎ 2466 8463; St Francis St, Wan Chai; MTR Central) French wine is the passion of Les Q's manager and ex-sommelier, hence the focused selection of it here.

Margaret River Wine Shop (Map p72; ☎ 2575 6770; Ground fl, 3 St Francis St, Wan Chai) Excellent Australian wines from the Margaret River region, expertly chosen and recommended by the knowledgeable owner in this ever-smarter corner of Wan Chai.

Oliver's the Delicatessen (Map p67; ☎ 2810 7710; 2nd fl, Princes Bldg, Central; MTR Central) A good, well-located alternative to specialists such as Watson's, this foodie haven offers a solid selection of fine wines and champagnes.

Ponti Wine Cellars (Map p67; ☎ 2810 1000; Basement, Alexandra House, 16-20 Chater Rd, Central; MTR Central) Sells premium and boutique wines from around the world.

Tsim Sha Tsui (Map p104; ☎ 2730 3038; 15 Ashley Rd; ☾ noon-2am Sun-Thu, noon-3am Fri & Sat, happy hour 4-9pm).

OLD CHINA HAND Map p74   Bar
☎ 2865 4378; 104 Lockhart Rd, Wan Chai; ☾ 8am-5am, happy hour noon-10pm; MTR Wan Chai (exit C)

This place is hardly recognisable as the gloomy old dive where the desperate-to-drink (no one we know) used to find themselves unhappy but never alone at 3am. Now it has a generous happy hour, internet access and cheap set lunches.

SKITZ Map p74   Bar
☎ 2866 3277; www.skitzbar.com; 5th fl, Phoenix Bldg, 21-25 Luard Rd, Wan Chai; MTR Wan Chai (exit C)

Hong Kong's most convenient sports bar screens big sporting events on its massive plasmas. There are also pool tables and dartboards, and (depending on the night) a DJ on the decks.

DELANEY'S Map p74   Bar, Pub
☎ 2804 2880; Ground & 1st fl, One Capital Place, 18 Luard Rd, Wan Chai; ☾ noon-2.30am Sun-Thu, noon-3am Fri & Sat, happy hour noon-9pm; MTR Wan Chai (exit C)

At this immensely popular Irish watering hole you can choose between the black-and-white-tiled pub on the ground floor and a sports bar and restaurant on the 1st

floor. The food is good and plentiful; the kitchen allegedly goes through 400kg of potatoes a week. There's also a branch on Peking Rd in Tsim Sha Tsui (p214).

CLASSIFIED Map p72   Bar, Restaurant
☎ 2528 3454; 31 Wing Fung St; ☾ 5pm-2am; MTR Admiralty (exit F)

This tiny little bar with a large, scrubbed wood table opens right onto the street and styles itself as a mozzarella bar. It's an ideal place to quaff a glass of wine accompanied by a few slices of quality cheese.

PAWN Map p74   Bar, Restaurant
☎ 2866 3444; 62 Johnston Rd, Wan Chai; ☾ 11am-late; MTR Wan Chai (exit B2)

Downstairs from the Pawn's gastropub, the beaten-up sofas with space to sprawl, plus great little terrace spaces overlooking the tram tracks, make the ideal location to sample a great selection of lagers, bitters and wine at this excellent Wan Chai newcomer.

DEVIL'S ADVOCATE Map p74   Pub
☎ 2865 7271; 48-50 Lockhart Rd, Wan Chai; ☾ noon-late Mon-Sat, 1pm-late Sun, happy hour noon-10pm; MTR Wan Chai (exit C)

This pleasant pub in the thick of things is as relaxed as they come. The bar spills onto the pavement and staff are charming. 'Devilling Hour' (5pm to 7pm) is even cheaper than happy hour, and there are cheap drinks on Wednesday night.

GAY HONG KONG

Hong Kong's once rather hangdog gay scene gets better by the year with smart new bars and clubs catering to an increasingly discerning set of customers.

While it may not have the vibrancy or wider-scale visibility of cities like Sydney, the scene has made huge strides in recent years. Two decades ago, when homosexual acts between consenting adults over the age of 21 (it's 16 for heterosexuals and lesbians) were finally decriminalised, it had no more than a couple of grotty speakeasies.

Today Hong Kong counts more than two dozen bars and clubs – with more than a third in Central and Tsim Sha Tsui – and just as many gay-oriented saunas scattered throughout the territory. Grab a copy of G, a bimonthly gay-centric listings publication brought to you by the same people who publish HK Magazine, or check out the GayStation (www.gaystation.com.hk) or Gay HK (www.gayhk.com) websites. Some places to check out:

DYMK (Map p67; ☎ 2868 0626; 16 Arbuthnot Rd, Central; ☾ 6pm-4am; MTR Central, exit D2) An excellent, upmarket gay-friendly newcomer, DYMK (or 'does your mother know?') caters to a discerning crowd of professionals who lounge in the dimly but stylishly lit booths. There's an extensive wine list and cocktails including the Thai Me Up and the Pinch My Peach. Reach it through the basement staircase in Eden, the organic bistro next door.

New Wally Matt Lounge (Map p104; ☎ 2721 2568; www.wallymatt.com; 5A Humphreys Ave; ☾ 5pm-4am, happy hour 5-10pm; MTR Tsim Sha Tsui, exit A2) The name comes from the old Waltzing Matilda pub, which was one of the daggiest gay watering holes in creation. But New Wally Matt is an upbeat and busy place and actually more a pub than a lounge.

Causeway Bay

BRECHT'S CIRCLE Map p85   Bar
☎ 2576 4785; www.brechts.net; Ground fl, Rita House, 123 Leighton Rd; 4pm-2am Mon-Thu, 4pm-4am Fri & Sat, happy hour 4-8pm Mon-Sat; MTR Causeway Bay (exit F)
A small and fairly unusual bar with an arty edge, Brecht's is given more to intimate, cerebral conversation than raging. Thankfully the decor has been upgraded to this century.

DICKENS BAR Map p85   Bar
☎ 2837 6782; Basement, Excelsior Hong Kong, 281 Gloucester Rd; 11am-1am Sun-Thu, 11am-2am Fri & Sat, happy hour 5-8pm; MTR Causeway Bay (exit D1)
This place has been popular with expats and Hong Kong Chinese for decades. In truth the atmosphere is nothing special and the real draw is the big-screen sports coverage.

EXECUTIVE BAR Map p85   Bar
☎ 2893 2080; 7th fl, Bartlock Centre, 3 Yiu Wa St, Causeway Bay; 5pm-1am Mon-Sat; MTR Causeway Bay (exit A)
You won't be served if you just turn up at this clubby, masculine bar high above Causeway Bay – it's by appointment only. Odd perhaps, but worth the trip if you are serious about whisky and bourbon. Several dozen varieties are served here, in large brandy balloons with huge ice 'cubes' designed by the Japanese proprietor to maximise the tasting experience.

EAST END BREWERY & INN SIDE OUT Map p85   Pub
☎ 2895 2900; Ground fl, Sunning Plaza, 10 Hysan Ave; 11.30am-1am Sun-Thu, 11.30am-1.30am Fri & Sat, happy hour 2.30-8.30pm; MTR Causeway Bay (exit F)
These two related pubs flank a central covered terrace where you can while away the hours on a warm evening, sipping beers and throwing peanut shells on the ground. East End has imported microbrews, and also has a branch at Quarry Bay (below).

Island East & Island South

EAST END BREWERY Map pp62-3   Bar
☎ 2811 1907; 23-27 Tong Chong St, Quarry Bay; 11.30am-2am, happy hour 4-8pm; MTR Quarry Bay (exit B)
This place out in Quarry Bay is a beer lover's must-visit. You can choose from more than 30 beers and lagers from around the world, including a couple of local microbrews. There's wi-fi access, too. The branch at Causeway Bay (above) serves up much the same beer and fodder if you can't make it this far out.

PARADISO LOUNGE Map pp62-3   Bar
☎ 2809 2080; Ground fl, Government Bldg, Shek O Main Beach, Shek O; noon-1am; 9
If you want to drink with the sand between your toes and a towel around your waist, this relaxed beach spot, with a marine theme including a fish tank and sea shells,

---

Propaganda (Map p78; ☎ 2868 1316; Lower Ground fl, 1 Hollywood Rd, Central; 9pm-4am Tue-Thu, 9pm-6am Fri & Sat, happy hour 9pm-1.30am Tue-Thu; MTR Central, exit D2) Despite more gay-friendly venues out there today, Propaganda remains Hong Kong's default gay dance club and meat market. It's free from Tuesday to Thursday, but cover charges ($120 to $160) apply on Friday and Saturday (which also get you into Works, below, on Friday). Enter from Ezra's Lane, which runs between Pottinger and Cochrane Sts.

Tony's Bar (Map p104; ☎ 2723 2726; www.tonys-bar.com; Ground fl, 7-9 Bristol Ave; 5.30pm-4am, happy hour 5.30-10pm; MTR Tsim Sha Tsui, exit D2) This low-key, anonymous and – it has to be said – very down-at-heel gay-friendly bar just behind Mirador Mansion (see the boxed text, p242) is a relaxed place to come for a drink, with none of that 'last chance for romance' tension found in some other gay venues.

Volume (Map p80; ☎ 2857 7683; 83-85 Hollywood Rd, Central; 6pm-4am, happy hour 7.30-9.30pm; 26) This swanky, kitsch, mirror-lined, late-night cocktail bar pumps out a range of sounds, from cheesy '80s hits to cutting-edge dance genres, to a mixed crowd of gay and expat locals.

Works (Map p78; ☎ 2868 6102; 1st fl, 30-32 Wyndham St, Central; 7pm-2am, happy hour 7-10.30pm Mon-Fri; MTR Central, exit D2) Sister club to Propaganda (above), Works is where most gay boyz out on the town start the evening, and sees some heavy FFFR (file-for-future-reference) cruising till it's time to move on to the P. There's a cover charge ($60 to $100) on the weekend.

will oblige. At night it gets dressier and the dance floor fills up.

SMUGGLERS INN Map p96 · Pub
☎ 2813 8852; Ground fl, 90A Stanley Main St, Stanley; ⏰ 10am-2am, happy hour 6-9pm; 🚌 6, 6A, 6X or 260
This scruffy but good-natured place is arguably the most popular pub on the Stanley waterfront, offering perhaps the closest thing to an English pub in Hong Kong.

KOWLOON
Tsim Sha Tsui

FELIX Map p104 · Bar
☎ 2315 3188; 28th fl, Peninsula Hong Kong, Salisbury Rd; ⏰ 6pm-2am; MTR Tsim Sha Tsui (exit E)
Enjoy the fabulous view at this Philippe Starck–designed bar in Hong Kong's poshest hotel. Guys, the view from the urinals in the gents' is just one reason to fill your bladders.

SPASSO Map p104 · Bar, Restaurant
☎ 2730 8027; Level 4, Ocean Centre, Harbour City; ⏰ 6pm-2am, happy hour 5.30-7.30pm; ⛴ Star Ferry
Fantastic harbour views and alfresco drinking are the main reasons to head to this upmarket bar above Ocean Centre's vast shopping malls. The drinks list is long on cocktails and wine, less so on beer. Arrive early on weekends if you want to snag a spot outdoors.

DELANEY'S Map p104 · Pub
☎ 2301 3980; Basement, Mary Bldg, 71-77 Peking Rd; ⏰ 9am-3am, happy hour 5-9pm; MTR Tsim Sha Tsui (exit E)
This Irish-themed pub has lots of dark wood, green felt and a long bar that you can really settle into. It serves a decent pint of Guinness, too.

Tsim Sha Tsui East & Hung Hom

BALALAIKA Map p106 · Bar
☎ 2312 6222; 2nd fl, 10 Knutsford Tce, Tsim Sha Tsui; ⏰ 5pm-midnight Sun-Thu, 5pm-1am Fri & Sat; MTR Tsim Sha Tsui (exit B1)
Russian theming – from the dacha-style walls to the music, the food and, of course,

the vodka – set a fun tone here. Don a fur hat and coat and step into the ice bar if you really want to go to extremes.

BIERGARTEN Map p106 · Bar
☎ 2721 2302; 5 Hanoi Rd; ⏰ 10am-3am Mon-Fri, noon-2am Sat & Sun, happy hour 4-9pm; MTR Tsim Sha Tsui (exit G)
This clean, modern place rubbing shoulders with the expanding Minden Rd car and club hotspot has a jukebox full of hits (and misses) and Bitburger on tap. It's popular with visiting Germans and others who hanker after such hearty and filling nosh as pork knuckle and sauerkraut.

CHILLAX Map p106 · Bar
☎ 2722 4338; 8 Minden Ave; ⏰ 6pm-3am Mon-Sat; MTR Tsim Sha Tsui (exit G)
This tiny space lit by candles and mainly patronised by young locals is good for simply sitting, slumping and taking refuge from a day spent dodging through Tsim Sha Tsui. Things get livelier later when the DJ gets going.

DADA Map p106 · Bar
☎ 3763 8778; 2nd fl, Luxe Manor, 39 Kimberley Rd, Tsim Sha Tsui; ⏰ 11am-2am Mon-Sat, 11am-1am Sun; MTR Tsim Sha Tsui (exit X)
Upstairs in the strikingly styled Luxe Manor hotel, Dada is an attractive, intimate cocktail bar decked out with florid wallpaper, bold purple and silver, and a couple of real Dalí paintings. The crowd is creative, professional mid-30s and the vibe is jazzy.

INTERCONTINENTAL LOBBY LOUNGE Map p106 · Bar
☎ 2721 1211; 18 Salisbury Rd, Hotel InterContinental Hong Kong; ⏰ 24hr; MTR East Tsim Sha Tsui (exit J)
Soaring plate glass and an unbeatable waterfront location make this one of the best spots to soak up that Hong Kong Island skyline and take in the busy harbour, although you pay for the privilege. It's an ideal venue from which to watch the evening lightshow at 8pm.

MARTINI BAR Map p106 · Bar
☎ 2733 2995; Royal Garden Hotel, 69 Mody Rd; ⏰ noon-2am; MTR Tsim Sha Tsui East (exit P2)
In the plush Royal Garden Hotel, the Martini Bar is one of Hong Kong's premier cocktail lounges for well-mixed drinks and

swift service. Ideal for low-key drinks away from the crowds, it also boasts its own cigar lounge.

WHERE Map p106 — Bar

☎ 2135 9999; 4th fl, Century House, 3-4 Hanoi Rd; ⏰ 5pm-2am, happy hour 5-9pm; MTR Tsim Sha Tsui East (exit P3)

Occupying a floor above this increasingly interesting corner of TST, it's worth seeking this place out for its stylish white couches, softly lit interior, mellow music and leafy, spacious terrace, ideal for alfresco drinking. Look for the neon Hollywood Game Zone sign and take the lift up.

DECK 'N BEER Map p106 — Pub

☎ 2723 9227; Tsim Sha Tsui East Promenade; ⏰ 11am-1am, happy hour 5-9pm; MTR Tsim Sha Tsui (exit P1)

Offering exactly what it promises on its neon sign, this excellent new bar with no theme or fuss offers a deck, drinks including a good range of bottled beers and not much else – oh, apart from those spectacular waterfront views.

NEW TERRITORIES
Sai Kung Town

POETS Map p130 — Pub

☎ 2791 7993; 55 Yi Chun St; ⏰ 5pm-1am Mon-Fri, 3-4pm-2am Sat & Sun, happy hour noon-9pm Mon-Fri; 🚌 92, 299

This friendly workaday pub with literary aspirations is a pleasant place for a pint and serves typical pub meals, such as pies, chips and beans for $58.

DUKE Map p130 — Pub

☎ 2791 6255; Ground fl, 42-56 Fuk Man Rd; ⏰ noon-2am, happy hour noon-9pm Mon-Fri, noon-7pm Sat & Sun; 🚌 92, 299

This popular pub, just up from the waterfront, has darts, free pool and sports on the TV. Cocktails range from $35 to $60 and there's snack food, such as curried fish balls ($25) and marinated chicken kidney ($30).

OUTLYING ISLANDS
Lamma

Yung Shue Wan has several cosy waterfront boozers worth checking out, which serve very much a local crowd in the evenings (mostly expats). In theory you may have to sign a members' book, as some operate on club licences.

DIESEL'S BAR Map p136 — Bar

☎ 2982 4116; 51 Main St, Yung Shue Wan; ⏰ 6pm-late Mon-Fri, noon-late Sat & Sun, happy hour 6-9pm Mon-Fri; 🚢 Lamma (Yung Shue Wan)

This place next to the Lamma Bistro attracts punters with big-screen TV during sports matches.

FOUNTAINHEAD DRINKING BAR
Map p136 — Bar

☎ 2982 2118; 17 Main St, Yung Shue Wan; ⏰ 5pm-2am Mon-Fri, 3pm-4am Sat & Sun, happy hour all day Mon-Fri; 🚢 Lamma (Yung Shue Wan)

The cheerfully no-frills Fountainhead has a good mix of Chinese and expats in regular attendance, decent music and beer at affordable prices.

ISLAND SOCIETY BAR Map p136 — Bar

☎ 2982 1376; 6 Main St, Yung Shue Wan; ⏰ 6pm-late Mon-Fri, noon-late Sat & Sun, happy hour 4-8pm; 🚢 Lamma (Yung Shue Wan)

The Island remains the bar of choice for long-term expats living on Lamma, so if you want the lowdown on what's up, head here.

Lantau

CHINA BEACH CLUB Map p143 — Bar

☎ 2983 8931; 18 Tung Wan Tau Rd; ⏰ noon-10pm Thu & Fri, 11.30am-10pm Sat & Sun, happy hour all day Thu-Sun; 🚢 Lantau

This pleasant bar-restaurant has a 185-sq-metre rooftop and an open-air balcony overlooking Silvermine Bay Beach. Staff are friendly and helpful, and the food is good as well. The two-for-one cocktail 'hour' can go on well into the night.

JK'S CLUB Map p140 — Bar

☎ 2984 0220; Ground fl, 20 Lo Wai Tsuen, Pui O; ⏰ 6pm-late Tue-Sat, 4pm-late Sun; 🚌 1, 2, 3M, 4 or A35

This place is conveniently located just off the main road in Pui O. The beach is right across the street.

CHINA BEAR Map p143 — Pub

☎ 2984 9720; Ground fl, Mui Wo Centre, Ngan Wan Rd; ⏰ 10am-2am, happy hour 5-9pm Mon-Fri, 5-8pm Sat & Sun; 🚢 Lantau

The China Bear is the most popular expat pub-restaurant in Mui Wo, with a wonderful open bar facing the water. It's right by the ferry terminal, making it the perfect spot for your first and last beer in Mui Wo, and for those in between perhaps.

NIGHTLIFE

Energetic Hong Kong has long enjoyed a big night out, and while the economic turmoil of recent years may have taken the edge off things, the locals party on. It's best to approach a night out in Hong Kong as a movable feast flitting between a number of intimate (and free) little bar-cum-club venues and then later on perhaps hitting some of the more traditional clubs that charge a door fee.

There's a good spread of clubs in Hong Kong, including in Wan Chai and Causeway Bay, although Central and Soho dominate for sheer number of venues.

Most of the club nights take place on Friday and Saturday, but there are some good midweek venues as well. Cover charges range from $100 to as high as $500 when a big-name foreign DJ is mixing or an internationally recognised band is on stage. On some nights you may get in free (or for a cheaper cover) if you are among the first 50 or so through the door, you're dressed in '70s gear (or whatever) on theme nights, or you're a woman.

Karaoke clubs are as popular as ever with the city's young citizens, with a sprinkling of clubs in Central and a clutch of smart places springing up on and around Minden Ave in Tsim Sha Tsui.

The aural wallpaper at these clubs is most often Cantopop covers, a genre often written about as if it's a separate, exotic, original music unique to Hong Kong. In reality it consists of Western-style pop melodies sung in Cantonese by local hunks and starlets. If you like pop music it might do for an evening, but don't expect any musical epiphanies.

As in any world-class city, the club scene in Hong Kong changes with the speed of summer lightning, so it would be in your interest to flip through *Time Out*, *HK Magazine* or *bc magazine* (see p206).

Live music, never a great scene in town, is enjoying growing interest of late – albeit from a modest base. Rock bands (both local and imported) have been playing more around town, and numerous bars have house bands that play dance music. Many hotel bars and clubs employ Filipino bands that can play 'Hotel California' and 'Love is a Many-Splendoured Thing' in their sleep (and yours).

HONG KONG ISLAND
Lan Kwai Fong & Soho

BEIJING CLUB Map p78   Bar, Club
☎ 2815 7919; 2-8 Wellington St, Central; ☾ 8pm-late; MTR Central (exit D2)
A wildly popular recent arrival on Hong Kong's nightlife scene, Beijing Club is often packed with hot and sweaty revellers attracted by the neon interior and the mix of R&B, hip hop and dance music. Dress up.

CLUB 97 Map p78   Bar, Club
☎ 2186 1897; Ground fl, Cosmos Bldg, 9-11 Lan Kwai Fong, Central; ☾ 6pm-2am Mon-Thu, 6pm-4am Fri, 8pm-4am Sat & Sun, happy hour 3-8pm; MTR Central (exit D2)
This schmoozy lounge bar has a popular happy hour (it's a gay event on Friday night) and there's reggae on Sunday. It has a members-only policy to turn away the underdressed; make an effort and you're in.

JOYCE IS NOT HERE Map p78   Bar, Live Music
☎ 2851 2999; 38-44 Peel St, Soho; ☾ 11am-late Tue-Fri, 10am-late Sat & Sun, happy hour 3.53-8.04pm; ☒ 13, 26, 40M
Cosy and friendly, this little cafe has something for everyone – from poetry readings and live music on Thursday to booze and Sunday brunch. It's seldom packed so it's best considered as a place to wind up (or down) for the night.

DROP Map p78   Club
☎ 2543 8856; www.drophk.com; Basement, On Lok Mansion, 39-43 Hollywood Rd, Central; ☾ 7pm-2am Mon & Tue, 7pm-3am Wed, 7pm-4am Thu, 7pm-5am Fri, 9pm-5am Sat, happy hour 7-10pm Mon-Fri; ☒ 26
Deluxe lounge action, excellent tunes and potent cocktails keep Drop strong on the scene. It's like walking into *Wallpaper** magazine, but the vibe here is unpretentiously inclusive and the crowd reaches a happy fever pitch on big nights. The members-only policy after 10pm Thursday to Saturday is (flexibly) enforced to keep the dance floor capacity at a manageable 'packed like sardines' level. Enter from Cochrane St.

HOMEBASE Map p78   Club
☎ 2545 0023; 2nd fl, 23 Hollywood Rd, Central; ☾ 10pm-3am Mon-Fri, 10pm-9am Sat, happy hour 10pm-midnight Mon-Thu & Sat, 8pm-midnight Fri; ☒ 26

A meet 'n' greet for the styled and beautiful early on, this place turns into a bump 'n' grind after hours (there's a cover charge of $100). It's one of the more popular after-hours venues and one of the few places that is still partying well after dawn in a city that does, in fact, sleep. Great house and breakbeat music and a small dance floor.

INSOMNIA Map p78　　　　　　Club
☎ 2525 0957; Lower Ground fl, Ho Lee Commercial Bldg, 38-44 D'Aguilar St, Central; ⏰ 9am-6am Mon-Sat, 2pm-5am Sun, happy hour 5-9pm; MTR Central (exit D2)
This is the place to come to when you can't sleep, as it fills up only when other nearby bars are starting to wind down. It's a people-watching place with a wide, open frontage, and there's a live Filipino band doing covers out the back. If the munchies strike in the witching hour, you can get food here, too.

YUMLA Map p78　　　　　　　　Club
☎ 2147 2382; Lower Basement, 79 Wyndham St; ⏰ 8am-1pm Mon-Thu, 8am-3am Fri & Sat, 8am-9pm Sun, happy hour 4-8pm; 🚌 26
Tucked away Yumla is worth seeking out not for its scruffy looks but rather for the relaxed vibe and DJs who spin an eclectic but cutting-edge mix of excellent dance, hip hop and guitar stuff.

BOHEMIAN LOUNGE Map p78　　Live Music
☎ 2526 6099; 3-5 Old Bailey St, Soho ⏰ 4.30pm-12.30am Mon-Wed, 4pm-2am or 3am Thu-Sun, happy hour 5-9pm; 🚌 26
This long, narrow watering hole is a great place for a libation anytime, but try to make it on Thursday after 9pm or Friday or Saturday after 10pm when live jazz kicks in.

CAVERN Map p78　　　　　　　Live Music
☎ 2121 8969; Shop 1, Lower Ground fl, Lan Kwai Fong Tower, 33 Wyndham St, Central; ⏰ 6pm-late Mon-Sat; MTR Central (exit D2)
Hong Kong's first (and only) supper club, the Cavern is effectively a showcase for two tribute bands: Sixties Mania Showband, done up in mop-top haircuts and bell-bottoms, and the Rolling Bones, a great Filipino band. Music starts at 9pm Monday to Saturday. There's food and the cover charge is $100. Enter from D'Aguilar St.

FRINGE GALLERY Map p78　　　　Live Music
☎ 2521 7251; www.hkfringe.com.hk; Ground fl, Fringe Club, 2 Lower Albert Rd, Central; ⏰ noon-midnight Mon-Thu, noon-3am Fri & Sat, happy hour 3-9pm Mon-Thu, 3-8pm Fri & Sat; MTR Central (exit D1)
The Fringe, a friendly and eclectic venue on the border of the Lan Kwai Fong quadrant, has original music in its gallery-bar from 10.30pm on Friday and Saturday, with jazz, rock and world music getting the most airplay. There's a pleasant rooftop bar open in the warmer months.

Admiralty & Wan Chai

1/5 Map p72　　　　　　　　　　Club
☎ 2520 2515; 1st fl, Starcrest Bldg, 9 Star St, Wan Chai; ⏰ 5pm-3am Mon-Thu, 5pm-4am Fri & Sat, 6pm-2am Sun, happy hour 6-9pm Mon-Fri; MTR Admiralty (exit F)
Pronounced 'one-fifth', this sophisticated lounge bar and club has a broad bar backed by a two-storey drinks selection from which bar staff concoct some of Hong Kong's best cocktails. It gets packed on the weekend with a dressy professional crowd, but it's still a good place to chill.

JOE BANANAS Map p74　　　　　　Club
☎ 2529 1811; Ground fl, Shiu Lam Bldg, 23 Luard Rd, Wan Chai; ⏰ noon-5am Mon-Thu, noon-6am Fri & Sat, 4pm-5am Sun, happy hour 11am-10pm; MTR Wan Chai (exit C)
JB's, in Wan Chai forever it seems, has dropped its long-standing wet T-shirt/boxers aesthetic and gone for more of a bamboo-bar feel. Unaccompanied females should expect a good sampler of bad pick-up lines; go with friends and have some un-PC fun. There are free drinks for women from 6pm to 3am on Wednesday, and 'Crazy Hour' (6pm to 8pm daily) is even more generous than happy hour.

NEW MAKATI PUB & DISCO Map p74　　Club
☎ 2866 3928; 1st fl, 94-100 Lockhart Rd; ⏰ 4pm-5am, happy hour 4-9pm; MTR Wan Chai (exit C)
It has to be said: you can't go lower than this sleazy pick-up joint, named after a Manila neighbourhood. Imagine dimly lit booths, Filipino *amahs* and middle-aged white male booze-hounds, who all just wanna have fun. In fact it is less wretched than this description might make it sound and it's a friendly, unpretentious place to dance the morning away.

CARNEGIE'S Map p74 — Live Music
☎ 2866 6289; Ground fl, 53-55 Lockhart Rd, Wan Chai; ☺ 11am-late Mon-Sat, 5pm-late Sun, happy hour 11am-9pm Mon-Sat; MTR Wan Chai (exit C)
The rock memorabilia festooning the walls makes it all seem a bit Hard Rock Café-ish, but this place is worth a look all the same. From 9pm on Friday and Saturday, Carnegie's fills up with revellers, many of whom will end up dancing on the bar. All good clean fun.

DUSK TILL DAWN Map p74 — Live Music
☎ 2528 4689; Ground fl, 76-84 Jaffe Rd, Wan Chai; ☺ noon-5am Mon-Fri, 3pm-7am Sat & Sun, happy hour 5-9pm; MTR Wan Chai (exit C)
There's live music from 10.30pm, with an emphasis on beats and vibes that will get your booty shaking. The dance floor can get packed but the atmosphere is more friendly than sleazy. The food here sticks to easy fillers, such as meat pies and burgers.

WANCH Map p74 — Live Music
☎ 2861 1621; 54 Jaffe Rd, Wan Chai; ☺ noon-2am Sun-Thu, noon-4am Fri & Sat, happy hour noon-10pm Mon-Thu, noon-8pm Fri-Sun; MTR Wan Chai (exit C)
This place, which derives its name from what everyone calls the district, has live music (mostly rock and folk with the occasional solo guitarist thrown in) seven nights a week from 9pm. Jam night is Monday from 8pm. If you're not here for the music, it can be a dubious scene – the Wanch can be a bit of a pick-up joint.

KOWLOON
Tsim Sha Tsui & Tsim Sha Tsui East

BAHAMA MAMA'S Map p106 — Club
☎ 9803 6650, 2368 2121; 4-5 Knutsford Tce, Tsim Sha Tsui; ☺ 5pm-3am Sun-Thu, 5pm-4am Fri & Sat, happy hour 5-9pm; MTR Tsim Sha Tsui (exit B1)
Bahama Mama's goes for a 'Caribbean island' feel, complete with palm trees and surfboards. It's a friendly spot and stands apart from most of the other late-night watering holes in this part of town. It's also the place to come for a *foosball* (table soccer) showdown. On Friday and Saturday nights there's a DJ spinning and a young crowd out on the bonsai-sized dance floor.

CLOUDNINE Map p106 — Club
☎ 2723 6383; 7 Minden Ave; ☺ 6pm-3am Mon-Sat; MTR Tsim Sha Tsui (exit G)
If you want to find out what the local kids do of an evening (or at least those with some cash to burn), step through the egg-shaped doorway of this stylish little bar-cum-karaoke joint, take a seat and listen to the Cantopop classics getting murdered.

HARI'S Map p104 — Live Music
☎ 2369 3111 ext 1345; Mezzanine, Holiday Inn Golden Mile, 50 Nathan Rd, Tsim Sha Tsui; ☺ 5pm-2am, happy hour 5-9pm Mon-Sat, 5pm-2am Sun; MTR Tsim Sha Tsui (exit G2)
Is it tacky or classy (or neither)? You decide after you've had a couple of specialty martinis (there are over a dozen to challenge

MAJOR VENUES
Hong Kong has at last arrived on the big-name concert circuit, and a growing number of internationally celebrated bands and solo acts – including the likes of REM, U2, Robbie Williams, Avril Lavigne, Norah Jones, Diana Krall, Sting and k.d. lang – perform in Hong Kong regularly.

Big concerts are usually held at either the 12,500-seat Hong Kong Coliseum (Map p106; ☎ 2355 7233, 2355 7234; 9 Cheong Wan Rd, Hung Hom; MTR Hung Hom), behind the MTR station, and Queen Elizabeth Stadium (Map p74; ☎ 2591 1346; www.lcsd.gov.hk/qes; 18 Oi Kwan Rd, Wan Chai). The sound is abysmal in the former, and you'd get better acoustics in an empty aircraft hanger than at the latter.

Two other venues are the HITEC Rotunda (Map pp100–1; ☎ 2620 2222, 2620 2838; www.hitec.com.hk; 1 Trademart Dr, Kowloon Bay; MTR Kowloon Bay) and the New Wing of the Hong Kong Convention & Exhibition Centre (HKCEC; Map p74; ☎ 2582 8888, bookings 2582 1111; www.hkcec.com; 1 Expo Dr, Wan Chai; bus 18, MTR Wan Chai). These are not huge venues, so the ticket prices are usually quite high.

Smaller acts are sometimes booked into the Ko Shan Theatre (Map pp100–1; ☎ 2740 9222; www.lcsd.gov.hk/kst; 77 Ko Shan Rd, Hung Hom; MTR Hung Hom). The sound at this venue isn't great either, but the back portion of the seating area is open air, and most of the seats offer a good view of the stage.

you). There's live music from 6.15pm weekdays, 8.45pm Saturday and 7.30pm Sunday.

THE ARTS

Local orchestras or a foreign ensemble perform classical music weekly, while Hong Kong is well served with cinema screens both mainstream and arthouse. Most show local films (with English subtitles) or Hollywood blockbusters dubbed into Cantonese. Cine-Art House (right) in Wan Chai, the Broadway Cinematheque (p220) in Yau Ma Tei and the AMC Pacific Place (Map p72; ☎ 2869 0322; 1st fl, 1 Pacific Pl, Admiralty; MTR Admiralty, exit F) in Admiralty screen more interesting current releases and art-house films.

Tickets cost between $65 and $100, but can be cheaper (around $50) at matinees, the last screening of the day on weekends and on holidays (usually 11.30pm), or on certain days of the week (eg Tuesday at the AMC cinema; Map p72).

Almost all Hong Kong films screening in Hong Kong have both Chinese and English subtitles. *Time Out*, *HK Magazine* and the *South China Morning Post* have listings for film screenings.

Local theatre groups (p35) mostly perform at the Shouson Theatre of the Hong Kong Arts Centre, the Academy for the Performing Arts, the Hong Kong Cultural Centre and Hong Kong City Hall. Performances are usually in Cantonese, though there are often summaries in English available. Smaller troupes occasionally present plays in English at one of the two theatres at the Fringe Club.

HONG KONG ISLAND

Some of the most important classical music venues are the Hong Kong Academy for the Performing Arts (Map p74; ☎ 2584 8500, bookings 3128 8288; www .hkapa.edu; 1 Gloucester Rd, Wan Chai; MTR Wan Chai, exit A1), Hong Kong City Hall (Map p67; ☎ 2921 2840, bookings 2734 9009; www.cityhall.gov.hk; 5 Edinburgh Place, Central; MTR Central, exit J3) and the Hong Kong Arts Centre (Map p74; ☎ 2582 0200, bookings 2734 9009; www.hkac.org.hk; 2 Harbour Rd, Wan Chai; MTR Wan Chai, exit A1).

Central

PALACE IFC CINEMA Map p67   Cinema
☎ 2388 6268; Podium L1, IFC Mall, 8 Finance St; MTR Hong Kong (exit F)
This new eight-screen cinema complex in the IFC Mall is arguably the most advanced and comfortable in the territory.

Admiralty & Wan Chai

Certain cultural organisations based in this area show foreign films from time to time, including the Alliance Française (Map p74; ☎ 2527 7825; 1st & 2nd fl, 123 Hennessy Rd, Wan Chai) and the Goethe-Institut (Map p74; ☎ 2802 0088; 13th & 14th fl, Hong Kong Arts Centre, 2 Harbour Rd, Wan Chai).

For both art-house and mainstream films, Wan Chai has two of the best and most comfortable cinemas in the territory.

AGNÈS B CINEMA
Map p72   Cinema
☎ 2582 0200; Upper Basement, Hong Kong Arts Centre, 2 Harbour Rd, Wan Chai; 🚌 18
This recently renamed cinema – it was the Lim Por Yen Theatre for years – is the place for classics, revivals, alternative screenings and travelling film festivals.

CINE-ART HOUSE Map p74   Cinema
☎ 2827 4820; Ground fl, Sun Hung Kai Centre, 30 Harbour Rd, Wan Chai; MTR Wan Chai (exit A5)
This alternative cinema specialises in English-language films.

PUNCHLINE COMEDY CLUB
Map p74   Comedy
☎ 2827 7777; 2nd fl, Sun Hung Kai Centre, 30 Harbour Rd, Wan Chai; 🚌 18, alight at Wan Chai Sports Ground
A veteran on the scene – in fact the only regular comedy venue for many years – the Punchline Comedy Club hosts local and imported acts every third Thursday, Friday and Saturday from 9pm to 11pm. Entry costs around $300.

TAKE OUT COMEDY CLUB
Map p78   Comedy
☎ 6220 4436; 34 Elgin St; www.takeoutcomedy .com; 🚌 26
Consistent stand-up and improv acts (in Cantonese and English) bring in the punters to this basement venue established by Chinese-American stand-up Jami Gong.

Causeway Bay & Island East

Causeway Bay is packed with cinemas, but with few exceptions most of them show Hollywood blockbusters and Hong Kong and mainland films. Further east is Hong Kong's most important film-watching venue, the Hong Kong Film Archive (p91).

CHINESE OPERA UNMASKED

The best time to see and hear Chinese opera – not the easiest form of entertainment to catch in Hong Kong these days – is during the Hong Kong Arts Festival (p15) in February/March and the Mid-Autumn Festival (p17), when outdoor performances are staged in Victoria Park. At other times, you might take your chances at catching a performance at the Temple Street Night Market (p109), but the most reliable venue for opera performances year-round is the Sunbeam Theatre (below) in North Point.

SUNBEAM THEATRE Map pp62-3   Theatre
☎ 2856 0161, 2563 2959; Kiu Fai Mansion, 423 King's Rd, North Point; tickets $40-320; MTR North Point (exit B1)
Cantonese and other Chinese opera (p35) are performed here through the year. Performances generally run for about a week, and are usually held five days a week at 7.30pm, with occasional matinees at 1pm or 1.30pm. The theatre is above the North Point MTR station (exit B1), on the north side of King's Rd, near the intersection with Shu Kuk St.

WINDSOR CINEMA Map p85   Cinema
☎ 2577 0783; 1st fl, Windsor House, 311 Gloucester Rd, Causeway Bay; Causeway Bay (exit E)
This comfortable cineplex with four screens is just west of Victoria Park.

Lan Kwai Fong & Soho

FRINGE STUDIO & THEATRE
Map p78   Theatre
☎ 2521 7251, bookings 3128 8288; www.hkfringe .com.hk; Ground & 1st fl, Fringe Club, 2 Lower Albert Rd; ◷ 8pm during performances (days vary), box office noon-10pm Mon-Sat; MTR Central (exit D2)
These intimate theatres, each seating up to 100 people, host eclectic local and international performances (average ticket price is $80) in English and in Cantonese.

KOWLOON
Tsim Sha Tsui

GRAND OCEAN CINEMA Map p104   Cinema
☎ 2377 2100; www.goldenharvest.com; Marco Polo Hong Kong Hotel Shopping Arcade, Zone D, Harbour City, 3 Canton Rd, Tsim Sha Tsui; ⚓ Star Ferry
The Grand Ocean Cinema screens the usual blockbusters.

HONG KONG CULTURAL CENTRE
Map p104   Classical Music
☎ 2734 2009; www.hkculturalcentre.gov.hk; 10 Salisbury Rd, Tsim Sha Tsui; MTR Tsim Sha Tsui

Many classical music performances are held at the Hong Kong Cultural Centre (just east of the Star Ferry terminal), also home to the Hong Kong Philharmonic and the Hong Kong Chinese Orchestra. It is well worth stopping by there to pick up a monthly schedule.

Yau Ma Tei & New Kowloon
AMC FESTIVAL WALK
Map pp100-1   Cinema
☎ 2265 8545; www.amccinemas.com.hk; Upper Ground fl & Levels 1 & 2, Festival Walk, 80-88 Tat Chee Ave, Kowloon Tong; MTR Kowloon Tong (exit C2)
This complex with 11 screens at Hong Kong's poshest mall is the largest cinema in the territory. The films are a mix of Chinese and Western. Check ahead as the latter are sometimes dubbed, rather than subtitled in Cantonese.

BROADWAY CINEMATHEQUE
Map p108   Cinema
☎ 2388 3188; Ground fl, Prosperous Garden, 3 Public Square St, Yau Ma Tei; MTR Yau Ma Tei
This is an unlikely place for an alternative cinema, but it's worth coming up for new art-house releases and rerun screenings. The Kubrick Bookshop Café next door serves good coffee and decent pre-flick food.

NEW TERRITORIES

The New Territories also has several important cultural centres:

Kwai Tsing Theatre (Map pp58–9; ☎ 2408 0128; www.lcsd .gov.hk/ktt; 12 Hing Ning Rd, Kwai Chung; MTR Kwai Fong)
Sha Tin Town Hall (Map p127; ☎ 2694 2550; www.lcsd.gov .hk/stth; 1 Yuen Wo Rd, Sha Tin; MTR Sha Tin, East Rail)
Tuen Mun Town Hall (Map pp58–9; ☎ 2450 4202; www .lcsd.gov.hk/tmth; 3 Tuen Hi Rd, Tuen Mun; MTR Tuen Mun)
Tsuen Wan Town Hall (Map p117; ☎ 2414 0144; www.lcsd .gov.hk/twth; 72 Tai Ho Rd, Tsuen Wan; MTR Tsuen Wan)
Yuen Long Theatre (Map pp58–9; ☎ 2476 1029, bookings 2477 1462; www.lcsd.gov.hk/ylt; 9 Tai Yuk Rd, Yuen Long; MTR Yuen Long)

SPORTS & ACTIVITIES

top picks

- Horse racing in Happy Valley (p230)
- Rugby Sevens (p230)
- Luxury spa escape (p222)
- Kayaking in Sai Kung (p227)
- Walking Hong Kong's trails (p225)
- Harbour cruising (p229)
- Waterside morning t'ai chi (p227)

Hong Kong's expansive and sparsely populated green spaces surprise many first-time visitors with both their proximity to the urban centre and amazing accessibility. Rugged outdoor options such as hiking, camping and mountain biking are plentiful. Messing about on boats, boards or skis is another obvious category of activity, given the ubiquity of both salt and fresh water.

Edgier thrills are there for those eager to tackle the area's granite rock faces, to indulge in paintball firefights in the country parks or to participate in the increasingly busy local adventure sports calendar.

It is, however, possible to raise your heart rate without leaving the urban centres. Shoehorned into the precious spaces between the concrete canyons you'll find a surprisingly good range of public facilities, from public basketball and tennis courts to swimming pools, parks and gardens.

In short, Hong Kong offers the type of facilities, clubs and classes for most of the activities you'd expect to find in any other major city, including 24/7 gyms, golf, yoga, dance classes and the full range of pampering options from a quickie foot rub to a full-blown spa resort package.

In the home town of so many legendary martial artists such as Bruce Lee and Jackie Chan, it's no secret that Chinese martial arts are also well represented, from the full contact variety to the slow-motion art of t'ai chi practised with balletic grace in the parks each morning.

If watching rather than doing is your thing, there's a busy spectator sports calendar, too, and often plenty of atmosphere to be found (especially where there's the possibility of having a flutter on the result, or a beer for that matter). Hong Kong's Rugby Sevens in particular have a legendary status among rugby fans worldwide, both as a sporting event and as an excuse for a raucously good-natured carnival atmosphere.

HEALTH & FITNESS

Hong Kong is bursting at the seams with gyms, yoga studios, spas and alternative health clinics offering everything from aromatherapy and foot care to homeopathy. And if your hotel doesn't have a swimming pool, there are three dozen public ones to choose from.

GYMS & FITNESS CLUBS

Getting fit is big business in Hong Kong, with the largest slices of the pie shared out among a few big names. The South China Athletic Association (Map p85; ☎ 2890 7736; 88 Caroline Hill Rd, So Kon Po; 🚇 Happy Valley) has a massive (1000 sq metre) gym, with modern exercise machinery and an aerobics room, as well as a sauna, a steam room and massage (monthly membership $250, or $50 per visit). The following two are notable in that they offer short-term memberships.

CALIFORNIA FITNESS Map p78

☎ 2522 5229; www.californiafitness.com; 1 Wellington St, Central; daily $150; ☯ 6am-midnight Mon-Sat, 8am-10pm Sun; MTR Central exit D2
Asia's largest health club has six outlets in Hong Kong, including a Wan Chai branch (Map p74; ☎ 2877 7070; 88 Gloucester Rd; MTR Wan Chai, exit A1), which keeps the same hours.

PURE FITNESS Map p78

☎ 2970 3366; www.pure-fit.com; 1st-3rd fl, Kinwick Centre, 32 Hollywood Rd, Soho; daily $200; ☯ 6am-midnight Mon-Sat, 8am-10pm Sun; Central Escalator
This favourite of the Soho set (entered from Shelley St) has a Central branch (Map p67; ☎ 8129 8000; 3rd fl, Two IFC Mall, 8 Finance St, Central; MTR Hong Kong Station), which is open the same hours.

SPA TREATMENTS & THERAPIES

Whether you want to be spoilt rotten by sleek Priestesses of Wellness applying thousand-dollar caviar and lotus flower facials, or have a simple foot rub to soothe those throbbing bunions, Hong Kong's extensive pampering sector can assist. Most of the top hotels in town operate their own spas, with some of them essentially mini resorts. For less elaborate treatments you'll find plenty of places in Central and (to a lesser extent) Kowloon, offering spa treatments, massages and reflexology.

DK Aromatherapy (Map p78; ☎ 2771 2847; www.aroma.com.hk; Ground fl, 16A Staunton St, Central; ☯ 11am-10pm; Central Escalator) Full body aromatherapy treatment $500 to $550.

Elemis Day Spa (Map p78; ☎ 2521 6660; www.elemisdayspa.com.hk; 9th fl, Century Sq, 1 D'Aguilar St, Central; MTR

Central, exit D2) Pampering and treatments range from basic facials to deep-tissue massage. There are separate sections (and treatment menus) for men and women.

Happy Foot Reflexology Centre (Map p78; ☎ 2544 1010; 6th, 11th & 13th fl, Jade Centre, 98-102 Wellington St, Central; ☺ 10am-midnight; MTR Central, exit D2) Foot/body massage starts at $198/250 for 50 minutes.

Healing Plants (Map p78; ☎ 2815 9448; info@ehealing plants.com; 13th fl, Capitol Plaza, 2-10 Lyndhurst Tce, Central; ☺ 10am-8pm Mon-Sat; Central Escalator) Acupuncture, reflexology, Swedish massage and homeopathic doctors at hand.

Spa at the Four Seasons (Map p67; ☎ 3196 8900; www .fourseasons.com/hongkong/spa.html; 8 Finance St, Central; ☺ 8am-11pm; Hong Kong MTR, exit F) A 20,00-sq-ft, ultra-high-end spa with a comprehensive range of beauty, massage and health treatments, plus ice fountain, hot cups, moxibustion and even a 'herbal cocoon room'.

SWIMMING POOLS

Hong Kong has 36 swimming pools that are open to the public. There are excellent pools in Tsim Sha Tsui's Kowloon Park (p102) and in Victoria Park (p86) in Causeway Bay. Many pools are closed between November and March, but heated indoor and outdoor pools, such as the Morrison Hill Public Swimming Pool (Map p74; ☎ 2575 3028; 7 Oi Kwan Rd, Wan Chai; adult/child $19/9) and the one in the basement of the South China Athletic Association (Map p85; ☎ 2577 6932; 88 Caroline Hill Rd, Causeway Bay; adult/child $22/10; ☒ Happy Valley) are open all year.

YOGA

Yoga remains as popular in Hong Kong as it is everywhere else in the world.

Yoga Central (Map p78; ☎ 2982 4308; www.yoga central.com.hk; 4th fl, 13 Wyndham St, Central; ☺ variable hr; Central MTR, exit D2) Well-established studio offering Hatha with an Iyengar spin, and Pilates. Beginner and intermediate classes Monday to Saturday cost from $140/200 for one/two hours.

Yoga Fitness (Map p78; ☎ 2851 8353; www.yoga-fit ness.com; 5th fl, Sea Bird House, 22-28 Wyndham St, Central; ☺ variable hr; Central MTR, exit D2) Hatha for $140 per class or from $500 for five classes in a month.

ACTIVITIES

Hong Kong offers countless ways to have fun and keep fit. From tennis and squash courts to cycling and hiking trails, you won't be stumped for something active to do during your visit.

Information & Venues

One excellent, all-round option is the South China Athletic Association (SCAA; opposite), east of the Happy Valley Racecourse and south of Causeway Bay. The SCAA has facilities for badminton, billiards, bowling, tennis, squash, table tennis, gymnastics, fencing, yoga, judo, karate and golf (among other activities), and short-term membership for visitors is $50 per month. Another good place is the nearby Hong Kong Amateur Athletic Association (☎ 2504 8215; www.hkaaa.com).

Hong Kong Outdoors (www.hkoutdoors.com) is an excellent website for all sorts of active pursuits.

BEACHES

The most accessible beaches are on the southern side of Hong Kong Island (see in particular Shek O, p96), but the best ones are on the Outlying Islands and in the New Territories. For a list of beaches deemed safe enough for swimming and their water-quality gradings, check the website of the Environmental Protection Department (www.info.gov.hk/epd).

Hong Kong's 41 gazetted beaches are staffed by lifeguards from 9am to 6pm daily from at least April to October (from 8am to 7pm on Saturday and Sunday from June to August). A few beaches, including Deep Water Bay and Clearwater Bay, have year-round lifeguard services. Shark nets are installed and inspected at 32 beaches. From the first day of the official swimming season until the last, expect the beaches to be chock-a-block on weekends and holidays. When the swimming season is officially over, the beaches become deserted – no matter how hot the weather.

At most of the beaches you will find toilets, showers, changing rooms, refreshment stalls and sometimes cafés and restaurants.

BIRD-WATCHING

Birders in Hong Kong will have their work cut out: some 450 species have been spotted in the territory. The best area is Mai Po Marsh (p120), but others include Tai Po Kau Nature Reserve (p125) and Po Toi (p152). The Hong Kong Bird-Watching Society (www.hkbws.org.hk) is a fount of information and can arrange organised visits to local birding venues. Ask for its free brochure Bird Watching in Hong Kong.

TENPIN BOWLING

Some of the best facilities are on the 1st floor of the Sports Complex at the SCAA (above). About

60 lanes are open from 10am to 12.30am Monday to Thursday, from 10am to 1.30am Friday, 9.30am to 1.30am Saturday and from 9am to 12.30am on Sunday and holidays. Games cost $18 to $30, depending on the time of day and day of the week. Try also Belair Bowling (Map p127; ☎ 2649 9022; Shop 4, Level 2, Phase 1, Belair Garden Shopping Arcade, 52 Tai Chung Kiu Rd, Sha Tin).

CYCLING

There are bicycle paths in the New Territories, mostly around Tolo Harbour. The paths run from Sha Tin to Tai Po and continue to Tai Mei Tuk. You can rent bikes in these places, but the paths get crowded on weekends. Rentals are also available at Shek O on Hong Kong Island and on Lamma, Cheung Chau and Lantau.

Although the Hong Kong Cycling Association (www .cycling.org.hk) mainly organises races, you can try it for information.

Mountain biking is no longer banned in Hong Kong's country parks and there is a fine, ever-growing network of trails available in 10 of them, including Sai Kung and Lantau South Country Parks. You must apply for a permit in writing, in person or by fax through the Country & Marine Parks Authority (Map pp100–1; ☎ 2150 6868;

HONG KONG FOR ADRENALINE JUNKIES

It may not threaten the world's great adrenaline sports centres just yet, but thrills and spills are there to be found if you know where to look. So, if going for a jog or racquet sports just don't do it for you, here are some ideas for getting into the zone. If you're living in Hong Kong and looking for adventure options in the wider region the Action Asia (www .actionasia.com) website is a good place to go for information and inspiration.

Adventure Racing

Fitness junkies: what better way to test yourself than outdoor action events combining several sports in a day's racing in teams of two or more, such as kayaking, running, swimming, climbing and mountain biking? Action Asia Events (www.actionasiaevents.com) publishes an events calendar.

Climbing

Hong Kong is peppered with excellent granite faces and volcanic rocks in some striking wilderness areas. The Hong Kong Climbing (www.hongkongclimbing.com) website is the best resource for climbers; it has some excellent and detailed downloadable PDF guides. According to these guys, Tung Lung Chau (p151) has the highest concentration of quality sport climbs in Hong Kong.

Fight Club

Spend a day with your mates and DEF Boxing (www.def.com.hk) learning how to punch and how to avoid being punched before being let loose on each other for some real live sparring. Prices start at about $1200 per person.

Flight Club

Wanna know what it was like landing at Hong Kong's old Kai Tak airport, when pilots had to squeeze between the washing lines of Kowloon's tenement blocks before chucking a hard right for the final approach? Then trying flying a virtual Boeing 737 on the route or hundreds of others with Flight Experience (Map pp100–1; ☎ 2359 0000; www .flightexperience.com.hk; Shop G20, Megabox, 38 Wang Chiu Rd, Kowloon Bay). Sweaty palms guaranteed.

Paintball

From around $250 you don camo gear, get a gun and 100 rounds of paint, and are let loose in a range of team games to splatter or get splattered in secluded parts of the Hong Kong countryside. Try Paintball Headquarters (Map pp100–1; ☎ 3106 0220; www.paintballhq.com.hk; Ground fl, Po Lung Centre; 11 Wang Chui Rd, Kowloon Bay) or YSO War Games (Map pp100–1; ☎ 9837 5764; www.ysowargames.com; Yung Shue O, Sai Kung) for more information.

Virtual speeding

Fancy yourself as the new Vin Diesel drifting your hot wheels around the streets? Then head to the Sideways Driving Club (Map p78; ☎ 2523 0983; 1-2 Chancery Lane, Central; www.sideways-driving-club.com) and its 13 advanced, hyper-realistic F1 racing simulators to see if you've got what it takes. Prices start at $550 per hour.

6th fl, 303 Cheung Sha Wan Rd; MTR Sham Shui Po, exit D2). For information check out the website of the Hong Kong Mountain Bike Association (www.hkmba.org); for equipment (and first-hand advice) talk to the helpful staff at the Flying Ball Bicycle Co (Map pp58–9; ☎ 2381 3661; Ground fl, 478 Castle Peak Rd, Cheung Sha Wan; ☺ 11am-8pm Mon-Sat; MTR Lai Chi Kok, exit B1).

FISHING

While there are almost no restrictions on deep-sea fishing, it's a different story at Hong Kong's 17 freshwater reservoirs, where the season runs from September to March and there are limits on the quantity and size of fish (generally various types of carp and tilapia) allowed. A licence from the Water Supplies Department (Map p74; ☎ 2824 5000; 48th fl, Immigration Tower, 7 Gloucester Rd, Wan Chai; Wan Chai MTR, exit A5) costs $24 and is valid for three years.

For something a little less, well, wild, head for the Tai Mei Tuk Fish Farm (Map pp58–9; ☎ 2662 6351; Tai Mei Tuk, Tai Po; weekday/weekend per hr $25/30, rods rental $10; ☺ 9am-10pm; ☐ 75K), a large artificial pond by the harbour stocked with freshwater fish.

GOLF

Most golf courses in Hong Kong are private but do open to the public at certain times – usually weekdays only. Greens fees for visitors vary, but range from $500 for two rounds at the nine-hole Deep Water Bay Golf Club (Map pp62–3; ☎ 2812 7070; 19 Island Rd, Deep Water Bay; ☐ 6, 6A) on Hong Kong Island to $1400 at its parent club, the Hong Kong Golf Club (Map pp58–9; ☎ 2670 1211; www.hkgolfclub.org; Fan Kam Rd, Sheung Shui, New Territories; Fanling MTR), which has three 18-hole courses. Nonmembers can play on weekdays only at both clubs.

One of the most dramatic links to play in Hong Kong – for the scenery if not the par – is the 36-hole Jockey Club Kau Sai Chau Public Golf Course (Map pp58–9; ☎ 2791 3388; www.kscgolf.com) on Kau Sai Chau, which is linked by ferry with Sai Kung town, northeast of Kowloon (see the boxed text, p131). Greens fees for 18 holes of play by adult nonresidents range from $690 on weekdays to $1130 on the weekend. You must be accompanied by a Hong Kong ID card holder on weekends; for weekdays be sure to bring your passport and handicap card. It costs from $160 per round to rent clubs and $35 to rent golf shoes; caddies are $175 for 18 holes.

Other courses in Hong Kong:

Clearwater Bay Golf & Country Club (Map pp58–9; ☎ 2335 3700; www.cwbgolf.org; 139 Tau Au Mun Rd, Clearwater Bay; greens fees $1800-2000; ☐ 91) A 27-hole course at the tip of Clearwater Bay in the New Territories.

Discovery Bay Golf Club (Map p140; ☎ 2987 7273; Valley Rd, Discovery Bay, Lantau; greens fees $1400; ☑ Discovery Bay) Perched high on a hill, this 27-hole course has impressive views of the Outlying Islands. Nonmembers Monday, Tuesday and Friday only.

Shek O Golf & Country Club (Map pp62–3; ☎ 2809 4458; 5 Shek O Rd, Shek O; greens fees $300-500; ☐ 3, 309) An 18-hole course located on the southeastern edge of Hong Kong Island. Nonmembers must be accompanied by a member.

If you're content with just teeing off (again and again), the Jockey Club Kau Sai Chau Public Golf Course has a driving range (☎ 2791 3341; per 30 min $35, club rental $15; ☺ 7am-8pm Mon, Wed & Thu, 11am-8pm Tue, 7am-10pm Fri-Sun). In addition it offers a variety of packages where you can practise putting, chipping and bunker shots.

For more information, contact the Hong Kong Golf Association (☎ 2504 8659; www.hkga.com).

HIKING

Many visitors are surprised to learn that Hong Kong is an excellent place for hiking. Lengthy wilderness trails criss-cross the territory and its islands through striking mountain, coast and jungle trails. The four main ones are the MacLehose Trail (p227), at 100km the longest in the territory; the 78km-long Wilson Trail (p227), which runs on both sides of Victoria Harbour; the 70km-long Lantau Trail (p227); and the Hong Kong Trail (p227), which is 50km long. Hong Kong's excellent public transport network makes it feasible to tackle these trails a section at a time.

For full details and advice on routes and suggested itineraries invest in one of the excellent hiking guides that are widely available in Hong Kong bookshops (also see the boxed text p226). Before heading out it's also a good idea to consult the official Hong Kong hiking website (www.hkwalkers.net) for updates on weather and the conditions of the trails (landslides can sometimes mean route closure or diversions).

Although these trails are seldom more than half a day's walk from settlements, this is still rugged country so go prepared with plenty of water. Other useful items include trail snacks, a weatherproof jacket, a sun hat, maps and a compass. Boots are not necessary; a good pair of running shoes should do.

Hikers should remember that the high humidity during spring and summer can be enervating. October to March is the best season for arduous treks. At high elevations, such as parts of the Lantau and MacLehose Trails,

WALKING & NATURE GUIDES TO LEAD THE WAY

Exploring Hong Kong's Countryside: A Visitor's Companion by Edward Stokes is a well-written illustrated 185-page guidebook distributed free by the HKTB. It provides excellent background information and the maps are good.

- Peter Spurrier's new *Hiker's Guide to Hong Kong* will guide you along the four main trails and introduce you to 10 shorter ones.
- *Hong Kong Hikes: The Twenty Best Walks in the Territory* by Christian Wright and Tinja Tsang is unique in that it consists of 20 laminated loose-leaf cards for hikes on Hong Kong Island, the Outlying Islands and the New Territories that can be unclipped and slotted into the transparent plastic folder provided.
- *Historic Hong Kong Hikes* is a mix of 15 country and urban walks with a historical theme.
- *Magic Walks*, which comes in four volumes and is good for 50 relatively easy hikes throughout the territory, is written by Kaarlo Schepel, almost a legend among Hong Kong walkers.
- *The Birds of Hong Kong and South China* by Clive Viney, Karen Phillips and Lam Chiu Ying is the definitive guide for spotting and identifying the territory's feathered creatures and an excellent guide to take along while hiking in the New Territories.
- *Ruins of War: A Guide to Hong Kong's Battlefields and Wartime Sites* by Ko Tim Keung and Jason Wordie is a specialist title but a welcome addition to Hong Kong's walking guides bookshelf. It includes a lot of walking in the countryside.

it can get very cold so it's essential to bring warm clothing.

Mosquitos are a nuisance in spring and summer, so a good mosquito repellent is necessary. Snakes are rarely encountered.

Maps

Good hiking maps will save you a lot of time, energy and trouble. The Map Publication Centres (p296) stock the excellent Countryside Series of topographical maps, as well as the unfolded hiking maps ($34) produced by the Country & Marine Parks Authority for each of Hong Kong's four main trails: the 1:15,000 *Hong Kong Trail*, the 1:35,000 *Wilson Trail*, the 1:25,000 *MacLehose Trail* and the 1:20,000 *Lantau Trail*. The four trail maps are also available from the Government Publications Office (p159) in Central. If you're heading to Lantau it's also worth picking up the Conservation Department's brochure *Hiking on Lantau Country Trails*, which gives updates on landslides, path changes and path closures.

Accommodation

The Country & Marine Parks Authority (☎ 2150 6868; www.parks.afcd.gov.hk) of the Agriculture, Fisheries & Conservation Department maintains 38 free, no-frills camp sites in the New Territories and Outlying Islands for use by hikers. They are clearly labelled on the Countryside Series and four trail maps. Camping is generally OK on more remote beaches.

You can camp at the hostels managed by the Hong Kong Youth Hostels Association (HKYHA; ☎ 2788 1638; www.yha.org.hk), with the exception of the Jockey Club Mount Davis hostel on Hong Kong Island and Bradbury Jockey Club Youth Hostel at Tai Mei Tuk in the New Territories. The fee, which allows you to use the hostel's toilet and washroom facilities, is $25 for HKYHA or Hostelling International (HI) members and $35 for nonmembers.

Organised Hikes

The Hong Kong Trampers (☎ 8209 0517; www.hktrampers .com) are worth checking and arrange informal walks on Sundays. Serious hikers might consider joining in the annual Trailwalker (www .oxfamtrailwalker.org.hk) event, a gruelling 48-hour race across the MacLehose Trail in the New Territories in November, organised since 1986 by Oxfam Hong Kong (☎ 2520 2525).

If you want to do some hiking in the countryside – either individually or in a group – but you would prefer to be shown the way, Walk Hong Kong (☎ 9187 8641; www.walkhongkong.com) takes guided nature walks on Hong Kong Island (eg the Peak to Aberdeen), the New Territories (eg Plover Cove and Sai Kung Country Parks) and Lantau. Half-/full-day walks cost from $300 to $600, including lunch.

Natural Excursion Ideals (☎ 9300 5197; www.kayak-and -hike.com) offers hiking and kayaking trips. Hikes take in such places as Plover Cove Country Park and the peak of Ma On Shan. On the water it has half-/full-day tours ($700/880) including the 'Power Boat, Kayak & Coral Explorer'. This will take you, by 'fast-pursuit craft', to the otherwise inaccessible Bluff Island and the fishing village of Sha Kiu Tau from where you can swim, snorkel and then kayak. All gear, including a mask and snorkel, is provided and the full-day tours include lunch.

Hong Kong Trail

Right on the city's doorstep, the Hong Kong Trail takes you swiftly into secluded hills, isolated woodland and high paths that afford amazing views of the rugged south and (eventually) glimpses of its surf-beaten shore once you've tackled the formidable Dragon's Back ridge. Starting from the Peak Tram upper terminus (Map pp62–3) on the Peak, the 50km-long Hong Kong Trail takes in Pok Fu Lam Reservoir near Aberdeen, before turning east and zigzagging across the ridges. The trail traverses four country parks including beautiful Tai Tam, with its dense emerald woods and trickling streams.

Lantau Trail

Arguably Hong Kong's most remote trail, the 70km-long Lantau Trail (Map p140) is tough but hugely rewarding, following the mountain tops from Mui Wo and then doubling back at Tai O and along some spectacular and sparsely populated coast to where it started. It takes just over 24 hours to walk in full, but the trail is divided into a dozen manageable stages ranging from 2.5km (45 minutes) to 10.5km (three hours).

MacLehose Trail

The 100km MacLehose Trail (Map pp58–9), the territory's longest hiking path, spans the New Territories from Tuen Mun in the west to Pak Tam Chung on the Sai Kung Peninsula in the east. The trail follows the ridge, goes over Tai Mo Shan, at 957m Hong Kong's highest peak, and passes close to Ma On Shan (702m), the territory's fourth-tallest mountain. The trail's 10 stages range in length from about 4.6km (1½ hours) to 15.6km (five hours). The highlight is the breathtaking and largely unspoiled Sai Kung Peninsula at the trial's eastern end.

Wilson Trail

Something of an oddity, the Wilson Trail (Map pp58–9), which is 78km long (or 82.5km if you include the MTR harbour crossing) is unusual in that its southern section (two stages, 11.4km, 4½ hours) is on Hong Kong Island, while its northern part (eight stages, 66.6km, 26½ hours) crosses the eastern harbour to Lei Yue Mun in New Kowloon and then carries on into the New Territories.

Parts of the Wilson Trail overlap with the Hong Kong Trail on Hong Kong Island and with the MacLehose Trail in the New Territories, particularly in the area east of Tai Mo Shan.

HORSE RIDING

The Hong Kong Jockey Club's Tuen Mun Public Riding School (Map pp58–9; ☎ 2461 3338; Lot No 45, Lung Mun Rd, Tuen Mun; ☉ 9am-6pm Tue-Sun; Tuen Mun MTR) in the New Territories offers private lessons for about $360 per hour, as does the club's Pok Fu Lam Public Riding School (Map p62–3; ☎ 2550 1359; 75 Pok Fu Lam Reservoir Rd) in southeastern Hong Kong Island.

KAYAKING & CANOEING

The Cheung Chau Windsurfing Water Sports Centre (Map p146; ☎ 2981 2772; www.ccwindc.com.hk) located at Tung Wan beach rents out single/double kayaks for $60/100 per hour. These are also available at the St Stephen's Beach Water Sports Centre (off Map p96; ☎ 2813 5407; Wong Ma Kok Path; ☉ closed Tue; ☒ 6, 6A, 6X) located in Stanley.

Canoeing facilities are available through the Tai Mei Tuk Water Sports Centre (Map pp58–9; ☎ 2665 3591; ☉ closed Wed; ☒ 75K) at Tai Mei Tuk in the New Territories. You can also enquire at the Wong Shek Water Sports Centre (Map pp58–9; ☎ 2328 2311; Wong Shek pier, Sai Kung; ☉ closed Tue; ☒ 92, 299) in the New Territories.

Natural Excursion Ideals (☎ 9300 5197; www.kayak-and-hike.com) has organised kayaking trips out of its base in Sai Kung in the New Territories from $700. Dragonfly (☎ 2111 8917; www.dragonfly.com.hk) has similar excursions on offer.

MARTIAL ARTS

The HKTB (☎ 2508 1234), through its Cultural Kaleidoscope program, offers free one-hour t'ai chi lessons at 8am on Monday, Wednesday, Thursday and Friday on the waterfront promenade outside the Hong Kong Cultural Centre (p99) in Tsim Sha Tsui. A further class runs at 9am on Saturday on the Peak Tower (p89) rooftop. On Sunday from 2.30pm to 4.30pm a display of traditional Chinese martial arts takes place at Kung Fu Corner near Sculpture Walk in Kowloon Park (p102).

Fightin' Fit (Map p78; ☎ 2526 6648; www.fightinfit.com.hk; 303a, 3rd fl, Peter Bldg, 56-62 Queens Rd, Central; MTR Central, exit D)

Hong Kong Chinese Martial Arts Association (☎ 2504 8164)

Hong Kong Tai Chi Association (☎ 2395 4884; www.hktaichi.com)

Hong Kong Wushu Union (☎ 2504 8226; www.hkwushuu.com.hk) Has classes for children.

KUNG FU & YOU

Chinese *gùng-fù* (kung fu) is the basis for many Asian martial arts. Hundreds of styles of martial arts have evolved since about AD 500, including *mō-seut,* which is full of expansive strides and strokes and great to watch in competition; *wing-chèun,* the late actor and martial-arts master Bruce Lee's original style, indigenous to Hong Kong, which combines blocks, punches and low kicks; and *taai-gik* (t'ai chi), the slow-motion 'shadow boxing' that has been popular for centuries.

As you can see every morning in the parks throughout Hong Kong, t'ai chi is the most visible and commonly practised form of kung fu today. Not only is it a terrific form of exercise, improving your muscle tone, developing breathing muscles and promoting good health in general, but it also forms a solid foundation for any other martial-arts practice. Its various forms are characterised by deep, powerful stances, soft and flowing hand techniques and relaxed breathing.

In China martial arts were traditionally passed down through patriarchal family lines and seldom taught to outsiders, as these skills were considered far too valuable to spread indiscriminately. During the Cultural Revolution, when all teachings outside Maoist philosophy were suppressed, the practise of innocuous-looking t'ai chi was allowed, helping kung fu to live on when so much traditional culture had disappeared.

Wan Kei Ho International Martial Arts Association (☎ 2544 1368, 9885 8336; www.kungfuwan.com)

Wing Chun Yip Man Martial Arts Athletic Association (Map p104; ☎ 2723 2306; Unit A, 5th fl, Alpha House, 27-33 Nathan Rd, Tsim Sha Tsui; MTR Tsim Sha Tsui, exit E) Charges $500 a month for three lessons a week (two or three hours each) and has a six-month intensive course (six hours a day, six days a week) for around $5000, depending on the student.

RUNNING

It's hot, humid, hilly, crowded, congested and the air quality can be shocking. Apart from that Hong Kong is a great place to run.

The best places to run on Hong Kong Island include Harlech and Lugard Rds on the Peak, Bowen Rd above Wan Chai, the track in Victoria Park and the Happy Valley racecourse (as long as there aren't any horse races on it!). In Kowloon a popular place to run is the Tsim Sha Tsui East Promenade. Lamma makes an ideal place for trail runners with plenty of paths and dirt trails, great views and, best of all, no cars.

For easy runs followed by brewskis and good company, contact the Hong Kong Hash House Harriers (www.hkhash.com), the main local branch of a lively organisation with members worldwide, or the Ladies' Hash House Harriers (www.hk ladieshash.com). The inappropriately named Ladies Road Runners Club (www.hklrrc.org) allows men to join in the fun. Another group that organises runs is Athletic Veterans of Hong Kong (www.avohk.org).

SCUBA DIVING

Hong Kong has some surprisingly worthwhile diving spots, particularly in the far northeast, and there is certainly no shortage of courses. One of the best sources of information for courses and excursions is Sai Kung–based

Splash Hong Kong (☎ 2792 4495, 9047 9603; www.splashhk .com). Other outfits giving lessons and organising dives:

Bunn's Divers (p164) Organises dives in Sai Kung on Sunday for about $500 (less for members).

Ocean Sky Divers (p169) This dive shop runs PADI courses and organises local dives from $270.

SKATING

There are several major ice-skating rinks in Hong Kong, the newest and flashiest being MegaIce, a 57m-long rink with spectacular harbour and city views.

Cityplaza Ice Palace (Map pp62–3; ☎ 2844 8688; www. icepalace.com.hk; 1st fl, Cityplaza 2, 18 Tai Koo Shing Rd, Tai Koo; admission Mon-Fri $45, Sat & Sun before/after 2.30pm $60/70; ☽ 9am-8.45pm Mon-Sat, 9am-6pm Sun; MTR Tai Koo, exit E)

Dragon Centre Sky Rink (Map pp100–1; ☎ 2307 9264; www.skyrinkhk.com; 8th fl, Dragon Centre, 37K Yen Chow St, Sham Shui Po, Kowloon; ☽ 9.30am-10pm Mon-Fri, 7.30am-10pm Sat, 12.30-7.30pm Sun; MTR Quarry Bay, exit B)

Festival Walk Glacier (Map pp100–1; ☎ 2544 3588; www.glacier.com.hk; 8th fl, Festival Walk Shopping Centre, 80 Tat Chee Ave, Kowloon Tong; admission Mon-Fri $40-50, Sat & Sun $60-70; ☽ 10.30am-10pm Mon, Wed-Fri, 10.30am-8pm Tue, 8.30am-10pm Sat, 1-5.30pm Sun; MTR Kowloon Tong, exit C2)

MegaIce (Map pp100–1; ☎ 2709 4020; www.megaice .com.hk; 10th fl, Megabox, Wang Chui Rd, Kowloon; admission Mon-Fri $40-50, Sat & Sun $60-70; ☽ 10am-8.30pm Mon-Thu, 10am-10.30pm Fri, 9.30am-9pm Sat, 9am-7.30pm Sun; MTR Kowloon Bay, exit A)

SQUASH

There are almost 80 squash centres scattered around the territory. The Hong Kong Squash Centre (Map p72; ☎ 2860 0229; 23 Cotton Tree Dr, Central; per

30min $27; ☺ 7am-11pm) has some of the most modern facilities, with 18 courts bordering Hong Kong Park in Central. There are three squash courts located at Queen Elizabeth Stadium (Map p74; ☎ 2591 1346; 18 Oi Kwan Rd, Wan Chai; ⊕ Morrison Hill Rd) and at Kowloon Park Sports Centre (Map p104; ☎ 2724 3344; 22 Austin Rd, Tsim Sha Tsui; MTR Jordan, exit C3).

TENNIS

The Hong Kong Tennis Centre (Map pp62–3; ☎ 2574 9122; 33 Wong Nai Chung Gap Rd, Happy Valley; per hr day/evening $42/57; ☺ 7am-11pm), with 17 courts, is on the spectacular pass in the hills between Happy Valley and Deep Water Bay on Hong Kong Island. It's usually easy to get a court only during working hours. Other courts available:

Bowen Road Sports Ground (Map p72; ☎ 2528 2983; Bowen Dr, Mid-Levels; ☺ 6am-7pm; MTR Admiralty) Four courts.

King's Park Tennis Courts (Map p108; ☎ 2385 8985; 15 King's Park Rise, Yau Ma Tei; ☺ 7am-11pm; MTR Yau Ma Tei, exit D) Six courts.

Victoria Park (Map p85; ☎ 2890 5824; Hing Fat St, Causeway Bay; ☺ 6am or 7am-11pm; MTR Causeway Bay, exit E) Fourteen courts.

WINDSURFING & WAKEBOARDING

Windsurfing is extremely popular in Hong Kong; the territory's only Olympic gold medal to date (Atlanta, 1996) was won in this sport. The best time for windsurfing is October to December, when a steady northeast monsoon wind blows. Boards and other equipment are available for rent at St Stephen's Beach Water Sports Centre (off Map p96; ☎ 2813 5407) in Stanley on Hong Kong Island, at the Windsurfing Centre (off Map p130; ☎ 2792 5605) in Sha Ha just north of Sai Kung in the New Territories, at the Cheung Chau Windsurfing Water Sports Centre (Map p146; ☎ 2981 2772; www.ccwindc.com.hk) on Cheung Chau and at Long Coast Seasports (Map p140; ☎ 2980 3222) on Lantau.

The Windsurfing Association of Hong Kong (☎ 2504 8255; www.windsurfing.org.hk) has some courses for juniors.

Wakeboarding has grown tremendously in popularity in recent years. Deep Water Bay is a popular area for the sport, but for other venues contact the Hong Kong Wakeboarding Association, which shares a website with the Hong Kong Water Ski Association (☎ 2504 8168; www.waterski.org.hk).

YACHTING & SAILING

Even if you're not a member, you can check with any of the following yachting clubs to see if races are being held and whether an afternoon's sail is possible.

Aberdeen Boat Club (Map p94; ☎ 2552 8182; www.abcclub-hk.com; 20 Shum Wan Rd, Aberdeen; ☒ 70, 73 & 793)

Aberdeen Marina Club (Map p94; ☎ 2555 8321; www.aberdeenmarinaclub.com; 8 Shum Wan Rd, Aberdeen; ☒ 70, 73 & 793)

Hebe Haven Yacht Club (Map pp58–9; ☎ 2719 9682; www.hhyc.org.hk; 10.5 Milestone, Hiram's Hwy, Pak Sha Wan; ☒ 92 or 299)

Royal Hong Kong Yacht Club (Map p85; ☎ 2832 2817; www.rhkyc.org.hk; Hung Hing Rd, Kellett Island, Causeway Bay)

A major sailing event in Hong Kong is the Hong Kong–Manila yacht race, which takes place every two years. Phone the Royal Hong Kong Yacht Club or contact the Hong Kong Sailing Federation (☎ 2504 8159; www.sailing.org.hk) for details.

If there is a group of you, you should consider hiring a junk for the day or evening. Eight hours of vessel hire (four hours for night trips), plus a captain and deck hand, are usually included in the price. Jubilee International Tour Centre (Map p67; ☎ 2530 0530; www.jubilee.com.hk; Room 2305-6, Far East Consortium Bldg, 121 Des Voeux Rd Central; ☺ 8.30am-5.30pm Mon-Fri, 8.30am-1pm Sat; MTR Sheung Wan, exit E3) hires out vessels for 10 to 25 people from $2000 on weekdays and $3000 on the weekend.

Jaspa's has six junks for hire carrying up to 40 people each. The minimum booking is for 14 guests. An evening or daytime party, including drinks and a full menu prepared and served on board, costs $600/200/100 for adults/children/infants. There must be a minimum of 14 passengers. The boat can pick up or drop off guests at either Sai Kung or Causeway Bay. Ring Jaspa's Party Junk (☎ 2869 0733; www.jaspasjunk.com) or consult the website for details.

SPECTATOR SPORTS

Sporting events are well covered in the sports section of Hong Kong's English-language newspapers. Many of the annual events don't fall on the same day or even in the same month every year, so contact the Hong Kong Tourism Board (HKTB; ☎ 2508 1234; www.discoverhongkong.com) for further information.

CRICKET

Hong Kong has two cricket clubs: the very exclusive Hong Kong Cricket Club (Map pp62–3; ☎ 3511 8668; www.hkcc.org; 137 Wong Nai Chung Gap Rd; ☒ 63), above Deep Water Bay on Hong Kong Island, and the Kowloon Cricket Club (Map p106; ☎ 3473 7000; www.kcc.org.hk; 10 Cox's Rd, Tsim Sha Tsui; MTR Jordan, exit E), where the Hong Kong International Cricket Sixes is held in late October or early November. This two-day event sees teams from Australia, New Zealand, Hong Kong, England, the West Indies, India, Pakistan, Sri Lanka and South Africa battle it out in a speedier version of the game. For info, contact the Hong Kong Cricket Association (☎ 2504 8102; www.hkca.cricket.org).

FOOTBALL (SOCCER)

Hong Kong has a fairly lively amateur soccer league. Games are played at the Happy Valley Sports Ground (Map p85; ☎ 2895 1523; Sports Rd, Happy Valley; ☒ Happy Valley), a group of pitches inside the Happy Valley Racecourse, and at Mong Kok Stadium (Map p111; ☎ 2380 0188; 37 Flower Market Rd, Mong Kok; MTR Prince Edward, exit B1). For match schedules and venues, check the sports sections of the English-language newspapers or contact the Hong Kong Football Association (☎ 2712 9122; www.hkfa.com). The big football event of the year is the Lunar New Year Cup, which is held on the first and fourth days of the Chinese New Year (late January/early February).

HORSE RACING

Horse racing is Hong Kong's biggest spectator sport, probably because until recently it was the only form of legalised gambling in the territory apart from the Mark Six Lottery, and no one likes to wager like the Hong Kong Chinese. There are about 80 meetings a year at two racecourses: one in Happy Valley (p90) on Hong Kong Island, with a capacity for 35,000 punters, and the newer and larger one at Sha Tin (p128) in the New Territories accommodating around 80,000.

The racing season is from September to June, with most race meetings at Happy Valley taking place on Wednesday at 7pm or 7.30pm and at Sha Tin on Saturday or Sunday afternoon. Check the website of the Hong Kong Jockey Club (HKJC; ☎ information hotline 1817; www.hkjc.com; Ground fl, Kin Lee Bldg, 130 Jaffe Rd, Wan Chai; MTR Central, exit J3) for details, or pick up a list of race meetings from any HKTB information centre.

top picks

ONLY IN HONG KONG

- Morning t'ai chi in the park (p227)
- Betting on the horses at uniquely urban Happy Valley (left)
- Cheers and beers at the Rugby Sevens (below)
- Watching (or joining in) the Dragon Boat Racing festival (p17)
- Hiking from city into jungle on the Hong Kong Trail (p227)

You have three choices if you want to attend a meeting. You can join the crowds and pay $10 to sit in the public area. Or, if you've been in Hong Kong for less than 21 days and are over 18 years of age, you can buy a tourist badge ($100 to $150, depending on the meeting), which allows you to jump the queue, sit in the members' area and walk around near the finish area. These can be purchased at the gate on the day, or up to 10 days in advance at any branch of the HKJC. Bring along your passport as proof. The last choice is to join one of the racing tours (p90) sponsored by the HKTB.

The HKJC maintains off-track betting centres around the territory, including a Central branch (Map p67; Unit A1, Ground fl, CMA Bldg, 64 Connaught Rd Central; MTR Central, exit J3), a Wan Chai branch (Map p74; Ground fl, Kin Lee Bldg, 130 Jaffe Rd; MTR Wan Chai, exit A1) and a Tsim Sha Tsui branch (Map p104; Ground fl, Eader Centre, 39-41 Hankow Rd; MTR Tsim Sha Tsui, exit E).

Red-letter days at the races include the Chinese New Year races in late January or early February, the Hong Kong Derby in March, the Queen Elizabeth II Cup in April and the Hong Kong International Races in December.

RUGBY

The Rugby World Cup Sevens (www.hksevens.com.hk) sees teams from all over the world come together in Hong Kong in late March for three days of lightning-fast 15-minute matches at the 40,000-seat Hong Kong Stadium (Map p85; ☎ 2895 7926; www.lcsd.gov.hk/stadium; ☒ Happy Valley) in So Kon Po, a division of Causeway Bay. Even nonrugby fans scramble to get tickets (adult/child $880/300), because the Sevens is a giant, international, three-day party. For inquiries and tickets, contact the Hong Kong Rugby Football Union (☎ 2504 8311; www.hkrugby.com).

SLEEPING

top picks

- Courtyard by Marriott Hong Kong (p237)
- The Four Seasons (p240)
- Golden Island Guesthouse (p247)
- Hotel Jen (p238)
- Mandarin Oriental (p240)
- Peninsula Hong Kong (p241)
- Putman (p239)
- Salisbury (p244)
- W Hong Kong (p245)

SLEEPING

In a city where a foot of land, as the saying goes, is worth an inch of gold, money makes all the difference when you're looking for a bed for the night. If you have cash, you'll be spoiled for choice, so wide is the range of luxurious places. The middle range of the price spectrum tends to be crowded with adequate but less inspiring options, while further down the price scale the pickings get thinner – the defining feature here is hostels and guesthouses with broom cupboard–sized rooms.

But things have been improving of late. Since the easing of cross-border travel restrictions by China in 2003, visitors from the mainland have overtaken travellers from Japan and the West to become the single largest market for Hong Kong. As many of these northern visitors come mainly to shop, they seek out affordable accommodations in central locations. The global recession also means that hotels and guesthouses have to work harder to attract customers. Many budget addresses have improved their standards, and many midrange places and even top-end hotels are offering big discounts (especially during the shoulder and low seasons) on their posted rates, which are the ones listed in this chapter. But whatever your budget, accommodation costs are generally higher in Hong Kong than most other Asian cities, but cheaper than those in Europe and the US.

The two high seasons of Hong Kong's hotels have traditionally been from March to April and October to November, though things can be tight around Chinese New Year (late January or February) as well. When big trade fairs come to town in January, April and October, accommodation in Wan Chai (and areas with easy access to Wan Chai, such as Tsim Sha Tsui) is very tight and prices rocket. Outside these periods, rates can drop – sometimes substantially.

Almost all midrange to top-end hotels, and most guesthouses, offer broadband and/or wi-fi access (often free at guesthouses and usually starting at $40 per hour in the hotels), as well as computers for guests' use. The only places reviewed in this chapter that have no internet access whatsoever are Causeway Bay Guest House (p240), Man Lai Wah Hotel (p249) and Mui Wo Inn (p250). Due to the economic downturn, the majority of the hotels reviewed offer long-stay discounts and/or packages, some available only with advanced booking, so remember to inquire when you reserve a room.

The accommodation options in this guide are listed by price and by area.

ACCOMMODATION STYLES
Hotels

Hong Kong's luxury hotels are locked in an arms race for the dollars of affluent travellers. Their weapons are superstar restaurants, a choice of airport transit by Rolls Royce Phantom or helicopter, lavish spa complexes and infinity pools. Then, of course, there's the silky-smooth service and attention to your most footling whims.

It doesn't come cheaply though. Prices for top-of-the-range hotels start from about $2600 per room. A few such hotels – the Four Seasons, Peninsula and Mandarin Oriental, for example – offer comfort, amenities and service that compete with or surpass that of the world's finest five-star hotels.

Top-end hotels, starting at a minimum of $1600, are in spiffy locations; they also have smart, comfortable rooms with a good variety of room-service options. Amenities include business facilities, bars and restaurants, and fluent English-speaking staff.

While midrange hotels used to be generic business and/or leisure establishments with little to distinguish one from another, many new places have sprung up that are uniquely cool to look at and easy on the pocket, with room rates hovering in the high hundreds and dipping to budget range in the low season. Rooms at these places tend to be small and come with limited cable TV, wireless broadband connection and room service.

The majority of Hong Kong's budget hotels are in Kowloon, with many on or near Nathan Rd. Though most budget hotel rooms are small, the places listed here are clean and cheerily shabby or neat and austere, rather than grim and grimy. All have air-con and most have TVs, phones and private bathrooms. Anything under $600 should be considered budget.

Hotels in Hong Kong add 10% service and 3% government tax to your bill, something guesthouses and hostels usually do not do. The rates quoted in this book do not include these charges.

Guesthouses

Dominating the lower end of the accommodation market are guesthouses, usually a block of tiny rooms squeezed into a converted apartment or two. Often several guesthouses operate out of the same building. Your options are greater if there are two of you; find a double room in a clean guesthouse for $200 to $250 and your accommodation costs will fall sharply. Some offer dormitory accommodation for those on very tight budgets.

Depending on the season and location, try to negotiate a better deal, as a lot of places will be eager to fill empty rooms. Most guesthouses offer some sort of internet access, from a single PC at reception to free wi-fi in your room.

Hostels & Camp Sites

The Hong Kong Youth Hostels Association (HKYHA; Map pp100–1; ☎ 2788 1638; www.yha.org.hk; Shop 118, 1st fl, Fu Cheong Shopping Centre, Shum Mong Rd, Sham Shui Po; MTR Nam Cheong, exit A) maintains seven hostels affiliated with Hostelling International (HI). It sells HKYHA and HI cards (p291). If you intend on buying a membership card at one of the hostels, be sure to take along a visa-sized photo and some identification.

All HKYHA hostels have separate toilets and showers for men and women, and cooking facilities. They provide blankets, pillows and sheet bags, though you may prefer to take your own. Most hostels have lockers available.

Prices for a bed in a dormitory range from $30 to $100 a night, depending on the hostel and whether you are a junior (under 18 years of age) or senior member.

Only two of the hostels are open daily. Jockey Club Mount Davis Hostel (p239) allows check-in from 3pm till 11pm daily, while Bradbury Jockey Club Youth Hostel (p248) is open to guests from 4pm to 11pm on weekdays and 3pm to 11pm on weekends and holidays. Travellers are not normally permitted to stay more than six nights, but this can be negotiated with the HKYHA.

If you're booking more than three days in advance, ring or email the HKYHA head office. International computerised bookings are also possible for Jockey Club Mount Davis Hostel and Bradbury Jockey Club Youth Hostel. To reserve a bed less than three days before your stay, call the particular hostel directly. The phone numbers of the individual hostels are listed in the relevant reviews in this chapter.

The Country & Marine Parks Authority (☎ 1823; www.afcd.gov.hk) maintains about 38 basic camp sites in the New Territories and Outlying Islands that are intended for walkers and hikers (see p226 for details).

Rental Accommodation

Those staying in Hong Kong for over a month may be interested in serviced apartments (see p234 for recommendations). Many hotels now also offer extraordinarily good-value, long-term packages at certain times throughout the year.

Other than that, a one-bedroom apartment in the Mid-Levels will cost anywhere from $10,000 a month. That same apartment will go for somewhat less in Tsim Sha Tsui or Wan Chai. The districts in eastern Hong Kong Island, western Hong Kong Island, and northeastern or northwestern Kowloon are more affordable – you may even find a one-bedroom apartment (roughly 60 sq metres) for as little as $5000 a month. A guide to prices and availability can be found on the website www.gohome.com.hk.

Apartments are generally rented out with little or no furniture, but used furnishings can easily be bought from departing foreigners. Check the noticeboards at pubs and supermarkets, particularly around expatriate housing areas. Also check the classified advertisements of the weekend English-language papers and HK Magazine or try the website www.asiaxpat.com. Estate agents usually take a fee equivalent to two weeks' rent. Other upfront expenses include a deposit, usually equal to two months' rent, and, of course, the first month's rent in advance.

Long-term accommodation on the Outlying Islands and in the Sai Kung area of the New Territories offers far better value than the equivalent on Hong Kong Island or in Kowloon. Things to weigh up, however, include transport costs and the time spent commuting. Though nowhere near as cheap, Discovery Bay on Lantau is another affordable option.

Price Guide

$$$$	More than $2600
$$$	$1600 to $2600
$$	$600 to $1600
$	Up to $600

RESERVATIONS

Making a reservation for accommodation is not essential outside peak periods, but it can save you a lot of time, hassle and, depending on the season, money. If you fly into Hong Kong without having booked anything, the Hong Kong Hotels Association (HKHA; Map p104; ☎ 2375 3838; www .hkha.org; 508-511 Silvercord Tower Two, 30 Canton Rd, Tsim Sha Tsui; 🚇 Star Ferry, MTR Tsim Sha Tsui, exit A1) has reservation centres located inside Halls A and B (level 5) of the Hong Kong International Airport. It can book you into a midrange or top-end hotel room for as much as 50% cheaper than if you were to walk in yourself.

Booking through a travel agent can garner substantial discounts – sometimes up to 40% off the walk-in price. If you're in Hong Kong and want to book a midrange or luxury hotel, contact Phoenix Services Agency (Map p106; ☎ 2722 7378; info@phoenixtrvl.com; Room 1404, 14th fl, Austin Tower, 22-26 Austin Ave, Tsim Sha Tsui; 🕘 9am-6pm Mon-Fri, 9am-4pm Sat) or Traveller Services (Map p104; ☎ 2375 2277; www.taketraveller.com; 1813 Miramar Tower, 132 Nathan Rd, Tsim Sha Tsui; 🕘 9am-6pm Mon-Fri, 9am-1pm Sat).

SERVICED APARTMENTS
Hong Kong Island

Ice House (p241) and the Putman (p239) also have serviced apartments available.

SHAMA Map p85 $$$$

☎ 2202 5555; www.shama.com; 7th fl, 8 Russell St, Causeway Bay; studios per month from $26,200, 1-/2-bedroom apt from $36,300/63,000; MTR Causeway Bay (exit A); 🖳

These are among the most attractive serviced apartments in Hong Kong, in a block opposite Times Square shopping mall. Ranging from fairly spacious studio flats to two-bedroom apartments, they're all tastefully furnished and exceedingly comfortable. Features and extras include broadband, DVD equipment, laundry facilities on each floor and membership to gyms. There are

Price Guide – One-Bedroom Apartments (Monthly)	
$$$$	More than $35,000
$$$	$25,000 to $35,000
$$	$15,000 to $25,000
$	Up to $15,000

also branches in Central, Soho, Wan Chai and Tsim Sha Tsui; contact the Shama main office (Map p78; ☎ 2522 3082; www.shama.com; 8th fl, Shama Pl, 30 Hollywood Rd, Central) for details.

HOME2HOME Map p78 $$$$

☎ 2165 1082; www.home2home.hk; 1704 Universal Trade Centre, 3 Arbuthnot Rd, Central; MTR Central (exit D)

This company has several properties with serviced studio flats and one-bedroom apartments, including Ovolo (Map p78; ☎ 3105 2600; 2 Arbuthnot Rd; 1-bedroom flats per month $38,000-55,000; MTR Central, exit D) in Central, and Erba (Map p80; ☎ 2910 0700; 284 Queen's Rd Central; studios per month $19,000-25,000, 1-bedroom flats per month $31,000-38,000; MTR Sheung Wan, exit A2) in Sheung Wan.

FRASER SUITES Map p74 $$$

☎ 3966 0000; 74-80 Johnston Rd; http://hongkong .frasershospitality.com; 1-bedroom apt per month from $29,800; MTR Wan Chai (exit B3); 🛜 🖳

The 87 one-bedroom units at this central place come with soundproof glass, laundry facilities, kitchenette and a large dose of Singaporean good manners. The apartments are modestly sized but pleasant. The rates include thrice-a-week cleaning, and use of the gym, Jacuzzi and swimming pool.

HANLUN HABITATS Map p78 $$$

☎ 2868 0168; www.hanlunhabitats.com; 21st fl, Winway Bldg, 50 Wellington St, Central; MTR Central (exit D2)

This agency has three properties with serviced and furnished flats within striking distance of each other in the Mid-Levels and accessible via the Central Escalator to Central and Soho. Daisy Court (Map p88; ☎ 2533 7203; 31 Shelley St, the Mid-Levels; MTR Central, exit D1; 🛜) has one-bedroom flats measuring about 46 sq metres from $22,000 a month. Peach Blossom (Map p88; ☎ 2234 8202; 15 Mosque St, the Mid-Levels; MTR Central, exit D1; 🛜) has one-bedroom flats of about 64 sq metres for $25,000. Lily Court (Map p88; ☎ 2822 9508; 28 Robinson Rd, the Mid-Levels; 🚌 26; 🛜) has one-bedroom flats of about 67 sq metres for around $28,000.

YWCA BUILDING Map p80 $$

☎ 2915 2345; www.ywca.org.hk; 38C Bonham Rd, the Mid-Levels; studios per month $7600-9200, 1-bedroom apt $16,800-18,800; 🚌 23, 40 or 40M

This large block of serviced apartments is not in the most convenient of locations, but it's accessible by bus from Admiralty and Central, open to men and women, and is reasonably cheap. There are TVs, phones and broadband in the rooms, a laundry and a decent coffee shop on the 1st floor. All rooms require a minimum stay of seven nights.

BAUHINIA FURNISHED SUITES
Map p80 $

☎ 2156 3000; www.apartments.com.hk; 119-120 Connaught Rd, Central; 1-bedroom flats per month $13,500-19,000, 2-bedroom flats $18,000-28,000; MTR Sheung Wan (exit A1)

This very central outfit has more than 110 furnished and serviced flats on offer. Prices usually depend on whether you want an open or enclosed kitchen, and include daily cleaning, wired broadband, cooking utensils and crockery, and laundry facilities. Enter from Man Wah Lane.

DOMUS MERCURY SERVICED APARTMENTS Map p85 $

☎ 3616 6000; www.domus.com.hk; 23 Mercury St; studios per month from $12,800; MTR Tin Hau (exit A1); 🖳 🛜

This place has modest (under 500 sq ft) studio apartments and two-bed flats (980 sq ft) furnished in white and glass. Units facing the harbour (west) get little reprieve from the sun from mid-afternoon till sunset. However, the special heat-insulated windows should keep the flats reasonably cool. There are fitness and self-service laundry facilities.

Kowloon

HAN RESIDENCE Map p104 $$

☎ 2878 2878; www.hanresidence.com; 14-16 Hankow Rd, Tsim Sha Tsui; studios per month from $17,500, 1-bedroom apt from $21,000; MTR Tsim Sha Tsui (exit E); 🛜

These pleasant studio and one-bedroom apartments are so new that you can still smell the paint. Some of the living rooms are a little dark and the views are nothing spectacular, but you can't beat the location. Long-stay discounts apply.

PINNACLE APARTMENT Map p106 $$

☎ 2734 8288; www.pinnacleapartment.com; 8 Minden Ave; 1-bedroom apt per month $18,600-30,000, 2-bedroom $24,200-39,100; MTR Tsim Sha Tsui (exit G)

This elegant block of serviced apartments has four different size apartments available,

Long-Term Hotel Deals

As well as the serviced apartments listed in this section, several hotels and guesthouses across the territory offer discounted rates for stays of a week or more.

- Anne Black YWCA (Mong Kok, p248)
- Bridal Tea House Hotel (Yau Ma Tei, p246)
- Caritas Lodge (Mong Kok, p248)
- City Garden Hotel Hong Kong (Fortress Hill, p241)
- Cityview (Yau Ma Tei, p246)
- Harbour View (Wan Chai, p236)
- Hotel Bonaparte (Causeway Bay, p240)
- Mingle Place at the Eden (Central, p241)
- Mingle Place by the Park (Wan Chai, p237)
- Silvermine Beach Hotel (Lantau, p250)
- Warwick Hotel (Cheung Chau, p250)
- Wesley Hong Kong (Admiralty, p237)

ranging in size from 47 to 90 sq metres. Some have harbour views. Staff here are delightful.

HONG KONG ISLAND

The lion's share of Hong Kong Island's luxury hotels is in Central and Admiralty, catering predominantly to the business market. A handful of good midrange options do exist though, so don't dismiss the idea of staying in Central if your budget can stretch beyond guesthouse levels.

ADMIRALTY & WAN CHAI

Admiralty is home to two of the best high-end hotels in Hong Kong and that's your lot. Wan Chai is generally all about midrange accommodation, with a sprinkling of cheaper guesthouses and a couple of high-end options at the Convention & Exhibition Centre.

GRAND HYATT HOTEL
Map p74 Luxury Hotel $$$$

☎ 2588 1234; www.hongkong.grand.hyatt .com; 1 Harbour Rd, Wan Chai; s/d/ste from $4500/4700/9500; 🚌 18, MTR Wan Chai (exit A5); 🖳 🛜 🖭

Vast and unrestrained luxury in the public and private areas is the defining characteristic here. Subtle it is not. The rooms are huge, sporting desks bristling with technology, marble-clad bathrooms and some great views. Its Champagne Bar (p211) is very classy and its Italian restaurant Grissini (p178) is one of the best in town. The stunning

Plateau, a 7500-sq-metre spa complex with every treatment imaginable, is an oasis on the 11th floor with its own zenlike residential rooms.

CONRAD HONG KONG
Map p72   Luxury Hotel $$$$

☎ 2521 3838; www.conradhotels.com; Pacific Pl, 88 Queensway, Admiralty; r/ste from $4400/7000; MTR Admiralty (exit F) via Pacific Pl; 🖳 🛜 🖳 (executive fl)
This elegantly unstuffy hotel above Pacific Pl gets enthusiastic reviews for its attention to business travellers' needs, despite its vast size, and for its eateries (Golden Leaf Restaurant and Nicholini's).

ISLAND SHANGRI-LA HONG KONG
Map p72   Luxury Hotel $$$$

☎ 2877 3838; www.shangri-la.com; Pacific Pl, Supreme Court Rd, Admiralty; s/d/ste from $4200/4500/7500; MTR Admiralty (exit F), via Pacific Pl mall; 🖳 🛜 🖳
The monolithic exterior does not prepare you for the sophistication waiting inside. The guestrooms are among the loveliest in Hong Kong and the public spaces almost match them. Take a quick ride up the bubble lift that links the 39th and 56th floors; you'll catch a glance of the hotel's signature 60m-high painting, a mountainous Chinese landscape said to be the largest in the world. Facilities include an outdoor spa, a 24-hour business centre and a good selection of food outlets.

RENAISSANCE HARBOUR VIEW
HOTEL Map p74   Luxury Hotel $$$$

☎ 2802 8888; www.marriott.com/hotel-search/china/; 1 Harbour Rd; r $3300-4100, ste from $5000; 🚌 18, MTR Wan Chai (exit A5); 🖳 🖳
This spectacular hotel with a cavernous marble lobby adjoins the Hong Kong Convention & Exhibition Centre, ensuring steady suit-and-tie custom and marvellous harbour views from 65% of the guestrooms. Leisure travellers will appreciate the good service, outdoor pool and activities complex with a golf driving range and tennis courts. Rates drop significantly in off-peak periods.

FLEMING Map p74   Business Hotel $$$

☎ 3607 2288; www.thefleming.com; 41 Fleming Rd; r $1880-2980; MTR Wan Chai (exit A2); 🖳 🛜
Forgive the new 'urban lifestyle concept' marketing drivel. This is just the kind of

stylish, small-ish hotel Wan Chai needs. Located on a quiet road set back from all the Wan Chai nighttime madness, the rooms strike a good balance between smart minimalism and cosy homeliness. Executive rooms come complete with a home office, kitchenette and yoga mats, and there's also a secure, women-only floor.

METROPARK HOTEL Map p74   Hotel $$$

☎ 2863 7330; www.metroparkhotelwanchai.com; 41-49 Hennessy Rd; r $1600-2200, ste from $3800; MTR Wan Chai (exit B); 🖳
This hotel had some unwanted publicity when it was shut down for seven days after one of its guests was found to be the carrier of Asia's first confirmed case of swine flu. But we don't think that should deter anyone from staying here. It's central, the rooms are spick and span, and the staff helpful.

EMPIRE HOTEL HONG KONG
Map p74   Hotel $$$

☎ 3692 2111; www.empirehotel.com.hk; 33 Hennessy Rd, Wan Chai; r/ste from $1600/2800; MTR Wan Chai (exit A2); 🖳 🖳
With its sunny staff, pleasant rooms, outdoor swimming pool and fitness centre on the 21st-floor terrace, the 360-room Empire is a good option and an easy hop from the Hong Kong Convention & Exhibition Centre. Enter from Fenwick St.

HARBOUR VIEW Map p74   Hotel $$$

☎ 2802 0111; www.theharbourview.com.hk; 4 Harbour Rd; r $1600, fortnightly/monthly packages from $7000/14,400; 🚌 18, MTR Wan Chai (exit A5); 🖳 🖳
Right next door to the Hong Kong Arts Centre and a mere stroll to the Hong Kong Convention & Exhibition Centre and Wan Chai ferry terminal, this 320-room, YMCA-run hotel is excellent value. It offers simply furnished but adequate rooms, and exceptionally friendly staff. Room rack rates can drop by as much as 45%.

CHARTERHOUSE HOTEL Map p74   Hotel $$

☎ 2833 5566; www.charterhouse.com; 209-219 Wan Chai Rd; s/d/ste from $1400/1700/2000; MTR Wan Chai (exit A3), 🚋 Morrison Hill Rd Tram; 🖳 On the leafy side of Wan Chai, you're almost getting top-end accommodation for mid-range rates (as little as $800 if it's quiet). The 'signature' floor is a rather bleak attempt at 'boutique'. The standard rooms, with quality fittings and restful decor, will do just fine.

GARDEN VIEW Map p72   Hotel $$

☎ 2877 3737; www.ywca.org.hk; 1 MacDonnell Rd, Central; r/ste from $1350/2500, weekly packages from $4200; 🚌 green minibus 1A; 🖳 🛎 Straddling the border of Central and the Mid-Levels, the YWCA-run Garden View, with 133 rooms, overlooks the Zoological & Botanical Gardens. Accommodation here is plain but comfortable enough and comes with an outdoor swimming pool. Daily rates drop substantially in the low season.

WESLEY HONG KONG Map p72   Hotel $$

☎ 3553 6861; www.hanglung.com; 22 Hennessy Rd; r $1150-2000, weekly packages $4550, monthly packages $12,800-17,800; MTR Admiralty (exit F); 🖳 The rooms look a bit tired and service is somewhat lax. But if price and location matter more than service, this is a good option – rates can dip to $700. There are renovated rooms upwards from the 15th floor.

JJ HOTEL Map p74   Hotel $$

☎ 2904 7300; www.jjhotel.com.hk; 9th fl, Lucky Centre, 165-171 Wan Chai Rd; r $600-800; MTR Wan Chai (exit A3); 🖳 📶 This place has 40 clean, basic rooms occupying four floors. Don't expect over-the-top trimmings, but your needs will be taken care of – the owner also has a restaurant, a mah-jong club, massage facilities and a bar on other floors. Press '9' for reception.

MINGLE PLACE BY THE PARK

Map p74   Boutique Hotel $$
☎ 2838 1109; www.mingleplace.com; 143 Wan Chai Rd; s $500-700, d $800-900, monthly packages $9000-20,000; MTR Wan Chai (exit A3); 🖳 📶 The most interesting of the Mingle Place chain, this five-storey hotel is housed in a restored 1960s tenement building with terrazzo staircase. The '60s paraphernalia and the decor are quirkily charming. Some rooms, including the cubicle-sized 'lite' rooms, have tiny balconies.

YING KING APARTMENT

Map p74   Guesthouse $
☎ 2573 2049; 9th fl, Mei Wah Mansion, 172-176 Johnston Rd; r $300; MTR Wan Chai (exit A3); 🖳 Marooned somewhat across from the business end of Wan Chai, this little place trims its prices accordingly. The rooms are squeaky clean, with air-con and bathrooms, and there is internet access in the lobby.

ISLAND WEST

Sheung Wan and to a lesser extent Western District are good options if you want to stay close to Central without the prices. They're served by the Sheung Wan MTR station, as well as trams and buses. The Hong Kong–Macau ferry terminal in the Shun Tak Centre has ferries departing for Macau and destinations in mainland China. Most large hotels in Western District have free shuttle-bus services to Central and further east.

ISLAND PACIFIC HOTEL Map p80   Hotel $$

☎ 2131 1188; www.islandpacifichotel.com.hk; 152 Connaught Rd W; r $1500-3000, ste $5200; 🚌 5 or 5B from Central; 🖳 📶 🛎 This hotel has a chandeliered marble lobby that strikes a contrast with the small rooms and the slow-moving lifts. The 'side harbour view' rooms face a side street and are very dark. We prefer the standard rooms. The pool with its views of looming buildings promises a surreal underwater experience.

RAMADA HONG KONG HOTEL

Map pp62-3   Hotel $$
☎ 3410 3333; www.ramadahongkong.com; 308 Des Voeux Rd W; r $1400, weekly/monthly packages from $2380/9800; 🚌 5B from Central; 🖳 📶 Above a lobby decked out in carpeted opulence are 300 stuffy-looking but adequate rooms. Sure, the mattresses could be softer and the shower stalls roomier, but you really can't beat the rates, which can drop to $440 when it's quiet. Ramada is 10 minutes by tram from Sheung Wan MTR station. There's an Airbus stop on Water St nearby.

COURTYARD BY MARRIOTT HONG KONG Map pp62-3   Business Hotel $$

☎ 3717 8888; www.marriott.com/hotel-search /china/; 167 Connaught Rd W; r $1300-1750, ste $2450; 🚌 5 or 5B from Central; 🖳 📶 This hotel juggles luxury with limited space and it works. The dark carpeting and marble counters of the lobby are tastefully echoed by the decor of the rooms and complemented by impeccable service. Bear in mind, however, that not all the 'Deluxe Harbourview' rooms have harbour views. There's an Airbus stop across the street.

HOTEL JEN Map pp62-3   Hotel $$

☎ 2974 1234; www.hoteljen.com; 508 Queen's Rd W, Western District; r $700-2500, ste $2500-4000, weekly packages from $4200; 🚌 5 or 10 from Central; 🖳 📶 🏊

The 280 rooms at this chic hotel feature nouveau-retro furnishings in pale wood and whites with orange accents. If going 'standard', request the helpful staff to give you a

room on the 16th or 17th floors. The vista of Kowloon Peninsula from the rooftop pool is quite breathtaking. Jen is 15 minutes by tram from Sheung Wan MTR station.

SOHOTEL Map p80   Boutique Hotel $$

☎ 2851 8818; www.sohotel.com.hk; 139 Bonham Strand; r $1000-1200, ste $1800; MTR Sheung Wan (exit A2); 🖳

Located 10 minutes from Soho, Sohotel reminds one of a love hotel, with its red and black reflective surfaces and heavy drapes. The rooms are clean and new, but the smallest ones are claustrophobic and the suites won't let you do cartwheels either. Rates include internet access and breakfast.

STANDBY HOTELS

At busy times, the best hotels can get booked out. The following are some standby, midrange alternatives that should have rooms available and will do if you get stuck without a bed for the night.

Hong Kong Island

Regal Hongkong Hotel (Map p85; ☎ 2890 6633; www.regalhongkong.com; 88 Yee Wo St; s & d $2000-5000, ste from $6000; MTR Causeway Bay, exit F; 🖳 📶 🏊) This Sino-baroque palace drips with gilt and has a rooftop Roman-style *piscina* (pool). Over the top in the nicest possible way. The new floors (31st to 33rd) offer more privacy. Deals are available if you book two or three weeks in advance.

Luk Kwok Hotel (Map p74; ☎ 2866 2166; www.lukkwokhotel.com; 72 Gloucester Rd, Wan Chai; s $1800-2400, d $2000-2600, ste from $4000; 🚌 18; 🖳 📶) Few frills but an attentive staff and you're close to the convention centre and the bustle (and hustle) of Wan Chai. Low-season deals from $1015.

Newton Hotel Hong Kong (Map p85; ☎ 2807 2333; www.newtonhk.com; 218 Electric Rd; r $1400-2400, ste $3500; MTR Fortress Hill (exit A); 🖳) A great little hotel – it's just a shame it's in less-than-sexy North Point. Fortress Hill MTR station is just opposite. Causeway Bay is a pleasant walk away through Victoria Park. Some rooms have broadband.

Walden Hotel (Map p74; ☎ 8200 3308; www.walden-hotel.com; 353 Hennessy Rd; r $960-1890; MTR Causeway Bay, exit C; 🖳) You may not like the corporate feel or the dim bathrooms, but you'll admit the rates and location are very competitive. Inquire about deals and long-stay packages.

Express by Holiday Inn (Map p85; ☎ 3558 6688; www.ichotelsgroup.com; 33 Sharp St E; r $780-1500; MTR Causeway Bay, exit A; 🖳) Delivers what it promises: consistent and affordable accommodation, and it's right next to the Times Square shopping mall.

Kowloon

Harbour Plaza Metropolis (Map p106; ☎ 3160 6888; www.harbour-plaza.com/hpme; 7 Metropolis Dr, Hung Hom; s $2000-2800, d $2100-2900, ste from $3200; 🚌 5C or 8, MTR Hung Hom, exit C; 🖳) Directly behind the Hong Kong Coliseum and just southeast of the Hung Hom train station, it's handy if you expect to be travelling into China at the crack of dawn.

Royal Pacific Hotel & Towers (Map p104; ☎ 2736 1188; www.royalpacific.com.hk; China Hong Kong City, 33 Canton Rd; r $1700-3500, ste from $4800; MTR Tsim Sha Tsui, exit E; 🖳) An easy stroll to Kowloon Park and the China and Macau ferry terminal. Reception is on the 3rd floor; service can be both slow and harried at times.

Newton Hotel Kowloon (Map p111; ☎ 2787 2338; www.newtonkln.com; 66 Boundary St, Mong Kok; r $1200; MTR Prince Edward, exit A; 🖳) It's in a noisy neighbourhood close to Prince Edward MTR and the Mong Kok market, clothes stalls and noodle shops. Reasonable value but no surprises.

PUTMAN Map p80
Serviced Apartments $$

☎ 2233 2233; www.theputman.com; 202-206 Queen's Rd Central; studios $800-1000, flats $2200, studios/flats per month from $21,000/45,000; MTR Sheung Wan (exit A or E); 🖳 🛜

This designer outfit near Soho has three airy, cool-toned studios, one with an electric stove and two without, and 25 one-bedroom flats, which can be rented by the day, week or month. Prices include membership at a gym nearby, daily cleaning, wi-fi and TV. For the same price as some hotels, you get space (flats are 1300 sq ft and rooms 335–420 sq ft), privacy (one flat to a floor) and impeccable taste. The kitchens come with designer cooking utensils, crockery, stemware and laundry facilities.

JOCKEY CLUB MOUNT DAVIS HOSTEL Map pp62-3
Hostel $

☎ 2817 5715; www.yha.org.hk; Mt Davis Path, Kennedy Town; dm members under/over 18 $65/100, 2-/4-/6-bed r members $280/420/620; 🚌 5, light bus 54; 🖳 🛜

Hong Kong Island's only official hostel is a very clean and quiet property occupying a prime spot atop Mt Davis, in the northwest part of the island. It has great views of Victoria Harbour and there are wireless, cooking and laundry facilities, plus a TV and recreation room and secure lockers. The only problem is that it's so far away from everything; call ahead to make sure there's a bed before you make the trek out. The hostel is open daily throughout the year; check-in time is from 3pm to 11pm. You can check out before 1pm any day of the week. Camping is prohibited.

Get there aboard the free hostel shuttle bus from the Shun Tak Centre (Map p80; 200 Connaught Rd Central, Sheung Wan). It departs seven times a day; the schedule may change so it is better to check the HKYHA website. Alternatively, you can catch bus 5 from Admiralty MTR station or light bus 54 from the Central ferry terminal and alight at Felix Villas, at the junction of Victoria and Mt Davis Rds. From there, walk back 100m. Look for the hostel association sign and follow Mt Davis Path (not Mt Davis Rd). The walk is about 2km. A taxi from Central costs about $40.

CAUSEWAY BAY
As well as some good-value midrange options, Causeway Bay is also relatively well served by inexpensive guesthouses, especially on or around Paterson St. During the low season, guesthouses often struggle to fill beds and rooms; most will offer discounts to anyone staying longer than a few nights.

PARK LANE HONG KONG
Map p85
Hotel $$$

☎ 2293 8888; www.parklane.com.hk; 310 Gloucester Rd; r $2500-4100, ste from $5500; MTR Causeway Bay (exit E); 🖳 🛜

With restful views of Victoria Park to the east and busy Causeway Bay to the west, the Park Lane is the perfect hotel for those who want to be both in and out of the action. The rooms are spacious, the fittings of good quality, and the decor in soothing greens and earth tones. There's also a large gym.

LANSON PLACE Map p85
Hotel $$$

☎ 3477 6888; www.lansonplace.com; 133 Leighton Rd; r $2500-3800, ste from $4800; MTR Causeway Bay (exit F); 🖳 🛜

This plush hotel is an oasis of calm and class amid the Causeway Bay din. The spacious rooms blend classic style with modern fittings on which money has been plentifully spent, including in the lavish bathrooms. There's plenty of public lounging space and a concierge service.

JIA Map p85
Boutique Hotel $$$

☎ 3196 9000; www.jiahongkong.com; 1-5 Irving St; r $2500, ste from $3500; MTR Causeway Bay (exit F); 🖳 🛜

At this chi-chi place conceived in part by French design guru Philippe Starck, every aspect right down to the staff's uniforms, modern baroque furnishings, and the latest in technology is designed to fit with its sleek, whimsical aesthetic. 'Home' (its name in Mandarin) is above all else a friendly place and the service here is great. Downsides? Well, you need to reserve a router when you book to use wi-fi, the rooms are what Monsieur Starck would call serré (cramped) and the location is traffic choked.

METROPARK HOTEL Map p85
Hotel $$$

☎ 2600 1000; www.metroparkhotel.com; 148 Tung Lo Wan Rd; r $1900-2300, ste from $3500; MTR Causeway Bay (exit E); 🖳 📺

This flashy tower overlooking Victoria Park makes the most of its easterly location, with 70% of its 243 rooms boasting sweeping city-harbour views through floor-to-ceiling windows. Bright, appealing open-plan rooms offer generous work space and broadband internet. Check the website for discounts and packages.

EMPIRE HOTEL Map p85   Hotel $$

☎ 3692 2888; www.empirehotel-hongkong.com; 8 Wing Hing St, Causeway Bay; r $1600; MTR Tin Hau (exit A1); ▣

Empire has quiet rooms and a subdued lobby that would make for a soothing and convenient stay. Rooms with numbers ending in 03 are more spacious. Prices can drop to $700 when it's quiet. It's served by an airport shuttle bus.

HOTEL BONAPARTE

Map p74   Boutique Hotel $$

☎ 3518 6688; www.hotelbonaparte.com.hk; 11 Morrison Hill Rd; r $988, weekly/monthly packages $4210/14,880; MTR Causeway Bay (exit A); ▣

This small boutique hotel has 82 tasteful but Bonaparte-sized rooms. In some, hand basins are outside bathrooms, closets are hanging and the only storage space is under the beds. However, this is compensated for by friendly service and good location. Computers in the cafe are for patrons only.

COSMOPOLITAN HOTEL Map p74   Hotel $$

☎ 3552 1111; www.cosmopolitanhotel.com.hk; 387-397 Queen's Rd E; r $900-1500, ste $1800-3500; MTR Causeway Bay (exit A); ▣ 🛜

This place has unusual views – a graveyard to the south and a racecourse to the east. If cemeteries spook you out, request a room with frosted windows, or for better feng shui, one facing the racecourse. Despite their tacky aesthetics, the rooms are decent.

ALISAN GUEST HOUSE

Map p85   Guesthouse $

☎ 2838 0762; http://home.hkstar.com/~alisangh; Flat A, 5th fl, Hoito Crt, 275 Gloucester Rd; s $280-320, d $350-450, tr $480-520; MTR Causeway Bay (exit D1); ▣ 🛜

This spotless family-run place has 21 rooms with air-con, bathrooms and free internet. The multilingual owners are very helpful and can organise China visas (see p287 for costs). There's a communal computer on the 5th floor. Enter from 23 Cannon St.

CAUSEWAY BAY GUEST HOUSE

Map p85   Guesthouse $

☎ 2895 2013; www.cbgh.net; Flat B, 1st fl, Lai Yee Bldg, 44A-D Leighton Rd; s/d/tr $250/350/450; MTR Causeway Bay (exit A)

On the south side of Causeway Bay and wedged between a pub and a church (enter from Leighton Lane), this comfortable, seven-room guesthouse can get booked up quickly, so phone ahead. All rooms are quite clean and have private bathrooms.

CHUNG KIU INN Map p85   Hostel $

☎ 2895 3304; www.chungkiuinn.com.hk; Flat P, 15th fl, Hong Kong Mansion, 1 Yee Wo St; s $220-280, d $280-350, tr $400-450; MTR Causeway Bay (exit E); ▣ 🛜

This hostel, with three-dozen rooms spread over the 9th and 15th floors of the same building, is tidy but the rooms are small and basic. Cheaper rooms with shared bathrooms are available. Communication might be difficult, as the owner speaks no English.

OTHER NEIGHBOURHOODS

FOUR SEASONS Map p67   Luxury Hotel $$$$

☎ 3196 8888; www.fourseasons.com/hongkong/; Finance St, Central; r/ste from $4200/8000; MTR Hong Kong (exit F); ▣ 🛜 🛋

The Four Seasons arguably edges into top place on the island for its amazing views, its location close to the Star Ferry and Hong Kong station, its palatial rooms, glorious pool and spa complex, and its Michelin three-starred Lung King Heen (p177) and two-starred Caprice (p176) restaurants.

MANDARIN ORIENTAL

Map p67   Luxury Hotel $$$$

☎ 2522 0111; www.mandarinoriental.com/hong kong/; 5 Connaught Rd, Central; r $3400-4300, ste from $5500, Landmark Oriental rooms d from $5200, ste $9300; MTR Central (exit J3); ▣ 🛜 🛋

The venerable Mandarin set the standard on the island and continues to be a contender for top spot, despite the competition from the likes of the Four Seasons. The styling, service, food and atmosphere are stellar throughout and there's a sense of gracious, old-world charm. It's also home to a great restaurant, Pierre (p177). The sleek Landmark Oriental, in the Landmark Building just across the way, offers more modern luxury, with rooms designed down to their door knobs.

HOTEL LKF Map p78   Hotel $$$$

☎ 3518 9688; www.hotel-lkf.com.hk; 33 Wyndham St, Central; r from $3500; MTR Central (exit D2); ▣ 🛜 (26th fl up)

A great upper-to-midrange addition to your options in Central, Hotel LKF is in the thick of the Lan Kwai Fong action (but far enough above it not to be disturbed by it), and has spacious rooms in muted tones that contain all the trimmings: fluffy dressing gowns, espresso machines and free bedtime milk and cookies. Staff are eager to please, and there's a plush spa and yoga studio in the building. Prices go down by 50% when it's quiet.

LAN KWAI FONG HOTEL
Map p80   Boutique Hotel $$$
☎ 3650 0000; www.lankwaifonghotel.com.hk; 3 Kau U Fong, Central; r/ste from $2400/7800; MTR Sheung Wan (exit E2); 🖳 🛜
Not to be confused with Hotel LKF, which is a notch up in terms of quality, service and location (this place is nowhere near Lan Kwai Fong), this hotel nonetheless offers good value if you can secure a better online deal than the rates published. The Chinese decor is done with a modern flair and the rooms are reasonably spacious.

BISHOP LEI INTERNATIONAL HOUSE
Map p88   Hotel $$
☎ 2868 0828; www.bishopleihtl.com.hk; 4 Robinson Rd, the Mid-Levels; s/d/ste from $1250/1480/2480; 🚌 23 or 40; 🖳 🖳
It's out of the way on the Mid-Levels and the rooms are neither large nor luxurious, but consider BLIH all the same for its good service, swimming pool and gym, and the proximity to the Zoological & Botanical Gardens. Rates can fall by more than half during low season.

ICE HOUSE Map p78   Serviced Apartments $$
☎ 2836 7333; www.icehouse.com.hk; 38 Ice House St, Central; studios per night $1000-1800; MTR Central (exit G)
Next to the Fringe Club and up the hill from Lan Kwai Fong, Ice House offers open-plan 'suites' spread over 13 floors that are bright, colourfully decorated and fitted with small kitchenettes and work areas. It's a favourite of visiting journalists. The down side is that some of the rooms on the top floors are very noisy, and service can be cavalier. Monthly rates start at $20,000.

CITY GARDEN HOTEL HONG KONG
Map pp62–3   Hotel $$
☎ 2887 2888; www.citygarden.com.hk; 9 City Garden Rd, Fortress Hill; r $850-2500; ste from $3000; MTR Fortress Hill (exit A); 🖳

It may be in gritty Fortress Hill, but readers have nice things to say about this exceptionally well-turned-out hotel, and not only for its service and generous discounting policy (fortnightly/monthly packages from $8200/13,800). Enter from the corner of Electric Rd and Power St.

MINGLE PLACE AT THE EDEN
Map p67   Boutique Hotel $$
☎ 2850 6289; www.mingleplace.com; 148 Wellington St, Central; s $600-900, d $750-1000, monthly packages s $13,000; MTR Central (exit D2); 🖳 🛜
It may call itself a 'boutique hotel in Central', but with rates posted as '3 hours extended session' and the like, we know what this place is up to... Still, it is probably the most luxurious knocking shop you'll stay in. Rooms are comfortable but small.

KOWLOON
Splendour rubs shoulders with squalor in Kowloon. Hong Kong's poshest hotel, the Peninsula, is here in Tsim Sha Tsui, within spitting distance of the (in)famous Chungking Mansions. A huge range of other hotels and guesthouses can be found in Kowloon, catering to all budgets between these two extremes.

Tsim Sha Tsui East, an area of reclaimed land northeast of Tsim Sha Tsui, is weighed down by mostly anonymous top-end hotels. It's served by the MTR East Rail (East Tsim Sha Tsui station) and most hotels run shuttles to Tsim Sha Tsui proper and/or to Central. You'll find many more top-end hotels lining Nathan Rd as it travels north from the harbour.

TSIM SHA TSUI
PENINSULA HONG KONG
Map p104   Luxury Hotel $$$$
☎ 2920 2888; www.peninsula.com; Salisbury Rd; r $4200-5800, ste from $6800; MTR Tsim Sha Tsui (exit E); 🖳 🛜 🖳
Lording it over the southern tip of Kowloon, Hong Kong's finest hotel evokes colonial elegance. Your main dilemma will be how to get here: landing on the rooftop helipad or arriving in one of the hotel's 14-strong fleet of Rolls Royce Phantoms. Some 300 classic European-style rooms boast wi-fi, CD and DVD players, as well as marble bathrooms. Many rooms in the Pen's 20-storey annexe offer spectacular harbour views; in the original building you'll have to make do with the

glorious interiors. There's a top-notch spa and swimming pool. Spring Moon (p191) is one of the best Cantonese restaurants in town.

SHERATON HONG KONG HOTEL & TOWERS Map p104 · Hotel $$$$

☎ 2369 1111; www.sheraton.com/hongkong; 20 Nathan Rd; s $3000-3600, d $3100-3700, ste hotel/towers from $6400/7300; MTR Tsim Sha Tsui (exit F); ▯ ▩

This large, very American hostelry at the start of Nathan Rd is as central as you'll find in Tsim Sha Tsui and offers a high level of comfort and great facilities. The tower rooms command superior harbour views (and higher prices). The Sky Lounge, on the 18th floor, is worth a visit for the stunning views and there's a rooftop pool and gym.

MIRA HONG KONG

Map p104 · Luxury Hotel $$$$

☎ 2368 1111; www.themirahotel.com; 118-130 Nathan Rd; r $3000-3500, ste $5700-9700; MTR Tsim Sha Tsui (exit B1); ▯ ⟩⟩ ▩

Dowdy Miramar has morphed into sexy Mira, with colour-themed rooms, designer chairs

BUDGET BLOCKS IN TSIM SHA TSUI
Chungking Mansions

Say 'budget accommodation' and 'Hong Kong' in one breath and everyone thinks of Chungking Mansions (Map p104; 36-44 Nathan Rd, Tsim Sha Tsui; MTR Tsim Sha Tsui, exit F). Built in 1961, CKM is a labyrinth of homes, guesthouses, Indian restaurants, souvenir stalls and foreign-exchange shops spread over five 17-storey blocks in the heart of Tsim Sha Tsui. According to Gordon Mathews, an anthropologist who studies the place, it has a resident population of about 4000 and an estimated 10,000 daily visitors. Over 120 different nationalities – predominantly South Asian and African – pass through its doors in a single year. CKM has a unique TV line-up, consisting of 16 stations, including Nepali, Indian, Pakistani, French (Le Monde, which many West Africans watch) and, interestingly, BBC but no CNN. No surprise CKM was named 'Best Example of Globalisation' by Time magazine in 2007.

Cultural diversity does not make for cleaner rooms or safer lockers, of course. There's always a queue for the coffin-sized lifts. Visitors have been harassed, swindled or worse. And only the most naive would think there are no illegal goings-on inside the building. So while some are charmed by CKM's chaotic ethics (and aesthetics), others avoid it like the plague.

But in all fairness, CKM has cleaned up much of its act since it changed management in the late '90s, to the extent that travellers who've known it since its days as a hippie haven are lamenting the loss of its charisma. Over 200 CCTVs are now installed throughout the building, and there are security guards and cleaners to make sure things are in order.

Though standards vary significantly, most of the guesthouses at CKM – including the ones recommended below – are clean and quite comfortable. It's worth bearing in mind, however, that rooms are usually the size of cupboards and you have to shower right next to the toilet. The rooms typically come with air-con and TV and, sometimes, a phone. Many guesthouses can get you a Chinese visa quickly, most have internet access and some have wi-fi and laundry service.

Bargaining for a bed or room is always possible, though you won't get very far in the high season. You can often negotiate a cheaper price if you stay more than, say, a week, but never try that on the first night – stay one night and find out how you like it before handing over more rent. Once you pay, there are usually no refunds.

Dragon Inn (☎ 2368 2007; dragoinn@netvigator.com; Flat B5, 3rd fl, B Block; s $200-300, d $200-500, tr $390) It's owned by the chairperson of the Incorporated Owners of CKM – a shrewd but helpful matron with the political correctness of a Ming emperor and a taste for florals. It has clean rooms with private bathrooms, drinking water and a hairdryer; there are discounts for students, seniors and repeat customers. (And, yes, the email address really is spelt dragoinn.)

Chungking House (☎ 2366 5362; chungkinghouse@yahoo.com.hk; 4th & 5th fl, A Block; s $200, d $250-350) Covering two floors with a total of 80 rooms, it's among the swishest in CKM – though standards have slipped a little of late. All rooms have private bathrooms.

Holiday Guesthouse (☎ 2316 7152, 9121 8072; fax 2316 7181; Flat E1, 6th fl, E Block; s/d $200/300; ▯ ⟩⟩) An upmarket Nepali-run place with 23 pleasant rooms.

Four Seasons Guesthouse (☎ 3523 1783, 9177 3177; Flat A1-A2, 14th fl, A Block; s & d $170-300; ▯) Run by the spritely Mrs Tsui, it has clean rooms with private bathrooms and wallpaper worthy of the other Four Seasons.

Tom's Guest House (☎ 2722 6035, 9194 5923; fax 2366 6706; Flat B7, 16th fl, B Block; s $150-160, d $150-250) This is a friendly and popular place, which can also be entered from C Block (Flat C1, 16th floor). There's another branch located in A Block (☎ 2722 4956; Flat A5, 8th fl).

Yan Yan Guest House (☎ 2366 8930, 9489 3891; fax 2721 0840; Flat E1, 8th fl, E Block; s $130, d $180-250; ⟩⟩) This is one of the last of the Chinese-owned guesthouses in the overwhelmingly subcontinental E Block. Wi-fi

SLEEPING KOWLOON

and an entrance so cool you'd expect to see a bouncer. Techies will drool over the gadgets, which include a mobile phone for local calls and a flat-screen TV you can use to surf the net. Even the staff are helpful in a (fashionably) informal kind of way. However, the walls are a wee bit thin for a luxury hotel.

LANGHAM HOTEL HONG KONG
Map p104   Luxury Hotel $$$$
☎ 2375 1133; www.langhamhotels.com/langham /hongkong; 8 Peking Rd; r/ste from $2800/4800; MTR Tsim Sha Tsui (exit E); 🖵 🛜 🖳

The renovated Langham continues to serve up five-star luxury in the heart of Tsim Sha Tsui. The rooms are classic and there's a 24-hour gym and open-air pool, as well as the famous Chinese restaurant T'ang Court (p191).

MARCO POLO HONGKONG HOTEL
Map p104   Luxury Hotel $$$
☎ 2113 0088; www.marcopolohotels.com; Harbour City, 3-9 Canton Rd; s/d/ste from $2450/2550/4900; 🚢 Star Ferry, MTR Tsim Sha Tsui (exit E); 🖵 🖳
This is the daddy of the Marco Polo Hotel group's Canton Rd trio. Closest to the Star

reception is better in the front rooms. New Yan Yan Guesthouse (☎ 2723 5671; Flat E5, 12th fl, E Block; 🛜), in the same block, is managed by the same people.

Beverly Guesthouse (☎ 2721 1758, 2722 1758, 9148 9787; fax 2368 3397; Flat B7, 8th fl, B Block; s/d $130/200) Has basic rooms with private bathrooms and is run by a laid-back owner. There's wi-fi in the lobby.

Garden Guest House (☎ 2368 0981, 9057 5265; Flat C5, 16th fl, C Block; s/d $120/180; 🛜) This clean, quiet place is much favoured by backpackers. There's another branch (☎ 2366 0169; Flat C5, 7th fl; 🛜) in the same block.

Park Guesthouse (☎ 2368 1689; fax 2367 7889; Flat A1, 15th fl, A Block; s with shared bathroom $108, r with private bathroom $100-150; 🛜) A basic but welcoming 45-room guesthouse that comes recommended by readers.

Travellers Hostel (☎ 2368 7710; mrspau@yahoo.com.hk; Flat A1-A4, 16th fl, A Block; dm $60-80, s & d with shared shower $100-140, d with private shower $150; 🖵) This 44-year-old joint may look a little scruffy, but it's a good place to meet fellow travellers. Owner Mr Chan is very nice, and cooking facilities, cable TV, student discounts and internet access are all available.

Mirador Mansion

Mirador Mansion (Map p104; 58-62 Nathan Rd, Tsim Sha Tsui; MTR Tsim Sha Tsui, exit D2), above an arcade of that name between Mody and Carnarvon Rds, is a 51-year-old residential building with a serene atmosphere. In fact it was Mirador Mansion – and not Chungking Mansions – where Wong Kar-wai filmed most of Chungking Express (1994). Strolling down the open corridors of Mirador Mansion on a breezy day will make you feel like you've retreated into a Tsim Sha Tsui that's disappeared.

Mei Lam Guest House (☎ 2721 5278, 9095 1379; fax 2723 6168; Flat D1, 5th fl; s/d from $160/200; 🖵) This excellent place has modern rooms packed with extras, including internet access.

Man Hing Lung Hotel (☎ 2722 0678, 2311 8807; http://home.hkstar.com/~mhlhotel; Flat F2, 14th fl; s $120-150, d $150-200, tr $210-240; 🖵 🛜) This is a decent place with over 40 clean if rather spartan rooms, wi-fi and laundry facilities.

Garden Hostel (☎ 2311 1183; fax 2721 2085; Flat F4, 3rd fl; dm $60, d with shared shower $180, s & d with shower $200; 🖵) It's on the scruffy side and the air-con seems to be rationed, but there are laundry facilities and the lockers are like Fort Knox. The living room doubles as the martial arts studio of the owner Sam Lau, a kung fu instructor who claims to have been Bruce Lee's classmate.

Cosmic Guest House (☎ 2369 6669; www.cosmicguesthouse.com; Flats A1-A2, F1-F4, 12th fl; dm $60, r $166-200, large d $220-240; 🖵) This very clean and quiet place has big and bright rooms and a very helpful owner. There's internet access in every room.

Besides CKM and Mirador Mansion, Golden Crown Court (Map p104; 66-70 Nathan Rd, Tsim Sha Tsui; MTR Tsim Sha Tsui, exit D1), opposite the southeast corner of Kowloon Park, has undergone a transformation in recent years and now offers a host of clean, smart guesthouses.

Ferry and the most highly priced, it has large and well-appointed rooms, and an outdoor pool that it shares with Gateway and Prince. The 433-room Marco Polo Gateway (Map p104; ☎ 2113 0888; 13 Canton Rd; s $2050-2350, d $2150-2450, ste from $3650; 💻 📶) and the smaller Marco Polo Prince (Map p104; ☎ 2113 1888; 23 Canton Rd; s $2400-2700, d $2500-2800, 1-/2-person ste from $3200/3300; 💻 📶) are both a step down in terms of luxury and room size, but both have good business facilities and some of the rooms in the Prince have harbour views. Rooms in all three hotels have wired internet access.

KOWLOON HOTEL HONG KONG
Map p104   Hotel $$$
☎ 2929 2888; www.thekowloonhotel.com; 19-21 Nathan Rd; s $2000-4400, d $2100-4600, ste from $3900; MTR Tsim Sha Tsui (exit E); 💻 📶
The Kowloon Hotel has a dated feel about it, with its 1990s techno aesthetic and views of the back of the Peninsula. Nevertheless, the hotel is popular for its unflappable service, central location and decent if rather small rooms. Rates drop dramatically off season.

BP INTERNATIONAL HOTEL
Map p104   Hotel $$
☎ 2376 1111; www.bpih.com.hk; 8 Austin Rd; r $1250-2600, ste from $3800; MTR Jordan (exit C); 💻 📶 (14th-17th fl)
This enormous hotel overlooks Kowloon Park and is relatively convenient to most places of interest in Tsim Sha Tsui. The rooms are of a reasonable standard and some of the more expensive ones have good harbour views. There are family rooms with bunk beds available, making this a good option if you're travelling with kids. Haggle before you book: depending on the season and day of the week, prices are often reduced by 50%.

SALISBURY Map p104   Hostel $, Hotel $$
☎ 2268 7000; www.ymcahk.org.hk; 41 Salisbury Rd; dm $240, s $700-950, d $700-1000, ste from $1450; 🚢 Star Ferry; 💻 📶 📶
If you can manage to book a room at the fabulously located, YMCA-run Salisbury, you'll be rewarded with professional service and excellent exercise facilities, including a swimming pool, a fitness centre and a climbing wall. The rooms and suites are comfortable but simple, so keep your eyes on the harbour: that view would cost you

five times as much at the Peninsula next door. The four-bed dormitory rooms are a bonus, but there are restrictions: check-in is at 2pm, no one can stay more than seven consecutive nights, and walk-in guests aren't accepted if they've been in Hong Kong for more than 10 days.

SEALAND HOUSE Map p104   Guesthouse $
☎ 2368 9522; www.sealandhouse.com.hk; Flat D, 8th fl, Majestic House, 80 Nathan Rd; s $320-380, d $350-480; MTR Tsim Sha Tsui (exit B2); 💻 📶
This eight-room place, towering above Nathan Rd, is small but clean and very bright. Wi-fi is included in the rates. Rooms without private bathrooms are a bit cheaper. Enter from Cameron Rd.

TSIM SHA TSUI EAST & HUNG HOM

INTERCONTINENTAL HONG KONG
Map p106   Luxury Hotel $$$$
☎ 2721 1211; www.hongkong-ic.intercontinental .com; 18 Salisbury Rd; r $4700, ste from $7800; MTR Tsim Sha Tsui (exit F); 💻 📶 📶
Occupying arguably the finest waterfront position in the territory, the InterContinental tilts at modernity while bowing to colonial traditions, such as a fleet of navy-blue Rolls Royces, doormen liveried in white, and incessant brass polishing. The emphasis on service ensures a lot of return customers, from rock stars to business VIPs. Restaurants such as the Steak House (p194), Nobu and Spoon are top class. The InterContinental Lobby Lounge (p214) bar has the best views in Hong Kong.

KOWLOON SHANGRI-LA
Map p106   Luxury Hotel $$$$
☎ 2721 2111; www.shangri-la.com; 64 Mody Rd, Tsim Sha Tsui East; s $3498-5048, d $3798-5348, ste from $5380; 🚌 5C or 8; 💻 📶 📶
Almost as swish as its sister hotel, Island Shangri-La Hong Kong (p236), in Admiralty, the views here and the bars and restaurants, including the Japanese food at Nadaman, are excellent. We love the enormous murals of imperial Chinese scenes in the lobby.

ROYAL GARDEN Map p106   Luxury Hotel $$$$
☎ 2721 5215; www.rghk.com.hk; 69 Mody Rd, Tsim Sha Tsui East; s $2900-3900, d $3100-4100, ste from $4800; 🚌 5C or 8; 💻 📶 📶
The 422-room Royal Garden is one of the best-equipped hotels in Tsim Sha Tsui East

and one of the territory's most attractive options. From the blonde-wood and chrome lobby and atrium to the rooftop sports complex (25m pool, putting green and tennis court with million-dollar views), the Royal Garden ticks all the boxes. The rooms are highly specced with plasma screens and large, comfortable beds. You should be able to secure large discounts off the quoted rates. Sabatini Italian (p194), on the 3rd floor, is one of the best Italian restaurants in Hong Kong.

PARK HOTEL Map p106   Hotel $$$
☎ 2731 2100; www.parkhotel.com.hk; 61-65 Chatham Rd S; s $2200-3500, d $2400-3700, ste from $5500; MTR Tsim Sha Tsui (exit B2); 🖳
The spacious rooms have a welcoming feel, a sense backed up by the warm service. The history and science museums are just over the road, and the hustle of Granville Rd is a block away. Enter from Cameron Rd.

BUTTERFLY ON PRAT Map p106   Hotel $$$
☎ 3962 8888; www.butterflyhk.com; 21 Prat Ave; r $1700-1900, ste from $2500; MTR Tsim Sha Tsui (exit A2); 🖳
Its lobby may look a little flighty – which can happen when nouveau baroque gets out of hand – but don't be put off. All 22 rooms are presentable, with matching fabrics, glass partitions, a queen-sized bed and a host of conveniences, including microwave oven, broadband and TV with 30 channels. Staff are very attentive, and guests get discounts at eateries nearby.

EMPIRE KOWLOON Map p106   Hotel $$$
☎ 3692 2222; www.empirehotel.com.hk; 62 Kimberley Rd; r $1600-2400, ste from $3000; MTR Tsim Sha Tsui (exit B1); 🖳 📺
This sister hotel of the Empire Hotel Hong Kong (p236) offers modern, comfortable rooms and an excellent indoor atrium swimming pool and spa. It's an easy stroll from here to just about anywhere in Tsim Sha Tsui. Check the website for promotions.

KIMBERLEY HOTEL Map p106   Hotel $$$
☎ 2723 3888; www.kimberleyhotel.com.hk; 28 Kimberley Rd; r $1500-2350, ste from $2800; MTR Tsim Sha Tsui (exit B1); 🖳
The Kimberley isn't a glamorous property, but it's one of the better midrange hotels in Tsim Sha Tsui East. You'll find assured staff and large, chintz-free rooms with good facilities. The hotel also has golf nets and a health spa. The lobby, a leafy and cool oasis

up from the bustle, is on the 2nd floor. Summer rates are half the quoted ones.

MINDEN Map p106   Hotel $$
☎ 2739 7777; www.theminden.com; 7 Minden Ave; r $900-1500, ste from $2500; MTR Tsim Sha Tsui (exit G); 🖳
This almost-boutique 64-room hotel, tucked away on relatively quiet Minden Ave, is one of our favourites. It's central, being well located for both Tsim Sha Tsui and Tsim Sha Tsui East stations, and very reasonable value. The lobby is stuffed with Chinese antiques and paintings, while the rooms are serene and comfortable, with all the amenities you'd expect included in the rates.

HOTEL PANORAMA Map p106   Hotel $$
☎ 3550 0388; www.hotelpanorama.com.hk; 8A Hart Ave; r $888-1488, ste $3180; MTR East Tsim Sha Tsui (exit N); 🖳
As its name suggests, you'll find panoramic views at this hotel – but only above the 17th floor. The lower rooms overlook old buildings nearby, which may not be everyone's cup of tea. That said, all rooms are tastefully furnished, and the breezy Sky Garden on the 40th floor offers some of the best vistas of Tsim Sha Tsui. The friendly tourist desk helps to organise China visas.

STAR GUEST HOUSE Map p106   Guesthouse $
☎ 2723 8951; www.starguesthouse.com; Flat B, 6th fl, 21 Cameron Rd; s & d with shared bathroom $300, s/d with private bathroom from $350/450, tr with private bathroom $550; MTR Tsim Sha Tsui (exit B2); 🖳 📶
This excellent guesthouse and its sister property just up the road, the Lee Garden Guest House (Map p106; ☎ 2367 2284; charliechan @iname.com; 8th fl, D Block, 36 Cameron Rd), with a total of 45 rooms, are owned by the charismatic Charlie Chan, who can arrange most things for you, including China visas. Long-term stayers get good discounts. The rooms at Star have satellite TV, while Lee Garden has a computer for guests' use.

KOWLOON WEST

W HONG KONG Map p108   Luxury Hotel $$$$
☎ 3717 2222; www.whotels.com; 1 Austin Rd W; r from $4500, ste $7800-45,000; MTR Kowloon (exit C1); 🖳 📶 📷
W features wow-worthy interiors created by an Australian and a Japanese designer, with rooms named after superlatives (wonderful,

spectacular, fantastic…). Very impressed we were by the aesthetics, the sleek gadgetry, the harbour views in the suites and the 'highest pool in the city' (72nd floor), but slightly less so by the service at both the hotel and its restaurants.

YAU MA TEI

Things start getting much cheaper up in this part of Kowloon. There are several midrange options, plus cheap, basic hotels and a good assortment of guesthouses, many of them occupying Alhambra Building (Map p108; 385 Nathan Rd, Yau Ma Tei) and New Lucky House (Map p108; 300-306 Nathan Rd, Yau Ma Tei), with its main entrance on Jordan Rd.

EATON HOTEL Map p108   Hotel $$$

☎ 2782 1818; www.eaton-hotel.com; 380 Nathan Rd; r $2250-3250, ste from $3250; MTR Jordan (exit B1); 🖳 🚇
Leave the chaos of Nathan Rd behind as you step into the Eaton's grand lobby. The rooms are large and comfortable, while the glass-fronted Planter's Bar on the 4th floor sits next to an improbably pleasant and leafy courtyard, given the proximity of all that traffic. Booking on the internet can halve the quoted rates. Enter from Pak Hoi St.

CITYVIEW Map p108   Hotel $$

☎ 2771 9111; www.thecityview.com.hk; 23 Waterloo Rd; r $1380, ste from $2180, monthly packages from $16,500; MTR Yau Ma Tei (exit A2); 🖳 🛜 🚇
The good old YMCA has glammed itself up. All 413 rooms are looking smart, with mellow tones and stylish bedding, and the service is excellent. The hotel occupies a quiet corner of Yau Ma Tei, yet is only a hop away from the nearest eatery. The City Cafe offers decent buffets.

NOVOTEL Map p108   Hotel $$

☎ 3965 8888; www.novotel.com; 348 Nathan Rd; r/ste $1100/3180; MTR Jordan (exit B2); 🖳 🛜
Although it claims to be located on the 'golden mile' of Tsim Sha Tsui, Novotel's actual address is nowhere near the harbour; rather, it's at the doorstep of Yau Ma Tei. It's also on Saigon St, not Nathan Rd. Despite its slightly misleading address, Novotel is a bright, contemporary hotel with a spacious lobby and 400 pleasant rooms that were renovated in 2008. They're the same size, but the more costly rooms boast better views and nicer decor.

NATHAN HOTEL Map p108   Hotel $$

☎ 2388 5141; www.nathanhotel.com; 378 Nathan Rd; r $1080-2480, ste from $1880; MTR Jordan (exit B1); 🖳 🛜 (9th-12th fl)
Surprisingly quiet and pleasant; even the cheapest of its 166 rooms are spacious, clean and serene. It's in a good location, right near the Jordan MTR station and Temple St, and we like the mustachioed and turbaned doorman. All in all it's good value for what you get. Enter from Pak Hoi St.

CARITAS BIANCHI LODGE
Map p108   Guesthouse $$

☎ 2388 1111; www.caritas-chs.org.hk/eng /bianchi_lodge.asp; 4 Cliff Rd; s/d/tr $920/1020/1220; MTR Yau Ma Tei (exit D)
This 90-room hotel-cum-guesthouse is run by a Catholic social-welfare organisation. Though it's just off Nathan Rd (and a goalie's throw from Yau Ma Tei MTR station), the rear rooms are very quiet and some have views of King's Park. All rooms have private bathroom and breakfast is included. Lodge manager Kevin Mak will give discounts to Lonely Planet readers.

CASA HOTEL Map p108   Hotel $$

☎ 3758 7777; www.casahotel.com.hk; 487-489 Nathan Rd; s/d/f $750/880/1380; MTR Yau Ma Tei (exit C); 🖳 🛜
Casa is pretty sleek for this price range and this part of town, with a fancy lobby featuring black tiles and a modern fish tank. The rooms are clean but be prepared to shower right next to the toilet. Try to secure a room ending in 04 or 09 between the 3rd and 8th floors – they're larger, but bear in mind that the 7th floor does not have wi-fi.

BOOTH LODGE Map p108   Guesthouse $$

☎ 2771 9266; http://boothlodge.salvation.org.hk; 11 Wing Sing La; r $620-1500; MTR Yau Ma Tei (exit D); 🖳 🛜
Run by the Salvation Army, this 53-room place is spartan but clean and comfortable. Promotional rates for rooms can drop to $500. Rates include breakfast. Reception is on the 7th floor.

BRIDAL TEA HOUSE HOTEL
Map p108   Hotel $

☎ 2388 9591; www.hkchhotel.com; 6 Arthur St; r from $500, monthly package from $7000; MTR Yau Ma Tei (exit C); 🖳

This is one of a large chain of cheap places that used to be a home for the elderly. The down side: rooms are tiny, service is minimal and the lift is slow. The up side: it's dirt-cheap and clean, showers are enclosed and rooms come with broadband internet. Long-stay discounts apply.

RENT-A-ROOM HONG KONG
Map p108   Guesthouse $

☎ 2366 3011, 9023 8022; www.rentaroomhk.com; Flat A, 2nd fl, Knight Garden, 7-8 Tak Hing St; dm $160-220, s $400-650, d $450-750, tr $750-1050, q $950-1300; MTR Jordan (exit E); 🖳
This fabulous place has 50 immaculate rooms in a block close to Jordan MTR station. Each room has a bathroom, TV, telephone (free local calls), high-speed internet and a fridge. But readers have told us that reservations are sometimes 'forgotten', so do confirm yours if possible.

HONG KONG STAR GUESTHOUSE
Map p108   Guesthouse $

☎ 9780 3737; Flat 8, 3rd fl, Alhambra Bldg, 385 Nathan Rd; s/d $250/300; MTR Yau Ma Tei (exit C); 🖳
The six rooms here are spick and span. If you need to use the computer, Ms Cheung has one in her home-cum-bone-setting clinic next door, where toddler-sized statues of Taoist deities look on from a large red shrine as you surf the net.

GOLDEN ISLAND GUESTHOUSE
Map p108   Guesthouse $

☎ 9583 5051, 2783 7952; www.gig.com.hk; Flat 1-2, 7th fl, Alhambra Bldg, 385 Nathan Rd; s $220-280, d $260-360, tr & q $380-480; MTR Yau Ma Tei (exit C); 🖳 📶
This 30-room guesthouse with an affiliated tour agency offers the best deal in the Alhambra Building. All rooms come with private bathrooms, toiletries, TV, phone and free wi-fi; some are locked with key-cards. It can also help you make ticket and day-tour arrangements. Jessie Fu, the young owner, is amiable and speaks good English. You can make reservations on its website.

OCEAN GUEST HOUSE
Map p108   Guesthouse $

☎ 2385 0125; fax 2771 4083; Flat G, 11th fl, New Lucky House, 300-306 Nathan Rd; s/d $250/300; MTR Jordan (exit B); 🖳 📶
All eight rooms in this rather comfy place have TV, phone, air-con and private shower.

HAKKA'S GUEST HOUSE
Map p108   Guesthouse $

☎ 2771 3656; fax 2770 1470; Flat 1, 3rd fl, New Lucky House, 300-306 Nathan Rd; s $200-250, d $250-300, tr $300-350; MTR Jordan (exit B1); 🖳
This is the most decent guesthouse in the building and each of the nine ultraclean guestrooms has a telephone, TV and shower. The affable owner, Kevin Koo, is a keen hiker and he'll invite guests out along with him for country walks on Sunday. Mr Koo sometimes sends spillovers to Ying Pin (☎ 2771 0888; 2nd fl, New Lucky House) downstairs, which offers basic accommodation.

MONG KOK
LANGHAM PLACE HOTEL
Map p111   Hotel $$$$

☎ 3552 3388; http://hongkong.langham placehotels.com; 555 Shanghai St; s $2600-3600, d $2800-3800, ste from $5100; MTR Mong Kok (exit C3); 🖳 📶 🛋
Peering out from one of the rooms of this colossal tower hotel, you'd never suspect for a moment that you were in Mong Kok. It's a triumph for the district. The special guest-room features include multifunction IP phones, DVD players, marble bathrooms and room safes that can fit (and recharge) a laptop. Reception is on the 4th floor and the hotel is linked to the Langham Place Mall (p170). The 20m rooftop pool, gym and spa all command great views over Kowloon.

ROYAL PLAZA HOTEL
Map p111   Hotel $$$

☎ 2928 8822; www.royalplaza.com.hk; 193 Prince Edward Rd W; s $1800-3200, d $2000-3400, ste from $4800; MTR Mong Kok East Rail; 🖳 📶 🛋
The plushness is a bit overdone, but the 671-room Royal Plaza is comfortable and central; the bird and flower markets are on the other side of Prince Edward Rd. The rooms are well equipped, with heated no-steam bathroom mirrors, and some have kitchenettes and wi-fi. The outdoor pool with underwater music is a lounge-lizard's nirvana. The Mong Kok KCR station is accessible through the adjoining Grand Century Place shopping centre, making this a handy spot if you've business in the New Territories or mainland China.

SUNNY DAY HOTEL
Map p111   Hotel $$

☎ 3760 8888; www.sunnydayhotel.cn; 419 Reclamation St; s/d $800/1100; MTR Mong Kok (exit C4); 📶
This 39-room hotel has small rooms overlooking Reclamation St and Langham Pl. The

warm russet walls in the lift lobbies are a nice touch, but the litter outside the windows is a reminder that this is Mong Kok. Staff are helpful. If you want to make reservations on the website, click 'reservations', then click the left orange box for this hotel (the right box will take you to another branch).

ANNE BLACK YWCA Map p111   Guesthouse $
☎ 2713 9211; www.ywca.org.hk; 5 Man Fuk Rd; r with shared bathroom $380, with private bathroom $900-1100, monthly packages from $6000; MTR Yau Ma Tei (exit D); 🖳 🛜
This YWCA-run guesthouse, which accommodates both women and men, is located near Pui Ching and Waterloo Rds in Mong Kok, behind and uphill from a petrol station. There are laundry facilities and a decent restaurant here. Conveniently, almost half of the rooms are singles.

CARITAS LODGE Map pp100-1   Guesthouse $
☎ 2339 3777; www.caritas-chs.org.hk; 134 Boundary St; s/d from $408/456, s weekly/monthly packages from $2387/6900, d from $2772/8910; MTR Mong Kok East (exit C or D)
With just 40 rooms, this place is just as nice as its sister guesthouse, Caritas Bianchi Lodge (p246), but the rooms are smaller and it's further afield. Still, you couldn't get much closer to the bird market, and the New Territories is (officially) just across the road. Breakfast is included in the price.

NEW TERRITORIES

The New Territories does not offer travellers a tremendous choice of accommodation, but there are five official and independent hostels, mostly in the more remote parts of the region. Remember, too, that walkers and hikers can pitch a tent at any one of 38 New Territories camp sites managed by the Country & Marine Parks Authority (☎ 1823; www.afcd.gov.hk).

TAI MEI TUK

BRADBURY JOCKEY CLUB YOUTH HOSTEL Map pp58-9   Hostel $
☎ 2662 5123; www.yha.org.hk; 66 Tai Mei Tuk Rd; dm members under/over 18 yr $65/100, d/q members $280/420; 🚌 75K
Bradbury Jockey Club Youth Hostel (not to be confused with Bradbury Hall Youth Hostel in Sai Kung) is the HKYHA's flagship hostel in the New Territories. It has 72 beds and is open daily year-round. Check-in is

from 4pm to 11pm (from 3pm on weekends and holidays). Bradbury is next to the northern tip of the Plover Cove Reservoir dam wall, a few hundred metres south of Tai Mei Tuk. Camping is not permitted. To get here take bus 75K (or 275R on Sundays and public holidays) from Tai Po Market KCR East station to the Tai Mei Tuk bus terminus. The hostel is on the road leading to the reservoir.

SHA TIN

HYATT REGENCY HONG KONG
Map pp58-9   Luxury Hotel $$$$
☎ 3723 1234; www.hongkong.shatin.hyatt.com; 18 Chak Cheung St; r $2500-3000, ste $3500-12,500; MTR University East Rail (exit B); 🖳 🛜 🎬
Despite an unremarkable exterior, the Hyatt Regency is the plushest hotel in the New Territories, and it makes the best of its location. Most rooms have peerless views overlooking Tolo Harbour or the rolling hills of Sha Tin. Guests won't be short of space to stretch their legs: there are gardens, a swimming pool and a tennis court. It's a five-minute walk from MTR University station.

REGAL RIVERSIDE HOTEL
Map p127   Hotel $$
☎ 2649 7878; www.regalriverside.com; 34-36 Tai Chung Kiu Rd; r $1300-1700, ste from $3800; 🚌 284, MTR Sha Tin Wai East Rail (exit A); 🖳 🛜 🎬
This enormous hotel is not very appealing from the outside, but inside the rooms are well decorated and surprisingly spacious for Hong Kong. Those overlooking the Shing Mun River have excellent views. MTR exit A is inside Shatin New Town Plaza (Map p127). Walk straight ahead for three minutes and you'll see, to your left, escalators going down to the bus terminus.

PILGRIM'S HALL Map p127   Hostel $
☎ 2691 2739; www.achouse.com; 33 Tao Fong Shan Rd; s/d with shared bathroom $240/360; MTR Sha Tin East Rail (exit B); 🖳
This cosy 18-room place affiliated with the Lutheran Church provides a nice escape from the city as it's set on a peaceful hillside above the town. To get here, take the MTR East Rail to Sha Tin station, leave via exit B and walk down the ramp, passing a series of old village houses on the left. To the left of these houses is a set of steps signposted 'To Fung Shan'. Follow the path all the way to the top and you'll see Pil-

grim's Hall. The walk should take around 20 minutes. A taxi from the nearest MTR station in Tai Wai will cost around $24. There are free shuttle buses running between Sha Tin and To Fung Shan two or three times daily (Monday to Saturday). The canteen serves simple and healthy meals (advance booking required).

OUTLYING ISLANDS

There are not many hotels per se on the Outlying Islands, though you'll find one each on Lamma and Cheung Chau and several on Lantau. There are guesthouses on these three islands as well.

During the warmer months and on the weekends throughout most of the year, estate agencies set up booking kiosks for rental apartments and holiday villas near the ferry piers on Cheung Chau and at Mui Wo (Silvermine Bay) on Lantau.

The HKYHA has two hostels on Lantau, and the Country & Marine Parks Authority (☎ 1823; www.afcd.gov.hk) maintains 10 basic camp sites for hikers along the Lantau Trail and a single one on Tung Lung Chau.

LAMMA

CONCERTO INN Map p136   Hotel $$
☎ 2982 1668; www.concertoinn.com.hk; 28 Hung Shing Yeh beach, Hung Shing Yeh; r Sun-Fri $400-800, r Sat & eve of public holidays $700-1200; 🚊 Lamma (Yung Shue Wan); 🛜
This cheerful beach-front hotel, southeast of Yung Shue Wan, is quite some distance from the action, so you should stay here only if you really want to get away from it all. Rooms for three or four people are actually doubles with a sofa bed or pull-out bed.

MAN LAI WAH HOTEL Map p136   Guesthouse $
☎ 2982 0220; manlaiwahhotel@yahoo.com; 2 Po Wah Garden, Yung Shue Wan; r Mon-Fri $400-450, Sat & Sun $550-600; 🚊 Lamma (Yung Shue Wan)
This guesthouse greets you as you get off the ferry and begin to walk up Main St. Rooms have air-con and private shower and some have balconies ($50 more).

JACKSON PROPERTY AGENCY
Map p136   Holiday Homes $
☎ 2982 0606, 9055 3288; fax 2982 0636; 15 Main St, Yung Shue Wan; 🚊 Lamma (Yung Shue Wan)

This property agency has studios and apartments for rent on Lamma. All of them have a TV, private bathroom, microwave and fridge. Rooms start at $300 per night for two people from Sunday to Friday and go up to between $450 and $550 on Saturday.

BALI HOLIDAY RESORT
Map p136   Holiday Homes $
☎ 2982 4580; fax 2982 1044; 8 Main St, Yung Shue Wan; s/d Sun-Fri $280/380, Sat $560/760; 🚊 Lamma (Yung Shue Wan)
An agency rather than a resort as such, Bali Holiday Resort has about 30 studios and apartments sprinkled around the island. All have a TV, fridge and air-con and some have sea views.

LANTAU

As on Lamma and Cheung Chau during the summer, and on weekends the rest of the year, you can rent holiday rooms and apartments from kiosks set up at the Mui Wo ferry pier.

The HKYHA (Map pp100–1; ☎ 2788 1638; www.yha. org.hk; Shop 118, 1st fl, Fu Cheong Shopping Centre, Shum Mong Rd, Sham Shui Po; MTR Nam Cheong, exit A) has two hostels on Lantau: one a stone's throw from the Tian Tan Buddha in Ngong Ping and the other in a remote area of the Chi Ma Wan Peninsula. The hostels are open to HKYHA/ HI cardholders only, but membership is available if you pay the nonmember's rate for six nights here or at other HKYHA hostels.

You can also find three other decent accommodation options along Silvermine Bay beach.

REGAL AIRPORT HOTEL
Map p140   Luxury Hotel $$$$
☎ 2286 8888; www.regalairport.com; 9 Cheong Tat Rd, Hong Kong International Airport; r/ste from $3200/8000; MTR Airport Express; 🖥 🛜 🚇
A simple undercover shuffle from the airport terminal is this stylish hotel with more than 1100 sleek and easily accessible rooms, many with futuristic runway views. There's a splashy indoor/outdoor pool complex and half a dozen restaurants. Soundproofing ensures the only noise is that of your own making. Rooms are also available for day use (five hours and more between 6am and 9pm) and cost from $880 for every five hours. Follow directions to the 'arrival hall' after getting off the Airport Express, then cross the pedestrian bridge to the hotel.

HONG KONG SKYCITY MARRIOTT
HOTEL Map p140   Business Hotel $$
☎ 3969 1888; www.marriott.com/hotel-search
/china; 1 Sky City Rd E, Hong Kong International Air-
port; r/ste from $1280/1588; MTR Airport Express;
🖥 🛜 🖳

This hotel near the airport greets travellers
with dignified but modern furnishings, miles
of meeting space, secretarial services and
a nine-hole golf course. The spacious and
well-appointed rooms come with views of
the golf course or the sea. Man Ho (☎ 3969 1888)
is one of the best Chinese restaurants on
Lantau. Follow directions to the 'arrival hall'
after getting off the Airport Express, then
cross the pedestrian bridge to the hotel.

SILVERMINE BEACH HOTEL
Map p143   Hotel $$
☎ 2984 8295; www.resort.com.hk; Tung Wan Tau
Rd, Silvermine Bay beach; r $1080-1580, monthly
packages from $9000; 🧍 Lantau; 🖥 🛜 🖳
This 128-room hotel has rooms that look out
to the hills, sideways to the bay and directly
onto the bay. Eschew the rooms in the South
Wing for those in the superior New Wing.
Rates are negotiable. There are computers
in the restaurant for patrons' use.

MUI WO INN Map p143   Hotel $
☎ 2984 7225; fax 2984 1916; Tung Wan Tau Rd,
Silvermine Bay beach; r Sun-Fri $400, Sat $600;
🧍 Lantau
This is the last hotel on the beach and can
be identified by the ring of faux-classical
statues at the front. It's a friendly place to
stay and rates include breakfast.

MUI WO ACCOMMODATION KIOSKS
Map p143   Holiday Homes $
Mui Wo Ferry Pier; 🧍 Lantau
Several kiosks (☎ 2984 8982, 2984 2282) run by
different outfits on the ferry pier let out
rooms and apartments and have photos
of them on display. Expect to pay $150 on
weekdays and $250 on the weekend for a
double room or studio. Not all the places
are within walking distance of the ferry pier.

HONGKONG BANK FOUNDATION SG
DAVIS HOSTEL Map p140   Hostel $
☎ 2985 5610; www.yha.org.hk; Ngong Ping; dm
members under/over 18 yr $65/100, nonmembers
from $30; 🚌 2, 21 or 23
This hostel is a 10-minute walk from the
bus stop near the Tian Tan Buddha statue
in Ngong Ping and is an ideal place to stay

if you want to watch the sun rise at Lantau
Peak. Check-in is from 4pm to 11pm (from
3pm on Saturday). From the Ngong Ping bus
terminus, take the paved path to your left as
you face the Tian Tan Buddha, pass the public toilets on your right and the Lantau Tea
Garden on your left and follow the signs to
the maze-like steps going up to the hostel.
If you visit in winter, be sure to bring warm
clothes for evenings and early mornings.

CHEUNG CHAU
Cheung Chau is not really well set up for over-
nighters. Depending on the day of the week and
the season, up to half a dozen kiosks opposite
the ferry pier rent studios and apartments.

WARWICK HOTEL Map p146   Hotel $$
☎ 2981 0081; www.warwickhotel.com.hk; Cheung
Chau Sports Rd, Tung Wan beach; s/d Mon-Fri
$900/1000, Sat & Sun $1200/1300, ste from $1600,
weekly/monthly packages from $5000/20,000;
🧍 Cheung Chau; 🖥
This 71-room carbuncle on the butt of
Tung Wan beach is the only game in town,
but it does offer wonderful views across
to Lamma and Hong Kong Island. Heavy
discounts are available, so call to check.

CHEUNG CHAU B&B Map p146   Guesthouse $
☎ 2986 9990; www.bbcheungchau.com.hk; 12-14
Tung Wan Rd; r Sun-Thu from $420, Fri/Sat from
$520/720; 🧍 Cheung Chau; 🛜
This is an alternative to the island's only
hotel and the rooms offered by kiosks.
The 16 rooms are well decorated and have
private bathrooms, although some are compact so you might want to look first. There's
a lovely terrace on the roof from where you
can catch sunset and sunrise. Get a room on
the lower floors for better wi-fi reception.

CHEUNG CHAU ACCOMMODATION
KIOSKS Map p146   Holiday Homes $
Cheung Chau Ferry Pier; 🧍 Cheung Chau
Agents with booking kiosks on the praya
(waterfront promenade) include Bela Vista
Miami Resort (☎ 2981 7299; www.miamicheungchau
.com.hk), Holiday Resort (☎ 2981 0093) and Sea
View Holiday Flats (☎ 2986 9368), but unless you
have a smattering of Cantonese or a Chinese friend, you may have difficulty getting
what you want at a fair price (though there
are photo albums illustrating what's on
offer). Expect to pay $200 to $250 a night
for a studio for two people from Sunday to
Friday, and $300 to $500 on Saturday.

DAY TRIPS & EXCURSIONS

contents

SHENZHEN (p252)
- Information (p256)
- Shopping (p257)
- Eating (p258)
- Drinking (p259)
- Sleeping (p259)

ZHUHAI (p259)
- Information (p261)
- Eating & Drinking (p262)
- Sleeping (p263)

GUANGZHOU (p263)
- Information (p267)
- Shopping (p267)
- Eating (p268)
- Drinking (p269)
- Entertainment (p269)
- Sleeping (p269)

Just across the border from Hong Kong and Macau is the Pearl River Delta in Guangdong, home to the world's most expansive manufacturing hub. This polluted delta chock-full of factories is certainly not a typical tourist draw, but if you are at all like many residents of Hong Kong and Macau, you'll be tempted to cross the border for bargain, well, pretty much everything: tailor-made clothes, electronics, honest massages, authentic dim sum, and even oil paintings. But Hong Kong's mainland neighbours, with their unique tales and many interesting sites, both old and new, are certainly worth visiting for more than just bargains.

It was here that the ancient Maritime Silk Road had its beginnings and here that foreign merchants first made contact with China. Guangdong was the birthplace of reform and revolution in the early 20th century, eventually guiding the fate of modern China. In the 1980s, the region was emblematic of China's modernity. Two out of five Special Economic Zones (SEZs) and trade links with Hong Kong were set up here under Deng Xiaoping, turning the region into a trailblazer for the mainland's transition from a planned socialist economy into a market-based system. The region is still taking a lead in steering 21st-century China.

The easiest places to visit for a day from Hong Kong and Macau, respectively, are the two SEZs – Shenzhen (below) and Zhuhai (p259). These two cities are among the most prosperous in China, and for residents of Hong Kong and Macau, they're an extended shopping mall, a manufacturing mecca in which you can bargain-hunt to your wallet's content.

More interesting is Guangzhou (p263), the capital of Guangdong, which is worth a weekend or longer. Apart from the Canton Trade Fair (p263), the country's largest trade event, this historic city boasts a number of well-preserved heritages houses that are worth strolling around.

The fast and efficient railway and other ground transportation networks make it a snap to get around. All of the destinations in this chapter lie within a 90-minute journey of Hong Kong.

SHENZHEN

Once you cross the border at Lo Wu, you'll gradually notice that Cantonese is no longer the lingua franca on the other side of the fence, even though you're technically in Guangdong. Shenzhen, with a population of 13 million people, has drawn a mix of businessmen, investors and migrant workers to its golden gates, all of them trying to find a place in China's economic miracle. When this once sleepy fishing village became a SEZ in 1980, capitalism took root. Developers added a stock market, luxury condominiums and office towers rivalling those of Hong Kong. In less than 30 years, it has become China's wealthiest and youngest city (the average age of its residents is just 29) and a get-rich-quick prototype for other Chinese cities.

Geographically, Shenzhen includes Shenzhen City (Shēnzhèn Shì in Mandarin), opposite the border crossing at Lo Wu (Luóhú), the Shenzhen SEZ and Shenzhen County (Shēnzhèn Xiàn), which extends several kilometres north of the SEZ. You can buy a five-day, Shenzhen-only visa at the border (Americans excluded, see p287).

For most day visitors, Shenzhen is mostly about shopping (possibly followed by a cheap massage or good dim sum). It doesn't matter whether goods are counterfeit or pirate, so long as the price is right. Sometimes, with a little patience and luck, you can actually find quality at rock-bottom prices; see p257. However, although the bargains are Shenzhen's main draws, the rise of the new, young and relatively rich middle class has energised this city with some edgy and fascinating cultural scenes that are gradually picking up steam. There are also a few theme parks worth checking out, some of which are new, and some dated.

A good introduction to this incredible city is the new, hulking complex of Shenzhen Museum (Shēnzhèn Bówùguǎn Xīnguǎn; 深圳博物馆新馆; ☎ 0755-8201 3036; www.shenzhenmuseum.com.cn; East Gate, Citizens' Centre, Fuzhong Sanlu, Futian; admission free; ☾ 10am-6pm Tue-Sun; Shìmín Zhōngxīn metro, exit B). It showcases the city's short yet dynamic history of social transformation before and after Deng Xiaoping's policies of *gǎigé kāifàng* (reform

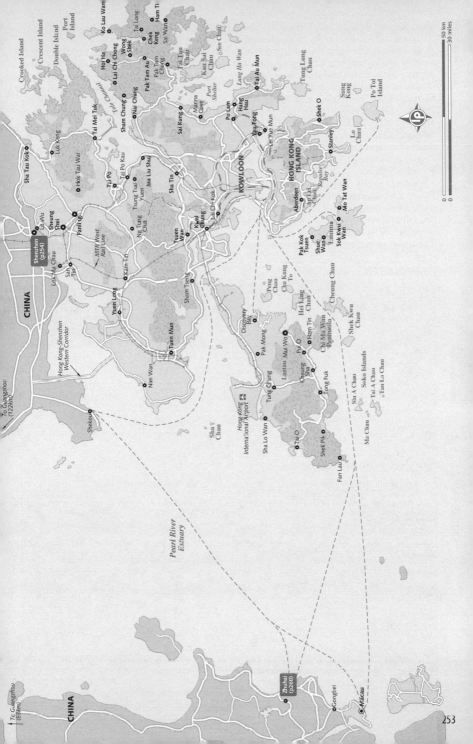

253

and opening) through spectacular life-sized dioramas and massive interactive multimedia presentations. The most interesting exhibits include the collections of propaganda art popular in the 1940s and the colourful scale models in the folk culture hall. The old Shenzhen Museum (Shēnzhèn Bówùguǎn Lǎoguǎn; ☎ 0755-8210 1036; Tongzin Lu, Futian; ☻ 9am-5pm; Kēxué Guǎn metro, exit A, ➌ 3, 12, 101, 102 or 104) in Litchi Park (Lìzhī Gōngyuán) has been converted into a museum of ancient arts that has less interesting displays of some 20,000 jade, porcelain and bronze artefacts.

Culture junkies rejoice: arts scenes are no longer a pipedream in this Temple of Mammon. For a complete list of museums, arts and cultural events, pick up a copy of the bimonthly *Life Art Map*, available at museums. The city's cultural ambition is obvious, espe-

cially in the Overseas Chinese Town, 15km west of Shenzhen City. The OCT-LOFT Art Terminal (Huáqiáochéng Chuàngyì Wénhuàyuán; 华侨城创意文化园; ☎ 0755-2691 5100; Enping Lu, Overseas Chinese Town; ☻ 10am-5.30pm Tue-Sun; Qiáochéng dōng metro, exit A) is an ambitious project intended to attract artists to gather and explore, discuss and consume. This excellent museum complex exhibits works of international and local contemporary Chinese artists. Some communist-era warehouses have been converted into artists' studios, hip cafes and bars.

Just one metro stop from the Art Terminal is He Xiangning Art Gallery (Héxiāngníng Měishùguǎn; ☎ 0755-2660 4540; www.hxnart.com; 9013 Shennan Lu; admission Y20, free on Fri; ☻ 10am-5.30pm Tue-Sun; Huáqiáochéng metro, exit C, ➌ 245 from Shenzhen Bay Port). It has an esoteric collection of hybrid Japanese/Chinese water paintings by the legendary late

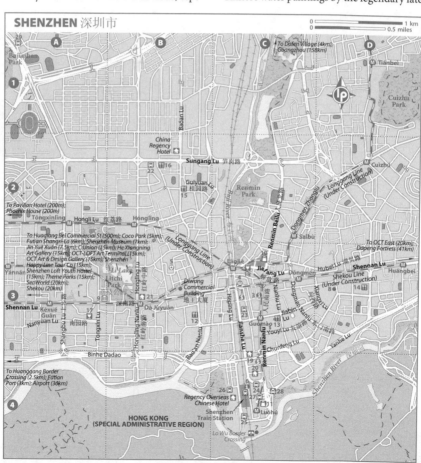

master of modern Chinese art, He Xiangning. Pick up a pamphlet in English at the ticket office, as there are no English descriptions by the displays. Adjacent is the Beijing Water Cube–like OCT Art & Design Gallery (Huá Měishùguǎn; 华美术馆; ☎ 0755-3399 3111; www.oct-and.com; 9009 Shennan Lu; adult/student Y18/8; ◷ 10am-5.30pm Tue-Sun). The focus of this new gallery is on fresh, mainland avant-garde designers. A marvellous collection of innovative design pieces in various art forms is on display. Exhibits change frequently.

Just a few minutes' walk from the gallery is a series of dated theme parks that are always packed with snap-happy Chinese tourists. They're fun destinations for a family day out. Window of the World (Shìjiè Zhīchuāng; 世界之窗; ☎ 0755-2690 2840, 0755-2660 8000; www.szwwco .com; adult/child under 12yr Y120/60; ◷ 9am-10.30pm; Shìjiè Zhīchuāng metro, exit J, 🚌 90 or 245 from Shenzhen Bay Port) hosts a collection of scale replicas of famous world monuments. Foreigners being misidentified as part of the exhibits is not unheard of.

Reverse roles at the adjacent Splendid China (Jǐnxiù Zhōnghuá; 锦绣中华; ☎ 0755-2660 0626; www .cn5000.com.cn; adult/child under 12yr incl entry to China Folk Culture Village Y120/60; ◷ 9am-6pm; Huáqiáochéng metro, exit B, 🚌 245 from Shenzhen Bay Port), home to miniature replicas of China's own famous sights. Included in the admission is China Folk Culture Village (Zhōngguó Mínsú Wénhuà Cūn; 中国民俗文化村; ☎ 0755-2660 0626; www.cn5000.com.cn;

adult/child under 12yr incl entry to Splendid China Y120/60; ◷ 9am-10pm; Huáqiáochéng metro, exit B), which has two-dozen faux minority villages complete with minority-culture demonstrations. A mini-monorail run by the Shenzhen Happy Line Tour Co links the three parks, along with several other sights.

Some 20km east of Shenzhen City, a whopping Y3.5 billion went into making OCT East (Dōngbù Huáqiáochéng; 东部华侨城; ☎ 0755-2503 1837; www.octeast.com; Dàméishā, Yantian District; admission Y200-229; ◷ 9.30am-6pm), an upmarket and incredibly beautiful theme-park-cum-resort that will certainly awe you. It feels like a supersized Universal Studios plus Chinese Disneyland, with a mock Swiss village, a golf complex, a tea valley and luxurious hotels to keep you entertained and pampered. The park offers some stunning views that make it worth a couple of days to explore, and you can rent a car from inside the park to tour around. To get here, an express bus (Y65, one hour) leaves hourly at exit E, Kowloon Tong MTR station in Hong Kong, between 8.15am and 5.15pm. In Shenzhen, Sightseeing Bus 1, which leaves from Window of the World, with stops at Diwáng Dàxià on Shennan Lu, goes to the park; get off at the last stop. A taxi from Luohu train station is about Y60.

Further to the east is Dapeng Fortress (Dàpéng Shǔochéng; 大鹏所城; ☎ 0755-8431 9269; Pengcheng Village, Dapeng Town, Longgang District; adult/student & senior Y20/10; ◷ 10am-6pm). This preserved walled

SHENZHEN

INFORMATION
Bank of China 中国银行分行 1 C3
Bank of China (Branch)
    中国银行分行.................................2 C4
China Travel Service Shenzhen
    深圳中国旅行社 3 C3
HSBC 汇丰银行 ....(see 20)
Luggage Storage 行李寄存......(see 27)
Post Office 邮局.................................4 C3
Public Security Bureau 公安局.....5 B3
Shenzhen Tourist Consultation
    Centre 深圳市游客咨询处 6 C4
Visa Office (Luohu)
    落地签证办公室（罗湖）...........7 C4

SIGHTS & ACTIVITIES
Queen's Spa & Dining 皇室假期... 8 D3
Shenzhen Museum (Old)
    深圳博物馆老馆......................9 A3

SHOPPING
Dongmen Market 东门市场........10 C3
Luohu Commercial City
    罗湖商业城...........................11 C4

Stephanie ....(see 11)

EATING 🍴
Belle Epoque............................(see 12)
Grand Prince 王子国宴.............12 B3
Laurel ....(see 19)
Laurel (Branch) 丹桂轩 ....(see 11)
Made in Kitchen 厨房制造........13 C3
Muslim Hotel Restaurant
    穆斯林宾馆大餐厅...............14 D3
Summer Tea House
    静颐茶馆...............................15 B2
West Lake Spring 西湖春天.......16 B2

DRINKING 🍷
Citic City Plaza
    中信城市广场........................17 A3
True Color 本色.........................18 C4

SLEEPING 🛏
Century Plaza Hotel
    新都酒店...............................19 C4
Shangri-La Hotel
    香格里拉大酒店.....................20 C4

Vision Fashion
Hotel
    深圳视界风尚酒店
    ....21 B3

TRANSPORT
Bus to Dafen
    Village ....(see 24)
Bus to Dapeng
    Fortress 22 B2
Buses to Shekou.......................23 C3
Local Bus Station
    公车站...................................24 C4
Local Minibuses
    本地中巴站............................25 C4
Long Distance Bus
    Station
    侨社客运站...........................26 C4
Luohu Bus Station
    罗湖汽车站............................27 C4
Taxi Stands...............................28 C4
Yinhu Bus Station
    银湖客运站............................29 A1

town, still a lively village, was built 600 years ago and was a key battle site in the Opium Wars in the 19th century. To get here, board bus 360 at Yinhu bus station; the bus also stops near China Regency Hotel at Sungang Lu. The journey takes about 90 minutes. Alight at Dapeng bus station (Dàpéng zǒngzhàn; 大鹏总站) and change to bus 966. Faster and easier is the Sha Tau Kok Express ($60, 90 minutes, hourly departure between 7am and 6.30pm) at Suffolk Rd (MTR Kowloon Tong, exit C). At the Dapeng bus station change to minibus 966.

Shenzhen offers all sorts of body-perfecting services, from massage to manicure. Try the Queen's Spa & Dining (Huángshì Jiàqí; ☎ 0755-8225 3888; B1-5th fl, Golden Metropolis Bldg, Chunfeng Lu; ☺ 24hr; Gúomào metro, exit B) near Guómào metro. This spa wonderland offers aromatherapy and different types of massages (Y168 to Y218; a minimum tip of Y30 is mandatory). The pools, fruit bar and sleeping capsules allow you to lose days inside.

INFORMATION

Hong Kong dollars are no longer accepted in Shenzhen, only Chinese Renminbi (or yuan, abbreviated as 'Y'). For around Y20 per hour, you can access the internet at most of the hotels listed in this chapter.

Bank of China (Zhōngguó Yínháng; 2022 Jianshe Lu; ☺ 8.30am-5pm Mon-Fri, 9am-4pm Sat, Sun & holidays) There's another branch on Renmin Nanlu (Zhōngguó Yínháng Fēnháng; 1st fl, Fángdìchǎn Dàxià), just behind New Century Hotel.

China Travel Service Shenzhen (CTS; Zhōngguó Lǚxíngshè Shēnzhèn; ☎ 0755-8225 8447; 6th fl, 3023 Renmin Nanlu; ☺ 9am-6pm)

HSBC (Ground fl, Shangri-La Hotel, 1002 Jianshe Lu; ☺ 9am-5pm Mon-Fri)

Luggage storage (piece per day approx Y10-20; ☺ 7.30am-10.30pm) Located next to the ticketing office in Luohu bus station.

Post office (Yóujú; ☎ 0755-2516 8326; 3040 Jianshe Lu; ☺ 8am-8pm)

Public Security Bureau (PSB; Gōng'ānjú; ☎ 0755-8446 3999; 4018 Jiefang Lu; ☺ 9am-noon & 2-6pm Mon-Fri)

Shenzhen Happy Line Tour Co (☎ 0755-2690 6000; tours adult/child under 12yr Y40/20; ☺ 10am-7pm; Huáqiáochéng metro)

Shenzhen Tourist Consultation Centre (Shēnzhènshì Yóukè Wènxúnchù; ☎ 0755-8232 3045; Ground fl, Shenzhen train station, east exit; ☺ 9am-6pm) Free and

TRANSPORT – SHENZHEN

For more detailed information about getting from Hong Kong to China, see p285.

Distance from Hung Hom station 35km

Direction from Hung Hom station North

Travel time from Hung Hom station 40 minutes by MTR train

Distance from Macau's Inner Harbour to Shékǒu About 115km

Direction from Macau's Inner Harbour to Shékǒu Northeast

Travel time from Macau's Inner Harbour to Shékǒu 90 minutes by ferry

To keep pace with Shenzhen's explosive growth, there is continual and rapid expansion of the area's transport services, especially the rail systems.

Boat There are seven jet-cat departures ($110 to $145, one hour) daily between Shekou port (☎ 0755-2669 1213) and Hong Kong between 7.45am and 10pm. Six go to the Macau ferry pier in Central, and one heads to the China ferry terminal in Kowloon. The same number of boats leave Hong Kong for Shékǒu between 7.45am and 8.30pm. Thirteen ferries go to Hong Kong airport (one way Y260 to Y290, round-trip Y360; 30 minutes one way) between 7.45am and 8.15pm. The same number of boats leave Hong Kong airport for Shékǒu between 9am and 9.20pm. Ten ferries a day also link Shékǒu with Macau; for details, see p351. You can also reach Zhuhai (Y80, one hour) from Shékǒu every half-hour from 7.30am to 8.30pm.

Bus Buses to the Huánggǎng border crossing run 24-hourly from various departure points in Hong Kong. There are also buses going to Shenzhen International Airport between 6.40am and 10.20pm. For details, see p285. With the opening of the Hong Kong–Shenzhen Western Corridor, buses go to Shenzhen Bay (深圳湾) at Shékǒu from a couple of departure points in Hong Kong. Operators such as Eternal East (☎ 3760 0888; www.eebus.com) have express buses running from reasonably detailed maps are available on request. There's another branch at Futian Port that keeps the same hours.

Visa offices Lo Wu (☎ 0755-8233 9585; ⌚ 9am-10pm); Huánggǎng (☎ 0755-8339 5171; ⌚ 9am-1pm & 2.30-5pm, border 24hr); Shékǒu (☎ 0755-2669 1848; ⌚ 8.45am-12.30pm & 2.30-5.30pm) You can buy a five-day visa on the spot (restricted to Shenzhen SEZ, excluding the Longgang and Bao'an Districts) at any of these offices (Y160 for most nationalities, Y469 for British citizens; US citizens must apply in advance for a full Chinese visa). Only Renminbi is accepted.

www.shenzhenparty.com For entertainment options in Shenzhen, check out this expat-run website.

www.shenzhentour.com A government-run website that contains fairly useful travel information.

SHOPPING

Shopping is the sole reason many people visit Shenzhen. An invaluable book to guide you is *Shop in Shenzhen: An Insider's Guide* (HK$95/US$12) by Ellen McNally, available in bookshops throughout Hong Kong and online from Amazon. Shoppers won't leave Shenzhen empty-handed, though the quality can vary. Be ready to haggle.

Dafen Village (Dàfēncūn; 大芬村; ☎ 0755-8473 2633; www.cndafen.com; Dafen, Buji, Longgang District)

It's easy to associate China with all kinds of counterfeits, including artwork, but this village is definitely eye-opening: 600 art-packed studios-cum-stores, 10,000 skilled artists and thousands of freshly painted *Mona Lisas*, and any other famous masterpieces you can imagine, every week. Prices range from Y200 to Y700. Bus 306 from Luohu takes you to the village in an hour. A taxi ride costs around Y40 to Y60.

Dongmen Market (Dōngmén Shìchǎng; Lǎojiē metro) This chaotic market is popular for tailored suits and skirts, electronic goods and cheap ready-to-wear clothes, at competitive prices. Most shops open from 10am to 10pm. Be extremely careful of pickpockets.

Huaqiang Bei Commercial St (Huáqiángběi Shāngyèjiē; Huáqiánglù metro, exit A) For electronics, Huaqiang Bei is a living, breathing eBay, with shops and malls for blocks on end selling the latest tech gadgets, hi-tech audiovisual equipment and computer components at rock-bottom prices.

Luohu Commercial City (Luóhú Shāngyè Chéng; ☎ 0/55-8233 8178; Renmin Nanlu; ⌚ 6.30am-midnight) The Hong Kong day-trippers' favourite. Over 700 shops sell heaps of goods. The 5th floor houses a cluster of fabric and tailor shops. Stephanie (www.shenzhen-tailor.com; Shop 5060A) has a

Grand Promenade, Sai Wan Ho (one way/round-trip $50, 65 minutes one way) and Dragon Centre, Sham Shui Po (one way/round-trip $35, 45 minutes one way) to Shenzhen Bay. New Lantao Bus and City Bus also operate bus B2 from Yuen Long MTR station ($11), B3 from Tuen Mun Ferry Pier bus terminus ($11) and B3X from Tuen Mun Town Centre ($11) to the bay. Travellers will find Shenzhen a stepping stone to other parts of China. Buses to other cities in Guangdong depart from Luohu bus station (Luóhú qìchēzhàn) beneath Luohu Commercial City, and there are departures to Guangxi from the bus station next to Regency Overseas Chinese Hotel. See Lonely Planet's *China* guide for more details. Shenzhen has a cheap and efficient network of buses and minibuses (tickets cost between Y1.50 and Y4).

Metro At present, Shenzhen has two metro lines (Y2 to Y5). Line 1 stretches from the Luohu border crossing to the Window of the World theme park. An extension to the airport is expected in 2011. Line 4 (lines 2 and 3 are under construction) has a station at Futian Port, where passengers can interchange from Lok Ma Chau station across the border in Hong Kong. This line will extend to the north to connect with a new train station in Bùjí that is scheduled to open in 2011.

More lines are in the works: the Shekou Line, expected in 2011, will run from Shekou ferry terminal to Luohu, with interchanges at Dàjùyuàn and Shìmín Zhōngxīn metros. Another line, also expected in 2011, will run from Futian District to Longgang District with stops in Bùjí and Dàfēn.

Taxi In Shenzhen, taxis (☎ 0755-8322 8000) cost Y12.50 (Y18.50 from 11pm to 6am) for the first 3km, with each additional 250m costing another Y0.60.

Train MTR's Lo Wu–bound or Lok Ma Chau–bound trains (1st/2nd class $69.50/36.50, 40 minutes) are the most convenient transport to Shenzhen from Hong Kong (p286). Both connect with the metro in Shenzhen once across the border. From Shenzhen there are frequent high-speed trains (Y75 to Y95, 60 to 70 minutes) to Guangzhou between 6.15am and 10.50pm. The Shenzhen–Guangzhou segment of the new Guangzhou–Shenzhen–Hong Kong Express Rail Link, expected in 2011, will reduce travel time to 40 minutes.

IS THE SEZ STILL SPECIAL?

It's hard to imagine that a decade ago there was an electrified fence bordering the northern part of the Special Economic Zone (SEZ) to prevent mass illegal migrations south to Shenzhen. Deng Xiaoping bestowed numerous favourable measures on the city, which during the '80s was at the forefront of capitalism in communist China. Today, cities like Shanghai and Chongqing are granted similar favours, sending waves of apprehension through Shenzhen, which is keen to safeguard its 'special' status.

Shenzhen is increasingly eager to merge with Hong Kong, both economically and physically, to retain its favoured status. A few years ago the megacity plan to integrate the two cities was still wishful thinking. But now, Shenzhen is actively (and unilaterally) preparing itself for the creation of a borderless megacity. The visa procedures for residents of Shenzhen to come into Hong Kong have been simplified, and a new direct express train linking the two cities is under construction.

While there is tremendous concern that this one-sided movement is a potential breach of the Sino-British Joint Declaration – which guarantees the autonomy of Hong Kong – some, especially those north of the border, are excited to see the arranged marriage between the SEZ and the SAR, arguing that 'one country, two systems' is a straitjacket for the economy of both cities.

As the migrant population outstrips the locals in Shenzhen, social problems arise. The minimum wage in Shenzhen is Y8.80 per hour, aggravating the imbalance of wealth. Human trafficking and labour disputes that result in violent suppression aren't uncommon, and the local police are severely understaffed, overworked and insufficiently trained.

The only way for this anomalous society to retain its status, according to a police officer and a TV producer we met, is integration with Hong Kong. 'We are ready to erase the border. Hong Kong police are welcome to combat crimes for us.' As we walked along an unruly street in Shenzhen, we sensed that Shenzhen is struggling to keep its special status. It looks north to the mainland and south to Hong Kong, and strives to remain the bridge between the two.

---

reputation for its workmanship and quality clothing. Most shops are open from 10.30am to 10pm.

EATING

Shenzhen's cultural diversity means it's not difficult to find a wide variety of both Chinese and international cuisines. The food courts in shopping malls like the MixC and Coco Park (Gòuwù Gōngyuán metro) have some decent options for budget travellers.

Belle Epoque (☎ 0755-8266 8880; Shop 299, 2nd fl, The MixC, Bao'an Nanlu; tea set Y68, lunch & dinner from Y258; ☼ noon-11pm Mon-Fri, 11.30am-11pm Sat & Sun; Dàjùyuàn metro, exit C3) This French restaurant, arguably the best in town, hits the mark with an interior that is both plush and comfortable, decor-wise.

Grand Prince (Wángzǐ Guóyàn; ☎ 0755-8269 0666; Shop 45, 5th fl, The MixC, Bao'an Nanlu; lunch Y38-50, dinner Y80-150; ☼ 9am-3pm & 5-10pm; Dàjùyuàn metro, exit C3) This classy restaurant serves up a wide variety of surprisingly affordable dishes from all over China in an impressive, spacious dining hall.

Jīn Yuè Xuān (金悦轩; ☎ 0755-8886 8880; 1st-4th fl, Seyou Bldg, 6013 Shennan Dadao; dim sum Y4.80-20.80, meals per person Y60-190; ☼ 11am-3pm, 5.30-10.30pm; Chēgōngmiào metro, exit C or D) The meticulous 200-item dim sum menu is amazing, as is Jīn Yuè Xuān's impressive interior.

Laurel (Dānguìxuān; ☎ 0755-8232 1888; 2nd fl, Century Plaza Hotel, 1 Chunfeng Lu; meals per person Y50-180; ☼ 7am-11pm) The Luohu branch (☎ 0755-8232 3668; Shop 5010, 5th fl, Luohu Commercial City; ☼ 7am-11pm) is a handy choice if you are shopping at Luohu Commercial City, but the main branch at the Century Plaza Hotel serves better dim sum.

Made in Kitchen (Chúfáng Zhìzào; ☎ 0755-8261 1639; 7th fl, Kingglory Plaza, 2028 Renmin Lu; appetisers Y15-95, mains Y55-208; ☼ 9.30am-11.30pm; Gúomào metro, exit A) The menu in this attractive, stylish fusion spot is a feast for the eyes and palate, with over 400 diverse choices, from pad thai noodles to sashimi to steak.

Muslim Hotel Restaurant (Músīlín Bīnguǎn Dàcānguǎn; ☎ 0755-8225 9664; 2nd fl, Muslim Hotel, 2013 Wenjing Nanlu; dishes Y28-68; ☼ 10am-11pm; ☒ minibus 430) If you fancy trying *huí* (Chinese Muslim) food, head for this halal restaurant, where you can sample various beef and mutton dishes.

Phoenix House (Fènghuánglóu; 凤凰楼; ☎ 0755-8207 6688, 0755-8207 6338; East Wing, Pavilion Hotel, 4002 Huaqiang Beilu; lunch Y60-80, dinner Y100-350; ☼ 7.30am-11pm; Huáqiánglù metro, exit A) The best Cantonese restaurant in town, but expect rowdy waits for 30 minutes or more after 11.30am.

Summer Tea House (Jīngyí Cháguǎn; ☎ 0755-2557 4555; 7th & 8th fl, Jīntáng Dàxià, 3038 Bao'an Nanlu; tea-tasting per person Y28, meals Y28-68; ☼ 10am-1am) Tucked away in an office building near Xīhú Bīnguǎn is this veggies' favourite in Shenzhen, with good-for-you ingredients, a relaxing tea-tasting area and a smoke-free dining hall (hurrah!). No English menu, but colourful pictures illustrate the dishes.

West Lake Spring (Xīhú Chūntiān; ☎ 0755-8211 6988; 2nd-3rd fl, Parkway Tower, 3019 Sungang Lu; dishes Y21-180; ⏱ 11am-2.30pm & 5-10pm; 🚇 18, get off at Xīhú Bīnguǎn) This Hángzhōu restaurant gets the thumbs-up from locals. There's an English-less menu with pictures. The signature dishes, Lóngjǐng Xiārén (龙井虾仁; stir-fried freshwater shrimp with Longjing tea leaves; Y78) and Sòngsǎo Yúgēng (宋嫂鱼羹; yellow croaker fish soup; small/large Y38/48), deserve savouring.

DRINKING

Finding a venue in Shenzhen for anything from a quiet drink to a raucous knees-up after a hard day of bargaining is easy. There are upmarket bars galore below Citic City Plaza (Zhōngxìn Chéngshì Guǎngchǎng), at Coco Park in Futian and SeaWorld (Hǎishàng Shìjiè; 海上世界) in Shékǒu. The following locals' favourites are also worth a shot.

C: Union (Yídùtáng; 一渡堂; Block F3, OCT-LOFT Art Terminal, Enping Lu, Huaqiaocheng; ⏱ 10am-2am; Qiáochéngdōng metro, exit A) This warehouse-turned-Bohemian-style drinking haunt is where rebellious local bands jam every night after 10pm. It has a good mix of blues and punk rock, and is absolutely pop-music-free.

True Colour (Běnsè; ☎ 0755-8230 1833; 4th fl, Golden World, 2001 Jiefang Lu; ⏱ 9am-1am; Lǎojiē metro, exit A) Clubbers should check out this night-time playground of young Shenzhenians. Its watering-hole-plus-dancefloor formula attracts city slickers and trendy young adults alike.

SLEEPING

Hotels in Shenzhen discount deeply during the week, slicing as much as 60% off the regular rack rate, though you should ask for a discount no matter when you go.

Shangri-La (Xiānggélǐlā Dàjiǔdiàn; ☎ 0755-8233 0888; www.shangri-la.com/shenzhen; 1002 Jianshe Lu; d Y1598-1950, ste Y2500; 🛜) This classic, luxurious hotel is one of the best places to stay in Luohu District that offers free wi-fi. Its new branch, Futian Shangri-La (Shēnzhèn Fútián Xiānggélǐlā Dàjiǔdiàn; 福田香格里拉大酒店; ☎ 0755-8828 4088; 4088 Yitian Lu; r Y1340-1988, ste Y2500; 🛜), in Futian District also has spacious and sparkling rooms.

Shenzhen Loft Youth Hostel (Shēnzhèn Qiáochéng Lǚyóu Guójì Qīngnián Lǚshè; 深圳侨城旅友国际青年旅舍; ☎ 0755-2694 9443; www.yhachina.com; 3 Enping Lu, Huaqiaocheng; dm Y60, d without bathroom Y138, s & d Y158; Qiáochéngdōng metro, exit A) This excellent hostel is located in a tranquil residential area behind the OCT-LOFT Art Terminal (p254). Rooms are spotless and the staff are helpful.

Vision Fashion Hotel (Shēnzhèn Shìjiè Fēngshàng Jiǔdiàn; ☎ 0755-2558 2888; www.visionfashionhotel.com; 5018 Shennan Donglu; r Y386-798; Dàjùyuàn metro, exit B) Inside a theatre complex is this new boutique hotel with many different interior designs in its range of rooms. Some are chic, some bizarre. Its prime location and quiet environment make it very good value.

ZHUHAI

Zhuhai, or 'pearl of the sea', is Shenzhen's little SEZ sister, with 1.5 million people, and is close enough to Macau for a day trip. It's as laid-back as its neighbour Macau and has the fewest maniacal drivers in China. Like many Hong Kongers visiting Shenzhen, residents of Macau come here on the weekends for cheap massages and lavish but affordable Cantonese feasts.

A small agricultural town into the 1980s, the Zhuhai of today has not only the usual SEZ skyline of glimmering five-star hotels and luxurious condos along the bay, but even its own ultramodern airport. Zhuhai is divided into three main districts: Gǒngběi, Jídà and Xiāngzhōu. Gǒngběi (拱北), adjacent to Macau, is the main tourist district, with restaurants and shops; Gongbei Port (Gǒngběi Kǒu'àn) is the large modern complex that visitors pass through en route from Macau. To the northeast is Jídà (吉大), with large waterfront hotels and resorts and Jiuzhou Harbour (Jiǔzhōu Gǎng; 九州港), where Hong Kong, Shenzhen and Guangdong passenger ferries arrive and depart. The northernmost district is Xiāngzhōu (香洲), which has government buildings and a busy fishing port.

Downtown, you can visit the recently renovated Zhuhai City Museum (Zhūhǎishì Bówùguǎn; ☎ 0756-332 4116; 191 Jingshan Lu; admission free; ⏱ 9am-5pm; 🚌 2, 30 or 26) in Jídà. It has 13 exhibition halls displaying old photos and the history of Zhuhai, as well as cannon batteries and stelae excavated around Zhuhai. The exhibits are not particularly attractive, but the meticulously arranged garden is charming amid the bustling downtown.

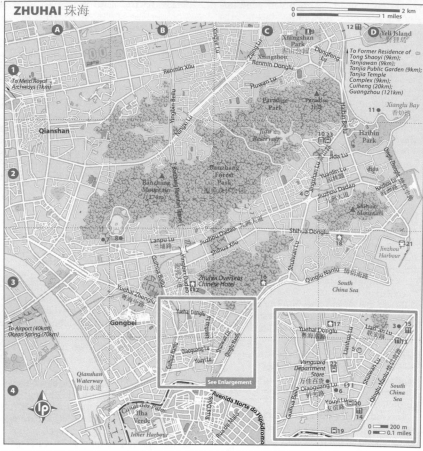

ZHUHAI 珠海

ZHUHAI

INFORMATION

Bank of China
中国银行 .... (see 17)
Bank of China
中国银行 1 D4
China Travel Service
Guangzhou Gongbei
中国旅行社广州拱北 2 B3
Cohiba 3 D3
Post Office 邮局 4 C2
Post Office 邮局 5 D4
Public Security Bureau
公安局 6 D4

SIGHTS & ACTIVITIES

Chinese Medicine
Valley 中药谷 7 A3
New Yuan Ming Palace
圆明新园 8 B3
Revolutionary Martyrs'
Memorial 烈士陵园 9 C1

Zhuhai City Museum
珠海市博物馆 10 D2
Zhuhai Fisher Girl
珠海渔女 11 D1

EATING 🍴

Déyuè Fǎng 得月舫 12 D1
Jīn Yué Xuān 金悦轩 13 D4
May Flower Restaurant
五月花酒家 14 D4
Rosa Chinensia 月季轩 15 D3
Tea Palace 茶皇殿 .... (see 17)

SLEEPING 🛏

Grand Bay View Hotel
珠海海湾大酒店 16 C3
Yindo Hotel 银都酒店 17 D3
Yong Tong Hotel
永通酒店 .... (see 20)
Youth Hostel
珠海国际学生旅馆 .... (see 18)

Zhuhai Holiday
Resort
珠海度假村 18 D3

TRANSPORT

CTS Bus Station 19 D4
Gongbei Coach
Station
拱北汽车总站 20 D4
Jiuzhou Harbour
Ferry Pier
九州港码头 21 D3
Kee Kwan Bus
Station
歧關站汽车站 .... (see 19)
Xinhe Bus Station
信禾客运站 .... (see 20)
Zhuhai Sightseeing
Bus Stop 22 D4
Zhuhai Sightseeing
Bus Terminal 23 D2

North of the museum at the eastern edge of Xiangshan Park (Xiāngshān Gōngyuán; Fenghuang Bei Lu), the austere Revolutionary Martyrs' Memorial (Lièshì Língyuán; ⏱ 5.30am-7pm; 🚌 3, 13 or 99) is dedicated to local victims of the Japanese forces during WWII.

In the bay between Haibin Park and Paradise Park is the Zhuhai Fisher Girl (Zhūhǎi Yúnǚ; Xianglu Bay; 🚌 99), an 8.7m-high statue of a dame holding a pearl, the symbol of the city.

Zhuhai has a number of lesser-known sites that nonetheless played vital parts in Guangdong's history. To the northwest of downtown is Meixi Royal Archways (Méixī Páifāng; 梅溪牌坊; ☎ 0756-865 9577; Meixi Village, Qianshan; admission Y50; ⏱ 8.30am-6pm; 🚌 99 or Line 1, Sightseeing Bus) at Qiánshān (前山), originally a residence of the legendary philanthropist Chen Fang. The archways were bestowed by Emperor Guangxu, but one was destroyed during the Cultural Revolution. The mansions beside them display wax works, archway models and photos.

To the north of Xiāngzhōu, two sites are worth discovering in the labyrinth-like suburb of Tángjiāwān (唐家湾). Tangjia Public Garden (Tángjiā Gònglèyuán; 唐家共乐园; ☎ 0756-338 8896; Eling, Tángjiāwān; adult/student Y20/10; ⏱ 8.30am-5.30pm) was a private estate of the first premier of the Republic of China, Tong Shaoyi, in 1900. Now it is a tranquil garden preserving various old growth and rare species from South China. Take bus 10 on Yingbin Dadao and alight at Tangjia Market (Tángjiāshìcháng). A taxi from Gōngběi to here is around Y60. The ticket to the garden includes admission to the nearby Former Residence of Tong Shaoyi (Táng Shàoyí Gùjū; 唐绍仪故居; 99 Fangshang Lu), where this statesman was born. It's accessible from the south gate of the garden.

In the same area is the 300-year-old Tangjia Temple Complex (Tángjiā Sānmiào; 唐家三庙; cnr Datong Lu & Xindizhi Jie, Tángjiāwān; admission free; ⏱ 8.30am-6pm; 🚌 10), dedicated to Lady Golden Flower (a local deity of marriage and pregnancy), the God of War and Literature, and the Buddha. The highlight is a grim-looking Buddha statue brought from India when the temple was founded. The temples are a bit difficult to find; just ask the friendly villagers where Sānmiào is.

The small village of Cuiheng (Cuīhēng; 翠亨), 33km north of the border with Macau, is the site of the Dr Sun Yat-sen Residence Memorial Museum (Sūn Zhōngshān Gùjū Jìniànguǎn; 孙中山故居纪念馆; ☎ 0760-550 1691; Culheng Dadao, Cuiheng; admission free; ⏱ 9am-5pm), where the revolutionary hero and founder of the Republic of China was born in 1866. A solemn place of pilgrimage for Chinese of all political persuasions, the museum recreates the house where Sun grew up, and the village compound includes a remarkable collection of period furniture. To get there, take bus 10 in Zhuhai on Yingbin Dadao. Alight at the terminus and change to bus 12. Or pay Y100 (one way) for a taxi from Gōngběi.

Two kilometres northwest of Gōngběi is a 'been there, done that' icon of Zhuhai, New Yuan Ming Palace (Yuánmíng Xīnyuán; ☎ 0756-861 0388; www.ymy.com.cn; cnr Jiuzhou Dadao & Lanpu Lu; adult/child Y120/80; ⏱ 9am-9pm; 🚌 1, 13, 60 or 99). This massive theme park is a reproduction of the original imperial Yuan Ming Palace in Beijing, destroyed by British and French forces during the Second Opium War.

Next door is Chinese Medicine Valley (Zhōngyàogǔ; ☎ 0756-866 1113; cnr Lanpu Lu & Baishi Lu; adult/child Y99/49), a resort where you can soak away your fatigue in pools filled with Chinese herbs, or just settle for a traditional massage. For a true hot-spring experience, the Ocean Spring (Hǎiquánwān; 海泉湾; ☎ 0756-726 7788; Pingsha, Zhuhai; admission Y168-252; ⏱ 8.30am-1.30am) resort in Dǒumén (斗门) has a huge oceanside open-air pool and rooms with their own hot-spring tubs.

INFORMATION

Bank of China (⏱ 9am-5pm Mon-Fri, 10am-4pm Sat & Sun) Yuehai Donglu branch (Zhōngguó Yínháng; cnr Yingbin Dadao & Yuehai Donglu); Lianhua Lu branch (Zhōngguó Yínháng Fēnháng; 41 Lianhua Lu) ATMs here and elsewhere are linked to the most common international money systems.

China Travel Service Guangzhou Gongbei (CTS; Zhōngguó Lǚxíngshè Guǎngzhōu Gōngběi; ☎ 0756-889 9228; 33 Yingbin Dadao; ⏱ 8am-8pm) This helpful office, next to Zhuhai Overseas Chinese Hotel, sells discounted tickets to a number of tourist sights.

Post office (⏱ 8am-8pm) Jingshan Lu branch (Yóujú; 57 Jingshan Lu); Yuehai Donglu branch (Yóujú; 1043 Yuehai Donglu)

Public Security Bureau (PSB; Gōng'ānjú; ☎ 0756-887 2872; 1038 Yingbin Dadao)

Visa offices Gongbei Port (2nd fl; ⏱ 8.30am-12.15pm, 1-6.15pm & 7-10.30pm); Jiuzhou Port (⏱ 8.30am-7pm) These offices issue Zhuhai-only visas valid for three days (Y160 for most nationalities, Y469 for British). US citizens must get a visa in advance in Macau (p355) or Hong Kong

TRANSPORT – ZHUHAI

Distance from Macau ferry pier 2km

Direction from Macau ferry pier North

Travel time from Macau ferry pier 20 minutes by bus

Distance from Hong Kong's Macau ferry pier in Central About 65km

Direction from Hong Kong's Macau ferry pier in Central West

Travel time from Hong Kong's Macau ferry pier in Central 70 minutes by high-speed ferry

Boat Jetcats between Zhuhai and Hong Kong (Y165, 70 minutes) depart seven times a day between 8am and 5.30pm from Jiuzhou Harbour (☎ 0756-333 3359, in Hong Kong 2858 3876) for the China ferry terminal in Kowloon, and nine times a day from 9am to 9.30pm for the Macau ferry pier in Central. Keep the ferry ticket and once you're in Zhuhai you're entitled to a free shuttle to Gongbei coach station between 8.50am and 7.50pm; the bus leaves every 30 minutes. High-speed ferries operate between Jiuzhou Harbour and Shenzhen's port of Shékǒu (Y95, one hour). There are departures every half-hour from 8am to 9.30pm. They leave from Shékǒu at the same frequency between 7.30am and 9.30pm. Local buses 3 (stopovers at Tángjiāwān and Jiuzhou City), 12 (departs from Fènghuángběi), 25 (departs from Nánpíng) and 26 (stopovers at Xiangzhou bus terminal) all go to the harbour.

Bus For transport options to the border gate (Portas do Cerco) in Macau, see p351. In Zhuhai, both Kee Kwan bus station (☎ 0756-818 6705) and CTS bus station have buses to Ocean Spring (Hǎiquánwān; one way/round-trip Y25/45; 1 hour one way) and Héngqín (Y15, 45 minutes), as well as buses to other parts of Guangdong. Gongbei coach station (☎ 0756-888 5218, 0756-888 8554; Youyi Lu) and the new Xinhe bus station (☎ 0756-211 6222) next to it have frequent buses to other points in China. Zhuhai's local buses are clean, efficient and, at Y1.50 to Y3 per trip, very cheap. The bus stop at Vanguard Department Store has a number of routes to most parts of the city. The Zhuhai Sightseeing Bus (☎ 0756-334 5605, 0756-337 8381) has two lines. Line 1 (Y2, every 20 minutes, 6.45am to 7pm) goes to the west and Line 2 (Y3, every 30 minutes, 7am to 7pm) to the east. Both take you to most of the sights, and depart from along Yingbin Dadao and the Zhuhai City Museum in Jida.

Light Rail A light-rail link from Gǒngběi to Guangzhou (Y55) is expected in 2010, shortening the travel time to 40 minutes. A light-rail line from the city centre to the airport is scheduled for 2011.

Taxi In Zhuhai, taxis (☎ 0756-863 2033) have meters; flagfall is Y10 for the first 3km and Y0.60 for each additional 250m. From the border with Macau, a taxi to Jiuzhou Harbour and to the airport costs around Y25 and Y140, respectively.

(p287). The border at Gongbei Port is open from 7.30am to midnight.

EATING & DRINKING

Déyuè Fǎng (☎ 0756-217 3298; Minting Garden, Yeli Island; mains Y38-78, seafood from Y138; ☹ 10am-3pm & 5-10.30pm Mon-Fri, 9am-3pm & 5-10.30pm Sat & Sun) Try the fried eel balls with almond at this faux-floating seafood restaurant moored off Yeli Island in Xiangzhou Harbour.

Jīn Yuè Xuān (☎ 0756-813 3133; 1st-3rd fl, Block B, 265 Rihua Commercial Sq, Qinglu Nanlu, Gǒngběi; dim sum Y6-20, meals per person Y32-100; ☹ 9am-10pm; ⊜ 4) For the best dim sum and classic Cantonese cuisine in Zhuhai, head to this elegant restaurant well before 11am to score a table.

May Flower Restaurant (Wǔyuèhuā Jiǔjiā; ☎ 0756-818 1111; 31 Shuiwan Lu; meals per person Y75-120; ☹ 7.30am-11pm) This place serves up elaborately pre-

pared Cantonese seafood as well as clay-pot dishes.

Rosa Chinensia (Yuèjìxuān; ☎ 0756-818 3382; 2nd fl, 305 Qinglu Nanlu; dim sum Y8-28, dishes from Y48-188; ☹ 8am-5pm) If you cannot get a table in Jīn Yuè Xuān, this is a good, affordable alternative. Apart from its many dim sum choices, it has a creative menu of Cantonese cuisine with a contemporary twist.

Tea Palace (Chá Huángdiàn; ☎ 0756-888 3388; Ground fl, Yindo Hotel, cnr Yingbin Dadao & Yuehai Lu; meals per person from Y85; ☹ 8am-5pm) This is a perfect place to chill out; it serves traditional Chinese brews and snacks.

Night owls will find Zhuhai's nightlife passable, with a stack of pubs on Shuiwan Lu. Cohiba (☎ 0758-889 2444; 203-209 Shuiwan Lu; ☹ 10am-3am; ⊜ 13 or 99) stands out. Drinks start at Y38. Nearby, Lianhua Lu has a cluster of open bar booths straddling the road where the drinks are cheap and the street-walkers rampant.

SLEEPING

With competition popping up left and right, most midrange to top-end hotels offer heavy discounts that can blur budget distinctions. Some hotels add a 10% to 15% levy to the bill.

Grand Bay View Hotel (Zhūhǎi Hǎiwān Dàjiǔdiàn; ☎ 0756-887 7998; fax 0756-887 8998; Shuiwan Lu; s & d Y930-1640, ste from Y1990) It's all in the name – the elegantly appointed rooms have great views over the bay, and the hillside rooms are equally impressive. Take bus 9 from Vanguard Department Store (see the map) to get here.

Yindo Hotel (Yíndū Jiǔdiàn; ☎ 0756-888 3388; www.yindo-ohm.com; cnr Yingbin Dadao & Yuehai Donglu; s & d Y860-1240, ste from Y1890) This is one of the best places to stay within striking distance of the Macau SAR border. Outlets in the hotel include the Tea Palace (opposite).

Yong Tong Hotel (Yǒngtōng Jiǔdiàn; ☎ 0756-888 8887; fax 0756-888 9342; 20 Youyi Lu; s & d Y388-438, ste Y538-558; 📶) This new budget hotel just above Gongbei coach station has reasonably clean rooms and free wi-fi. You might be able to talk staff down to Y220 for a two-bed room.

Zhuhai Holiday Resort (Zhūhǎi Dùjià Cūn; ☎ 0756-333 3838; www.zhuhai-holitel.com; 9 Shihua Donglu; s & d Y572-997, ste from Y1166) This five-star complex was once *the* place to stay in Zhuhai. It still has spacious rooms and villas. For budget travellers, the youth hostel (Zhūhǎi Gúojìxuéshēng Lǚguǎn) is also here, with two eight-bed dorms (Y60).

GUANGZHOU

Known to many in the West as Canton, Guangzhou, the capital of Guangdong province, is a sprawling city with 12 million people wrapped in a perpetual haze of pink smog and flashing neon lights. But that's slowly changing. To prepare for the Asian Games in November 2010, the city began to ameliorate the worst of its rampant urbanisation with a makeover that has resulted in tougher traffic-law enforcement and greener roadsides. Guangzhou remains as chaotic as ever, but you'll find it unique among China's metropolises. It just takes some time to grow on you. Many of its elegant churches and villas have been restored. More importantly, as home to a series of uprisings that changed the Middle Kingdom forever, Guangzhou's revolution-related sights unveil a vital part of China's modern history. And fittingly enough, in Guangzhou, where food is the centrepiece of any conversation, you'll find Cantonese cuisine cooked at its very best.

The biggest event in Guangzhou is the 15-day Canton Trade Fair (Zhōngguó Chūkǒu Shāngpǐn Jiāoyì Huì; ☎ 020-2608 8888; www.cantonfair.org.cn). It has been held twice yearly, usually in April and October, since 1957. Now the fair is held in complexes on Pazhou Island (Pázhōu) south of the river, accessible by metro.

Unlike the SEZs, you cannot get visas on the spot in Guangzhou. Get one in advance in Hong Kong or Macau.

Central Guangzhou is bounded by semicircular Huanshi Lu to the north and the Pearl River (Zhū Jiāng) to the south. If you arrive by train, your first encounter of Guangzhou will be the new commercial area, Tiānhé District. West of here is Yuèxiù District, with a cluster of high-end hotels and important sights, and the main train station. The east–west bound Zhongshan Lu is the boulevard that separates Yuèxiù from the old town, Lìwān District, that stretches from south of the road to the riverbank.

Begin your tour in Yuèxiù District and lose your sense of time in the Mausoleum of the Nanyue King (Nányuèwáng Mù; ☎ 020-8666 4920; 867 Jiefang Beilu; admission Y12, audioguide Y10; ☁ 9am-5.30pm), a superb mausoleum from the 2000-year-old Nanyue kingdom now turned into one of China's best museums. A highlight is the burial suit of Zhao Mo (second king of Nanyue), made of thousands of tiny jade tiles, gold jewellery and trinkets.

Near the mausoleum is Yuexiu Park (Yuèxiù Gōngyuán; 13 Jiefang Beilu; admission Y5; ☁ 6am-9pm). Within, you'll find Guangzhou's Five Rams Statue, a statue of the five immortals attributed to Guangzhou's founding. On top of a hill in the park is the red-walled, five-storey Zhenhai Tower (Zhènhǎi Lóu), which houses the Guangzhou City Museum (Guǎngzhōushì Bówùguǎn; ☎ 020-8355 0627; admission Y10; ☁ 9am-5.30pm; Yuèxiù Gōngyuán metro). The museum boasts an excellent collection of exhibits that trace the history of Guangzhou from the Neolithic period. On the east side of the tower is the Guangzhou Art Gallery (Guǎngzhōu Měishùguǎn), showcasing Cantonese embroidery, carved ivory decorations, and (oddly) displays outlining Guangzhou's trading history with the West.

Chen Clan Ancestral Hall (Chénjiā Cí; ☎ 020-8181 4559; 34 Enlongji Lu; admission Y10; ☁ 8.30am-5.30pm;

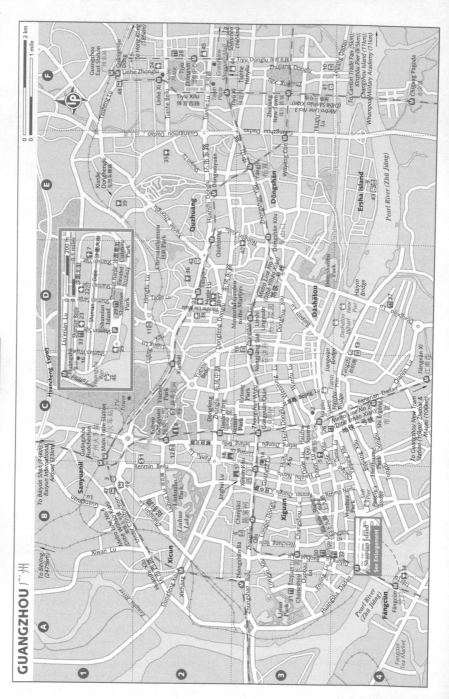

lonelyplanet.com

2 km
1 mile

To Beijing
(2475km)

To Baiyun Shan (4km);
Baiyun International
Airport (33km)

Guangzhou
Huochezhan

Main Train Station

Sanyuanli

Xicun

Xiwan Lu

Dongfeng Xilu

Xichang Lu

Xicun

Renmin Beilu

Liuhua
Lake

Liuhua
Park

Jinghui Lu

Chenjiaci
陈家祠

Xiguan

Changshou

Changshou Xilu

Qingping

Shamian Island

See Enlargement

Fangcun

Fangcun Tea Market

Pearl River (Zha Jiang)

People's
Bridge

Wenhua
Park

Huangsha Dadao

Yuexiu
Gongyuan

Yuexiu Park

Zhenhai
Tower

Dongfeng Xilu

Jiefang Beilu

Renmin
Park

Bei

Huanshi Xilu

Guangzhou
Dong

Guangzhou East Train Station
广州东站

To Hong Kong
(185km)

Linhe Zhonglu

Linhe Xi

Linhe Beilu

Tianhe Lu

Tianhe Nanlu

Tiyu Xilu
体育西路

Tianhe

Citic
Plaza

Tiyu
Donglu

Grand View
Plaza

Tianhe
Nanlu

Zhujiang Donglu

Zhujiang
New Town

Huanshi Donglu

Xianlie
Donglu
先烈东路

Dongshan

Dongfeng Donglu

Quzhuang

Huanshi Dong

Huanshi Zhong

Huaqiao Xincun

Memorial Garden
to the Martyrs

Metro Line No 1
Yuexiu Gongyuan

Metro Line No 1
Nong Jiangsuo

Nongjiang Suo

Lieshi
Lingyuan

Beijing Lu

Bei

Metro Line No 2
(Ditie Erhao Xian)

Shi Ergong

Haizhu
Square

Haizhu Nanlu

Haizhu Dadao

Haizhu
Bridge

Tianzi
Pier

Jiangwan
Bridge

Jiefang Nanlu

Jiefang Zhonglu

Renmin Nanlu

Tianzi
Bridge

Jiangnan Dadao

Jiangxi

Jiangwan Xi

To Guangzhou New Train
Station (5km); Zhuhai &
Macau (106km)

To Canton Trade Fair (5km);
Xinzhou (5km); Whampoa
Military Academy (11km)

Zhujiang
Dadao

Luhu
Park

Guangzhou Dadao

Dashatou

Dashatou
Wharf

Dashatou
New
Pier

Ersha Island

Pearl River (Zha Jiang)

Haiyin
Bridge

Dong-Shuimu
Park

Chigang Pagoda
赤岗塔

Dongxiao Lu

Fangcun
Pearl River (Zha Jiang)

DAY TRIPS & EXCURSIONS GUANGZHOU

264

GUANGZHOU

INFORMATION
Bank of China 中国银行 1 C2
China Travel Service Guangzhou
广州中国旅行社 2 C3
Post Office (Liuhua Post Office)
邮政总局 (流花邮局) 3 B1
Public Security Bureau
公安局 4 C3

SIGHTS & ACTIVITIES
Cathedral of the Sacred Heart
石室教堂 5 C3
Chen Clan Ancestral Hall
陈家祠 6 B3
Church of Our Lady of Lourdes
天主教露德圣母堂 7 D1
Five Rams Statue 五羊石像 8 C2
Guangdong Museum of Art
广东美术馆 9 E4
Guangdong Museum
广东省博物馆新馆 10 F3
Guangzhou Art Gallery
广州美术馆 .... (see 19)
Guangzhou City Museum
广州市博物馆 .... (see 19)
Guangzhou Museum of Art
广州艺术博物院 11 D2
Mausoleum of the Nanyue King
南越王墓 12 C2
Memorial Museum of Generalissimo
Sun Yat-sen's Mansion
孙中山大元帅府纪念馆 13 D4
Mosque Dedicated to the Prophet
怀圣寺 14 C3
Peasant Movement Institute
农民运动讲习所 15 D3

Shamian Traditional Chinese
Medical Center 沙面国医馆 16 C1
Temple of Bright, Filial and Piety
光孝寺 17 B3
Temple of the Six Banyan Trees
六榕寺 18 C2
Zhenhai Tower 镇海楼 19 C2

SLEEPING
7 Days Inn 7天连锁酒店 20 D2
Garden Hotel 花园酒店 21 D2
Guangdong Victory Hotel
(New Annexe)
胜利宾馆 (新楼) 22 D1
Guangdong Victory Hotel
胜利宾馆 23 D1
Guangzhou Riverside International
Youth Hostel
广州江畔国际青年旅舍 .... (see 34)
Westin Guangzhou
广州威斯汀酒店 24 F2
White Swan Hotel
白天鹅宾馆 25 D1

EATING
1920 Restaurant & Bar 26 C3
Bingsheng Restaurant
炳胜海鲜酒家 27 D4
Chuānguó Yǎnyì 川国演义 28 F2
La Seine 赛纳河法国餐厅 ...... (see 43)
Lucy's 露丝酒吧餐厅 29 D1
Nánxin 南信 30 B3
Panxl Restaurant 泮溪酒家 31 A3
Tao Tao Ju Restaurant 陶陶居 ... 32 B4
Thai Zhen Cow & Bridge
泰珍牛桥 33 D1

DRINKING
Baietan Bar Street
白鹅潭酒吧街 34 B4
C Union (Chéngshì Huì)
喜窝 (城市会) 35 E2
Overseas Chinese Village 36 D2
Paddy Field 37 D2
People's Café 38 D2
Ping Pong (Xinghai Conservatory)
乒乓空间(星海音乐学院) 39 E1
Wilber's 40 D3

ENTERTAINMENT
Guangzhou Opera House
广州歌剧院 41 F3
Velvet 42 D2
Xinghai Concert Hall
星海音乐厅 43 E4

SHOPPING
Liùyùn Xiǎoqū 六运小区 44 F2
Tiahe Computer Markets
天河电脑城 45 F2

TRANSPORT
Ferries to Bai'etan Bar Street
去白鹅潭酒吧街的渡船 46 C1
Guangdong Long-Distance Bus
Station 广东省汽车客运站 47 B1
Guangzhou Dongzhan Coach
Station 广州东站客运站 48 F2
Hotel Landmark Canton (Buses to
Hong Kong & Macau)
华厦大酒店
(往香港及澳门直通巴) .... (see 2)
Liuhua Bus Station 流花车站...... 49 B1

Chénjiācí metro) is a spectacular ancestral shrine built in 1894 by the residents of 72 villages in Guangdong, where the Chen lineage is the predominant family. The complex encompasses 19 buildings with exquisite carvings, statues and paintings. Throughout, ornate scrollworks depict stories from Chinese literature and folklore.

The Temple of the Six Banyan Trees (Liùróng Sì; 87-89 Liurong Lu; admission Y15; 8am-5pm; 56) was built in AD 537 to enshrine Buddhist relics brought over from India. Located about 400m west is the Temple of Bright, Filial and Piety (Guǎngxiào Chánsì; 109 Jinghui Lu; admission Y5; 6am-5pm; Xímén Kǒu metro), the oldest temple in Guangzhou, dating back to the 4th century. Many prominent monks came to teach here, including Bodhidarma, the founder of Zen Buddhism.

The Mosque Dedicated to the Prophet (Huáishèng Sì; 020-8333 3593; 56 Guangta Lu; Xímén Kǒu metro) dates from the Qing dynasty, but the original

building on the site is thought to have been established in AD 627 by Abu Waqas, one of the Prophet Mohammed's uncles, making it the first of its kind in China.

Cathedral of the Sacred Heart (Shíshì Jiàotáng; Yide Xilu; Hǎizhū Guǎngchǎng metro) is an impressive twin-spired Roman Catholic cathedral built between 1863 and 1888. It was designed by a French architect in the neo-Gothic style and built entirely of granite.

To the southwest of the city is the leafy oasis of Shamian Island (Shāmiàn Dǎo; Huángshā metro). It was acquired as a foreign concession in 1859 after the two Opium Wars and is now a peaceful respite from the city. Shamian Dajic, the main boulevard, is a gentle stretch of gardens, trees, and old men playing Chinese checkers. The Roman Catholic Church of Our Lady of Lourdes (Tiānzhǔjiào Lùdé Shèngmǔ Táng; Shamian Dajie; 8am-6pm), built by the French in 1892, is on the eastern end of the thoroughfare. Travellers recommend Shamian Traditional Chinese

Medical Centre (Shāmiàn Guóyīguǎn; ☎ 020-8121 8383; 85-87 Shamian Beijie; ⏳ 11am-2am), at the western end of the island, for its massage (Y68 per hour).

For buffs of modern Chinese history, Guangzhou has several significant 'revolutionary sights'. The recently restored Memorial Museum of Generalissimo Sun Yat-sen's Mansion (Sūnzhōngshān Dàyuánshuàifǔ Jìniànguǎn; ☎ 020-8900 2276; www.dyshf.com; 18 Dongsha Jie Fangzhi Lu, Haizhu District; adult/student Y10/5; ⏳ 9am-5pm Tue-Sun), on the other side of the river, was where Sun Yatsen lived when he established governments in Guangzhou in 1917 and 1923.

This beautiful complex consists of two Victorian-style buildings exhibiting the history of Guangzhou during the revolutionary era and Sun's office and living room. A taxi from Shamian Island is around Y20. Or take bus 182 on Zhongshan Wulu and get off after five stops. Change to bus 24 and then get off on Jiangbin Lu.

Much more interesting is Whampoa Military Academy (Huángpǔ Jūnxiào; 黄埔军校; ☎ 020-8820 3564; admission free; ⏳ 9am-5pm Tue-Sun) on Changzhou Island (Chángzhōu Dǎo; 长洲岛). Established in 1924 by Kuomintang, the academy trained a number of military elites for both Kuomintang and the Communist Party, who went on to fight in many subsequent conflicts and civil wars. The present structure houses a museum dedicated to the revolutionary history of modern China. Take metro line 2 to Chìgǎng station, then exit C1. Then board bus 262 on Xingang Zhonglu to Xīnzhōu Pier (新洲码头; Xīnzhōu Mǎtou). Ferries (Y1.50) to the academy depart every 40 minutes past the hour from between 6.40am and 8.40pm.

The communists had a stronghold here once. The Peasant Movement Institute (Nóngmín Yùndòng Jiǎngxísuǒ; ☎ 020-8333 3936; 42 Zhongshan Silu; admission free; ⏳ 9am-4.30pm Tue-Sun; Nóngjiǎng Suǒ metro) was established in 1924 by the Communist Party. Mao Zedong and Zhou Enlai both taught here, before the school closed in 1926. You can see Mao Zedong's recreated personal quarters.

East of the institute, on Zhongshan Sanlu, is the Memorial Garden to the Martyrs (Lièshì Língyuán; admission Y3; ⏳ 8am-7pm), dedicated to those killed on 13 December 1927 under the orders of Chiang Kaishek. The massacre occurred when a small group of workers, led by the Communist Party, were gunned down by Kuomintang forces; over 5000 lives were lost.

Art lovers may find Guangzhou disappointing, but the Guangzhou Museum of Art (Guǎngzhōu Yìshù Bówùguǎn; ☎ 020-8365 9337; 3 Luhu Lu; admission Y20;

TRANSPORT – GUANGZHOU

Distance from Hung Hom station 185km

Direction from Hung Hom station Northwest

Travel time from Hung Hom station 90 minutes by high-speed express train

Distance from Macau's Portas do Cerco to Tiānhé About 106km

Direction from Macau's Portas do Cerco to Tiānhé North

Travel time from Macau's Portas do Cerco to Tiānhé 2½ hours

Bus There are three useful stations clustered around the main train station. These are the Liuhua bus station (Liúhuā Chēzhàn; ☎ 020-8668 4259), the Guangdong long-distance bus station (Guǎngdōng shěng qìchē kèyùnzhàn; ☎ 020-8666 1297; Huanshi Xilu) and another long-distance bus station (Guǎngzhōu qìchē kèyùnzhàn; ☎ 020-8668 4259) over the footbridge leading from the train station. They all have frequent departures to most parts of Guangdong and Guangxi. The new Guangzhou Dongzhan Coach Station (Guǎngzhōu Dōngzhàn Kèyùnzhàn; ☎ 020-8755 5009; Linhe Xilu) beside Guangzhou east train station is also good for destinations within Guangdong (except for Cháozhōu and Shàntóu). For further details, see Lonely Planet's *China* guide. The easiest way to get to Hong Kong is by the deluxe buses that ply the Guangzhou–Shenzhen freeway. The trip takes three hours, tickets cost Y100 (Y250 to Hong Kong International Airport) and buses leave from Garden Hotel and the Hotel Landmark Canton. The latter hotel also has direct buses to Macau (Y70, 2½ hours). Guangzhou has a large network of motor buses and electric trolleybuses (Y2 to Y5). Unfortunately, the network is overstretched and the buses are usually very crowded and slow.

Metro At the time of writing, Guangzhou had four metro lines in full service. Line 1 runs from Guangzhou east train station in the northeast and across the Pearl River in the southwest. It goes by many of the city's major sights along Zhongshan Lu, and is also a convenient way to get to Shamian Island and Fāngcūn. Line 2 runs more or less north–south from Pázhōu station in the south to the main train station in the northeast. It's good for

9am-5pm Tue-Fri, 9.30am-4.30pm Sat & Sun; 🚌 10 or 63) and Guangdong Museum of Art (Guǎngdōng Měishùguǎn; ☎ 020-8735 1468; www.gdmoa.org; 38 Yanyu Lu; admission Y15; 🕙 9am-5pm Tue-Sun; 🚌 12, 18 or 89) are good places to see contemporary Chinese artworks. A new Guangdong Museum south of Tiānhé will be open by press time.

The northern bank of the Pearl River is an interesting area filled with people and dilapidated buildings. The Guangzhou Star Cruises Company (☎ 020-8333 2222) has evening cruises on the Pearl River (Y50 to Y128, 1½ hours) between 6.30pm and 10pm. Boats leave from the Tianzi Pier (Tiānzì Mǎtou; Beijing Lu), just east of Haizhu Bridge (Hǎizhū Qiáo; catch metro line 2 from Hǎizhū Guǎngchǎng metro), and head downriver as far as Ersha Island (Èrshā Dǎo). Guangzhou Passenger Ship Company (☎ 020-8101 3912) also has evening cruises (Y23 to Y38, 1½ hours) from 7.30pm to 9.50pm leaving from Xidi Pier (Xīdī Mǎtou; Yanjiang Xilu).

INFORMATION

You can access the internet at most of the hotels listed in the Sleeping section.

Bank of China (Zhōngguó Yínháng; ☎ 020-8334 0998; 698 Renmin Beilu; 🕙 9am-6pm Mon-Fri, to 4pm Sat & Sun)

China Travel Service (CTS; Zhōngguó Lǚxíngshè; ☎ 020-8333 6888; 8 Qiaoguang Lu; 🕙 8.30am-6pm Mon-Fri, 9am-5pm Sat & Sun) Located next to Hotel Landmark Canton, it offers various tours and books tickets.

Post office (Yóujú; Huanshi Xilu; 🕙 8am-8pm) Conveniently located next to the train station.

Public Security Bureau (PSB; Gōng'ānjú; ☎ 020-8311 5800/8; 155 Jiefang Nanlu; 🕙 8-11.30am & 2.30-5pm) Helps with the needs of all 'aliens'. Between Dade Lu and Daxin Lu.

www.lifeofguangzhou.com Online yellow pages for visitors and expats in Guangzhou.

SHOPPING

Guangzhou is a terrific place for cheap and cheerful shopping, and almost each market or area has its speciality. Prices are reasonably cheap, and you can unearth some real treasures among the overwhelming variety of goods.

Běijīng Lù (Gōng Yuánqián metro) One of Guangzhou's favourite shopping spots, this is a 300m pedestrian street crammed full of shops, big and small, selling virtually everything imaginable. The weekends are crowded here, but that's part of the fun.

many of the sights around Yuexiu Park, and the Canton Trade Fair at Pázhōu. The two lines intersect at Gōngyuán Qián station. Line 3 also goes north–south from Pānyú Guǎngchǎng in the south, alternating at the north end between Guangzhou east station and Tianhe Coach Terminal. Line 4 begins at Wànshèngwéi, east of Pázhōu, and goes south to Jīnzhōu. It links the islands on the Pearl River to Pānyú District. More lines are in the works: Line 5, linking the pier at Hua'ngpǔ to the border with Fóshān via the main train station, should be complete by 2010. Line 2 will extend further to the south, connecting with the new train station in Pānyú, and Line 3 will extend north to the airport. A separate metro line linking Guangzhou to Fóshān is also expected by 2010. Depending on the line, the metro runs from about 6.20am to just before 11pm. Fares are between Y2 and Y8. A better deal for getting around is to buy a transit pass (Yáng chéng tōng; 羊城通), which can be bought from kiosks inside metro stations. Passes start at Y50 and require a Y30 deposit, which can be refunded in Gōngyuán Qián station. The pass can be used for all public transport except taxis.

Taxi Most taxi drivers in Guangzhou are migrant workers (ie they don't know the city well). If possible, flag down the rare yellow or red cabs, which are driven by local drivers. The flagfall is Y7. There is an additional Y1 added on for a fuel surcharge. A trip from the main train station to Shamian Island should cost between Y20 and Y30. A taxi to/from the airport will cost about Y140.

Train Guangzhou's current main train station is chaotic. Note that this train station will be moved to outlying Pānyú in late 2010. An express rail link, expected in 2011, will connect Guangzhou with Hong Kong and Shenzhen in just 40 minutes; and a light rail linking Zhuhai will be complete by the same time. More efficient is the Guangzhou east train station, which serves more far-flung destinations. There is a separate ticketing booth (🕙 7.30am-9pm) for trains to Hung Hom, in Hong Kong's Kowloon (Y167/HK$190, 1¾ hr), and a dozen fast trains a day between 8.19am and 9.32pm. A cheaper and popular way to get from Hong Kong to Guangzhou is to board a bullet train once you go across the border to Shenzhen. They run frequently between Guangzhou east train station and Shenzhen (Y75 to Y109, 52 minutes to 1¼ hours) from 5.35am to 10.50pm.

Fangcun Tea Market (Fāngcūn Cháyè Shìchǎng; Fangcun Dadao; Fāngcūn metro) A sprawling block-after-block market with tea shops and malls selling tea and teapots. Most target wholesale traders but retail is often possible.

Haizhu Square (Hǎizhū Guǎngchǎng; Hǎizhū Guǎngchǎng metro) Haizhu Square has always been a popular spot for discounted clothing and other merchandise.

Xiguan Antique Street (Xīguān Gǔwán Chéng; Lizhiwan Lu) If it's antiques you're after, there's no better place to head than in the Xīguān area, which has shops selling everything from ceramic teapots to Tibetan rugs.

Tianhe computer markets (Tiānhé Diànnǎochéng; east end of Tianhe Lu; Shípáiqiáo or Gāngdǐng metro) A supersized version of Huaqiang Bei St in Shenzhen. Tons and tons of electronics and gadgets are sold in shops and malls straddling a few kilometres of the east end of Tianhe Lu.

Wéndé Lù, east of Beijing Lu, is a less touristy area that hosts an array of Chinese fine-art shops and galleries selling calligraphy, paintings and antique books.

Xià Jiǔlù/Shàng Jiǔlù ('Up Down Nine Street') is another pedestrian shopping street that has a bit more character. It's in one of the oldest parts of the city, where the buildings retain elements of both Western and Chinese architecture. It's a good place to look for discounted clothing.

Huálè Lù, located behind the Garden Hotel, and Liùyùn Xiǎoqū, a leafy residential area clustered with trendy boutiques and cafes off Tianhe Nanyilu, are fashion destinations with the hottest looks at a fraction of the cost. To get to Liùyùn Xiǎoqū, enter from the alley next to the 7-Eleven store on Tianhe Nanyilu.

EATING

Guangzhou is especially famous for its dim sum. In Xīguān District there are many tiny restaurants featuring some locally well-known Xīguān Xiǎochī (snacks and dessert), where you can bump elbows with the locals. A large expat population means that there are also many other types of restaurants that serve international cuisines.

1920 Restaurant & Bar (Kāfēitīng; ☎ 020-8333 6156; 183 Yanjiang Xilu; mains from Y78, beer from Y30; ☯ 11am-2am) Offers casual German fare and is a nice place to enjoy an imported beer on the riverfront. The menu includes sausages, meatballs and even stuffed goose.

Bingsheng Restaurant (Bǐngshàng Hǎixiān Jiǔjiā; ☎ 020-3428 6910; 33 Dongxiao Lu; dishes from Y48; ☯ 11am-midnight) Bingsheng has a handful of branches in Guangzhou, but the mammoth flagship beneath Haiyin Bridge remains the best. Its sea bass sashimi with Shùndé flavour (hǎilú cìshēn; 海鲈刺身) and bean curd with crab roe (dòufuhuā zhēngxiègāo; 豆腐花蒸蟹羔) are outstandingly tasty. There is no English menu, so try to grab a Chinese friend to communicate. Reservations are impossible.

Chuāngguó Yānyì (☎ 020-3887 9878; Nanfang Securities Bldg, 140-148 Tiyu Donglu; dishes from Y35; ☯ 10am-2pm & 5-9pm) If you like your food hot, this restaurant will fry your tastebuds with its authentic Sichuan cuisine, served with plenty of hot peppers. The fiery Sichuan hotpot is the best in Guangzhou.

Nánxìn (☎ 020-8138 9904; 47 Dishipu Lu; dessert Y5-12, dishes Y8-15; ☯ 10am-midnight) A specialist in Xīguān Xiǎochī, this busy restaurant is a very popular pit stop for Cantonese desserts and is located near the Xià Jiǔlù/Shàng Jiǔlù shopping quarter. Try the steamed egg whites with milk (shuāngpínǎi; 双皮奶).

La Seine (Sàinàhé Fǎguó Cāntīng; ☎ 020-8735 2531; 33 Qingbo Lu; mains Y96-258; ☯ 11am-2.30pm & 5-10.30pm) For authentic nouvelle cuisine try this French restaurant on the 1st floor of the Xinghai Concert Hall.

Lucy's (Lùsī Jiǔbā Cāntīng; ☎ 020-8121 5106; 3 Shamian Nanjie; dishes Y28-40; ☯ 11am-2am) Western carnivores seeking comfort food should try this favourite on Shamian Island. Enjoy decent burgers, buffalo wings, and beer for Y16 a pint (happy hour is from 4pm to 6pm).

Panxi Restaurant (Pānxī Jiǔjiā; ☎ 020-8172 1328; 151 Longjin Xilu; dishes from Y36; ☯ 7.30am-midnight) The majestic garden in this restaurant is as impressive as its dim sum and dishes like sautéed clam and fish with vegetables.

Tao Tao Ju Restaurant (Táotáojū Jiǔjiā; ☎ 020-8139 6111; 20 Dishipu Lu; dishes from Y35; ☯ 6.45am-midnight) This restaurant is housed in an academy dating back to the 17th century. It's a bit more expensive than other Canto diners, but the fabulous 200-item dim sum menu makes up for it. Getting a table here is impossible after 11am.

Thai Zhen Cow & Bridge (Tàizhēn Niú Qiáo; ☎ 020-8121 9988; 54 Shamian Beijie; mains Y58-78; ☯ 11am-11pm) Though bizarrely named, the Thai Zhen Cow & Bridge serves up the best Thai food in Guangzhou. The red and green curries are superb.

DRINKING

Guangzhou has a number of international-style bars where, in addition to sinking chilled Tsingtao and imported beers, you can scoff pizza, burgers, rice or noodles.

People's Cafe (☎ 020-8376 6677; 35 Jianshe Wumalu; coffee from Y22, sandwiches from Y30; ⏱ 7.30am-2.30pm) This popular cafe run by two Korean sisters has had a very smart facelift after its relocation. Best are the homemade pastries and tasty sandwiches. At night it turns into a cheerful drinking spot.

C Union (Xīwǒ; ☎ 020-3584 0144; Ground fl, Chéngshì Huì, 115 Shuiyin Lu; ⏱ 7pm-2am) Live music is the principal attraction at this unpretentious boozer. It hosts a good mix of local bands, from R&B to reggae.

Paddy Field (☎ 020-8360 1379; Westin Guangzhou, 6 Linhe Zhonglu; ⏱ 6.30pm-3am) This famous (and pricey) Irish pub is one of the expats' favourite drinking haunts for top-notch beer. It cranks up on Saturdays for the salsa party.

Ping Pong (☎ 020-2829 6306; Starhouse 60, 60 Xianlie Donghenglu; ⏱ 6pm-2am) This speakeasy-like bohemian watering hole hosts live music from time to time and offers a mix of theatre and exhibitions. It's a bit tricky to get here, though. Flag down a yellow taxi and tell the driver to drop you behind Xinghai Conservatory (Xīnghǎi Yīnyuè Xuéyuàn Hòumiàn; 星海音乐学院后面).

Wilber's (☎ 020-3761 1101; 62 Zhusigang Frmalu; ⏱ 5pm-midnight Sun-Thu, to 2am Fri & Sat) Wilber's is a gem that is hidden down an alley in a historical villa. It has something for everyone: the patio is popular with ladies looking for a quiet natter, indoors is a gay-friendly drinking den, and upstairs is a fine-dining restaurant. It serves the best martinis and margaritas in town.

Other watering holes include the bars at Baie-tan Bar Street (Bái'étán Jiǔbā; ⏱ 7pm-2.30am), located along the Pearl River, next to the Guangzhou Riverside International Youth Hostel. The Overseas Chinese Village (Heping Lu) and nearby Huanshi Donglu have a string of bars catering to foreigners and trendy locals.

ENTERTAINMENT

The free monthly entertainment guide *That's PRD* (http://guangzhou.urbanatomy.com), which is available at most top-end hotels and international-style bars and restaurants, is an invaluable source of information for what's going on around town. The 1800-seat Guangzhou Opera House will be the premier performance venue of Guangdong and China's third-largest theatre after its completion in 2010.

Velvet (Sīróngbā; ☎ 020-8732 1139; Ground fl, International Electronic Tower, 403 Huanshi Donglu; beer Y55, cocktails Y50; ⏱ 7.30pm-3am) Guangzhou's most famous club, popular with local and international DJs. With a full range of tunes to suit everybody, it's one of the best bets for a good night out.

Xinghai Concert Hall (Xīnghǎi Yīnyuè Tīng; ☎ 020-8735 2766; 33 Qingbo Lu) Ersha Island houses the city's premier venue for classical music, and this concert hall is home to the Guangzhou Symphony Orchestra.

SLEEPING

Hotels in Guangzhou are expensive. Prices rise even higher during the Canton Trade Fair in spring and autumn. Despite the horror of posted rates, most hotels offer 50% discounts, depending on the season. Top-end places add a 15% service charge to the quoted room rate. Most hotels offer in-room broadband internet access.

7 Days Inn (Qītiān Liánsuǒ Jiǔdiàn; ☎ 020-8364 4488; fax 020-8364 4477; 32 Huale Lu; r Y189-229) This chain hotel is the cheapest (but very decent) option in the five-star enclave in Yuèxiù District.

Westin Guangzhou (Guǎngzhōu Tiānyú Wēisītíng Jiǔdiàn; ☎ 020-2886 6868; www.starwoodhotels.com; 6 Linhe Zhonglu; s & d from Y1260, ste from Y2076) The luxurious Westin is the best place to stay in Tiānhé, if not in Guangzhou. Staff are very welcoming and efficient, rooms are spacious and sparkling, and the location near the east train station is terrific.

Garden Hotel (Huāyuán Jiǔdiàn; ☎ 020-8333 8989; www .thegardenhotel.com.cn; 368 Huanshi Donglu; s & d US$160-260, ste from US$450) This lavish five-star hotel will impress you with its grand lobby, spiralling staircases, garden, elegant rooms and the impeccable service.

Guangzhou Riverside International Youth Hostel (Guǎngzhōu Jiāngpàn Guójì Qīngnián Lǚguǎn; ☎ 020-2239 2500; fax 020-2239 2548; 15 Changdi Lu; dm Y50, s Y108-138, d Y148-198, ste Y268; Fāngcūn metro, exit B) Located in Fāngcūn next to a bar street, this emerging backpacker hub has spotless rooms. Ferries depart frequently from Huángshā pier on Shamian Island to Fāngcūn pier right in front of the hostel.

Guangdong Victory Hotel (Shènglì Bīnguǎn; ☎ 020-8121 6688; www.vhotel.com; 53 & 54 Shamian Beijie) There are two branches of the Victory Hotel on Shamian Island, an older branch at 54 Shamian Beijie (enter from 10 Shamian Sijie) with adequate rooms between Y300 and Y420, and a newer wing at 53 Shamian Beijie, with better-value doubles costing between Y480 and Y800.

White Swan Hotel (Báitiān'é Bīnguǎn; ☎ 020-8188 6968; www.whiteswanhotel.com; 1 Shamian Nanjie; r Y1300-1500, ste from Y3100) With 843 rooms, this hotel is considered the most prestigious of Guangzhou's hotels, complete with a waterfall and fish pond in the lobby, plus an excellent range of rooms and outlets.

TRANSPORT

Amazingly well connected, Hong Kong's international sea, air, road and rail links make getting there and away easy and largely stress free. Equally, its excellent infrastructure makes it a breeze to get around within the Special Administrative Region (SAR), whether by bus, taxi, ferry, tram or train. Flights, tours and rail tickets can be booked online at www.lonelyplanet.com/travel_services.

AIR

Hong Kong's importance as an international hub for China and much of East and Southeast Asia ensures excellent international air connections, and competition keeps the fares relatively low to most places – except China.

A proliferation of budget airlines in recent years has only increased competition and downward pressure on many shorter-haul fares in particular. Specific information on air travel to and from Macau and China can be found on p350 and p285, respectively.

Tickets are normally issued the day after booking, but you can usually pick up really cheap tickets (actually group fares) at the airport from the 'tour leader' just before the flight. Check these tickets carefully as there may be errors (eg the return portion of the ticket being valid for only 60 days from when you paid for a ticket valid for six months).

You can generally get a good idea of what fares are available at the moment by looking in the classified section of the *South China Morning Post*. Otherwise, check out any of the following websites:

Bargain Holidays (www.bargainholidays.com)

ebookers (www.ebookers.com)

Last Minute (www.lastminute.com)

Skyscanner (www.skyscanner.net)

Travelocity (www.travelocity.com)

You'll find travel agencies everywhere in Hong Kong, but the following are among the most reliable and offer the best deals on air tickets:

Concorde Travel (Map p78; ☎ 2526 3391; www. concorde-travel.com; 1st fl, Galuxe Bldg, 8-10 On Lan St, Central; ☺ 9am-5.30pm Mon-Fri, 9am-1pm Sat) This is a long-established and highly dependable agency owned and operated by expats.

THINGS CHANGE...

The information in this chapter is particularly vulnerable to change. Check directly with the airline or a travel agent to make sure you understand how a fare (and ticket you may buy) works and be aware of the security requirements for international travel. Shop carefully. The details given in this chapter should be regarded as pointers and are not a substitute for your own careful, up-to-date research.

Natori Travel (Map p78; ☎ 2810 1681; fax 2810 8190; www.natoritvl.com; Room 2207, Melbourne Plaza, 33 Queen's Rd Central; ☺ 9am-7pm Mon-Fri, 9am-4pm Sat) Readers have long used and recommended this place.

Phoenix Services Agency (Map p106; ☎ 2722 7378; Room 1404, 14th fl, Austin Tower, 22-26 Austin Ave, Tsim Sha Tsui; ☺ 9am-6pm Mon-Fri, 9am-4pm Sat) Phoenix is one of the best places in Hong Kong to buy air tickets, get China visas and seek travel advice. It is also the Hong Kong agent for the student and discount-travel company STA Travel.

Traveller Services (Map p104; ☎ 2375 2222; www. taketraveller.com; 1813 Miramar Tower, 132 Nathan Rd, Tsim Sha Tsui; ☺ 9am-6pm Mon-Fri, 9am-1pm Sat) Very reliable for good-value air tickets.

Airlines

More than 70 international airlines operate between Hong Kong International Airport and some 130 destinations around the world. You can check flight schedules and real-time flight information for both Macau and Hong Kong airports at www.hktimetable.com.

Regional short-haul operators flying to Hong Kong include Singapore-based Jetstar (www.jetstar.com), which flies to Jakarta and Singapore.

Major airlines serving Hong Kong:

Air New Zealand (NZ; Map p67; ☎ 2862 8988; www. airnewzealand.com.hk; Suite 1701, 17th fl, Jardine House, 1 Connaught Pl, Central)

British Airways (BA; Map p67; ☎ 3071 5083; www. britishairways.com; 24th fl, Jardine House, 1 Connaught Pl, Central)

China Eastern (MU; Map p67; ☎ 2861 1898; www.ce-air. com; Unit B, 31st fl, United Centre, 95 Queensway, Admiralty)

TRANSPORT AIR

CLIMATE CHANGE & TRAVEL

Climate change is a serious threat to the ecosystems that humans rely upon, and air travel is the fastest-growing contributor to the problem. Lonely Planet regards travel, overall, as a global benefit, but believes we all have a responsibility to limit our personal impact on global warming.

Flying & Climate Change

Pretty much every form of motor transport generates carbon dioxide (the main cause of human-induced climate change) but planes are far and away the worst offenders, not just because of the sheer distances they allow us to travel, but because they release greenhouse gases high into the atmosphere. The statistics are frightening: two people taking a return flight between Europe and the US will contribute as much to climate change as an average household's gas and electricity consumption over a whole year.

Carbon Offset Schemes

Climatecare.org and other websites use 'carbon calculators' that allow travellers to offset the greenhouse gases they are responsible for with contributions to energy-saving projects and other climate-friendly initiatives in the developing world – including projects in India, Honduras, Kazakhstan and Uganda.

Lonely Planet, together with Rough Guides and other concerned partners in the travel industry, supports the carbon offset scheme run by climatecare.org. Lonely Planet offsets all of its staff and author travel.

For more information check out our website: www.lonelyplanet.com.

TRANSPORT AIR

China Southern Airlines (CZ; Map p67; ☎ 2929 5033; www.cs-air.com; Unit B1, 9th fl, United Centre, 95 Queensway, Admiralty)

Dragonair (KA; Map p104; ☎ 3193 3888; www.dragon air.com/hk; Suite 1808, 18th fl, Tower 6, The Gateway, Harbour City, 9 Canton Rd, Tsim Sha Tsui)

Hong Kong Express (UO; Map p74; ☎ 3923 7399; www. hongkongexpress.com; 28th fl, Bank of East Asia Harbour View Centre, 56 Gloucester Rd, Wan Chai)

Northwest Airlines (NW; ☎ 2810 4288; www.nwa.com/hk)

Qantas Airways (QF; Map p67; ☎ 2822 9000; www. qantas.com.au; 24th fl, Jardine House, 1 Connaught Pl, Central)

Singapore Airlines (SQ; Map p72; ☎ 2520 2233; www. singaporeair.com.hk; 17th fl, United Centre, 95 Queensway, Admiralty)

Virgin Atlantic Airways (VS; Map p67; ☎ 2532 6060; 8th fl, Alexandra House, 16-20 Chater Rd, Central)

Airport

Hong Kong International Airport (Map p140; ☎ 2181 0000; www.hkairport.com), which was the world's largest civil engineering project when it opened in mid-1998, is on Chek Lap Kok, a largely man-made island off the northern coast of Lantau. It is connected to the mainland by several spans. Among them is the 2.2km-long Tsing Ma Bridge, which is one of the world's largest suspension bridges and is capable of supporting both road and rail transport, including

the 34km-long Airport Express high-speed train from Hong Kong Island to Chek Lap Kok via Kowloon.

The futuristic passenger terminal, designed by British architect Sir Norman Foster, consists of eight levels, with check-in on level seven, departures on level six and arrivals on level five. Outlets (including bank branches, moneychangers and five ATMs) total 150, and there are more than 30 cafes, restaurants and bars, and more than 280 check-in counters.

The Hong Kong Tourism Board (HKTB; ☎ 2508 1234; www.discoverhongkong.com) maintains information centres on level five. On the same level you'll also find branches of China Travel Service (CTS; ☎ 2261 2472, 2261 2062; www.ctshk.com; ☯ 8.45am-10pm), which can issue China visas, and counters run by the Hong Kong Hotels Association (HKHA; ☎ 2383 8380, 2769 8822; www.hkha.org; ☯ 6am-midnight); for details see Reservations, p234. Be advised that the HKHA deals with midrange and top-end hotels only and does not handle hostels, guesthouses or other budget accommodation.

If you are booked on a scheduled (but *not* a charter) flight and are taking the Airport Express to the airport, most airlines allow you to check in your bags and receive your boarding pass a day ahead of your flight at the in-town check-in counters at the Hong Kong Island or Kowloon Airport Express stations between 5.30am and 12.30am. You are required, however, to check yourself in at least 90 minutes before your flight. Some airlines, including Cathay Pacific Airways, China Airlines and Thai Airways, allow check-in a full day before your flight. See the airport's website for details.

DEPARTURE TAX

Hong Kong's airport departure tax – $120 for everyone over the age of 12 – is always included in the price of the ticket. Those travelling to Macau by helicopter (see p350) must pay the same amount.

To/From the Airport

The Airport Express line of the Mass Transit Railway (MTR) is the fastest – and most expensive – way to get to and from Hong Kong International Airport. A gaggle of much cheaper buses connects the airport with Lantau, the New Territories, Kowloon and Hong Kong Island.

AIRPORT EXPRESS

Airport Express (AEL; ☎ 2881 8888; www.mtr.com.hk) has trains departing from Hong Kong station in Central every 10 to 12 minutes from 5.50am to 12.48am, calling at Kowloon and Tsing Yi stations before arriving at Airport station. The last train leaves the airport for all three stations at 12.48am. Running at speeds of up to 135km/h, trains make the journey from Central/Kowloon/Tsing Yi in only 24/21/13 minutes.

From Central/Kowloon/Tsing Yi one-way adult fares are $100/90/60, with children three to 11 years paying half-fare. Adult return fares, valid for a month, are $180/160/110. A same-day return is equivalent to a one-way fare.

Airport Express has two shuttle buses on Hong Kong Island (H1 and H2) and five in Kowloon (K1 to K5), with free transfers for passengers between Hong Kong and Kowloon stations and major hotels. The buses run every 12 to 20 minutes between 6.12am and 11.12pm. Schedules and routes are available at Airport Express and MTR stations and on the Airport Express website.

BOAT

High-speed ferries run by Fortune Ferry Co (☎ 2994 8155; www.fortuneferry.com.hk) link Tung Chung New Development ferry pier opposite the airport (and accessible from the terminal on bus S56) with Tuen Mun in the New Territories. Ferries depart from Tuen Mun between 7am and 7pm; the first ferry from Tung Chung pier leaves at 7.30am and the last

at 7.30pm and the journey takes 30 minutes (one way $18).

A fast ferry service called the Skypier (☎ 2307 0880) links Hong Kong airport with five Pearl River Delta destinations: Shekou near Shenzhen, Shenzhen Fuyong, Humen in Dongguan, Zhongshan and Macau. At the time of writing, the Turbojet service linking Hong Kong International Airport with Shenzhen Airport was suspended. For updates call the hotline (☎ 2859 3333).

One of the companies operating from the Skypier is Turbojet Sea Express (☎ 2859 3333; www.turbojetseaexpress.com.hk), sailing six to eight times daily to Macau (adult/child weekdays $134/123, weekends $146/131).

Another operator, Chu Kong Passenger Transportation Company (☎ 2858 3876; www.cksp.com.hk), sails 13 times daily to Shenzhen Shekou (economy class/1st class $220/240) and six times daily to Shenzhen Fuyong (economy class/1st class/ VIP room $295/325/355).

The service enables travellers to board ferries directly without clearing Hong Kong customs and immigration. Book a ticket prior to boarding from the ticketing desks located in the transfer area on Arrivals level five close to the immigration counters. An air-side bus then takes you to the ferry terminal. Ferries to Humen depart five times daily and take an hour ($290/340/390), while ferries to Zhuhai depart three times daily and take 50 minutes ($260/315/345). Once a day, a ferry sails to Zhongshan, taking one hour ($250/280/300).

BUS

Most major areas of Hong Kong Island, Kowloon, the New Territories and Lantau are connected to the airport by buses, of which there is a huge choice. The buses are run by quite a few different companies.

The most useful for travellers are the Citybus 'airbuses' A11 ($40) and A12 ($45), which go to or near the major hotel and guesthouse areas on Hong Kong Island; and the A21 ($33), which serves similar areas in Kowloon. These buses have plenty of room for luggage, and announcements are usually made in English, Cantonese and Mandarin notifying passengers of hotels at each stop. But they are also the most expensive; there are cheaper options, such as taking 'external' bus E11 ($21) to Hong Kong Island, or 'shuttle' bus S1 ($3.50) to Tung Chung and then the MTR to Kowloon or Central. There are also quite a few night buses (designated 'N'); tickets cost between $20.90 and $31.

Bus drivers in Hong Kong do not give change, but it is available at the ground transportation centre at the airport, as are Octopus cards (p284). Normal returns are double the one-way fare. Unless otherwise stated, children aged between three and 11 years and seniors over 65 pay half-fare.

Some of the New Territories buses terminate at MTR stations, from where you can reach destinations in Kowloon and on Hong Kong Island at a lower cost than the more direct buses. You can also reach Shenzhen and other points in southern China directly from the airport (p285).

The following lists give the bus numbers, service providers, routes, one-way fares and frequencies for the airport buses most useful for visitors. For full route details, check out www.citybus.com.hk.

Buses to Hong Kong Island:

A11 (Citybus) Sheung Wan, Central, Admiralty, Wan Chai, Causeway Bay and North Point Ferry pier; $40; every 20 to 25 minutes from 6.10am to midnight.

A12 (Citybus) Tsing Ma, Kowloon Station, Wan Chai, North Point, Quarry Bay, Sai Wan Ho, Shau Kei Wan, Chai Wan and Siu Sai Wan; $45; every 20 to 25 minutes from 6am to 12.10am.

E11 (Citybus) Tung Chung, Tsing Ma, Kowloon Station, Sheung Wan, Central, Admiralty, Wan Chai, Causeway Bay and Tin Hau MTR; $21; every 12 to 20 minutes from 5.20am to midnight.

N11 (Citybus) Same routing as E11; $31; every 30 minutes from 12.50am to 4.50am.

Buses to Kowloon:

A21 (Citybus) Sham Shui Po, Mong Kok, Yau Ma Tei, Jordan, Tsim Sha Tsui MTR, Tsim Sha Tsui East and Hung Hom MTR; $33; every 10 to 20 minutes from 5.30am to midnight.

N21 (Citybus) Tung Chung, Mei Foo Sun Chuen, Lai Chi Kok MTR, Mong Kok and Tsim Sha Tsui Star Ferry pier; $23; every 20 minutes from 12.20am to 4.40am.

Buses to Lantau:

A35 (New Lantao) Tong Fuk village and Mui Wo; $15 ($25 on Sunday and public holidays); every 40 to 60 minutes from 6.25am to 11.30pm.

DB02R (Discovery Bay Transportation Services) Discovery Bay; $32; every 30 minutes, 24 hours.

N35 (New Lantao) Same routing as A35; $21 ($32 on Sunday and public holidays); departures at 1.30am and 4.30am.

S1 (Citybus) Tung Chung MTR; $3.50; every five to 10 minutes from 5.30am to midnight.

S56 (Citybus) Tung Chung New Development pier (ferries to/from Tuen Mun); $3.50; every 30 minutes from 5.55am to 11.25pm.

Buses to the New Territories:

A31 (KMB) Tsing Yi, Kwai Chung, Tsuen Wan MTR; $17.80; every 15 to 20 minutes from 6am to midnight.

N31 (KMB) Same routing as A31; $20.90; every 30 minutes from 12.30am to 5am.

TAXI
In addition to the fares listed, passengers taking a taxi to or from the airport at Chek Lap Kok are required to pay the $30 toll for using the Lantau Link road and bridge network in both directions.

Destination	Fare ($)
Aberdeen (Hong Kong Island)	310
Causeway Bay (Hong Kong Island)	280
Central (Hong Kong Island)	280
Kwun Tong MTR (Kowloon)	260
Mui Wo (Lantau)	125
Sai Kung (New Territories)	350-370
Sha Tin (New Territories)	250
Tsim Sha Tsui Star Ferry (Kowloon)	225
Tsuen Wan (New Territories)	180-190
Tung Chung (Lantau)	35-45

There are limousine service counters in the arrivals hall and at the ground transportation centre, including Parklane Limousine Service (☎ 2261 0303; www.hongkonglimo.com) and Intercontinental Hire Cars (☎ 3193 9333; www.trans-island.com.hk). In a car seating up to four people, expect to pay from $550 to destinations in urban Kowloon and from $700 to Hong Kong Island.

BICYCLE
Cycling in urbanised Kowloon or Hong Kong Island would be suicide, but in the quiet areas of the islands (including southern Hong Kong Island) and the New Territories, a bike can be a lovely way to get around. It's more recreational than a form of transport, though – the hilly terrain will slow you down (unless you're mountain biking). Be advised that bicycle-rental shops and kiosks tend to run out of bikes early on weekends if the weather is good (see p224).

BOAT
Despite Hong Kong's comprehensive road and rail public-transport system, the territory still relies very much on ferries to get

across the harbour and to reach the Outlying Islands.

Hong Kong's cross-harbour ferries are faster and cheaper than buses and the MTR. They're also great fun and afford stunning views. Since the opening of the Lantau Link, ferries are not the only way to reach Lantau, but for the other Outlying Islands they remain the only game in town.

Smoking is prohibited on all ferries inside or out; the fine is a hefty $5000. With the exception of Star Ferry services from Central to Hung Hom and Wan Chai to Hung Hom, the cross-harbour ferries ban the transport of bicycles. You can, however, take bicycles on the ordinary ferries to the Outlying Islands.

Star Ferry

You can't say you've 'done' Hong Kong until you've taken a ride on a Star Ferry (☎ 2367 7065; www.starferry.com.hk), that wonderful fleet of electric-diesel vessels with names like *Morning Star*, *Celestial Star* and *Twinkling Star*. Try to take your first trip on a clear night from Kowloon to Central. It's not half as dramatic in the opposite direction.

The Star Ferry operates on four routes, but the most popular one is the run between Tsim Sha Tsui and Central (pier 7). The coin-operated turnstiles do not give change, but you can get it from the ticket window (unnecessary, of course, if you're carrying an Octopus card, p284).

Star Ferry routes:

Central (Star Ferry pier 7)–Tsim Sha Tsui Adult lower/upper deck $1.80/2.30, child $1.30/1.40, seniors free; nine minutes; every six to 12 minutes from 6.30am to 11.30pm.

Central (Star Ferry pier 8)–Hung Hom Adult/child/senior $6/3/free; 15 minutes; every 15 to 22 minutes from 7.18am to 8pm Monday to Friday, every 20 to 22 minutes from 7am to 7pm Saturday and Sunday.

Wan Chai–Hung Hom Adult/child/senior $6/3/free; 10 minutes; every 15 to 22 minutes from 7.08am to 8.10pm Monday to Friday, every 20 to 22 minutes from 7.08am to 7.10pm Saturday and Sunday.

Wan Chai–Tsim Sha Tsui Adult/child/senior $2.30/1.40/free; eight minutes; every eight to 20 minutes from 7.30am to 11pm Monday to Saturday, every 12 to 20 minutes from 7.40am to 11pm Sunday.

Other Cross-Harbour Ferries

Two other ferry companies operate cross-harbour ferries: New World First Ferry (☎ 2131 8181; www.nwff.com.hk) has ferries from North Point to Hung Hom and Kowloon City; and the Fortune Ferry Co (☎ 2994 8155; www.fortuneferry.com.hk) has a service linking North Point and Kwun Tong.

North Point–Hung Hom Adult $4.50, child and senior $2.30; eight minutes; every 30 minutes from 7.23am to 7.23pm.

North Point–Kowloon City Adult $4.50, child and senior $2.30; 14 minutes; every 30 minutes from 7.17am to 7.17pm.

North Point–Kwun Tong Adult $5, child and senior $2.50; 12 to 15 minutes; every 30 minutes from 7am to 7.30pm.

FERRY ANGRY

The Star Ferry is an institution dear to the hearts of its passengers. Mess with it and you risk getting Hong Kong's ordinarily phlegmatic folk worked up into a fury.

Take 1966, for example, when Communist China was in the grip of the Cultural Revolution. Agitators used the ferry company's fare increase of 5¢ as a pretext for fomenting violent demonstrations. The disturbances continued for almost a year.

More recently, the demolition in 2006 of the rather functional, but nonetheless iconic, 1950s Central ferry pier to make way for new development and land reclamation provoked more fury. In the days running up to the pier's demolition, thousands of emotional Hong Kong residents arrived to post banners and plead for the conservation of a rare piece of Hong Kong's historical architecture. Their efforts were in vain.

Mention of the Star Ferry service between Pedder's Wharf (now reclaimed land) and Tsim Sha Tsui first appeared in an 1888 newspaper article. At that time, boats sailed 'every 40 minutes to one hour during all hours of the day', except on Monday and Friday when they were billeted for coal delivery. Service has continued ever since, with the only major suspension occurring during WWII. The Star Ferry was something of a war hero: during the Japanese invasion, boats were used to evacuate refugees and Allied troops from the Kowloon peninsula before the service was suspended for more than four years.

Until the Cross-Harbour Tunnel opened in 1978 and the first line of the MTR two years later, the Star Ferry was the only way to cross the harbour. At rush hour long queues of commuters would back up as far as the General Post Office on the Hong Kong Island side and Star House in Kowloon.

New Territories Ferries
SAI KUNG PENINSULA & TAP MUN CHAU

Tsui Wah Ferry Service (☎ 2527 2513, 2272 2022; www.traway.com.hk) boats link the east-central New Territories near Chinese University with the Sai Kung Peninsula and Tap Mun Chau. From the pier at Ma Liu Shui, ferries cruise through Tolo Harbour to Tap Mun Chau and back, calling at various villages on the Sai Kung Peninsula both outbound and inbound.

Ferries leave Ma Liu Shui at 8.30am and 3pm daily, arriving at Tap Mun Chau at 10am and 4.20pm respectively, from where they continue on to Ko Lau Wan, Chek Keng and Wong Shek (weekdays/weekend $18/28). They leave for Ma Liu Shui at 11.10am and 5.30pm. On Saturday, Sunday and public holidays an extra ferry leaves Ma Liu Shui at 12.30pm, arriving and departing from Tap Mun Chau at 1.45pm.

An easier – and faster – way to reach Tap Mun Chau, with many more departures, is by *kaido* (p279) from Wong Shek pier, which is the last stop on bus 94 from Sai Kung town. The *kaido*, operated by Tsui Wah Ferry Service, run about once every two hours (there's a total of six sailings, with two callings at Chek Keng) from 8.30am to 6.30pm Monday to Friday ($9.50), and hourly (there are 12 sailings, with two stops at Chek Keng) between 8.30am and 6.35pm on the weekend and on public holidays ($14). Be aware that the last sailing back from Tap Mun Chau is at 6pm from Monday to Friday and 6.05pm at the weekend.

If you've missed the boat or can't be bothered waiting for the next, the private sampans at Wong Shek pier, which seat up to three people in addition to the driver, charge from $70 per trip to or from the island.

TUNG PING CHAU

You can reach Tung Ping Chau from Ma Liu Shui, near the Chinese University, on ferries operated by Tsui Wah Ferry Service (☎ 2527 2513; www.traway.com.hk), but only on the weekend and on public holidays. The Sunday morning ferry could well be booked out, so call ahead to check availability. The Ma Lui Shui-Tung Ping Chau ferry (adult return $90, 1¾ hours) departs at 9am and returns at 5.15pm.

Outlying Islands Ferries

Regular ferry services link the main Outlying Islands to Hong Kong. Fares are cheap and the ferries are comfortable and usually air-conditioned. They have toilets, and some have a basic bar that serves snacks and cold drinks. The ferries can get very crowded on Saturday afternoon and all day Sunday, especially in the warmer months. They depart early and return in the evening.

There are two types of ferries: the large 'ordinary ferries' that, with the exception of those to Lamma, offer ordinary and deluxe classes; and the smaller 'fast ferries' that cut travel time by between 10 and 20 minutes, but cost between 50% and 100% more. 'Weekday' fares apply from Monday to Saturday; prices are higher on Sunday and public holidays. Unless stated otherwise, children aged three to 11 years, seniors over 65 years and people with disabilities pay half-fare on both types of ferries and in both classes. Return is double the single fare.

The main operator serving the Outlying Islands is New World First Ferry (NWFF; ☎ 2131 8181; www.nwff.com.hk). NWFF boats sail to/from Cheung Chau, Peng Chau and Lantau, and connect all three via an interisland service. The Hong Kong & Kowloon Ferry Co (HKKF; ☎ 2815 6063; www.hkkf.com.hk) serves destinations on Lamma only and also has a customer service centre (Map p67; pier 4, Outlying Islands ferry pier; ☼ 9am-6pm).

Ferry timetables are subject to slight seasonal changes. They are prominently displayed at all ferry piers, or you can read them on the ferry companies' websites.

Tickets are available from booths at the ferry piers, but avoid queuing at busy times by using an Octopus card or putting the exact change into the turnstile as you enter.

If your time is limited, you can go on an organised tour (p298) or even hire your own junk (p229).

LAMMA

For travelling to/from Central, both Yung Shue Wan and Sok Kwu Wan are served by HKKF ferries from pier 4 (Map p67) at the Outlying Islands ferry pier in Central. The Aberdeen to Lamma ferry services are run by Tsui Wah Ferry Service (☎ 2272 2022) linking the pier at Aberdeen Promenade with Yung Shue Wan, via Pak Kok Tsuen. There is also a smaller ferry – more like a *kaido*, really – run by Chuen Kee Ferry (☎ 2982 8225, 2375 7883; www.ferry.com.hk) between Aberdeen and Sok Kwu Wan; all but two stop at Mo Tat Wan along the way.

A sampan from Aberdeen to Sok Kwu Wan/Yung Shue Wan will cost from $100 during the day and double that or more in the wee hours, when drunken revellers who have missed the last ferry back from Central are trying to get home. If you should be in the same boat – as it were – don't panic; there's usually at least one other person willing to split the cost.

Central–Yung Shue Wan Adult $14.50 ($20 on Sunday and public holidays); 30 to 35 minutes; departures approximately every half-hour to an hour (with additional sailings around 8am and 6pm) from 6.30am to 12.30am. The last boat to Central from Yung Shue Wan departs at 11.30pm.

Central–Sok Kwu Wan Adult $17.70 ($25 on Sunday and public holidays); 40 minutes; departures every 1½ hours or so from 7.20am to 11.30pm. The last ferry to Central from Sok Kwu Wan is at 10.40pm.

Aberdeen–Yung Shue Wan Adult $17.50, via Pak Kok Tsuen ($7.50); departures 10 times a day from 5.20am to 8.35pm Monday to Saturday (Sunday from 7.20am to 6.20pm). The last ferry for Aberdeen departs Yung Shue Wan at 9.15pm and Pak Kok Tsuen at 9.30pm Monday to Saturday (on Sunday the last departure is at 7pm from Yung Shue Wan and 7.15pm from Pak Kok Tsuen).

Aberdeen–Mo Tat Wan Adult $9.20; 23 minutes; up to 13 departures daily from 6.45am to 10.50pm, every 30 minutes from 7am to 7.30pm (on Sundays and public holidays there are 19 departures from 6.40am to 10.50pm).

CHEUNG CHAU

For travelling to/from Central, ordinary and fast ferries run by New World First Ferry for Cheung Chau depart from pier 5 (Map p67) at the Outlying Islands ferry pier in Central.

As well as the services listed below, an interisland ferry ($11.10 for all sectors) links Cheung Chau with Mui Wo (usually via Chi Ma Wan on Lantau) and Peng Chau seven days a week. The first ferry leaves Cheung Chau at 6am, and the last ferry is at 10.50pm; boats depart approximately every 1¾ hours. From Cheung Chau, it takes 20 minutes to reach Chi Ma Wan, 30 to 45 minutes to Mui Wo and 50 to 75 minutes to Peng Chau.

Central–Cheung Chau (ordinary ferry) Adult ordinary/deluxe class $11.50/18 ($16.80/26.20 on Sunday and public holidays), 55 to 60 minutes; departures approximately every half-hour from 6.10am. The last boat to Central from Yung Shue Wan departs at 11.30pm.

Central–Cheung Chau (fast ferry) Adult $22.50 ($32.20 on Sunday and public holidays); 35 minutes.

LANTAU

The main entry port for vessels serving Lantau proper is Mui Wo, which is known as Silvermine Bay in English. You can, however, also reach Lantau destinations from other ports: Discovery Bay from Central; the Chi Ma Wan Peninsula from Cheung Chau; the Trappist Monastery from Peng Chau; and Tai O and Tung Chung from Tuen Mun in the New Territories.

For travelling between Mui Wo and Central, both ordinary and fast ferries run by New World First Ferry depart for Mui Wo from pier 6 (Map p67) at the Outlying Islands ferry pier in Central. Ferries run by Peng Chau Kaito (☎ 9033 8102, 2983 8617) depart from Mui Wo for Discovery Bay.

To/from Discovery Bay, high-speed ferries run by the Discovery Bay Transportation Service (☎ 2987 7351; www.hkri.com) leave from pier 3 (Map p67) at the Outlying Islands ferry pier in Central.

Central–Mui Wo (ordinary ferry) Adult ordinary/deluxe class $13/21.70 ($19.20/31.70 on Sunday and public holidays); 50 to 55 minutes; departures around every half-hour from 6.10am (from 7am Sunday and public holidays). The last ferry from Mui Wo to Central departs at 11.30pm.

Central–Mui Wo (fast ferry) Adult $25.50 ($36.70 on Sunday and public holidays); 31 minutes; see timetable for departure times.

Central–Discovery Bay Adult $31; 25 to 30 minutes; departures approximately every half-hour from 6.30am to 1am. The last ferry from Mui Wo to Central departs at 11.30pm.

Mui Wo–Discovery Bay Adult $12 ($15 on Sunday and public holidays); 20 minutes; departures from 7.45am to 6.45pm. The last ferry from Mui Wo to Central departs at 11.30pm.

Tuen Mun–Tung Chung Adult $18; 30 minutes; departures 7am, 8am, 4pm and 7pm (7am and 7pm on Sunday and public holidays).

The ordinary interisland ferry ($11.10) links Mui Wo with Cheung Chau (via Chi Ma Wan mostly) and Peng Chau 20 times a day. The first ferry leaves Mui Wo for Cheung Chau at 6am and for Peng Chau at 6.30am; the last ferry to Cheung Chau is at 10.20pm and to Peng Chau at 11.20pm. From Mui Wo it takes 20 minutes to reach Peng Chau, 20 minutes to Chi Ma Wan and 30 to 50 minutes to Cheung Chau.

For travelling to/from Chi Ma Wan, the ordinary interisland ferry ($11.10) linking Cheung Chau and Mui Wo calls at the Chi Ma Wan ferry pier on the northeastern corner of the peninsula six times a day heading for Cheung Chau (with the first at 6.15am and the last at 8.30pm), and five times a day going to Mui Wo (the first at 6.52am and the last at 7.05pm), from where it carries on to Peng Chau.

For details on how to reach the Trappist Monastery on Lantau's northeast coast, see below. The same section has details on reaching Discovery Bay from Peng Chau.

To/from Tai O, there are ferries run by Fortune Ferry Co (☎ 2994 8155; www.fortuneferry.com. hk) linking the Tai O berthing pier on Wing On St and Tuen Mun in the New Territories (via Sha Lo Wan and the Tung Chung New Development pier on Lantau's north coast) daily at 10am, 4pm and 6pm. Ferries sail at 9.30am, 11.30am, 2pm, 4pm and 6pm from Tai O on Sunday. The trip takes between 50 minutes and an hour and costs $25 ($30 on Sunday).

MA WAN

For travelling to/from Central, ferries run by Park Island Transport (☎ 2946 8888; www.pitcl.com. hk), which essentially service the high-end residential community on Ma Wan, depart from pier 2 (Map p67) at the Outlying Islands ferry pier in Central every 15 to 30 minutes from 7am to midnight, then overnight ferry service is replaced by hourly bus service from 12.30am until the normal schedule resumes. The one-way fare is $20 and the trip takes 30 minutes.

To/from Tsuen Wan, boats run by Park Island Transport leave the ferry pier in Tsuen Wan (which is due south of the MTR West Rail's Tsuen Wan West station in the New Territories) for Ma Wan every 17 to 35 minutes between 5.57am and 1.02am (5.40am to 12.45am from Ma Wan to Tsuen Wan). The one-way fare is $8 and the trip takes just 12 minutes.

PENG CHAU

Ordinary and fast ferries run by Hong Kong & Kowloon Ferry Co leave for Peng Chau from pier 6 (Map p67) at the Outlying Islands ferry pier in Central.

Central–Peng Chau (ordinary ferry) Adult $12 ($18.50 on Sunday and public holidays); 38 minutes; departures from 7am to 12.30am (7am and 7pm on Sunday and public holidays). The last ferry from Peng Chau to Central departs at 11.30pm (11.35pm on Sunday).

Central–Peng Chau (fast ferry) Adult $24.80 ($36 on Sunday and public holidays); 25 to 30 minutes.

An ordinary interisland ferry ($11.10) run by NWFF links Peng Chau with Mui Wo and (frequently) Chi Ma Wan on Lantau, as well as Cheung Chau, up to 10 times a day. The first ferry leaves Peng Chau at 5.40am for all three destinations; the last ferry to Mui Wo is at 11.40pm. Boats take 20 to 30 minutes to reach Mui Wo, 35 to 50 minutes to Chi Ma Wan and 45 to 75 minutes to Cheung Chau.

Peng Chau is the main springboard for the Trappist Monastery, with up to 10 sailings a day. Peng Chau Kaito (☎ 9033 8102, 2983 8617) sails sampans to Tai Shui Hang pier from the auxiliary pier southeast of the main Peng Chau ferry pier daily between 7.45am and 5pm. They return from the monastery between 8.10am and 5.10pm. The same company links Peng Chau with Discovery Bay every 30 minutes to 90 minutes, with up to 20 sailings a day between 6.30am and 10pm, from the pier southeast of the main Peng Chau ferry. The last boat from Discovery Bay sails at 10.15pm.

TUNG LUNG CHAU

On the weekend only, ferries run by Lam Kee Kaido (☎ 2560 9929) heading for Joss House Bay on the Clearwater Bay Peninsula from Sai Wan Ho, east of Quarry Bay on Hong Kong Island, stop at Tung Lung Chau en route. On Saturday boats sail from Sai Wan Ho at 9am, 10.30am, 3.30pm and 4.45pm, departing from Tung Lung Island a half-hour later. On Sunday and public holidays there are boats from Sai Wan Ho at 8.30am, 9.45am, 11am, 2.15pm, 3.30pm and 4.45pm; they return from Tung Lung Island at 9am, 10.20am, 1.45pm, 3pm, 4pm and 5.30pm. The trip takes a half-hour, and the round-trip fare is $28/14 for adults/children under 12.

To catch the ferry, take the MTR's Island line to Sai Wan Ho and then use exit A. Follow Tai On St north until you reach the quayside. The ride to Joss House Bay from Tung Lung Island is significantly shorter than the one from Sai Wan Ho. If you're in a hurry coming back, get off there and catch bus 91 to the Choi Hung MTR station.

PO TOI ISLAND

A ferry run by Tsui Wah Ferry Service (☎ 2527 2513, 2272 2022; www.traway.com.hk) leaves Aberdeen for Po Toi on Tuesday and Thursday at 10am, returning from the island at 2pm. On Saturday boats sail from Aberdeen at 10am and 3pm, and return from 2pm and 4pm; there is a boat departing from Po Toi at 12.40pm to Stanley Blake Pier. On Sunday a single boat leaves Aberdeen at 8.15am, but there are also departures at 10am, 11.30am, 3.30pm and 5pm from Blake Pier (off Map p96; near Murray House,

Stanley Plaza) in Stanley. Boats return from Po Toi at 3pm, 4.30pm to Stanley and at 6pm to Aberdeen. A same-day return fare is $40 and the journey takes about 30 to 50 minutes.

Other Boats

Sea and harbour transport is not limited to scheduled ferries in Hong Kong. You may encounter several other types of boats as you travel further afield.

Kaido (small- to medium-sized 'ferries') are able to make short runs on the open sea. Only a few *kaido* routes operate on regular schedules (eg from Peng Chau to the Trappist Monastery and Discovery Bay, and from Aberdeen to Sok Kwu Wan on Lamma); most simply adjust supply to demand. *Kaido* run most frequently on weekends and public holidays.

Sampans are motorised launches that can only accommodate a few (usually four) people. Sampans are generally too small to be considered seaworthy, but they can safely zip you around typhoon shelters like the ones at Aberdeen and Cheung Chau.

Bigger than a sampan but smaller than a *kaido, walla wallas* (water taxis that operate in Victoria Harbour) are a dying breed. Most of the customers are sailors stationed on ships anchored in the harbour. On Hong Kong Island look for them at Queen's pier on the east side of the Star Ferry pier. On the Kowloon side, they can sometimes be found southeast of the Star Ferry pier in Tsim Sha Tsui.

BUS

Hong Kong's extensive bus system offers a bewildering number of routes that will take you just about anywhere in the territory. Since Kowloon and the northern side of Hong Kong Island are so well served by the MTR, most visitors use the buses primarily to explore the southern side of Hong Kong Island and the New Territories.

Although buses pick up and discharge passengers at stops along the way, on Hong Kong Island the most important bus stations are the bus terminus below Exchange Square in Central (Map p67; at the time of writing there were plans to move the terminus to Sheung Wan in 2009) and the one at Admiralty (Map p72). From these stations you can catch buses to Aberdeen, Repulse Bay, Stanley and other destinations on the southern side of Hong Kong Island. In Kowloon the bus terminal at the Star Ferry pier in Tsim Sha Tsui (Map p104) is the most important, with buses to

Hung Hom station and points in eastern and western Kowloon. Almost all New Towns in the New Territories are important transport hubs, though Sha Tin is particularly so, with buses travelling as far afield as Sai Kung, Tung Chung and Tuen Mun.

Fares range from $1.90 to $52, depending on the destination and how many sections you travel. Fares for night buses cost from $6.70 to $32.20. Payment is made into a fare box upon entry, so unless you're carrying an ever-so-convenient Octopus card (p284), have plenty of coins handy, as the driver does not give change.

Hong Kong's buses are usually double-deckers. Many buses have easy-to-read LCD displays of road names and stops in Chinese and sometimes in English, and TV screens to entertain (or annoy) you as you roll along. Buses serving the airport and Hung Hom train station have luggage racks.

Hong Kong's buses are run by half a dozen private operators, carrying more than four million passengers a day. Though it's much of a muchness as to who's driving you from A to B, you may want to check routes online.

Citybus (☎ 2873 0818; www.citybus.com.hk)

Discovery Bay Transportation Services (☎ 2987 7351; www.hkri.com)

Kowloon Motor Bus Co (☎ 2745 4466; www.kmb.com.hk)

Long Win Bus Co (☎ 2261 2791; www.kmb.com.hk)

New Lantao Bus Company (☎ 2984 9848; www.newlantaobus.com)

New World First Bus Services (☎ 2136 8888; www.nwfb.com.hk)

Routes & Schedules

There are no good bus maps and, because buses are run by so many different private operators, there is no longer a comprehensive directory for the whole territory. Your best option is Universal Publications' *Hong Kong Public Transport Atlas* ($50).

The HKTB has useful leaflets on the major bus routes, and the major bus companies detail all of their routes on their websites.

Minibuses

Minibuses are vans with no more than 16 seats. They come in two varieties: red and green. The red minibuses are cream-coloured with a red roof or stripe, and they pick up and discharge passengers wherever they are hailed or asked to stop (but not in restricted zones or at busy bus stops). Maxicabs, commonly known as 'green minibuses', are also cream-coloured but with a green roof or stripe, and they operate on fixed routes. As with red minibuses there are set stops for green minibuses (where circumstance allows and no traffic restrictions apply); you may also flag one down. There are 4350 minibuses running in the territory. About 40% are red and 60% green.

RED MINIBUSES

Red minibuses can be handy for short distances, such as the trip from Central to Wan Chai or Causeway Bay, and you can be assured of a seat – by law, passengers are not allowed to stand. The destination is displayed on the front in large Chinese characters, usually with a smaller English translation below.

Minibus fares range from $2 to $22. The price to the final destination is displayed on a card propped up on the windscreen, but this is often only written in Chinese numbers. Fares are equal to or higher than those on the bus, and drivers often increase their fares on rainy days, at night and during holiday periods. You usually hand the driver the fare when you get off, and change is given. You can use your Octopus card on certain routes.

If you're in Central, the best place to catch minibuses to Wan Chai and other points east is the Central bus terminus below Exchange Square (Map p67). If heading west towards Kennedy Town, walk to Stanley St, near Lan Kwai Fong.

There are a few minibuses that cross the harbour late at night, running between Wan Chai and Mong Kok. In Wan Chai, minibuses can be found on Hennessy and Fleming Rds. In Kowloon you may have to trudge up Nathan Rd as far as Mong Kok before you'll find one. Minibuses to the New Territories can be found at the Jordan and Choi Hung MTR stations in Kowloon.

GREEN MINIBUSES

Green minibuses operate on some 352 routes, more than half of which are in the New Territories, and serve designated stops. Fares range from $2.50 to $24, according to distance. You must put the exact fare in the cash box as you descend (no change is given) or, on some routes, you can use your Octopus card.

Night Buses

Most buses run from about 5.30am or 6am until midnight or 12.30am, but there are a

handful of useful night-bus services in addition to the ones linking the airport with various parts of the territory. Citybus' N121, which operates every 15 minutes between 12.45am and 5am, runs from the Macau ferry bus terminus through Central and Wan Chai on Hong Kong Island and through the Cross-Harbour Tunnel to Chatham Rd North in Tsim Sha Tsui East before continuing on to eastern Kowloon and Ngau Tau Kok ($13.40).

Bus N122, also run by Citybus with the same fare and schedule, runs from North Point ferry bus terminus on Hong Kong Island, through the Cross-Harbour Tunnel to Nathan Rd and on to Mei Foo Sun Chuen in the northwestern part of Kowloon. You can catch these two buses near the tunnel entrances on either side of the harbour.

Other useful night buses that cross the harbour include the N118, which runs from Siu Sai Wan in the northeastern part of Hong Kong Island to Sham Shui Po in northwest Kowloon via North Point and Causeway Bay ($13.40); and the N170, which runs from Wah Fu, a large estate near Aberdeen in the southwest of Hong Kong Island, through Wan Chai and Causeway Bay before crossing over to Kowloon and travelling as far as Sha Tin in the New Territories ($24).

Useful night buses on Lantau run by New Lantao Bus Co include the N1 ($16; $27 on Sunday and public holidays) linking Mui Wo and Tai O at 3.45am and the N35 ($21; $32 on Sunday and public holidays) between Mui Wo (3.15am and 4.20am) and the airport (1.30am and 4.30am).

CAR & MOTORCYCLE

It would be sheer madness for a newcomer to consider driving in Hong Kong. Traffic is heavy, the roads can get hopelessly clogged and the ever-changing network of highways and bridges with its new numbering system is complicated in the extreme. And if driving the car doesn't destroy your holiday sense of spontaneity, parking the damn thing will. If you are determined to see Hong Kong under your own steam, do yourself a favour and rent a car with a driver.

Driving Licence & Permits

Hong Kong allows most foreigners over the age of 18 to drive for up to 12 months with a valid licence from home. It's still a good idea to carry an International Driving

Permit (IDP) as well. This can be obtained from your local automobile association for a reasonable fee.

Anyone driving in the territory for more than a year will need to get a Hong Kong licence, which will be valid for 10 years ($900). Apply to the Licensing Division of the Transport Department (Map p72; ☎ 2804 2600; www.info.gov.hk/td; 3rd fl, United Centre, 95 Queensway, Admiralty; ⏱ 9am-5pm Mon-Fri).

Hire

Car-hire firms accept IDPs or driving licences from your home country. Drivers must usually be at least 25 years of age. Daily rates for small cars start at just under $700, but there are weekend and weekly deals available. For example, Avis (Map p106; ☎ 2890 6988; www.avis.com.hk; Ground fl, Shop 46, Peninsula Centre, 67 Mody Sq, Tsim Sha Tsui East; ⏱ 8am-7pm Mon, 9am-7pm Tue-Fri, 9am-4pm Sat & Sun) will rent you a Toyota Corolla or Honda Civic for the weekend (from noon on Friday to 10.00am Monday) for $1600; the same car for a day/week costs $760/3500. Rates include unlimited kilometres.

If you're looking for a car with a driver, Avis has chauffeur-driven cars for $350 to $1000 per hour, with a minimum of three hours.

Road Rules

Vehicles drive on the left-hand side of the road in Hong Kong, as in the UK, Australia and Macau, but *not* in mainland China. Seat belts must be worn by the driver and all passengers, in both the front and back seats. Police are strict and give out traffic tickets at the drop of a hat.

TAXI

Hong Kong taxis are a bargain compared with those in other world-class cities. With more than 18,000 cruising the streets of the territory, they're easy to flag down.

When a taxi is available, there should be a red 'For Hire' sign illuminated on the meter that's visible through the windscreen. At night the 'Taxi' sign on the roof will be lit up as well. Taxis will not stop at bus stops or in restricted zones where a yellow line is painted next to the kerb.

The law requires that everyone in a vehicle wears a seat belt. Both driver and passenger(s) will be fined if stopped by the police, and most drivers will gently remind you to buckle up before proceeding.

'Urban taxis' – those in Kowloon and on Hong Kong Island – are red with silver roofs. New Territories taxis are green with white tops, and Lantau taxis are blue.

Hong Kong Island and Kowloon taxis tend to avoid each others' turf as the drivers' street knowledge on the other side of the harbour can be pretty shaky. Hong Kong Island and Kowloon taxis maintain separate ranks at places such as Hung Hom train station and the Star Ferry pier, and will sometimes refuse to take you to the 'other side'. In any case, if you're travelling from Hong Kong Island to Kowloon (or vice versa), choose the correct taxi as you'll save on the tunnel toll. New Territories taxis are not permitted to pick up passengers in Kowloon or on Hong Kong Island at all.

The rate for taxis on Hong Kong Island and Kowloon is $18 for the first 2km and $1.50 for every additional 200m; waiting costs $1.50 per minute. In the New Territories it's $14.50 for the first 2km and $1.30 for each additional 200m; waiting costs $1.30 per minute. On Lantau the equivalent charges are $13 and $1.30, and $1.30 per minute for waiting. There is a luggage fee of $4 to $5 per bag, but (depending on the size) not all drivers insist on this payment. It costs an extra $4 to $5 to book a taxi by telephone. Try to carry smaller bills and coins; most drivers are hesitant to make change for anything over $100. You can tip up to 10%, but most Hong Kong people just leave the little brown coins and a dollar or two.

Passengers must pay the toll if a taxi goes through the many Hong Kong harbour or mountain tunnels or uses the Lantau Link to Tung Chung or the airport. Though the Cross-Harbour Tunnel costs only $10, you'll have to pay $20 if, say, you take a Hong Kong taxi from Hong Kong Island to Kowloon. If you manage to find a Kowloon taxi returning 'home', you'll pay only $10. (It works the other way round as well, of course.) If you cross the harbour via the Western Harbour Tunnel, you must pay the $40 toll plus $15 for the return unless you can find a taxi heading for its base. Similarly, if you use the Eastern Harbour Crossing, you may have to pay the $25 toll plus $15.

There's no way of avoiding the whopping great toll of $30 in both directions when a taxi uses the Lantau Link.

There is no double charge for the other roads and tunnels: Aberdeen ($5), Lion Rock ($8), Shing Mun ($5), Tate's Cairn ($14), Tai Lam ($30) and Tseung Kwan O ($3).

You may have some trouble hailing a taxi during rush hour, when it rains or during the driver shift-change period (around 4pm daily). Taxis are also in higher demand after midnight. There are no extra late-night charges and no extra passenger charges, though some taxis are insured to carry four passengers and some five. You can tell by glancing at the licence plate.

Some taxi drivers speak English well; others don't know a word of the language. It's never a bad idea to have your destination written down in Chinese.

Though most Hong Kong taxi drivers are scrupulously honest, if you feel you've been ripped off, take down the taxi or driver's licence number (usually displayed on the sun visor in front) and call the Transport Complaints Unit hotline (☎ 2889 9999), the police report hotline (☎ 2527 7177) or the Transport Department hotline (☎ 2804 2600) to lodge a complaint. Be sure to have all the relevant details: when, where and how much. If you leave something behind in a taxi, ring the Road Co-op Lost & Found hotline (☎ 187 2920); most drivers turn in lost property.

TRAIN

The Mass Transit Railway (MTR; ☎ 2881 8888; www.mtr.com.hk) is the name for Hong Kong's rail system comprising underground, overland and light rail (slower tram-style) services. Universally known as the 'MTR', it is a phenomenon of modern urban public transport. Sleek, pristine and *always* on time, it is also rather soulless.

Though it costs more than bus travel in Hong Kong, the MTR is the quickest way to get to most destinations in the urban areas, and in fact it is sensational value by Western standards.

Should you leave something behind on the MTR, you can contact the lost property office (☎ 2861 0020; ◷ 8am-8pm) at Admiralty MTR station.

Underground Lines

The core of the MTR network comprises seven largely underground lines, including the Airport Express and the new Disneyland Resort line. It serves 53 stations and carries 2.3 million passengers a day. Trains run every two to 12 minutes from around 6am to sometime between 12.30am and 1am.

The Island line (blue) extends along the northern coast of Hong Kong Island, from Sheung Wan in the west to Chai Wan in the east. The Tsuen Wan line (red) runs from Central

station and travels alongside the Island line as far as Admiralty, where it crosses the harbour and runs through central Kowloon, terminating at Tsuen Wan in the New Territories.

The Kwun Tong line (green), which begins at Yau Ma Tei, shares that and two subsequent stations with the Tsuen Wan line; at Prince Edward it branches off and heads for eastern Kowloon, crossing the MTR East Rail line at Kowloon Tong before joining the Tseung Kwan O line at Yau Tong and terminating at Tiu Keng Leng in the southeastern New Territories.

The Tseung Kwan O line (purple) starts at North Point and hits Quarry Bay before crossing the eastern harbour and terminating at Po Lam in the southeastern New Territories. The Tung Chung line (orange) shares the same rail lines as the Airport Express, but stops at two additional stations in Kowloon (Kowloon and Olympic) along the way. It terminates at Tung Chung, a New Town on Lantau that offers cheaper transport options to and from the airport.

The MTR connects with the overland services of the MTR East Rail line at Tsim Sha Tsui and Kowloon Tong stations. It meets the MTR West Rail line at Nam Cheong and Mei Foo.

For short hauls, the MTR is pricey. If you want to cross the harbour from Tsim Sha Tsui to Central, for example, at $8.50/4 per adult/child (or $7.70/3.90 with an Octopus card) the MTR is more than four times the price of the Star Ferry, with none of the views, and the journey is only marginally faster. If your destination is further away – North Point, say, or Kwun Tong – the MTR is considerably faster than a bus or minibus and about the same price. If possible, it's best to avoid the rush hours: 7.30am to 9.30am and 5pm to 7pm weekdays and Saturday morning, when 85% of the 1050 MTR carriages are in use.

Travelling by the MTR is so easy: everything from the ticket-vending machines to the turnstiles is automated. The system uses the stored-value Octopus card (p284), really the only way to go, and single-journey tickets with a magnetic coding strip on the back. When you pass through the turnstile, the card is encoded with the station identification and time. At the other end, the exit turnstile sucks in the ticket, reads where you came from, the time you bought the ticket and how much you paid. If everything is in order, it will let you through. If you have underpaid (by mistake or otherwise), you can make up the difference at an MTR service counter; there are no fines since no one gets out without paying. Once you've passed through the turnstile to begin a journey you have 90 minutes to complete it before the ticket becomes invalid.

Ticket prices range from $4 to $23.50 ($3.60 and $20.70 with an Octopus card); children and seniors pay between $3 and $11.50 ($2.30 and $10.40 with a card), depending on the destination. Ticket machines accept $10 and $20 notes and $10, $5, $2, $1 and 50c coins, and they dispense change. The machines have a touch screen with highlighted destinations. You can also buy tickets from MTR service counters and get change from the Hang Seng Bank branches located in most stations.

Smoking, eating and drinking are not permitted in MTR stations or on the trains, and violators are subject to a fine of $5000. You are not allowed to carry large objects or bicycles aboard trains either, though backpacks and suitcases are fine.

There are no toilets in any of the MTR stations. Like the 90-minute limit on a ticket's validity, the reasoning behind this is to get bodies into stations, bums on seats (or hands on straps) and bodies out onto the street again as quickly as possible. The system works, and very few people complain.

MTR exit signs use an alphanumerical system and there can be as many as a dozen to choose from. We give the correct exit for sights and destinations wherever possible, but you may find yourself studying the exit table from time to time and scratching your head. There are always maps of the local area at each exit.

Overland Lines

The overland network (formerly known as the Kowloon-Canton Railway or KCR) is made up of two lines. The MTR East Rail, which commenced in 1910, is a single-line, 43km-long commuter railway running from the new East Tsim Sha Tsui station in southern Kowloon to Lo Wo on the border with mainland China, plus a new spur to Lok Ma Chau (also on the border). The terminus of the new spur connects to the new Shenzhen Metro system at Huanggang station via a pedestrian bridge across the Shenzhen River.

The tracks are the same as those used by the express trains to cities in Guangdong province, as well as to Shanghai and Beijing, but the trains are different and look more like MTR carriages. Ma On Shan Rail, which branches off from the MTR East Rail at Tai Wai and serves nine stations, opened in December 2004 but is of limited use to travellers.

The 30.5km MTR West Rail line links Nam Cheong station in Sham Shui Po with Tuen Mun via Yuen Long, stopping at nine stations. It is linked to the MTR East Rail at East Tsim Sha Tsui and Austin (from where it's also possible to connect to Kowloon station for the Airport Express and Tung Chung lines).

The overland lines of the MTR make a quick way to get to the New Territories, and the ride offers some nice vistas, particularly between the Chinese University and Tai Po Market stations on the MTR East Rail. You can transfer from the MTR underground lines to the MTR East Rail at Tsim Sha Tsui and Kowloon Tong stations. On the MTR West Rail, there is interchange with the Tung Chung MTR line at Nam Cheong, with the Tsuen Wan line at Mei Foo and with the Light Rail (see below) at Yuen Long, Tin Shui Wai, Siu Hong and Tuen Mun.

Overland trains run every four to 14 minutes, except during rush hour when they depart every three to eight minutes. The first MTR East Rail train leaves East Tsim Sha Tsui at 5.28am and the last departs from Lo Wu at 12.30am. The MTR West Rail runs from 6am to sometime between 12.15am and 12.45am. The trip from Nam Cheong to Tuen Mun on the MTR West Rail takes 32 minutes.

Overland fares are cheap, starting at $3.50, with a 42-minute ride to Sheung Shui from East Tsim Sha Tsui costing just $11.50 (1st class is $23) and the 48-minute trip to Lo Wu $36.50 (1st class $73). Children and seniors pay reduced fares of between $1.50 and $18. Paying with an Octopus card brings down fares considerably.

The MTR runs some 129 feeder buses on 18 routes via its MTR Bus Service (☎ 2881 8888; www.mtr.com.hk), but these are generally of interest only to residents of housing estates within striking distance of the MTR East and West Rails and the Light Rail.

Light Rail Lines

The MTR's Light Rail system began operations in 1988 and has been extended several times since. It is rather like a modern, air-conditioned version of the trams in Hong Kong, but it's much faster, reaching speeds of up to 70km/h. It runs along 36km of track parallel to the road and stops at 68 designated stations, carrying some 320,000 passengers a day.

Until recently, only those travellers visiting the temples of the western New Territories made much use of the Light Rail, as it essentially was just a link between the New Towns of Tuen Mun and Yuen Long. But with the opening of the MTR West Rail, it is an important feeder service for the MTR.

There are 11 Light Rail lines connecting various small suburbs with Tuen Mun to the south and Yuen Long to the northeast, both of which are on the MTR West Rail. The system operates from about 5.30am to between 12.15am and 1am. Trams run every four to 12 minutes, depending on the line and time of day. Fares are $4 to $5.80, depending on the number of zones (from one to five) travelled; children aged three to 11 and seniors over 65 pay from $2 to $2.90. If you don't have an Octopus card, you can buy single-journey tickets from vending machines on the platforms.

The system of fare collection is unique in Hong Kong: there are no gates or turnstiles and customers are trusted to validate their ticket or Octopus card when they board and exit. That trust is enforced by frequent spot checks, however, and the fine is 50 times the maximum adult fare – $290 at present.

TRAM

Hong Kong's venerable old trams, operated by Hongkong Tramways Ltd (☎ 2548 7102; www.hktramways. com), are tall and narrow double-decker streetcars, the only all double-deck wooden-sided tram fleet in the world. They roll (and rock) along the northern coast of Hong Kong Island on 16km of track, carrying some 240,000 passengers daily.

The electric tramline first began operating in 1904 on what was then the shoreline of Hong Kong Island. This helps explain why roads curve and dogleg in ways that don't seem quite right. Try to get a seat at the front window on the upper deck for a first-class view while rattling through the crowded streets: tall passengers will find it uncomfortable standing up as the ceiling is low, but there is more space at the rear of the tram on both decks.

Trams operate from 6am to midnight and arrive every couple of minutes. The six routes from west to east are: Kennedy Town–Western Market, Kennedy Town–Happy Valley, Kennedy Town–Causeway Bay, Sai Ying Pun (Whitty St)–North Point, Sheung Wan (Western Market)–Shau Kei Wan, and Happy Valley–Shau Kei Wan.

Peak Tram

The Peak Tram (☎ 2522 0922, 2849 7654; www.thepeak. com.hk; one way/return adult $22/33, child 3-11yr $8/15, senior

over 65yr $8/15) is not really a tram but a cable-hauled funicular railway that has been scaling the 396m ascent to the highest point on Hong Kong Island since 1888. It is thus the oldest form of public transport in the territory.

While a few residents on the Peak and in the Mid-Levels actually use it as a form of transport – there are four intermediate stops before you reach the top – the Peak Tram is intended to transport visitors and locals to the attractions, shops and restaurants in the Peak Tower and Peak Galleria (p89).

The Peak Tram runs every 10 to 15 minutes from 7am to midnight, making between one and four stops (Kennedy Rd, MacDonnell Rd, May Rd and Barker Rd) along the way in about seven minutes. It's such a steep ride that the floor is angled to help standing passengers stay upright. Running for more than a century, the tram has never had an accident – a comforting thought if you start to have doubts about the strength of that vital cable. It carries 8500 passengers a day.

The Peak Tram lower terminus (Map p67) is behind the St John's Building. The upper tram terminus is in the Peak Tower (off Map p67; 128 Peak Rd). Avoid going on Sunday and public holidays when there are usually long queues. Octopus cards can be used.

Between 10am and 11.55pm, open-deck (or air-conditioned) bus 15C takes passengers between the Star Ferry pier and Pedder St in Central and the lower tram terminus.

TRAVEL & TOURIST PASSES

The Octopus card (☎ 2266 2222; www.octopuscards.com), originally designed for the MTR and seven other forms of transport (thus the eight-armed 'octopus' connection), is valid on most forms of public transport in Hong Kong and will even allow you to make purchases at retail outlets across the territory (such as 7-Eleven convenience stores and Wellcome supermarkets). All you do is touch fare-deducting processors installed at stations and ferry piers, on minibuses, in shops etc with the Octopus card and the fare is deducted, indicating how much credit you have left.

The Octopus card comes in three basic denominations: $150 for adults, $100 for students aged 12 to 25, and $70 for children aged three to 11 and seniors ('elders' here) over 65. All cards include a refundable deposit of $50. If you want to add more money to your card, just go to one of the add-value machines or the ticket offices located at every MTR station.

The maximum amount you can add is $1000, and the card has a maximum negative value of $30, which is recovered the next time you reload (thus the $50 deposit). Octopus fares are between 5% and 10% cheaper than ordinary fares on the MTR, Light Rail systems and certain green minibuses.

You can purchase Octopus cards at ticket offices or customer service centres in MTR and LRT stations, New World First Bus customer service centres as well as Outlying Islands ferry piers on both sides.

The much-advertised Airport Express Tourist Octopus card is not really worth the microchip embedded into it. The card costs $220 (including $50 deposit) and allows one trip on the Airport Express and three days of unlimited travel on the MTR (except Airport Express, Light Rail, MTR Bus, East Rail Line First Class, Lo Wu and Lok Ma Chau stations). Value can be added to the ticket for travel on other major means of transport. For $300 you get two trips on the Airport Express and the same benefits. At the end of your trip you can claim your deposit back (plus any part of the 'remaining value' added still on the card). For shorter stays there's the Tourist MTR 1-Day Pass ($55), valid on the MTR for 24 hours.

TRANSPORT TO/FROM MAINLAND CHINA

Air

Competition (of sorts) is driving prices down slightly, but expect to pay a premium to fly between Hong Kong and the mainland as the government regulates the prices. Depending on the season, seats can be difficult to find due to the enormous volume of business travellers and Chinese tourists, so book well in advance. Destinations and sample adult return fares valid for a year from Hong Kong are Beijing ($4290), Chengdu ($4650), Kunming ($2840) and Shanghai ($3060). One-way fares are a bit more than half the return price.

You should be able to do better than that, however, on both scheduled and charter flights, especially in summer. Also note that you can save at least 30% on the above fares by heading for Shenzhen by bus or ferry and boarding the aircraft at Huangtian airport there.

Land

The only way in and out of Hong Kong by land is to cross the 30km border with mainland China. The options for surface travel to and from China have increased dramatically since the handover, with buses and trains departing throughout the day to destinations as close as Shenzhen and as far as Beijing. Travellers should be aware that, although the Hong Kong Special Administrative Region (SAR) is an integral part of China, visas are still required to cross the border to the mainland (see p287).

The border crossing at Lo Wu opens at 6.30am and closes at midnight. The crossing at Lok Ma Chau is open around-the-clock. The terminus of the new MTR spur line connects to the new Shenzhen Metro system at Huanggang station via a pedestrian bridge across the Shenzhen River.

BUS

You can reach virtually any major destination in neighbouring Guangdong province by bus from Hong Kong. Mainland destinations and one-way fares from Hong Kong include Dongguan ($100), Foshan ($100), Guangzhou ($60 to $90), Huizhou ($100), Kaiping ($120 to $150), Shantou ($120 to $200), Shenzhen's Huangtian airport ($90 to $160), Xiamen ($310 to $348) and Zhongshan ($100).

Buses are run by a multitude of transport companies and depart from locations around the territory; the list that follows is a sample. Schedules vary enormously according to carrier and place, but buses leave throughout the day and departures are frequent.

CTS Express Coach (☎ 2764 9803, 2365 0118; http://cts bus.hkcts.com) Buses depart from locations throughout Hong Kong, including the CTS Wan Chai branch (Map p74; ☎ 2832 3888; Southern Centre, 130 Hennessy Rd) on Hong Kong Island and from just south of the CTS Mong Kok branch (Map p111; ☎ 2789 5888; 62-74 Sai Yee St) in Kowloon.

Eternal East Cross Border Coach (Map p104; ☎ 3412 6677, 3760 0888; 13th fl, Kai Seng Commercial Centre, 4-6 Hankow Rd, Tsim Sha Tsui; ⏰ 7am-8pm) Buses leave from just outside the Hang Seng Bank next door.

Motor Transport Company of Guangdong and Hong Kong (GDHK; ☎ 2317 7900; www.gdhkmtc.com) Buses bound for destinations throughout Guangdong leave from the Cross-Border Coach Terminus (Map p104; Ground fl, Hong Kong Scout Centre, 8 Austin Rd, Tsim Sha Tsui; ⏰ 6.30am-7pm), which is entered from Scout Path.

Trans-Island Chinalink (Map p111; ☎ 2336 1111; www.trans island.com.hk) Buses depart from Prince Edward MTR next to the Metropark Hotel. Cars and vans leave from Portland St opposite the Hotel Concourse Hong Kong.

In addition, at Chek Lap Kok buses run by China Travel Tours Transportation Services HK Ltd (☎ 2261 2472/2147; http://ctsbus.hkcts.com), Eternal East Cross Border Coach (☎ 2261 0176) and Trans-Island (☎ 2261 0296; www.trans-island.com.hk) link Hong Kong International Airport with many points in southern China, including Dongguan ($200 to $230), Foshan ($250), Guangzhou ($250) and Shenzhen ($150 to $180).

TRAIN

You can book cross-border train tickets online via the website of MTR (☎ 2947 7888; www.it3.mtr.com.hk). You have to sign up, but it's a useful service. Reaching Shenzhen is a breeze. Just board the MTR East Rail at East Tsim Sha Tsui station (1st/2nd class $73/36.50) or at any other MTR East Rail station along the way (such as Hung Hom, Kowloon Tong or Sha Tin) and ride it to Lo Wu; the mainland is a couple of hundred metres away. The first train to Lo Wu leaves East Tsim Sha Tsui station at 5.28am, the last at 11.05pm, and the trip takes about 48 minutes. For more details on MTR services, see p282.

The most comfortable way to reach Guangzhou by land is via the Kowloon-Guangzhou express train (usually via Dongguan), which covers the 182km route in approximately 1¾ hours. High-speed intercity trains leave Hung Hom station for Guangzhou East train station 12 times a day between 7.25am and 7.24pm, returning from that station the same number of times from 8.19am to 9.32pm. One-way tickets cost $230/190 in 1st/2nd class for adults and $115/95 for children aged five to nine. Adults/children are allowed one piece of luggage, weighing up to 20/10kg. Additional bags cost $3.90 per 5kg.

There are also direct rail links between Hung Hom and both Shanghai and Beijing. Trains to Beijing West train station (hard/soft sleeper from $574/934, 24 hours) depart on alternate days at 3.15pm and travel via Guangzhou East, Changsha and Wuhan, arriving at 2.51pm the following day. Trains to Shanghai (hard/soft sleeper from $508/825, 20 hours) also depart on alternate days at 3.15pm and pass through Guangzhou East and Hangzhou East stations, arriving at 11.10am the following day.

There is one daily departure to Zhaoqing (adult/child $235/117.50) via Dongguan, Guangzhou East and Foshan at 10.42am, arriving in Zhaoqing at 2.29pm. The train departs Zhaoqing at 3.10pm, reaching Hung Hom at 6.49pm.

Immigration formalities at Hung Hom are completed before boarding; you won't get on the train without a visa for China. Passengers are required to arrive at the station 45 minutes before departure. To reach Hung Hom station from Tsim Sha Tsui by public transport, take the MTR East Rail for one stop, bus 5C from the Star Ferry pier, or the green minibus 6 or 8 from Hankow Rd.

One-way and return tickets can be booked 60 days in advance through CTS, including at CTS Hung Hom station branch (Map p106; ☎ 2334 9333; ☾ 6.30am-8pm) and at MTR East Rail stations in Hung Hom, Mong Kok, Kowloon Tong and Sha Tin. Tickets booked with a credit card via the Tele-Ticketing Hotline (☎ 2947 7888) must be collected at least one hour before departure.

A cheaper but much less convenient option is to take the MTR East Rail train to Lo Wu (or to the Shenzhen Metro via Lok Ma Chau), cross through immigration into Shenzhen and catch a local train from there to Guangzhou. There are frequent high-speed trains (Y75 to Y101; 60 to 90 minutes) that run throughout the day.

Sea

Regularly scheduled ferries link the China ferry terminal (Map p104; 33 Canton Rd, Tsim Sha Tsui) in Kowloon and/or the Macau ferry pier (Map p80; 200 Connaught Rd, Sheung Wan) on Hong Kong Island with a string of towns and cities on the Pearl River Delta – but not central Guangzhou or Shenzhen. For sea transport to/from Macau, see p351.

CMSE Passenger Transport (☎ 2858 0909) runs some seven Jetcats (day/night sailing $110/145, 50 minutes) that link Hong Kong with Shekou (a port about 20km west of Shenzhen town and easily accessible by bus or taxi to the town centre) from 7.45am to 9pm daily. One of these (1.30pm) leaves from the China ferry terminal in Kowloon, while the rest (7.45am to 8.30pm) go from the Macau ferry pier on Hong Kong Island. Return sailings from Shekou are from 7.45am to 9pm.

Zhuhai can also be reached from Hong Kong on seven ferries a day ($178, 70 minutes) from the China ferry terminal in Tsim Sha Tsui (from 7.30am to 5.45pm) and on the same number of ferries from the Macau ferry pier in Sheung Wan (8.40am to 9.30pm) on ferries operated by the Chu Kong Passenger Transportation Company (☎ 2858 3876; www.cksp.com.hk). The 14 return sailings from Zhuhai ($175) run between 8am and 9.30pm.

Chu Kong also has ferries from the China ferry terminal to a number of other ports in southern Guangdong province, including Shunde (G class/F class/VIP class $195/220/240, 115 minutes, six sailings between 7.30am and 6pm) and Zhongshan ($195/225/245, 90 minutes, eight or nine sailings from 7.30am to 8pm).

Ferries run by Expert Fortune (☎ 2375 0688, 2517 3494) link the China ferry terminal with Nansha (standard/1st class/VIP class $160/210/260, five sailings daily between 8am and 3.50pm), with return sailings ($140/195/245) between 9.30am and 5.30pm. One daily ferry departs from the Macau ferry pier at 11.30am.

DEPARTURE TAX

The $15 to $26 departure tax levied when leaving Hong Kong by sea varies according to the destination and is usually included in the ticket price.

Visas

Everyone except Hong Kong Chinese residents must have a visa to enter mainland China. At the time of writing, holders of Canadian, Australian, New Zealand and most EU passports – but *not* USA ones – can get a single visa on the spot for $150 at the Lo Wu border crossing, the last stop on the MTR's East Rail. This particular visa limits you to a maximum stay of seven days within the confines of the Shenzhen Special Economic Zone (SEZ).

The queues for these visas can be interminable, so it is highly recommended that you shell out the extra money and get a proper China visa before setting off, even if you're headed just for Shenzhen.

If you would like to arrange your visa yourself, you can go to the Visa Office of the People's Republic of China (Map p74; ☎ 3413 2424; www. fmcoprc.gov.hk; 7th fl, Lower Block, China Resources Centre, 26 Harbour Rd, Wan Chai; ⏶ 9am-noon & 2-5pm Mon-Fri). Double-entry visas processed in one/two/three days for 'reciprocal countries', such as the UK, cost $920/820/670. Visas for double/multiple entry valid for six months cost $220/400. If you require express/urgent service, the double-entry visa costs $370/470 and the multiple entry valid for six months is $550/650. You must supply two photos, which can be taken at photo booths in the MTR (though not all stations have photo booths) or at the visa office for $40. Any photo-processing shop can also oblige.

Visas can be arranged by China Travel Services (CTS, ☎ 2851 1700, 2315 7188; www.ctshk.com), the mainland-affiliated agency; a good many hostels and guesthouses; and most Hong Kong travel agents, including those listed on p271.

CHINA TRAVEL SERVICES OFFICES

There are almost three dozen CTS offices in Hong Kong, including those listed below.

Offices on Hong Kong Island:

Causeway Bay (Map p85; ☎ 2808 1131; Room 606, 6th fl, Hang Lung Centre, 2-20 Paterson St; ⏶ 9am-8.30pm Mon-Fri, 10am-7pm Sat)

Central (Map p67; ☎ 2522 0450; Ground fl, China Travel Bldg, 77 Queen's Rd Central; ⏶ 9am-7.30pm Mon-Fri, 9am-5pm Sat)

Wan Chai (Map p74; ☎ 2832 3888; Ground fl, Southern Centre, 130 Hennessy Rd; ⏶ 9am-7pm Mon-Fri, 9.30am-6pm Sat)

Offices in Kowloon:

Mong Kok (Map p111; ☎ 2789 5888; 1st & 2nd fl, Tak Po Bldg, 62-74 Sai Yee St; ⏶ 9am-7pm Mon-Fri, 9am-5pm Sat, 9.30am-12.30pm & 2-5pm Sun)

ADDRESSES

Addresses in Hong Kong are fairly straightforward. In general, the apartment (or office) number and floor precede the name of the building, street address and district. There are no postal codes. In Hong Kong (and in this book), the 1st floor is the floor above the ground floor. Virtually every business and residential building here has a guard or concierge and a table displaying the names of the occupants.

About the only problem you may have in finding your way around Hong Kong is determining the appropriate exit for your destination from the Mass Transit Railway (MTR; p282).

BUSINESS

Hong Kong is not all about business, but it remains an important aspect of its ethos and character. Some useful business contacts:

American Chamber of Commerce (Map p67; ☎ 2530 6900; www.amcham.org.hk; Room 1904, 19th fl, Bank of America Tower, 12 Harcourt Rd, Central) The most active overseas chamber of commerce in Hong Kong.

Chinese General Chamber of Commerce (Map p67; ☎ 2525 6385; www.cgcc.org.hk; 4th fl, Chinese General Chamber of Commerce Bldg, 24-25 Connaught Rd, Central) Authorised to issue Certificates of Hong Kong origin for trade.

Chinese Manufacturers' Association of Hong Kong (Map p67; ☎ 2545 6166; www.cma.org.hk; 3rd fl, CMA Bldg, 64-66 Connaught Rd, Central) Operates testing laboratories for product certification and can also issue Certificates of Hong Kong origin.

Hong Kong General Chamber of Commerce (Map p72; ☎ 2529 9229; www.chamber.org.hk; 22nd fl, United Centre, 95 Queensway, Admiralty) Services for foreign executives and firms, such as translation, serviced offices, secretarial help and printing.

Hong Kong Labour Department (Map p67; ☎ 2717 1771; www.labour.gov.hk; 16th fl, Harbour Bldg, 38 Pier Rd, Central) Contact this department for labour-relations problems and queries.

Hong Kong Trade & Industry Department (Map p111; ☎ 2392 2922; www.tid.gov.hk; Room 908, Trade & Industry Department Tower, 700 Nathan Rd, Mong Kok) This department is a key source for trade information, statistics, government regulations and product certification. Enter from Fife St.

Hong Kong Trade Development Council (HKTDC; Map p74; ☎ 1830 668; www.tdctrade.com; 38th fl, Office Tower, Convention Plaza, 1 Harbour Rd, Wan Chai) Cosponsors and participates in trade fairs, and publishes a wealth of material on Hong Kong markets.

TDC Business InfoCentre (Map p74; ☎ 2248 4000; http://infocentre.tdctrade.com; New Wing, Hong Kong Convention & Exhibition Centre, 1 Expo Dr, Wan Chai; ☼ 10am-7pm Mon-Fri, 10am-5pm Sat) Run by the HKTDC, the centre is well stocked with relevant books, periodicals and reference materials.

BUSINESS HOURS

Office hours in Hong Kong are from 9am to either 5.30pm or 6pm on weekdays and often (but increasingly less so) from 9am to noon or 1pm on Saturday. The weekday lunch hour is usually from 1pm to 2pm. Banks are open from 9am to 4.30pm or 5.30pm weekdays and 9am to 12.30pm on Saturday.

Shops that cater to tourists keep longer hours, but almost nothing opens before 9am. As a rule of thumb, assume a place will be open from 10am to 7pm daily. For specifics, see p154.

Museums are generally open from 10am to between 5pm and 9pm and are closed one day a week (usually Monday, Tuesday or Thursday).

Restaurants in Hong Kong are generally open from noon to 3pm; dinner is usually from 6pm to 11pm.

CHILDREN

Hong Kong is a great travel destination for kids (see the boxed texts, p92 and p168), though the crowds, traffic and pollution might be off-putting to some parents. Food and sanitation is of a high standard, and the territory is jam-packed with things to entertain the young 'uns. As a starting point, get a copy of the *Hong Kong Family Fun Guide* from the Hong Kong Tourism Board (HKTB) or download it from the HKTB website (www.discoverhongkong.com /eng/travelneeds/family/index.jhtml).

Lonely Planet's *Travel with Children*, written by Brigitte Barta et al, includes all sorts of useful advice for those travelling with their little ones.

Most public transport and museums offer half-price fares and admission fees to children under the age of 12, but combination family tickets are rare. Hotels can recommend baby-sitters if you've got daytime appointments or want a night out sans child. Otherwise, call Rent-A-Mum (☎ 2523 4868; www.rent-a-mum.com; per hr $110-140); transport charges may be added, depending on the location.

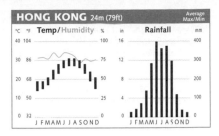

CLIMATE

Both Hong Kong and Macau have a subtropical climate characterised by hot and humid summers and cool, relatively dry winters.

October, November and most of December are the best months to visit. Temperatures are moderate, the skies are clear and the sun shines. January and February are cloudy and cold but dry. It's warmer from March to May, but the humidity is high, and the fog and drizzle can make getting around difficult. The sweltering heat and humidity from June to August can make sightseeing a sweaty proposition, and it is also the rainy season. September is a grand month if you like drama: the threat of a typhoon seems to loom every other day.

The very informative Hong Kong Observatory (Map p106; ☎ 2926 8200; www.hko.gov.hk; 134A Nathan Rd, Tsim Sha Tsui) issues weather reports on ☎ 1878 200 and on its website. The hotline for cyclone warnings is ☎ 2835 1473.

COURSES

The Community Advice Bureau (Map p67; ☎ 2815 5444; www.cab.org.hk; Room 16C, Right Emperor Commercial Bldg, 122-126 Wellington St, Central; 🕒 9.30am-4.30pm Mon-Fri) is a fabulous source of information on courses of all kinds in Hong Kong. The YMCA

TYPHOON!

Typhoons – massive tropical cyclones often tens of kilometres high and hundreds of kilometres wide – sometimes hit Hong Kong. When they hit, the place all but shuts down. Flights are grounded, ferries are cancelled, shops and offices close (although happily a handful of enterprising bars have been known to stay open).

Cyclones can last for as long as a few weeks, but not all will mature into typhoons. Feeding off moisture, tropical cyclones can only survive over warm oceans – once typhoons hit land, they quickly die out. The 'eye' of the cyclone is generally tens of kilometres wide and is basically a column of descending air, which is much calmer than the surrounding vortex.

Only about half the cyclones in the South China Sea ever reach typhoon ferocity. The gradation of tropical cyclones ascends as follows: tropical depression (with winds up to 62km/h); tropical storm (up to 87km/h); severe tropical storm (up to 117km/h); and typhoon (118km/h or more).

About a dozen typhoons develop in the South China Sea each year, but Hong Kong is a small target, so the chances of a direct hit – within 100km – are reasonably slim.

There is a numbering system to warn of typhoons broadcast on all media. No 1 (its visual symbol being the letter 't') means that a tropical cyclone is within 800km of Hong Kong. No 3 (an upside-down 't') – there is no No 2 – warns that winds of up to 62km are blowing, or expected to blow, generally in Hong Kong near sea level, and there is a risk of Hong Kong being hit and that people should take precautions such as securing flower pots on balconies and terraces. The system then jumps to No 8 (a triangle), which means that there are sustained winds of between 63km/h and 117km/h. People are instructed to stay indoors and to fix adhesive tape to exposed windows to reduce the damage caused by broken glass, while businesses shut down and ferries stop running. No 9 (a double triangle) warns that gale- or storm-force winds are increasing, and No 10 (a cross) is the most severe, with winds reaching upwards of 118km/h and gusts exceeding 220km/h.

Only 13 typhoons have reached No 10 since the end of WWII. The most famous ones in recent years were Typhoon Wanda (1962), the most ferocious of all, delivering hourly mean wind speeds of 133km/h and peak gusts of 259km/h; Typhoon Ellen (1983), which killed 22 people and injured over 300; and Typhoon York (1999), which had the No 10 signal up the longest of any typhoon – 11 hours.

Rain, which can fall so heavily in Hong Kong that it sounds like a drum roll as it hits the pavement, can cause deadly landslips. Hong Kong also has a 'heavy rain warning system' that is colour-coded – in ascending degrees of severity – amber, red and black.

(☎ 2771 9111; www.ymca.org.hk) and the YWCA (☎ 3476 1300; www.ywca.org.hk) both offer a range of cultural classes and three-month courses, from basic Cantonese and mah-jong to yoga and t'ai chi.

For visual arts, check with the Hong Kong Museum of Art (☎ 2721 0116), the Hong Kong Visual Arts Centre (☎ 2521 3008) or the Hong Kong Arts Centre (☎ 2582 0200). The Fringe Club (☎ 2521 7251; www .hkfringe.com.hk; 2 Lower Albert Rd, Central) offers any number of courses and workshops.

The Cultural Kaleidoscope Meet the People programme organised by the HKTB (☎ 2508 1234; www.discoverhongkong.com) will whet your appetite for everything from Chinese tea and opera to t'ai chi and jade. It is unique in that it allows you to visit galleries, antique shops, jewellers to grade pearls and jade, teahouses, t'ai chi classes and even a feng shui master's studio. It's an excellent way to learn first-hand about Hong Kong Chinese culture. For details on times and locations, see the HKTB website.

Cooking

There's a huge choice of cookery courses in the city. You'll find a list of bilingual courses in the Eating chapter, p175.

Language

The New-Asia-Yale-in-China Chinese Language Centre at the Chinese University of Hong Kong (Map pp58–9; ☎ 2609 6727; www.cuhk.edu.hk/clc; Fong Shu Chuen Bldg, Ma Liu Shui, New Territories) offers regular courses in Cantonese and Mandarin. There are four terms a year: four- and 11-week summer sessions and two regular 15-week terms in spring and autumn. The cost of the four-week summer term is $8850, the 11-week session $21,050, and the 15-week semesters are $26,200. In addition there are shorter two-week introductory courses such as Elementary Cantonese for $5400.

Another good place for learning Cantonese, Mandarin and other Asian languages is the School of Professional and Continuing Education at Hong Kong University (Map pp62–3; ☎ 2559 9771; www.hkuspace.hku.hk; Room 304, 3rd fl, TT Tsui Bldg, Pok Fu Lam Rd, Pok Fu Lam).

A number of private language schools cater to individuals or companies. These schools offer more flexibility and even dispatch teachers to companies to teach the whole staff. For one-on-one instruction, expect to pay from $200 per hour. The following are language schools to consider.

Essential Chinese Language Centre (Map p67; ☎ 2544 6979; http://eclc.com.hk; 8th fl, Man On Commercial Bldg, 12-13 Jubilee St, Central)

Hong Kong Institute of Languages (Map p78; ☎ 2877 6160; www.hklanguages.com; 6th fl, Wellington Plaza, 56-58 Wellington St, Central)

These centres also offer language courses:

Alliance Française (Map p74; ☎ 2527 7825; www .alliancefrancaise.com.hk; 1st & 2nd fl, 123 Hennessy Rd, Wan Chai) This place has a library and offers a wide range of cultural activities.

Goethe-Institut (Map p74; ☎ 2802 0088; www.goethe .de/hongkong; 14th fl, Hong Kong Arts Centre, 2 Harbour Rd, Wan Chai) German classes, films, exhibitions and lectures.

CUSTOMS REGULATIONS

Even though Hong Kong is a duty-free port, there are items on which duty is still charged. Import taxes apply on cigarettes and spirits, although wine and beer imports are now free of these taxes.

The duty-free allowance for visitors arriving in Hong Kong (including those coming from Macau and mainland China) is 60 cigarettes (or 15 cigars or 75g of tobacco) and 1L of spirits. Apart from these limits there are few other import taxes, so you can bring in reasonable quantities of almost anything.

Firecrackers and fireworks are banned in Hong Kong but not in Macau and mainland China, and people crossing the border are sometimes thoroughly searched for these. Customs officers are on high alert for drug smugglers. If you're arriving from Thailand or Vietnam, be prepared for a rigorous examination of your luggage.

DISCOUNT CARDS
Hong Kong Museums Pass

This pass allows multiple entries to six of Hong Kong's museums: Hong Kong Museum of Coastal Defence (p91) on Hong Kong Island; the Hong Kong Science Museum (p107), Hong Kong Museum of History (p107), Hong Kong Museum of Art (p98) and Hong Kong Space Museum (excluding Space Theatre; p103) in Kowloon; and the Hong Kong Heritage Museum (p128) in the New Territories. Passes valid for seven consecutive days cost $30. Passes are available from HKTB outlets and participating museums. Note that these six museums are all free on Wednesdays.

Hostel Card

A Hostelling International (HI) card, or the equivalent, is of relatively limited use in Hong Kong, as there are only seven HI-affiliated hostels here, and most are in remote locations in the New Territories. If you arrive without a card and want to stay in one of these hostels, you can buy one from the Hong Kong Youth Hostels Association (HKYHA; Map pp100–1; ☎ 2788 1638; www.yha .org.hk; Room 225-227, Block 19, Shek Kip Mei Estate, Kowloon; HI card under/over 18yr $50/110).

You are allowed to stay at any of Hong Kong's HKYHA hostels without a membership card, but you will have to buy a 'Welcome Stamp' ($30) for each night of your stay. Once you've stayed six nights, you are issued your own card.

Seniors Card

Many attractions in Hong Kong offer discounts for people aged over 60 or 65. Most of Hong Kong's museums are either free or half-price for those over 60, and most forms of public transport offer a 50% discount to anyone over 65. A passport or ID with a photo should be sufficient proof of age.

Student, Youth & Teacher Cards

The International Student Identity Card (ISIC), a plastic ID-style card with your photograph, provides discounts on some forms of transport and cheaper admission to museums and other sights. If you're aged under 26 but not a student, you can apply for an International Youth Travel Card (IYTC) issued by the Federation of International Youth Travel Organisations (FIYTO), which gives much the same discounts and benefits. Teachers can apply for the International Teacher Identity Card (ITIC).

Hong Kong Student Travel, based at Sincerity Travel (Map p104; ☎ 2735 6668; Room 833-834, Star House, 3 Salisbury Rd, Tsim Sha Tsui; ⏰ 10am-7pm Mon-Sat), can issue you any of these cards instantly for $100. Make sure you bring your student ID or other credentials along with you.

ELECTRICITY

The standard is 220V, 50Hz AC. Hong Kong's plug and socket system can be a bit confusing at first. The vast majority of electricity outlets are designed to accommodate the British three square pins, but some take three large round prongs, and others take three small pins. Unsurprisingly, inexpensive plug adaptors are widely available in Hong Kong, even in supermarkets.

EMBASSIES & CONSULATES

Hong Kong is definitely one of the world's most consulate-clogged cities. You'll find a complete list of consulates in the *Yellow Pages*.

Australia (Map p74; ☎ 2827 8881; 23rd fl, Harbour Centre, 25 Harbour Rd, Wan Chai)

Canada (Map p67; ☎ 3719 4700; One Exchange Sq, 8 Connaught Pl, Central)

France (Map p72; ☎ 3196 6100; 26th fl, Tower II, Admiralty Centre, 18 Harcourt Rd, Admiralty)

Germany (Map p72; ☎ 2105 8788; 21st fl, United Centre, 95 Queensway, Admiralty)

Ireland (Map p72; ☎ 2527 4897; Suite 1408, Two Pacific Place, 88 Queensway, Wan Chai) Honorary consulate.

Japan (Map p67; ☎ 2522 1184; 46th-47th fl, One Exchange Sq, 8 Connaught Pl, Central)

Netherlands (Map p67; ☎ 2522 5127; Room 5702, 57th fl, Cheung Kong Centre, 2 Queen's Rd Central, Central)

New Zealand (Map p74; ☎ 2877 4488; Room 6508, 65th fl, Central Plaza, 18 Harbour Rd, Wan Chai)

South Africa (Map p74; ☎ 2577 3279; Rooms 2706-2710, 27th fl, Great Eagle Centre, 23 Harbour Rd, Wan Chai)

UK (Map p72; ☎ 2901 3000; 1 Supreme Court Rd, Admiralty)

USA (Map p67; ☎ 2523 9011; 26 Garden Rd, Central)

EMERGENCY

Hong Kong is generally a very safe place, but as everywhere, things can go awry. Although it is safe to walk around just about anywhere in the territory after dark, it's best to stick to well-lit areas. Tourist districts, such as Tsim Sha Tsui, are heavily patrolled by the police. In the event of an emergency, ring ☎ 999.

Hong Kong has its share of local pickpockets and thieves. Carry as little cash and as few valuables as possible, and if you put a bag down, keep an eye on it. This also applies to restaurants and pubs, particularly in touristy areas such as the Star Ferry piers and the Peak Tram. If your bag doesn't accompany you to the toilet, don't expect to find it when you return.

If you are robbed, you can obtain a loss report for insurance purposes at the police station in the area in which the crime occurred. For locations and contact details of police stations in Hong Kong, visit www.info.gov.hk/police and click on 'Contact Us' and then 'Report Rooms'.

If you run into legal trouble, call the Legal Aid Department (☎ 2537 7677; www.lad.gov.hk; ☼ 24hr hotline), which provides residents and visitors with representation, subject to a means and merits test. Other important numbers include the following:

Auxiliary Medical Service (AMS) hotline (☎ 2762 2033)

Bushfire Control Centre hotline (☎ 2720 0777)

Police (☎ 2527 7177)

St John Ambulance Brigade Hong Kong Island (☎ 2576 6555); Kowloon (☎ 2713 5555); New Territories (☎ 2639 2555)

Tropical Cyclone Warning (☎ 2835 1473)

GAY & LESBIAN TRAVELLERS

Those travelling to Hong Kong will find a small but vibrant and growing gay-and-lesbian scene in the Special Administrative Region (SAR). It may not compete with the likes of London or Sydney, but Hong Kong has come a long way all the same.

It was, after all, only in 1991 that the Crimes (Amendment) Ordinance removed criminal penalties for homosexual acts between consenting adults over the age of 18. Since then, gay groups have been lobbying for legislation to address the issue of discrimination on the grounds of sexual orientation. Despite these changes, however, Hong Kong Chinese society remains fairly conservative, and it can still be risky for gays and lesbians to come out to family members or their employers.

Useful organisations:

Chi Heng Foundation (☎ 2517 0564; www.chihengfoundation.com; GPO Box 3923, Central, Hong Kong) Umbrella unit for gay and lesbian associations and groups in Hong Kong and an AIDS-prevention organisation.

Horizons (☎ 2815 9268, 9776 6479; www.horizons.org.hk; GPO Box 6837, Central, Hong Kong; ☼ hotline 7.30-10.30pm Tue & Thu) A phone service that provides information and advice to local and visiting gays, lesbians and bisexuals.

HEALTH

The occasional avian or swine flu outbreak notwithstanding, health conditions in the region are good. Travellers have a low risk of contracting infectious diseases, apart from travellers' diarrhoea, which is common throughout Asia. The health system (p296) is generally excellent.

Diseases
DENGUE FEVER

Dengue is a viral disease transmitted by mosquitoes, and there are occasional outbreaks in Hong Kong. Unlike the malaria mosquito, the *Aedes aegypti* mosquito, which transmits the dengue virus, is most active during the day, and is found mainly in urban areas, in and around human dwellings. Signs and symptoms of dengue fever include a sudden onset of high fever, headache, joint and muscle pains (hence its old name, 'breakbone fever'), and nausea and vomiting. A rash of small red spots sometimes appears three to four days after the onset of fever.

You should seek medical attention as soon as possible if you think you may be infected. A blood test can exclude malaria and indicate the possibility of dengue fever. There is no specific treatment for dengue. Aspirin should be avoided, as it increases the risk of haemorrhaging. The best prevention is to avoid mosquito bites at all times by covering up, using insect repellents containing the compound DEET and mosquito nets.

GIARDIA

This is a parasite that often jumps on board when you have diarrhoea. It then causes a more prolonged illness with intermittent diarrhoea or loose stools, bloating, fatigue and some nausea. There may be a metallic taste in the mouth. Avoiding potentially contaminated foods and always washing your hands can help prevent giardia.

HEPATITIS A

Hepatitis A is a virus common in Hong Kong and Macau, and is transmitted through contaminated water and shellfish. It is most commonly caught at local island seafood restaurants. Immunisation and avoiding local seafood restaurants should prevent it.

HEPATITIS B

While this is common in the area, it can only be transmitted by unprotected sex, sharing needles, treading on a discarded needle, or receiving contaminated blood in very remote areas of China.

INFLUENZA

Hong Kong has a bad flu season over the winter months from December to March. Symptoms include a cold (runny nose etc) with a high fever and aches and pains. You should wash your hands frequently, avoid anybody you know who has the flu and consider getting a flu shot before you travel.

TRAVELLERS' DIARRHOEA

To prevent diarrhoea, avoid tap water unless it has been boiled, filtered or chemically disinfected (eg with iodine tablets); only eat fresh fruits and vegetables if they're cooked or peeled; be wary of dairy products that might contain unpasteurised milk; and be highly selective when eating food from street vendors.

If you develop diarrhoea, be sure to drink plenty of fluids, preferably an oral rehydration solution containing lots of salt and sugar. A few loose stools doesn't mean you require treatment, but if you start experiencing more than four or five stools a day, you should start taking an antibiotic (usually a quinolone drug) and an anti-diarrhoeal agent (such as loperamide). If diarrhoea is bloody, or persists for more than 72 hours, or is accompanied by fever, shaking chills or severe abdominal pain, you should seek medical attention.

Environmental Hazards

INSECTS

Mosquitoes are prevalent in Hong Kong. You should always use insect repellent and if you're bitten use hydrocortisone cream to reduce swelling. Lamma Island is home to large red centipedes, which have a poisonous bite that causes swelling and discomfort in most cases, but can be more dangerous (and supposedly in very rare cases deadly) for young children.

MAMMALS

Wild boars and aggressive dogs are a minor hazard in some of the more remote parts of the New Territories. Wild boars are shy and retiring most of the time but are dangerous when they feel threatened, so give them a wide berth and avoid disturbing thick areas of undergrowth.

SNAKES

There are many snakes in Hong Kong, and some are deadly, but you are unlikely to encounter any. Still, always take care when bushwalking, particularly on Lamma and Lantau Islands. Go straight to a public hospital if bitten; private doctors do not stock antivenin.

WATER

Avoid drinking the local water, as its quality varies enormously and depends on the pipes in the building you're in. Bottled water is a safer option, or you can boil tap water for three minutes.

Online Resources

The World Health Organization (WHO) publishes a superb book called *International Travel and Health*, which is revised annually and is available online at www.who.int/ith for free.

Recommended Immunisations

There are no required vaccinations for entry into Hong Kong or Macau unless you have travelled from a country infected with yellow fever. In this case, you will have to show your yellow-fever vaccination certificate. Hong Kong is a highly developed city and, as such, immunisations are not really necessary unless you will be travelling to the mainland or elsewhere in the region.

Since most vaccines don't produce immunity until at least two weeks after they're given, visit a physician four to eight weeks before departure. Ask your doctor for an International Certificate of Vaccination (or 'yellow booklet'), which will list all of the vaccinations you've received.

If your health insurance doesn't cover you for medical expenses abroad, consider supplemental insurance (check out www.lonelyplanet.com/bookings/insurance.do for more information).

HOLIDAYS

Western and Chinese culture combine to create an interesting mix – and number – of public holidays in Hong Kong and Macau. Determining the exact date of some of them is tricky, as there are traditionally two calendars in use: the Gregorian solar (or Western) calendar and the Chinese lunar calendar.

The following are public holidays in both Hong Kong and Macau (unless otherwise noted). For Macau-specific holidays, check out p353.

New Year's Day 1 January

Chinese New Year 14 February 2010, 3 February 2011

Easter 2 to 5 April 2010, 24 to 27 April 2011

Ching Ming 5 April

Labour Day 1 May

Buddha's Birthday 21 May 2010

Dragon Boat (Tuen Ng) Festival 16 June 2010, 6 June 2011

Hong Kong SAR Establishment Day 1 July (not in Macau)

Mid-Autumn Festival 22 September 2010, 12 September 2011

China National Day 1 October

Cheung Yeung 16 October 2010, 5 October 2011

Christmas Day 25 December

Boxing Day 26 December

IDENTITY CARD

Hong Kong residents are required to carry a government-issued Hong Kong Identity Card with them at all times and this rule is strictly enforced. As a visitor, you are required to carry your passport; it is the only acceptable form of identification as far as the police are concerned.

Anyone over the age of 11 who stays in Hong Kong for longer than 180 days must apply for a Hong Kong ID. Inquire at the ID-issuing office of the Hong Kong Immigration Department (Map p74; ☎ 2824 6111; www.immd.gov.hk; 2nd fl, Immigration Tower, 7 Gloucester Rd, Wan Chai; 8.45am-4.30pm Mon-Fri, 9-11.30am Sat). Make sure you take your passport and other documents along with you.

INTERNET ACCESS

Long since fully cabled with broadband, getting online in Hong Kong should be a breeze. Wi-fi is increasingly available in hotels and public areas, including in all of the major shopping malls.

The most-used internet service providers (ISPs) in Hong Kong include PCCW's Netvigator (☎ 183 3833; www.netvigator.com), HKNet (☎ 2110 2288; www.hknet.com), CPCNet (☎ 2331 8930; www.cpcnet-hk.com) and Yahoo (☎ 2895 5769; www.yahoo.hk).

Most hotels and hostels have internet access either through terminals or by offering wireless access to hook your own machines up to. You'll also be able to log on for free at major MTR stations (eg Central and Causeway Bay) and many public libraries, including

the Causeway Bay branch of the Central Library (Map p85; ☎ 3150 1234; www.hkpl.gov.hk; 66 Causeway Rd; 10am-9pm Thu-Tue, 1-9pm Wed, 10am-7pm some public holidays; Shau Kei Wan). All it takes to log on to one of the terminals at the Pacific Coffee Company (www.pacificcoffee.com) or the many Mix (www.mix-world.com) juice bars is the purchase of a drink.

The following are among the best private internet cafes (ie they have fast machines, good locations and lots of terminals):

Cyber Pro Internet (Map p85; ☎ 2836 3502; Basement, 491-499 Lockhart Rd, Causeway Bay; per hr 11am-midnight/midnight-7am Sun-Thu $16/10, Fri & Sat $18/13; 11am-7am) This huge place is packed with young 'uns playing games.

IT. Fans (Map p67; ☎ 2542 1868; Ground & Cockloft, Man On Commercial Bldg, 12-13 Jubilee St, Central; membership $10, per hr members/nonmembers Mon-Thu $16/20, Fri-Sun $18/22; 10am-5am) This massive and very central place has 100 monitors and serves food.

Pacific Coffee Company (Map p104; ☎ 2735 0112; www.pacificcoffee.com; Shop G31-G32A, Miramar Shopping Centre, 132 Nathan Rd, Tsim Sha Tsui; 7am-midnight Mon-Thu, 7am-1am Fri & Sat, 8am-midnight Sun) Internet is free for customers. There are dozens of other branches throughout Hong Kong.

Wi-Fi & Wireless Broadband Access

One of the most wired cities on earth, Hong Kong has lately been going wireless. You'll find excellent wi-fi connectivity in urban areas, and an increasing number of hotels and bars offer free access, along with almost every shopping mall in Tsim Sha Tsui and on Hong Kong Island, often only requiring registration and possibly an email address. Many chains of coffee and juice shops, such as Pacific Coffee Company (www.pacificcoffee.com) offer free wi-fi. For a comprehensive list of wireless locations, try Hotspot Locations (www.hotspot-locations.com).

Most of the mobile-phone-network operators in town now offer USB 'dongles' that use a mobile phone SIM card as a data link for your laptop; some also offer these on pay-as-you-go plans that do not require a contract (and thus proof of residency). The cost (around $900) of these contract-free units will doubtless fall in time, but they are probably only worth considering if you are staying several nights or longer in town and your hotel charges a daily rate for internet connections. If you have a dongle of your own, see if you can use it here. Many overseas dongles are locked to their original country of use, so insist on the shop trying out your unit in store before you buy.

LAUNDRY

Laundries are easy to find everywhere in Hong Kong – hey, this *is* China – though they're *never* self-service. Most hotels, guesthouses and even some hostels have a laundry service. Prices at local laundries are normally $28 to $35 for the first 3kg, and then $8 to $12 for each additional kilogram.

Dry cleaners are easy to spot and some laundries also offer a dry-cleaning service. Both prices and quality vary enormously, but expect to pay from $25 for a dress shirt, from $35 for a skirt and from $60 for a suit. Try Martinizing (Map p78; ☎ 2525 3089; Ground fl, 7 Glenealy, Central; ☑ 8.30am-7pm Mon-Sat).

LEFT LUGGAGE

There are left-luggage lockers in major MTR train stations, including the Hung Hom station; the West Tower of the Shun Tak Centre in Sheung Wan, from where the Macau ferry departs; and the China ferry terminal in Tsim Sha Tsui. Luggage costs between $20 and $30 for up to two hours (depending on the locker size) and between $25 and $35 for every 12 hours after that.

The Hong Kong Airport Express station has a left-luggage office that's open from 6am to 1am. There's also a counter on Level 5 (arrivals hall) at Hong Kong International Airport (☎ 2261 0110; ☑ 5.30am-1.30am). Storage here costs $35 for up to three hours, $50 for up to 24 hours and $120 for up to 48 hours. It's $80 for each 24-hour period after that.

Generally the machines don't use keys but spit out a numbered ticket when you have deposited your money and closed the door. You have to punch in this number when you retrieve your bag, so keep it somewhere safe or write the number down. Some lockers have a maximum storage time of three days, so read the instructions carefully.

If you're going to visit Macau or the mainland and you'll be returning to Hong Kong, most hotels and even some guesthouses and hostels have left-luggage rooms and will let you leave your gear behind, even if you've already checked out and won't be staying on

your return. There is usually a charge for this service, so be sure to inquire first.

LEGAL MATTERS

Hong Kong has a serious drug problem, much of it supplied by the Triads. There are estimated to be more than 40,000 drug addicts in Hong Kong, 75% of whom are hooked on heroin, which they generally smoke – the process is called 'chasing the dragon' – rather than inject. Some female addicts finance their habit by working in the sex industry; others resort to pickpocketing, burglary and robbery.

Professional smugglers often target Westerners to carry particular goods into countries like Vietnam and India, where those goods are prohibited or the import taxes are high. The theory is that customs agents are less likely to stop and search foreigners. These small-time smuggling expeditions, or 'milk runs', either earn the Westerner a fee or a free air ticket to another destination. But smuggling is very, very risky.

Most foreigners who get into legal trouble in Hong Kong are involved in drugs. *All* forms of narcotics are illegal in Hong Kong. It makes no difference whether it's heroin, opium, 'ice', ecstasy or marijuana – the law makes no distinction. If police or customs officials find dope or even smoking equipment in your possession, you can expect to be arrested immediately. If you do run into legal trouble, contact the Legal Aid Department (☎ 2537 7677; ☑ 24hr hotline).

LIBRARIES

Hong Kong has an extensive public library system – some 66 libraries in total – and you can find the list at www.hkpl.gov.hk. The most useful for travellers is the City Hall Public Library (Map p67; ☎ 2921 2555; ☑ 10am-7pm Mon-Thu, 10am-9pm Fri, 10am-5pm Sat, Sun & some public holidays), spread over eight floors of the High Block of City Hall, opposite Queen's Pier in Central. With a passport and a deposit of $130 per item, foreign visitors can get a temporary library card (on the 3rd floor), which allows them to borrow up to six books and other materials from the library for 14 days at any one time.

In Causeway Bay the even larger Central Library (Map p85; ☎ 3150 1234; 66 Causeway Rd; ☑ 10am-9pm Thu-Tue, 1-9pm Wed, 10am-7pm some public holidays) has lending sections, children's and young-adult libraries, some two dozen terminals with internet available to the public, and a wonderful reading room on the 5th floor with around 4000 international periodicals.

MAPS

Decent tourist maps are easy to come by in Hong Kong, and they're usually free. The HKTB hands out copies of *The Hong Kong Map*, which is bimonthly, at its information centres. It covers the northern coast of Hong Kong Island from Sheung Wan to Causeway Bay and part of the Kowloon peninsula, and has inset maps of Aberdeen, Hung Hom, Kowloon City, Kowloon Tong, Sha Tin, Stanley and Tsuen Wan.

Universal Publications (UP; www.up.com.hk) produces many maps of Hong Kong, including the 1:80,000 *Hong Kong Touring Map* and the 1:9000 *City Map of Hong Kong & Kowloon*. It publishes detailed street maps of Hong Kong Island and Kowloon ($22 each), with scales below 1:8000.

The *Hong Kong Official Guide Map* ($45), produced by the Survey and Mapping Office of the Lands Department (www.info.gov.hk/landsd/mapping), has both street and district maps and is available from most bookshops.

If you're looking for greater detail, topographical accuracy and good colour reproduction, it's worth investing in the *Hong Kong Guidebook* ($60), a street atlas to the entire territory published by UP and updated annually. Compiled in English and Chinese, it also includes useful information on public transport and a host of other listings. A larger format version of this, the *Hong Kong Directory* ($70) is available, as well as the pocketsized *Palm Atlas of Hong Kong* ($42). The *Public Transport Atlas* ($50) shows detailed information on all land public transport routes in Hong Kong, displaying all of the stops on maps.

Along with everything from flying charts to plans of the New Towns in the New Territories, the Survey and Mapping Office produces a range of *Countryside Series* maps that are useful for hiking in the hills and country parks. They are available from two Map Publication Centres: the North Point branch (Map pp62–3; ☎ 2231 3187; 23rd fl, North Point Government Offices, 333 Java Rd; ☺ 9am-5.30pm Mon-Fri) and the Yau Ma Tei branch (Map p108; ☎ 2780 0981; 382 Nathan Rd; ☺ 9am-5.30pm Mon-Fri).

Each of the *Countryside Series* maps is 1:25,000, with larger-scale inset maps. One of them covers Hong Kong Island and surrounds: *Hong Kong Island & Neighbouring Islands* ($50). Three maps are devoted to the New Territories: *North-West New Territories* ($62), *North-East & Central New Territories* ($50) and *Sai Kung & Clearwater Bay* ($50). For the islands, there's *Outlying Islands* ($45), with large-scale maps of Cheung Chau, Lamma, Peng Chau, Ma Wan, Tung Lung Chau and Po Toi; and *Lantau Island & Neighbouring Islands* ($62), essentially a 1:25,000-scale map of Hong Kong's largest island, with several larger-scale inset maps.

Most bookshops stock UP's 1:32,000-scale *Lantau Island, Cheung Chau & Lamma Island* ($25), which is laminated and contains useful transport information, and its 1:54,000 *Tseung Kwan O, Sai Kung, Clearwater Bay* ($25).

If you're heading for any of Hong Kong's four major trails, you should get a copy of the trail map produced by the Country & Marine Parks Authority, which is available at the Map Publication Centres.

MEDICAL SERVICES

The standard of medical care in Hong Kong is generally excellent but expensive. Always take out travel insurance before you travel. Healthcare is divided into public and private, and there is no interaction between the two. In the case of an emergency, all ambulances (☎ 999) will take you to a government-run public hospital where, as a visitor, you will be required to pay a hefty fee for using emergency services. Treatment is guaranteed in any case; people who cannot pay immediately will be billed later. While the emergency care is excellent, you may wish to transfer to a private hospital once you are stable.

There are many English-speaking general practitioners, specialists and dentists in Hong Kong, who can be found through your consulate (p291), a private hospital or the *Yellow Pages*. If money is tight, take yourself to the nearest public-hospital emergency room and be prepared to wait. The general inquiry number for hospitals is ☎ 2300 6555.

Public and private hospitals with 24-hour accident and emergency departments:

HONG KONG ISLAND

Hong Kong Central Hospital (Map p78; ☎ 2522 3141; 1 Lower Albert Rd, Central) Private.

Matilda International Hospital (Map pp62–3; ☎ 2849 0111; 41 Mt Kellett Rd, the Peak) Private.

Queen Mary Hospital (Map pp62–3; ☎ 2855 3838; 102 Pok Fu Lam Rd, Pok Fu Lam) Public.

KOWLOON

Hong Kong Baptist Hospital (off Map pp100–1; ☎ 2339 8888; 222 Waterloo Rd, Kowloon Tong) Private.

Princess Margaret Hospital (Map pp58–9; ☎ 2990 1111; 2-10 Princess Margaret Hospital Rd, Lai Chi Kok) Public.

Queen Elizabeth Hospital (Map p108; ☎ 2958 8888; 30 Gascoigne Rd, Yau Ma Tei) Public.

NEW TERRITORIES

Prince of Wales Hospital (Map p127; ☎ 2632 2211; 30-32 Ngan Shing St, Sha Tin) Public.

There are many pharmacies in Hong Kong and Macau. They bear a red-and-white cross outside and there should be a registered pharmacist available inside. Though in Hong Kong many medications can be bought over the counter without a prescription, you should always check it is a known brand and that the expiry date is valid. Birth-control pills, pads, tampons and condoms are available over the counter in these dispensaries, as well as in stores such as Watson's and Mannings.

MONEY

Consult the inside front cover for a table of exchange rates and refer to the boxed text on p18 for information on costs.

ATMs

Automated Teller Machines (ATMs) can be found almost everywhere in Hong Kong and are almost always linked up to international money systems such as Cirrus, Maestro, Plus and Visa Electron. Some HSBC so-called Electronic Money machines offer cash withdrawal facilities for Visa and MasterCard holders; American Express (Amex) cardholders have access to Jetco ATMs and can withdraw local currency and travellers cheques at Express Cash ATMs in town.

Changing Money

Hong Kong has no currency controls; locals and foreigners can bring, send in or take out as much money as they like.

Banks in Hong Kong generally offer the best rates, though two of the biggest ones – Standard Chartered Bank and Hang Seng Bank – levy a $50 commission for each transaction for those who don't hold accounts. Avoid HSBC,

where this charge is $100. If you're changing the equivalent of several hundred US dollars or more, the exchange rate improves, which usually makes up for the fee.

Licensed moneychangers, such as Chequepoint, abound in touristed areas, including Tsim Sha Tsui. While they are convenient (usually open on Sundays, holidays and late into the evenings) and take no commission per se, the less-than-attractive exchange rates offered are equivalent to a 5% commission. These rates are clearly posted, though if you're changing several hundred US dollars or more you might be able to bargain for a better rate. Before the actual exchange is made, the moneychanger is required by law to give you a form to sign that clearly shows the amount due to you, the exchange rate and any service charges. Try to avoid the exchange counters at the airport or in hotels, which offer some of the worst rates in Hong Kong.

No foreign-currency black market exists in Hong Kong. If anyone on the street does approach you to change money, assume it's a scam.

Credit Cards

The most widely accepted credit cards in Hong Kong are Visa, MasterCard, Amex, Diners Club and JCB – and pretty much in that order. It may be an idea to carry two, just in case.

Some shops in Hong Kong add a surcharge to offset the commission charged by credit companies, which can range from 2.5% to 7%. In theory, this is prohibited by the credit companies, but to get around this many shops will offer a 5% discount if you pay with cash. It's your call.

If a card is lost or stolen, you must inform both the police (☎ 2527 7177) and the issuing company as soon as possible; otherwise, you may have to pay for the purchases that the unspeakable scoundrel has racked up on your card. Some 24-hour numbers for cancelling cards:

American Express (☎ 2811 6122)

Diners Club (☎ 2860 1888)

MasterCard (☎ 800 966 677)

Visa (☎ 800 900 782)

The Visa contact might be able to help you (or at least point you in the right direction) should you lose your Visa card, but in general you must deal with the issuing bank in the case of an emergency. Round-the-clock emergency bank numbers:

Citibank (☎ 2860 0333)

HSBC (☎ 2233 3000)

Standard Chartered Bank (☎ 2886 8888)

Currency

The local currency is the Hong Kong dollar (HK$), which is divided into 100 cents. Bills are issued in denominations of $10, $20, $50, $100, $500 and $1000. There are little copper coins worth 10¢, 20¢ and 50¢, silver-coloured $1, $2 and $5 coins, and a nickel and bronze $10 coin.

Three local banks issue notes: HSBC (formerly the Hongkong & Shanghai Bank), the Standard Chartered Bank and the Bank of China (all but the $10 bill).

For exchange rates see the inside front cover, or check out www.xe.com.

Travellers Cheques & Cards

Travellers cheques and their modern equivalent, ATM-style cards that can be credited with cash in advance, offer protection from theft but are becoming less common due to the preponderance of ATMs. Most banks will cash travellers cheques, and they all charge a fee, often irrespective of whether you are an account holder or not.

If any cheques go missing, contact the issuing office or the nearest branch of the issuing agency immediately. American Express (☎ 3002 1276) can usually arrange replacement cheques within 24 hours.

NEWSPAPERS & MAGAZINES

The main English-language newspaper in the city is the daily broadsheet *South China Morning Post* (www.scmp.com), which has always toed the government line, both before and after the handover. It has the largest circulation and is read by more Hong Kong Chinese than expatriates. The livelier and slightly punchier tabloid *Hong Kong Standard* (www.thestandard.com.hk), published from Monday to Saturday (weekend edition), is harder to find. The Beijing mouthpiece *China Daily* (www.chinadaily.com.cn) also prints a Hong Kong English-language edition of its paper.

The *Asian Wall Street Journal* and regional editions of *USA Today*, the *International Herald Tribune* and the *Financial Times* are printed in Hong Kong.

Hong Kong has its share of English-language periodicals, including a slew of home-grown (and Asian-focused) business-related magazines. *Time, Newsweek* and the *Economist* are all available in their current editions.

ORGANISED TOURS

Despite its size, a profusion of organised tours operates in Hong Kong. There are tours available to just about anywhere in the territory and they can make good options if you only have a short time in Hong Kong or don't want to deal with public transport. Some tours are standard excursions covering major sights on Hong Kong Island, such as the Peak and Hollywood Rd, while other tours take you on harbour cruises, out to the islands or through the New Territories. For tours to Macau, see p313.

Air

If you hanker to see Hong Kong from on high – and hang the expense – Heliservices (☎ 2802 0200; www.heliservices.com.hk) has chartered Aerospatiale Squirrels for up to five passengers available for $6600/10,000 for 15-/30-minute periods. They depart from rooftop helipads at the Peninsula Hong Kong (p241) annexe.

Boat

Several operators offer harbour tours. If you're on a budget, the HKTB (p302) offers a one-hour free ride on the *Duk Ling,* a traditional Chinese junk complete with red triangular sails, that departs Kowloon public pier at 2pm and 4pm on Thursday and 10am and noon on Saturday. It also picks up from Central pier 9 at 3pm and 5pm on Thursday, and at 11am and 1pm on Saturday.

The easiest way to see the full extent of Victoria Harbour from sea level is to join a circular Star Ferry Harbour Tour (☎ 2118 6201/2; www.starferry .com.hk/tour.html), of which there are a number of different options. A single daytime round trip, departing hourly from the Star Ferry pier in Tsim Sha Tsui between 2.05pm and 5.05pm daily, costs $50/45 for adult/concession (children aged three to 12 years and seniors over 65). A full-/half-day hopping pass, available from 11.05am to 7.05pm/5.05pm, respectively, costs $170/75 for adults and $153/68 for concessions. At night, a two-hour round trip (at 7.05pm and 9.05pm) is $100/90 for adult/concession. A single night ride taken between 6.05pm and 11.05pm costs $95/85. There are also departures from the piers at Central, Wan Chai and Hung Hom; see the website for details.

Many agents, including Gray Line (☎ 2368 7111; www.grayline.com.hk), Splendid Tours & Travel (☎ 2316 2151; www.splendidtours.com) and Hong Kong Dragon Cruise (☎ 2131 8181; www.nwft.com.hk), run by New World First Travel, offer tours of Victoria and Aberdeen Harbours, but the company with the longest experience in these is Watertours (Map p104; ☎ 2926 3868; www.watertours.com.hk; Unit 1023A, 10F, Star House, 3 Salisbury Rd, Tsim Sha Tsui; ☿ 9am-9pm). Some eight different tours of the harbour and the Outlying Islands, as well as dinner and cocktail cruises, are available. Prices range from $230 ($135 for children aged two to 12 years) for the Morning Harbour & Noon Day Gun Firing Cruise to $400 ($370 for children) for the Harbour Lights & Lei Yue Mun Seafood Village Dinner Cruise.

For the Outlying Islands, HKKF Travel (☎ 2815 6063; www.hkkf.com.hk) has a five-hour Outlying Islands Escapade ($370) that takes in Cheung Chau and Lamma Island. Departure is from pier 4 at the Outlying Islands ferry terminal in Central.

Bus

A good way to get your bearings in the city centre is on the hop-on, hop-off, open-topped double-deckers run by the Big Bus Company (☎ 2723 2108; www.bigbustours.com; tours adult/child $320/200), which runs two tours. The Blue Tour takes in much of the Tsim Sha Tsui and Hung Hom waterfront, and the Red Tour explores Central, Admiralty, Wan Chai and Causeway Bay.

For first-time visitors to Hong Kong eager to explore further afield, Splendid Tours & Travel (☎ 2316 2151; www.splendidtours.com) runs some interesting 'orientation' tours of Hong Kong Island, Kowloon and the New Territories. The tours last four to five hours and cost $320/220 per adult/child aged three to 12 years. Another tour company to try is the old stalwart Gray Line (☎ 2368 7111; www.grayline.com.hk), which has a five-hour tour ($320/215) taking in Man Mo Temple, Victoria Peak, Aberdeen and Repulse Bay.

Some of the most popular surface tours of the New Territories are offered (or subcontracted) by the HKTB (p302). The ever-popular Land Between Tour takes in the Yuen Yuen Institute temple complex (p117) in Tsuen Wan and Tai Mo Shan lookout (p118), as well as sev-

eral other sights. The full-day tour (adult/child under 16 or senior over 60 $420/370) takes 6½ hours and includes lunch; the half-day tour ($320/270) is five hours, without lunch. The five-hour Heritage Tour ($320/270), which does not include lunch, takes in New Territories sights such as Man Mo Temple (p124) in Tai Po, the Tang Chung Ling Ancestral Hall in Leung Yeuk Tau village and the walled settlement of Lo Wai. Contact the HKTB tours reservation hotline (☎ 2368 7112; ☿ 7am-9pm) for information and bookings.

Walking

For tailor-made, personal walking tours of both urban and rural Hong Kong, contact Walk Hong Kong (☎ 9187 8641; www.walkhongkong .com), which is run by a couple of long-term expatriates. For other walking tours, see the Neighbourhoods & Islands chapter (p54).

PHOTOGRAPHY

Almost everything you could possibly need in the way of photographic accessories is available in Hong Kong. Stanley St on Hong Kong Island is the place to look for reputable camera shops catering to both digital and film photography.

Photo developing from digital or from film is relatively inexpensive; it costs from $5 per digital file to print, and to develop a roll of 36 exposures and have them printed costs from $55 for size 3R and from $65 for size 4R. Processing and mounting slide film is $50. Most photo shops will take four passport-sized photos of you for around $50. Some of the best photo-processing in town is available at Color Six (Map p78; ☎ 2526 0123; www.colorsix.com; Ground fl, 28A Stanley St, Central; ☿ 8.30am-7pm Mon-Fri, 8.30am-4pm Sat). Not only can colour slides be professionally processed in just three hours, but many special types of film, unavailable elsewhere in Hong Kong, are on sale here. Most photography shops are well geared up for printing from digital formats and for copying onto CDs.

POST

Hong Kong Post (☎ 2921 2222; www.hongkongpost.com) is generally excellent; local letters are often delivered the same day they are sent and there is Saturday delivery. The staff at most post offices speak English, and the lavender-coloured mail boxes with lime-green posts are clearly marked in English.

Receiving Mail

If a letter is addressed c/o Poste Restante, GPO Hong Kong, it will go to the GPO on Hong Kong Island. Pick it up at counter No 29 from 8am to 6pm Monday to Saturday only. If you want your letters to go to Kowloon, have them addressed as follows: c/o Poste Restante, Tsim Sha Tsui Post Office, 10 Middle Rd, Tsim Sha Tsui, Kowloon. Mail is normally held for two months.

Sending Mail

On Hong Kong Island, the General Post Office (Map p67; 2 Connaught Pl, Central; 8am-6pm Mon-Sat, 9am-2pm Sun) is just west of the Star Ferry pier. In Kowloon, the Tsim Sha Tsui Post Office (Map p104; Ground fl, Hermes House, 10 Middle Rd, Tsim Sha Tsui; 9am-6pm Mon-Sat, 9am-2pm Sun) is just east of the southern end of Nathan Rd. Post office branches elsewhere keep shorter hours and usually don't open on Sunday.

You should allow five days for delivery of letters, postcards and aerogrammes to the UK, Continental Europe and Australia, and five to six days to the USA.

COURIER SERVICES

Private companies offering courier delivery service include the following:

DHL International (2400 3388)

Federal Express (2730 3333)

TNT Express Worldwide (2331 2663)

UPS (2735 3535)

All four companies have pick-up points around the territory. Many MTR stations have DHL outlets, including the MTR Central branch (2400 3388) next to exit F, and the MTR Admiralty branch (2529 5778) next to exit E.

POSTAL RATES

Local mail is $1.40 for up to 30g. Airmail letters and postcards for the first 20/30g are $2.40/4.50 to Asia (excluding Japan) and $3/5.30 elsewhere, and $75/95 respectively per kilogram. Aerogrammes are a uniform $2.30.

SPEEDPOST

Letters and small parcels sent via Hong Kong Post's Speedpost (2921 2288; www.hongkongpost. com/speedpost) should reach any of 210 destinations worldwide within four days and are automatically registered. Speedpost rates vary enormously according to destination;

every post office has a schedule of fees and a timetable.

RADIO

Hong Kong's most popular English-language radio stations are RTHK Radio 3 (current affairs and talkback; 567AM, 1584AM, 97.9FM and 106.8FM); RTHK Radio 4 (classical music; 97.6-98.9FM); RTHK Radio 6 (BBC World Service relays; 675AM); AM 864 (hit parade; 864AM); and Metro Plus (news; 1044AM). The *South China Morning Post* publishes a daily schedule of radio programmes.

RELOCATING

Several companies offer relocation services in Hong Kong. One of the larger ones is Santa Fe Transport (2574 6204; www.santaferelo.com), which operates in cities around Asia and also offers online quotations. For a more comprehensive list of relocation agents, see yp.com.hk.

See also the sections in this book on working in Hong Kong (p304) and long-term-rental accommodation options (p233).

TAXES & REFUNDS

There is no sales tax in Hong Kong. The only 'visible' tax that visitors are likely to encounter is the 3% government tax on hotel rates.

TELEPHONE
International Calls & Rates

Hong Kong's 'country' code is 852. To call someone outside Hong Kong, dial 001, then the country code, the local area code (you usually drop the initial zero if there is one) and the number. Country codes:

Australia (61)

Canada (1)

China (mainland 86)

France (33)

Germany (49)

Japan (81)

Macau (853)

Netherlands (31)

New Zealand (64)

South Africa (27)

UK (44)

USA (1)

Remember that phone rates in Hong Kong are cheaper from 9pm to 8am on weekdays and throughout the weekend. If the phone you're using has the facility, dial ☎ 0060 first and then the number; rates will be cheaper at any time.

You can make International Direct Dial (IDD) calls to almost anywhere in the world from most public telephones in Hong Kong, but you'll need a phonecard, available from most phone service providers, such as PCCW's Hello card. You can buy phonecards at any PCCW branch, at 7-Eleven and Circle K convenience stores, Mannings pharmacies or Wellcome supermarkets.

PCCW (☎ 2888 2888; www.pccw.com) has retail outlets called i.Shops (☎ 2888 0008; www.pccwshop.com) throughout the territory, where you can buy phonecards, mobile phones and accessories. The most convenient shop for travellers is the Central branch (Map p67; Ground fl, 113 Des Voeux Rd Central; ☽ 10am-8pm Mon-Sat, noon-7pm Sun). There's also a Causeway Bay branch (Map p85; G3, Ground fl, McDonald's Bldg, 46-54 Yee Wo St; ☽ 10am-10pm Mon-Sat, 11am-9pm Sun).

Local Calls & Rates

All calls made from private phones in Hong Kong are local calls and therefore free. From public pay phones calls cost $1 for five minutes. Pay phones accept $1, $2, $5 and $10 coins. Hotels charge from $3 to $5 for local calls.

All landline numbers in the territory have eight digits (except ☎ 800 toll-free numbers and specific hotlines), and there are no area codes.

Mobile Phones

Hong Kong locals are addicted to their mobile telephones, which work everywhere, including in the harbour tunnels and on the MTR. Any GSM-compatible phone can be used here.

PCCW i.Shops have mobile phones and accessories along with rechargeable SIM chips for sale from $45. Local calls work out to cost between 30¢ and 50¢ a minute (calls to the mainland are about $1 to $2 a minute) and top-up cards are $88 or $180. Handsets can be hired for as little as $35 a day from Hong Kong CSL (☎ 2888 1010; www.hkcsl.com), which maintains 1010 outlets in Hong Kong, including a 1010 CSL Central branch (Map p78; ☎ 2918 1010; 4th fl, Century Sq, 1-13 D'Aguilar St; ☽ 8.30am-11pm) and a 1010 CSL Tsim Sha Tsui branch (Map p104; ☎ 2910 1010; 122-126 Canton Rd; ☽ 8.30am-10pm). CSL's prepaid SIM cards come in a variety of price options, depending

on if and where you need roaming services; top-up cards are also available at 7-Eleven and Circle K convenience stores.

Useful Numbers

The following are some important telephone numbers and codes; for emergency numbers, see p291. Both the telephone directory and the *Yellow Pages* can be consulted online at www.yp.com.hk.

Coastal Waters & Tidal Information (☎ 187 8200)

International Dialling Code (☎ 001)

International Directory Inquiries (☎ 10015)

International Fax Dialling Code (☎ 002)

Local Directory Inquiries (☎ 1081)

Reverse-Charge/Collect Calls (☎ 10010)

Time & Temperature (☎ 18501)

Weather (☎ 187 8200)

TELEVISION

Hong Kong's four free terrestrial TV stations are run by two companies: TV Broadcasts (TVB) and Asia TV (ATV). Each runs a Cantonese-language channel (TVB Jade and ATV Home) and an English one (TVB Pearl and ATV World). Programmes are listed daily in the *South China Morning Post* and in a weekly Sunday supplement.

The better hotels in town (although not usually the guesthouses) offer a wider array of cable channels and a variety of satellite channels.

TIME

Hong Kong does not have daylight-saving time. Hong Kong time is eight hours ahead of GMT and London; 13 hours ahead of New York; 16 hours ahead of San Francisco; the same time as Singapore, Manila and Perth; and two hours behind Sydney.

TIPPING

Hong Kong isn't particularly conscious of tipping and there is no obligation to tip, say, taxi drivers; just round the fare up, or you can throw in a dollar or two more. It's almost mandatory to tip hotel staff $10 to $20, and if you make use of the porters at the airport, $2 to $5 a suitcase is normally expected. The porters putting your bags on a push cart at Hong Kong or Kowloon Airport Express station do not expect a gratuity, though; it's all part of the service.

Most hotels and many restaurants add a 10% service charge to the bill. Check for hidden extras before you tip; some midrange hotels charge $3 to $5 for each local call when they are actually free throughout the territory, and some restaurants consistently get the bill wrong. If using the services of a hotel porter, it's customary to tip them at least $10.

TOILETS

Hong Kong has never had as many public toilets as other world-class cities, but that is changing rapidly, with new ones being built and old ones refurbished and reopened. They are always free to use. Almost all public toilets have access for people with disabilities, and baby-changing shelves in both men's and women's rooms. Equip yourself with tissues, though; public toilets in Hong Kong are often out of toilet paper.

TOURIST INFORMATION

The enterprising and energetic Hong Kong Tourism Board (HKTB; ☎ 2508 1234; www.discoverhongkong.com) is one of the most helpful and useful tourist organisations in the world. Staff are welcoming and have reams of information. Most of its literature is free, though it also sells a few useful publications and books, as well as postcards, T-shirts and souvenirs.

Before you depart, check the comprehensive HKTB website. While on the ground in Hong Kong, phone the HKTB Visitor Hotline (☎ 2508 1234; ☺ 8am-6pm) if you have a query, a problem or you're lost. Staff are eager to help.

HKTB Visitor Information & Service Centres can be found on Hong Kong Island, in Kowloon, at Hong Kong International Airport on Lantau Island, and in Lo Wu, which is on the border with the mainland. Outside these centres and at several other places in the territory you'll be able to find iCyberlink screens, from which you can conveniently access the HKTB website and database 24 hours a day.

Hong Kong International Airport HKTB Centres (Map p140; Chek Lap Kok; ☺ 7am-11pm) There are centres in Halls A and B on the arrivals level and the E2 transfer area.

Hong Kong Island HKTB Centre (Map p85; Causeway Bay MTR station, near exit F; ☺ 8am-8pm)

Kowloon HKTB Centre (Map p104; Star Ferry Concourse, Tsim Sha Tsui; ☺ 8am-8pm)

Lo Wu HKTB Centre (Map pp58–9; 2nd fl, Arrival Hall, Lo Wu Terminal Bldg; ☺ 8am-6pm)

TRAVELLERS WITH DISABILITIES

People with disabilities have to cope with substantial obstacles in Hong Kong, including the stairs at many MTR stations, as well as pedestrian overpasses, narrow and crowded footpaths, and steep hills. On the other hand, some buses are accessible by wheelchair, taxis are never hard to find, most buildings have lifts (many with Braille panels) and MTR stations have Braille maps with recorded information. Wheelchairs can negotiate the lower decks of most ferries.

For further information about facilities and services in Hong Kong for travellers with disabilities, contact either of the following:

Hong Kong Paralympic Committee & Sports Association for the Physically Disabled (☎ 2602 8232; www.hkparalympic.org)

Joint Council for People with Disabilities (Map p74; ☎ 2864 2931; www.hkcss.org.hk; 11th-13th fl, Duke of Windsor Bldg, 15 Hennessy Rd, Wan Chai)

UNIVERSITIES

Hong Kong has a total of eight universities. Hong Kong University (Map pp62–3; ☎ 2859 2111; www.hku.hk), established in 1911, is the oldest and most difficult to get into. Its campus is in Pok Fu Lam on the western side of Hong Kong Island. The Chinese University of Hong Kong (Map pp58–9; ☎ 2609 6000; www.cuhk.edu.hk), established in 1963, is most applicants' second choice. It is situated on a beautiful campus at Ma Liu Shui, which is north of Sha Tin in the New Territories.

The Hong Kong University of Science & Technology (Map pp58–9; ☎ 2358 6000; www.ust.hk) admitted its first students in 1991, and it is situated at Tai Po Tsai in Clearwater Bay in the New Territories.

The other five universities are based in Kowloon, and include the Hong Kong Polytechnic University (Map p106; ☎ 2766 5111; www.polyu.edu.hk) in Hung Hom, which was set up in 1972.

USEFUL ORGANISATIONS

Hong Kong Consumer Council (☎ 2929 2222; www.consumer.org.hk) Can help with complaints about dishonest shopkeepers and other rip-offs.

Royal Asiatic Society (☎ 2813 7500; www.royalasiaticsociety.org.hk; GPO Box 3864, Central) Organises lectures, field trips of cultural and historical interest and puts out publications.

Royal Geographical Society (☎ 2583 9700; www .rgshk.org.hk; GPO Box 6681, Central) Organises lectures by high-profile local and foreign travellers, as well as hikes and field trips.

World Wide Fund for Nature Hong Kong (WWFHK; ☎ 2526 1011; www.wwf.org.hk; 1 Tramway Path, Central)

VISAS & PASSPORTS

A passport is essential for visiting Hong Kong, and if yours is within six months of expiration, get a new one. If you'll be staying for some time in Hong Kong, it's wise to register with your consulate. This makes the replacement process much simpler if you lose your passport or it is stolen.

Hong Kong residents are required to carry an officially issued identification card at all times (p294). Visitors should carry their passports with them at all times, as the immigration authorities do frequent spot checks to catch illegal workers and those who overstay their visas, and this is the only form of identification acceptable to the Hong Kong police.

The vast majority of travellers, including citizens of Australia, Canada, the EU, Israel, Japan, New Zealand and the USA, are allowed to enter the Hong Kong SAR without a visa and stay for 90 days. Holders of British passports can stay up to 180 days without a visa, but British Dependent Territories and British Overseas citizens not holding a visa are only allowed to remain 90 days. Holders of many African (including South African), South American and Middle Eastern passports do not require visas for visits of 30 days or less.

If you do require a visa, you must apply beforehand at the nearest Chinese consulate or embassy; for addresses and contact information, consult the website www.immd.gov .hk/e html/embassy.htm.

If you plan on visiting mainland China, you must have a visa, and US citizens must apply for their visas prior to crossing the border; for further details, see p287.

Visitors may have to prove they have adequate funds for their stay (a credit card should do the trick) and that they hold an onward or return ticket. Ordinary visas cost $160 (or the equivalent in local currency), while transit visas are $90.

Visitors are not permitted to take up employment, establish any sort of business or enrol as students while visiting on a tourist visa. If you want to work or study, you must apply for an employment or student visa beforehand. It is very hard to change your visa status after you have arrived in Hong Kong. Anyone wishing to stay longer than the visa-free period must apply for a visa before travelling to Hong Kong. For details on applying for a work permit, see p304.

Visa Extensions

In general, visa extensions ($160) are not readily granted unless there are special or extenuating circumstances, such as cancelled flights, illness, registration in a legitimate course of study, legal employment, or marriage to a local.

For more information contact the Hong Kong Immigration Department (Map p74; ☎ 2824 6111; www .immd.gov.hk; 2nd fl, Immigration Tower, 7 Gloucester Rd, Wan Chai; ☻ 8.45am-4.30pm Mon-Fri, 9-11.30am Sat).

VOLUNTEERING

Being small and developed, the scope for volunteering in Hong Kong is limited. Volunteer abroad.com contains a handful of listings for Hong Kong aimed at incoming volunteers. Ho-Sum ('Good Heart'; www.ho-sum.org) lists scores of schemes, most of them more short-term volunteering projects aimed at local residents.

WEIGHTS & MEASURES

Although the international metric system (see the inside front cover) is in official use in Hong Kong, traditional Chinese weights and measures are still common. At local markets, meat, fish and produce are sold by the *léung*, equivalent to 37.8g, and the *gàn* (catty), which is equivalent to about 600g. There are 16 *léung* to the *gàn*. Gold and silver are sold by the *tael*, which is exactly the same as a *léung*.

WOMEN TRAVELLERS

Respect for women is deeply ingrained in Chinese culture. Despite the Confucian principle of the superiority of men, women in Chinese society often call the shots and can wield a tremendous amount of influence at home, in business and in politics.

Hong Kong is a safe city for women, though common-sense caution should be observed, especially at night. Few women – visitors or residents – complain of bad treatment, intimidation or aggression. Having said that, some Chinese men regard Western women as 'easy'. If you are sexually assaulted, call the Hong Kong Rape Hotline (☎ 2375 5322). A useful organisation for women is the Hong Kong Federation of Women (Map p74; ☎ 2833 6131; hkfw.org; Ground fl, 435 Lockhart Rd, Wan Chai).

WORK

Travellers on tourist visas are barred from accepting employment in Hong Kong. It is possible to obtain work 'under the table', but there are stiff penalties for employers who are caught hiring foreigners illegally. Still, to earn extra money many foreigners end up teaching English or doing some other kind of work – translating, modelling, acting in Chinese films, waiting on tables or bartending. These days, few – if any – restaurants or bars will take the risk and hire you if you don't have a Hong Kong ID card (p294).

For professional jobs, registering with Hong Kong personnel agencies or head-hunters is important; check out Jobs DB (www.jobsdb.com /hk). Drake International (Map p67; ☎ 2848 9288; www .drakeintl.com; Room 1308, 13th fl, 9 Queen's Rd, Central) is an international employment agency that often advertises work in Hong Kong. You can always check the classified advertisements in the local English-language newspapers. The Thursday and Saturday editions of the *South China Morning Post* or the Friday edition of the *Hong Kong Standard* are particularly helpful. *HK Magazine* also has a jobs section.

Recruit (www.recruit.com.hk) and *Jiu Jik* (Job Finder; www.jiujik.com) are free job-seeker tabloids available on Wednesdays and Fridays at the majority of MTR stations. There are also the *Job Market Weekly* (www .jobmarket.com.hk) and *Career Times* (www

.careertimes.com.hk), which are for sale at most newsagents.

Work Permits

To work legally here you need to have a work permit. Hong Kong authorities require proof that you have been offered employment, usually in the form of a contract. The prospective employer must show the work you plan to do cannot be performed by a local person. If you're planning on working or studying in Hong Kong, it could be helpful to have copies of transcripts, diplomas, letters of reference and other professional qualifications at hand.

In general, visitors must leave Hong Kong in order to obtain a work permit, returning only when it is ready; unfortunately Macau and the mainland do not qualify as interim destinations. Exceptions can be made, however, especially if the company urgently needs to fill a position. Work visas are generally granted for between one and three years. Extensions should be applied for at least a month before the visa expires.

From overseas, applications for work visas can be made at any Chinese embassy or consulate. In Hong Kong, contact the Hong Kong Immigration Department (Map p74; ☎ 2824 6111; www .immd.gov.hk; 2nd fl, Immigration Tower, 7 Gloucester Rd, Wan Chai; ☺ 8.45am-4.30pm Mon-Fri, 9-11.30am Sat) for information on how to apply.

top picks

- Ruins of the Church of St Paul (p317)
- Monte Fort (p319)
- Avenida da República (p323)
- A-Ma Temple (p323)
- Portuguese and Macanese soul food (p334)
- Taipa House Museum (p327)
- Coloane Village (p331)
- Casinos (p341)

Macau, the first European enclave in Asia – established by the Portuguese and now a Special Administrative Region (SAR) of China – is a cultural two-face with a more laidback and hedonistic streak than its sister SAR of Hong Kong. It is uniquely Chinese, but with an amicable Mediterranean charm.

In the last five years gambling in Macau has taken off like wildfire, drawing millions of Chinese punters to spend money in the only place where casinos are legal in China. It is now commonplace to refer to Macau as the Vegas of the East. Indeed, Macau has long since surpassed its American rival in gambling income. But Macau is much more than casinos. The 450-year Portuguese influence is still vivid: cobbled backstreets, baroque churches, ancient stone fortresses, art deco apartment buildings, and restful parks and gardens are everywhere, intermixed with numerous Chinese temples and shrines along the way. It's a unique fusion of East and West that has been recognised by Unesco, which in 2005 named 30 buildings and squares collectively as the Historic Centre of Macau World Heritage Site.

This arresting clash certainly reveals an impressive history, but Macau is not about spending all its time living on a bygone era. Big-name entertainers not only bring gaming tables to Macau, but also other forms of entertainment and cultural festivals, ambitiously positioning Macau to become Asia's leading arts and conference destination.

Long before the arrival of the city's own Michelin guide, which sparks controversies and gourmet tourism, food was always one of the prime motives for gourmets to make the trip to Macau. Apart from the new fine-dining scenes that have sprung up in big resorts, the unpretentious restaurants that serve hearty and home-style Portuguese and Macanese dishes are still the culinary drawcard.

Macau is just 65km west of Hong Kong, making it the closest getaway for Hong Kong residents. Travel between the two territories has never been easier, with high-speed ferries running about every 15 minutes (as well as frequent helicopter services). With time and patience you will be rewarded with something new at each step and on every visit, but even spending just a night or two will allow you to discover this hybrid city's unique lifestyle, temperament and cuisine that make it so much fun.

BACKGROUND
HISTORY
Early Settlement

Archaeological finds from digs around Hác Sá and Ká Hó Bays on Coloane Island suggest that Macau has been inhabited since Neolithic times (from 4000 BC). Before the arrival of the Portuguese, Macau had a relatively small number of inhabitants, mainly Cantonese-speaking farmers and fisherfolk from Fujian.

The Arrival of the Portuguese

In 1510 and 1511 the Portuguese routed Arab fleets at Goa on the west coast of India and Malacca on the Malay Peninsula. At Malacca they encountered several junks with Chinese captains and crews. Realising that the so-called Chins – about whom Portuguese mariners and explorers had heard reports of

a century earlier – were not a mythical people but natives of 'Cathay' (the land that Marco Polo had visited and written about 2½ centuries earlier), a small party sailed northwards to try to open up trade with China.

The first Portuguese contingent, led by Jorge Álvares, set foot on Chinese soil in 1513 at a place they called Tamaõ, today known as Shangchuan Island, about 80km southwest of the mouth of the Pearl River. However, it wasn't until 1553 that an official basis for trading was set up between the two countries, and the Portuguese were allowed to settle on Shangchuan. The exposed anchorage there forced the Portuguese traders to abandon the island that same year, and they moved to Lampacau, an island closer to the Pearl River estuary.

To the northeast of Lampacau was a small peninsula where the Portuguese had frequently dropped anchor. Known variously as Amagau, Aomen and Macau (see the boxed text, opposite), the peninsula had two natural harbours – an

WHAT'S IN A NAME?

The name Macau is derived from the name of the goddess A-Ma, better known in Hong Kong as Tin Hau. At the south-western tip of Macau Peninsula stands the A-Ma Temple, which dates back to the early 16th century. Many people believe that when the Portuguese first arrived and asked the name of the place, 'A-Ma Gau' (Bay of A-Ma) was what they were told.

According to legend, A-Ma, a poor girl looking for passage to Guangzhou, was turned away by wealthy junk owners. Instead, a poor fisherman took her on board; shortly afterwards a storm blew up, wrecking all the junks but leaving the fishing boat unscathed. When it returned to the Inner Harbour, A-Ma walked to the top of nearby Barra Hill and, in a glowing aura of light, ascended to heaven. The fisherman built a temple on the spot where they had landed (which was, in fact, on the water's edge until land reclamation early in the last century set it further inland).

In modern Cantonese, Macau is Ou Mun (Aomen in Mandarin), meaning Gateway of the Bay.

inner one on the Qianshan waterway facing the mainland, and an outer one in a bay on the Pearl River – and two sheltered islands located to the south. In 1557 officials at Guangzhou let the Portuguese build temporary shelters on the peninsula in exchange for customs dues and rent. The Portuguese also agreed to rid the area of the pirates that were endemic at the time.

A Trading Powerhouse

Macau grew rapidly as a trading centre, largely due to the fact that Chinese merchants were forbidden to leave the country by imperial decree. Acting as agents for the Chinese merchants, Portuguese traders took Chinese goods to Goa and exchanged them for cotton and textiles. The cloth was then taken to Malacca, where it was traded for spices and sandalwood. The Portuguese would then carry on to Nagasaki in Japan, where the cargo from Malacca was exchanged for Japanese silver, swords, lacquerware and fans that would be traded in Macau for more Chinese goods.

During the late 16th century the Portuguese in Macau were at the forefront of all international commerce between China and Japan. Macau's growing status was evidenced when the Holy See established the bishopric of Macau in 1576, which included both China and Japan under its jurisdiction. By 1586 Macau was important enough for the Portuguese Crown to confer upon it the status of a city: Cidade de Nome de Deus (City of the Name of God).

The Golden Years

By the beginning of the 17th century, Macau supported several thousand permanent residents, including about 900 Portuguese. The rest were Christian converts from Malacca and Japan and a large number of slaves from colonial outposts in Africa, India and the Malay Peninsula. Many Chinese had moved to Macau from across the border, and they worked there as traders, craftspeople, hawkers, labourers and coolies; by the close of the century, their numbers had reached about 40,000.

Besides trading, Macau had also become a centre of Christianity in Asia. Priests and missionaries accompanied Portuguese ships, although the interests of traders and missionaries were frequently in conflict.

Among the earliest missionaries was Francis Xavier (later canonised) of the Jesuit order, who spent two years (1549 to 1551) in Japan attempting to convert the local population before turning his attention to China. He was stalled by the Portuguese, who feared the consequences of his meddling in Chinese affairs, but made it as far as Tamaõ, where he developed a fever and died in December 1552 at the age of 46.

The Portuguese who stayed in Macau, along with their Macanese descendants, created a home away from home. Their luxurious villas overlooking the Praia Grande, now the enclosed Baia da Praia, and splendid baroque churches were paid for with the wealth generated by their monopoly on trade with China and Japan. These buildings included the Jesuit Church of Madre de Deus (later the Church of St Paul, p317), hailed as the greatest monument to Christianity in the Far East when it was dedicated in 1602.

Portuguese Decline

Portugal's decline as an imperial power came as quickly as its rise. In 1580 Spanish armies occupied Portugal and for more than 60 years three Spanish kings ruled over the country and its empire. In the early years of the 17th century, the Dutch, embroiled in the Thirty

Years' War with Spain, moved to seize the rich Portuguese enclaves of Macau, Nagasaki and Malacca. In June 1622 some 13 Dutch warships carrying 1300 men attacked Macau, but retreated when a shell fired by a Jesuit priest from one of the cannons on Monte Fort hit a stock of gunpowder and blew the Hollanders out of the water.

The Japanese soon became suspicious of Portuguese and Spanish intentions and closed its doors to foreign trade in 1639. Two years later, Dutch harassment of Portuguese commerce and trading interests ended with the capture of Malacca. The Portuguese would no longer be able to provide the Chinese with the Japanese silver needed for their silk and porcelain or with spices from the Malay Peninsula.

A Change of Status

A flood of refugees unleashed on Macau when the Ming dynasty was overthrown in 1644. In 1684 the most corrupt of the new Manchu rulers, the so-called *hoppo* (*hói poi* in Cantonese) – the customs superintendent who held the monopoly on trade with foreigners – set up an office in the Inner Harbour.

At the same time religious infighting weakened the status of Macau as a Christian centre. In what became known as the Rites Controversy, the Jesuits maintained that central aspects of Chinese belief – such as ancestor worship and Confucianism – were not incompatible with the Christian faith. The Dominicans and Franciscans, equally well represented in Macau, disagreed. It took an edict by Pope Clement XI in 1715 condemning the rites as idolatrous to settle the matter and this stopped further missionary expansion into China.

In the mid-18th century Chinese authorities created the *cohong*, a mercantile monopoly based in Guangzhou that dealt with foreign trade. Numerous restrictions were placed on Western traders, including limitations on the amount of time they could reside in Guangzhou. Macau in effect became an outpost for all European traders in China, a position it held until the British took possession of Hong Kong in 1841.

Until the mid-19th century the history of Macau was a long series of incidents involving the Portuguese, Chinese and British, as the Portuguese attempted to maintain a hold on the territory. But as time progressed and the troublesome British wrested concession after concession out of China, the Portuguese grew bolder.

The Treaty of Nanking (1842) ceded the island of Hong Kong in perpetuity to the British; the Treaty of Tientsin (1860) gave them Kowloon on the same terms. The Portuguese felt that they, too, should take advantage of China's weakness and push for sovereignty over the territory they had occupied for three centuries. Negotiations began in 1862, although it was not until 1887 that a treaty was signed in which China effectively recognised Portuguese sovereignty over Macau forever.

With the advent of the steamship, there were fewer trans-shipments from Chinese ports through Macau and more direct transactions between the mainland and Hong Kong. Macau's future economy was greatly assisted by the legalisation of gambling in the 1850s, but by the close of the 19th century the ascent of the British colony and the decline of the Portuguese territory had become irreversible.

Macau in the 20th Century

By the turn of the 20th century Macau was little more than an impoverished backwater, its glory days all but forgotten. It did, however, continue to serve as a haven for Chinese refugees fleeing war, famine and political oppression. Among them was Sun Yat-sen, founder of the Republic of China, who lived in Macau before the 1911 revolution. Even the birth of the Portuguese republic in 1910 had little effect on the sleepy outpost.

In the mid-1920s large numbers of Chinese immigrants doubled the number of Macau residents to 160,000. A steady stream of refugees from the Sino-Japanese War meant that by 1939 the population had reached 245,000. During WWII many people from Hong Kong and China, as well as Asian-based Europeans, took refuge in Macau, as the Japanese respected Portugal's neutrality; by 1943 the population stood at 500,000. There was another influx of Chinese refugees in 1949 when the Communists took power in China. Macau was made an overseas province of Portugal in 1951, and from 1978 until about 1981 it was a haven for Vietnamese boat people.

Macau's last great upset occurred in 1966 and 1967, when China's Cultural Revolution spilled over into the territory. Macau was stormed by Red Guards, and violent riots resulted in some of them being shot and killed by Portuguese troops. The government proposed that Portugal abandon Macau forever, but China refused to hear of it, fearing the loss of foreign trade through the colony.

In 1974 a revolution restored democracy in Portugal and the new left-wing government began to divest Portugal of the last remnants of its empire, including Mozambique and Angola in Africa and East Timor in the Indonesian archipelago. Powerbrokers in Lisbon tried to return Macau to China as well, but the word from Beijing was that China wished Macau to remain as it was – at least for the time being.

The End of Portuguese Rule

Once the Joint Declaration over Hong Kong had been signed by Britain and China in 1984, the latter turned its attentions to the future of Macau. Talks began in 1986 and an agreement was signed the following April.

Under the so-called Sino-Portuguese Pact, Macau would become a Special Administrative Region of China. The date set was 20 December 1999, ending 442 years of Portuguese rule. Like Hong Kong, the Macau SAR would enjoy a 'high degree of autonomy' for 50 years in all matters except defence and foreign affairs, under the slogan 'one country, two systems'.

The basic law for Macau differed from its Hong Kong equivalent in that holders of foreign passports were not excluded from holding high-level posts in the post-handover administration (apart from the position of chief executive). There was also no stipulation that China would station troops of the People's Liberation Army (PLA) in Macau after the return of the territory to China, though it did just that.

Macau had directly elected some of the members of its Legislative Assembly since the assembly's founding in 1976, but unlike Hong Kong it did not rush through proposals to widen the franchise or speed up democratisation at the last minute. The existing legislature continued to serve throughout the handover, unlike that in the British territory.

But not everything went so smoothly. Macau residents were pleased when Portugal gave everyone born in Macau the right to a Portuguese passport, allowing them to live anywhere in the EU – something the UK had refused Hong Kong Chinese people. However, not everyone in Macau benefited from Portugal's move. Until 1975 any Chinese refugee reaching Macau could obtain residency. As a result, as much as 70% of the population had not actually been born in Macau and therefore didn't qualify for Portuguese citizenship.

The years 1996 to 1998 were a grim showdown for Macau and its all-important tourism industry – an escalating number of gangland killings took place. Some 40 people were killed as senior Triad leaders jostled for control of the lucrative gambling rackets, and one international hotel was raked with AK-47 gunfire. On 8 May 1998 alone, 14 cars and motorcycles and a couple of shops were engulfed in flames when Triad members, protesting the arrest of their boss, Wan Kwok 'Broken Tooth' Koi, let off a string of firebombs. The violence scared tourists off in a big way; arrivals fell by some 36% in August 1997.

As the handover approached, China put pressure on Portugal to clean up its act. The government issued a new anti-Triad law calling for a lengthy prison term for anyone found to be a senior leader. Koi was arrested and sentenced to 15 years, and many other Triad members fled overseas.

The Handover & Macau after 1999

The handover ceremony on 20 December 1999 was as stage-managed as the one held 2½ years earlier in Hong Kong. The following day 500 PLA soldiers drove down from Zhuhai. There are now an estimated 10,000 troops stationed here, though they are not responsible for internal security.

The most significant change since 1999 has been the liberalisation of casino licences in 2001, when the rule of Stanley Ho, previously Macau's sole casino magnate, came to an end. Following an invasion of mostly American casinos, in 2006 Macau supplanted Las Vegas as the world's gambling capital, bringing about a drastic socio-economic shift. The casino industry is now the primary driver of economic activity (see p311). Demand for service labour in the expanding casino industry initially caused a labour shortage – and associated degradation of services – across many sectors elsewhere in Macau. Unfortunately, the boom didn't benefit some local workers, as developers usually hired cheap illegal labourers for construction. A labour protest on May Day in 2007 that resulted in brutal police suppression reflected the undercurrents of dissatisfaction in the city.

Recently, though, the boom has stalled. The global credit crisis and travel restrictions imposed by China to mainland visitors in 2008 have dealt a double blow to Macau's economy, knocking it off track from its galloping growth.

The casino boom also had a corrupting influence on the city. The notorious Ao Man Long graft scandal, in which the former transportation minister was convicted of taking 800 million patacas in bribes from a number of public-works projects, is believed to be just the tip of the iceberg.

Macau's image has been further tarnished by the enactment of the controversial national security legislation and the barring of democratic activists and politicians from entering the territory, suggesting a gradual 'mainlandisation' is underway.

In the past decade or so, Macau has launched a series of enormous public works and land-reclamation projects. These include a US$11.8 billion airport built in 1995, and Cotai – a reclaimed area almost the size of Taipa with a six-lane highway. But the most ambitious project by far is the proposed 29km-long, US$5.47 billion, six-lane cross-delta bridge linking Macau and Zhuhai with Hong Kong via Tai O on Lantau Island. The construction is expected to commence in 2010. The Y-shaped bridge would reduce the present four-hour journey by car between Zhuhai and Hong Kong to 20 minutes. Other projects include an ocean theme park in northwestern Taipa and a new campus for the University of Macau on Zhuhai's Hengqin Island, Macau's future concession.

ARTS
Painting

Macau can lay claim to having spawned or influenced a number of artists. Their work is on display in the Gallery of Historical Pictures of the Macau Museum of Art (p322).

The most important Western artist to have lived in Macau was George Chinnery (see the boxed text, below). Other influential European painters who spent time in Macau include the Scottish physician Thomas Watson (1815–60), who was a student of Chinnery and lived in Macau from 1845 to 1856; Frenchman Auguste Borget (1808–77), who spent some 10 months in 1838 and 1839 painting Macau's waterfront and churches; and watercolourist Marciano António Baptista (1856–1930), who was born in Macau.

Guan Qiaochang (1825–60), another of Chinnery's pupils, was a Chinese artist who painted in the Western style and worked under the name Lamqua. His oil portraits of mandarins and other Chinese worthies are particularly fine.

Two of the best galleries for viewing contemporary Macau and other art are Tap Seac Gallery (p325) and Ox Warehouse (p325). The emerging art hubs in St Lazarus District (p325) are also worth a visit.

Architecture

Portuguese architectural styles reflect a variety of forms, from Romanesque and Gothic through to baroque and neoclassical, and these are best seen in Macau's churches. Two excellent examples are the Chapel of St Joseph Seminary (p321), completed in 1758, and the Church of St Dominic (p320), a 17th-century replacement of a chapel built in the 1590s.

Civic buildings worth close inspection are the Leal Senado (p317), erected in 1784 but rebuilt after it was damaged by a typhoon

---

GEORGE CHINNERY: CHRONICLER OF MACAU

Though George Chinnery may enjoy little more than footnote status in the history of world art, as a chronicler of his own world (colonial Macau) and his times (the early 19th century) he is without peer. In the absence of photography, taipans ('big bosses' of large companies) and mandarins turned to trade art (commissioned portraiture), and Chinnery was the master of the genre. Today he is known less for his formal portraits and paintings of factory buildings and clipper ships than for his landscapes and sometimes fragmentary sketches of everyday life.

Chinnery was born in London in 1774 and studied at the Royal Academy of Arts before turning his hand to portrait painting in Dublin. He sailed for India in 1802 and spent the next 23 years in Madras and Calcutta, where he earned substantial sums (up to UK£500 a month) as a popular portrait painter to British colonial society and spent most of it on his opium addiction. He fled to Macau in 1825 to escape spiralling debts, Calcutta's 'cranky formality' and his wife (whom he described as 'the ugliest woman I ever saw in my life'), and took up residence at 8 Rua de Inácio Baptista (Map p318), just south of the Church of St Lawrence. He lived at this address until his death from stroke in 1852.

Although Chinnery is sometimes 'claimed' by Hong Kong (the Mandarin Oriental hotel even has a bar named after him), he visited the colony only once, during the hot summer of 1846. Although he was unwell and did not like it very much, he managed to execute some vivid sketches of the place.

a century later; and the Government House (p321), dating from 1849.

Macau has seen a surge of skyscrapers go up, changing its skyline drastically. The tallest one is Macau Tower (p323), a 338m-tall copy of the Sky Tower in Auckland, New Zealand. The landmark Grand Lisboa Casino (p342), an ugly, 52-storey, lotus-shaped golden structure, is the second tallest and visible even from Coloane.

The feverish construction in Macau has also given rise to a public outcry for heritage conservation, especially as the Unesco-protected Guia Lighthouse (p324) is almost overshadowed by skyscrapers in the NAPE area.

Literature

Macau's home-grown writers are not insignificant; you can sample their work at the Macau Museum (p320).

First and foremost in literature was Portugal's national poet, Luís de Camões (1524–80), who was banished from Portugal to Goa and then apparently went to Macau in the 16th century. He is said to have written part of his epic poem *Os Lusiadas* (The Lusiads), which recounts the 15th-century voyage of Vasco da Gama to India, during the two years he lived in the enclave, but there is no firm evidence that he was ever in Macau.

The teacher, judge, opium addict and Symbolist poet Camilio de Almeida Pessanha (1867–1926), author of such works as *Clepsidra*, lived in Macau for the last 30 years of his life; he is buried in the Cemetery of St Michael the Archangel (p324).

Local-born writers include Henrique de Senna Fernandes (1923–), author of the *Nam Wan* collection of short stories and the novel *The Bewitching Braid;* and the much-beloved Macanese writer José dos Santos Ferreira (1919–93), also known as Adé, who wrote in *patuá*, a dialect forging Portuguese and a melange of Southeast Asian languages, as well as Cantonese. A statue in honour of Adé, who wrote plays, operettas and poems, stands in the Jardim des Artes along Avenida da Amizade, opposite the Landmark Macau building, and in the Macau Museum you can listen to a recording of him reading his poetry.

CULTURE

Traditional culture among the Chinese of Macau is almost indistinguishable from that of Hong Kong. However, the Portuguese

POPULATION & PEOPLE

Macau's population is approximately 549,200, with an annual growth rate of 2%. Population density is more than 18,428 people per sq km. While the northern part of the peninsula is one of the most densely populated areas, Coloane Island has remained essentially rural, but Taipa is rapidly becoming an urban extension of Macau Peninsula.

The population is about 95% Chinese. Fewer than 2% of Macau residents are Portuguese and the rest are Macanese (people of mixed Portuguese, Asian and/or African blood) or Filipino.

minority has a vastly different culture that has evolved under a number of different influences through the centuries. Colonial Portuguese architecture survives throughout Macau, and Portuguese food is found in abundance.

Macanese culture is different again. Unlike the Portuguese and Chinese communities elsewhere in the world, the Macanese community – a tiny community of the descendents of intermarriages between Portuguese and Asians – is very distinct and exists almost solely in Macau. The Macanese have a unique cuisine, set of festivals and traditions, and even their own dialect called *patuá*. The *do* (traditional woman's outfit) has long disappeared, though you may catch a glimpse of it at certain festivals.

Portuguese and Chinese – Cantonese being the more widely spoken dialect – are both official languages of Macau. For key phrases, see p356.

For the vast majority of Macau Chinese people, Taoism and Buddhism are the dominant religions. Four-and-a-half centuries of Portuguese Christian rule left its mark, however, and the Roman Catholic Church is very strong in Macau, with an estimated 30,000 adherents (about 6% of the population). Macau consists of a single diocese, directly responsible to Rome.

ECONOMY

Tourism and gambling still drive Macau's economy, and the latter remains Macau's major cash cow despite a revenue slump in 2008. Today, gambling concessions contribute some 75% of government revenue through betting tax.

Tourism usually generates almost half of Macau's GDP, and about a third of the labour

MACAU CALENDAR

You're likely to find a festival or some special event taking place in Macau no matter what time of the year you visit. Chinese New Year (see the boxed text, p16) is chaotic in Macau, and hotel rooms are a prized commodity during this period. Still, it's a colourful time to visit, as the city literally explodes with bangers and fireworks – they're legal here – and the streets are filled with a carnival atmosphere. The Macau Formula 3 Grand Prix (opposite) is also a peak time for visitors to Macau. The website of the Macau Government Tourist Office (MGTO; www.macautourism.gov.mo) has a list of events that take place in Macau. For dates of Macau's public holidays, check out p353. For information on festivals and events that are celebrated both here and in Hong Kong, have a look at p15.

February/March

Procession of the Passion of Our Lord A 400-year-old tradition on the first Saturday of Lent in which a colourful procession bears a statue of Jesus Christ from Macau's Church of St Augustine to Macau Cathedral, where it spends the night and is carried back the following day.

April/May

A-Ma Festival This festival honours Tin Hau (known here as A-Ma), the patron of fisherfolk and one of the territory's most popular goddesses. The best place to see the festival is at the A-Ma Temple in the Inner Harbour. This festival will fall on 6 May in 2010, 25 April in 2011 and 13 April in 2012.

Birthday of the Lord Buddha/Feast of the Drunken Dragon Buddha's statue is taken from monasteries and temples around Macau and ceremoniously bathed in scented water on this day. The day also marks the Feast of the Drunken Dragon, which features dancing dragons in the streets of the Inner Harbour area along with a lot of legless merrymakers enjoying the celebrations. Festivities will take place on 21 May in 2010, on 10 May in 2011 and on 28 April in 2012.

Procession of our Lady of Fatima The procession goes from Macau Cathedral to the Chapel of Our Lady of Penha to commemorate a series of apparitions by the Virgin Mary to three peasant children at Fatima in Portugal in 1917. This falls on 13 May each year.

Macau Arts Festival (www.icm.gov.mo) Macau's red-letter arts event kicks off the cultural year with music, drama and dance from both Asia and the West.

---

force works in some aspect of it. In 2008 Macau welcomed some 22 million tourists and visitors, a decrease of 15.1% from the previous year, owing to China's travel curbs. But visitors from the mainland still accounted for 51% of total arrivals, with most of the balance coming from Hong Kong, Taiwan, Japan and the USA. As a result of this phenomenal boost, Macau's economy expanded a record 13.2% in 2008.

Macau has some light industries, such as textile, garment, toy and fireworks production, but factories have slowed down and many companies have moved across the border. Unemployment in Macau is currently around 3.3%.

GOVERNMENT & POLITICS

The executive branch of the Macau SAR government is led by the chief executive, who is chosen by an electoral college made up of 200 local representatives. Fernando Tsui, the sole candidate for Macau's second chief executive, was 'elected' to a five-year term of office in 2009.

The Legislative Assembly, which sits in its own purpose-built assembly hall on reclaimed land in the Nam Van Lakes area, now permanently consists of 29 members, 12 of whom are directly elected in geographical constituencies, 10 chosen by interest groups and seven appointed by the chief executive.

Like Hong Kong, Macau has primary courts, intermediate courts and a Court of Final Appeal.

NEIGHBOURHOODS

Tiny Macau is amazingly packed with many important cultural and historical sights, including eight squares and 22 historic buildings that have collectively been named the Historic Centre of Macau World Heritage Site by Unesco. The best way to see the city and to feel its uniqueness is to stroll in the narrow

June

Dragon Boat Festival This festival is also known as Tuen Ng (Double Fifth), as it falls on the fifth day of the fifth moon. It commemorates the death of Qu Yuan, a poet-statesman of the 3rd century BC who hurled himself into the Mi Lo River in Hunan province to protest against a corrupt government; dragon-boat races take place and traditional rice dumplings are eaten in memory of the event. The festival will fall on 16 June in 2010, 6 June in 2011 and 23 June in 2012.

Macau Lotus Flower Festival The symbol of Macau is the focus of this festival, which sees lotuses blossoming in parks and gardens throughout Macau.

July

FIVB Women's Volleyball Grand Prix (www.sport.gov.mo) This is one of the most important women's volleyball tournaments in the region.

September/October

Macau International Fireworks Display Contest This event, the largest of its kind in the world, adds a splash of colour to the Macau night sky in autumn.

Macau Open Golf Tournament (www.sport.gov.mo) Part of the Asian PGA Tour, this event is held at the Macau Golf & Country Club on Coloane and attracts the region's best golfers.

October/November

Macau International Music Festival (www.icm.gov.mo) This two-week festival is a heady mix of opera, musicals, visiting orchestras and other musical events.

Macau Formula 3 Grand Prix (www.macau.grandprix.gov.mo) Around 30 national championship drivers compete to take the chequered flag in Macau's premier sporting event. The Grand Prix is held in the third week of November.

December

Macau International Marathon (www.sport.gov.mo) Like its Hong Kong counterpart, this event, which takes place on the first Sunday in December, also includes a half-marathon.

alleys and squares. Pick up the excellent series of pamphlets produced by the Macau Government Tourist Office (MGTO; p354) before you set off.

Macau is divided into three main sections: the Macau Peninsula, which is attached to mainland China to the north; the middle island of Taipa, directly south of the peninsula and linked to it by the 2.5km-long Ponte Governador Nobre de Carvalho (Macau–Taipa Bridge), the 4.5km-long Ponte da Amizade (Friendship Bridge) and the 2.2km-long covered, typhoon-proof Sai Van Bridge; and Coloane Island, which is south of Taipa and connected to it by Cotai, a recent massive land-reclamation project.

ORGANISED TOURS

Tours booked on the ground in Macau are generally much better value than those booked in Hong Kong, though the latter include transportation to and from Macau.

Tours from Hong Kong are usually one-day whirlwind tours, departing for Macau in the morning and returning to Hong Kong on the same evening. Gray Line (☎ in Hong Kong 01-2368 7111; www.grayline.com.hk) offers such a tour for HK$690/720 on weekdays/weekends.

Quality Tours organised by the MGTO and tendered to agents such as Gray Line (Map p318; ☎ 2833 6611; Rua do Campo; adult/child under 10yr incl admission to museum & Macau Tower MOP$350/300; ⏱ 9.30am-6.30pm Mon-Sat) take around 6½ hours.

The Tour Machine, run by Avis Rent A Car (Map pp314–15; ☎ 2833 6789; www.avis.com.mo; Room 1022, Ground fl, Macau ferry terminal; adult/child under 12yr MOP$150/80; ⏱ 8am-7pm), is a replica 1920s-style English bus that seats nine people and runs on fixed routes in about two hours past some of Macau's most important sights. You're allowed to disembark, stretch your legs and take photos along the way. There are two departures a day (11am and 3pm) from the Macau ferry terminal.

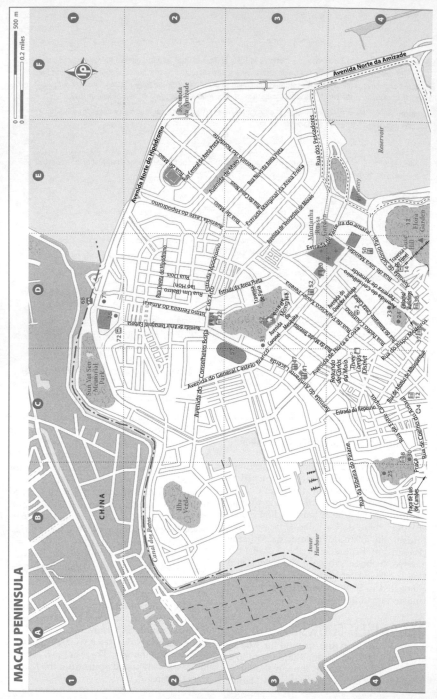

MACAU PENINSULA

CHINA

Canal dos Patos

Ilha Verde

Sun Yat Sen Memorial Park

Inner Harbour

Avenida de Artur Tamagnini Barbosa

Avenida do Conselheiro Borja

Avenida do General Castelo Branco

Avenida do Almirante Lacerda

Rua da Ribeira do Patane

Praça de Luis de Camões

Avenida Norte do Hipódromo

Avenida Leste do Hipódromo

Avenida de Venceslau de Morais

Estrada Marginal da Areia Preta

Rua Nova da Areia Preta

Avenida de Maio

Rua Central da Areia Preta

Avenida do Hipódromo

Avenida do Nordeste

Rotunda do Amizade

Avenida Norte da Amizade

Rua dos Pescadores

Reservoir

Cemetery

Flora Garden

Montanha Russa Garden

Estrada de Ferreira do Amaral

Travessa de Paria

Estrada da Areia Preta

Estrada do Hipódromo

Rua Direita do Hipódromo

Rua Um (Bairro Iao Hon)

Rua Dois

Avenida de Sidónio Ferreira do Amaral

Rua de Francisco Xavier Pereira

Avenida do Coronel Mesquita

Rua de Pedro Coutinho

Rua do Ouvidor Arriaga

Rua de Manuel Dos Reis

Avenida de Horta e Costa

Rotunda de Carlos da Maia

Three Lamps District

Estrada do Repouso

Rua do Bispo Medeiros

Rua de Manduco de Albuquerque

Rua de Coelho do Amaral

Estrada do Arco

Avenida de Almeida Ribeiro

Avenida de Sílvia Mendes

Avenida do Conselheiro Ferreira de Almeida

Cathedral Buildings

500 m

0.2 miles

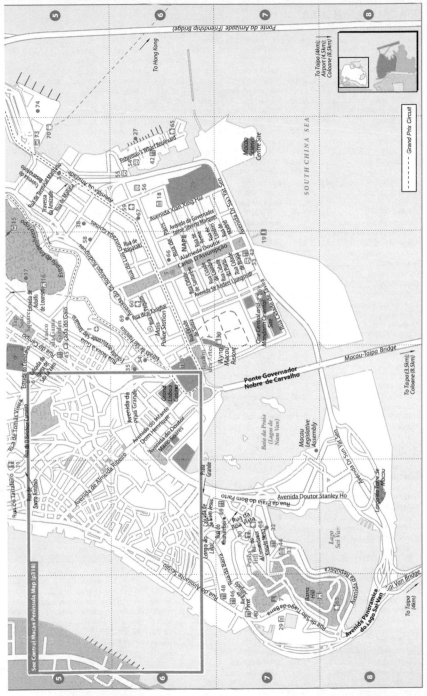

SOUTH CHINA SEA

Ponte da Amizade (Friendship Bridge)

To Hong Kong

To Taipa (4km);
Airport (4.5km);
Coloane (8.5km)

- - - - Grand Prix Circuit

Macau Science
Centre Site

Fisherman's Wharf Boulevard

Avenida Xian Xing Hai

Avenida do Governador
Jaime Silverio Marques

NAPE

Alameda Doutor
Carlos D'Assumpção

Avenida Sir Anders Ljungstedt

One Central and
Mandarin Oriental
Site

Wynn
Macau
Resort

Jardim
das Artes

Police Station

Macau-Taipa Bridge

To Taipa (3.5km);
Coloane (8.5km)

Ponte Governador
Nobre de Carvalho

Grand
Lisboa
Casino

Avenida da
Praia Grande

Avenida do Infante
Dom Henrique

Avenida do Doutor
Mario Soares

Baía da Praia
Lagoa de
Nam Van

Macau
Legislative
Assembly

Avenida da Praia do Bom Parto

Praia
Grande

See Central (Macau Peninsula Map (p318)

Estrada do Cemitério

Rua de Tomás Vieira

Rua de Pedro Coutinho

Ruína de
Santo António

Avenida de Almeida Ribeiro

Praça Tarrafeiro

Largo do
Lilau

Rua Central

Rua da
Boa Vista

Avenida Doutor Stanley Ho

Lago Sai Van

Lago
Sai Van

Barra
Hill

Avenida da Republica

Rua de São Tiago da Barra

Avenida Panorâmica
do Lago Sai Van

To Taipa
(4km)

Sai Van Bridge

MACAU PENINSULA

INFORMATION
Bloom .... (see 6)
Conde Saõ Januário Central
  Hospital 山頂醫院 1 D5
CTM Main Office
  澳門電訊總店 2 D4
Immigration Department
  澳門入境處 3 E5
Kiang Wu Hospital 鏡湖醫院 4 C4
MGTO Branch
  澳門旅遊諮詢處 ....(see 70)
MGTO Branch
  澳門旅遊諮詢處 ....(see 16)
Post Office 郵局 ....(see 70)
Unesco Internet Café
  澳門教科文中心國際互聯網
  咖啡廊 5 D6

SIGHTS   (pp317-26)
Albergue da Santa Casa da
  Misericórdia (Old Ladies'
  House) 仁慈堂婆仔屋 6 C5
A-Ma Temple 媽閣廟 7 A7
Avis Rent A Car ....(see 70)
Bishop's Palace 主教府 ....(see 10)
Casa Garden
  東方基金會會址 8 C4
Cemetery of St Michael the
  Archangel 西洋墳場 9 C5
Chapel of Our Lady of Guia
  聖母雪地殿聖堂 ....(see 16)
Chapel of Our Lady of Penha
  主教山小教堂 10 B7
Chapel of St Michael
  聖彌額爾小堂 ....(see 9)
Church of St Anthony
  聖安多尼教堂 11 B5
Fire Services Museum
  消防博物館 12 C4
Flora Garden 二龍喉公園 13 E4
Grand Prix Museum
  大賽車博物館 ....(see 38)
Guia Cable Car Lower
  Terminus 東望洋纜車 14 D4
Guia Cable Car Upper
  Terminus 纜車站 15 E5
Guia Fort 東望洋松山燈塔 16 D5
Guia Hill Air Raid Shelter
  防空洞 17 D5
Guia Lighthouse 松山燈塔 ....(see 16)
Handover of Macau Gifts
  Museum
  澳門回歸賀禮陳列館 18 E6
Kun Iam Statue &
  Ecumenical Centre 觀音像 ...19 D7
Kun Iam Temple 觀音堂 20 D3
Lin Fung Temple 蓮峰廟 21 D2
Lin Zexu Memorial Hall
  林則徐紀念館 22 D2
Lou Lim Ioc Garden
  盧廉若公園 23 D4
Lou Lim Ioc Garden Pavilion
  盧廉若公園 24 D4
Luís de Camões Garden &
  Grotto 白鴿巢公園 25 B4

Macau Convention &
  Entertainment Centre
  澳門旅遊塔會展及娛樂
  中心 .... (see 28)
Macau Cultural Centre
  澳門文化中心 26 E6
Macau Fisherman's
  Wharf 漁人碼頭 27 E6
Macau Museum of Art
  澳門藝術博物館 ....(see 26)
Macau Security Forces
  Museum
  澳門保安部隊博物館 ....(see 34)
Macau Tea Culture House
  澳門茶文化館 ....(see 24)
Macau Tower
  澳門旅遊塔 28 B8
Macau Wine Museum
  葡萄酒博物館 ....(see 38)
Maritime Museum
  海事博物館 29 A7
MGTO Ferry Terminal
  Branch
  澳門旅遊局諮詢處 ....(see 70)
Old Protestant Cemetery
  基督教墳場 30 C4
Oriental Foundation
  東方基金會 ....(see 8)
Ox Warehouse 牛房倉庫 31 D3
Residence of the
  Portuguese Consul
  General 葡國領事官邸 32 B7
Santa Sancha Palace
  禮賓府 33 B7
St Francis Barracks
  加思欄炮台 34 C6
St Francis Garden
  加思欄花園 35 C6
Sun Yat Sen Memorial
  Home 澳門國父紀念館 36 D4
Tap Seac Gallery
  塔石藝文館 37 D4
Tourist Activities Centre
  旅遊活動中心 38 E5

SHOPPING   (pp333-4)
Wynn Macau 永利門 39 D7

EATING   (pp334-8)
A Lorcha 船屋 40 A7
Almirante Lacerda City
  Market 紅市場 41 C3
Camões 賈梅士葡國餐廳 42 E6
Fat Siu Lau 2 佛笑樓 43 D7
Henri's Galley
  美心亨利餐廳 44 B7
Il Teatro 帝雅廷 ....(see 39)
La Paloma 芭朗瑪餐廳 ....(see 63)
Lai Kei 禮記 45 C5
Litoral 海灣餐廳 46 A7
Locanda ....(see 6)
Long Wa 龍華茶樓 47 C3
O Porto Interior
  內港餐廳 48 A7
Portas Do Sol 葡京日麗 ....(see 51)

Praia Grande
  美麗灣葡式餐廳 49 B7
Riquexó 利多自助餐廳 50 D4
Robuchon a Galera 51 C6
Rossio 盛事 ....(see 61)
Serrdura 沙厘娜 52 D3
Wing Lei 永利軒 ....(see 39)

ENTERTAINMENT   (pp341-5)
Aba Bar ....(see 61)
Casablanca Café 53 D7
Cinnebar 霞 ....(see 39)
DD3 ....54 E6
Fashion Club 55 E6
MGM Grand Casino
  澳門美高梅金殿 ....(see 61)
Russian Room 魚子屋 ....(see 61)
Sands Macau
  金沙娛樂場 56 E6
Veuve Clicquot Lounge
  凱歌吧 ....(see 61)
Wynn Macau Casino
  永利娛樂場 ....(see 39)

SPORTS & ACTIVITIES   (pp345-6)
Canidrome 逸園狗場 57 C3
Macau Sports Institute
  澳門體育學院 58 D5

SLEEPING   (pp347-8)
Grand Lapa Hotel
  金麗華酒店 59 E6
Metro Park Hotel
  維景酒店 60 D6
MGM Grand Macau
  澳門美高梅金殿 61 D7
Pousada de Mong Há
  望廈賓館 62 D3
Pousada de Saõ Tiago
  聖地牙哥酒店 63 A8
Riviera Hotel Macau
  濠璟酒店 64 B7
Rocks Hotel 萊斯酒店 65 E6
Wynn Macau 永利澳門 ....(see 39)

TRANSPORT   (pp350-2)
Air Macau 澳門航空 66 D6
Avis Rent A Car ....(see 70)
Avis Rent A Car 67 E6
Border Gate (Portas de
  Cerco) 關閘 68 D1
China Travel Service
  中旅社 69 D6
Ferry Terminal
  澳門外港碼頭 70 E5
Free casino shuttle buses 71 D1
Free casino shuttle buses 72 D1
Free casino shuttle buses 73 E5
Happy Rent A Car ....(see 70)
Heliport 直升機 74 F5
Public bus and minibus
  terminal
  關閘巴士及小巴總站 75 D1

Cotai Strip Travel (Map p328; ☎ 8118 2930; www.vene
tianmacao.com; Shop 1028, Venetian Macao Resort Hotel, Estrada da Baía de Nossa Senhora da Esperança; adult/child under
11yr/infant MOP$250/200/free; ☼ 9am-9pm) runs a daily
tour to Taipa and Coloane Villages that begins
at 9.15am and finishes at 1pm.

MACAU PENINSULA

You'll find the lion's share of Macau's museums, churches, gardens, old cemeteries and
important colonial buildings on the peninsula. In 2005, Unesco recognised this wealth
by adding the Historic Centre of Macau, comprising 30 sites, to its World Heritage list.
If you're after more active pursuits, such as
cycling, hiking and swimming, head for the
islands (p345).

Central Macau Peninsula

Avenida de Almeida Ribeiro – called San Ma
Lo (New St) in Cantonese, together with its
southern extension, Avenida do Infante Dom
Henrique – is the peninsula's main thoroughfare. It effectively divides the narrow southern
peninsula from central and northern Macau.
In the centre of this long thoroughfare is the
cobbled square, Largo do Senado. Bus 3 brings
you to the city centre. The free casino shuttle to
Grand Lisboa is a viable alternative. The sights
are within walking distance from the casino.

RUINS OF THE CHURCH OF ST PAUL
Map p318
**Ruinas de Igreja de São Paulo; Travessa de São
Paulo; admission free**
The most treasured icon in Macau, the
facade and stairway are all that remain of
this early-17th-century Jesuit church, called
Tai Sam Ba in Cantonese. With its statues,
portals and engravings that effectively
make up a 'sermon in stone' and a *Biblia
pauperum* (Bible of the poor), the church
was one of the greatest monuments to
Christianity in Asia, intended to help the
illiterate understand the Passion of Christ
and the lives of the saints.

The church was designed by an Italian
Jesuit and completed by early Japanese
Christian exiles and Chinese craftsmen in
1602. It was abandoned after the expul-
sion of the Jesuits in 1762 and a military
battalion was stationed here. In 1835 a
fire erupted in the kitchen of the barracks,
destroying everything, except what you see
today.

At the top is a dove, representing the
Holy Spirit, surrounded by stone carvings
of the sun, moon and stars. Beneath the
Holy Spirit is a statue of the infant Jesus
surrounded by stone carvings of the
implements of the Crucifixion (the whip,
crown of thorns, nails, ladder and spear).
In the centre of the third tier stands the
Virgin Mary being assumed bodily into
heaven along with angels and two flowers:
the peony, representing China, and the
chrysanthemum, a symbol of Japan. To
the right of the Virgin is a carving of the
tree of life and the apocalyptic woman
(Mary) slaying a seven-headed hydra; the
Japanese *kanji* next to her reads: 'The holy
mother tramples the heads of the dragon'.
To the left of the central statue of Mary, a
'star' guides a ship (the Church) through
a storm (sin); a carving of the devil is to
the left.

The fourth tier has statues of four Jesuit
doctors of the church (from left to right):
Blessed Francisco de Borja; St Ignatius
Loyola, the founder of the order; St Francis
Xavier, the apostle of the Far East; and
Blessed Luís Gonzaga.

MUSEUM OF SACRED ART & CRYPT
Map p318
**Museu de Arte Sacra e Cripta; Travessa de São
Paolo; admission free; ☼ 9am-6pm**
This small museum behind the ruins of
the Church of St Paul contains polychrome
carved wooden statues, silver chalices,
monstrances and oil paintings, including a
copy of a 17th-century painting depicting
the martyrdom of 26 Japanese Christians
by crucifixion at Nagasaki in 1597. The
adjoining crypt contains the remains of the
martyrs, as well as those of Vietnamese and
other Japanese Christians killed in the 17th
century. Also here is the recently unearthed
tomb of Alessandro Valignano, the Jesuit
who founded the College of the Mother
of God and is credited with establishing
Christianity in Japan.

LEAL SENADO Map p318
163 Avenida de Almeida Ribeiro
Facing Largo do Senado to the west is
Macau's most important historical building,
the 18th-century 'Loyal Senate', which now
houses the Instituto para os Assuntos Cívi-
cos e Municipais (IACM; Civic and Municipal
Affairs Bureau). It is so named because

CENTRAL MACAU PENINSULA

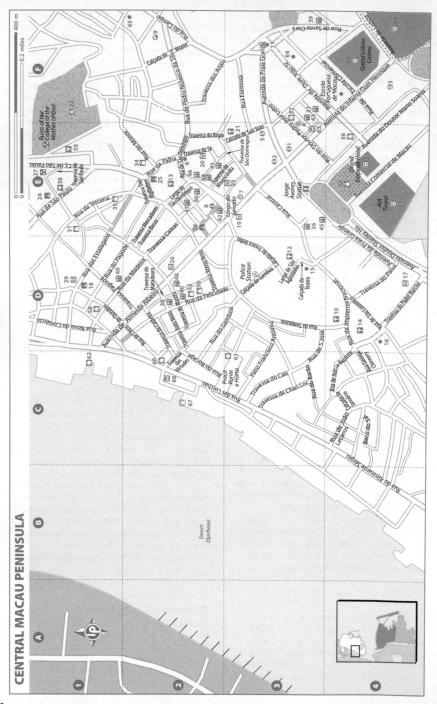

Inner Harbour

CENTRAL MACAU PENINSULA

INFORMATION

Banco Comercial de Macau
澳門國際銀行 1 E3
Banco Nacional Ultramarino
大西洋銀行 2 E3
Bank of China 中國銀行大廈 3 F4
CTM Branch 澳門電訊 4 E2
HSBC 匯豐銀行 5 E3
Livararia Portuguesa
葡文書局 6 E2
Main Post Office 郵政總局 7 E3
MGTO Branch 旅遊諮詢處 8 E2
MGTO Branch 旅遊諮詢處 ....(see 27)
Portuguese Consulate
葡萄牙領事館 9 F2

SIGHTS   (pp317-22)

Chapel of St Joseph
Seminary
聖約翰修院及聖堂 10 D4
Chinese Reading Room
八角亭圖書館 11 F3
Church of St Augustine
聖奧斯定教堂 12 D3
Church of St Dominic 玫瑰堂 13 E2
Church of St Lawrence
聖老楞佐教堂 14 D4
Cultural Club 文化會館 ....(see 26)
Dom Pedro V Theatre
崗頂劇院 15 D3
George Chinnery House
錢納利故居 16 D4
Government House
特區政府總部 17 D4
Hong Kung Temple 康公廟 18 D1
IACM Gallery
民政總署展覽館 ....(see 19)
Leal Senado 民政總署 19 E3
Lou Kau Mansion 盧家大屋 20 E2
Macau Cathedral 大堂
(主教座堂) 21 E3
Macau Museum 澳門博物館 ....(see 22)
Monte Fort 中央大炮台 22 F1
Museum of Sacred Art &
Crypt
天主教藝術博物館與墓室 ......(see 27)

Museum of the Holy House of
Mercy 仁慈堂博物館 23 E3
Na Tcha Temple 哪吒廟 24 E1
Nu Wa Temple 女媧廟 25 E2
Pawnshop Museum
典當業展示館 26 D2
Ruins of the Church of St Paul
大三巴 27 E1
Sam Kai Vui Kun Temple
三街會館 28 E2
Senate Library
民政總署圖書館 ....(see 19)
Sound of the Century
Museum (Tai Peng
Electronics)
留聲歲月音響博物館
(太平電器) 29 D1
Treasury of Sacred Art
聖物寶庫 ....(see 13)

SHOPPING   (pp333-4)

Choi Heong Yuen 咀香園 30 D2
Flea Market 跳蚤市場 31 E1
Koi Kei 鉅記 32 D2
Main Post Office 郵政總局 ......(see 7)
New Yaohan 新八佰伴 33 E4
Pun Veng Kei 潘榮記 34 E2
St Dominic Market 營地街市 ...(see 47)
Traditional Shops 35 E1

EATING   (pp334-8)

Afonso III 亞豐素三世餐廳 36 E3
Caravela 金船餅屋 37 F3
Cheong Kei 祥記 38 D2
Clube Militar de Macau
陸軍俱樂部 39 F3
Don Alfonso 1890
當奧豐素1890 ....(see 54)
Eight 8餐廳 ....(see 54)
Fat Siu Lau 佛笑樓 40 D2
La Bonne Heure
良辰法國餐廳 41 E2
Long Kei 龍記 42 E2
Margaret's Café e Nata
瑪嘉烈蛋撻店 43 F3
New Yaohan 新八佰伴 ....(see 33)

Ou Mun Café 44 E2
Pavilions Supermercado
百利來超級市場 45 E3
Platão 九如坊 46 E2
St Dominic Market
營地街市 47 D1
Tou Tou Koi 陶香居酒家 48 D2
U Tac Hong 頤德行 49 D1
Wong Chi Kei 黃枝記 50 E2

ENTERTAINMENT   (pp341-5)

Corner's Wine Bar & Tapas
Café 三角落 51 E1
Crazy Paris Cabaret
瘋狂巴黎艷舞團 ....(see 54)
D2 ....52 E4
Emperor Palace Casino
英皇宮殿娛樂場 53 E4
Grand Lisboa Casino
新葡京 54 F4
Lisboa Casino 葡京 55 F4
Macau Soul 澳感廊 56 E1

SLEEPING   (pp347-8)

Augusters Lodge 57 F3
East Asia Hotel 東亞酒店 58 D1
Hotel Sintra 新麗華酒店 59 E4
Hou Kong Hotel 濠江酒店 60 C2
Ole London Hotel
澳萊英京酒店 61 C3
Sofitel Macau at Ponte 16
澳門十六浦索菲特
大酒店 62 C1

TRANSPORT   (pp350-2)

Buses to Islands
往離島巴士 63 E3
China National Aviation
Corporation 中國航空 64 F3
Gray Line 65 F2
Kee Kwan Motor Road Co
歧關客運站 66 C2
Pier 11A 粵通碼頭 67 C2
Viva Macau 非凡航空 ....(see 52)

the body sitting here refused to recognise Spain's sovereignty during the 60 years that it occupied Portugal.

In 1654, a dozen years after Portuguese sovereignty was re-established, King João IV ordered a heraldic inscription to be placed inside the senate's entrance hall, and this can still be seen today. To the right of the entrance hall is the IACM Gallery (☎ 8988 4100; admission free; ⏰ 9am-9pm Tue-Sun), which features changing exhibits. On the 1st floor is the Senate Library (☎ 2857 2233; admission free; ⏰ 1-7pm Mon-Sat), which has a collection of some 18,500 books, and

wonderful carved wooden furnishings and panelled walls.

MONTE FORT Map p318

Fortaleza do Monte; ⏰ 7am-7pm
Accessible by an escalator just east of the ruins of the Church of St Paul, Monte Fort was built by the Jesuits between 1617 and 1626 as part of the College of the Mother of God. Barracks and storehouses were designed to allow the fort to survive a two-year siege, but the cannons were fired only once: during the aborted attempt by the Dutch to invade Macau in 1622 (see p307).

ONE-DAY ITINERARY

If you only have a day in Macau, start by following the Macau Peninsula walking tour (p326) to get a feel for the lie of the land and Macau's living history. Spend an hour or so in the Macau Museum (below) to answer all the questions you'll now have, and walk to the ruins of the Church of St Paul (p317). In the afternoon, hop on a bus for Taipa (p327) and stroll through the village to Avenida da Praia and the three-part Taipa House Museum (p327). In the evening you should also walk along peninsula Macau's more dramatic Avenida da Praia Grande, stopping for a while at the Grand Lisboa Casino (p342) to see what all the fuss is about. Complete the trip with a dinner at the atmospheric Clube Militar de Macau (p336) before catching the ferry back to Hong Kong.

MACAU MUSEUM Map p318

Museu de Macau; ☎ 2835 7911; Praceta do Museu de Macau, Fortaleza do Monte; adult/child under 11, student & senior over 60 MOP$15/8, 15th of month admission free; ☿ 10am-6pm Tue-Sun
To interactively grab the essence of the history of Macau, head to this excellent museum housed in the Monte Fort.

On the first level, the Genesis of Macau exhibit takes you through the early history of the territory, with parallel developments in the East and the West compared and contrasted. The highlight here is the elaborate section devoted to the territory's religions.

On the second level (Popular Arts & Traditions of Macau), you'll see and hear everything from a re-created firecracker factory and a *chá gordo* (fat tea) of 20 dishes enjoyed on a Sunday, to the recorded cries of street vendors selling items such as brooms and scrap metal. Do not miss the recording of the Macanese poet José dos Santos Ferreira (1919–93), known as Adé, reading from his work in the local dialect.

The top-floor Contemporary Macau exhibit focuses on the latest architecture and urban-development plans.

MACAU CATHEDRAL Map p318

A Sé Catedral; Largo da Sé; ☿ 8am-6pm
East of Largo do Senado is the cathedral, a not particularly attractive structure consecrated in 1850 and completely rebuilt in 1937. It has some notable stained-glass windows and is very active during major Christian festivals and holy days in Macau.

MUSEUM OF THE HOLY HOUSE OF MERCY Map p318

Núcleo Museológico da Santa Casa da Misericórdia; ☎ 2857 3938; 2 Travessa da Misericórdia; adult/student & senior over 65 MOP$5/free; ☿ 10am-5.30pm Mon-Sat
In the heart of Largo do Senado is the oldest social institution in Macau, established in

1569, which served as a home to orphans and prostitutes in the 18th century. Today it's a museum containing items related to the House, including religious artefacts; Chinese, Japanese and European porcelain; the skull of its founder and Macau's first bishop, Dom Belchior Carneiro; and a portrait of Martha Merop, an orphan who became a tycoon and a patron of the House. The restaurant (☎ 2833 5220; ☿ 10am-6pm Mon-Sat) in the basement serves very affordable and decent meals during lunch time.

CHURCH OF ST DOMINIC Map p318

Igreja de São Domingos; Largo de São Domingos; ☿ 10am-6pm
Northeast of Largo do Senado, this 17th-century baroque church is a replacement of a chapel built in the 1590s. Today it contains the Treasury of Sacred Art (Tresouro de Arte Sacra; ☎ 2836 7706; admission free; ☿ 10am-6pm), an Aladdin's cave of ecclesiastical art and liturgical objects exhibited on three floors.

LOU KAU MANSION Map p318

Casa de Lou Kau; ☎ 8399 6699; 7 Travessa da Sé; admission free; ☿ 9am-7pm Tue-Sun & public holidays
This well-preserved, Cantonese-style mansion was built in 1889. It belonged to tycoon Lou Wa Sio (aka Lou Kau), who made his fortunes in the opium trade and gambling during the 19th century. The mansion has kept its elaborate brick relief and lattice carvings on the windows, and some hybrid East-West architecture. Interestingly, there is no kitchen in the mansion, as the owner's concubines were supposed to bring him pleasure rather than cook.

DOM PEDRO V THEATRE Map p318

Teatro Dom Pedro V; ☎ 2893 9646; Calçada do Teatro
Opposite the Church of St Augustine, this colonnaded, neoclassical theatre built in

1858 is the oldest European theatre in China. It opens during cultural performances.

CHURCH OF ST LAWRENCE Map p318
Igreja de São Lourenço; Rua de São Lourenço;
🕒 **10am-4pm**
The original church was built out of wood in the 1560s but was rebuilt in stone in the early 19th century. It has a magnificent painted ceiling and one of the church towers once served as an ecclesiastical prison. Enter from Rua da Imprensa Nacional.

CHAPEL OF ST JOSEPH SEMINARY
Map p318
Capela do Seminário São José; Rua do Seminário;
🕒 **10am-5pm**
Southwest of Dom Pedro V Theatre is the Chapel of St Joseph, consecrated in 1758 as part of a Jesuit seminary. Its 19m-high domed ceiling has superb acoustics, and the church is used as a concert venue.

CHURCH OF ST AUGUSTINE Map p318
Igreja de Santo Agostinho; Largo de São Agostinho;
🕒 **10am-6pm**
Southwest of Largo do Senado via Rua Central is the Church of St Augustine. Its foundations date from 1586, but the present church was built in 1814. The high altar has a statue of Christ bearing the cross, which is carried through the streets during the Procession of the Passion of Our Lord on the first Saturday of Lent (p312). During research, the church was closed for maintenance.

SAM KAI VUI KUN TEMPLE Map p318
Sam Kai Vui Kun; Rua Sui do Mercado de São Domingos; 🕒 **8am-6pm**
Literally 'a community hall for three streets', this temple was a meeting place for merchants and then an adjudication court before the Chinese Chamber of Commerce came into existence in 1912. The temple is dedicated to Kwan Yu, the god of war and justice. It gets particularly busy in May, June and July when locals celebrate three festivals in the god's honour.

TEMPLES
Macau has some interesting Chinese temples dedicated to important but lesser-worshipped deities. Na Tcha Temple (Map p318; Nat Tcha Miu; Rua de São Paolo; admission free; 🕒 8am-5pm), sitting quietly beside the Ruins of the Church of St Paul, was built in 1888 and dedicated to the child god of war to halt the plague occurring at that time. The Nu Wa Temple (Map p318; Nui Wo Miu; cnr Rua das Estalagens & Travessa Dos Algibebes; admission free; 🕒 9am-5pm), a family shrine-like temple in a faded yellow building, also built in 1888, was consecrated to the Chinese equivalent of Gaia. The 200-year-old Hong Kung Temple (Map p318; Hong Kung Miu; cnr Rua das Estalagens & Rua de Cinco de Outubro; 🕒 8am-6pm) is for worshipping Li Lie, a Han-dynasty general. The boat-shaped sculpture in the middle of the main hall is for offering wine to the deities during religious festivities.

GOVERNMENT HOUSE Map p318
Sede do Governo; cnr Avenida da Praia Grande & Travessa do Padré Narciso
South of the Church of St Lawrence is the headquarters of the Macau SAR government. This pillared, rose-coloured building was erected in 1849 for a Portuguese noble. It's open to the public for only one day a year, usually in September or October.

CHINESE READING ROOM Map p318
Rua de Santa Clara; 🕒 **9am-noon & 7-10pm Tue-Sat, 9am-10pm Sun**
This attractive octagonal structure, with its double stone staircase and little round tower, is the wonderful mix of Chinese and Portuguese styles found only in Macau.

PAWNSHOP MUSEUM Map p318
Casa de Penhores Tradicional; ☎ **2892 1811; 396 Avenida de Almeida Ribeiro; admission MOP$5;** 🕒 **10.30am-7pm, closed 1st Mon of month**
This museum is housed in the former pawnshop built in 1917, with the fortress-like eight-storey granite tower and slotted windows, where goods were stored on racks or in safes. Sharing the same building is the Cultural Club (Clube Cultural; ☎ 2892 1811; www.culturalclub.net; 390 Avenida de Almeida Ribeiro; admission free; 🕒 10.30am-8pm), which claims to look at various aspects of everyday life in Macau but is little more than a souvenir shop.

SOUND OF THE CENTURY MUSEUM
Map p318
☎ **2892 1389; www.tai-peng.com/antique; 3rd fl, 13-15 Rua das Estalagens; admission MOP$30;** 🕒 **11am-5pm**
From antique phonographs to tourna-phones and echophones dating back to as

early as 1882, the private collections of the owner of Tai Peng Electronics will definitely wow you, no matter if you are a phonograph enthusiast or not. Prior appointment is required.

Southern Macau Peninsula

Southern Macau Peninsula is growing. To the southernmost is a rectangle of reclaimed land called NAPE, where reclamation hasn't stopped yet. A new science museum is expected to be complete in 2010. This part of the peninsula also encompasses two more areas: that around the Macau Forum (a conference and exhibition space) and Tourist Activities Centre housing two museums; and the southwest corner of the peninsula. Buses 8, 12 and 17 – leaving from Ilha Verde, the ferry terminal and Luís de Camões Garden, respectively – will take you to NAPE, but the free casino shuttles provided by Sands, Babylon, Wynn Macau and MGM Grand are an alternative.

MACAU CULTURAL CENTRE Map pp314-15
Centro Cultural de Macau; ☎ 2870 0699, 2855 5555; www.ccm.gov.mo; Avenida Xian Xing Hai; ◯ 9am-7pm Tue-Sun
This US$100 million centre is the territory's prime venue for theatre, opera and other cultural performances.

MACAU MUSEUM OF ART Map pp314-15
Museu de Arte de Macau; ☎ 8791 9814; www.artmuseum.gov.mo; Avenida Xian Xing Hai; adult/child under 12 & student/senior over 65 MOP$5/3/free, Sun admission free; ◯ 10am-7pm Tue-Sun
This five-storey complex within the Macau Cultural Centre is one of the best museums in Macau, and houses some excellent exhibits and collections of Chinese traditional art and paintings by Western artists who lived in Macau, such as George Chinnery (see the boxed text, p310).

KUN IAM STATUE Map pp314-15
Estátua de Kun Iam; Avenida Dr Sun Yat Sen
This 20m-high bronze figure, emerging Virgin Mary–like from a 7m-high lotus in the outer harbour, is probably the only statue in the world of the goddess of mercy that is not facing the sea. The Kun Iam Ecumenical Centre (Centro Ecuménico Kun Iam; ☎ 2875 1516; admission free; ◯ 10am-6pm Sat-Thu) in the Kun Iam's 'blossom' has information on Buddhism, Taoism and Confucianism.

GRAND PRIX MUSEUM Map pp314-15
Museu do Grande Prémio; ☎ 8798 4108; Basement, CAT, 431 Rua de Luís Gonzaga Gomes; adult/child under 11 & senior over 60/child under 19 MOP$10/free/5, adult incl Macau Wine Museum MOP$20; ◯ 10am-6pm Wed-Mon
Cars from the Macau Formula 3 Grand Prix, including the bright-red Triumph TR2 driven by Eduardo de Carvalho that won the first Grand Prix in 1954, are on display, while simulators let you test your racing skills.

MACAU SECURITY FORCES MUSEUM Map pp314-15
Museu das Forças de Segurança de Macau; ☎ 2855 9999; Calçada dos Quartéis; admission free; ◯ 9am-5.45pm Mon-Fri, 9am-5pm Sat & Sun
Housed in the 17th-century St Francis Barracks (Quartéis de São Francisco), this museum has two rooms of exhibits relating to the police and their work. The building is set in the lovely St Francis Garden (Jardim de São Francisco).

MACAU WINE MUSEUM Map pp314-15
Museu do Vinho de Macau; ☎ 8798 4188; Basement, CAT, 431 Rua de Luís Gonzaga Gomes; adult/child under 11 & senior over 60/child under 19 MOP$15/free/5, adult incl Grand Prix Museum MOP$20; ◯ 10am-6pm Wed-Mon
This is probably the only museum in Macau where beverages are allowed. More than 1300 types of wines on display are available for tasting, which is included in the entry fee. There is also a rundown of Portugal's various wine regions, but the display of wine racks, barrels, presses and tools is rather bland.

MACAU FISHERMAN'S WHARF Map pp314-15
Doca dos Pescadores; www.fishermanswharf.com.mo
Bordering the east of NAPE is Macau Fisherman's Wharf, a tacky 'theme park' built on reclaimed land. It combines attractions, hotels, shops and restaurants, and is divided into three sections. Tang Dynasty focuses on Chinese history and culture; East Meets West is a 30m-high working volcano, an Africa Fort funfair for kids, and the Greek Square leisure and performance park; and Legend Wharf features landmarks from around the world. The new phase of the park, which includes a couple of luxurious resorts, is still under construction.

HANDOVER OF MACAU GIFTS MUSEUM Map pp314-15

Museu das Ofertas sobre a Transferência de Soberania de Macau; ☎ 8791 9800; Avenida Xian Xing Hai; admission free; ☺ 10am-7pm Tue-Sun

Next to the Macau Cultural Centre is this major attraction to visitors from the mainland. It displays (kitschy) art pieces and handicrafts presented by China's various provinces to Macau to mark the return of Chinese sovereignty in 1999.

SOUTHWEST CORNER

The southwestern tip of the Macau Peninsula has a number of important historical sights, as it was the first area of the territory to be settled.

A-MA TEMPLE Map pp314-15

Templo de A-Ma; Rua de São Tiago da Barra; ☺ 7am-6pm; ☒ 1, 1A, 5

North of Barra Hill is a temple dedicated to the goddess A-Ma and Macau's namesake – called Ma Kok Miu in Cantonese. She is better known as Tin Hau (see the boxed text, p331). This is the oldest temple in Macau and was probably standing when the Portuguese arrived, although the present one may only date back to the 17th century. At the entrance is a large boulder with a coloured relief of a *lorcha* (a traditional sailing vessel of the South China Sea). During the A-Ma Festival (p312) sometime between late April and early May, it is crowded with pilgrims. If you can only visit one temple in Macau, make it this one.

AVENIDA DA REPÚBLICA Map pp314-15

Avenida da República along the northwest shore of Sai Van Lake is the oldest Portuguese section of Macau. Here are several grand colonial villas not open to the public. The former Bela Vista Hotel, one of the most-storied hotels in Asia, is now the residence of the Portuguese consul general. Nearby is the ornate Santa Sancha Palace (Palacete de Santa Sancha; Estrada de Santa Sancha), once the residence of Macau's Portuguese governors and now used to accommodate state guests.

PENHA HILL Map pp314-15

Colina da Penha

Towering above the colonial villas along Avenida da República is Penha Hill, the most tranquil and least visited area of the peninsula. From here you'll get excellent views of the central area of Macau. Atop

the hill is the Bishop's Palace (built in 1837) and the Chapel of Our Lady of Penha (Capela de Nostra Señora da Penha; ☺ 9am-5.30pm), once a place of pilgrimage for sailors.

MARITIME MUSEUM Map pp314-15

Museu Marítimo; ☎ 2859 5481; 1 Largo do Pagode da Barra; adult/child 10-17/senior over 65 Mon & Wed-Sat MOP$10/5/free, Sun MOP$5/3/free; ☺ 10am-5.30pm Wed-Mon

Opposite the A-Ma Temple, the Maritime Museum has interesting boats and artefacts from Macau's seafaring past, a mock-up of a Hakka fishing village and displays of the long, narrow boats that are raced during the Dragon Boat Festival (p313) in June.

MACAU TOWER Map pp314-15

Torre de Macau; ☎ 2893 3339; www.macautower .com.mo; Largo da Torre de Macau; ☺ 10am-9pm Mon-Fri, 9am-9pm Sat & Sun; ☒ 9A, 32, AP1

Macau Tower, at 338m, is the 10th-tallest freestanding structure in the world; it stands on the narrow isthmus of land southeast of Avenida da República. The squat building at its base is the Macau Convention & Entertainment Centre.

The tower houses observation decks (adult/child 3-12 & senior over 85 MOP$90/45) on the 58th and 61st floors, and restaurants and bars such as the revolving 360° Café (☺ 11.30am-3pm, 3.30-4.15pm & 6-11pm) on the 60th floor, and the 180° Lounge (minimum charge MOP$60; ☺ noon-1am) one floor below it.

If none of this takes your fancy, you might be interested in the activities of the New Zealand–based extreme-sports company AJ Hackett (☎ 8988 8656), which organises all kinds of adventure climbs up and around the tower.

The intrepid will go for the Mast Climb (MOP$1688), in which you go up and down the mast's 100m of vertical ladders to the top in two hours. Skywalk X (MOP$588) is a rail less walk around the *outer* rim, some 233m high, on the 61st floor. Bungy (MOP$1488) is the world's highest free fall, from a 233m-high platform. Sky Jump (MOP$888) or Tandem Sky Jump (MOP$1688 per two people) are slower versions of Bungy.

Northern Macau Peninsula

This area encompasses everything northwards from the Luís de Camões Garden in the west and Guia Fort in the east to the border with the mainland in the northern part of Macau. It's a mix of industrial areas and densely populated residential buildings, dotted with a few historic sites and splendid gardens. Tourists are scant and wandering around the sites is pleasant.

GUIA FORT Map pp314-15
Colina da Guia

This fortress atop the highest point on the peninsula was built in 1638 to defend the border with China. Storm warnings were sounded from the bell in the Chapel of Our Lady of Guia (Capela de Nostra Señora da Guia; ☽ 10am-5pm Tue-Sun), built in 1622. The walls of the little church have interesting frescoes discovered recently, and there's a colourful choir loft above the main entrance. On the floor below is a tombstone with the inscription (in Latin): 'Here lies at this gate the remains of a Christian, by accident, for his body does not deserve such an honourable sepulchre'. It's believed the deceased was buried here in 1687. The 15m-tall Guia Lighthouse (Farol da Guia; 1865) is the oldest lighthouse on the China coast. It's open on 18 May annually. On clear days you can see Lantau Island from the fort, but the new skyscrapers in NAPE now block some of the views.

The 52m-long Guia Hill Air Raid Shelter (Abrigos Antiaéreos da Colina a Guia; ☽ 10am-5pm Tue-Sun), an old military installation, was constructed in 1931 and was off-limits until 1962. Photos of the history of the shelter and an electricity generator used during WWII are on display.

The easiest way to reach the top of Guia Hill is to hop on the little Guia Cable Car (Teleférico da Guia; one way/return MOP$2/3) that runs from 8am to 6pm Tuesday to Sunday from just outside the entrance of the attractive Flora Garden (Rua do Túnel; ☽ 6am-7pm), off Avenida de Sidónio Pais.

OLD PROTESTANT CEMETERY
Map pp314-15
15 Praça de Luís de Camões; ☽ 8.30am-5.30pm

Some of the better-known early Anglophone residents of Macau are interred here, like George Chinnery (see the boxed text, p310) and Robert Morrison (1782–1834), the first Protestant missionary to China and author of the first Chinese-English dictionary.

As church law forbade the burial of non-Catholics on hallowed ground, there was nowhere to inter Protestants who died here. Finally the governor allowed the British East India Company to establish the cemetery

in 1821. A number of old graves were then transferred to the cemetery, which explains the earlier dates on some of the tombstones.

CASA GARDEN Map pp314-15
13 Praça de Luís de Camões; ☒ 8A, 12, 26

Quietly sitting east of the Luís de Camões Garden is this beautiful colonial villa, once the headquarters of the British East India Company when it was based in Macau in the early 19th century. Today the villa houses the Oriental Foundation (Fundação Oriente; ☎ 2855 4699; www.foriente.pt), an organisation that promotes Portuguese culture worldwide, and an exhibition gallery (☎ 8398 1126; admission free; ☽ 10am-5.30pm Mon-Fri, 10am-7pm daily during special exhibitions), which houses exhibits of Chinese antiques, porcelain and contemporary art.

CEMETERY OF ST MICHAEL THE ARCHANGEL Map pp314-15
Cemitério de São Miguel Arcanjo; 2A Estrada do Cemitério; ☽ 8am-6pm

This cemetery, northeast of Monte Fort, contains tombs and sepulchres that can only be described as baroque ecclesiastical works of art. Near the main entrance is the Chapel of St Michael (Capela de São Miguel; ☽ 10am-6pm), a doll-sized, pea-green church with a tiny choir loft and pretty porticoes.

LOU LIM IOC GARDEN Map pp314-15
Jardim de Lou Lim Ioc; 10 Estrada de Adolfo de Loureiro; ☽ 6am-9pm; ☒ 12

This picturesque Chinese garden was originally owned by Lou Wa Sio back in the 19th century and later inherited by his son Lou Lim Ioc. Now it's open to the public and local people use the park to practise t'ai chi or play traditional musical instruments. It contains huge shady trees, lotus ponds, golden bamboo groves, grottoes and a bridge with nine turns (since evil spirits can only move in straight lines).

The Victorian-style Lou Lim Ioc Garden Pavilion (Pavilhão do Jardim de Lou Lim Ioc; ☎ 8988 4128; admission free; ☽ 9am-9pm Tue-Sun) was where the Lou family received guests, including Dr Sun Yat-sen, and is now used for exhibits and for recitals during the Macau International Music Festival (p313) in late October/November.

Adjacent to the garden is the Macao Tea Culture House (Caultura do Chá em Macau; ☽ 9am-7pm Tue-Sun), displaying the local tea culture with exhibits of various teapots.

SUN YAT SEN MEMORIAL HOME
Map pp314-15

Casa Memorativa de Doutor Sun Yat Sen; ☎ 2857 4064; 1 Rua de Silva Mendes; admission free; ⏱ 10am-5pm Wed-Mon

Near Lou Lim Ioc Garden, this Moorish-style house was once a residence of Lu Muzhen, the first wife of the founder of the Chinese Republic, Dr Sun Yat-sen (1866–1925). She died in the upstairs back bedroom in 1952. This house replaced the original house, which blew up in 1930. Now it's a museum dedicated to Dr Sun, though he had never lived here. You'll find a collection of flags, photos and documents relating to the life and times of the 'Father of the Nation'.

ST LAZARUS DISTRICT Map pp314-15
Calçada da Igreja de São Lázaro; www.macauart.net /ts; 95 Avenida Conselheiro Ferreira de Almeida; ⏱ 10am-6pm Tue-Sun; ☒ 9, 12

Looking for a cheerful rest area amid densely populated northern Macau? Head to this beautiful district not far from the Cemetery of St Michael the Archangel. The cobbled streets and historic houses of this district offer a little taste of the sleepy Macau of old. The highlight here is the Albergue da Santa Casa da Misericórdia (aka Old Ladies' House), home to a group of avant-garde designers working in a variety of media. It also houses the cheerful Locanda (p336) Italian restaurant in its courtyard.

TAP SEAC GALLERY Map pp314-15
Galeria Tam Seac; www.macauart.net/ts; 95 Avenida do Conselheiro Ferreira de Almeida; ⏱ 10am-6pm Tue-Sun; ☒ 9, 12

Housed in a Moorish-style mansion dating back to the 1920s, this gallery is arguably the best place to view contemporary art in Macau, and exhibitions change regularly. Check its website for details. The gallery keeps the original patio in the middle of the house, which creates a light-filled, relaxed setting.

OX WAREHOUSE Map pp314-15
Armazem de Boi; ☎ 2853 0026; oxwarehousenews .blogspot.com; cnr Avenida do Coronel Mesquita & Avenida do Almirante Lacerda; ⏱ noon-7pm Wed-Mon; ☒ 1A, 12

Local Chinese artists have their own studios near the Canidrome called Ox Warehouse. Once a slaughterhouse, it is now a colourful quarter for artists and hosts avant-garde installations and performances. Between 3pm and 7pm on the weekends the rest area on the 2nd floor turns into a cafe, serving passable coffee.

LIN FUNG TEMPLE Map pp314-15
Lin Fung Miu; Avenida do Almirante Lacerda; ⏱ 10am-6.30pm; ☒ 12

Once Taoist but now dedicated to Kun Iam, this temple (built in 1592) was where people from Guangdong province would stay when they visited Macau, including Lin Zexu, the commissioner charged with stamping out the opium trade, who stayed here in September 1839. The Lin Zexu Memorial Hall (Museu de Lin Zexu; ☎ 2855 0166; tourist/local adult MOP$10/5, child under 8 & senior over 65 MOP$3; ⏱ 9am-5pm Tue-Sun), with its old photographs, a model of a Chinese war junk and opium-smoking paraphernalia, recalls his visit.

KUN IAM TEMPLE Map pp314-15
Kun Iam Tong; Avenida do Coronel Mesquita; ⏱ 10am-6pm; ☒ 1A, 12

This is probably the most active temple in Macau and is also dedicated to the goddess of mercy. It dates from 1627 and its most historic moment was in 1844, when the first treaty of trade and friendship between the USA and China was signed on a stone table in the terraced gardens at the back. Unfortunately some of the reliefs were damaged during the Cultural Revolution.

LUÍS DE CAMÕES GARDEN Map pp314-15
Jardim de Luís de Camões; Praça de Luís de Camões; ⏱ 6am-10pm; ☒ 8A

This garden is popular with locals practising Cantonese opera or playing Chinese chequers. In the centre of the park is the Camões Grotto (Gruta de Camões), which contains a 19th-century bust of the one-eyed national poet of Portugal, Luís de Camões.

CHURCH OF ST ANTHONY Map pp314-15
Igreja de Santo António; cnr Rua de Santo António & Rua do Tarrafeiro; ⏱ 7.30am-5.30pm

Outside Casa Garden and next to the roundabout, this church, built from 1558 to 1608, was the Jesuits' earliest headquarters. The local Portuguese used to hold wedding ceremonies here, hence its name in Cantonese: Fa Vong Tong (Church of Flowers). It burnt down three times and the present architecture is a restoration from 1930.

FIRE SERVICES MUSEUM Map pp314-15

Museu de Bombeiros; ☎ 2857 2222; 2-6 Rua de Coelho do Amaral; admission free; ☼ 10am-6pm; 🚌 8

Housed in the former HQ of the Macau fire brigade, the museum holds a small but interesting collection of old fire trucks from the 1940s and '50s, a manual pump from 1877, and lots of helmets and boots.

MACAU PENINSULA WALKING TOUR

1 Largo do Senado Begin in the beautiful 'Square of the Senate' in the heart of Macau, which is accessible from the ferry terminal on bus 3. On the south side of the square facing Avenida de Almeida Ribeiro is the main post office, built in 1931, and nearby is the restored Museum of the Holy House of Mercy (p320). From here, walk to the northeastern end of the square.

2 Church of St Dominic Overlooking Largo de São Domingos is this church (p320), with its distinctive green shutters and doors.

3 Macau Cathedral On the southern side of the square, you'll spot a narrow road called

WALK FACTS

Start Largo do Senado
End Maritime Museum
Distance 4km
Duration Three to four hours
Fuel Stops Many along the way

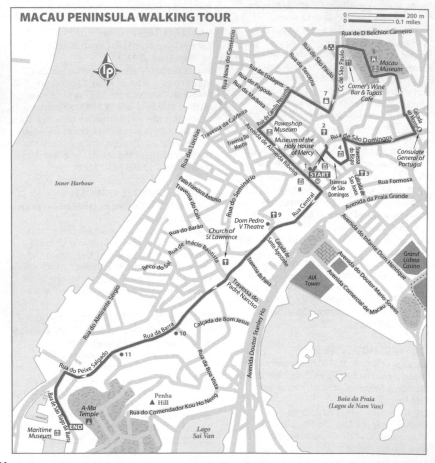

MACAU PENINSULA WALKING TOUR

Travessa de São Domingos. Follow this up to Largo da Sé and Macau Cathedral (p320).

4 Lou Kau Mansion Housed on Travessa da Sé is Lou Kau Mansion (p320), built in 1889. The street leads down into Rua de São Domingos. Take a right at the bottom of the hill and follow Rua de São Domingos and its extension, Rua de Pedro Nolasco da Silva, to the corner with Calçada do Monte. Just visible across the garden to the east is the Consulate General of Portugal, housed in an exquisite colonial mansion.

5 Monte Fort Begin climbing up Calçada do Monte, and once you reach Travessa do Artilheiros, turn left. A cobbled path leads up to Monte Fort (p319) and the Macau Museum (p320).

6 Ruins of the Church of St Paul Take the escalator down from the museum and walk west to the facade of the Church of St Paul (p317); there's a platform offering stunning views over the town on the north side leading to the former choir loft.

7 Antique & Chinese Shops Walk down the stone steps in front of the facade. If you're peckish, stop for tapas at Corner's Wine Bar and Tapas Café (p344). Continue south along Cç de São Paolo, which is lined with antique shops (p333). Turn right onto Rua das Estalagens, which is full of traditional Chinese shops and, once you reach Rua de Camilo Pessanha, turn left. At the western end of this street, turn left again into Avenida de Almeida Ribeiro and on your left you'll pass the Pawnshop Museum (p321).

8 Leal Senado Continue along Avenida de Almeida Ribeiro. After passing the Leal Senado (p317), take a right turn onto Rua Central, which changes names several times as it heads southwest for the Inner Harbour.

9 Church of St Augustine Towering above this end of Rua Central is the Church of St Augustine (p321) and opposite that the Dom Pedro V Theatre (p320).

10 Largo do Lilau Follow Rua Central's extensions, Rua de São Lourenço and Rua da Barra, passing the Church of St Lawrence (p321) and Largo do Lilau; according to folklore, should you drink from the fountain in this romantic square, it's a given that you'll return to Macau one day.

11 Moorish Barracks Further on are these enormous barracks, completed in 1874 and now housing the offices of the maritime police. Rua do Peixe Salgado (Street of Salted

Fish) debouches into Rua do Almirante Sérgio, where you should turn left. A short distance south is the ever-active A-Ma Temple (p323) and opposite, across Rua de São Tiago da Barra, is the Maritime Museum (p323). From here, you can follow Avenida da República to Avenida da Praia Grande and Avenida de Almeida Ribeiro or hop on bus 5 or 7.

TAIPA & COLOANE ISLANDS

Taipa and Coloane are oases of calm and greenery, with colonial villas, quiet lanes, decent beaches and fine Portuguese and Macanese restaurants. They are connected to Macau by three bridges and joined together by Cotai, an ever-growing area of reclaimed land, with several new megacasinos sprouting up.

Taipa Island

Taipa (Tam Chai in Cantonese, Tanzai in Mandarin) was actually two islands joined together by silt from the Pearl River. Reclamation has succeeded in doing the same thing to Taipa and Coloane.

Taipa has rapidly urbanised and it's hard to imagine that just a few decades ago it was an island of duck farms and boat yards, with small fireworks factories. Now it boasts major casino-hotels, a university, a racecourse and stadium, high-rise apartments, a new ferry terminal and an airport. But a parade of baroque churches, Portuguese buildings, Chinese temples and lethargic settlements means it's still possible to experience the traditional charms of the island. Buses 11 and 28A leave from A-Ma Temple and the ferry terminal, respectively, and have stops at most sights in Taipa. They also stop along Avenida do Infante Dom Henrique.

TAIPA VILLAGE Map p328
The historical part of Taipa is best preserved in this village in the south of the island. With a tidy sprawl of traditional Chinese shops and some excellent restaurants, the village is punctuated by grand colonial villas, churches and ancient temples. Avenida da Praia, a tree-lined esplanade with wrought-iron benches, is perfect for a leisurely stroll.

TAIPA HOUSE MUSEUM Map p328
Casa Museum da Taipa; ☎ 2882 7103; Avenida da Praia; adult/child under 12 & senior over 65/student MOP$5/free/2, Sun admission free; ☯ 10am-6pm Tue-Sun
The most beautiful sight on Taipa is this unusual museum, formed by five lime-green

TAIPA

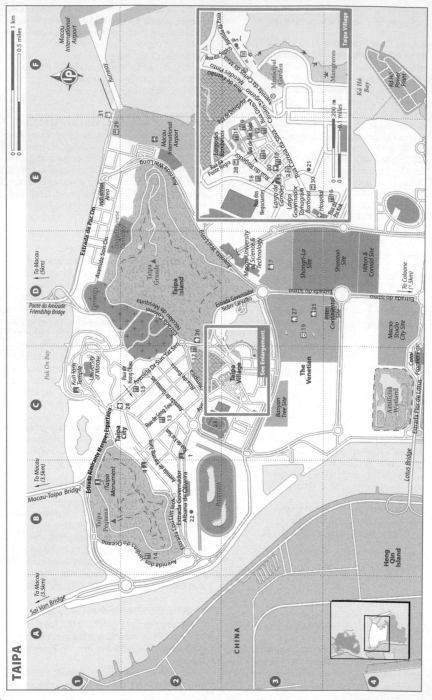

Macau International Airport

Macau International Airport

Runway

Taipa Island

Taipa City

Taipa Monument

Taipa Grande

Taipa Pequena

CHINA

Heng Qin Island

The Venetian

Taipa Village

See Enlargement

Macau University of Science & Technology

United Chinese Cemetery

Cemetery

Kun Iam Temple

University of Macau

Pok On Bay

Ká Hó Bay

Ká Hó Power Plant

Mangroves

Taipa Village

Municipal Garden

Macau-Taipa Bridge

Sai Van Bridge

Ponte da Amizade Friendship Bridge

Lotus Bridge

Artificial Wetland

Shangri-La Site

Sheraton Site

Hilton & Conrad Site

Inter Continental Site

Macau Studio City Site

Banyan Tree Site

Estrada da Baía de Nossa Senhora da Esperança

To Macau (5km)

To Macau (3.5km)

To Macau (3.5km)

To Coloane (1.5km)

Riverfront

Estrada do Istmo

Estrada do Istmo

Estrada Flor de Lotus

Estrada Governador Albano de Oliveira

Estrada Almirante Marques Esparteiro

Estrada de Pac On

Industrial Area

Avenida Son On

Avenida Wai Long

Estrada Coronel Nicolau de Mesquita

Estrada Governador Nobre Carvalho

Avenida dos Jardins do Oceano

Rua de Hong Chau

Avenida da Dr Sun Yat Sen

Rua de Seng Tou Seang

Rua de Fui Sing

Rua do Pai Kok

Ká Hó

Coloane

Frontier Post

TAIPA

SIGHTS	(pp327-9)
Cotai Strip Travel	
路氹金光大道旅遊有限公司 ..... (see 27)	
Four-Faced Buddha Shrine	
四面佛 1 C2	
Museum of Taipa & Coloane	
History 路氹歷史館 2 E3	
Pak Tai Temple 北帝廟 3 E3	
Pou Tai Temple 菩提禪院 4 B2	
Reception House	
龍環葡韻住宅博物館 5 F3	
Taipa House Museum	
龍環葡韻住宅博物館 6 F3	

SHOPPING	(pp333-4)
City of Dreams 新濠天地 7 D3	
Grand Canal Mall	
大運河購物中心 ....(see 27)	

EATING	(pp338-40)
A Petisqueira 葡國美食天地 8 E3	
Amagao 阿馬交美食 9 F3	
António 安東尼奧餐廳 10 E3	
Canton 喜粵 ....(see 20)	
Cozinha Pinocchio	
木偶葡國餐廳 11 E3	
Galo 公雞餐廳 12 E3	
Gourmet Fine Foods 13 C2	

Hyper Gourmet 14 B2
Kapok Cantonese
Restaurant 六棉酒家 15 C2
La Cucina Italiana
我的意大利廚房 16 E4
O Manel
阿曼諾葡國餐 17 C2
Portofino
碧濤意式漁宴 ....(see 27)
Pou Tai Temple
Restaurant ....(see 4)
Serrdura 沙厘娜 18 E3
Tenmasa 天政 ....(see 24)
Ying 帝影樓 ....(see 24)

ENTERTAINMENT	(pp341-5)
38 ....(see 24)	
Dragone Show ....(see 7)	
McSorley's Ale House	
麥時利愛爾蘭酒吧 ....(see 20)	
Old Taipa Tavern	
好客鄉村餐廳 19 E3	
Plaza Casino	
百利沙娛樂場 ....(see 25)	
Venetian Macao	
Casino	
威尼斯人娛樂場 20 D3	
Zaia 太陽劇團 ....(see 27)	

SPORTS & ACTIVITIES	(pp345-6)
Iao Kei 有記單車 21 E3	
Macau Jockey Club	
澳門賽馬會 22 B2	
Macau Stadium	
澳門奧林匹克運動場 23 C2	
Si Toi 時代租單車 ....(see 3)	

SLEEPING	(pp348-9)
Altira Macau 新濠鋒酒店 24 C1	
Four Seasons Hotel	
四季酒店 25 D3	
Hotel Taipa	
澳門格蘭酒店 26 D2	
Venetian Macao Resort	
Hotel	
澳門威尼斯人渡假村酒店	
.................................27 D3	

TRANSPORT	(pp350-2)
Bus Stop 巴士站 28 E3	
Free shuttle buses to	
Cotai Strip 29 E1	
Main Bus Stop 巴士總站 30 E3	
Taipa Temporary Ferry	
Terminal	
氹仔臨時客運碼頭 31 F1	

villas. The villas were summer residences built in 1921 by wealthy Macanese. Three hold permanent exhibitions, while the other two are used for receptions and special exhibitions.

The House of the Regions of Portugal (Casa das Regiões de Portugal) has costumes and examines traditional Portugal. The House of the Islands (Casa das Ilhas) looks at the history of Taipa and Coloane, with displays devoted to the islands' traditional industries: fishing and the manufacture of oyster sauce, shrimp paste and fireworks. The last is the Macanese House (Casa Macanese), a residence in local style; it looks like the *dom e doña* (husband and wife) living here just left. The furnishings – blackwood furniture and Chinese cloisonné with statues and pictures of saints and the Sacred Heart – offer a snapshot of life here in the early 20th century.

MUSEUM OF TAIPA & COLOANE HISTORY Map p328
Museu da História da Taipa e Coloane; ☎ 2882 7103; Rua Correia da Silva; adult/student & senior MOP$5/2, Tue admission free; ☽ 10am-6pm Tue-Sun
This museum is built on the remnants of the former Island Municipal Council and tries to be a mini–Macau Museum, although the collections are not as good as those on Monte Fort. There's a display of excavated

relics and other artefacts on the 1st floor that represent the earlier cultural history of Taipa and Coloane, while the 2nd floor contains religious objects, handicrafts and architectural models.

POU TAI TEMPLE Map p328
Pou Tai Un; 5 Estrada Lou Lim Ieok; ☽ 9am-6pm
This is the largest temple complex on the islands. The main hall, dedicated to the Three Precious Buddhas, contains an enormous bronze statue of Lord Gautama, and there are prayer pavilions and orchid greenhouses scattered around the complex. There's also a popular vegetarian restaurant (p340).

FOUR-FACED BUDDHA SHRINE Map p328
O Buda de Quatro Faces; cnr Estrada Governador Albano de Oliveira & Rua de Fat San
Northeast of the Macau Jockey Club racetrack's main entrance is this Buddhist shrine guarded by four stone elephants and festooned with gold leaf and Thai-style floral bouquets. It's a popular place to pray and make offerings before race meetings.

Coloane Island
The small island of Coloane (Lo Wan in Cantonese) is a world away from Macau peninsular, atmosphere-wise. The tallest buildings here

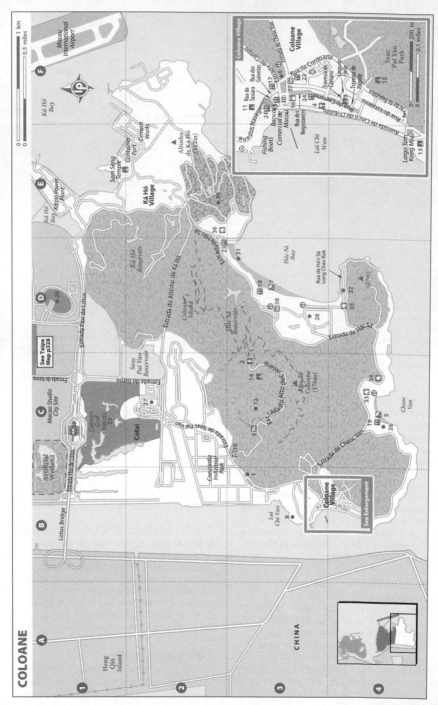

COLOANE

COLOANE

SIGHTS	(pp329-32)
A-Ma Cultural Village	
媽祖文化村	(see 14)
A-Ma Ornamental Entrance	
Gate 媽祖文化村石牌坊	1 B3
A-Ma Statue & Temple	
媽祖像及媽祖廟	2 C3
Aviary 小鳥天堂	3 C3
Chapel of St Francis Xavier	
聖方濟各教堂	4 F3
Cheoc Van Beach 竹灣海灘	5 C4
Coloane Market 路環街市	6 F3
Hác Sá Beach 黑沙海灘	7 D3
Junk-Building Sheds 造船廠	8 B3
Kun Iam Temple 觀音廟	9 F4
Museum of Nature &	
Agriculture	
土地灣自然博物館	10 C3
Sam Seng Temple 三聖邑	11 F3
Seac Pai Van Park 石排灣公園	12 C3
Tam Kong Temple 譚公廟	13 E4
Tian Hou Temple 天后廟	14 C3
Tin Hau Temple 天后廟	15 F4

SHOPPING	(pp333-4)
Asian Artefacts	16 F3

EATING	(pp340-1)
Espaço Lisboa	
里斯本地帶餐廳	17 F3
Fernando 法蘭度餐廳	18 D3
Kwun Hoi Heen 觀海軒	(see 36)
La Gondola 陸舟餐廳	19 C4
Lord Stow's Bakery	
安德魯餅店	20 F3
Lord Stow's Cafe	
澳門澳門安德魯餅店	21 F3
Lord Stow's Garden Café	
安德魯花園咖啡	22 F3
Miramar	23 D2
Nga Tim Café	
雅憩花園餐廳	24 F3

DRINKING	(p349)
Café Panorama	
全景咖啡廳	(see 36)

SPORTS & ACTIVITIES	(pp345-6)
Caesars Golf Macau	25 C1
Cheoc Van Swimming Pool	
竹灣泳池	26 C4
Coloane Kartodrome	
高卡車場	27 C2

Hác Sá Sports & Recreation	
Park	
黑沙綜合康樂及體育中心	28 D3
Macau Dome 澳門蛋	29 D1
Macau Golf & Country Club	
澳門鄉村俱樂部	30 E2
Water Sports Equipment	
Hire 水上運動器材出租處	31 D3
Water Sports Equipment	
Hire 水上運動器材出租處	32 D4

SLEEPING	(pp348-50)
Pousada de Coloane	
路環竹灣酒店	33 C4
Pousada de Juventude de	
Cheoc Van 竹灣青年旅舍	34 C4
Pousada de Juventude de	
Hác Sá 黑沙青年旅舍	35 D4
Westin Resort Macau	
威斯汀度假酒店	36 E2

TRANSPORT	(pp350-2)
Bus Stop 巴士站	37 F3
Bus Stop 巴士站	38 D3
Cotai Frontier Post	39 C1

are only a couple of storeys. It was a haven for pirates until 1910, when the Portuguese fought off the last pirate assault on the South China Sea. Today Coloane retains Macau's old way of life and being, though some quaint residential quarters were demolished to make way for luxurious villas. To visit Coloane Island board bus 21A at A-Ma Temple or bus 25 at Portas do Cerco (border crossing). Both head to Hác Sá beach and have stops at Avenida do Infante Dom Henrique and Coloane Village.

COLOANE VILLAGE Map p330

Tourism has given the economy in Coloane Village a big boost, but it is still a sleepy fishing village in character. The narrow lanes flanked by temples still ooze old-world charm and make strolling a joy.

The bus drops you off in the village's attractive main square; Coloane market is on the eastern side. To the west is the waterfront. From here a sign points the way north to the Sam Seng Temple (2 Rua dos Navegantes), a small, family altar-like temple. Just past the temple is a quaint old wharf and beyond that, about a dozen junk-building sheds, although a fire in 1999 destroyed many of the sheds.

CHAPEL OF ST FRANCIS XAVIER Map p330

Capela de São Francisco Xavier; Avenida de Cinco de Outubro; ☼ 10am-8pm

This chapel was built in 1928 to honour St Francis Xavier, a missionary in Japan. It has little architectural style but don't be disappointed. It's a delightful church painted in yellow and embellished with red lanterns. The inside contains an interesting portrait of a bodhisattva-like Virgin Mary. A fragment of the saint's arm bone was once kept in the chapel, but it has now been moved to St Joseph Seminary on the Macau Peninsula.

In front of the chapel are a monument and fountain surrounded by four cannonballs that commemorate the successful – and final – routing of pirates in 1910.

TEMPLES Map p330

Southeast of the Chapel of St Francis Xavier, between Travessa de Caetano and Travessa de Pagode, is a small Kun Iam Temple – just an altar inside a little walled compound. If you walk just a little further to the southeast, you'll find a newly renovated Tin Hau temple up in Largo Tin Hau Miu.

At the south end of Avenida de Cinco de Outubro in Largo Tam Kong Miu, Tam Kong Temple is dedicated to a Taoist god of seafarers. To the right of the main altar is a long whale bone, which has been carved into a model of a boat, with a dragon's head and a crew of men in pointed hats. To the left of the main altar is a path leading to the roof, which has views of the village and waterfront.

HÁC SÁ BEACH Map p330

Hác Sá (Black Sand) is the most popular beach in Macau. The sand is indeed a grey to blackish colour and makes the water look somewhat dirty (especially at the tide line), but it's perfectly clean. Lifeguards keep the same schedule here as on Cheoc Van beach.

A-MA STATUE Map p330

Estátua da Deusa A-Ma; Estrada do Alto de Coloane
Atop Alto de Coloane (176m), this 20m-high white jade statue of the goddess who gave Macau its name (see the boxed text, p307) was erected in 1998. Below it is Tian Hou Temple (☎ 8am-7.30pm), which, together with the statue, form the core of A-Ma Cultural Village, a religious complex with a museum, retreat and medical centres, plus a vegetarian restaurant. It's popular with Fujianese and Taiwanese worshippers, and is rather commercial. You'll probably see traders selling stuff supposedly meant to bring luck and wealth, including birds and turtles. Still, it's a good spot to get a bird's-eye view of Hác Sá beach on a clear day.

A free bus runs from the A-Ma ornamental entrance gate on Estrada de Seac Pai Van half-hourly from 8am to 6pm. You can also reach both by following the Coloane Trail (Trilho de Coloane; p346) from Seac Pai Van Park.

CHEOC VAN BEACH Map p330

Estrada de Cheoc Van
About 1.5km down Estrada de Cheoc Van, which runs east and then southeast from Coloane Village, is the beach at Cheoc Van

(Bamboo Bay). There are changing rooms and toilets and, in season, lifeguards (☺ 10am-6pm Mon-Sat, 9am-6pm Sun May-Oct) on duty.

SEAC PAI VAN PARK Map p330

☎ 2887 0277; Estrada de Seac Pai Van; admission free; ☺ 9am-6pm Tue-Sun
At the end of Cotai, this 20-hectare park, built in the wooded hills on the western side of the island, has somewhat unkempt gardens sprouting species of plants and trees from around the world, a children's zoo, a lake with swans and other waterfowl, and a walk-through aviary (☺ 9am-5pm Tue-Sun), which contains rare birds. The Museum of Nature & Agriculture (Museu Natural e Agrário; ☎ 2882 7277; admission free; ☺ 10am-6pm Tue-Sun) has traditional farming equipment, dioramas of Coloane's ecosystem and displays cataloguing a wide range of the island's fauna and flora.

TAIPA WALKING TOUR

1 Taipa House Museum Bus 28A from the ferry terminal will take you to Taipa. Begin your tour by visiting this beautiful Macanese villa built in 1921, which is now converted to the Taipa House Museum (p327).

WALK FACTS

Start Taipa House Museum
End Largo de Camões
Distance 1km
Duration One to 1½ hours
Fuel Stops Many along Rua do Regedor

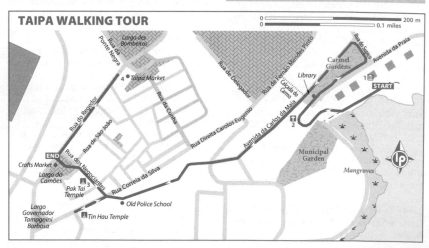

TAIPA WALKING TOUR

MACAU NEIGHBOURHOODS

2 Church of Our Lady of Carmel Walk up the steps to the 1885 Church of Our Lady of Carmel from the western end of Avenida da Praia. The colonial library, opposite, is a recent reproduction, replacing the original that had been pulled down illegally. Surrounding it are the pretty Carmel Gardens and just north is Calçada do Carmo, a positively delightful stepped lane lined with ancient banyans.

3 Temples Following Avenida de Carlos da Maia will take you past an old police school and into Rua Correia da Silva, which leads to a small early-19th-century Tin Hau temple on Largo Governador Tamagnini Barbosa. Northeast, just off Rua do Regedor, is Pak Tai Temple, dedicated to the Taoist god of the sea who became the 'Emperor of the North'.

4 Markets There is a weekly crafts market (🕑 noon-9pm Sun) in Largo de Camões. The Taipa market is housed in a building at the end of Rua do Regedor.

SHOPPING

Macau is not really a shopping destination, but you'll find a variety of shops straddling Avenida do Infante Dom Henrique and Avenida de Almeida Ribeiro in Macau Peninsula. Other shopping zones include Rua da Palha, Rua do Campo and Rua Pedro Nolasco da Silva.

There is a growing number of luxury outlets catering to high-end fashion shoppers. The massive Venetian Macao Resort Hotel (Map p328) has the huge Grand Canal mall, which extends to the Four Seasons Hotel and is well stocked with familiar international brand names. Similar, yet smaller, shopping complexes include City of Dreams (Map p328) and Wynn Macau (Map pp314–15; Rua Cidade de Sintra, NAPE).

New Yaohan (Map p318; Avenida Comercial de Macau), located behind the Grand Emperor Hotel, is a large, multistorey, family-oriented department store.

ANTIQUES & CURIOS

You'll stumble across bustling markets and traditional Chinese shops in Macau's back lanes, including the charming market street of Rua da Madeira that has shops selling carved Buddha heads and other religious items.

Rua dos Mercadores, which leads up to Rua da Tercena, will lead you past tailors, tiny jewellery stores, incense and mah-jong

shops, and other traditional businesses (Map p318). At the far end of Rua da Tercena, where the road splits, is a flea market (Map p318), where you can pick up baskets and other rattan ware, plus jade pieces and old coins.

Great streets for antiques, ceramics and curios (eg traditional Chinese kites) are Rua de São Paulo, Rua das Estalagens and Rua de São António, and the lanes off them; most shops are open from 10.30am or 11am to 6pm or 7pm, with a one-hour lunch some time between 12.30pm and 2pm.

Coloane Village has a few shops selling bric-a-brac, traditional goods and antiques. Asian Artefacts (Map p330; ☎ 2888 1022; 9 Rua dos Negociantes; 🕑 10am-7pm) is recommended.

CLOTHING

For cheap clothing, go to the St Dominic Market (Map p318), in an alley just north of Largo do Senado, or the Three Lamps District (Map pp314–15), especially around Rotunda de Carlos da Maia near the Almirante Lacerda City Market in northern Macau Peninsula.

SPECIALITY FOODS

On Rua de Felicidade – the 'street of happiness' but more commonly known as 'street of souvenirs' – a cluster of shops sell Chinese pastries original to Macau. Koi Kei (Map p318; 74 Rua de Felicidade) specialises in phoenix rolls (shredded pork wrapped with seaweed) and peanut candies. Choi Heong Yuen (Map p318; ☎ 2835 5966; 70-72 Rua de Felicidade), going strong for over 70 years, is Macau's most popular place for *hang-yàn-béng* (almond-flavoured biscuits). Both shops have numerous outlets, but Felicidade has the more elaborate choices. Other Macau specialities you might want to try include nougats, preserved apricots and *yuk-gàwn*, dried sweet strips of pork and other meats. The shops usually open from 10am to 10pm.

Pun Veng Kei (Map p318; ☎ 2833 5177; 1B Rua do Monte; 🕑 noon-6pm), just below the Ruins of São Paulo, is a humble but beloved pastry shop selling freshly made aromatic *kam chin béng* (egg crisps). Mr Pun's son also sells the egg crisps from the cart in front of the Museum of the Holy House of Mercy.

STAMPS

Macau produces some wonderful postage stamps: real collector's items that include images of everything from colonial landmarks to roulette tables. Mint sets and first-day covers are available from counters 17 and 18 at the main post office (Map p318) facing Largo do Senado.

EATING

While the new mega-resorts boast high-end international cuisines that have changed the food culture in the city, Macau's own fare is still alive and well preserved. Be it Portuguese cuisine, Macanese 'soul food', Cantonese dim sum or the special treats from street stalls, eating is often the prime motive for making a trip to Macau.

The most popular tipple in Macau is *vinho verde*, a crisp, dry, slightly effervescent 'green' wine from Portugal that goes down a treat with salty Portuguese food and spicy Macanese dishes. You may also try one of the fine wines from Dão, Douro or Alenquer.

Portuguese & Macanese Cuisine

Portuguese cuisine is meat-based and not always particularly refined. It makes great use of olive oil, garlic and *bacalhau* (dried salted cod), which can be prepared in many different ways. The cuisine sometimes combines meat and seafood in one dish, such as *porco à Alentejana*, a tasty casserole of pork and clams. Some favourite dishes are *caldo verde* (a soup of green kale – a type of cabbage – thickened with potatoes), *pastéis de bacalhau* (codfish croquettes), *sardinhas grelhadas* (grilled sardines) and *feijoada* (a casserole of beans, pork, spicy sausages, potatoes and cabbage).

Macanese food borrows a lot of its ingredients and tastes from Chinese and other Asian cuisines, as well as from those of former Portuguese colonies in Africa and India. Dishes are redolent of coconut, tamarind, chilli, jaggery (palm sugar) and shrimp paste.

The most famous Macanese speciality is *galinha á Africana* (African chicken), in which

the bird is prepared in coconut, garlic and chillies. As well as cod, there are plenty of other fish and seafood: shrimps, prawns, crabs, squid and white fish. Sole, a tongue-shaped flat fish, is a Macanese delicacy. The contribution from the former Portuguese enclave of Goa, on the west coast of India, is spicy prawns.

Other Macanese favourites include *casquinha* (stuffed crab), *porco balichão tamarino* (pork cooked with tamarind and shrimp paste), *minchi* (minced beef or pork cooked with potatoes, onions and spices), and baked rice dishes made with cod, prawns or crab. Macanese desserts include *pudim*, which is basically crème caramel; *pastéis de nata*, a scrumptious egg-custard tartlet eaten warm; and *serradura*, a calorie-rich 'sawdust' pudding made with crushed biscuits, cream and condensed milk. If you want to try the latter while touring around, visit the mistakenly spelled Serrdura (p338).

Dining in Macau (www.dininginmacau.com) is a quarterly advertorial freebie, but a good source of information about restaurants nonetheless.

Other Cuisines

Some people swear that the dim sum here is far better than anything you'll find in Hong Kong. Japanese and other European fare are expertly prepared in most top-end hotels in the casino strips and the Cotai area. Excellent Thai food can be found in the area just east of the Cemetery of St Michael the Archangel, and Burmese cuisine is commonly available in the Three Lamps District, a contribution of the sizeable Burmese community living there.

MACAU PENINSULA

Whether it's Chinese, Portuguese or Macanese cuisine you're after, making reservations is a must in midrange and fine-dining restaurants. Places are often booked solid on the weekends (thanks to the arrival of the controversy-stirring Michelin guide). Most restaurants open from noon to around 3pm, and re-open again at 6pm till 11pm. Good news for foodies is the 5% government tax levied on food and beverages in restaurants has been lifted.

Macau Peninsula's *dqai pàai dawng* (open-air street stalls) serve up excellent stir-fry dishes; try any of those along Rua do Almirante Sérgio or those on the 3rd floor of St Dominic Market (Mercado de São Domingos; Map pp314–15; Rua Oeste do Mercado de São Domingos; ⊙ 7am-6pm).

Macau has about 10 *mercados* (markets) selling fresh fruit, vegetables, meat and fish from 6am to 8pm daily. The largest is the

---

PRICE GUIDE

This price guide is for the approximate cost of a two-course meal, with drinks.

$$$$	More than MOP$1200 a meal
$$$	MOP$400-1200
$$	MOP$150-400
$	Up to MOP$150

Almirante Lacerda City Market (Mercado Municipal Almirante Lacerda; Map pp314–15; 130 Avenida do Almirante Lacerda), in northern Macau, commonly known as the Red Market. The historical St Lawrence City Market (Mercado Municipal de São Lourenço) on Rua de João Lecarosin in the south was demolished in 2006, but a new market complex at the same location was under construction at the time of writing.

Pavilions Supermercado (Map p318; ☎ 2833 3636; 421 Avenida da Praia Grande; ☉ 10am-9pm Mon-Sat, 11am-8pm Sun), a supermarket in the centre of the Macau Peninsula, has a wide selection of imported food and drinks, including a Portuguese section in the basement. The supermarket on the 7th floor of New Yaohan (Map p318; ☎ 2872 5338; Avenida Comercial de Macau; ☉ 10.30am-10pm) beside Nam Van Lake also has great choices of imported Japanese and international food. Hyper Gourmet (Map p328; ☎ 2881 3452; Ground fl, Magnolia Court, Ocean Gardens, Avenida dos Jardins do Oceano, Taipa; ☉ 10am-10pm), another supermarket on Taipa, and Gourmet Fine Foods (Map p328; ☎ 2884 1436; Ground fl, Block 25, Nava Taipa Garden, 393 Rua de Seng Tou, Taipa; ☉ 10am-9pm), a deli-style store, both feature Portuguese, French and Italian foods.

ROBUCHON A GALERA
Map pp314-15 French $$$$

☎ 2888 3888; 3rd fl, New/West Wing, Lisboa Hotel, 2-4 Avenida de Lisboa; starters MOP$190-290, mains MOP$330-570; ☉ noon-2.30pm & 6.30-10.30pm

What else do you expect from an institution created by Joël Robuchon, the most Michelin-starred chef on the planet? As Macau's only holder of three Michelin stars, this restaurant features haute cuisine and world-class wines. For an ultimate fine-dining experience, try the 12-course tasting menu for MOP$2100. Even if you don't win big at the casinos, the three-course set lunch for MOP$398 is still affordable.

DON ALFONSO 1890 Map p318 Italian $$$$
☎ 8803 7722; Grand Lisboa, Avenida de Lisboa; starters MOP$180-230, mains from MOP$510; ☉ noon-2.30pm & 6.30-10.30pm

Classically decorated with red crystal chandeliers, and with a posh ambience, this opulent restaurant opened by another colourful Michelin-starred chef, Alfonso Iaccarino, ensures the most authentic cucina Italiana in the high-end culinary world. The dégustation menu is MOP$1390, but you don't need to break the bank for its two-course lunch at MOP$280.

top picks

MACAU RESTAURANTS

- Robuchon a Galera (left)
- António (p339)
- Amagao (p340)
- Eight (p336)
- Fernando (p341)

LA PALOMA
Map pp314-15 Spanish, Mediterranean $$$

☎ 2837 8111; Pousada de São Tiago, Avenida da República; mains MOP$360-720; ☉ 7am-11.30pm

You might go inside this restaurant just for a cup of coffee on its terrace, and no one could blame you, as its romantic ambience is unbeatable. The tapas and paella are fabulous. For a less decadent meal, try its afternoon tea set (MOP$118), served from 3pm to 6pm.

IL TEATRO Map pp314-15 Italian $$$
☎ 8986 3663; 1st fl, Wynn Macau, Rua Cidade de Sintra, NAPE; mains MOP$260-650; ☉ 5.30pm-11.30pm Tue-Sun

Overlooking the spectacular performance lake in the resort, this sumptuously designed restaurant has a tempting range of Italian cuisine and Sicilian fare. Chefs are visible through the full-length glass of the kitchen. The service is attentive.

TOU TOU KOI Map p318 Cantonese $$$
☎ 2857 2629; 6-8 Travessa do Mastro; mains MOP$68-175, seafood MOP$178-520; ☉ 8am-3pm & 5pm-midnight

Located down the alley just opposite the Pawnshop Museum, this nominally Chinese restaurant serves some traditional Cantonese dishes you can no longer find in other Chinese restaurants. Among the wide range of sumptuous dishes is its signature deep-fried stuffed crab with shrimp.

WING LEI Map pp314-15 Chinese $$$
☎ 8986 3688; Ground fl, Wynn Macau, Rua Cidade de Sintra, NAPE; dim sum MOP$28-102, mains MOP$110-520; ☉ 11am-3pm & 6-11pm

This restaurant is decked out with an iconic crystal dragon, which some love, but some find gaudy. But its dim sum menu, featuring contemporary Cantonese with a Shanghai twist, is certainly outstanding, and also surprisingly affordable.

EIGHT Map p318 — Cantonese $$$

☎ 2888 3838; 2nd fl, Grand Lisboa, Avenida de Lisboa; dim sum MOP$25-120, mains MOP$150-200; ⏰ 11.30am-2.30pm & 6.30-10.30pm
Elegantly designed in black, the main dining hall will impress you at first sight with its water-lily pool. Getting a table is next to impossible if you don't have a reservation. The dim sum menu is not as elaborate as its competitors', but its solid food quality and the chef's creativity will win your heart.

ROSSIO Map p318 — International $$$

☎ 8802 3888; MGM Grand Macau, Grand Praça; mains MOP$250-630; ⏰ 7am-11pm
Rossio's spacious dining hall, integrated with waterfalls and granite stones, exudes a soothing ambience. And the open kitchen is made to be photographed. Sunday brunch (11am to 3pm; MOP$380) is an impressive spread of buffet items with a focus on seafood, Indian, Portuguese and Mediterranean cuisines; it comes highly recommended.

CLUBE MILITAR DE MACAU
Map p318 — Portuguese $$

☎ 2871 4000; 975 Avenida da Praia Grande; starters MOP$56-112, mains MOP$148-264, lunch buffet MOP$118; ⏰ noon-3pm & 7-11pm
Housed in Macau's most distinguished colonial building, with ceiling fans spinning lazily above, the Military Club is for those who romanticise about days gone by. The food here is much better than it used to be and the place has some excellent Portuguese wines. Be sure to dress smartly.

LITORAL Map pp314-15 — Macanese, Portuguese $$

☎ 2896 7878; 261A Rua do Almirante Sérgio; starters MOP$68-120, mains MOP$98-450; ⏰ noon-3pm & 6-10.30pm
This restaurant has a cheerful ambience that attracts locals and tourists alike. Apart from the authentic Macanese fare, including baked duck rice, it's renowned for its homemade shrimp soup served in a bread bowl.

CAMÕES Map pp314-15 — Portuguese $$

☎ 2872 8818; 1st fl, 3 Lisboa Bldg, Fisherman's Wharf; starters MOP$48-180, mains MOP$98-178; ⏰ noon-3pm & 6-11.30pm

Camões is the best place to dine on the Fisherman's Wharf. The menu features a wide range of *bacalhau* dishes to suit everybody's fancy. It also has a kid-friendly menu. Ask for a table on the balcony.

LOCANDA Map pp314-15 — Italian $$

☎ 2833 1785; 8 Calçada da Igreja de São Lazaro; starters MOP$58-78, mains MOP$88-128; ⏰ noon-3pm & 6-10pm
Tucked away in the historical Old Ladies' House, Locanda's Italian dishes may not be the best in town, but it has a peerless location that provides an excellent outdoor dining opportunity on its leafy patio. Travellers recommend the pizzas here.

AFONSO III Map p318 — Portuguese $$

☎ 2858 6272; 11A Rua Central; starters MOP$68-110, mains MOP$98-210; ⏰ noon-3pm & 6.30-10.30pm Mon-Sat
A short stroll southwest of the Leal Senado is this tiny restaurant that has won a well-deserved reputation among the Portuguese community in Macau. Tables are often in short supply, so phone ahead.

LA BONNE HEURE Map p318 — French $$

☎ 2833 1209; 12A-B Travessa de São Domingos; starters MOP$56-120, mains MOP$98-260; ⏰ noon-3pm & 5.30-10pm Sun-Wed, 5.30-11.30pm Thu-Sat
This brasserie is just up from the Largo do Senado. The bar area extends its opening hours until 1.30am on Fridays. Upstairs there's a tiny gallery (tall people mind your heads!) with artwork from local young artists.

PRAIA GRANDE
Map pp314-15 — Portuguese, Macanese $$

☎ 2897 3022; 10A Praça Lobo d'Avila; starters MOP$48-78, mains MOP$98-260; ⏰ noon-11pm Mon-Fri, 11.45am-11pm Sat & Sun; 🚍 6, 9, 32
Get a table by the window upstairs for a view of the boulevard. This stylish place is beautifully decorated with a Portuguese motif and serves adequate Portuguese dishes on the historic Praia Grande.

PLATÃO Map p318 — Portuguese $$

☎ 2833 1818; www.plataomacau.com; 3 Travessa de Sao Domingos; starters MOP$28-40, mains MOP$94-248; ⏰ noon-11pm Tue-Sun
This restaurant is renowned for its chef, who once worked for the governors of

Macau. Dishes worth trying include the baked duck rice and the rack of lamb with mustard. The giant *serradura* (MOP$52) is a must.

A LORCHA Map pp314-15 — Portuguese $$

☎ 2831 3193; 289A Rua do Almirante Sérgio; starters MOP$52-78, mains MOP$78-180; ⏰ 12.30-3pm & 6.30-11pm Wed-Mon

'The Sailboat' is arguably the best casual Portuguese eatery on the peninsula. Try the pork-ear salad and deep-fried *bacalhau*. It's also listed in every guide book, so you get lots of tourists.

O PORTO INTERIOR
Map pp314-15 — Macanese, Portuguese $$

☎ 2896 7770; 259B Rua do Almirante Sérgio; mains MOP$65-180; ⏰ noon-11.30pm

If you can't get a table at A Lorcha, this lovely restaurant is a good alternative for both Portuguese and Macanese fare. The juicy African chicken deserves savouring.

HENRI'S GALLEY Map pp314-15 — Macanese $$

☎ 2855 6251; 4G-H Avenida da República; starters MOP$52-84, mains MOP$75-240; ⏰ 11am-10pm

The wonderful Macanese chef Henri Wong is the soul of this 34-year-old institution. Mr Wong expertly prepares Macanese specialities like African chicken and Macau sole with a unique recipe. The Sai Van Lake setting is superb.

FAT SIU LAU
Map p318 — Macanese $$

☎ 2857 3580; cnr Rua da Felicidade & Travessa do Mastro; mains MOP$88-156; ⏰ noon-11pm

At least three generations in Macau would have heard about this charming century-old Macanese institution. Try its signature roasted pigeon. The chic Fat Siu Lau 2 (Map pp314-15; ☎ 2872 2922; Ef Vista Magnifica Ct, Avenida Dr Sun Yat Sen; ⏰ noon-3pm & 6.30pm-midnight), its first and only branch after a century, has some fusion innovations in its menu.

PORTAS DO SOL Map pp314-15 — Cantonese $$

☎ 2888 3888; 2nd fl, East Wing, Lisboa Hotel; dim sum MOP$18-48, mains MOP$88-240; ⏰ 9.30am-3pm & 6.30-11.30pm

Portas do Sol is best known for its ever-changing dim sum menu that surprises anew every visit. Make sure you have a reservation if you go on the weekend as it gets pretty full when families get together for dim sum.

LONG KEI Map p318 — Cantonese $$

☎ 2858 9508; 7B Largo do Senado; dishes MOP$68-230; ⏰ 11.30am-3pm & 6-11.30pm

In the heart of Largo do Senado, this unpretentious restaurant has an assortment of Cantonese dishes (300-plus items on the menu!). It's a handy choice for a delectable seafood experience.

OU MUN CAFÉ Map p318 — Cafe $

☎ 2837 2207; 12 Travessa de São Domingos; sandwiches MOP$20-35, set lunches MOP$80, dishes MOP$60; ⏰ 9am-10pm Tue-Sun

This much-loved Macanese cafe closed down for a while, but it has come back with a modern facelift, decorated with colourful stained glass. The freshly made Portuguese pastries and chocolates are still here.

CARAVELA Map p318 — Cafe $$

☎ 2871 2080; Ground fl, Kam Loi Bldg, 7 Pátio do Comandante Mata e Oliveira; cakes MOP$25-45, set lunch MOP$75; ⏰ 8am-10.30pm

Hidden in a charmless backstreet north of Avenida de Dom João IV is this excellent *pastelaria* (pastry shop), a popular hangout for Portuguese residents on the peninsula. Grab a *befe a Caravela* (Caravela beef) if you're craving something more substantial.

RIQUEXÓ Map pp314-15 — Macanese, Cafeteria $

☎ 2856 5655; 69 Avenida Sidónio Pais; dishes MOP$33-70, set meals from MOP$58; ⏰ noon-10pm

This unpretentious eatery near the reservoir is one of the best kept secrets among the local Macanese community. Choices are sparse, but its homemade Macanese dishes like *feijodo* (pork with black beans) and *minchi,* as well as its flan, deserve a thumbs-up.

LONG WA Map pp314-15 — Cantonese, Tea House $

☎ 2857 4456; 3 Avenida do Almirante Lacerda; dim sum MOP$7, dishes MOP$12-25; ⏰ 7am-2pm

Next to the Red Market, this rare survivor of traditional Cantonese tea houses in Macau has a nostalgic charm, with age-old tiling on the floors and flights. There is no English menu. Just help yourself to the tea and grab what you want from the dim sum carts. No smoking here.

WONG CHI KEI Map p318   Cantonese $

☎ 2833 1313; 17 Largo do Senado; rice & noodle dishes MOP$21-45; ⏰ 8am-midnight

Decked out with traditional furniture, this eatery is where tourists and locals like to congregate for good, cheap noodle soup with wonton.

CHEONG KEI Map p318   Cantonese $

☎ 2857 4310; 68 Rua da Felicidade; noodle dishes MOP$18-30; ⏰ 12.30pm-1.30am

Peak-time queues at the door are a clue that this long-standing noodle joint on the 'street of happiness' has a loyal following. Try the stewed noodles with jelly fish (*hoi chik lou mein;* 海蜇撈麵). There are just a few communal tables; be prepared to trade elbows with the locals.

MARGARET'S CAFÉ E NATA Map p318   Cafe

☎ 2871 0032; Rua Alm Costa Cabral; cakes & sandwiches MOP$6-25; ⏰ 6.30am-8pm Mon-Sat, 9am-7pm Sun

If you want to try the legendary Macanese egg tarts but don't want to go all the way to Lord Stow's (see p341) in Coloane, this busy cafe is famous for its meltingly sweet, rich egg tarts and good-value sandwiches.

SERRDURA Map pp314-15   Macanese Dessert $

☎ 2833 2880; Ground fl, Tin Fok Bldg, 15 Avenida do Coronel Mesquita; ⏰ noon-11pm

This shop sells bite-sized (MOP$11) and large (MOP$88) versions of *serradura,* a rich local dessert made with crushed biscuits, cream and condensed milk. It also has a branch in Taipa Village (Map p328; ☎ 2833 2880; Rua do Regedor; ⏰ noon-10pm).

LAI KEI Map pp314-15   Dessert $

☎ 2837 5781; 12-12A Avenida Conselheiro Ferreira de Almeida; ice cream MOP$7-16; ⏰ 12.30-10pm

This ice-cream parlour oozes nostalgia for Macau in the 1960s, and indeed, the menu and prices haven't changed for decades. The simplicity of the food conjures up bitter-sweet feelings of childhood. Fans of retro must try the perennial favourite wafer Neapolitan ice-cream sandwiches.

U TAC HONG Map p318   Cantonese Dessert $

☎ 2892 0598; 19D Rua da Madeira; snacks & drinks MOP$4-10; ⏰ 8am-7pm

Also known as Lee Hong Kee, U Tac Hong is a tiny local place that has been selling soya-bean products for 50 years, and is reputable for its silky *tofufa* (sweet bean-curd with evaporated milk; 豆腐花加奶; MOP$4) and soya-bean milk.

TAIPA & COLOANE ISLANDS

The arrival of hotel-casino-mall complexes in the Cotai strip usher in a host of new fine-dining scenes in Taipa, tripling the number of eateries in just a few short years. While restaurants serving international cuisine keep popping up, Portuguese and Macanese food is still a key drawcard in Taipa. You'll also find some excellent Cantonese restaurants here, too.

Coloane is not the treasure trove of restaurants and other eateries that Taipa is, but there are a few decent options offering a variety of cuisines at various price levels.

Taipa Island

TENMASA Map p328   Japanese $$$$

☎ 8803 6611; 11th fl, Altira Macau, Avenida de Kwong Tung; lunch MOP$300-520, dinner MOP$480-2200; ⏰ noon-2.30pm & 6-10.30pm

For those who fancy Japanese delicacies, Tenmasa should top your must-try list. It is one of the best and most impressive Japanese restaurants in town, serving exceptional tempura. Sashimi quality here is also exemplary.

YING Map p328   Cantonese $$$$

☎ 8803 6600; 11th fl, Altira Macau, Avenida de Kwong Tung; dim sum MOP$28-88, mains MOP$90-690; ⏰ 9.30am-4.30pm & 6-10.30pm

Ying is as notable for its terrific view of Macau Peninsula as it is for dim sum, both of which are spectacular. Try the lobster and coconut roll (MOP$48). The interior is beautifully decorated with crystal beaded curtains, making it an excellent choice for classy Chinese dining.

PORTOFINO Map p328   Italian $$$$

☎ 8118 9950; Shop 1039-1040, Venetian Macao Resort Hotel, Estrada da Baía de Nossa Senhora da Esperança; starters MOP$75-128, mains MOP$95-380; ⏰ 11am-3pm & 6-11pm

For a true Italian splurge, head to this newbie in the Venetian's high-end dining row. With generous spacing between tables and vast views of the swimming pools from the terrace, this is a wonderful (and rare) spot for alfresco dining in this mega-resort complex.

MACAU EATING

CANTON Map p328   Chinese $$$$

☎ 8118 9930; Shop 1018, Venetian Macao Resort Hotel, Estrada da Baía de Nossa Senhora da Esperança; mains MOP$90-285; ⏲ 11am-3pm & 6-11pm
Don't be misled by the name of this restaurant. Apart from an extensive choice of Cantonese dishes and dim sum, classy Canton serves some carefully and healthily prepared food from different regions in China, and sometimes with a fusion flair. The problem is getting there – it's on the casino floor. If you are going with kids, call ahead and staff will show you a secret entrance.

ANTÓNIO Map p328   Portuguese $$$

☎ 2899 9998; 3 Rua dos Negociantes; starters MOP$68-158, mains from MOP$128; ⏲ noon-3pm & 6-11pm
It's hard not to fall in love with António. The cosy mahogany-framed dining room, the meticulously thought-out menu, and the entertaining and celebrated chef

SAMPLING THE MENU

These are a few of the dishes you're likely to encounter on your travels through Macau.

Entradas
chouriço assado
croquetes de carne
pastéis de bacalhau

Appetisers
grilled Portuguese sausage
minced-beef croquettes
dried Portuguese cod cakes

Sopas
caldo verde
sopa de marisco

Soups
Portuguese kale soup with *chouriço,* thickened with potato
seafood soup

Marisco
açorda de marisco
ameijoas 'Bulhão Pato'
arroz de marisco
camarão frito com alho e piri-piri
caril de carangueijo
casquinha

Shellfish
seafood and mashed-bread casserole
clams with garlic, coriander and olive oil
mixed-seafood rice
deep-fried prawns with garlic and chilli
crab curry
stuffed crab

Peixe
bacalhau á 'Brás'
bacalhau á 'Zé do Pipo'
lulas recheadas
sardinhas na brasa

Fish
sautéed *bacalhau* with potatoes and egg
baked, dried cod with mashed potato
stuffed squid
grilled sardines

Carne
bife de vitela grelhado na brasa com batata frita
caldeirada de borrego
carne de porco à Alentejana
coelho á caçadora
feijoada
galinha á Africana
minchi
porco balichão tamarino

Meat
grilled veal steak and chips
lamb, potato and white wine stew
sautéed pork and clams
rabbit stew
pork knuckle, *chouriço,* red-bean and cabbage stew
grilled chicken cooked with coconut, garlic and chillies
minced beef or pork cooked with potato, onions and spices
pork cooked with tamarind and shrimp paste

Sobremesas
fatias de tomar
pudim de ovos
serradura

Desserts
cake-like dessert made with egg yolks and syrup
caramel egg pudding
cream and condensed-milk pudding topped with crumbled biscuits

António Coelho all make this *the* place to go for all of your traditional Portuguese favourites. If you can only try one Portuguese restaurant in Macau, make it this one. You shouldn't miss the gratinated goat cheese with olive oil and honey, and the flaming Portuguese sausage.

A PETISQUEIRA Map p328 Portuguese $$
☎ 2882 5354; 15A-B Rua de São João; starters MOP$25-85, mains MOP$98-198; ⏰ noon-2.30pm & 7-10.15pm Tue-Fri, noon-2.45pm & 7-10.15pm Sat & Sun
'The Snackery' is an amicable place with a myriad of Portuguese choices set in a little alley that is easy to overlook. It serves its own *queijo fresca da casa* (homemade cheese). Try the baked seafood with rice.

LA CUCINA ITALIANA Map p328 Italian $$
☎ 2882 7818; 6-12 Rua do Pai Kok; starters MOP$38-88, mains MOP$88-188; ⏰ noon-10pm Wed-Mon
This low-key restaurant in Taipa Village is full of locals in the evenings, drawn by carefully prepared pastas and toothsome tiramisu. It has a great selection of Italian wines that go perfectly with the fresh seafood dishes.

AMAGAO Map p328 Macanese $$
☎ 2882 7627; Rua Ho Lin Vong; starters MOP$38-84, mains MOP$78-185; ⏰ 6-10pm Thu-Tue
Make your way to Amagao and let the chef heal you if you are sick of flash eateries and crying out for a good honest meal. Located down a side alley off Rua da Cunha, this 10-seat family style Macanese restaurant is probably the best in Macau. The fabulously flavourful Portuguese chicken (MOP$98) is exceptional.

O MANUEL Map p328 Portuguese $$
☎ 2882 7571; 90 Rua de Fernão Mendes Pinto; starters MOP$40-56, mains MOP$78-154; ⏰ noon-3.30pm & 6-10.30pm Wed-Mon
A family-run restaurant, though a bit isolated from Taipa Village, it still attracts both locals and expats alike with its splendid Portuguese dishes such as grilled *bacalhau*.

KAPOK CANTONESE RESTAURANT
Map p328 Cantonese $$
☎ 2883 3333; 60 Rua de Hong Chau, Hoi Yee Garden; mains MOP$60-150; ⏰ 11am-3pm & 5.30-11pm Mon-Sat, 9am-3pm & 5.30-11pm Sun

This crowd-pleaser behind the Crown has quality dim sum in a more casual setting. It's always full during lunch hours and on the weekends.

COZINHA PINOCCHIO
Map p328 Macanese $$
☎ 2882 7128; 4 Rua do Sol; starters MOP$68-88, mains MOP$65-168; ⏰ 11.45am-10.30pm
After moving back to its original location in a newly renovated building, Cozinha Pinocchio's food has improved a lot and its size doubled. On the weekends it's packed with tourists enjoying the stir-fried curried crab.

GALO Map p328 Macanese, Portuguese $$
☎ 2882 7423; 45 Rua da Cunha; starters MOP$35-65, mains MOP$56-148; ⏰ 11am-3pm & 6-10.30pm
You can easily recognise this place by the picture of a red-combed *galo* (rooster) above the door. The food is adequate and the service flawless.

POU TAI TEMPLE RESTAURANT
Map p328 Chinese, Vegetarian $
☎ 2893 0321; 5 Estrada Lou Lim leok; dishes MOP$36-55; ⏰ 11am-8pm Mon-Sat, 9am-9pm Sun
If you get tired of the meat-laden Portuguese cuisine, this strictly vegetarian restaurant, set in a Buddhist temple in northern Taipa, is a great find for the health conscious. No frills here.

Coloane Island
ESPAÇO LISBOA Map p330 Portuguese $$
☎ 2888 2226; 8 Rua dos Gaivotas; starters MOP$89-250, mains MOP$120-350; ⏰ noon-3pm & 6.30-10pm Tue-Fri, noon-10.30pm Sat & Sun
Located in a charming village house with white stuccoed walls, the 'Lisbon Space' restaurant is perfect if you want a quiet, romantic evening with your partner. Get a table on the balcony and try the carefully prepared Portuguese dishes such as grilled sardines.

MIRAMAR Map p330 Portuguese $$
☎ 2888 2663; Zona Norte de Praia de Hac Sa; starters MOP$40-98, mains MOP$118-248; ⏰ 7-11pm Tue-Fri, noon-11pm Sat & Sun
Miramar is one of the best kept secrets among the Portuguese community in Macau. Just next to the Westin, this seaside restaurant serves magnificent Portuguese

food with a Mozambique flavour. Try the curry with shrimp and wash it down with *vinho verde*. It has indoor and outdoor dining areas, and is equipped with shower facilities for beachgoers. The restaurant is really out of the way. Call for a free pick-up service from anywhere in Taipa.

KWUN HOI HEEN Map p330 Cantonese $$
☎ 8899 1320; 3rd fl, Westin Resort Macau, 1918 Estrada de Hác Sá; rice & noodle dishes MOP$40-89, mains MOP$48-280; ⏲ lunch 11am-3pm Mon-Fri, 9.30am-4pm Sat & Sun, dinner 6.30-11pm nightly
Though it boasts alfresco dining and sumptuous views, it's the superb Cantonese cuisine that makes Kwun Hoi Heen stand out among the hotel restaurants on Coloane Island.

LA GONDOLA Map p330 Italian $$
☎ 2888 0156; Cheoc Van beach; mains MOP$80-240; ⏲ 11am-11pm
For a weekend getaway, head to this beachside eatery next to the swimming pool at Cheoc Van beach. It offers excellent pizza cooked in a wood-fired oven.

FERNANDO Map p330 Portuguese $$
☎ 2888 2264; 9 Hác Sá beach; starters MOP$58-78, mains MOP$88-198; ⏲ noon-9.30pm
Fernando is probably the most famous restaurant in Coloane. It has a devoted clientele and is famed for its seafood. The easy-breezy atmosphere makes it perfect for a protracted lunch by the sea. The bar stays open till midnight.

NGA TIM CAFÉ
Map p330 Cantonese, Macanese $
☎ 2888 2086; 1 Rua do Caetano; mains from MOP$68; ⏲ 11am-1am
Although the food here is so-so, the great view and a laidback and unique setting make this cafe a winner. Enjoy the scene of the Chapel of St Francis Xavier just in front of it. The amusing Macanese owner Mr Wong loves playing guitar to his guests in the evenings.

LORD STOW'S CAFÉ Map p330 Cafe $
☎ 2888 2174; 9 Largo do Matadouro; sandwiches & quiches MOP$36-54, desserts MOP$10-26; ⏲ 10.30am 7pm
Though the celebrated English baker Andrew Stow passed away, his cafe and Lord Stow's Bakery (☎ 2888 2534; 1 Rua da Tassara;

⏲ 7am-10pm Thu-Tue, 7am-7pm Wed) keeps his memory well alive by serving his renowned *pastéis de nata,* a warm egg-custard tart (MOP$6) and cheesecake (MOP$14) in unusual flavours, including black sesame and green tea. The Lord Stow's Garden Café (☎ 2888 1851; 105 Rua da Cordoaria; ⏲ 10.30am-7pm) near the Coloane bus stop has a very relaxed atmosphere on its patio.

ENTERTAINMENT
Macau has ambitions to reshape itself as an artistic destination in Asia, but it certainly has some way to go. The Macau Cultural Centre (p322) is the territory's premier venue for cultural performances such as opera and classical music. To book tickets, ring ☎ 2855 5555 (in Hong Kong ☎ 2380 5083) or check www.ccm .gov.mo. The mammoth Venetian Macao Resort Hotel (p349) has a 15,000-seat indoor arena, which is a great place for live music performances and has drawn the likes of Celine Dion and Avril Lavigne. Check www.cotaiticketing. com for event listings.

CCM+, a bimonthly, and *Destination Macau*, a monthly magazine, have useful entertainment listings. They're free and available at MGTO outlets and larger hotels.

CASINOS
As of mid-2009, Macau had 31 casinos. Most of them are located in big hotels on the 'casino strip' along Avenida da Amizade and Cotai Strip in Taipa. All provide frequent free shuttle service (⏲ 9.30am-midnight) to and from both the ferry terminal and Portas do Cerco. All casinos are open 24 hours.

The legal gambling age in Macau is 18 years (21 for Macau residents). Photography is absolutely prohibited inside the casinos. Men cannot wear shorts nor a singlet (undershirt) unless they have a shirt over it. Women wearing shorts or sleeveless tops are refused entry, as is anyone wearing thongs (flip-flops).

Even if you don't fancy playing the tables, it's worth taking a look around, enjoying the free shows and just watching the way these temples of Mammon operate.

EMPEROR PALACE CASINO Map p318
☎ 2888 9988; 299 Avenida Comerical De Macau, Grand Emperor Hotel, Macau Peninsula
With a faux-antique interior complete with portraits of British royalty, and a

SOME FUN & GAMES IN MACAU

Baccarat

Also known as *chemin de fer* (railroad), baccarat has become the card game of choice for the upper crust of Macau's gambling elite. Baccarat rooms are always the classiest part of any casino, and the minimum wager is high – MOP$1000 at some casinos. Two hands are dealt simultaneously: a player hand and a bank hand. Players can bet on either (neither is actually the house hand), and the one that scores closest to nine is the winner. The casino deducts a percentage if the bank hand wins, which is how the house makes its profit. If the player understands the game properly, the house enjoys only a slightly better than 1% advantage over the player.

Blackjack

Also known as 21, this is an easy game, although it requires some skill to play it well. The dealer takes a card and gives another to the players. Face cards count as 10 and aces either one or 11. Cards are dealt one at a time – the goal is to get as close as possible to 21 (blackjack) without going over. If you go over 21 you 'bust', or lose. Players are always dealt their cards before the dealer, so if they bust they will always do so before the dealer does. This is what gives the casino the edge over the player. If the dealer and player both get 21, it's a tie and the bet is cancelled. If players get 21, they win even money plus a 50% bonus. Dealers must draw until they reach 16, and stand on 17 or higher. The player is free to decide when to stand or when to draw.

Boule

Similar to roulette, except that boule is played with a ball about the size of a billiard ball, and there are fewer numbers – 24 numbers plus a star. The payoff is 23 to one on numbers. On all bets (numbers, red or black, odd or even) the casino has a 4% advantage over players.

---

pair of rather unconvincing Queen's Irish Guards standing sentry outside, this place is a scream. The princely concourse, with marble columns and pure gold bricks on the floor, is where you'll find the art of feng shui to make fortunes, if not to show off.

GRAND LISBOA CASINO Map p318

☎ 2838 2828; Avenida de Lisboa, Macau Peninsula
Connected to its little sister (Lisboa Casino) by a footbridge is the plush Grand Lisboa, with its glowing golden-bulb exterior and a truly kitsch flaming-torch-shaped towering structure. The interior ventilation works much better than Lisboa Casino and people are gaming with slightly more manners here. The famous Crazy Paris Cabaret (🕒 4.30pm-12.30am), featuring a multitude of leggy women onstage strutting around in a couple of beads and a feather, is also held here.

LISBOA CASINO Map p318

☎ 2837 5111; Hotel Lisboa, 2-4 Avenida de Lisboa, Macau Peninsula
With cigarette smoke for ambience and little effort at decor, this once-monopolistic old-timer nevertheless is still the best-known casino in Asia for its faded '60s glamour.

Those days are gone, but the tightly packed baccarat tables still live on.

MGM GRAND CASINO Map pp314-15

☎ 8802 1888; www.mgmgrandmacau.com; Avenida Dr Sun Yat Sen, NAPE, Macau Peninsula
This MGM Grand is much smaller than its mother in Vegas, but its gentility and modern design with innovative lighting make it a casino with taste and class. It's more for unruffled high-rollers, meaning it has a more relaxing atmosphere.

PLAZA CASINO Map p328

☎ 2881 8888; www.fourseasons.com/macau; Four Seasons Hotel, Estrada da Baía de Nossa Senhora da Esperança, Taipa
If you want a quieter gaming time, head to the secluded Plaza. Hidden in the Four Seasons Hotel, the Plaza cannot compete with other casinos listed here in terms of size, but its decor is marvellously impressive, making it one of the classiest casinos in Macau. Its location suggests that tourist groups do not venture here.

SANDS MACAU Map pp314-15

☎ 2888 3377; www.sands.com.mo; 23 Largo de Monte Carlo, Macau Peninsula

Daai-sai

Cantonese for 'big little', this game is also known as *sìk-bó* (dice treasure) or *chàai sìk* (guessing dice) and remains popular in Macau. Three dice are placed in a covered glass container, the container is then shaken and you bet on whether the toss will be from three to nine (small) or 10 to 18 (big). However, you lose on combinations where all three dice come up the same (2-2-2, 3-3-3 etc) unless you bet directly on three of a kind. For betting *daai-sai* the house advantage is 2.78%. Betting on a specific three of a kind gives the house a 30% advantage.

Fàan-tàan

This ancient Chinese game is practically unknown in the West. The dealer takes an inverted silver cup and plunges it into a pile of porcelain buttons, then moves the cup to one side. After all bets have been placed, the buttons are counted out in groups of four. You have to bet on how many will remain after the last set of four has been taken out.

Pàai-gáu

This is a form of Chinese dominoes similar to mah-jong. One player is made banker and the others compare their hands against the banker's. The casino doesn't play, but deducts a 5% commission from the winnings for providing the gambling facilities.

Roulette

The dealer spins the roulette wheel in one direction and tosses a ball the other way. Roulette wheels have 36 numbers plus a zero, so your chance of hitting any given number is one in 37. The payoff is 35 to one, which is what gives the casino its advantage. Rather than betting on a single number, it's easier to win if you bet odd versus even, or red versus black, which only gives the house a 2.7% advantage. If the ball lands on zero, everyone loses to the house (unless you also bet on the zero).

Run by the consortium from Vegas leading Macau's gambling business renaissance, the Sands has a spacious atrium allowing natural lighting, together with a fantastic array of crystal chandeliers. Expect throngs of gamblers from the mainland.

VENETIAN MACAO CASINO Map p328
☎ 2882 8888; www.venetianmacao.com; Venetian Macao Resort Hotel, Cotai Strip
As the world's largest casino and three times the size of its Vegas counterpart, you're guaranteed to get lost in this behemoth. Gambling tables are omnipresent and time is irrelevant in this labyrinth. Like the Sands, this is a must-see destination for mainland tourists and is packed 24/7.

WYNN MACAU CASINO Map pp314-15
☎ 2888 9966; Wynn Macau, Rua Cidade de Sintra, NAPE, Macau Peninsula
Mimicking its counterpart in Vegas, Wynn is one of the major players on the casino strip in Macau, emphasising themes, elegance, fine dining, upmarket shopping and, of course, gambling. It has a hedonistic atmosphere and is the first casino with a non-smoking gambling hall.

Gambling

In 2006, Macau's gambling revenue reached US$7.2 billion, overtaking Las Vegas as the world's casino capital. The story begins with the end of a casino monopoly held by Stanley Ho's Sociedade de Turismo Diversoes de Macau (STDM) in 2002. The gambling industry was shaken up with the subsequent arrival of consortiums from Las Vegas.

Despite the global credit crisis in 2008 that put casino operators under serious threat, the revenue from gambling still rose to more than US$14 billion. The passing of the baton to Macau resulted in a drastic increase of addicted gamblers in Macau and China, and very little has been done to curb this. Other side effects, such as money laundering, domestic violence and prostitution, have also shot up.

Although the games in Macau are somewhat different from those played in Las Vegas and elsewhere (see the boxed text, opposite), the same basic principles apply. No matter what the game, the casino enjoys a built-in mathematical advantage. In the short term, anyone can hit a winning streak and get ahead, but the longer you play, the more certain it is that the odds will catch up with you.

CLUBBING

Most of the trendiest bars-cum-clubs with live music are in the newer casino hotels. There are also many choices for clubbing around the NAPE area, including those listed here.

D2 Map p318

☎ 2872 3777; 2nd fl, AIA Tower, 301 Avenida Comercial de Macau, Macau Peninsula; ☺ 10pm-7am, happy hour 11pm-2am

This two-storey bar and dance club is where to strut your stuff. Downstairs there's loud dance music, a dance floor and a bar-lounge area; upstairs there are fashionable booth seats and a terrace overlooking the dance floor. Its sister club DD3 (Map pp314–15; ☺ 4pm-12am) at the Fisherman's Wharf is also a throbbing, groovy spot to revel and to flirt.

FASHION CLUB Map pp314-15

☎ 2872 8922, 2889 9999; Block 1, Trinidad, Fisherman's Wharf, Macau Peninsula; ☺ 10pm-6am

This glitzy bar is where partiers dress to impress or be impressed. But pick your night carefully as it can be dead mid-week, but on a good night there's a great mix of tunes and a fun vibe. The indoor-outdoor combo is perfect, and makes it the best place on the wharf.

DRINKING

Despite an economic downturn, larger casino resorts still have thriving bar and music scenes. The southern end of the NAPE area on Macau Peninsula (what locals call Lan Kwai Fong) is also where to head for pub crawls.

Drinks-wise, Macau Beer has a couple of its own brews: the citrus-tasting Blond Ale and the Amber Ale, which is quite hoppy. All sorts of 'ruby' ports are available in Macau – the Parador is particularly fine – but go for something different, such as the evocatively named Lágrima do Christo (Tears of Christ), a white port. Some Portuguese *aguardentes* (brandies) are worthwhile, such as Adega Velha and Antqua VSOP Aliança.

38 Map p328 Bar

☎ 2886 8888; 38th fl, Altira Macau, Avenida de Kwong Tung, Taipa; ☺ 24hr

The latest incarnation of the famous Crystal Club, this bar sits atop the hotel tower with a terrific outdoor terrace that offers spectacular vistas of the harbour and Macau Peninsula. Combine this with its extensive wines and whisky selection and you get one of the best drinking haunts on Taipa.

CASABLANCA CAFÉ Map pp314-15 Bar

☎ 2875 1281; Ground fl, Vista Magnífica Court Bldg, Avenida Dr Sun Yat Sen, Macau Peninsula; ☺ 6pm-4am, happy hour 6-8pm

Casablanca is a favourite hang-out for the Portuguese in Macau's Lan Kwai Fong. It has a long list of cocktails, plays cold jazz in the background and is considered the best spot to chill out in NAPE.

CINNEBAR Map pp314-15 Bar

☎ 8986 3838; Ground fl, Wynn Macau, Rua Cidade de Sintra, NAPE, Macau Peninsula; ☺ 3pm-midnight

Cinnebar is a good place to go for a quiet natter. It has a fantastic combination of swish and casual: upmarket and classy surroundings indoor and a relaxed, amicable atmosphere in its outdoor seating area around the swimming pool and the garden. Some exotically blended cocktails and homemade snacks are served in this lobby bar.

CORNER'S WINE BAR & TAPAS CAFÉ
Map p318 Bar, Cafe

☎ 2848 2848; 3 Travessa de São Paulo, Macau Peninsula; ☺ cafe noon-5pm, wine bar 5pm-midnight Sun-Thu, 5pm-1am Fri & Sat

This popular rooftop bar and tapas joint attracts the cool, arty-inclined crowd. It has a great location just across from the cathedral ruins, and is dominated by pink comfy couches. At night it's a perfect place for chilled-out drinks amid soft lighting and soothing music.

MACAU SOUL Map p318 Cafe, Lounge

☎ 2836 5182; www.macausoul.com; 31A Rua de São Paulo, Macau Peninsula; ☺ 9.30am-8.30pm Mon-Thu, 9.30am-midnight Fri-Sun

Run by two English retirees, this low-key spot is a hidden gem just down the hill from St Paul's ruins. The ground floor is elegantly decked out with wooden furniture and stained-glass windows that ooze a comfy, easygoing feel. The basement gets very crowded when it is transformed into a live venue for jazz, blues and country bands. The opening hours vary, so phone ahead before you go.

MCSORLEY'S ALE HOUSE Map p328   Bar

☎ 2882 8198; Shop 1038, Venetian Macao Resort Hotel, Estrada da Baía de Nossa Senhora da Esperança, Taipa; ☯ 11am-2.30am

This cosy tavern-style watering hole in the Venetian is a genial spot that attracts rugby and soccer fanatics watching footy on the telly with its live-satellite broadcasts of European matches. The selection of imported beers and pub grub is extensive and reasonably priced.

MGM GRAND MACAU Map pp314-15   Bar

☎ 8802 3888; Grande Praça, Avenida Dr Sun Yat Sen, Macau Peninsula

If you can't make up your mind where to sip in the city, MGM Grand has several excellent bars that offer a bit of something for everyone. The handsome Veuve Clicquot Lounge (☎ 8802 3888; ☯ 6pm-4am) is decked out with whimsically designed loveseats and populated mostly by yuppies and after-work suits enjoying the pricey champagnes. The sleek, high-up Aba Bar (☎ 8802 2533; ☯ 5pm-2am) has a beautiful glass cellar stored with a variety of wines that attracts beautiful urbanities at all times. Next door is the Russian Room (☎ 8802 2374; ☯ 5pm-2am), a sparkling and splendidly designed pub for the high-heeled types to wash down the caviar with the expertly selected vodka.

OLD TAIPA TAVERN Map p328   Bar, Live Music

☎ 2882 5221; Rua dos Negociantes, Taipa; ☯ noon-1am, happy hour 5-8pm

Known as 'OTT', its location near the Pak Tai Temple at Taipa Village makes this delightful bar a sublime spot to watch the comings and goings in the centre of the village. A wonderful live band plays on Saturday.

THEATRE

Apart from the floorshows in the casinos, authentic theatre in Macau has begun to take off, with Cirque du Soleil taking the lead.

ZAIA Map p328

☎ 2882 8818; www.cotaiticketing.com; Venetian Macao Resort Hotel, Estrada da Baía de Nossa Senhora da Esperança, Taipa; adult MOP$388-788, child MOP$194-394

Cirque du Soleil has already put up its big top in the Venetian, ushering in the next big entertainment scene in Macau (apart from gambling, of course). *Zaia*, the nightly resident show, is a spectacular mix of high-wire acrobatics and choreographed dances. Up to 40% discounts for tickets are often available.

DRAGONE SHOW Map p328

☎ 8868 6888; Bubble Theatre, City of Dreams, Taipa

Though not many details were revealed at the time of writing, this water-themed megashow just across the road on the Cotai is designed to rival *Zaia*, and is scheduled to commence in early 2010.

SPORTS & ACTIVITIES
ACTIVITIES
Cycling

You can rent bicycles (MOP$15 to MOP$20 per hour) in Taipa Village from Si Toi (Map p328; Largo do Camões; ☯ 10am-10pm), next to Pak Tai Temple, and Iao Kei (Map p328; ☎ 2882 7975; 36 Largo Governador Tamagini Barbosa; ☯ 10am-7.30pm), next to the Don Quixote restaurant.

Cycling across the Macau–Taipa bridges is prohibited.

Go-Karting

The Coloane Kartodrome (Map p330; ☎ 2888 2126; Estrada de Seac Pai Van; ☯ 11.30am-7pm Mon-Fri, 11am-8.30pm Sat & Sun) is the region's most popular venue for go-karting. There's a choice of seven circuits. It costs MOP$100/200 for 10/25 minutes; a two-seater is MOP$150 for 10 minutes. Races are held on Sunday.

Golf

The 18-hole, par-71 course at Macau Golf & Country Club (Map p330; ☎ 2887 1188; www.macaugolfandcountry club.com; 1918 Estrada de Hác Sá), connected to the Westin Resort Macau on Coloane by walkway on the 9th floor, is open to foreigners through the hotel. Green fees are MOP$1550/2880 on weekdays/weekends, and you must have a handicap certificate to tee off. There's also a driving range (☎ 2887 1111; per 40 balls MOP$45), from where you drive balls into the ocean.

Acquired by the casino giant Harrah's in 2007, Caesars Golf Macau (Map p330; ☎ 2888 0123; www .harrahs.com/golf/macau-orient-golf; Estrada de Seac Pai Van, Taipa) on the Cotai is an 18-hole, par-72 course. The first phase, completed in 2008, includes a golf school and a newly refurbished driving range. Green fees are MOP$1620/2120 on weekdays/weekends.

Hiking

There are two trails on Guia Hill (Map pp314–15), in central Macau Peninsula, which are good for a stroll or jog. The Walk of 33 Curves (1.7km) circles the hill; inside this loop is the shorter Fitness Circuit Walk, with 20 exercise stations. You can access these by the Guia Cable Car.

The Little Taipa Trail (Trilho de Taipa Pequena; Map p328) is a 2km long circuit around a hill (111m) of that name in northwestern Taipa, reachable via Estrada Lou Lim Ieok. The 2.2km-long Big Taipa Trail (Trilho de Taipa Grande; Map p328) rings Taipa Grande, a 160m-high hill at the eastern end of the island. You can access the trail via a short paved road off Estrada Colonel Nicolau de Mesquita.

Coloane's longest trail, the Coloane Trail (Trilho de Coloane; Map p330), begins at Seac Pai Van Park and is just over 8km long; the main trailhead is called the Estrada do Alto de Coloane. The shorter Northeast Coloane Trail (Trilho Nordeste de Coloane), near Ká Hó, runs for about 3km. Other trails that offer good hiking include the 1.5km-long Altinho de Ká Hó Trail and the 1.5km-long Hác Sá Reservoir Circuit (Circuito da Barragem de Hác Sá), which both loop around the reservoir to the northwest of Hác Sá beach.

Water Sports

The Hác Sá Sports & Recreation Park (Map p330; ☎ 2888 2296; Estrada Nova de Hác Sá, Coloane; ◷ 8am-9pm Sun-Fri, 8am-11pm Sat), by the beach, has an outdoor swimming pool (adult/child/student MOP$15/5/7; ◷ 8am-noon & 1-9pm Sun-Fri, 8am-noon & 1-11pm Sat).

The Cheoc Van swimming pool (Map p330; ☎ 2887 0277), which costs the same for entry and keeps the same hours as the Hác Sá pool, is at the southern end of the beach.

There are watersports equipment stands, where you can hire windsurfing boards, jet skis and water scooters, at either end of Hác Sá beach.

SPECTATOR SPORTS

The Macau Stadium (Estádio de Macau; Map p328; ☎ 2883 8208; www.sport.gov.mo; Avenida Olímpica), next to the Macau Jockey Club on Taipa Island, seats 16,250 people and hosts international soccer matches and athletics competitions. On the first Sunday in December the Macau International Marathon starts and finishes here. The impressive Macau Dome (Map p330) on Coloane was built to host the 2005 East Asian Games and the 2007 Indoor Asian Games. Its main arena seats more than 7000 spectators.

For details of forthcoming events, contact the Macau Sports Institute (Instituto do Desporto de Macau; Map pp314–15; ☎ 2858 0762, 2888 1836; Macau Forum, Avenida do Doutor Rodrigo Rodrigues).

Dog Racing

Macau's Canidrome (Map pp314–15; ☎ 2822 1199, racing information hotline 2833 3399, Hong Kong hotline 800 932 199; www.macauyydog.com; Avenida do General Castelo Branco; admission MOP$10; ☐ 1, 1A, 3, 25), in the northern part of the Macau Peninsula, is the only facility for greyhound racing in Asia. Greyhound races are held on Monday, Thursday, Saturday and Sunday at 7.30pm. There are 16 races per night, with six to eight dogs chasing a mechanical rabbit around the 455m oval track at speeds of up to 60km/h. If you want to sit in the members' stands, it costs MOP$80 on weekdays and MOP$120 on the weekend.

Grand Prix

The biggest sporting event of the year is the Macau Formula 3 Grand Prix, held in the third week of November. The 6.2km Guia circuit starts near the Lisboa Hotel and follows the shoreline along Avenida da Amizade, going around the reservoir and back through the city. It is a testing series of twists and turns – including the infamous Melco hairpin – that calls on the drivers' reserves of skill and daring.

Certain zones in Macau are designated as viewing areas for the races. Streets and alleys along the track are blocked off, so it's unlikely that you'll be able to find a decent vantage point without paying for it. Seats in the Reservoir Stand range from MOP$200 to MOP$350, and at the Lisboa and Grand Stands range from MOP$450 to MOP$900. To watch just the practice days and qualifying events costs MOP$50. For ticket inquiries and bookings call ☎ 2855 5555 or consult www.macau.grandprix.gov.mo.

Horse Racing

Regular flat racing takes place at the Taipa racetrack (Hipodromo da Taipa) of the Macau Jockey Club (Jockey Clube de Macau; Map p328; ☎ 2882 1188, racing information hotline 2882 0868, Hong Kong hotline 800 967 822; www.macauhorse.com; Estrada Governador Albano de Oliveira; admission MOP$20; ☐ 11, 15, 22) through most of the year, usually on Saturday or Sunday from 2pm, and midweek (generally Tuesday or Wednesday) from 5pm. Summer recess lasts from late August to mid-September.

SLEEPING

Welcome to the city of hotels. Luxurious hotels have been springing up in Macau over the last eight years, targeting high-rollers, but the recent financial hit means that some great rooms are substantially discounted. Discounts of 30% or more are available for hotels of three stars and above if you book through a travel agency. In Hong Kong many of these agents are at the Shun Tak Centre (Map p80; 200 Connaught Rd Central, Sheung Wan), from where the ferries to Macau depart. You can book your room upon arrival at one of the many hotel desks in the ferry terminal pier in Macau, but be aware that hotel prices can double or even treble on the weekend, on public holidays or during the summer high season.

Most large hotels add a 10% service charge and 5% government tax to the bill. Prices listed here are the rack rates quoted to walk-in customers.

MACAU PENINSULA

Macau has a range of choices to suit every taste and pocket. Big names like Sofitel and MGM Grand are in full swing. A new Mandarin Oriental should be ready by late 2009. The Oceanus complex, Stanley Ho's latest megaproject, is scheduled to open in mid-2010, but it was still very quiet at the time of writing.

WYNN MACAU Map pp314-15   Hotel $$$$
☎ 2888 9966; www.wynnmacau.com; Rua Cidae de Sintra, NAPE; r MOP$3000-3700, ste from MOP$7800; 📶 🏊
This five-star, American-style resort has charming rooms and suites with high ceilings, and almost everything automated. Bonuses include its superb outdoor swimming pool and some very serious restaurants.

POUSADA DE SÃO TIAGO
Map pp314-15   Hotel $$$$
☎ 2837 8111; www.saotiago.com.mo; Avenida da República; ste from MOP$5800; 🏊
Built into the ruins of the 17th-century Barra Fort, the landmark São Tiago is the most romantic place to stay in Macau. No other hotels in Macau can boast such a rich history. All 12 rooms are recently renovated and upgraded to elegantly furnished suites, and it still has an old-world grandeur. The chapel attached to the hotel is also well restored.

PRICE GUIDE

Below is the price guide for rooms in Macau. Breakfast is usually included with hotels marked $$ and $$$.

$$$$	More than MOP$2500
$$$	MOP$1650-2500
$$	MOP$500-1650
$	Up to MOP$500

MGM GRAND MACAU
Map pp314-15   Hotel $$$
☎ 8802 1888; www.mgmgrandmacau.com; Avenida Dr Sun Yat Sen, NAPE; r MOP$1678-2129, ste from MOP$5280; 📶 🏊
The obvious reason for staying in this hotel is the optically fantastic spa. The gallery-like hotel lobby with Dale Chihuly's spectacular glass installation will impress you at first sight, as will the chic, luxurious rooms straddling the curly corridors. Choose the seaside rooms for the sweeping harbour views. The on-site restaurants and pubs (p345) give you all the excitement you need right at one address.

GRAND LAPA HOTEL
Map pp314-15   Hotel $$$
☎ 2856 7888; www.mandarinoriental.com/grand lapa; 956-1110 Avenida da Amizade; r MOP$1288-2788, ste from MOP$5300
Compared to its glossy neighbours on the casino strip, the rooms in Grand Lapa (formerly Mandarin Oriental) are a bit outdated, but its superlative service and superb spa complex with impressive natural surroundings win the hearts of its loyal clientele. It's always full during the weekends.

ROCKS HOTEL Map pp314-15   Hotel $$$
☎ 2878 2782; www.rockshotel.com.mo; Macau Fisherman's Wharf; r MOP$1880-2580, ste from MOP$4080; 🖥
This elegant Victorian-style boutique hotel is set amid a tribal-hut African restaurant and Babylon Casino, reminding you that you're in the middle of a theme park. All rooms feature a balcony and most have a view of the waterfront. It also has affordable shuttle services with its Nissan Cefiro (MOP$30/60/90 to Macau/Taipa/Coloane) and Benz-Mercedes (MOP$150/250/350 to Macau/Taipa/Coloane).

SOFITEL MACAU AT PONTE 16
Map p318 · Hotel $$$
☎ 8861 0016; www.sofitel.com; Rua do Vis-
conde Paço de Arcos; r MOP$1420-2220, ste from
MOP$4220; 🛜
This reasonably priced luxury hotel from a
high-end chain offers some atmospheric
views of the sleepy Inner Harbour and the
ruins of São Paulo on the other side. Rooms
are modern and large, and beds are comfy.
The bathrooms have L'Occitane toiletries.

METRO PARK HOTEL Map pp314-15 Hotel $$
☎ 2878 1233; www.metroparkmacau.com;
199 Rua de Pequim; r MOP$1680-2300, ste from
MOP$2800
Rooms are small and the service so-so,
but this is a good-value casino-free option
along the casino strip. A plus is a regular
substantial discount (60% or more). Cross-
border buses to China also leave from here.

HOTEL SINTRA Map p318 Hotel $$
☎ 2871 0111; www.hotelsintra.com; Avenida de
Dom João IV; r MOP$650-1200, ste from MOP$1400
This centrally located three-star hotel is a
better place to stay than Metro Park. Rooms
are spotless, but those facing Grand Emperor Hotel may find the big LED screen
disturbing. It provides a shuttle service to
the ferry terminal every 15 minutes.

RIVIERA HOTEL MACAU
Map pp314-15 Hotel $$
☎ 2833 9955; www.rivierahotel.com.mo; 11-13
Rua do Comendador Kou Ho Neng; r MOP$1080-
1180, ste from MOP$2080
If you want to stay away from the casinos
and prefer somewhere more secluded, head
to this renovated hotel near the legendary
Bela Vista. Most rooms have wonderful
views of the historic Avenida da República
and Sai Van Lake from the balconies.

POUSADA DE MONG HÁ
Map pp314-15 Inn $$
☎ 2851 5222; www.ift.edu.mo; Colina de Mong
Há; r Mon-Thu MOP$480-680, Fri MOP$580-760, Sat
& Sun MOP$800-960, ste Mon-Thu MOP$960, Fri
MOP$1160, Sat & Sun MOP$1360; 🖳
Sitting atop Mong Há Hill near the ruins of
a fort built in 1849 is this traditional-style
Portuguese inn run by students at the
Instituto de Formação Turística (Institute for
Tourism Studies). Rooms are well appointed

(some equipped with computers) and service attentive. Rates include breakfast. The
restaurant here is open from 12.30pm to
3pm for lunch on weekdays and from 7pm
to 10.30pm on Friday for a Macanese buffet
(MOP$180). Afternoon tea (3pm to 6pm) is
served in its atmospheric cafe.

OLE LONDON HOTEL Map p318 Hotel $
☎ 2893 7761; fax 2893 7790; 4-6 Praça de Ponte
e Horta; d MOP$390-480
This Victorian-style inn near the Inner Harbour was extensively renovated with a pink-
ish facade and smart, spotless rooms. They
are small, but given its location and rates you
can't really complain. You can get greater
discounts if you book via www.macau.com.

HOU KONG HOTEL Map p318 Hotel $
☎ 2893 7555; www.houkonghotel.com; Travessa
das Virtudes; s/tw/tr MOP$310/400/580
Just opposite Kee Kwan Motor Road Company in the historic Porto Interior area, the
newly refurbished Hou Kong retains its
wonderful old facade but now offers surprisingly modern rooms for the money. Check a
few rooms – some don't have windows. You
may get better deals mid-week.

EAST ASIA HOTEL Map p318 Hotel $
☎ 2892 2433; fax 922 431; 1A Rua da Madeira; s
MOP$270-370, d MOP$400-500, ste MOP$720
The East Asia is housed in a classic green-
and-white colonial-style building and,
though it's been remodelled, has not lost
all of its charm. The rooms are simple but
spacious.

AUGUSTERS LODGE Map p318 Guesthouse $
☎ 2871 3242; www.augusters.de; Flat 3J, Block
4, Edif Kam Loi, 24 Rua do Dr Pedro José Lobo; dm
MOP$125, d MOP$260, tr MOP$390; 🚌 3, 3A, 10,
10A, 10B, AP1; 🖳
Though not atmospheric, this backpacker-
friendly guesthouse, located above the CTM
shop, has basic and clean rooms with shared
bathrooms. It's the most central option for
budget travellers (so it's always full).

TAIPA & COLOANE ISLANDS
The land-reclamation projects on the Cotai
strip straddling Taipa and Coloane have
brought in a bunch of top-end accommodation options. While the new Crown Towers,
Hard Rock and Grand Hyatt were opened

on schedule in mid-2009, consortiums have halted most of the other developments, including Banyan Tree, Marriott and Ritz-Carlton, due to the global financial slowdown. There is also the half-built Sheraton, Shangri-La, Hilton, Conrad and InterContinental resort complex on Cotai across the street from the Venetian. Coloane offers quite a diversity of places to stay – from two budget hostels to a 'cosy' inn to the territory's most exclusive resort.

Taipa Island & Cotai Strip

FOUR SEASONS HOTEL
Map p328 — Hotel $$$$

☎ 2881 8888; www.fourseasons.com/macau; Estrada da Baía de Nossa Senhora da Esperança; r MOP$2700-4200, ste from MOP$5100

Four Seasons is a newcomer to the luxury stakes on the Cotai. There aren't many great views from the rooms as its surroundings were still under construction at the time of writing. But inside, especially by the leafy outdoor pools and waterfalls, it truly is a city oasis. You feel very royal once you step into its lobby. Services are attentive and impeccable, and rooms are beautifully appointed.

ALTIRA MACAU Map p328 — Hotel $$$$
☎ 2886 8888; www.altiramacau.com; Avenida de Kwong Tung; r MOP$3080, ste from MOP$4180; 🖥 🛜 🍴

A change of name (it was formerly the Crown) hasn't changed its quality service. The massive rooms are in muted earth tones embellished with flowers, exuding a refreshing ambience, and the 3m plate-glass windows offer breathtaking sea views. Its best features are the rooftop bar and terrace, as well as the award-winning restaurants.

VENETIAN MACAO RESORT HOTEL
Map p328 — Hotel $$$

☎ 2882 8888; www.venetianmacao.com; Estrada da Baía de Nossa Senhora da Esperança; ste MOP$1600-4500; 🛜 🍴

Well, you need a map to navigate this elephantine resort complex, and getting lost is not unheard of! With 3000 lavishly decorated suites in its 32-storey tower, this man-made wonderland has countless amenities catering to luxury over hedonism. It's worth checking its website for packages that often come with complimentary ferry tickets.

HOTEL TAIPA Map p328 — Hotel $$
☎ 2882 1666; www.hoteltaipa.com; 822 Estrada Governador Nobre Carvalho; r MOP$1280-2080, ste MOP$2680-4880

This Best Western chain is a decent place to stay, though it's lacking in character. It's an aircrew's favourite and has less tourist groups staying here. A nice 60% discount is usually on offer.

Coloane Island

WESTIN RESORT MACAU
Map p330 — Hotel $$$

☎ 2887 1111; www.westin.com/macau; 1918 Estrada de Hác Sá; r MOP$2200-2700, ste from MOP$5000; 🍴

Each room has a large terrace in this 'island resort' complex, boasting excellent vistas of the mountains and Hác Sá beach. The attached 18-hole golf course (p345), two swimming pools and an outdoor spa allow you to soak up the ample sun and the relaxing country club atmosphere. Enjoy a sundowner at its delightful Café Panorama (☎ 8899 1020; 🕐 11am-1am).

POUSADA DE COLOANE Map p330 — Inn $$
☎ 2888 2143; www.hotelpcoloane.com.mo; Estrada de Cheoc Van; r MOP$780-880; 🍴

We've got mixed reports about this inn. While some rooms are nicely furnished, others are poorly maintained. Check the rooms before you check in. For the nice ones you'll swear you've landed in an inn in Lisbon. Rooms are decorated with fantastic Portuguese-style tiles and furniture, as well as whirlpool bathtubs. The location above Cheoc Van beach is about as chilled as you'll find. The attached Portuguese restaurant has a great bar area. Midweek, rooms are discounted to MOP$580.

POUSADA DE JUVENTUDE DE CHEOC VAN Map p330 — Hostel $
☎ 2888 2024; Rua de António Francisco; dm/d Sun-Fri MOP$20/50, Sat MOP$30/80

To stay either here or at the hostel at Hác Sá (p350), you must book through the Education & Youth Services Department (☎ 2855 5533; www.dsej .gov.mo) and have a Hostelling International (HI) card. During the high season (summer and holidays), competition for beds is high and it might be shut altogether in August. The hostel has a garden and a small kitchen for making hot drinks.

POUSADA DE JUVENTUDE DE HÁC SÁ

Map p330   Hostel $

☎ 2888 2701; Rua de Hác Sá Long Chao Kok; dm/d Sun-Fri MOP$20/50, Sat MOP$30/80

This circular, grey-tiled building, at the southern end of Hác Sá beach, is more modern than the Cheoc Van hostel, though it's sometimes reserved for groups only.

TRANSPORT
MACAU TO HONG KONG
Air

Travel to Macau by helicopter is a viable option and is becoming increasingly popular for residents and visitors alike.

Sky Shuttle (☎ in Hong Kong 2108 9898; www.skyshuttle hk.com) runs a 16-minute helicopter shuttle service between Macau and Hong Kong (HK$2300, tax included) with up to 28 daily flights leaving between 9am and 11pm. Flights arrive and depart in Macau from the roof of the ferry terminal (Map pp314–15; ☎ 8790 7240). In Hong Kong departures are from the helipad atop the ferry pier that is linked to the Shun Tak Centre (Map p80; ☎ 2859 3359; 200 Connaught Rd Central) in Sheung Wan.

Sea

The vast majority of people make their way from Macau to Hong Kong by ferry. The journey takes just an hour and there are frequent departures throughout the day, with reduced service between midnight and 7am.

TurboJet (☎ 8790 7039, in Hong Kong information 2859 3333, bookings 2921 6688; www.turbojet.com.hk) operates three types of vessels (economy/superclass Monday to Friday MOP$142/244, Saturday and Sunday MOP$154/260, and night crossing MOP$176/275), from the ferry terminal in Macau and the Shun Tak Centre in Hong Kong, which take 65 minutes.

New World First Ferry (NWFF; ☎ 2872 7676, in Hong Kong 2131 8181; www.nwff.com.hk) operates high-speed catamarans from the Macau ferry terminal every half-hour or so between 7am and 10.30pm. In Hong Kong they leave the China ferry terminal (Map p104; Canton Rd, Tsim Sha Tsui) on the half-hour from 7am to 10.30pm. The trip takes 60 to 75 minutes and tickets cost HK$140/175 on weekdays/nights (6pm to 10.30pm), and HK$155/175 on weekends/public holidays. Deluxe class is HK$245/275 on weekdays/nights and HK$260/275 on weekends/public holidays.

CotaiJet (☎ 2885 0595, in Hong Kong 2359 9990; www .cotaijet.com.mo) has high-speed catamarans leaving from Taipa Temporary Ferry Terminal (Map p328; ☎ 2885 0595) to the Shun Tak Centre in Hong Kong every half-hour between 7.30am and 8.30pm. In Hong Kong they leave from the ferry terminal in the Shun Tak Centre every half-hour between 7am and 7pm. Tickets can also be purchased at Sands and the Venetian in Macau, and at the ticketing office of Chu Kong Passenger Transport (Map p80; ☎ 2857 6625; Shop 305N, Shun Tak Centre, Sheung Wan) in Hong Kong. Prices are the same as TurboJet's. Getting a membership to Sands (it's free and issued on the spot) entitles you to complimentary ferry tickets, subject to conditions that change from time to time. Check its website (www.sands .com.mo) or simply ask the help desk in Sands or the Venetian. Free shuttles at the ferry terminal in Taipa will take you to destinations along the Cotai Strip.

Macao Dragon (☎ in Hong Kong 3972 3600; www.macao dragon.com) was supposed to operate the same route as CotaiJet by its own fleet of catamarans, but at the time of writing it was not yet in service.

Macau is also linked directly to Hong Kong International Airport by the TurboJet Sea Express (☎ 2859 3333; www.turbojetseaexpress.com.hk), which has nine ferries operating between 8.15am and 8.15pm. It costs MOP$235/180/128 per adult/child/infant and takes 45 minutes.

The Macau Express Link (☎ 2886 1111, in Hong Kong 2859 3401), run by TurboJet and seven airlines operating in Macau, connects Macau International Airport to Hong Kong. Passengers can check in and transit straight through to Macau from Shop G02 at the ferry terminal at the Shun Tak Centre. Make sure you arrive at the ferry terminal three hours before flight departure. You'll be given a temporary boarding pass after you check in. When you arrive at the ferry terminal in Macau, you do not need to go through immigration; instead, proceed to the Express Link waiting room at Berth 2, and a transit bus (four daily from 11.50am to 6.45pm; from Macau airport, five departures between 11.30am and 6.10pm) will take you directly to the airport. The fare is the same as the normal TurboJet service.

Tickets can be booked up to 90 days (Turbo Jet) and 28 days (NWFF and CotaiJet) in advance at the ferry terminals, many travel agencies or online. You can also simply buy tickets on the spot, though advance booking is recommended if you travel on weekends or public holidays. There is a standby queue for passengers wanting to travel before their ticketed sailing. You need to arrive at the pier at least 15 minutes before departure, but you should allow 30 minutes because of occasional long queues at immigration.

You are limited to 10kg of carry-on luggage in economy class, but oversized or overweight bags can be checked.

MACAU TO CHINA

Nationals of Australia, Canada, EU, New Zealand and most other countries (but not US citizens) can purchase their visas at the border with Zhuhai, but it will ultimately save you time if you buy one in advance. These are available in Hong Kong (see p287) or in Macau from China Travel Service (CTS; Map pp314–15; ☎ 2870 0888; 207 Avenida do Dr Rodrigo Rodrigues, Nam Kwong Bldg; ☺ 9am-6pm), usually in one day.

Air

Air Macau (NX; Map pp314–15; ☎ 8396 5555; www.air macau.com.mo; Ground fl, Nam Ngan Garden Bldg, 398 Alameda Doutor Carlos d'Assumpção; ☺ 9am-6pm) and several carriers of the China National Aviation Corporation (CNAC; Map p318; ☎ 2878 8034; fax 2878 8036; 5th fl, Iat Teng Hou Bldg, Avenida de Dom João IV) group link Macau International Airport (Map p328; ☎ 2886 1111; www.macau -airport.gov.mo) with at least five flights a week to Beijing, Chengdu, Fuzhou, Guilin, Hangzhou, Kunming, Nanjing, Shanghai, Xiamen and Xian. The departure tax for adults is MOP$80 and for children aged two to 12 it's MOP$50.

Sky Shuttle (☎ in Hong Kong 2108 9898; www.skyshuttle hk.com) has a helicopter shuttle linking Macau with Shenzhen five times a day from 9.45am to 7.45pm (11.45am to 8.30pm from Shenzhen) for HK$2400 (HK$2490 from Shenzhen). The trip takes 15 minutes.

Land

Macau is an easy gateway by land into China. Simply take bus 3, 5 or 9 to the border gate (Portas do Cerco; Map pp314–15; ☺ 7am-midnight) and walk across. A second – and much less busy crossing – is the Cotai Frontier Post (Map p330; ☺ 9am-8pm) on the causeway linking Taipa and Coloane, which allows visitors to cross over the Lotus Flower Bridge by shuttle bus (MOP$4) to Hengqin in Zhuhai. Buses 15, 21 and 26 will drop you off at the crossing.

If you want to travel further afield in China, buses run by the Kee Kwan Motor Road Co (Map p318; ☎ 2893 3888; ☺ 7.15am-9pm) leave the bus station

on Rua das Lorchas. Buses for Guangzhou (MOP$77, 2½ hours) depart about every 15 minutes, and for Zhongshan (MOP$38, one hour) every 20 minutes between 8am and 6.30pm. There are many buses to Guangzhou (MOP$77) and Dongguan (MOP$100) from Macau International Airport.

Sea

TurboJet has 10 departures daily to the port of Shekou in Shenzhen between 9.45am and 8.45pm. The journey takes 60 minutes and it costs between MOP$171 and MOP$271. The same number of ferries come back from Shekou between 8.15am and 7.30pm.

Yuet Tung Shipping Co (☎ 2857 4478) also has ferries connecting Macau with Shekou. The boat departs from Macau at 10am, 2pm, 4.30pm, 6.45pm and 8.15pm and takes 1½ hours; it returns from Shekou at 8.15am, 9.45am, 11.45am, 3.45pm and 6.30pm. Tickets (one way/return MOP$155/227) can be bought up to three days in advance from the point of departure, which is pier 11A (Map p318) in the Inner Harbour. A departure tax of MOP$20 applies.

There is a boat that leaves for Jiangmen (one way/return MOP$62/103) daily at 3.20pm and returns at 9am. The journey takes 70 minutes.

Ferries also leave from the same pier for Wanzai (one way/return MOP$12/20) on the mainland, crossing the Inner Harbour. Departures are every half-hour between 8am and 4.15pm, returning a half-hour later.

MACAU TO ASIA PACIFIC

Air Macau and other budget airlines like AirAsia (www.airasia.com) and Viva Macau (ZG; Map pp314–15; ☎ 2871 8883; www.flyvivamacau.com; 12th fl, AIA Tower, 251A-301 Avenida Comercial De Macau; ☺ 9am-6pm) have frequent service to destinations including Bangkok, Jakarta, Kaohsiung, Kota Kinabalu, Kuala Lumpur, Osaka and Taipei. There are also flights to Ho Chi Minh City, Kuching, Manila, Okinawa, Penang, Sydney and Tokyo. Jetstar (3K; ☎ in Hong Kong 800 962 808; www.jetstar .com) and Tiger Airways (www.tigerairways.com) operate flights to Perth and Singapore. The departure tax for adults is MOP$130 and for children aged two to 12 it's MOP$80.

CAR & MOTORCYCLE

The streets of Macau Peninsula are a gridlock of cars and mopeds that will cut you off at every turn. A Moke (a brightly coloured Jeep-like convertible) can be a convenient way to explore the islands, as can a motorbike.

Hire

Happy Rent A Car (Map pp314–15; ☎ 2872 6868; fax 2872 6888; Room 1025, arrivals hall, Macau ferry terminal) has four-person Mokes for hire for MOP$500 a day. Avis Rent A Car (Map pp314–15; ☎ 2872 6571; www .avis.com.mo; Room 1022, Ground fl, Macau ferry terminal; ☒ 8am-7pm), which also has an office at the Mandarin Oriental hotel car park, hires out cheap Suzuki Vitaras for MOP$700/850 per day on weekdays/weekends.

PUBLIC TRANSPORT

Public buses and minibuses run by TCM (☎ 2885 0060) and Transmac (☎ 2877 1122) operate on 40 routes from 6.45am till shortly after midnight. Fares – MOP$3.20 on the peninsula, MOP$4.20 to Taipa Village, MOP$5 to Coloane Village and MOP$6.40 to Hác Sá beach – are dropped into a box upon entry (exact change needed), or you can pay with a Macau Pass, which can be purchased in numerous supermarkets and all Circle K convenience stores. There's a refundable deposit of MOP$30. A minimum of MOP$50 is required to add money to the card each time.

The *Macau Tourist Map* (opposite) has a full list of both bus companies' routes, or you can check the routes online (www.i-busnet.com /macau/). The two most useful buses on the peninsula are buses 3 and 3A, which run between the ferry terminal and the city centre, near the post office. Both continue up to the border crossing with the mainland, as does bus 5, which can be boarded along Avenida Almeida Ribeiro. Bus 12 runs from the ferry terminal, past the Lisboa Hotel and then up to Lou Lim Ioc Garden and Kun Iam Temple.

The best services to Taipa and Coloane are buses 21, 21A, 25 and 26A. Bus 22 goes to Taipa, terminating at the Macau Jockey Club. Buses to the airport are AP1, 26, MT1 and MT2.

Macau is suffering from a severe shortage of drivers, so you may have to wait at least 20 minutes for a bus. Expect buses to be very crowded. Hopping aboard the free casino shuttles (p341) to some of the sights is a viable alternative. The shuttles depart from both the ferry terminal and Portas do Cerco every 10 minutes between 9.30am and midnight. Originally they were designed to bring Hong Kong and mainland gamblers to spend money, but in reality nobody checks whether you go gambling or not, and now Macau citizens use them regularly instead of waiting for the never-coming buses. Bear in mind that all passengers must be over 18 years of age.

TAXI

Flag fall is MOP$13 for the first 1.6km and MOP$1.50 for each additional 230m. There is a MOP$5 surcharge to go to Coloane; travelling between Taipa and Coloane is MOP$2 extra. Journeys starting from the airport incur an extra charge of MOP$5. A taxi from the airport to the town centre should cost about MOP$80. Large bags cost an extra MOP$3. For yellow radio taxis call ☎ 2851 9519 or ☎ 2893 9939.

DIRECTORY

Much of the advice given for Hong Kong applies to Macau as well. If you find any sections missing here, refer to those in the Hong Kong Directory chapter (p288).

BOOKS

Macau: The Imaginary City: Culture and Society, 1577 to Present, by Jonathan Porter, provides a vivid account of Macau's history. Novels set in Macau are rare, but Austin Coates' *City of Broken Promises,* a fictionalised account of 18th-century Macanese trader Martha Merop (see Museum of the Holy House of Mercy, p320), is a classic. *Lights and Shadows of a Macao Life: the Journal of Harriett Low, Travelling Spinster,* by Harriett Low Hillard, is an American woman's account of Macau from 1829 to 1834. For short stories, you won't do better than *Visions of China: Stories from Macau,* edited by David Brookshaw, which includes works by writers with strong Macau connections, including Henrique de Senna Fernandes. If you want to learn more about Macau's distinctive hybrid cuisine, try Annabel Jackson's *Taste of Macau: Portuguese Cuisine on the China Coast.*

These books can be found at Livararia Portuguesa (Map p318; ☎ 2856 6442; 18-20 Rua de São Domingos; ☒ 11am-7pm Mon-Sat) and Bloom (Map pp314–15; ☎ 2892 0121; 8 Calçada da Igreja de São Lázaro; ☒ 2-7pm Sat & Sun).

BUSINESS HOURS

Most government offices are open from 9am to 1pm and 2.30pm to 5.30pm (or 5.45pm) on weekdays. Banks normally open from 9am to 5pm weekdays and to 1pm on Saturday.

CLIMATE

Macau's climate is similar to Hong Kong's (p289), with one major difference: there is a delightfully cool sea breeze on warm summer evenings along the waterfront.

CUSTOMS REGULATIONS

Customs formalities are virtually nonexistent here, but customs in Hong Kong only allow you to import small amounts of duty-free tobacco and alcohol (see p290).

DISCOUNT CARDS

The Macau Museums Pass – a card allowing you entry to the Grand Prix Museum, the Macau Wine Museum, the Maritime Museum, Lin Zexu Memorial Hall in Lin Fung Temple, the Macau Museum of Art and the Macau Museum – is valid for five days. It costs MOP$25/12 for adults/concessions, and is available from the MGTO or any participating museum.

EMERGENCY

In the event of any emergency, phone the central SOS number (☎ 999) for the fire services, police or an ambulance. Important numbers:

Ambulance (☎ 2837 8311)

Consumer Council (☎ 8988 9315)

Fire service (☎ 2857 2222)

Police (☎ 2857 3333)

Tourist Assistance Hotline (☎ 2834 0390; ☉ 9am-6pm)

HOLIDAYS

In Macau, half-days are allowed on the day before the start of Chinese New Year and on the day of New Year's Eve. For holidays celebrated in both Hong Kong and Macau, see p293. The following are public holidays in Macau only:

All Souls' Day 2 November

Feast of the Immaculate Conception 8 December

Macau SAR Establishment Day 20 December

Winter Solstice 22 December

INTERNET ACCESS

In NAPE, you can check your email at the Unesco Internet Café (Map pp314–15; ☎ 2872 7066; Alameda Doutor Carlos d'Assumpção; per 30/60min MOP$5/10;

☉ noon-8pm Wed-Mon), and for free at two terminals located in the MGTO (Map p318; ☎ 8397 1120; ☉ 9am-6pm) at Largo do Senado.

LEFT LUGGAGE

There are electronic lockers on both the arrivals and departure levels of the Macau ferry terminal. They cost MOP$20 or MOP$25, depending on the size, for the first two hours and MOP$25/30 for each additional 12-hour period. There is also a left-luggage office on the departures level that's open from 6.45am to midnight daily. It charges MOP$10 for the first six hours and another MOP$10 till midnight. Each additional day costs MOP$10.

MAPS

The MGTO distributes the excellent (and free) *Macau Tourist Map*, with major tourist sights and streets labelled in English, Portuguese and Chinese characters, small inset maps of Taipa and Coloane, and bus routes marked.

MEDICAL SERVICES

Macau's two hospitals both have 24-hour emergency services.

Conde São Januário Central Hospital (Map pp314–15; ☎ 2831 3731; Estrada do Visconde de São Januário) Southwest of Guia Fort.

Kiang Wu Hospital (Map pp314–15; ☎ 2837 1333; Rua de Coelho do Amaral) Northeast of the ruins of the Church of St Paul.

MONEY

Macau's currency is the pataca (MOP$), which is divided up into 100 avos. Bills are issued in denominations of MOP$10, MOP$20, MOP$50, MOP$100, MOP$500 and MOP$1000. There are little copper coins worth 10, 20 and 50 avos, and silver-coloured MOP$1, MOP$2, MOP$5 and MOP$10 coins.

The pataca is pegged to the Hong Kong dollar at the rate of MOP$103.20 to HK$100. As a result, exchange rates for the pataca are virtually the same as for the Hong Kong dollar. Hong Kong bills and coins (except the $10 coins) are accepted everywhere in Macau. When you spend Hong Kong dollars in big hotels, restaurants and department stores, usually your change will be returned in that currency. Try to use up all your patacas before leaving Macau.

Most ATMs allow you to choose between patacas and Hong Kong dollars, and credit cards are readily accepted at Macau's hotels, larger restaurants and casinos. You can also change cash and travellers cheques at the banks lining Avenida da Praia Grande and Avenida de Almeida Ribeiro, as well as at major hotels.

Banco Comercial de Macau (Map p318; ☎ 2879 1000; 572 Avenida da Praia Grande; 9am-5pm Mon-Fri, 9am-12.30pm Sat)

Banco Nacional Ultramarino (Map p318; ☎ 2835 5111; 22 Avenida de Almeida Ribeiro; 9am-5.30pm Mon-Fri)

Bank of China (Map p318; ☎ 2878 1828; Avenida do Doutor Mario Soares; 9am-5pm Mon-Fri)

HSBC (Map p318; ☎ 2855 3669; 639 Avenida da Praia Grande; 9am-5pm Mon-Fri, 9am-1pm Sat)

POST

Correios de Macau, Macau's postal system, is efficient and inexpensive.

The main post office (Map p318; ☎ 2832 3666; 126 Avenida de Almeida Ribeiro; 9am-6pm Mon-Fri, 9am-1pm Sat) faces Largo do Senado; pick up poste restante from counter one or two. There are other post offices in Macau Peninsula, including a Macau ferry terminal branch (Map pp314–15; ☎ 2872 8079; 10am-7pm Mon-Sat).

Domestic letters cost MOP$1.50/2 for up to 20/50g, while those to Hong Kong are MOP$2.50/4. For international mail, Macau divides the world into zones: zone 1 (MOP$4/5 for up to 10/20g) is east and Southeast Asia; zone 2 (MOP$5/6.50) is everywhere else except for the mainland, which is MOP$3.50/4.50, and Portugal (MOP$4/5.50).

EMS Speedpost (☎ 2859 6688) is available at the main post office. Other companies that can arrange express forwarding are DHL (☎ 2837 2828), Federal Express (☎ 2870 3333) and UPS (☎ 2875 1616).

TELEPHONE

Macau's telephone service provider is Companhia de Telecomunicações de Macau (CTM; ☎ inquiry hotline 1000; www.ctm.net). Note that from 2009, all numbers in Macau, except emergency numbers, turned to eight digits. The initial digits of '28' were added to all six-digit telephone numbers and fax numbers, '8' was added to all seven-digit numbers and '6' was added to mobile phone numbers.

Local calls are free from private telephones, while at a public pay phone they cost MOP$1 for five minutes. Most hotels will charge you at least MOP$3. All pay phones permit International Direct Dialling (IDD) using a phonecard available from CTM for MOP$50 or MOP$100. Rates are cheaper from 9pm to 8am during the week and all day Saturday and Sunday. Prepaid SIM cards are also available from CTM for MOP$50 (for local calls) and MOP$100 (with IDD and international roaming).

The international access code for every country, except Hong Kong, is ☎ 00. If you want to phone Hong Kong, dial ☎ 01 first, then the number you want; you do not need to dial Hong Kong's country code (☎ 852). To call Macau from abroad – including Hong Kong – the country code is ☎ 853.

Convenient CTM branches in Macau include the following:

CTM branch (Map p318; 22 Rua do Doutor Pedro José Lobo; 10.30am-7.30pm) South of Avenida da Praia Grande.

CTM main office (Map pp314–15; 25 Rua Pedro Coutinho; 10.30am-7.30pm) Two blocks northeast of the Lou Lim loc Garden.

Useful Numbers

The following is a list of some important telephone numbers. For numbers to call in the case of an emergency, see p353.

International directory assistance (☎ 101)

Local directory assistance (☎ 181)

Macau ferry terminal (☎ 8790 7240)

New World First Ferry (☎ 2872 6301)

Tourist Hotline (☎ 2833 3000)

TurboJet (☎ 8790 7039)

TOURIST INFORMATION

The Macau Government Tourist Office (MGTO; ☎ 2831 5566; www.macautourism.gov.mo) is a well-organised and helpful source of information. It has a half-dozen outlets scattered around town, including ones in the Largo do Senado (Map p318; ☎ 8397 1120; 9am-6pm), at the Guia Lighthouse (Map pp314–15; ☎ 2856 9808; 9am-1pm & 2.15-5.30pm), at the ruins of the Church of St Paul (Map p318; ☎ 2835 8444; 10am-6pm) and in the Macau ferry terminal (Map pp314–15; ☎ 2872 6416; 9am-10pm). Its dispenses information and a large selection of free literature, including pamphlets on everything from Chinese temples and Catholic churches to fortresses, gardens and walks. The MGTO also runs a tourist assistance unit (☎ 2834 0390; 9am-6pm) to help travellers who run into trouble.

MGTO also has a Hong Kong branch (Map p80; ☎ 2857 2287; 11th fl, Yue Thai Commercial Bldg, 128 Connaught Rd Central, Sheung Wan, Hong Kong; ⊙ 9am-1pm & 2.15-5.30pm).

VISAS

Most travellers, including citizens of the EU, Australia, New Zealand, the USA, Canada and South Africa, can enter Macau with just their passports for between 30 and 90 days.

Travellers who do require them can get visas valid for 30 days on arrival in Macau. They cost MOP$100/50/200 for adults/children under 12 years/families.

You can get a single one-month extension from the Macau Immigration Department (Map pp314–15; ☎ 2872 5488; Ground fl, Travessa da Amizade; ⊙ 9am-5pm Mon-Fri).

WEBSITES

Useful Macau websites:

Cityguide (www.cityguide.gov.mo) A good source of practical information, such as transport routes.

Macau Cultural Institute (www.icm.gov.mo) Macau's cultural offerings month by month.

Macau Government Information (www.macau.gov.mo) The number-one source for nontourism information about Macau.

Macau Government Tourist Office (www.macautourism .gov.mo) The best source of information for visiting Macau.

Macau Yellow Pages (www.yp.com.mo) Telephone directory with maps.

LANGUAGE

The Official Languages Ordinance of 1974 names Hong Kong's two official languages as English and Cantonese, while Macau's official languages are Portuguese and Cantonese. Cantonese, a southern Chinese dialect (or language, depending on your definition), is spoken throughout most of Guangdong and Guangxi provinces on the mainland. Cantonese preserves many archaic features of spoken Chinese that date back to the Tang dynasty, which is why Tang and Sung dynasty poetry can sound better in Cantonese than in Mandarin.

While Cantonese is used in Hong Kong in everyday life by the vast majority of the population, English remains the lingua franca of commerce, banking and international trade, and is still used in the law courts. But there has been a noticeable decline in the level of English-speaking proficiency in the territory due to emigration and the switch by many secondary schools to

Chinese vernacular education. Still, some schools see it as a sign of prestige to keep teaching English, and many parents believe it is better for their children to have learnt English. In general, most Hong Kong Chinese, even those taught in English, cannot hold a candle to their English-proficient cousins in Singapore.

At the same time, the ability to speak Mandarin is on the increase in both Hong Kong and Macau due to the political realities. Also, for a Cantonese native speaker, Mandarin is far easier to learn than English. It's not uncommon these days to hear Cantonese and Mandarin being mixed in conversation.

Get Some Lingo

It's true – anyone can speak another language. Don't worry if you haven't studied languages before or that you studied a language at school for years and can't remember any of it. It doesn't even matter if you failed English grammar. After all, that's never affected your ability to speak English! The key to picking up a language in another country is just to start speaking.

Learn a few key phrases before you go. Write them on pieces of paper and stick them on the fridge, by the bed – anywhere that you'll see them often.

You'll find that locals appreciate travellers trying their language, no matter how muddled you may think you sound. If you want to learn more Cantonese than we've included here, pick up a copy of Lonely Planet's comprehensive and user-friendly *Cantonese Phrasebook*.

PRONUNCIATION
Vowels & Vowel Combinations

a	as the 'u' in 'but'
eu	as the 'er' in 'fern'
ew	as in 'blew' (short and pronounced with tightened lips)
i	as the 'ee' in 'deep'
o	as in 'go'
u	as in 'put'
ai	as in 'aisle' (short sound)
au	as the 'ou' in 'out'
ay	as in 'pay'
eui	as in French *feuille* (eu with i)
iu	as the 'yu' in 'yuletide'
oy	as in 'boy'
ui	as in French *oui*

Consonants

In Cantonese, the ng sound can appear at the start of the word. Practise by saying 'sing along' slowly and then do away with the 'si' at the beginning.

Note that words ending with the consonant sounds p, t, and k must be clipped in Cantonese. This happens in English as well – say 'pit' and 'tip' and listen to how much shorter the p sound is in 'tip'.

Many Cantonese speakers, particularly young people, replace an n sound with an l if it begins the word – náy (you) is often heard as láy. Where relevant, this change is reflected in the words and phrases in this language guide.

Tones

The use of tones in Cantonese can be quite tricky for an English speaker. The 'tone' is the pitch value of a syllable when you pronounce it. The same word, pronounced with different tones can have a very different meaning, eg gwat means 'dig up' and gwàt means 'bones'.

In our simplified pronunciation guide there are six tones: high, high rising, level, low falling, low rising and low. They can be divided into two groups: high and low pitch. High-pitch tones involve tightening your vocal muscles to get a higher note, whereas lower-pitch tones are made by relaxing the vocal chords to get a lower note. These tones are represented as accents and diacritics as shown in the list below; the low tones are all underlined in the Romanisations. Tones in Cantonese fall on vowels (a, e, i, o, u) and on n.

à	high
á	high rising
a	level
à̱	low falling
á̱	low rising
a̱	low

SOCIAL
Meeting People
Hello.
你好。　　　　láy·hó
How are you?
你幾好啊嗎?　　láy gáy hó à maa
Fine, and you?
幾好，你呢?　　gáy hó láy lè
Good morning.
早晨。　　　　jó·sàn
Goodbye/Bye.
再見。/拜拜。　joy·gin/bàai·baai
What's your name?
你叫乜嘢名?　　láy giu màt·yé méng aa
My name is …
我叫…　　　　ngáw giu …
Please …
唔該…　　　　ng̱·gòy …
Thank you.
唔該。　　　　ng̱·gòy
多謝。(for a gift)　dàw·je̱
You're welcome.
唔駛客氣。　　　ng̱·sái haak·hay
Yes.
係。　　　　　ha̱i
No.
唔係。　　　　ng̱·ha̱i
Excuse me. (to get attention)
對唔住。　　　deui·ng̱·je̱w
Excuse me. (to get past)
唔該借借。　　ng̱·gòy je·je

I'm sorry.
對唔住。　　　deui·ng̱·je̱w
Do you speak (English)?
你識唔識講　　láy sìk·ng̱·sìk gáwng
(英文)啊?　　(yìng·mán) aa
Do you understand?
你明唔明啊　　láy mìng·ng̱·mìng aa
Yes, I do understand.
明白。　　　　mìng·ba̱ak
No, I don't understand.
我唔明。　　　ngáw ng̱ mìng

Could you please …?
唔該你…?　　ng̱·gòy láy …
　repeat that
　再講一次　　joy gáwng yàt chi
　write it down
　寫落嚟　　　sé la̱wk là̱i

Going Out
What's on …?
…有乜嘢活動?　… yáu màt·yé wu̱t·du̱ng
　locally
　呢度附近　　là̱y·do̱ fu̱·ga̱n
　this weekend
　呢個週末　　là̱y·gaw jàu·mu̱t
　today
　今日　　　　gàm·ya̱t
　tonight
　今晚　　　　gàm·máan

I feel like going to (a/the) …
我想去…　　　ngáw séung heui …
Where can I find …?
邊度有…?　　bìn·do̱ yáu …
　clubs
　夜總會　　　ye̱·júng·wúi
　gay venues
　同志吧　　　tu̱ng·ji·bàa
　places to eat
　食飯嘅地方　sik·fa̱an ge da̱y·fàwng
　pubs
　酒吧　　　　jáu·bàa

Is there a local entertainment guide?
有冇本地娛樂指南?
yáu mó bún·da̱y ye̱w·la̱wk jí·là̱am

Local Lingo
Beautiful!	靚啊!	leng aa
Excellent!	冇得頂!	mó·dàk·díng
Great!	冇得頂!	mó·dàk·díng
It's OK.	OK。	ò·kày
Maybe.	可能。	háw·là̱ng

357

| No way! | 無得傾！ | mó·dàk·kìng |
| No problem. | 無問題。 | mó·man·tài |

PRACTICAL

Accommodation
Where's a …?

邊度有…?   bìn·do yáu …

  guest house

  賓館   bàn·gún

  hostel

  招待所   jiù·doy·sáw

  hotel

  酒店   jáu·dim

Do you have a … room?

有冇…房?   yáu·mó … fáwng

  double

  雙人   sèung·yàn

  single

  單人   dàan·yàn

How much is it per (night/person)?

一(晚/個人)幾多錢?

yàt (máan/gaw yàn) gáy·dàw chín

Banking
Where can I …?

我喺邊度可以…?

ngáw hái bìn·do háw·yí …

I'd like to …

我要…

ngáw yiu …

  cash a cheque

  兌一張支票   deui yàt jèung jì·piu

  change money

  換錢   wun chín

Where's the nearest …?

最近嘅…喺邊度?

jeui kán ge … hái bìn·do

  ATM

  自動提款機   ji·dung tài·fún·gày

  foreign exchange office

  換外幣嘅   wun ngoy·bai ge

  地方   day·fàwng

Days
Monday	星期一	sìng·kày·yàt
Tuesday	星期二	sìng·kày·yi
Wednesday	星期三	sìng·kày·sàam
Thursday	星期四	sìng·kày·say
Friday	星期五	sìng·kày·ńg
Saturday	星期六	sìng·kày·luk
Sunday	星期日	sìng·kày·yat

Internet
Where's the local internet cafe?

附近有冇網吧?

fu·gan yáu·mó máwng·bàa

I'd like to …

我想…

ngáw séung …

  check my email

  睇下我嘅電子信箱

  tái háa ngáw ge din·jí yàu·sèung

  get internet access

  上網

  séung·máwng

Numbers
0	零	lìng
1	一	yàt
2	二	yi
3	三	sàam
4	四	say
5	五	ńg
6	六	luk
7	七	chàt
8	八	baat
9	九	gáu
10	十	sap
11	十一	sap·yàt
12	十二	sap·yi
13	十三	sap·sàam
14	十四	sap·say
15	十五	sap·ńg
16	十六	sap·luk
17	十七	sap·chàt
18	十八	sap·baat
19	十九	sap·gáu
20	二十	yi·sap
21	二十一	yi·sap·yàt
22	二十二	yi·sap·yi
30	三十	sàam·sap
40	四十	say·sap
50	五十	ńg·sap
60	六十	luk·sap
70	七十	chàt·sap
80	八十	baat·sap
90	九十	gáu·sap
100	一百	yàt·baak
200	兩百	léung·baak
1000	一千	yàt·chìn
10,000	一萬	yàt·maan

Phones & Mobile Phones
Where's the nearest public phone?

呢度附近有冇公眾電話呀?

làu·do fu·gan yáu·mó gùng·jung din·wáa aa

I want to ...
我想…　　　　　ngáw séung …
　buy a phonecard
　買張電話卡
　máai jèung dịn·wáa·kàat
　call (Singapore)
　打電話去(新加坡)
　dáa dịn·wáa heui (sàn·gaa·bàw)

I'd like a ...
我想買個…
ngáw séung máai gaw …
　charger for my phone
　手機充電器
　sáu·gày chùng·dịn·hay
　mobile/cell phone for hire
　出租手機
　chèut·jò sáu·gày
　prepaid mobile/cell phone
　預付手機
　yẹw·fụ sáu·gày
　SIM card for your network
　你地網絡用嘅SIM卡
　láy·dạy máwng·làwk yụng ge sím·kàat

Post

Where is the post office?
郵局喺邊度?　　　yàu·gúk hái·bìn·dọ

I want to send a ...
我想…　　　　　ngáw séung …
　parcel
　寄包裹　　　　gay bàau·gwáw
　postcard
　寄明信片　　　gay mịng·seun·pín

I want to buy a/an ...
我想買…　　　　ngáw séung máai …
　envelope
　個信封　　　　gaw seun·fùng
　stamp
　張郵票　　　　jèung yàu·piu

Shopping

I'd like to buy ...
我想買…　　　　ngáw séung máai …
I'm just looking.
睇下。　　　　　tái hạa
How much is it?
幾多錢?　　　　gáy·dàw chín
Can I pay by credit card?
可唔可以用　　　háw·ṅg·háw·yí yụng
信用卡　　　　　seun·yụng·kàat
埋單呀?　　　　mạai·dàan aa

less
少啲　　　　　siú dì
more
多啲　　　　　dàw dì
bigger
更大　　　　　gang dạai
smaller
細啲　　　　　sai dì

Transport

Where's the...?
…喺邊度?　　　… hái bìn·dọ
　airport
　機場　　　　gày·chẹung
　bus stop
　巴士站　　　bàa·sí·jaam
　China Ferry terminal
　中國客運碼頭　jùng·gawk haak·wạn
　　　　　　　máa·tàu
　subway station
　地鐵站　　　dạy·tit·jaam

Is this the ... to (...)?
呢班…係唔係去(…)㗎?
lày bàan … hai·ṅg·hại heui (…) gaa
Which ... goes to (...)?
去(…)坐邊班…?
heui (…) cháw bìn·bàan …
　bus
　巴士　　　　bàa·sí
　ferry
　渡輪　　　　dọ·lèun
　minibus
　小巴　　　　siú bàa
　train
　火車　　　　fáw·chè
　tram
　電車　　　　dịn·chè

What time does it leave?
幾點鐘出發?
gáy·dím jùng chèut·faa
How much is a (soft-seat) fare to ...?
去…嘅(軟座飛)幾多錢?
heui … ge (yẹwn·jaw fày) gáy·dàw chín
I'd like to get off at (Panyu).
我要喺(番禺)落車。
ngáw yiu hái (pùn·yèw) lạwk·chè
Please stop here. (eg taxi, minibus)
唔該有落。
ṅg·gòy yau lawk
Tell me when we arrive at (Causeway Bay).
唔該喺　　　　ṅg·gòy hái
(銅鑼灣)叫　　(tùng làw wàn) giu
我落車。　　　ngáw lawk chè

Where is …?

…喺邊度? … hái·bìn·do

How far is it?

有幾遠? yáu gáy yéwn

By …

…去。 … heui

bus

坐車 cháw·chè

foot

行路 hàang·lo

train

坐地鐵 cháw dai·tit

Can you show me (on the map)?

你可唔可以 láy háw·ǹg·háw·yí

(喺地圖度)指俾 (hái day·to do) jí báy

我睇我喺 ngáw tái ngáw hái

邊度 bìn·do

EMERGENCIES

Help!

救命 ! gau·meng

Could you please help?

唔該幫幫忙? ǹg·gòy bàwng bàwng
màwng

Call an ambulance!

快啲叫救傷車 ! faai·dì giu
gau·sèung·chè

Call a doctor!

快啲叫醫生 ! faai·dì giu yì·sàng

Call the police!

快啲叫警察 ! faai·dì giu gíng·chaat

HEALTH

Where's the nearest …?

最近嘅…喺邊度? jeui kán ge … hái bìn·do

dentist

牙醫 ngàa·yì

doctor

醫生 yì·sàng

hospital

醫院 yì·yéwn

pharmacist

藥房 yeuk·fàwng

I'm sick.

我病咗。 ngáw beng·jáw

I need a doctor (who speaks English).

我要睇 ngáw yiu tái

(識講英文 (sìk gáwng yìng·mán

嘅)醫生。 ge) yì·sàng

Symptoms

I have (a/an) …

我有… ngáw yáu …

asthma

哮喘 hàau·chéwn

diarrhoea

肚痾 tó·ngàw

fever

發燒 faat·siù

headache

頭痛 tàu·tung

sore throat

喉嚨疼 hàu·lùng·tung

FOOD & DRINK
Useful Phrases

Where would you go for (a) …?

你會去邊度…? láy wuí heui bìn·do …

cheap meal

食平嘢 sik pèng·yé

local specialities

食地方小食 sik day·fàwng siú·sik

yum cha

飲茶 yám·chàa

Can you recommend a …?

有乜好…介紹? yáu màt hó … gaai·xiu

bar

酒吧 jáu·bàa

cooked food stall

熟食檔 suk·sik·dawng

(大排檔) (daai pàai dawng)

restaurant

茶樓 chàa·làu

tea cafe

茶餐廳 chàa chàan·tèng

I'd like …, please.

唔該我要… ǹg·gòy ngáw yiu …

the bill

埋單 màai·dàan

a fork

叉 chàa

a knife

刀 dò

a menu (in English)

(英文)菜單 (yìng·màn) choy·dàan

the set lunch

套餐 to·chàan

a table for (five)

(五位) 嘅檯 (ńg wái) ge tóy

I'd like a local speciality.
我想食地方風味菜。
ngáw séung sik day·fàwng fùng·may choy

What would you recommend?
有乜嘢好介紹？
yáu màt·yé hó gaai·siu

I'm (a) vegetarian.
我係食齋嘅。
ngáw hai sik jàai ge

Food Glossary

FISH & SHELLFISH

bàau·yew   鮑魚
abalone

daai·hàa   大蝦
prawn

hàa   蝦
shrimp

hò   蠔
oyster

lùng hàa   龍蝦
rock lobster

yàu·yéw   魷魚
squid

yèw   魚
fish

yéw chi   魚翅
shark's fin

yéw dáan   魚蛋
fish balls, usually made from pike

MEAT & POULTRY

gài   雞
chicken

jèw sáu   豬手
pork knuckle

jèw·yuk   豬肉
pork

ngáap   鴨
duck

ngàu yuk   牛肉
beef

ngáw   鵝
goose

pàai guàt   排骨
pork spareribs

yéw jèw   乳豬
suckling pig

RICE & NOODLE DISHES

baak·faan   白飯
steamed white rice

cháau faan   炒飯
fried rice

cháau·min   炒麵
fried noodles

faan   飯
rice

fán·sì   粉絲
cellophane noodles or bean threads

háw·fán   河粉
wide, white, flat rice noodles that are
usually pan-fried

jùk   粥
congee

min   麵
noodles

sìn·hàa hàa wàn·tàn   鮮蝦餛飩
wontons made with prawns

wàn·tàn min   餛飩麵
wonton noodle soup

yáu·jaa·gwái   油炸鬼
'devils' tails'; dough rolled and fried in
hot oil

SAUCES

gaai laat   芥辣
hot mustard

hò yàu   蠔油
oyster sauce

laat jiù jeung   辣椒醬
chilli sauce

si yàu   豉油
soy sauce

SOUPS

áai yuk sùk mái gàng   蟹肉粟米羹
crab and sweet corn soup

baak·choy tàwng   白菜湯
Chinese cabbage soup

dáan fàa·tàwng   蛋花湯
'egg flower' (or drop) soup; light stock
into which a raw egg is dropped

dùng·gwàa tàwng   冬瓜湯
winter-melon soup

wàn·tàn tàwng   餛飩湯
wonton soup

yèw·chi tàwng   魚翅湯
shark's-fin soup

yin wàw gàng   燕窩羹
bird's-nest soup

VEGETARIAN DISHES

chùn géwn   春卷
vegetarian spring rolls

gài ló máy   雞濾味
mock chicken, barbecued pork or roast
duck

gàm gù sún jìm   金菇筍尖
braised bamboo shoots and black
mushrooms

la̱w hon jàai 羅漢齋
braised mixed vegetables
la̱w hon jàai yì mi̱n 羅漢齋伊麵
fried noodles with braised vegetables

CANTONESE DISHES

ba̱ak cheuk hàa 白灼蝦
poached prawns served with dipping
sauces
chàa siù 叉燒
roast pork
chìng cháau gàai láan 清炒芥蘭
stir-fried Chinese broccoli
chìng jìng ye̱w 清蒸魚
whole steamed fish served with spring
onions, ginger and soy sauce
gèung chùng cháau ha̱ai 薑蔥炒蟹
sautéed crab with ginger and spring
onions
ha̱ai yu̱k pàa da̱u miu̱ 蟹肉扒豆苗
sautéed pea shoots with crab meat
hò̱ yàu choi sàm 蠔油菜心
choisum with oyster sauce
hò̱ yàu ngàu yu̱k 蠔油牛肉
deep-fried spare ribs served with coarse
salt and pepper
jaa jí gài 炸子雞
crispy-skin chicken
jiù yìm yàu·yéw 椒鹽魷魚
squid, dry-fried with salt and pepper
mu̱i choi kau yu̱k 霉菜扣肉
twice-cooked pork with pickled cabbage
sài làan fàa daai jí 西蘭花帶子
stir-fried broccoli with scallops
siù ngáap 燒鴨
roast duck
siù yéw gaap 燒乳鴿
roast pigeon
siù yéw jèw 燒乳豬
roast suckling pig
yìm gu̱k gài 鹽焗雞
salt-baked chicken, Hakka-style

DIM SUM

chàa siù bàau 叉燒包
steamed barbecued-pork buns
chéung fán 腸粉
steamed rice-flour rolls with shrimp, beef
or pork
chìng cháau sì choi 清炒時菜
fried green vegetable of the day
chiu̱·jàu fán gwáw 潮州粉果
steamed dumpling with pork, peanuts and
coriander
chùn géwn 春卷
fried spring rolls

fán gwáw 粉果
steamed dumplings with shrimp and
bamboo shoots
fu̱ pày géwn 腐皮卷
crispy tofu rolls
fu̱ng jáau 鳳爪
fried chicken feet
hàa gáau 蝦餃
steamed shrimp dumplings
la̱w ma̱i gài 糯米雞
sticky rice wrapped in a lotus leaf
pàai gwa̱t 排骨
small braised spare ribs with black beans
sàan jùk ngàu yu̱k 山竹牛肉
steamed minced-beef balls
siù máai 燒賣
steamed pork and shrimp dumplings

CHIU CHOW DISHES

bìng fàa gwùn yin 冰花官燕
cold, sweet bird's-nest soup served as
a dessert
chiu̱·jàu ló séui ngáw 潮州滷水鵝
Chiu Chow braised goose
chiu̱·jàu yéw tòng 潮州魚湯
aromatic fish soup
chiu̱·jàu yì mi̱n 潮州伊麵
pan-fried egg noodles served
with chives
dung jìng ha̱ai 凍蒸蟹
cold steamed crab
jìn hò̱ béng 煎蠔餅
oyster omelette
se̱k láu gài 石榴雞
steamed egg-white pouches filled with
minced chicken
ti̱m·sèwn hùng·siù hàa/ha̱ai kàu 甜酸紅燒蝦/蟹球
prawn or crab balls with sweet, sticky
dipping sauce

NORTHERN DISHES

bàk·gìng tìn ngáap 北京填鴨
Peking duck
chòng bàau yèung yu̱k 蔥爆羊肉
sliced lamb with onions served on
sizzling platter
gàau·ji 餃子
dumplings
gòn cháau ngàu yu̱k sì 乾炒牛肉絲
dried shredded beef with chilli sauce
hàau yèung·yu̱k 烤羊肉
roast lamb
sèwn la̱at tòng 酸辣湯
hot-and-sour soup with shredded pork
(and sometimes congealed pig's blood)

SHANGHAINESE DISHES

baat bó faan 八寶飯
steamed or pan-fried glutinous rice with
'eight treasures', eaten as a dessert

chòng yáu béng 蔥油餅
pan-fried spring onion cakes

chùng·jí wòng yéw 松子黃魚
sweet-and-sour yellow croaker with
pine nuts

daai jaap háai 大閘蟹
hairy crab (an autumn and winter dish)

fu gwai gài/hàt yì gài 富貴雞 / 乞丐雞
'beggar's chicken'; partially deboned
chicken stuffed with pork, Chinese pickled
cabbage, onions, mushrooms, ginger and
other seasonings, wrapped in lotus leaves,
sealed in wet clay or pastry and baked for
several hours in hot ash

gòn jìn say gwai dáu 乾煎四季豆
pan-fried spicy string beans

hung·siù sì·jí·tàu 紅燒獅子頭
Braised 'lion's head meatballs' – oversized
pork meatballs

jeui gài 醉雞
drunken chicken

lùng jéng hàa jàn 龍井蝦仁
shrimps with 'dragon-well' tea leaves

seung·hói chò cháau 上海粗炒
fried Shanghai-style (thick) noodles with
pork and cabbage

siú lùng bàau 小籠包
steamed minced-pork dumplings

SICHUAN DISHES

ching jiu ngau yok si 青椒牛肉絲
sautéed shredded beef and green pepper

daam daam mìn 擔擔麵
noodles in savoury sauce

gòng baau gài ding 宮爆雞丁
sautéed diced chicken and peanuts in
sweet chilli sauce

jèung chàa hàau ngáap 樟茶烤鴨
duck smoked in camphor wood

máa ngái séung sew 螞蟻上樹
'ants climbing trees'; cellophane noodles
braised with seasoned minced pork

màa pàw dau fù 麻婆豆腐
stewed tofu with minced pork and chilli

say·chèwn mìng hàa 四川明蝦
Sichuan chilli prawns

wuì gwàw yuk 回鍋肉
slices of braised pork with chillies

yèw hèung ké jí 魚香茄子
sautéed eggplant in a savoury, spicy sauce

GLOSSARY

amah – literally 'mummy'; a servant, traditionally a woman, who cleans houses, sometimes cooks, and looks after the children

arhats – Buddhist disciple freed from the cycle of birth and death

Bodhisattva – Buddhist striving towards enlightenment

chàa chàan-tèng – local tea cafes serving Western-style beverages and snacks and/or Chinese dishes

chàu – Cantonese for 'island'

cheongsam – a fashionable, tight-fitting Chinese dress with a slit up the side (*qípáo* in Mandarin)

chìm – bamboo sticks shaken out of a cylindrical box, usually at temples, and used to divine the future

chop – see *name chop*

daai-pàai-dawng – open-air eating stalls, especially popular at night, but fast disappearing in Hong Kong

dim sum – literally 'touch the heart'; a Cantonese meal of various titbits eaten as breakfast, brunch or lunch and offered from wheeled steam carts in restaurants; see also *yum cha*

dragon boat – long, narrow skiff in the shape of a dragon, used in races during the Dragon Boat Festival

feng shui – Mandarin spelling for the Cantonese *fung sui* meaning 'wind water'; the Chinese art of geomancy that manipulates or judges the environment to produce good fortune

gàwn-buì – literally 'dry glass'; 'cheers' or 'bottoms up'

godown – a warehouse, originally on or near the waterfront but now anywhere

gùng-fù – Chinese for 'kung fu'

gwái-lò/-páw (m/f) – literally 'ghost person'; a derogatory word for 'foreigner', especially a Caucasian Westerner, but now used jocularly

Hakka – a Chinese ethnic group who speak a different Chinese language than the Cantonese; some Hakka people still lead traditional lives as farmers in the New Territories

hell money – fake-currency money burned as an offering to the spirits of the departed

HKTB – Hong Kong Tourism Board

Hoklo – boat dwellers who originated in the coastal regions of present-day Fujian province

II – illegal immigrant

incense sticks – incense

junk – originally Chinese fishing boats or war vessels with square sails; diesel-powered, wooden pleasure yachts, which can be seen on Victoria Harbour

kaido – small- to medium-sized ferry that makes short runs on the open sea, usually used for nonscheduled services between small islands and fishing villages; sometimes spelled *kaito*

KCR – Kowloon-Canton Railway

KMB – Kowloon Motor Bus Company

kung fu – the basis of many Asian martial arts

LRT – Light Rail Transit; former name for the KCR's Light Rail system

màai-dàan – bill (in a restaurant)

mah-jong – popular Chinese game played among four persons using tiles engraved with Chinese characters

name chop – carved seal; the stamp it produces when dipped into red-ink paste often serves as a signature

nullah – uniquely Hong Kong word referring to a gutter or drain and occasionally used in place names

PLA – People's Liberation Army

PRC – People's Republic of China

Punti – the first Cantonese-speaking settlers in Hong Kong

sampan – motorised launch that can only accommodate a few people and is too small to go on the open sea; mainly used for interharbour transport

SAR – Special Administrative Region of China; both Hong Kong and Macau are now SARs

SARS – Severe Acute Respiratory Syndrome

SEZ – Special Economic Zone of China that allows more unbridled capitalism but not political autonomy

shroff – Anglo-Indian word meaning 'cashier'

sitting-out area – Uniquely Hong Kong word meaning open space reserved for passive or active recreation

snakehead – a smuggler of *IIs*

si-yàu sai-chaan – 'soy sauce Western'; a cuisine that emerged in the 1950s featuring Western dishes of various origins prepared in a Chinese style

t'ai chi – slow-motion shadow-boxing and form of exercise; also spelt *tai chi*

tai tai – any married woman but especially the leisured wife of a businessman

taijiquan – Mandarin for *t'ai chi;* usually shortened to *taiji*

Tanka – Chinese ethnic group that traditionally lives on boats

Triad – Chinese secret society originally founded as patriotic associations to protect Chinese culture from the influence of usurping Manchus, but today Hong Kong's equivalent of the Mafia

wàan – bay

walla walla – motorised launch used as a water taxi and capable of short runs on the open sea

wet market – local word for an outdoor market selling fruit, vegetables, fish and meat

yum cha – literally 'drink tea'; common Cantonese term for *dim sum*

BEHIND THE SCENES

THIS BOOK

This edition of *Hong Kong & Macau* was written by Andrew Stone, Chung Wah Chow and Piera Chen; Andrew and Chung Wah wrote the previous edition along with Reqqie Ho. This guidebook was commissioned in Lonely Planet's Oakland office and produced by the following:

Commissioning Editor Emily K Wolman

Coordinating Editors Carolyn Boicos, Simon Williamson

Coordinating Cartographers Mark Griffiths, Corey Hutchison

Coordinating Layout Designer Jacqui Saunders

Senior Editors Helen Christinis, Katie Lynch

Managing Cartographers David Connolly, Alison Lyall

Managing Layout Designer Sally Darmody

Assisting Editors Pete Cruttenden, Cathryn Game

Assisting Cartographers Enes Basic, Eve Kelly

Assisting Layout Designers Jim Hsu, Indra Kilfoyle

Cover research Paul Mosij, lonelyplanetimages.com

Internal image research Sabrina Dalbesio, lonelyplanet images.com

Language Content Laura Crawford

Project Manager Chris Love

Thanks to Lucy Birchley, David Carroll, Daniel Corbett, Rebecca Lalor, Raphael Richards, Sarah Sloane, Ji Yuanfang

Cover photographs Lippo Centre in Admiralty, Hong Kong, Michael Coyne/LPI (top); opera performer, Hong Kong, Glow Images/Photolibrary (bottom).

Internal photographs Bohemian Nomad Picturemakers/ Corbis p12 (#1); David Crausby/Alamy p49 (middle); dbimages/Alamy p12 (#2); ImageState/Alamy p9 (#2); Rudy Sulgan/Corbis p4 (#1). All other photographs by Lonely Planet Images: Andrew Burke p50 (top); Michael Coyne p5 (#5), p8 (#1), p8 (#3), p51; Greg Elms p2, p3, p4 (#2), p6, p7 (#2), p7 (#3), p7 (#4), p9 (#1), p9 (#3), p10 (#1), p10 (#2), p11 (#5), p11 (#6), p45, p49 (bottom), p52 (bottom); Manfred Gottschalk p10 (#3); Christopher Groenhout p50 (bottom); Richard I'Anson p7 (#5), p49 (top); Ray Laskow- itz p5 (#4), p47 (top), p52 (middle); Holger Leue p11 (#4); Chris Mellor p46 (bottom); Geoff Stringer p5 (#3), p7 (#6), p46 (top); Jane Sweeney p48 (bottom), p52 (top); Phil Weymouth p47 (bottom); Brent Winebrenner p48 (top); Lawrence Worcester p8 (#2).

All images are copyright of the photographer unless otherwise indicated. Many of the images in this guide are available for licensing from Lonely Planet Images: www .lonelyplanetimages.com.

THANKS
ANDREW STONE

My fellow authors Chung Wah and Piera helped me out in so many ways on this title with ideas, suggestions, contacts, enthusiasm and hard work. I am indebted to them. Thanks guys. Thanks also to my commissioning editors Rebecca Chau and Emily Wolman for their patience and help throughout. To Ling Lui, John Wong and everyone else who were so generous with their time and assistance. To Jaki Doreen and Marianne, my love and thanks for

THE LONELY PLANET STORY

Fresh from an epic journey across Europe, Asia and Australia in 1972, Tony and Maureen Wheeler sat at their kitchen table stapling together notes. The first Lonely Planet guidebook, *Across Asia on the Cheap*, was born.

Travellers snapped up the guides. Inspired by their success, the Wheelers began publishing books to Southeast Asia, India and beyond. Demand was prodigious, and the Wheelers expanded the business rapidly to keep up. Over the years, Lonely Planet extended its coverage to every country and into the virtual world via lonelyplanet.com and the Thorn Tree message board.

As Lonely Planet became a globally loved brand, Tony and Maureen received several offers for the company. But it wasn't until 2007 that they found a partner whom they trusted to remain true to the company's principles of travelling widely, treading lightly and giving sustainably. In October of that year, BBC Worldwide acquired a 75% share in the company, pledging to uphold Lonely Planet's commitment to independent travel, trustworthy advice and editorial independence.

Today, Lonely Planet has offices in Melbourne, London and Oakland, with over 500 staff members and 300 authors. Tony and Maureen are still actively involved with Lonely Planet. They're travelling more often than ever, and they're devoting their spare time to charitable projects. And the company is still driven by the philosophy of *Across Asia on the Cheap*: 'All you've got to do is decide to go and the hardest part is over. So go!'

SEND US YOUR FEEDBACK

We love to hear from travellers – your comments keep us on our toes and help make our books better. Our well-travelled team reads every word on what you loved or loathed about this book. Although we cannot reply individually to postal submissions, we always guarantee that your feedback goes straight to the appropriate authors, in time for the next edition. Each person who sends us information is thanked in the next edition and the most useful submissions are rewarded with a free book.

To send us your updates – and find out about Lonely Planet events, newsletters and travel news – visit our award-winning website: lonelyplanet.com/contact.

Note: We may edit, reproduce and incorporate your comments in Lonely Planet products such as guidebooks, websites and digital products, so let us know if you don't want your comments reproduced or your name acknowledged. For a copy of our privacy policy visit lonelyplanet.com/privacy.

everything during write-up in Sydney. Finally, thanks to Tonya for a fun time at the end of the trip, hope Hong Kong was everything you hoped it would be.

PIERA CHEN

I extend my gratitude to friends who've helped to make my first Lonely Planet guide stronger than I could have made it on my own, in particular to Chan Wing-chiu, Lee Cheuk-to, Ho Wai-leng, Winnie Fu, Leung Ping-kwan, Herman Lee, Suyin Mak, Gérard Henri, Lydia Ngai, Phoebe Wong, Conita Leung, Gordon Mathews, Aloysius Lee and Susanna Eusantos. Thanks also to my editor Emily Wolman, to coordinating author Andrew Stone, and to Simon

Williamson and Corey Hutchison at Lonely Planet. Finally I must acknowledge my husband Sze Pang-cheung, whose assistance and love have been crucial in ways too numerous to mention.

CHUNG WAH CHOW

Many people deserve thanks and appreciation for this project. Liz Lam and Teresa Costa Gomes from MGTO have been an invaluable source for my research by being available at any time, despite their hectic schedule. I am equally grateful for the wonderful suggestions and ideas of Calvin Kok, Teresa Freitas and António Falcão in Macau, and Jesse Warren, Thomas O'Connor, Angelo Chiu and David Abrahamson in China, and to Trey and Hera Menefee and Chiu Yi Ting for putting me up and keeping me company. Thanks also to fellow author Andrew Stone, Emily Wolman and David Connolly from Lonely Planet, as well as all those involved in completing this book. Finally a big hug and thanks to my partner, David Rheinheimer, for his endless love and support.

OUR READERS

Many thanks to the travellers who used the last edition and wrote to us with helpful hints, useful advice and interesting anecdotes:

Joe Alvaro, Thaddeus Beebe, David Berg, Brett Bundale, Hannah Chaplin, Franzine Co, Joseph Cowl, Chris Doherty, Vinod Goonmeter, Elisabeth Heimdal, Brian Henthorn, Alanna Jeayes, Christian Klausener, Ryan Macdicken, Julia Milne, Kazuya Miyashita, Bernhard Moestl, David Morrison, Jens Müller, Barbara Nardelli, Don Nguyen, Sarah Olthof, Sunil Pakalpati, Margarita Passion, John Rai, David Rheinheimer, Jim Rogers, Annett Schlenker, First Sequenz, PC Shum, Russell Smith, Julie Stapleton, Michael Sumpter, Francisco Velastegui, Lauren Wistrom.

Notes

Notes

Notes

INDEX

See also separate
indexes for:

Eating	p378
Entertainment	p381
Shopping	p382
Sights	p383
Sleeping	p385
Sports & Activities	p387
Top Picks	p387

A

Aberdeen 92-5, 189-91, **94**
accessories, *see* Shopping *subindex*
accommodation 232-50, *see also* Sleeping *subindex, individual neighbourhoods & towns*
  Admiralty 235-7
  campsites 233
  Causeway Bay 239-40
  Central 240-1
  costs 234, 347
  guesthouses 233
  Hong Kong Island 234-40
  hostels 233, 291
  hotels 232-3
  Hung Hom 244-5
  Kowloon 238, 241-8
  Macau 347-50
  Mid-Levels 241
  Mong Kok 247-8
  New Territories 248-9
  rental accommodation 233
  reservations 234-5
  serviced apartments 234-5
  Sha Tin 248-9
  Tsim Sha Tsui 241-4
  Tsim Sha Tsui East 244-5
  Wan Chai 235-7
activities 222-30, 345-6, *see also* Sports & Activities *subindex*

000 map pages
000 photographs

Admiralty 70-6, **72**
  accommodation 235-7
  clubs & live music 217-18
  entertainment 219
  food 178-81
  shopping 163-4
  transport 73
air travel 271-4
  airlines 271-2
  airports 272
  departure taxes 273
  to/from Hong Kong 273-4
  to/from Macau 350-1
  to/from mainland China 285
Alliance Française 290
Álvares, Jorge 21, 306
A-Ma Festival 312
A-Ma Temple 323
ambulance 291-2
antiques 155-6, 333, *see also* Shopping *subindex*
Ap Lei Chau 94-5
architecture 37-9, 310-11
area codes, *see inside front cover*
art, *see* Shopping *subindex*
art galleries, *see* Sights *subindex*
arts 31-9, 219-20, 310-11, *see also individual arts*
ATMs 297
auction houses 158-9
Avenue of the Stars 106, **52**

B

baccarat 342
bakeries, *see* Eating *subindex*
bargaining 154
bars, *see* Entertainment *subindex*
bathrooms 302
beaches 223, *see also* Sights *subindex*
bicycle travel, *see* cycling
bird-watching 223
Birthday of Lord Buddha 17, 312, 317
Birthday of Tin Hau 16
blackjack 342
boat travel, *see* ferry travel

books, *see also* literature, Shopping *subindex*
  hiking 226
  history 27
  Macau 352
boule 342
boxing 224
British rule
  colonisation 22-4
  handover 25-6, 27-8
buildings, *see* Sights *subindex*
bungy-jumping 323
bus travel 279-80
  to/from Macau 351
  to/from mainland China 285-6
  within Macau 352
business hours 288, *see also inside front cover*
  bars 207
  Macau 352
  restaurants 175
  shops 154

C

cafes, *see* Eating & Entertainment *subindexes*
campsites 233
canoeing 227-8, *see also* Sports & Activities *subindex*
Canton Trade Fair 263
car travel 280-1, 351-2
carpets 158
casinos 341-3
cathedrals, *see* Sights *subindex*
Causeway Bay 84-7, **85**
  accommodation 239-40
  drinking 213
  entertainment 219-20
  food 186-7
  shopping 166-7
  transport 84
cell phones 301
cemeteries, *see* Sights *subindex*
Central 61-70, **67**
  accommodation 240-1
  drinking 207-8
  entertainment 219
  food 176-8

shopping 157-63
transport 66
walking tour 70, **70**
Chai Wan 92
Chan, Luis 33
Chang, Eileen 37
changing money 297
Chau, Carrie 48
Chek Keng 131-2
cheongsam 160
Cheung Chau 145-8, **146**, **50**
  accommodation 250
  food 203-4
  walking tour 148-9, **149**
Cheung Chau Bun Festival 16, 145
Cheung Chau Village 148
Cheung Yeung 17
Chi Ma Wan 142
children, travel with 288-9
children's attractions, *see* Sights *subindex*
children's goods, *see* Shopping *subindex*
Chinese civil war 24
Chinese medicine 44, 82
Chinese New Year 15, 16
Chinese opera 36, 220
Chinese University of Hong Kong 126
Chinese zodiac 42
Chinnery, George 310
Chow, Stephen 32
Chow Yun Fat 137
Chungking Mansions 242
churches, *see* Sights *subindex*
cigars 166
cinema 31-3, *see also* Entertainment *subindex*
classical music, *see* Entertainment *subindex*
Clearwater Bay Peninsula 133
climate 15, 289, 353
climate change 272
clothing 156, 333, *see also* Shopping *subindex*
clubs 216-19, 344, *see also* Entertainment *subindex*

INDEX

Coloane Island 329-32, **330**
    accommodation 349-50
    food 340-3
Coloane Village 331, **10**
colonisation
    Hong Kong 22-4
    Macau 306-8
comedy clubs 219
computers 156, *see
    also* Shopping *subindex*
congee, *see* Eating *subindex*
conservation 3
consulates 291
cooking courses 175
costs 17-18, 290-1, 353
    accommodation 234, 347
    food 176, 334
    freebies & bargains 71
    taxes 287, 300
    tipping 176, 301-2
Cotai Strip 349
courses 289-90
    cooking 175
    language 290
credit cards 297-8
cricket 230
curios, *see* antiques
customs regulations 290, 353
cycling 224-5, 274, 345

D
dai pai dongs 174-6, **46**,
    see also Eating *subindex*
Deep Water Bay 97, 191
democratic reform 29-30, 43
Deng Xiaoping 25, 28
dengue fever 292
department stores, *see*
    Shopping *subindex*
departure taxes 273, 287
Diamond Hill 114-15, 198
diarrhoea 293
dim sum 173, **2**, *see also*
    Eating *subindex*
disabilities, travellers
    with 302
Discovery Bay 144, 203
dog racing 346
dolphins 142
Dragon Boat Festival
    17, 313
drinking 207-16, 344-5,
    see also Entertainment
    subindex
    business hours 207
drinks, *see* Shopping
    subindex

driving, *see* car travel
driving licences 280-1

E
economy 2-3, 22, 24-5,
    39-40, 288, 307, 309-10,
    311-12
electricity 291
electronic goods 257
Elliot, Captain Charles 22
embassies 291
emergencies 291-2, 353,
    see also inside front cover
entertainment, *see* Enter-
    tainment *subindex*
environmental issues 41-3,
    135, 142, 272
etiquette 30, 175
events, *see* festivals &
    events
exchange rates, *see inside
    front cover*

F
Fan Lau 142
Fanling 122-3
fashion 44
Feast of the Drunken
    Dragon 312
feng shui 42
ferry travel 274-9
    Star Ferry 275, **7**
    to/from Hong Kong
        Island 275
    to/from Macau 350-1
    to/from mainland China
        286-7
    to/from New Territories
        276
    to/from Outlying Islands
        276-9
festivals & events 15-17,
    312, *see also* sporting
    events
    A-Ma Festival 312
    Birthday of Lord Buddha
        17, 312, 317
    Birthday of Tin Hau 16
    Cheung Chau Bun
        Festival 16, 145
    Cheung Yeung 17
    Dragon Boat Festival
        17, 313
    Feast of the Drunken
        Dragon 312
    Hong Kong Arts
        Festival 15

Hong Kong Artwalk 16
Hong Kong City Fringe
    Festival 15
Hong Kong Fashion
    Week 17
Hong Kong International
    Film Festival 16, 32-3
Hong Kong International
    Jazz Festival 35
Hong Kong Winterfest 17
Hungry Ghost Festival 17
Le French May 17
Macau Arts Festival 312
Macau International
    Fireworks Display
    Contest 313
Macau International
    Music Festival 313
Macau Lotus Flower
    Festival 313
Mid-Autumn Festival 17
Procession of our Lady of
    Fatima 312
Procession of the Passion
    of Our Lord 312
Spring Lantern
    Festival 16
film 31-3
fishing 225
fitness 222-3
FIVB Women's Volleyball
    Grand Prix 313
florists 166
food 172-204, *see also*
    Eating & Shopping
    *subindexes, individual
    neighbourhoods & towns*
    Aberdeen 189-91
    Admiralty 178-81
    business hours 175
    Causeway Bay 186-7
    Central 176-8
    cooking courses 175
    costs 176, 334
    culture 172-3
    dai pai dongs 174-6, **46**
    dim sum 173, **2**
    etiquette 175
    history 172-3
    Hong Kong Island 176-91
    Hung Hom 194-6
    Kowloon 191-8
    Kowloon City 197-8
    Lan Kwai Fong 181-4
    language 339
    Macanese cuisine 334
    Macau 334-41

Mid-Levels, the 184-5
Mong Kok 196-7
Mui Wo 202-3
New Kowloon 197-8
New Territories 198-201
Portuguese cuisine
    334, **11**
reservations 176
self-catering 176
Sha Tin 199-200
Sheung Wan 184-5
smoking 176
Soho 181-4
soy sauce Western
    173-4
Stanley 190-1
sweets 193
tea cafes 174
tipping 176, 302
Tsim Sha Tsui 191-4
Tsim Sha Tsui East 194-6
vegetarian 182
Wan Chai 178-81
football 230
Fortress Hill 241
forts, *see* Sights *subindex*
free attractions 71

G
galleries, *see* Sights
    subindex
gambling 341-3
gardens, *see* Sights
    subindex
gay travellers 212-13, 292
gems 156
geography 40
giardia 292
Goethe-Institut 290
go-karting 345
golf 225, 345, *see
    also* Sports & Activities
    subindex
government 43, 312
Guangzhou 263-70, **264**
    accommodation 269-70
    drinking 269
    food 268
    shopping 267-8
    transport 266-7
guesthouses 233, *see
    also* Sleeping *subindex*
Guia Fort 324
gyms 222

H
Hakka people 21
Happy Valley 90, 188

Happy Valley Racecourse
  90, **5**
health 292-3
Hebe Haven 129-30
hepatitis 292
herbalism 44, 82
hiking 225-7, 346, *see*
  also Sports & Activities
  subindex
history 20-31, 306-10
  books 27
  democratic reform
    29-30, 43
  food 172-3
  Hong Kong handover
    25-6, 27-8
  Macau 306-10
  Macau handover 309-10
  Opium Wars 22, 23
  WWII 23-4, 308
Hoi Ha 131-2
holidays 293-4, 353
  Birthday of Lord
    Buddha 17, 312
  Chinese New Year 15, 16
homewares, *see* Shopping
  subindex
Hong Kong Arts Festival 15
Hong Kong Artwalk 16
Hong Kong City Fringe
  Festival 15
Hong Kong Consumer
  Council 157
Hong Kong Fashion Week 17
Hong Kong Immigration
  Department 303
Hong Kong International
  Airport 272-3
Hong Kong International
  Cricket Sixes 17
Hong Kong International
  Film Festival 16, 32-3
Hong Kong International
  Jazz Festival 35
Hong Kong Island 61-97,
  62-3
  accommodation 234-40
  clubs & live music 216-18
  drinking 207-14
  entertainment 219-20
  food 176-91
  shopping 157-67
Hong Kong Marathon 15
Hong Kong Park 71, 73

Hong Kong Rugby World
  Cup Sevens 16
Hong Kong Trail 227
Hong Kong Winterfest 17
horse racing 90, 230, 346,
  see also Sights *subindex*
horse riding 227, *see*
  also Sports & Activities
  subindex
hospitals 296-7, 353
hostels 233, 291, *see*
  also Sleeping *subindex*
hotels 232-3, *see*
  also Sleeping *subindex*
Hui, Ann 32, 52
Hui, Michael 31
Hung Hom 104-8, **106**
  accommodation 244-5
  drinking 214-15
  food 194-6
  shopping 167-9
  transport 107
Hung Shing Yeh 202
Hungry Ghost Festival 17

identity cards 294
immunisations 293
incense 81-2
influenza 293
insect bites 293
internet access 294-5, 353
internet resources 18, 355
Island East 90-2
  drinking 213-14
  entertainment 219-20
  food 188-9
  transport 91
Island South 92-7
  drinking 213-14
  food 189-91
  transport 93
Island West 237-9
itineraries 14, 56-7, 320

Jet Li 31
jewellery 156, *see*
  also Shopping *subindex*

Kam Tin 121-2
Kat Hing Wai 121-2
Kau Sai Chau 131
kayaking 227-8, *see*
  also Sports & Activities
  subindex

Kiu Tsui Chau 131
Kowloon 98-115, **100-1**
  accommodation 238,
    241-8
  clubs & live music
    218-19
  drinking 214-15
  entertainment 220
  food 191-8
  shopping 167-70
  walking tour 110-12,
    112
Kowloon City 113-14,
  197-8
Kowloon Tong 113, 197
Kowloon West 245-6
kung fu 228

Lamma 134-7, **136**, **9**, **50**
  drinking 215
  food 201-2
Lan Kwai Fong 77-9, **78**, **3**
  clubs & live music 216-17
  drinking 208-10
  entertainment 220
  food 181-4
  shopping 157-63
  transport 77
landmarks, *see* Sights
  subindex
language 356-64, *see also*
  inside front cover
  courses 290
  food 339
Lantau 137-45, **140**, **9**
  accommodation 249-50
  drinking 215-16
  food 202-3
Lantau Peak 139
Lantau Trail 227
laundries 295
Le French May 17
leather goods 156-7
Lee, Bruce 27, 31
legal matters 295
Lei Yue Mun 115, 198
Leng Kwok Hung 49
lesbian travellers
  212-13, 292
Leung Ping-kwan 37, 38,
  173, 174
Leung Shuen Wan 131
libraries 295-6
literature 36-9, 311, *see*
  also books
Liu Yichang 37

live music 216-19, *see*
  also Entertainment *subindex*
luggage
  left 295, 353
  shopping 156-7
Lui Shou-kwan 33

M
Ma Wan 150-1
Macanese cuisine 334
Macau 306-55, **10**
  accommodation 347-50
  activities 345-6
  arts 310-11
  attractions 312-32
  books 352
  business hours 352
  casinos 341-3
  clubs 344
  culture 311
  drinking 344-5
  economy 311-12
  festivals 312
  food 334-41
  history 306-10
  shopping 333-4
  tours 313-17
  transport 350-2
Macau Arts Festival 312
Macau Formula 3 Grand
  Prix 313, 346
Macau International Fire-
  works Display Contest 313
Macau International
  Marathon 313
Macau International Music
  Festival 313
Macau Lotus Flower
  Festival 313
Macau Open Golf
  Tournament 313
Macau Peninsula 317-27,
  314-15
  accommodation 347-8
  food 334-8
  walking tour 326-7, **326**
MacLehose Trail 227
magazines 43-4, 298
Mai Po Marsh 120-1
malls, *see* Shopping
  subindex
maps 159, 226, 296, 353
markets, *see* Eating, Shopping, Sights *subindexes*
martial arts 227-8, *see*
  also Sports & Activities
  subindex

000 map pages
000 photographs

massage 222-3
measures, *see inside front cover*
medical services 296-7, 353
medicine, Chinese 44, 82
metric conversions, *see inside front cover*
Mid-Autumn Festival 17
Mid-Levels, the 87-9
    accommodation 241
    food 184-5
    transport 88
Mirador Mansion 243
Mo Tat Wan 202
mobile phones 301
monasteries, *see Sights subindex*
money 290-1, 297-8, 353-4
Mong Kok 110, **111**
    accommodation 247-8
    food 196-7
    shopping 170
    transport 110
monuments, *see Sights subindex*
mosques, *see Sights subindex*
motorcycle travel 280-1, 351-2
mountain biking, *see cycling*
Mui Wo 143-4, 202-3
museums 290, *see also Sights subindex*
music 35, *see also Entertainment, Shopping subindexes*

N

nature reserves, *see Sights subindex*
New Kowloon 112-15
    entertainment 220
    food 197-8
    shopping 170
New Territories 116-33
    accommodation 248-9
    drinking 215
    entertainment 220
    food 198-201
newspapers 43-4, 298
Ngong Ping 203
Ngong Ping 360 138
Ngong Ping Plateau 138-9
Ngong Ping Village 138
nightlife 216-19, *see also Entertainment subindex*

noodles, *see Eating subindex*
North Point 90-1
numerology 42
nunneries, *see Sights subindex*

O

opening hours 288
opera, Chinese 36, 220
opium 22
Opium Wars 22, 23
outdoor gear, *see Shopping subindex*
Outlying Islands 134-52
    accommodation 249-50
    drinking 215-16
    food 201-4

P

paintball 224
painting 33
Pak Sha Chau 131
Pak Tam Chung 130-1
parks, *see Sights subindex*
passports 294, 303
Patten, Chris 27
Peak, the 89-90, **4**
    food 187-8
    transport 89
Peng Chau 149-50, 204, **150**
photographic equipment 157, *see also Shopping subindex*
photography 33-4, 299
Ping Kong 123
planning 18, 56-7
Plover Cove 124-5
Po Toi 152, 204
politics 43, 312
pollution 41-3
population 40
Portuguese cuisine 334, **11**
Portuguese rule of Macau
    colonisation 306-8
    handover 309-10
postal services 299-300, 354
Procession of our Lady of Fatima 312
Procession of the Passion of Our Lord 312
pubs, *see Entertainment subindex*
Pui O 141

Q

Quarry Bay 90-1

R

racecourses, *see Sights subindex*
radio 300
relocation to Hong Kong 300
rental accommodation 233, *see also Sleeping subindex*
Repulse Bay 97, 191
responsible travel 18-19
restaurants, *see Eating subindex*
rock carvings, *see Sights subindex*
rock climbing 224
roulette 343
rugby 230
running 228

S

Sai Kung Peninsula 129-32, 200-1, **8**
Sai Kung Town 129, 215, **130**
Sai Wan Ho 91
sailing 229
sampans 93, 148
scuba diving 228, *see also Sports & Activities subindex*
seafood, *see Eating subindex*
senior travellers 291
serviced apartments 234-5, *see also Sleeping subindex*
Sha Tin 126-9, **127**
    accommodation 248-9
    food 199-200
Sham Shui Po 112-13, 197
Sham Wan 136
Shamian Island 265, **12**
Shau Kei Wan 91-2
Shek O 96-7, 191
Shenzhen 252-9, **254**
    accommodation 259
    drinking 259
    food 258-9
    shopping 257-8, **12**
    transport 256-7
Sheung Shui 122-3
Sheung Wan 80-3, **80**
    accommodation 237, 240
    drinking 210
    food 184-5

shopping 164-6
transport 81
walking tour 83-4, **83**
shopping 154-70, 333-4, *see also Shopping subindex, individual neighbourhoods*
    Admiralty 163-4
    bargaining 154
    business hours 154
    Causeway Bay 166-7
    Central 157-63
    Hong Kong Island 157-67
    Hung Hom 167-9
    Kowloon 167-70
    Lan Kwai Fong 157-63
    Macau 333-4
    refunds & exchanges 155
    scams 157
    Sheung Wan 164-6
    Soho 157-63
    Tsim Sha Tsui 167-9
    Tsim Sha Tsui East 167-9
    Wan Chai 163-4
    warranties & guarantees 155
shrines, *see Sights subindex*
Shui Tau Tsuen 122
skating 228
sleeping, *see Sleeping subindex*
smoking 176
snakes 138, 293
soccer, *see football*
Soho 77-9, **78**
    clubs & live music 216-17
    drinking 208-10
    entertainment 220
    food 181-4
    shopping 157-63
    transport 77
Sok Kwu Wan 135, 202, **50**
South Lantau Rd 203
souvenirs, *see Shopping subindex*
soy sauce Western food 173-4
spas 222-3, 256
Special Economic Zone (SEZ) 258
sporting events
    FIVB Women's Volleyball Grand Prix 313
    Hong Kong International Cricket Sixes 17
    Hong Kong Marathon 15
    Hong Kong Rugby World Cup Sevens 16

sporting events *continued*
Macau Formula 3 Grand
Prix 313, 346
Macau International
Marathon 313
Macau Open Golf
Tournament 313
sporting goods, *see*
Shopping *subindex*
sports 222-30, 346, *see
also* Sports & Activities
subindex
Spring Lantern Festival 16
squares, *see* Sights *subindex*
squash 228-9
St Lazarus district 325
stamps 333-4
Stanley 95-6, 190-1, **96**
Star Ferry 275, **7**
statues, *see* Sights *subindex*
streets, notable, *see* Sights
subindex
structures, *see* Sights
subindex
Sun Yat-sen 88, 261,
266, 325
sustainable travel 18-19
swimming 223, 346, *see
also* Sports & Activities
subindex
Symphony of the Stars 106
synagogues 88-9

T

Tai Long 131-2
Tai Mei Tuk 248
Tai Mo Shan 118-19
Tai O 139-41, 203
Tai Po 123-4, 199, **124**
Tai Po Kau 125-6
Tai Wan 152
Taipa Island 327-9, **328**
accommodation 349
food 338
walking tour 332-3, **332**
Taipa Village 327
Tap Mun Chau 132, 201
taxes 287, 300
departure 273, 287
duty free 154-5
taxis 281-2, 352
tea cafes & houses 174, *see
also* Eating *subindex*
telephone services 300-1, 354

000 map pages
000 photographs

Temple Street Night Market
109, **7**
temples, *see* Sights *subindex*
tennis 229
tenpin bowling 223-4
theatre 35-6, 345, *see
also* Entertainment,
Sights *subindexes*
theme parks, *see* Sights
subindex
Tian Tan Buddha 138, **9**
Tiananmen Square 26
time 301
tipping 176, 301-2
To, Johnnie 32
To Kwa Wan 198
toilets 302
Tong Fuk 142
tourist information 302,
354-5
tourist passes 284-5
tours 298-9, 313-17, *see
also* walking tours
Pearl River 267
sailing 229
sampans 93
trails, *see* Sights *subindex*
train travel 282-4
to/from mainland China
286
trams 284
travellers cheques 298
Triads 29
Tsang, Donald 29-30
Tsim Sha Tsui 98-104, **104**
accommodation 241-4
clubs & live music 218-19
drinking 214
entertainment 220
food 191-4
shopping 167-9
transport 103
Tsim Sha Tsui East 104-8,
106
accommodation 244-5
clubs & live music 218-19
drinking 214-15
food 194-6
shopping 167-9
transport 107
Tsim Sha Tsui East
Promenade 106
Tsing Yi 151
Tsui Hark 31, 32
Tsuen Wan 116-18, **117**, **8**
Tuen Mun 119-20, 198
Tung Chee Hwa 27, 29

Tung Chung 144-5
Tung Lung Chau 151-2
Tung O Wan 137-8
Tung Ping Chau 132-3
turtles 135
TV 301
typhoons 289

U

universities 87, 126, 302

V

vacations, *see* holidays
vaccinations 293
vegetarian travellers 182,
see also Eating *subindex*
Victoria Peak 89
viewing points, *see* Sights
subindex
visas 287, 303, 355
volunteering 303

W

wakeboarding, *see* wind-
surfing & wakeboarding
walking tours, *see
also* hiking
Central 70, **70**
Cheung Chau 148-9, **149**
Kowloon 110-12, **112**
Macau Peninsula 326-7,
326
Sheung Wan 83-4, **83**
Taipa Island 332-3, **332**
Wan Chai 76-7, **76**
Wan Chai 70-7, **74**
accommodation 235-7
clubs & live music 217-18
drinking 210-12
entertainment 219
food 178-81
shopping 163-4
transport 77
walking tour 76-7, **76**
watches 157, 163
waterfalls 119, 144
weather 15, 289, 353
weights 303, *see also inside
front cover*
Western Districts 87, 184-5
wet markets 176, **5**, **47**, **51**
wildlife 41
Wilson Trail 227
windsurfing & wakeboarding
147, 229, *see also* Sports
& Activities *subindex*
wine 211, 322
bars 210

women travellers 303
Wong, Suzie 160
Wong Kar-wai 32
Wong Shek 131-2
Wong Tai Sin 114
Wong Yan-kwai 33
work 304
WWII 23-4, 308

X

Xavier, Francis 307
Xi Xi 37

Y

yachting 229
Yau Ma Tei 108-10, **108**
accommodation 246-7
entertainment 220
food 196-7
shopping 170
transport 109
Yeung Chau 131
Yim Tin Tsai 131
yoga 223
Yuen Long 120, 198-9
Yung Shue Ha 137
Yung Shue Wan 135, 201-2

Z

Zhuhai 259-63, **260**
accommodation 263
attractions 259-61
drinking 262-3
food 262-3
transport 262
zodiac, Chinese 42
zoos, *see* Sights *subindex*

EATING

AMERICAN
Flying Pan 183
Union J 183

ASIAN
Concerto Inn 202
International Curry House
180-1
Peak Lookout 188
Sevva 177

AUSTRIAN
Mozart Stub'n 181

BAKERIES
Ali Oli Bakery Cafe 200
Choi Heong Yuen 333

INDEX

Koi Kei 333
Lord Stow's Bakery 341
Pumpernickel Cafe 187
Pun Veng Kei 333
Sai Kung Cafe & Bakery 201
Tai Cheong Bakery 184

BARBECUE

Gallery Bar & Restaurants 203
Hemingway's by the Bay 203

CAFES

Bookworm Café 201
Cafe Merlion 199
Caravela 337
Deli Lamma Cafe 201
Hometown Teahouse 203
Lord Stow's Café 341
Lord Stow's Garden Café 341
Margaret's Café e Nata 338
Ou Mun Café 337
Riquexó 337

CANTONESE

Chan Kun Kee 199
Cheong Kei 338
Chuen Kee Seafood Restaurant 200
City Hall Maxim's Palace 178
Eight 336
Fook Lam Moon 194
Forum 186
Fung Shing Restaurant 188
Gi Kee Seafood Restaurant 188
Golden Valley 188
Happy Seafood Restaurant 199
Hing Kee Restaurant 196
Island Tang 177
Jīn Yuè Xuan (Zhuhai) 262
Joy Hing Food Shop 181
Jumbo Kingdom Floating Restaurant 190
Kam Kau Kee Seafood Restaurant 200
Kapok Cantonese Restaurant 340
Kin's Kitchen 189
Kwun Hoi Heen 341
Kwun Kee Restaurant 185
Lamcombe Seafood Restaurant 201-2

Lei Garden 195
Lin Heung Tea House 178
Long Kei 337
Long Wa 337
Luk Yu Tea House 182
Lung King Heen 177
Lung Wah Hotel Restaurant 199-200
Mak's Noodle 184
May Flower Restaurant 262
Nang Kee Goose Restaurant 198
New Hon Kee 201
Nga Tim Café 341
Ngau Kee Food Cafe 185
Phoenix House 258
Portas do Sol 337
Rosa Chinensia 262
Ser Wong Fun 184
Sha Tin 18 199
Shek O Chinese & Thai Seafood 191
Spring Moon 191
Sun Chiu Kee 189
T'ang Court 191
Tao Tao Ju Restaurant 268
Tim's Kitchen 185
Toby Inn 190-1
Tou Tou Koi 335
Tung Po Seafood Restaurant 189
U Tac Hong 338
Vbest Tea House 183
Veggie Palace 180
Victoria City 180
Wang Fu 184
West Villa 187
Wong Chi Kei 338
Ying 338
Yung Kee Restaurant 183

CARIBBEAN

Hemingway's by the Bay 203

CHINESE

Bay Phoon Town 199
Bingsheng Restaurant 268
Bo Innovation 178
Canton 339
Chi Lin Vegetarian (Long Men Lou) 198
Chun Chun 202
Golden Bull 186
Goldfinch 187
Grand Prince 258
Islam Food 197

Kung Wo Tofu Factory 195
Mido Cafe 196
Ming Kee Seafood Restaurant 204
Mui Wo Cooked Food Centre 202
New Baccarat 203-4
Pat Heung Kwun Yum Temple 199
Pou Tai Temple Restaurant 340
Pure Veggie House 180
Queen's Cafe 197
Rainbow Seafood Restaurant 202
Shu Zhai 190
Sosam Tea House 198
Tai Ping Koon 186-7
Tai Yuen Restaurant 202
Wing Lei 335-6
Yee Heung Bean Products 198
Yin Yang 179

CHINESE MUSLIM & HALAL

Islam Food 197
Muslim Hotel Restaurant 258

CHIU CHOW

Chong Fat Chiu Chow Restaurant 197
Leung Hing Chiu Chow Seafood Restaurant 185
Pak Lok Chiu Chow Restaurant 186

CONGEE

Hong Kee Congee Shop 189
King's Palace Congee & Noodle Bar 197
Nathan Congee & Noodle 196
Sweet Dynasty 193-4

DAI PAI DONG

Ap Lei Chau Market Cooked Food Centre 190
Chan Kun Kee 199
Fok Loi Kui Seafood Restaurant 196
Gi Kee Seafood Restaurant 188
Hing Kee Restaurant 196
Tak Chai Kee 202-3

Tak Fat Beef Balls 193
Tung Po Seafood Restaurant 189

DESSERTS

Honeymoon Dessert (Sai Kung) 200-1
Honeymoon Dessert (Sha Tin) 199
Hop Shing Chiu Chow Dessert 193
Kin Hing Tofu Dessert 202
Lai Kei 338
Nánxin 268
Serrdura 338
Sweet Auntie 193
Sweet Dynasty 193-4
Tiffin Lounge 193
U Tac Hong 338
Vero Lounge 193
XTC 193

DIM SUM

City Hall Maxim's Palace 178
Fook Lam Moon 194
Forum 186
Hong Kong Old Restaurant 192
Island Tang 177
Jīn Yuè Xuān (Shenzhen) 258
Jīn Yuè Xuān (Zhuhai) 262
Laurel 258
Lei Garden 195
Lin Heung Tea House 178
Luk Yu Tea House 182
Lung King Heen 177
Pak Lok Chiu Chow Restaurant 186
Panxi Restaurant 268
Spring Moon 191
T'ang Court 191
West Villa 187
Wu Kong Shanghai Restaurant 192
Yè Shanghai 192
Yung Kee Restaurant 183

EGYPTIAN

Habibi 178

ENGLISH

Pawn 180

EUROPEAN
Ali Oli Bakery Cafe 200
Amber 176
Crown Wine Cellars 189-90
Press Room 185
Pumpernickel Cafe 187
Swiss Chalet 194

FILIPINO
Mang Ambo's Filipino
Restaurant 181

FRENCH
Amigo 188
Belle Epoque 258
Bonheur 184-5
Caprice 176-7
Chez Les Copains 200
La Bonne Heure 336
La Seine 268
L'Atelier de Joël Robuchon
177
Le Marron 186
Petrus 179
Pierre 177
Robuchon a Galera 335

FUJIANESE
Mun Nam Restaurant 189

FUSION
Made in Kitchen 258
Sosam Tea House 198

GERMAN
920 Restaurant & Bar 268

HAKKA
Dah Wing Wah 200

HANGZHOU
Hang Zhou Restaurant 179
Tin Heung Lau 194
West Lake Spring 259

HUNANESE
Hunan Garden 178

INDIAN
Branto 192
Chungking Mansions 192

Gaylord Indian Restaurant
192
International Curry House
180-1
Khana Khazana 181
Koh-i-Noor 182
Woodlands 195

INDONESIAN
Indonesian Restaurant
1968 186

INTERNATIONAL
Amigo 188
Cafe Deco 187-8
Life Cafe 183
Lucy's 190
Peak Lookout 188
Pizza Express 190
Rossio 336
Sevva 177
Steak House 194
Top Deck 190
Verandah 191
Windsurfing Watersports
Centre & Cafe 204
World Peace Cafe 181

ITALIAN
Cecconi's Italian 181-2
Cine Città 179
Da Domenico 186
Don Alfonso 335
Gaia Ristorante 184
Grissini 178-9
Il Teatro 335
La Cucina Italiana 340
La Gondola 341
Locanda 336
Portofino 338
Rughetta 183
Sabatini Italian 194

JAPANESE
Hokahoka 194
Inagiku 177
Ippei-An 195
June Japanese
Restaurant 188
Sushi Hiro 186
Sushi Kuu 182
Tenmasa 338
Tonkichi Tonkatsu Seafood
187
Yakitoritei 189
Yokozuna 196-7
Zuma 177-8

KOREAN
Chang Won Korean
Restaurant 194
Hansung Co 195

LEBANESE
Assaf 182

MACANESE
Amagao 340
Cozinha Pinocchio 340
Fat Siu Lau 337
Galo 340
Henri's Galley 337
Litoral 336
Nga Tim Café 341
Nino's Cozinha 180
O Porto Interior 337
Praia Grande 336
Riquexó 337
Serrdura 338

MALAYSIAN
Prawn Noodle Shop 178
Sabah 181
Yeoh's Bah Kut Teh 185

MARKETS
Almirante Lacerda City
Market 335
wet markets 176, **5**, **47**, **51**

MEDITERRANEAN
Cococabana 191
La Paloma 335
Stoep Restaurant 203

NOODLES
Cheong Fat 197
Hong Kong Congee Shop 189
Ippei-An 195
Kau Kee Restaurant 185
King's Palace Congee &
Noodle Bar 197
Mak's Noodle 184
Man Fai 187
Nathan Congee & Noodle
196
Prawn Noodle Shop 178
Ruamjai Thai Restaurant
197
Shan Loon Tse Kee Fish
Ball 190
Tak Fat Beef Balls 193
Yokozuna 196-7

NORTHERN CHINESE
American Restaurant 180
Crystal Jade 193
Din Tai Fung 193
Hutong 191
Peking Dumpling Shop 195
Peking Restaurant 196
Sha Tin 18 199
Spring Deer 195
Wat Yat 195-6

PIGEON
Han Lok Yuen 202

PIZZA
Pizza Express 190
Shakey's Pizza Restaurant
199

PORTUGUESE
A Lorcha 337
A Petisqueira 340
Afonso III 336
António 339-40
Camões 336
Clube Militar de Macau 336
Espaço Lisboa 340
Fernando 341
Galo 340
Litoral 336
Miramar 340-1
Nino's Cozinha 180
O Manuel 340
O Porto Interior 337
Platão 336-7
Praia Grande 336

SANDWICHES
Tim Kee French
Sandwiches 196

SEAFOOD
Ap Lei Chau Market Cooked
Food Centre 190
Chuen Kee Seafood
Restaurant 200
Déyuè Fǎng 262
Fok Loi Kui Seafood
Restaurant 196
Happy Seafood
Restaurant 199
Kam Kau Kee Seafood
Restaurant 200
Lamcombe Seafood
Restaurant 201-2

000 map pages
000 photographs

Lung Mun Seafood Restaurant 198
Lung Yue Restaurant 198
May Flower Restaurant 262
Ming Kee Seafood Restaurant 204
New Baccarat 203-4
New Hon Kee 201
Rainbow Seafood Restaurant 202
Sam Ka Tsuen Seafood Precinct 115
Sea King Garden Restaurant 198
Tai Yuen Restaurant 202

SHANGHAINESE
Crystal Jade 193
Delicious Kitchen 187
Din Tai Fung 193
Hang Zhou Restaurant 179
Hong Kong Old Restaurant 192
Kung Tak Lam 192
Liu Yuan Pavilion 179
Shanghai Xiao Nan Guo 199
Tin Heung Lau 194
Wat Yat 195-6
Wing Lai Yuen (Yeung's Kitchen) 196
Wu Kong Shanghai Restaurant 192
Yè Shanghai 192
Yellow Door Kitchen 183

SICHUANESE
Chuānguó Yǎnyì 268
Da Ping Huo 182
Golden Valley 188
Wing Lai Yuen (Yeung's Kitchen) 196
Yellow Door Kitchen 183

SOUTH AFRICAN
Stoep Restaurant 203

SOY SAUCE WESTERN
Goldfinch 187
Queen's Cafe 197
Tai Ping Koon 186-7

SPANISH
La Paloma 335
Olé Spanish Restaurant & Wine Bar 182

STEAKHOUSES
Lardos Steak House 201
Steak House 194

SUPERMARKETS
Gourmet Fine Foods 335
Hyper Gourmet 335
New Yaohan 335
Pavilions Supermercado 335

SWISS
Swiss Chalet 194

TEA CAFES & HOUSES
Honolulu Coffee Shop 180
Kam Fung Cafe 181
Lan Fong Yuen 184
Lock Cha Tea Shop 179-80
Long Wa 337
Mido Cafe 196
Pak Kung Cafe 198
Star Cafe 193
Sun Chiu Kee 189
Tea Palace 262
Wah Nam Cafe Shop 197

THAI
Bon Appetit 183
Cheong Fat 197
Chung Shing Thai Restaurant 199
O Sip Hah 182-3
Ruamjai Thai Restaurant 197
Shek O Chinese & Thai Seafood 191
Thai Zhen Cow & Bridge 268

TOFU
Kung Wo Tofu Factory 195
Yee Heung Bean Products 198

TURKISH
Bahçe 202

VEGETARIAN
Bookworm Café 201
Branto 192
Chi Lin Vegetarian (Long Men Lou) 198
Khana Khazana 181
Kung Tak Lam 192
Life Cafe 183
Lock Cha Tea Shop 179-80

Po Lin Vegetarian Restaurant 203
Pou Tai Temple Restaurant 340
Pure Veggie House 180
Summer Tea House 258-9
Veggie Palace 180
Woodlands 195
World Peace Cafe 181

VIETNAMESE
Bon Appetit 183
Chun Chun 202
Golden Bull 186
Saigon Pho 181

WESTERN
Bay 202
Café Too 179
Concerto Inn 202
Lucy's 268

XIN JIANG
Bi Yi Restaurant 185

ENTERTAINMENT
BARS
38 344
Baietan Bar Street 269
Balalaika 214
Bar 109 210
Bar 1911 208
Barco 208
Beijing Club 216
Biergarten 214
Bit Point 208-9
Brecht's Circle 213
Bridge 210
C Union 269
C: Union 259
Cage 210
Captain's Bar 207
Casablanca Café 344
Champagne Bar 211
Chillax 214
China Beach Club 215
Chinatown 211
Cinnebar 344
Classified 212
Club 71 209, 49
Club 97 216
Corner's Wine Bar & Tapas Café 344
Dada 214
Deck 'n Beer 215

Delaney's 212
Dickens Bar 213
Diesel's Bar 215
Dragon-I 209
East End Brewery 213
Executive Bar 213
Felix 214
Finds 209
Fountainhead Drinking Bar 215
Intercontinental Lobby Lounge 214
Island Society Bar 215
JK's Club 215
Joyce is Not Here 216
La Dolce Vita 209
Lei Dou 209
Martini Bar 214 15
McSorley's Ale house 345
Mes Amis 211-12
MGM Grand Macau 345
MO Bar 207
Old China Hand 212
Old Taipa Tavern 345
Overseas Chinese Village 269
Paradiso Lounge 213-14
Pawn 212
Peak Cafe Bar 209
People's Cafe 269
Philia 209
Ping Pong 269
Red Bar 208
Skitz 212
Soho Wines & Spirits 210
Solas 209
Sparkz 210
Spasso 214
Tivo 209
True Colour 259
Where 215
Wilber's 269
Yun Fu 209-10

CAFES
Corner's Wine Bar & Tapas Café 344
Lobby Lounge 207
Macau Sou 344
Mix 207
Naturo 207
Salon de Thé de Joël Robuchon 207

CASINOS
Emperor Palace Casino 341-2
Grand Lisboa Casino 342, 10

Lisboa Casino 342
MGM Grand Casino 342
Plaza Casino 342
Sands Macau 342-3
Venetian Macao Casino 343
Wynn Macau Casino 343

CINEMAS
Agnès B Cinema 219
Alliance Française 219
AMC Festival Walk 220
Broadway Cinematheque 220
Cine-Art House 219
Goethe-Institut 219
Grand Ocean Cinema 220
Palace IFC Cinema 219
Windsor Cinema 220

CLASSICAL MUSIC & CULTURAL CENTRES
Hong Kong Cultural Centre 220
Kwai Tsing Theatre 220
Sha Tin Town Hall 220
Tsuen Wan Town Hall 220
Tuen Mun Town Hall 220
Xinghai Concert Hall 269
Yuen Long Theatre 220

CLUBS
1/5 217
Bahama Mama's 218
Beijing Club 216
Cloudnine 218
Club 97 216
D2 344
Dragon-I 209
Drop 216
Fashion Club 344
Homebase 216-17
Insomnia 217
Joe Bananas 217
New Makati Pub & Disco 217
Velvet 269
Yumla 217

COMEDY
Punchline Comedy Club 219
Take Out Comedy Club 219

000 map pages
000 photographs

GAY & LESBIAN VENUES
DYMK 212
New Wally Matt Lounge 212
Propaganda 213
Tony's Bar 213
Volume 213
Works 213

LIVE-MUSIC VENUES
Bohemian Lounge 217
Carnegie's 218
Cavern 217
Dusk till Dawn 218
Fringe Gallery 217
Hari's 218-19
HITEC Rotunda 218
Hong Kong Coliseum 218
Hong Kong Convention & Exhibition Centre 218
Joyce is Not Here 216
Ko Shan Theatre 218
Old Taipa Tavern 345
Queen Elizabeth Stadium 218
Wanch 218

LOUNGES
Gecko Lounge 210
Macau Sou 344

PUBS
China Bear 215-16
Cohiba 262-3
Delaney's (Tsim Sha Tsui) 214
Delaney's (Wan Chai) 212
Devil's Advocate 212
Duke 215
East End Brewery & Inn Side Out 213
Paddy Field 269
Poets 215
Smugglers Inn 214
Whiskey Priest 210

THEATRE
Dragone Show 345
Fringe Studio & Theatre 220
Sunbeam Theatre 220
Zaia 345

WINE BARS
Gecko Lounge 210
Staunton's Wine Bar & Café 210

WINE-TASTING
Tastings 211
Watson's Wine Cellar 211

SHOPPING
ANTIQUES
Amours Antiques 158
Arch Angel Antiques 157
Chine Gallery 158
Hobbs & Bishops Fine Art 157-8
Honeychurch Antiques 158
Karin Weber Gallery 164-5
Tai Sing Fine Antiques 158
Teresa Coleman Fine Arts 158
Wattis Fine Art 158
Xiguan Antique Street 268

ART
Dafen Village 257
Wéndé Lù 268

AUCTION HOUSES
Christie's 158-9

BOOKS
Bloomsbury Books 159
Bookazine 159
Cosmos Books 163
Dymocks 159
Government Publications Office 159
Hong Kong Book Centre 159
Indosiam 165
Joint Publishing 159
Kelly & Walsh 159
Page One 159
Swindon Books 159
Tai Yip Art Book Centre 159

CARPETS
Chine Gallery 158

CHILDREN'S GOODS
Kitty House Gift Shop 168
Little Misses & Mini Masters 168
Toy Museum 168
Wise Kids 168

CIGARS
Cigarro 166

CLOTHING & ACCESSORIES
45R Jeans 163
Amours Antiques 158
Beatniks 168
Blanc de Chine 159
Dada Cabaret Voltaire 166
D-Mop 166
Granville Rd 168
H&M 159-60
Huálè Lù 268
Jilian, Lingerie on Wyndham 160
Joyce 160
Kent & Curwen 163
LCX 166
Linva Tailor 160
Liùyùn Xiǎoqū 268
Lulu Cheung 160
Luohu Commercial City 257-8
Miu Miu 160
Muji 168
Pacific Custom Tailors 163
Ranee K 165
Sam's Tailor 168
Shanghai Tang 161
Sister 166
Sonjia 163
Trendy Zone 170
Vintage HK 161
Vivienne Tam 163-4
Walter Ma 166-7
www.izzue.com 168

COMPUTERS
Golden Computer Arcade 170
In Square 167
Mong Kok Computer Centre 170
New Capital Computer Plaza 170
Star Computer City 168-9
Tianhe computer markets 268
Wan Chai Computer Centre 164

DEPARTMENT STORES
Chinese Arts & Crafts 164
Harvey Nichols 161
Lane Crawford 161
Sogo 167
Swank 161

INDEX

Wing On 165
Yue Hwa Chinese Products Emporium 170

ELECTRONICS
Huaqiang Bei Commercial St 257

EYEWEAR
Ocean Optical 161

FLORISTS
Anglo-Chinese Florist 166
Armani Fiori 166
Mandarin Oriental Flower Shop 166

FOOD & DRINK
Cova 166
Fook Ming Tong Tea Shop 161
Lock Cha Tea Shop 165
Olympia Graeco-Egyptian Coffee 161
Three Sixty 161

GIFTS & SOUVENIRS
Alan Chan Creations 169
Curio Alley 169
Design Gallery 164
Liuligongfang 161
Mountain Folkcraft 162
Picture This 162
Wah Tung China Arts 162

HERBAL PRODUCTS
Good Spring Co 82

HOMEWARES
Addiction 165
Frols 165
Homeless 165
Muji 168
Sonjia 163

INCENSE
Queen's Road West incense shops 81-2

JEWELLERY
King Fook 162
King Sing Jewellery 169

Om International 169
Premier Jewellery 169
Rock Candy 162
Tse Sui Luen 162

MALLS
Beverley Commercial Centre 165
Cat Street Galleries 82
Cityplaza 167
Delay No Mall 167
Festival Walk 170
Harbour City 169
IFC Mall 162-3
Island Beverley 165
Landmark 163
Langham Place Mall 170
Pacific Place 164
Prince's Building 163
Rainbow City 167
Rise Commercial Centre 165
Times Square 167
Trendy Zone 170
Up Date Mall 165

MAPS
Government Publications Office 159

MARKETS
Apliu St 112-13, 158
Dongmen Market 257
Fangcun tea market 268
Four Lane Sq 158
Jardine's Bazaar 158
Sheung Shui market 122
Stanley Market 95, 158
Tai Po Market 124
Tianhe computer markets 268
Tung Choi St market 158

MUSIC
HMV 162
Hong Kong Records 164

OUTDOOR GEAR
Chamonix Alpine Equipment 170
Giga Sports 169
Mountaineering Services 167
Sunmark Camping Equipment 164
Travelmax 169
Wise Mount Sports 170

PHOTOGRAPHIC EQUIPMENT
David Chan Photo Shop 169
Everbest Photo Supplies 162
Photo Scientific 162

SHOES
Coup de Foudre 167
Pedder Red 162

SPORTING GOODS
Bunn's Divers 164
KHS Bicycles 170
KS Ahluwalia & Sons 169
Kung Fu Supplies 164
Ocean Sky Divers 169
Po Kee Fishing Tackle 165-6

WATCHES
City Chain 163

WINE
Les Q 211
Margaret River Wine Shop 211
Oliver's the Delicatessen 211
Ponti Wine Cellars 211

SIGHTS
BEACHES
Afternoon Beach 147
Big Wave Bay 97
Cheoc Van 332
Cheung Sha 141
Clearwater Bay First 133
Clearwater Bay Second 133
Hác Sá 332
Hung Shing Yeh 135
Lo So Shing 136
Mo Tat Wan 136
Nam Tam Wan 147
Pak Tso Wan 147-8
Silvermine Bay 143
Silverstrand 133
St Stephen's 96
Tung Wan 147

BUILDINGS & STRUCTURES
55 Nam Koo Terrace 77
Bank of China Buildings 66

Bishop's Palace 323
Central District Police Station 77
Central Plaza 73, **47**
Chinese Reading Room 321
Crown Wine Cellars 39
Former French Mission Building 66-7
Former KCR Clock Tower 99
Former Marine Police Headquarters 102, **7**
Former Residence of Tong Shaoyi 261
Government House (Hong Kong) 67
Government House (Macau) 321
Guia Hill Air Raid Shelter 324
Guia Lighthouse 324
High Island Reservoir 131
Hong Kong Academy for the Performing Arts 73
Hong Kong Arts Centre 73
Hong Kong City Hall 67-8
Hong Kong Convention & Exhibition Centre 73
Hong Kong Cultural Centre 99
HSBC Building 61, 64
International Commerce Centre 70
Jardine House 68
Kap Shui Mun Bridge 151
Leal Senado 317, 319
Legislative Council Building 68, **49**
Lou Kau Mansion 320
Macau Tower 323
Maryknoll Convent School 39
Meixi Royal Archways 261
Murray House 95
Old Stanley Police Station 95
Old Wan Chai Post Office 76
One & Two International Finance Centre 69-70
Pawn 39
Peninsula Hong Kong 102
Plover Cove Reservoir 125
Repulse Bay, the 97
Shek Kip Mei Estate, Mei Ho House 39
Tsing Ma Bridge 151
Yi Tai Study Hall 122
Yuen Yuen Institute 117

INDEX

CEMETERIES
Cemetery of St Michael the Archangel 324
Old Protestant Cemetery 324
Stanley Military Cemetery 96

CHILDREN'S SIGHTS
Children's Discovery Gallery 128
Hong Kong Toy Story 128
Lions Nature Education Centre 130

CHURCHES & CATHEDRALS
Cathedral of the Sacred Heart 265
Chapel of Our Lady of Guia 324
Chapel of Our Lady of Penha 323
Chapel of St Francis Xavier 331, **10**
Chapel of St Joseph Seminary 321
Chapel of St Michael 324
Church of Our Lady of Lourdes 265
Church of St Anthony 325
Church of St Augustine 321
Church of St Dominic 320
Church of St Lawrence 321
Macau Cathedral 320
Ruins of the Church of St Paul 317, **10**
St John's Cathedral 68-9

FORTS
Butterfly Hill Watchtower 144
Dapeng Fortress 255-6
Fan Lau Fort 142
Guia Fort 324
Luk Tei Tong Watchtower 144
Monte Fort 319, **11**
Tung Chung Battery 145
Tung Chung Fort 145
Tung Lung Fort 152

GALLERIES & ART SPACES
10 Chancery Lane Gallery 34
Amelia Johnson Contemporary 34
Cattle Depot Artist Village 34
Chao Shao-an Gallery 128
Edge Gallery 34
Fotan Art Studios 34
Grotto Fine Art 34
Guangzhou Art Gallery 263
Hanart TZ Gallery 34
He Xiangning Art Gallery 254-5
Hong Kong Planning & Infrastructure Exhibition Gallery 67-8
Hong Kong Visual Arts Centre 73
Jockey Club Creative Arts Centre 34
KS Lo Gallery 73
OCT Art & Design Gallery 255
OCT-LOFT Art Terminal 254
Osage Gallery 34
Ox Warehouse 325
Pao Sui Loong & Pao Yue Kong Galleries 73
Para/Site Artspace 34
Schoeni Art Gallery 34
Sin Sin Fine Art 34
Tap Seac Gallery 325
TT Tsui Gallery of Chinese Art 128
YY9 Gallery 34

HISTORIC SITES
Dapeng Fortress 255-6
Kat Hing Wai 121-2
Ping Kong 123
Shui Tau Tsuen 122

LANDMARKS
Amah Rock 127-8
Ap Lei Chau 94-5
Causeway Bay Typhoon Shelter 87
Cheung Chau Ferry Pier 148
Cheung Po Tsai Cave 148
Lam Tsuen Wishing Tree 123-4
Lantau Peak 139
Lover's Rock 76

Noonday Gun 84, 86
Tsim Sha Tsui East Promenade 106, **7**, **52**
Victoria Peak 89

MARKETS
Apliu St 112-13, 158
Cat St 82
Fanling market 122-3
Goldfish Market 111
Graham St Market 65
Jade Market 109-10
Sheung Shui market 122
Stanley Market 95, 158
Tai Po Market 124
Temple Street Night Market 109, **7**
Wan Chai Market 76
Western Market 82
Yuen Po Street Flower Market 110

MONASTERIES & NUNNERIES
10,000 Buddhas Monastery 126-7
Chi Lin Nunnery 39, 114-5
Chuk Lam Sim Monastery 118
Miu Fat Monastery 119-20
Po Lam Monastery 139
Po Lin Monastery 138
Trappist Monastery 143
Western Monastery 117-18

MOSQUES
Kowloon Mosque & Islamic Centre 103
Mosque Dedicated to the Prophet 265

MUSEUMS
Chinese University of Hong Kong Art Museum 126
Dr Sun Yat Sen Museum 88
Dr Sun Yat-sen Residence Memorial Museum 261
Fire Services Museum 326
Flagstaff House Museum of Tea Ware 71
Grand Prix Museum 322
Guangdong Museum of Art 267
Guangzhou City Museum 263
Guangzhou Museum of Art 266-7

Handover of Macau Gifts Museum 323
Hong Kong Correctional Services Museum 95
Hong Kong Film Archive 91
Hong Kong Heritage Museum 128
Hong Kong Maritime Museum 95
Hong Kong Museum of Art 98-9, **48**
Hong Kong Museum of Coastal Defence 91-2
Hong Kong Museum of History 107
Hong Kong Museum of Medical Sciences 88
Hong Kong Racing Museum 90
Hong Kong Railway Museum 123
Hong Kong Science Museum 107-8
Hong Kong Space Museum & Theatre 103
Law Uk Folk Museum 92
Lei Cheng Uk Han Tomb Museum 113
Macau Museum 320, **11**
Macau Museum of Art 322
Macau Security Forces Museum 322
Macau Wine Museum 322
Maritime Museum 323
Mausoleum of the Nanyue King 263
Memorial Museum of Generalissimo Sun Yat-sen's Mansion 266
Museum of Nature & Agriculture 332
Museum of Sacred Art & Crypt 317
Museum of Taipa & Coloane History 329
Museum of the Holy House of Mercy 320
Old Shenzhen Museum 254
Pawnshop Museum 321
Police Museum 90
Sam Tung Uk Museum 118-19
Shenzhen Museum 252, 254
Sheung Yiu Folk Museum 130-1
Sound of the Century Museum 321-2

000 map pages
000 photographs

Sun Yat Sen Memorial
Home 325
Taipa House Museum 327,
329, **11**
Wan Chai Livelihood
Museum 76
Whampoa Military
Academy 266
Zhuhai City Museum 259

**NATURE
RESERVES &
TRAILS**
Clearwater Bay Country
Park 133
Family Trail 134
Hoi Ha Wan Marine Park
131-2
Lions Nature Education
Centre 130
Mai Po Nature Reserve 120-1
Pak Tam Chung Nature Trail
130-1
Pat Sin Leng Nature Trail 125
Plover Cove Country Park 132
Tai Po Kau Nature Reserve
125-6

**PARKS &
GARDENS**
Casa Garden 324
Cheung Kong Garden 66-7
Hong Kong Park 71, 73
Hong Kong Wetland Park
119, **8**
Hong Kong Zoological &
Botanical Gardens 65-6
Kadoorie Farm & Botanic
Gardens 119
Kowloon Park 102-3
Kowloon Walled City Park
113-14
Lou Lim Ioc Garden 324
Luís de Camões Garden 325
Lung Tsai Ng Garden 139
Ma On Shan Country
Park 129
Ma Wan Park 151
Nan Lian Garden 39
Seac Pai Van Park 332
Tak Wah Park 116
Tangjia Public Garden 261
Victoria Park 86, **52**

RACECOURSES
Happy Valley Racecourse
90, **5**
Hipodromo da Taipa 346
Sha Tin Racecourse 128-9

ROCK CARVINGS
Big Wave Bay 97
Cheng Chau 148
Clearwater Bay Peninsula
133
Lantau 142
Po Toi 152

SHRINES
Chen Clan Ancestral Hall
263, 265
Four-Faced Buddha Shrine
329
Hung Shing shrine 95
Kwun Yam Shrine 97
Tai Wong shrine 96
Tang Ching Lok Ancestral
Hall 122
Tang Kwong U Ancestral
Hall 122

**STATUES &
MONUMENTS**
A-Ma Statue 332
Five Rams Statue 263
Golden Bauhinia 73
Hong Kong
Observatory 108
Kun Iam Statue 322
Memorial Garden to the
Martyrs 266
Revolutionary Martyrs'
Memorial 261
Tian Tan Buddha 138, **9**

**STREETS,
SQUARES &
PRECINCTS**
Avenida da República 323
Cat St 82
Chung On St 116
Exchange Square 66, **48**
Festival Walk 113
Ice House St 79
Largo do Senado 326
Li Yuen St East & West 77
Lower Albert Rd 79-80
Man Wa Lane 82
Nanking St 108
Nathan Rd 99, 102
Ning Po St 108
Possession St 82
Saigon St 108
Sam Ka Tsuen Seafood
Precinct 115
Shanghai St 108

Star St 77
Statue Sq 64-5

SYNAGOGUES
Ohel Leah Synagogue 88-9

TEMPLES
A-Ma Temple 323
Che Kung Temple 128
Ching Chung Temple 120
Fung Ying Sin Temple 122
Hau Wong Temple 145
Hong Kung Temple 321
Hung Shing Temple 73
Kun Iam Temple 325
Kwun Yam Temple 96
Lin Fung Temple 325
Man Mo temple (Mui
Wo) 144
Man Mo temple (Sheung
Wan) 80-1
Man Mo temple (Tai Po) 124
Na Tcha Temple 321
Nu Wa Temple 321
Pak Tai Temple 147
Pou Tai Temple 329
Sam Kai Vui Kun Temple 321
Sik Sik Yuen Wong Tai Sin
Temple 114, **6**
Tai Miu Temple 133
Tai Ping Shan Temples 82-3
Tam Kong Temple 331
Tangjia Temple Complex 261
Temple of Bright, Filial &
Piety 265
Temple of the Six Banyan
Trees 265
Tian Hou Temple 332
Tin Hau temple
(Aberdeen) 95
Tin Hau temple
(Causeway Bay) 87
Tin Hau temple (Coloane
Island) 331
Tin Hau temple (Peng
Chau) 150
Tin Hau temple (Ping
Kong) 123
Tin Hau temple (Shui Tau
Tsuen) 122
Tin Hau temple (Stanley) 96
Tin Hau temple (Tap Mun
Chau) 132
Tin Hau temple (Tung Ping
Chau) 132-3
Tin Hau temple (Yung Shue
Wan) 135

Tin Hau temples (Cheung
Chau) 148

THEATRES
Dom Pedro V Theatre 320-1

THEME PARKS
China Folk Culture
Village 255
Hong Kong Disneyland 144
Macau Fisherman's Wharf
322
New Yuan Ming Palace 261
Noah's Ark 151
Ocean Park 93, **4**
OCT East 255
Splendid China 255
Window of the World 255

UNIVERSITIES
Chinese University of Hong
Kong 126
Hong Kong University 87

VIEWING POINTS
Finger Hill 150
Lantau Link Visitors Centre
viewing platform 151
Lantau Peak 139
Macau Tower 323
Ocean Terminal 103-4
Peak Galleria 89
Peak Tower 89-90
Penha Hill 323

WATERFALLS
Ng Tung Chai Waterfall 119
Silvermine Waterfall 144

ZOOS & AVIARIES
Edward Youde Aviary 71
Hong Kong Zoological &
Botanical Gardens 65-6
Seac Pai Van Park 332

SLEEPING
**BOUTIQUE
HOTELS**
Hotel Bonaparte 240
Jia 239
Lan Kwai Fong Hotel 241
Mingle Place at the Eden
241

Mingle Place by the Park 237
Sohotel 238

BUSINESS HOTELS
Courtyard by Marriott Hong Kong 237-8
Fleming 236
Hong Kong Skycity Marriott Hotel 250

GUESTHOUSES
Alisan Guest House 240
Anne Black YWCA 248
Augusters Lodge 348
Beverly Guesthouse 243
Booth Lodge 246
Caritas Bianchi Lodge 246
Caritas Lodge 248
Causeway Bay Guest House 240
Cheung Chau B&B 250
Chung Kiu Inn 240
Chungking House 242
Cosmic Guest House 243
Dragon Inn 242
Four Seasons Guesthouse 242
Garden Guest House 243
Golden Crown Court 243
Golden Island Guesthouse 247
Hakka's Guest House 247
Holiday Guesthouse 242
Hong Kong Star Guesthouse 247
Man Lai Wah Hotel 249
Mei Lam Guest House 243
Ocean Guest House 247
Park Guesthouse 243
Rent-a-Room Hong Kong 247
Sealand House 244
Star Guest House 245
Tom's Guest House 242
Yan Yan Guest House 242-3
Ying King Apartment 237

HOLIDAY HOMES
Bali Holiday Resort 249
Cheung Chau Accommodation Kiosks 250

000 map pages
000 photographs

Jackson Property Agency 249
Mui Wo Accommodation Kiosks 250

HOSTELS
Bradbury Jockey Club Youth Hostel 248
Garden Hostel 243
Guangzhou Riverside International Youth Hostel 269
Hongkong Bank Foundation SG Davis Hostel 250
Jockey Club Mount Davis Hostel 239
Pilgrim's Hall 248-9
Pousada de Juventude de Cheoc Van 349
Pousada de Juventude de Hác Sá 350
Salisbury 244
Shenzhen Loft Youth Hostel 259
Travellers Hostel 243

HOTELS
Altira Macau 349
Bishop Lei International House 241
BP International Hotel 244
Bridal Tea House Hotel 246-7
Butterfly on Prat 245
Casa Hotel 246
Charterhouse Hotel 237
City Garden Hotel Hong Kong 241
Cityview 246
Concerto Inn 249
Cosmopolitan Hotel 240
East Asia Hotel 348
Eaton Hotel 246
Empire Hotel 240
Empire Hotel Hong Kong 236
Empire Kowloon 245
Express by Holiday Inn 238
Four Seasons Hotel 349
Futian Shangri-La 259
Garden Hotel 269
Garden View 237
Grand Bay View Hotel 263
Grand Lapa Hotel 347

Guangdong Victory Hotel 269-70
Harbour Plaza Metropolis 238
Harbour View 236
Hotel Jen 238
Hotel LKF 240-1
Hotel Panorama 245
Hotel Sintra 348
Hotel Taipa 349
Hou Kong Hotel 348
Island Pacific Hotel 237
JJ Hotel 237
Kimberley Hotel 245
Kowloon Hotel Hong Kong 244
Langham Place Hotel 247
Lanson Place 239
Luk Kwok Hotel 238
Man Hing Lung Hotel 243
Metro Park Hotel 348
Metropark Hotel 239-40
MGM Grand Macau 347
Minden 245
Mui Wo Inn 250
Nathan Hotel 246
Newton Hotel Hong Kong 238
Newton Hotel Kowloon 238
Novotel 246
Ole London Hotel 348
Park Hotel 245
Park Lane Hong Kong 239
Pousada de São Tiago 347
Ramada Hong Kong Hotel 237
Regal Hongkong Hotel 238
Regal Riverside Hotel 248
Riviera Hotel Macau 348
Rocks Hotel 347
Royal Pacific Hotel & Towers 238
Royal Plaza Hotel 247
Shangri-La 259
Sheraton Hong Kong Hotel & Towers 242
Silvermine Beach Hotel 250
Sofitel Macau at Ponte 16 348
Sunny Day Hotel 247-8
Venetian Macao Resort Hotel 349
Vision Fashion Hotel 259
Walden Hotel 238
Warwick Hotel 250

Wesley Hong Kong 237
Westin Guangzhou 269
Westin Resort Macau 349
White Swan Hotel 270
Wynn Macau 347
Yindo Hotel 263
Yong Tong Hotel 263

INNS
7 Days Inn 269
Pousada de Mong Há 348

LUXURY HOTELS
Conrad Hong Kong 236
Four Seasons 240
Grand Hyatt Hotel 235-6
Hyatt Regency Hong Kong 248
InterContinental Hong Kong 244
Island Shangri-La Hong Kong 236
Kowloon Shangri-La 244
Langham Hotel Hong Kong 243
Mandarin Oriental 240
Marco Polo Hongkong Hotel 243-4
Metropark Hotel 236
Mira Hong Kong 242-3
Peninsula Hong Kong 241-2, **7**
Regal Airport Hotel 249
Renaissance Harbour View Hotel 236
Royal Garden 244-5
W Hong Kong 245-6

RESORTS
Zhuhai Holiday Resort 263

SERVICED APARTMENTS
Bauhinia Furnished Suites 235
Domus Mercury Serviced Apartments 235
Fraser Suites 234
Han Residence 235
Hanlun Habitats 234
Home2home 234
Ice House 241
Pinnacle Apartment 235
Putman 239
Shama 234
YWCA Building 234-5

SPORTS & ACTIVITIES

BUNGY-JUMPING
Macau Tower 323

CRICKET
Hong Kong Cricket Club 230
Kowloon Cricket Club 230

CYCLING
Flying Ball Bicycle Co 225

DOG RACING
Canidrome 346

FISHING
Tai Mei Tuk Fish Farm 225

FOOTBALL
Happy Valley Sports Ground 230
Hong Kong Football Association 230
Mong Kok Stadium 230

GOLF
Caesars Golf Macau 345
Clearwater Bay Golf & Country Club 225
Deep Water Bay Golf Club 225
Discovery Bay Golf Club 225
Hong Kong Golf Club 225
Jockey Club Kau Sai Chau Public Golf Course 131, 225
Macau Golf & Country Club 345
Shek O Golf & Country Club 225

GYMS
California Fitness 222
Pure Fitness 222
South China Athletic Association 222

HIKING
Hong Kong Trampers 226
Natural Excursion Ideals 226
Walk Hong Kong 226

HORSE RACING
Happy Valley Racecourse 90, 5
Hipodromo da Taipa 346
Sha Tin Racecourse 128-9

HORSE RIDING
Pok Fu Lam Public Riding School 227
Tuen Mun Public Riding School 227

KAYAKING & CANOEING
Cheung Chau Windsurfing Water Sports Centre 227
Dragonfly 227
Natural Excursion Ideals Centre 227
St Stephen's Beach Water Sports Centre 227
Tai Mei Tuk Water Sports Centre 227
Wong Shek Water Sports Centre 227

MARTIAL ARTS
Fightin' Fit 227
Hong Kong Chinese Martial Arts Association 227
Hong Kong Tai Chi Association 227
Hong Kong Wushu Union 227
Wan Kei Ho International Martial Arts Association 228
Wing Chun Yip Man Martial Arts Athletic Association 228

RUGBY
Hong Kong Rugby Football Union 230
Rugby World Cup Sevens 230

SCUBA DIVING
Bunn's Divers 228
Ocean Sky Divers 169, 228
Splash Hong Kong 228

SKATING
Cityplaza Ice Palace 228
Dragon Centre Sky Rink 228
Festival Walk Glacier 228
Megalce 228

SPAS & MASSAGES
Chinese Medicine Valley 261
DK Aromatherapy 222
Elemis Day Spa 222-3
Happy Foot Reflexology Centre 223
Healing Plants 223
Ocean Spring 261
Queen's Spa & Dining 256
Shamian Traditional Chinese Medical Centre 265-6
Spa at the Four Seasons 223

SQUASH
Hong Kong Squash Centre 228-9
Kowloon Park Sports Centre 229
Queen Elizabeth Stadium 229

SWIMMING
Cheoc Van swimming pool 346
Hác Sá Sports & Recreation Park 346
Kowloon Park Swimming Complex 103
Morrison Hill Public Swimming Pool 223
South China Athletic Association 223
Victoria Park 86

TENNIS
Bowen Road Sports Ground 229
Hong Kong Tennis Centre 229
King's Park Tennis Courts 229
Victoria Park 229

TENPIN BOWLING
Belair Bowling 224

WINDSURFING & WAKEBOARDING
Cheung Chau Windsurfing Water Sports Centre 229
Long Coast Seasports Water Sports Centre 229
St Stephen's Beach Water Sports Centre 229
Windsurfing Association of Hong Kong 229
Windsurfing Centre 229

YACHTING & SAILING
Aberdeen Boat Club 229
Aberdeen Marina Club 229
Hebe Haven Yacht Club 229
Royal Hong Kong Yacht Club 229

YOGA
Yoga Central 223
Yoga Fitness 223

TOP PICKS
accommodation 231
attractions 53
eating 171, 335
entertainment 205
Macau 305, 335
shopping 153
sports & activities 221

INDEX

Published by Lonely Planet Publications Pty Ltd
ABN 36 005 607 983

Australia (Head Office)
Locked Bag 1, Footscray, Victoria 3011,
☎ 03 8379 8000, fax 03 8379 8111,
talk2us@lonelyplanet.com.au

USA 150 Linden St, Oakland, CA 94607,
☎ 510 250 6400, toll free 800 275 8555,
fax 510 893 8572, info@lonelyplanet.com

UK 2nd fl, 186 City Rd, London, EC1V 2NT,
☎ 020 7106 2100, fax 020 7106 2101,
go@lonelyplanet.co.uk

© Lonely Planet 2010
Photographs © as listed (p365) 2010

Printed by Fabulous Printers Pte Ltd,
Singapore.

MAP LEGEND

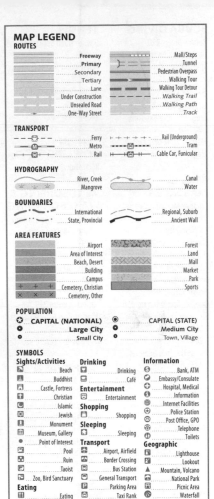

Mixed Sources
Product group from well-managed
forests and other controlled sources
www.fsc.org Cert no. SGS-COC-005002
© 1996 Forest Stewardship Council

FSC

64821828R00099

Made in the USA
Middletown, DE
30 August 2019

A Culture of Excellence!

A Culture of Excellence!

THE ART, PRACTICE, AND DISCIPLINE

OF BREAKTHROUGH LEADERSHIP

Fardad Fateri & James E. York

HARVARD SHUSTER

ISBN-13: 978-0-69209537-9

Acknowledgements

Writing this book was not a project for us but a ten-year journey of passion. It didn't take us ten years to write this book but our book is the emerging property of a ten-year incubation in organizational learning, organizational culture, and leadership. There are hundreds of people who have contributed to the growth and development of our work and all these individuals are worthy of acknowledgement relative to capturing the core principles of our framework.

First and foremost, I want to acknowledge my co-author, Jim York, who did a yeoman's job in being the key ambassador of our work. Jim has been using many parts of this book in workshops, seminars, webinars, and conferences. He not only "gets it" but he lives every part of our framework.

I want to extend my heartfelt gratitude to my colleagues in our trusted inner circle who spent many hours reading our work and providing honest, substantive, and meaningful feedback so our content is delivered cohesively and thoughtfully.

I also want to recognize many of our colleagues at various locations across the United States, including my colleagues in my "CEO Mentorship Program," for their insights, observations, suggestions, and feedback. We certainly learned from everyone and did our best to integrate guidance to make the book useable, understandable, and powerful.

ONWARD and UPWARD!

Fardad Fateri

Contents

Foreword and Introduction by Fardad Fateri 13

Chapter One: Culture Is a State of Mind...........21

How International Education
Corporation Defined Its Culture.......................25
How to Cultivate Your Culture
(Should We Say, "Culture-Vate"?) 30
    Get Everyone on Board 31
    Plan for a Revolution!...............................32
    Expect and Celebrate Redundancy............33
    Strive to Become an
    Organization of Excellence........................34
Excellence Is the Driving Force of Successful
Organizational Culture 35
    A Culture of Excellence
    Demands Leaders of Excellence.................37

Chapter Two: Leaders of Excellence 39

Be the CEO of Your Position!............................41
    Leaders of Excellence Take Ownership..... 44
    Communicate Expectations
    and Needs of the Team 46
    Celebrate the Team's Successes 48
    Confront Team Members
    When They Fall Short..............................49

Chapter Three: Values of Leadership Excellence .. 53

What Are the Values of
Leadership Excellence? 55
    Creating Urgency 56
    Utilizing Intuition 58
    Expressing Curiosity 60
    Instilling Accountability 62
    Using Perspective 67
    Working Hard 69
    Operating with Humility 73
    Utilizing Wisdom 76
    Giving Respect 80
    Acting with Courage 85
    Understanding Kindness
    versus Weakness 88
    Always Be Consistent 92
    Expressing Authenticity 93
    Types of Employees 95

Chapter Four: Putting Values into Action 99

Putting Values into Action 101
    Surrounding Yourself with Top Talent..... 101
    What Exactly Is Top Talent? 104
    How Can You Ensure That
    You Have Top Talent? 106
    Communicating Objectives
    of Excellence 111
    An IEC Case Study 114
    What Is Timely Communication? 117
    Be Sure to Prioritize 120
    Focusing on Planning, Then Executing ...124
    Driving BHAGS 126
    Don't Allow Bureaucracy
    to Get in the Way....................................129
    Trusting Your Superstars 130
    Always Focusing on Solutions 133
    Keeping Your Focus on
    Customer Service 135
    Seek First to Understand 138
    Always Seeking to Learn 140
    Holding Regular One-on-One
    Steering Meetings 145
    Asking Yourself the Tough Questions 147
    Positive Messaging 149

Catching People in the Act
of Doing Something Right 156
Keeping an Eye on the Financials 158
Driving Results through
Strategic Focus 161

Wrapping Up 165

Epilogue 169

References 174

Appendix A 175

Foreword and Introduction
by Fardad Fateri

What is leadership? What does breakthrough leadership look like? What is organizational culture, and why is it important? Why does culture matter? Why is culture the most important pillar of the best organizations in the world? What are the values that separate great organizations from those that continually struggle? What empowers people to produce peak performers when many others can only produce mediocrity? What behaviors separate ordinary people from extraordinary superstars? What helps some organizations to survive and excel over time while many others fail?

These questions have remained at the core of my academic and professional careers for the past thirty-five years. I have always been a student of leadership and culture, and I have had the privilege

to study and to work under several of the greatest scholars and organizational leaders in the United States. I learned a great deal from the very best.

I have always known that when leadership and culture are effectively leveraged, they can create sustained organizational greatness. My deepest interest was in developing people and allowing them to test their capacity to create the best versions of themselves. I knew that, within the appropriate culture, people with passion, bandwidth, and ambition would excel, and when people excel, an organization consistently achieves its objectives.

We've created an amazing environment at International Education Corporation (IEC)! Our culture has allowed us to grow dramatically—more than many similar organizations in the same economic sector—and to survive periods of turbulence and extreme difficulty. We're able to continuously reinvent ourselves to get better over time. While many of our competitors were shutting down, declaring bankruptcy, and dismantling, we continued to thrive.

IEC is perfectly imperfect. Though we face challenges, mistakes, and problems, we continue to learn, evolve, and improve every single day. We are a true learning organization committed to our core values, to our thesis, and to our customers.

It's not magic, and it's certainly not luck. Our success comes from our organizational culture. It's what separates failing or mediocre organizations from those that survive, persist, and sustain greatness regardless of economic conditions. Greatness is not about financial prowess—it's about survival, consistency, and persistence during economic and societal turbulence.

In the following chapters of this book, my colleague and I explore, identify, and explain what helped International Education Corporation develop a culture where people come together and create a platform for continuous quality and process improvement. I know our experiences, learning, and attributes will provide insight to readers both personally and professionally.

Before joining IEC in January 2008, I was the chief academic officer at one of the largest market-funded higher education corporations in North America. I had a prestigious and powerful position matched by few others in the country. I was generously compensated, and my company's reputation was one of the best in the nation. But I was unhappy. I felt I didn't have purpose. I wanted to lead a professional life that truly mattered. So in 2007, I decided to leave.

In my search for purpose, I came across a small career education company with only nine campuses. It was in such serious financial trouble that it struggled to meet payroll every two weeks. However, I didn't let the small size or the poor financial health of this organization stop me from assessing its overall potential. I decided to visit all the campuses and meet the staff and faculty who had committed their professional careers to this organization. After visiting the campuses and meeting the people, I fell in love with the organization because it had passion. It was small, but it had a heart bigger than most conglomerates. I saw tremendous potential and an extraordinary future. Therefore, I decided to leave my prestigious post to work at IEC and make it my new home.

My friends and colleagues seriously questioned my judgment for making such a poor career move. Some even wondered about my sanity! Who would leave a prestigious senior executive position at a multibillion-dollar corporation to join a small and almost bankrupt organization? But I made the life-changing decision to join IEC because I knew then what I know now: that IEC would allow me to have purpose and to create a culture where I and others like me could lead lives that truly matter.

Since January 2008, IEC has been through several dramatic architectural transformations; we had to reinvent ourselves multiple times to remain relevant and current. Although our name hasn't changed in the past ten years, we have evolved materially every year to survive. We went from a small organization struggling to meet payroll to one of the largest systems of private postsecondary career education in North America.

Neither I nor anyone else at IEC will ever claim that we are great or are the best; these are unacceptable words at IEC. We strive to become the best, though we know that's an unreachable destination for those who want to remain in business for decades. Over the years, remaining humble has made us vulnerable, and that vulnerability has allowed us to accept the brutal facts, learn continuously, enjoy the leadership of new top talent, and grow with quality and integrity—no stories, no excuses, no finger pointing, and no fluff.

Everything we've achieved at IEC was made possible only because of our culture, a culture we all built together. Our values and our identity allowed us to ascend through the good times and to survive during turbulent times. We are not smarter or better or more talented than anyone else, but at

IEC, we all share values that have empowered each of us to be the CEO of our position.

And here's the secret: anyone can build a culture that fuels success and breakthrough. I really mean that. It's why we wrote this book. In the coming chapters, you will learn the key values that can create and sustain greatness within any organization. We won't discuss any fancy theories or formulas but will instead focus on actual concepts that have helped IEC become an amazing organization and our people become breakthrough leaders. We will give you real-life examples of how our values have helped us get through very difficult times and leverage opportunities to achieve peak performance.

If you choose to adopt these lessons, values, and habits, you too can transform yourself personally and professionally to become the architect of your future. In almost every case, you have the choice to become accountable for the success of your department, your unit, your division, your region, your organization, and your own life. You can choose to be awesome!

Are you ready to embark on a path of personal and professional reinvention? Join us in this journey of discovery.

Onward and upward!

1

Culture Is a
State of Mind

Culture Is a State of Mind

Welcome! The first step of this journey is to define *culture*. Culture can mean a lot of different things to different people. To one person, it is how to hold the wine glass during a wine-tasting event. To another, it means knowing how to dress to "fit in" with one's peers.

Culture is as much a state of mind as it is anything else. It is how we think, act, and breathe. If we want to see personal or professional transformation, we have to create a culture of excellence—for ourselves, for our families, for our work teams, for our organization.

Many times, we think of culture as a *passive* concept, something that just *is*. It's something that we experience as a set of norms established by something or someone else. We operate within a particular culture without giving it much thought.

After all, the only important thing is that we follow the rules. Right?

Don't be fooled! We can create our own culture. Culture is a state of mind that we create, nurture, and preserve. We all have the opportunity to create the culture we live in by cultivating new norms for how we act, think, and behave.

If an organization can create its own culture of excellence, so can you!

Merriam-Webster's online dictionary defines *culture* as "the integrated pattern of human knowledge, belief, and behavior that depends on the capacity for learning and transmitting knowledge to succeeding generations" and "the set of shared attitudes, values, goals, and practices that characterize an organization."[1]

Without a doubt, organizational culture is one of the most important components and drivers of greatness. Top talent, viable strategy, and a thoughtful business thesis are great, but without a unified culture that colleagues believe in, organizations fail. On the flip side, organizations that have

---

1   *Merriam-Webster,* s.v. "culture," accessed April 10, 2018, https://www.merriam-webster.com/dictionary/culture.

a culture everyone understands often become the most reputable and successful organizations in their field! It is not about good or bad, right or wrong; it's all about sharing critical values that define the organization and encourage every single colleague to act and behave as one.

In organizations of excellence, leaders focus on cultural fit before any other consideration. When we interview leadership candidates for a position with IEC, the discussion revolves around their ability to thrive in our professional culture. Of course, the candidates must have the basic experience and expertise to do the job, but that's secondary to ensuring they'll be a good fit in the environment. Leaders understand it's essential for a candidate to support their organizational culture; if they don't, they will fail. Again, and we can't re-iterate enough: it's not about right or wrong, good or bad, it's about cultural fit.

For example, if a candidate has an autocratic, top-down, dictatorial leadership style, they most likely will not fit in a very inclusive, participatory, and communicative culture. The breakthrough organization and everyone in it is committed to their core values! Leaders must work tirelessly to make sure their values cascade down to all levels of the

organization and are practiced consistently by every team member.

Now, let's take a peek at a little background so we can "set the stage" for our discussion.

How International Education Corporation Defined Its Culture

It's difficult to say exactly when we realized we had something special going on at IEC. At some point, though, we recognized there was something unique and powerful about our culture. Something was happening that we hadn't experienced in other organizations. The colleagues of IEC were all fully engaged in the success of our customers and our campuses. Was it passion? Was it spirit? Was it commitment? What was it, exactly? It seemed so elusive at the time! No one had taught us how to capture a culture, so we became culture pioneers.

We knew we had to find a way to "bottle" our culture to make sure we could share its uniqueness with all our employees, particularly new colleagues. We had to somehow capture and define the magic that was happening. That wasn't an easy task, I can assure you!

Our initial method was to bring our IEC leadership team together from across the company; we came together to define the uniqueness of the organization. We all got together in a comfortable and quiet location and examined the qualities that

25

made us different from any organization any of us had ever worked with before.

The outcome was an extraordinary set of values, principles, and concepts that we captured in a statement called "We the People of IEC." This document is posted on the organization's internal website and still serves as a guide to each and every member of the organization, regardless of experience, title, or location. In short, every single member of the IEC team is exposed to our culture from day one!

Following is an excerpt from the document (see Appendix A for the full statement):

- We lead through recognition, gratitude, appreciation, praise, and inspiration.
- We have heart.
- We love to serve.
- We manage and lead by example.
- We regularly measure and monitor all we do in order to achieve top performance.
- We make thoughtful but quick decisions, and we take action.
- We are flexible, agile, and nimble, and we exhibit structure and discipline in all we do.

- We are passionate about student success.
- We embrace teamwork and strongly encourage open communication.
- We integrate regulatory compliance in all we do and never treat it as an event.
- We care deeply about the success of our students and our colleagues.
- We have a strong commitment to excellence and will never settle for less.
- We have an appetite for growth with quality and integrity.
- We are always hungry for more.
- We will never be perfect and know we can always improve.
- We learn and grow from our mistakes.
- We always embrace greatness.
- We make grassroots investments that lead to student and employee success.
- We have a sense of urgency.
- We take personal accountability and look within for solutions.
- We attract, hire, and develop the best talent.
- We seek support and assistance when needed.
- We promote from within.

- We empower "all" of our people to take ownership and serve.
- We praise in public and coach in private.
- We are close to our business and we know the numbers.
- We have enterprise-wide transparency.
- We face and accept the brutal facts and take action to address them effectively.
- We follow up and follow through on our commitments, priorities, and responsibilities.
- Our team at the corporate office is aligned to serve and to support the campuses.
- We are mindful of the big picture, which keeps us focused at all times.
- We exhibit determination in all we do; we never give up.
- We demonstrate strong communication at all times with no silos.
- We focus on all levels of the educational model to provide a top-quality student experience.
- We have fun as a team and enjoy what we do.
- We focus on fundamentals.

- We are deliberate in our actions and are always focused on results.
- We are high-energy.
- We have a positive attitude.
- We have caring, supportive, and nurturing environments.
- We are super competitive.
- We always focus on our competencies, keeping students at the heart of our enterprise.
- We take deliberate steps to celebrate achievements regularly.
- We operate under "One Standard of Excellence" in all we do within all departments.
- We take pride in our work.
- We are 24/7.
- We are "grown-ups."
- We are respectful.
- We are professional.

How to Cultivate Your Culture
(Should We Say, "Culture-Vate"?)

Because culture is a state of mind, it is accessible to anyone. Our experience in driving an enterprise-wide culture can be applied to both individual and organizational success. By paying attention to certain concepts and principles, such as humility, ownership, accountability, and more, you too can create a successful environment. You can impact your own future. You can even influence an entire organization!

We promise that if you implement the values, concepts, and principles we present in this book, you will not only enjoy a renewed sense of hope for your future, you will actively create your future! You will create a culture of excellence. There are some foundational things you need to commit to when you embark on designing and implementing culture in your own organization.

Get Everyone on Board

At the organizational level, it's essential that you get buy-in from everyone. In a multisite- and multistate-distributed organizational structure such as ours (or indeed in many other organizations in today's changing marketplace) it is absolutely vital that each and every one of our colleagues is on board with the direction of the organization. How do you achieve that? Certainly by having robust processes and procedures. But the most essential component we've realized is you need to have team members be a part of—*rather than apart from*—all the decisions made and actions taken.

Plan for a Revolution!

We would also be a bit remiss if we didn't warn you: plan for a revolution! Once your team members and employees adopt these concepts, they can't help but act as change agents for them! You will see. They are really very simple, and they make sense. If we can do it, so can you!

Expect and Celebrate Redundancy

As you read through the material, you'll notice that certain themes seem to appear more than once. You might think to yourself, *Didn't we just discuss this?* You're absolutely correct! A culture of excellence requires attention to detail, certainly, but it also requires redundancy. Frequent repetition of core practices and concepts is vital in order to energize your role, your team, your organization, your company, and your enterprise! So when you say to yourself, "Hmm . . . I've seen that before," you're probably right! Just remember, it is by design, not by accident.

Ask yourself what values, practices, beliefs, and behaviors should be repeated in your own team, department, and organization. How can you use redundancy to your advantage as you cultivate a culture of excellence?

Strive to Become an Organization of Excellence

At IEC, we are an organization of excellence.

Organizations of excellence care deeply about their culture and take many deliberate steps to ensure all core values are alive and well. Our experience has been that culture is by far the number one predictor of organizational success.

As you read through these concepts, take the time to digest them and self-reflect. For many of us, our natural tendency is to read or listen to guidance and then agree that the people around us are not behaving as expected. But leadership excellence does not allow for us to be a critic or spectator! In what ways can you more fully embody the values of your organizational culture? First, hold yourself personally accountable to produce necessary changes in your approach! Then you'll be in a position to hold your organizational leaders to the same rigorous standards.

We know that an organization is a living, dynamic, collective entity made up of the values and colleagues within that organization. We might even think of organization as an extension of an organism in that it is "alive" and vital. It requires a nurturing and healthy environment in which to thrive!

Excellence Is the Driving Force of Successful Organizational Culture

We've been using the word *excellence* a lot in only a short time. That's because excellence is the driving force of successful organizational culture. Raise the standards of your values to the highest level and enforce those standards consistently across all levels of the organization. This is what it means to hold values of excellence. And a culture of excellence is what drives success.

You might have heard of the adage, "The true measure of a person's character is what they do when no one is looking." We know that effective leaders perform with integrity, whether others see it or not! So then we might adjust the adage to say, "The true measure of a good leader is what they do when no one is looking!"

What about you? Do you consistently embody your organization's values with integrity? Do you strive to be an effective leader? Think of specific examples, of a time no one was watching but you did the right thing. Think of a time you failed to achieve your highest standards and what you learned from that experience. It is important to be honest with yourself on both accounts. Successful

leaders are brutally honest with themselves! This is how, day after day, they hold themselves and their teammates to the highest standards.

A Culture of Excellence
Demands Leaders of Excellence

A culture of excellence requires—in fact, demands—leaders of excellence. You can't achieve the one without the other. Jim Collins refers to such leaders as "breakthrough leaders" (Collins & Porras, 1994). For the purposes of our discussion, the term "breakthrough leaders" is synonymous with our own term, "leaders of excellence."

An organization's leaders of excellence fuel these cultural values over time. But being a leader of excellence is more than just having high standards. How exactly does a person become a respectable leader able to guide others and direct the course of organizational culture over time and distance?

2

Leaders of
Excellence

Be the CEO of Your Position!

We like to say that being a leader of excellence means becoming the "CEO of your position." Being the CEO of your position is something anyone can do. In fact, it's essential in order for their organization to thrive.

It sounds pretty lofty, doesn't it? But what does it mean to be the CEO of your position? After all, how many of us have ever considered ourselves a CEO?

The key to embodying this mindset is *ownership*. Own it! Create your own destiny! Take charge! Be accountable! At the end of the day, you are the one accountable to yourself, your team, your family. *You* are the one in charge.

Being the CEO of your position means you authentically own your responsibilities, you refuse to accept mediocrity, and you take swift but

thoughtful action at all times to influence favorable change and to meet and exceed expectations.

When you are the CEO of your position, you are a breakthrough leader! Breakthrough leaders don't do things to please others. Breakthrough leaders want to produce peak performance in all areas to meet the high standards they hold for themselves (Collins & Porras, 1994).

Leaders of excellence are tougher on themselves than on anyone else. They rate themselves every day and every week by asking themselves honest questions. Most importantly, they always face the brutal facts and take deliberate action to achieve organizational expectations. Breakthrough leaders don't wait for greatness to knock on their doors, they create greatness! So don't wait. Be powerful, be bold, and be audacious. Create your own destiny!

Organizations often tell their leaders in the field that they are in charge, but they don't actually let those leaders make any real decisions! Why does that happen? The organization doesn't fully trust its leaders, or it feels it will have greater control by micromanaging. The consequence is that it does not give field leaders the chance to be excellent. To be clear, excellence does not mean perfection.

An organization of excellence expects its leaders to make mistakes or to fail from time to time. That is how we learn and grow as an organization. On the other hand, an organization of excellence does not allow mistakes and failures to persist over time without seeking solutions or improved results.

Leaders of excellence thrive on autonomy, opportunity, and the chance to prove they can be the CEO of their position. These proven leaders don't allow results to suffer. As they overcome failure and learn from mistakes, the organization learns and grows too.

So leverage these concepts of autonomy, opportunity, and excellence to produce peak performance. Be assertive, aggressive, in charge, and in control. Don't focus on excuses about why you can't be the best. Focus on solutions that will make you the best! Regardless of your job title, be the CEO of your position and you'll thrive.

Leaders of Excellence
Take Ownership

Leaders of excellence treat their colleagues and teams as owners of their business and expect their behavior to reflect true ownership. Ownership is not about power and control but about caring for your business, your team members, and your results. Ownership means being very hands-on with everything that happens in your business. Leaders do whatever it takes to achieve expected results with quality and integrity; no stories, no excuses, and no fluff.

A breakthrough leader isn't passive; he or she strives to optimize processes and achieve the best outcomes. A breakthrough leader maintains a sense of urgency to move agendas forward and maximize productivity with tasks, projects, initiatives, and assignments. He or she is organized, structured, timely, and disciplined and always expects the same of others.

By maintaining extreme focus on your mission, goals, and priorities, you ensure the best chance of reaching your goals. Then set expectations for your team members, who will follow your lead. A central responsibility of leaders of excellence

is managing their teams. This requires a robust and compassionate approach. What are some essential aspects of managing your teams well?

Communicate Expectations and Needs of the Team

As leaders of excellence, we understand expectations. Expectations help us define the direction our colleagues must take. We make these expectations very clear so that colleagues can fully understand what our common goals are, what is important, and what is not. We over-communicate outcomes, results, and expectations to our colleagues at all times. We expect that others do the same with their team members at their sites, offices, regions, divisions, and organizations.

We expect top performers to help their peers achieve the same, and we expect those struggling with results to reach out to peers at other sites, offices, and regions to solicit help. Pride and ego must not prevent us from raising our hands and asking our colleagues to help. Our top priority is to focus on our customers; we truly admire colleagues who have the courage to ask for help because that's a selfless act.

We always look at quantitative results to gauge effective management and leadership. Our saying, "fewer words and more numbers," can describe effective leadership. Results are the emerging

outcomes of hundreds of decisions and actions. Results speak volumes about our work ethic, focus, ability, experience, vigor, commitment to excellence, accountability, pride, passion, sense of urgency, and leadership.

Celebrate the Team's Successes

We love what we do! Our focus is always on making sure we have the best learning communities, we have the best staff and colleagues, and that we serve our customers at the highest level. We expect the same from others.

Organizations of excellence thrive through hard work, passion, vigor, focus, ownership, ambition, personal accountability, and leadership! Top quantitative results are outcomes of a superior culture, one that is anchored in personal accountability, a sense of urgency, true ownership, hard work, competitiveness, passion, regulatory compliance, teamwork, a strong appetite for winning, integrity, and an environment that cares deeply about customer and colleague success. We all must always achieve top results!

And when your organization achieves top results, NEVER forget to celebrate them! Much good can come from simply letting others know when they are successful. Announce the victory! Use the team's achievement to develop momentum and continue their current trajectory of success! After all, what can be more motivating than truly succeeding . . . than truly making a difference?

Confront Team Members
When They Fall Short

As leaders of excellence, of course we want to inspire and motivate our colleagues publicly through repeated words of recognition and praise. However, should there be issues with performance and behavior, we coach our colleagues in private. Remember to praise in public and to coach in private.

As leaders of excellence, we know that no one is exempt from living the values and behaviors of a culture of excellence. If *we* think our boss or another executive is not following or living our values, might it be possible that our own direct reports are saying the very same thing about *us*? Ironically, in many cases it is those very same managers who complain about their supervisors, often getting the same complaints from their own direct reports! Let us all be real and act accordingly.

One of the more difficult roles you will have as a leader of excellence is to "confront the brutal facts." This sometimes requires difficult but respectful one-on-one communication with colleagues. While this can be a difficult process, it is also a very important component of effective leadership. Colleagues need to know where they stand.

That being said, colleagues also deserve to know what changes have to be made in order for them to be successful in the organization. After all, why wouldn't we want each and every colleague in our organization to be successful . . . ? Of course we do! But it requires effort and attention. This is something leaders of excellence do not shy away from. Leaders of excellence confront the brutal facts.

If you are reading this material, you are on the way to becoming a leader of excellence! To becoming the CEO of your position!

Leaders of excellence don't require additional or unnecessary attention from others in the organization. They know they need to produce at the highest level, and they monitor their own performance and the outcomes of their team. Strong leaders develop and empower strong teams through consistent and compassionate communication, celebration, and confrontation.

Being a leader of excellence means you authentically own your responsibilities, refuse to accept mediocrity, and take swift but thoughtful action at all times to influence favorable change beyond expectations. Leaders of excellence don't do things to please others; they want to produce peak performance in all areas to please themselves

because their standards are much higher than others'.

Above all, leaders of excellence look to the organization's culture to guide them. Leaders rely on the organization's core values to inform others of their goals, priorities, processes, and behaviors.

3

Values of Leadership Excellence

What Are the Values of Leadership Excellence?

Each of us is capable of being a leader of excellence. But in order to be the CEO of your position, you must embody values that set you apart from your teammates. What are the values that make a leader of excellence?

Becoming a true leader of excellence starts with identifying who you are, what you stand for, and what you are about. It is about focusing on your DNA, your internal code, your values system of success. In the following pages, we'll share our IEC values system with you. As you explore what makes us leaders of excellence, ask yourself what attributes resonate with you? Which ones don't? What's missing from our list that you feel is at the top of your list of essential values?

Creating Urgency

Having a sense of urgency is a critical part of becoming a leader of excellence. You must have a clear timeline for your projects and you must feel a sense of internal pressure to complete tasks on time. Not only that, you feel the responsibility to create accurate, thoughtful, consistent, high-quality work. You don't just aim to meet deadlines—you strive to beat them! You make a habit of exceeding customer and organizational expectations. Leaders of excellence make sure they remain focused on work until the job is done right.

What separates average performers from great performers? The answer is always the same: hard work! Talent, skills, abilities, and aptitude are critical, but they aren't unique. It's hard work that delineates average performers from top performers. Nothing can ever replace hard work. You've heard the saying, "The harder I work, the luckier I get." It's true! Hard work, productivity, and performance are positively and strongly correlated, which means the harder you work, the more you will accomplish and the more successful you will be in achieving desired results. Hard work doesn't necessarily mean how many hours you spend in the office or what

time you clock in or clock out; it's about what you do and the results you achieve while you are working!

Utilizing Intuition

Leaders of excellence carry a "no limits" mentality. They don't see any ceilings above them. They operate in a wide-open, spacious, and highly charged atmosphere. Ask these leaders for one, and they'll give you ten!

Don't allow anyone or anything to limit your thinking! Not only is this about numbers; it's also about taking initiative. Intuitive leaders see a need and work to find solutions. They don't let problems linger, they don't do only the minimum requirements, and they don't wait for someone else to notice a need. If they see room for improvement, they work to make it happen.

Think of the last time you asked someone to do something for you. Let's go with raking leaves, for example. You put in extra hours at work, you were exhausted, and you just needed some downtime. But it was late when you pulled into the driveway after work on Friday evening, and you saw the yard was a mess. Leaves were everywhere. Your community is under a "no-burn" ordinance, so you can't burn the leaves. The neighbors' yards looked green and perfect. The wind was blowing your leaves into their yards. The special Saturday

trash pickup was the very next afternoon. The work had to get done, but you were out of energy. You were done. You were over it.

You asked your teenage son to rake the leaves as a special favor to you. He said he would after he got a few things from the store. Oh, boy. You had heard this before! You just knew nothing would get done.

Exhausted, you fell asleep for several hours, only to wake up, look out the window, and find that the yard was spotless! Not one leaf remained. There were no lawn bags left anywhere. Your front yard looked like a perfectly manicured golf course!

Upon investigation, you find out that your son's trip to the store was to get special lawn bags to get the yard done. Not only did he rake and bag the leaves, he took them to the local dump to dispose of them so you wouldn't have to worry about it. And he got the lawn mower and trimmers out to make sure the lawn looked just right.

He was acting as a leader of excellence! He was being intuitive and observant. He knew what had to be done and he accomplished his assignment and more! He went above and beyond. Just raking the leaves would have been a mediocre performance. Bagging, dumping, mowing, and trimming made

it an excellent performance! No one asked him to go above and beyond. He just did it.

That's what leaders of excellence do. They don't brag about their initiative; they don't run around reporting what a great job they did. They get the work done, and then they move on to the next challenge.

The next time you are asked to perform a function, whether it be at work or at home, give your boss more than they asked for! Be a leader of excellence! Perform without limits.

Expressing Curiosity

Leaders of excellence are always curious. They wonder if their processes are effective. Is their work-flow at peak efficiency? How might they improve their management approach to raise team morale? This quality also gives rise to tenacity. Just because something has "always been done this way," it does not mean it has always been done the *right* way. When a strong leader sees an opportunity for improvement, they take the risk. Sometimes this requires speaking up when things do not seem right.

Do not accept a result if it seems wrong. Be willing to take the risk to raise the bar of achievement.

Being curious means asking a lot of questions! However, this doesn't mean that it's okay to be rude, disrespectful, or unprofessional. This is unacceptable behavior from a leader. Leaders set the tone for their team, department, and organization. As long as you act professionally and respectfully, you should never fear sacrificing what is right for your team or your business for fear of hurting feelings, making someone upset, and/or crossing chains of command. What you should fear is failure and defeat. So ask the questions that *matter*. This allows your colleagues to know that you care.

If you want results in a certain area, that's where you should direct your focus and curiosity. Interest from a leader signals team members to follow suit.

Instilling Accountability

Lead, follow, or get out of my way! Pretty strong words, right? Certainly passionate, to say the least!

Indeed, the importance of passion in leaders of excellence cannot be disregarded! Leaders of excellence are humble, communicative, consistent, respectful, and are team players . . . and they never wait to be told what to do! In a culture of excellence, superstars abound! They know what has to be done, and they go about doing it! They own it! They are accountable, so they get on with it! They ask for help when needed, but they are very clear that, when all is said and done, they are responsible for their own success and the success of their colleagues.

No exceptions! None! Zero!

A culture of excellence demands it!

Many who consider themselves accountable for outcomes and objectives often point the finger at other people's shortcomings when they fail. Truly accountable leaders accept the responsibility for getting the job done. No stories, no excuses, and no fluff. When leaders are accountable, they authentically feel like true owners of their positions, departments, stores, locations, regions, or

sites. Leaders of excellence teach accountability by modeling it through ownership. If you don't point the finger, blame, tell stories, or make excuses, your team members won't either. You reinforce in your words and your actions the kinds of behaviors that are and aren't appropriate.

It is fine to make mistakes, but own mistakes and learn from them. Never criticize your colleagues for being weak or incapable; that's not the way to solve the problem. Leaders of excellence look within and master their responsibilities first before disciplining others.

Being personally accountable is a huge factor in separating leaders and organizations. An attitude of accountability demands action. It demands the leader be hands-on and engaged. There's a fine balance, but leaders of excellence know how to delegate. They trust their team, they don't micromanage, and they share responsibility to get things done. You are in charge and you know how to do the work. You are not a broker. You are not a consultant. When you are truly the CEO of your position, others around you will understand what the role really means and will learn from your behavior.

Leaders of excellence lead primarily by example. They don't feel the need to brag about being

accountable and they don't micromanage! Their behavior, actions, and qualities speak for themselves. You may hear people expressing how "accountable" they are, but later they're the ones complaining to coworkers or blaming others for their failures. Have you ever had that experience?

Complaining to peers may be therapeutic and perhaps even reassuring, but it produces negativity, discomfort, and low confidence. So if you feel down on some days, go in front of a mirror and say, "It is all the boss's fault because they just don't get it, and . . . plus . . . I am awesome!" Then, once you are done, get on with it! Leaders who are powerful, assertive, and strong make decisions, take action, and execute plans. Everything else is just fluff.

Leaders of excellence take action and do not wait or hope and pray for something or someone to save the day. When dealing with issues, problems, and opportunities that manifest themselves in the form of inferior quantitative results, it is more important to take action and make a mistake than to be a passive leader. When your teammates observe a leader's inaction and see him or her hoping and praying for miraculous improvements without some kind of intervention, they lose confidence.

When you observe results below expected

levels, that's your cue to take action. It is okay to make a mistake, but inaction will lead to failure and defeat. You might have observed that some team members are more afraid of making a mistake than they are afraid of actually failing. Unfortunately, due to their fear of making a mistake, they fail by way of inaction! When faced with these two options, always take the former. Take action!

In an organization of excellence, being accountable for making a mistake earns the respect of colleagues. Ownership is an important pillar of a culture of excellence. Owning the mistake provides a level of humility and vulnerability, both of which require strength of character. Leaders of excellence have strength of character.

A great example of this concept of accountability played out in our organization. One member of the IEC team had heard the phrase, "No stories, no excuses, no fluff" several times. She was certain that she knew exactly what it meant until she stumbled and failed on a project. She was used to being a superstar, a winner, and now suddenly she didn't feel as if she was winning! Ouch! She spent time justifying it to herself with excuses like, "I did not get stupid overnight, so it cannot be my fault." She spent more time further explaining to

herself why she failed, who was to blame, and so on, rather than focusing on what resources and partnerships she needed in order to be successful. She was more interested in sharing all of the "he said she said" stories than focusing on a plan to achieve the outcomes.

Her supervisor asked her, "What does it matter who is right and who is wrong if you are not winning? The world is not fair! Life is not fair! Business is not fair! Sometimes we have to make decisions that are in the best interest of the customer and the organization and not what is in the best interest of one given person. Do you want to be right, or do you want to win?"

The colleague soon discovered it was time to start winning rather than focusing on being "right." She realized if she wanted to win, she must not worry about the problems so much as she should solutions so as to leverage resources and partnerships to achieve the best outcome. That is accountability.

Using Perspective

It is likely you work in a "team" industry. It doesn't matter how an *individual* performs if the *team* fails. For example, you may have one fantastic sales professional who consistently does very well, but if all others on the team do not contribute proportionately then the team will fail. On a different level, a department may do very well, but if other departments do not then the bigger team will fail. A leader of excellence has a sense of perspective. They care not only about their own success but also about the success of their division, region, and company as a whole, and they strive to optimize performance beyond themselves to ensure the success of the organization.

For example, a sales team may perform well, but if your product or service is not packaged in a timely manner, if your customers don't have a positive experience and decide to do business with another company, then the larger team will fail. A leader of excellence will focus on areas and outcomes that display the company's success! Leaders of excellence are thoughtful about not functioning within silos; they seek to work collaboratively across all boundaries. Everyone—every single

colleague—must work together to ensure the organization functions as ONE. Leaders need to own the success of their colleagues within every department, every site, every location, and every region. Please remember, to all outsiders, the company must appear as ONE. Leaders of excellence act and behave as one!

Working Hard

Work ethic, pride, and care are subjective values; they are relative and based on personal experience. Leaders of excellence have an unwavering commitment to a common standard, a common set of processes of excellence across the enterprise. At IEC, we refer to this as "One Standard of Excellence"— one standard—to aspire to, a common standard across the organization measured by quantitative benchmarks. Those who meet and exceed expectations and work hard have pride in what they do. They simply care more than others. All fantastic ideas, processes, tools, and resources can only be meaningful when grouped with hard work, pride, and care.

People may tell you they work hard, they have pride, and they care a great deal. That may very well be the case! But these attributes can only be shown through meeting an organization's quantitative expectations. So if you, your teams, or your departments are not meeting expectations and standards of excellence then you must work harder, you must show more pride, and you must care more.

Working in your field of choice can be extremely rewarding! It may be that your role is your

passion; perhaps it is your calling. Maybe you hold a unique and unusual position that requires a great deal more effort, passion, care, sacrifice, commitment, and sweat equity than those of your peers. Whatever the case, be the CEO of your position. Own it. Do your work with excellence!

Let's look at an example to illustrate the difference between caring and caring more.

You are the customer representative in a large building supplies store. This store caters to both women and men who love to come in and dream of home improvement. Every aisle has a surprise! Every aisle contains something they could use. A person could spend an afternoon here. It is one of a national chain of such stores and it is well known for quality and for having a HUGE inventory.

As the customer representative, your job is to walk the store and see if you can help customers with their needs. After all, if they are looking for a specific size of nuts and bolts, for example, it could literally take the customer half an hour just to find the right section!

Customer Evelyn has two children with her. One of them is in a baby carrier; the other is a two-year-old. Evelyn looks harried and confused, so you quickly approach her and ask how you can help.

Good for you! You think to yourself, *what great service I provide!*

Evelyn asks you where she can find a specific set of nuts and bolts. Her husband is in the middle of a big project at home and has asked her to hurry over to the store and pick these up for him so the project can continue. He is short on time, so this is very important for the timely finish of the project.

Proving what a great customer rep you are, you point Evelyn to Aisle 14, where all of the nuts and bolts are! You even brag about the thousands and thousands of sizes and shapes of nuts and bolts you have in inventory. Surely she will find what she needs. You feel good about helping her as she walks toward Aisle 14 with one kid in hand and one kid in tow. You're proud of yourself—you did your job. You showed how much you care!

But . . . were you a leader of excellence? Did you act as the CEO of your position? Well, don't feel too good just yet! A leader of excellence goes above and beyond.

To care is good. To care more is excellent.

To care is to tell Evelyn which aisle the nuts and bolts are in and point her and the young kids in the right direction. To care is to be courteous, respectful, and informative. However, a leader of

excellence cares more. To care more is to walk with Evelyn over to the exact section in Aisle 14 and to stay and answer any questions she may have. To care more is to help her pick out the nuts and bolts she needs or to call for an expert in the department to assist if you do not have the required knowledge to do so. You are available in case she needs to call her husband and ask questions about exactly what is needed. You can see this is really important to them!

Leaders of excellence care *more*. We create an atmosphere where the customer doesn't feel like they are bothering us. To care more is to make them comfortable enough to allow you to assist them.

See the difference?

Leaders of excellence care more because their organization of excellence cares more.

Operating with Humility

Often, when we think of humility, we imagine someone understated, quiet, and reserved—maybe even weak. But that is not our definition of humility. And that is certainly not the role of humility in a culture of excellence!

Humble leaders are successful leaders because they make themselves vulnerable to honest and continuous self-assessment and feedback from others. They never become victims of ego given to delusions of grandeur. Authentically humble leaders are never satisfied with being awesome yesterday or today! They are obsessed with continuous learning to ensure excellence at all times.

Leaders of excellence are never satisfied with just being good or with just meeting expectations; they always want to WIN in everything they do. They understand that self-improvement is the path to exceeding expectations. Leaders of excellence think like this: *Well, I agree that we are good, but we need to do a lot more to be great.* That's humility in action! Certainly, leaders of excellence are high achievers and don't confuse being good with being great.

Humility is a learned trait of courageous

leaders. Humility is learned when character is tested against difficult struggles. Humility allows us to learn, to sympathize, to empathize, to grow, to influence, to make mistakes, to admit to our faults, to collaborate, to be inclusive, and to earn the respect of our colleagues. This trait will let others inside and outside of the organization know that the leadership of the organization is approachable and human. Superstars want to follow leaders they respect and look up to.

When you think about it, accepting the gift of humility will free you from the curse of excessive ego! When your state of mind is one of humility then focusing on creating solutions and serving your customers take center stage. That's where every leader should strive to be. Focus on solutions and not problems. Being humble will allow you to be in the proper state of mind to learn, solve difficult problems, and chase excellence.

To position yourself effectively as a leader of excellence, you must have the courage, confidence, and mental strength to be humble. With humility, you will have the opportunity to be thoughtful, respectful, and inclusive. Your management style will leave room for the input of others and you will lead with compassion. Always remember that

sarcasm, disrespect, rudeness, and authoritarian behavior in your management style are properties of arrogance and insecurity. These are all learned behaviors. Leaders of excellence must be humble but confident, treating customers and colleagues in alignment with the values of high-performing cultures.

Leaders of excellence create and enjoy an office and campus climate anchored in discipline, structure, achievement, and fun! Enjoy your high-performing culture! Embrace high expectations! Have fun!

Utilizing Wisdom

You have likely encountered a situation where you knew you were right and the other person was wrong, and you felt compelled to "make it right." You needed to let them know you were in the right and they were in the wrong. Wouldn't it be great to satisfy your ego? To go tell them where they were wrong? To put them in their place? Yes, indeed that would feel good! But is that the best thing?

Let's look at an example. Imagine you are a regional manager for an auto parts company across three states. You have an excellent sales director, Sandra, in one of your stores. Sandra is always at the top of the list. She is your number one! She is driven, successful, and a great leader of her sales team. Her processes are compliant. She has outstanding integrity. She loves her team and she loves the organization. Customers love her. Sandra does everything right. What a fantastic situation for both Sandra and the company!

At Sandra's recommendation, her daughter (Gina) applies to an entry-level administrative job at another location (the organization does not allow family members to report to each other). After all, like mother, like daughter, right? Wrong! The other

location really doesn't care for Gina. The interview doesn't go well. Gina is discouraged, upset, and doesn't understand why she wasn't successful in the interview. After all, her parent is successful! Why isn't Gina?

Gina confides in Sandra. Or, more importantly, child confides in parent. Sandra, the parent, gets upset and threatens to quit the company if Gina isn't hired. As the regional manager, you might be offended. You may think, *Are you kidding me? Really? Who do you think you are?* You might take it personally and think to yourself, *Go ahead then! Quit! Who are you to tell me what to do?*

You feel quite self-righteous! After all that you have done for Sandra, how could she do this to you?

However, let's slow down and think about this for a minute. Would you rather be right, or would you rather have the best outcome? Let's decide by exploring the possible scenarios.

Scenario #1: We tell Sandra to go ahead and quit. Consider the consequences of that action:

- You lose your number-one sales director.
- Sandra is angry, resentful, and feels very

justified. She goes to your competitor and starts taking customers away from you.

- You have to find a replacement for Sandra. You'll have to take the time to train the new employee. In the meantime, you risk losing customers.
- Sandra's team is demoralized and becomes distracted.
- Sandra's team worries that her replacement won't be as supportive as Sandra.
- Sandra's team worries that something bad will happen to them too.
- You take the chance of Sandra calling members of your team to come over to her new company.
- The other location has to keep looking to fill the minor administrative position at the other location.

Scenario #2: Hire Gina for the entry-level administrative position at the other location. What are the possible consequences?

- You take the chance of frustrating the hiring manager of the other location.
- Sandra is happy, and her daughter is

happy. After all, it is an entry-level administrative position.

Of course, this is an imperfect scenario. You'll need to forgive its simplicity. But the concept holds true.

Leaders of excellence check their ego at the door. They always search for and work to achieve the best outcome!

As you read through the material, be sure to run this very important concept through your mind from time to time. Use it at home, use it at school, use it at work—even use it on your vacation! Don't we all love to be right? But if being "right" costs you in the long run, you need to weigh the damage to your ego against what best suits your family, your team, or your future!

As the CEO of your position, you must always seek the best outcome. The results will speak for themselves. You don't always have to prove that you're right!

Giving Respect

Another very important trait of a leader of excellence is respect.

Respect is the foundation of customer service. You cannot serve genuinely and fully when you don't respect your customers.

Leaders of excellence respect their colleagues, customers, and vendors alike, and hold them in the highest regard. There are no exceptions to this rule. Titles do not give anyone the right to be sarcastic, rude, degrading, and disrespectful in their communication or behavior. Titles do not define leaders of excellence; rather, behaviors and actions do.

Your colleagues may not always do everything as expected, but they all deserve to be treated with dignity, professionalism, and respect. Don't lower or dilute your expectations, but always approach customers and colleagues with the same respect and professionalism you would ask from them. Commit to following the golden rule: treat others as you would have them treat you. The golden rule still applies! Do unto others as you would have them do unto you.

You show respect—or lack of respect—in the way you approach someone, the way you

communicate with individuals or a group, the way you make a person feel when he or she hasn't met expectations, and the process you use to make decisions. These are just a few of many actions and behaviors that determine your level of respect for those around you.

If comments from fellow colleagues and customers suggest you are not being true to your culture, it is vital to immediately examine your behaviors and attitudes. When your actions and behaviors don't match your stated values then your fellow colleagues and customers will question your true intentions. Leaders of excellence strive to be consistent in what they say and do. As the CEO of your position, you have to walk the walk.

At IEC, we frequently hear it said by organizational colleagues that "we manage and lead through praise and recognition and not fear and intimidation." Remember, a title does not define you—your behaviors and actions do.

You don't have to be perfect, but recognize that you're on a journey of continual improvement. Each of us is a work in progress, and as long we do not fall victim to ego and arrogance and instead yield to learning, we allow ourselves the opportunity to grow and improve.

In some organizations some leaders may be rude, disrespectful, mean, hurtful, and degrading to other team members during calls or in meetings. Feedback may come with words like "bullying," "loud," and "humiliating." Some leaders may gossip about other leaders, managers, and team members. Confidential and private information might be shared with those who should not be privy to that information. It doesn't matter if this is widespread or not; if even one, two, or three leaders do it, that is excessive. This must not be allowed in a culture of excellence!

Of course, it is difficult to be great and to do great; it's hard to strive for excellence at all times. Producing and exceeding expected results is tough! It is also difficult to observe and to tolerate colleagues who don't work hard, those who do not care, or those who do not seek to achieve at a high level. But it is not acceptable to blame and point fingers at others. It is never acceptable to treat colleagues with disrespect, to embarrass them, or to humiliate them for underperforming or for failing to meet expectations.

For a variety of reasons, some organizations operate in such a manner and support a top-down cultural architecture. The "higher-ups" need to

prove that they are the bosses. They walk around, chests puffed out, putting a show on, making sure everyone knows who the bosses are.

In a culture of excellence, however, everyone already knows who the boss is; no one needs to prove it. The boss is the one supporting the team and each colleague, encouraging them, mentoring them, empowering them, trusting them, and engaging them! They are the primary motivators.

Imagine that a boss is introduced to a subordinate colleague's family at a company event. Rather than saying, "I'm Gary's boss," the leader of excellence says, "You must be so proud of Gary. We love him around here! We can always count on him giving us new ideas, helping others, and being a very positive example for us!"

There is no mention of who is boss and who is not. Imagine how that must make Gary feel! Imagine how his family must feel. It's that simple. That is how a leader of excellence embodies respect.

Always know and remember: the organization should act and behave as one. Also trust that no one is above it all; this conversation applies to the top level of the organization as well, where the leader should constantly be recalibrating so he or she is more and does more.

Time for some brutal honesty with yourself! Read, self-reflect, digest, and visualize the guidance below, and please be very mindful of how all of these matters apply to you.

The message here is that we must always be respectful and kind. We should not say things that are hurtful and we should not say things in a hurtful manner. We must not dilute our high expectations. Note that we don't ever want to imply that we should be weak. That is the furthest thing from our point here. But we must always honor the dignity of those around us. Everyone (and we mean everyone) deserves to be and must be respected at all times, regardless of their title, function, gender, race, ethnicity, age, sexual orientation, and national origin. Our titles and positions do not define us or separate leaders; our behaviors do. No one shows up to work to be disrespected, no matter what the circumstance. So let us all be mindful of how we behave and how we are perceived. Please trust that our colleagues watch our behaviors and actions at all times.

Acting with Courage

Leaders of excellence have the courage to take action to improve themselves and their teams and to exceed expectations as opposed to hoping, praying, and waiting for some outside force to prod them to get better! It takes courage to make mistakes and learn from them and become stronger. Leaders have the courage to authentically accept responsibility for all that goes wrong, and they certainly have the courage not to blame others and point fingers when issues and problems arise.

It is equally important that leaders have the courage to give credit to team members who go above and beyond to produce peak performance.

We can use our own experience at IEC as a case study in how leaders can act with courage in line with their values when facing difficult times. Every organization encounters periods of turmoil during change, whether it be an internal realignment or pressure from outside forces in the marketplace. IEC is no different in that respect. Change must take place in order for individuals, leaders, and organizations to properly evolve.

Several years ago, IEC went through a very difficult transition because of major,

sweeping changes in the business and education sector. During this period of uncertainty, some IEC campuses had to slow down their operations until certain remediation could be developed. Although Dr. Fateri (IEC's CEO and one of the authors of this book) was not involved in the issue at the campus level, he later stood in front of several hundred colleagues at a company function and admitted that he "owned" the mistake. Dr. Fateri said it had taken place on his watch and that he'd let his colleagues down because he didn't forecast the changes. To this day, IEC colleagues still talk about the time Dr. Fateri owned the problem. He did not blame a campus; he did not blame a colleague; he did not blame a situation; he did not blame the sector; he did not point a finger at anything or anyone. The CEO completely owned the failure. All of it. He was humble. He made himself vulnerable. Out of that courageous act, Dr. Fateri earned the respect of every single colleague in the organization. That single act contributed greatly to the phenomenal culture of excellence colleagues of IEC still enjoy today.

Out of humility, out of vulnerability, out of honesty, comes courage. Comes strength. Comes respect. Comes honor.

As goes the leader, so goes the team. If you want a team of courageous men and women, model by being a courageous leader.

Understanding Kindness versus Weakness

Never mistake kindness for weakness! Leaders of excellence are courageous and charge forward with incredible vigor and zeal. They are positive, motivated, committed, and passionate!

Think about it. Everyone in the office knows who the boss is. Does the boss need to prove that he or she is the boss? In a culture of excellence, that is absolutely unnecessary. An organization of excellence operates with respect, for every single colleague seeks to honor what the boss asks the team members to do! That being said, when leaders have to make difficult decisions, they operate with respect and dignity for everyone involved. If, for example, leaders have to provide negative feedback to someone (no matter what level or in what situation), they aren't rude, demeaning, or dismissive, but they have to take care of business. They take care of business in a kind, respectful, and dignified manner.

In a culture of excellence, leaders encourage team members to be productive through praise, appreciation, and recognition—not through fear, intimidation, and bullying. And they ensure this

value is upheld across teams, departments, and organizations. There are no exceptions. Leaders of excellence are always respectful and professional, and they expect the same of everyone else! No one should mistake kindness for weakness. Organizations of excellence have very high expectations for top performance, but they expect to achieve superior results through acceptable behaviors.

Let's look at an example to illustrate the point.

There is a job that must be accomplished, and it is on a tight timeline. Consider the approaches Supervisors #1 and #2 take to motivate Bob to get the job done.

Supervisor #1: "Bob, get this project done or I will write you up!"

Supervisor #2: "Bob, I know this is a huge project. We are all here to support you and you have resources at your disposal. What is it you need? As CEO of your position, I trust you will take charge of the project and let us know how to support you."

Which of these approaches will motivate Bob more? Which would motivate *you* more?

In both cases, it goes without saying that Bob needs to get the project done. In all likelihood, the supervisor will have to perform some kind of

written counseling or guidance if the project is not finished. We can be pretty sure Bob is aware of that possibility, right? He is already under pressure to get this done.

Of course we all read this and hope Bob finished on time! But let's say Bob didn't.

For whatever reason, he didn't finish on time. Now what?

Yep. We have to provide written feedback. It is never easy to give critique; it's distasteful for many. But a leader of excellence knows it has to be done. Follow-through is necessary.

The good news is that it can be done in a respectful and constructive manner. If the supervisor has to create a write-up, he or she can do it with kindness, dignity, and respect.

The chances that Bob comes to work intending to fail are virtually nonexistent. We have yet to meet the colleague who comes to work and seeks failure. Bob will feel the failure even more if the write-up is confrontational and negative. Do we want Bob demoralized, or do we want him to learn from the mistake?

Are leaders of excellence top-down, negative bullies, or are they strong, encouraging, and kind?

Leaders do what must be done! They never

shirk their responsibilities, no matter how uncomfortable! But leaders of excellence always act in a dignified, respectful manner.

Always Be Consistent

We often say that the mother of excellence is consistency. All of us have enjoyed moments of greatness when we have achieved the extraordinary; it is truly an amazing feeling. But not many can consistently produce peak performance because that requires us to be at our best at all times—and that's hard even for the most worthy. Therefore, consistency is what separates good from great and ensures excellence. Chasing excellence is what strong leaders do. They exceed expectations consistently.

Many organizational leaders know how difficult it is to get to the Super Bowl. Only leaders of excellence know what it takes to repeat the Super Bowl time and time again.

Expressing Authenticity

Leaders of excellence understand that clear and continuous communication between manager and supervisor is critical to in order to establish an honest and fair professional relationship. When leaders are clear about expectations, they help their team members become accountable and push them toward becoming CEOs of their positions. Conversely, when leaders ignore and avoid direct and clear communication of expected results, they hurt team members' development, and the organization suffers. Know and trust that a culture of excellence doesn't recognize or promote a team member unless that team member has a history of exceeding expectation. Leaders must always help team members understand expectations and have an accurate awareness of their level of performance.

It's also vital to maintain authentic communication across the organization for a culture of excellence to flourish.

Examples of IEC enterprise-wide authentic communication include the following:

- State of the Company calls on a regular basis
- CEO "brown bag" lunch calls

- Leadership workshops and conferences
- Regular accountability meetings with the operations and executive teams
- Regular recognition programs and calls

There are many types of communication calls and meetings that take place in an organization of excellence. The point is to have them consistently and to ensure depth and content. The practices listed above are just a few examples among many possibilities that, when properly and consistently performed, will support a culture of excellence.

Types of Employees

An organization of excellence will typically have two types of employees with management/leadership titles:

- **Type 1**: Managers who are negative, unhappy, journalists, record keepers, historians, skeptics, spectators, cynics, brokers, critics, and powerless victims.
- **Type 2**: Managers who exhibit competitiveness, problem-solving ability, energy, tenacity, accountability, passion, fun, care, hard work, a sense of urgency, excellence, ownership, integrity, belief, and a hunger for peak performance.

Type 2 managers and leaders survive and excel in an organization of excellence. And type 1 managers and colleagues? Well, not so much.

Be honest with yourself. Which type are you? Ask your colleagues how they perceive you. Invite genuine feedback and critique.

Think about this for a minute: if you believe you have type 2 attributes but your boss doesn't support you, then you are in type 1.

If you have the courage and self-awareness to realize you have become a type 1 manager, someone who is a broker, a spectator, and a consultant, then it is time to recalibrate. If you catch yourself becoming cynical, negative, and skeptical, then you have work to do to become more self-aware. Perform deep self-assessment, and then get on with it! Get over yourself!

Ask yourself, *Am I doing well in quantitative results? Am I producing peak results with integrity and quality? Am I a great role model for the customers and colleagues around me? What am I doing to be part of the solution? What am I doing to significantly contribute to the greater good of my team, my department, my site, my store, my organization?* Should you truly want to grow as a manager and a leader, ask those around you to give you an objective assessment of you!

Whatever the results, understand the issue of cultural fit is not about who is good or bad—it doesn't matter who is right or wrong. Leadership excellence is all about serving customers with excellence and meeting expected results.

With this feedback in hand, design practices and routines to be the best type 2 leader of excellence you can be. Be truly and authentically

accountable for your business. Take charge of your own destiny. Create greatness. Be an ambassador of excellence for every single customer and colleague around you! You are responsible for embodying these vitally important leadership behaviors and actions every single day. No stories, no excuses, and no fluff!

Being a leader of excellence, a superstar, a breakthrough leader, and the CEO of your position is all about how much you want to take charge of your life and your career. Are you strong enough to be accountable for your values and your performance? Do you understand the values required of a leader of excellence? And do you have what it takes to turn those values into action?

4

Putting Values
into Action

Putting Values into Action

Now that we've identified the values that make leaders of excellence, let's look at how they put that magic into action!

Surrounding Yourself with Top Talent

The first step to turning your values into action is to surround yourself with top talent. The highest priority is to have the right people on board in the first place. Too many companies don't understand that the success of the organization is not so much about policy or even about strategy; rather, successful and sustaining organizations have and maintain the right culture, and culture consists of like-minded people, not just people who need work. We are talking about people who understand a cause. We are talking about people who

have passion, integrity, and the drive to be the best. These are people with a purpose. It's hard to execute your values if you're the only one upholding those standards.

Organizations of excellence recruit top talent for every role, team, and department across their enterprise. In his book *Good to Great,* Jim Collins suggests that good to great leaders, "first [get] the right people on the bus, (and the wrong people off the bus) and then figured out where to drive it" (Collins, 2001 p41.) It only makes sense, doesn't it? If we have a mediocre team, how can we expect exceptional outcomes? It just isn't possible!

For example, think of a sports team. Pick your favorite! If that team has mediocre talent, can we possibly expect them to win a championship series? To take a medal in the Olympics? Again, it just isn't possible! Winning championships takes the best of the best colleagues with talent and ability.

Organizations of excellence recruit top talent. They *require* it. They position themselves for success. They don't accept anything less, and neither should you!

It seems obvious that an organization of excellence requires the right kind of people to support it. An organization is only as good as the people

in it. Hiring top talent should be an obsession for every leader, no matter their position or title! This is the first action leaders of excellence take to achieve objectives.

Leaders of excellence ask themselves the following questions:

- What am I doing to develop my team members?
- What am I doing to produce peak performance in every single aspect of the department so we can exceed expectations?
- What am I doing to improve the customer experience, the customer journey, and customer retention as well as all business measurements?
- What am I doing to ensure accurate customer feedback in each product or service?
- If it is a functional role, what am I doing to exceed the expectations of my customers in other departments or outside agencies?

Questions should also be geared toward uncovering empirical evidence of the organization's effectiveness! Remember, as CEO of your position, you own it—no matter what "it" is!

What Exactly Is Top Talent?

The term *top talent* may mean different things to different people. At the very core, a highly talented individual is a person with a demonstrable history of consistently achieving peak measurable performance in a specific area/department at a comparably sized organization offering similar programs, products, or services, and moving at the same or a higher pace.

A highly talented superstar is ambitious, competitive, and very hardworking. He or she is solutions-focused, accountable, tenacious, positive, hands-on, humble, and has a sense of urgency. Talented team members are passionate and committed to excellence, quality, industry compliance, and customer success.

It is not easy to find a team of such dedicated people! It can be difficult to find top talent: that's the reason we are igniting your obsession.

We promise it's not magic—it is leadership. But the first step is to face the brutal facts and then take deliberate and definitive steps to upgrade. If you realize you're not surrounded by top talent and your organization, productivity, and customer service suffer because of it, it's time to make a change.

Your customers deserve the best. It is your responsibility to provide it.

How Can You Ensure That You Have Top Talent?

Organizations of excellence are always searching for top talent and do not (and cannot) treat staff/management recruitment as an event. Good managers and supervisors should always be building a bench for every single position on the team. Organizations should upgrade and replace poor- and average-performing team members with talented professionals who have a history of peak performance. There should never be open positions, especially in areas critical to the management of the business.

Do you now have open positions on your team? Have you had areas and departments with poor, average, or below-average performance for months? Do you have poor performers on your teams and are you waiting, hoping, and praying for those team members to miraculously transform into superstars? Have you avoided facing the brutal fact that you have poor performers on your team?

Whether you're sweeping them under the rug or ignoring them altogether, it doesn't matter. Everyone around you will be aware that you have poor performers on your team, and that reflects badly on you as a leader. Recognize that accepting

and dealing with poor performers is very difficult, but building a strong team is one of your top priorities as a leader.

Hiring top talent should be part of who you are. So transform this practice from an "event-driven" activity to an ongoing part of your culture.

How do you find top talent? How do you interview top talent?

Here are a few pointers to guide you:

1. Always be in charge of the search; do not delegate the responsibility to anyone else.

2. Have a committee on-site, at the store, region, department, and/or division level to review, discuss, and plan for searches for open positions.

3. Once the position is open, advertise it on LinkedIn, Indeed.com, and other recruiting sites. Ask colleagues to share your post to widen your network.

4. Email position openings to all internal contacts and ask for their referrals. For example, if you are in search of a production specialist, email all production specialists in the organization.

5. Using this method, you will generate

many resumes. If the position reports directly to you, review all resumes yourself. Remember, this is about accountability.

6. Set interviews as qualified resumes come in. Top talent candidates want to be treated with urgency, respect, and professionalism. Don't wait. Make the candidate feel important. Communicate with them on a regular basis.

7. When searching for top talent, review resumes for direct and relevant experience. Look for individuals who advance vertically within the same function. Do not search for potential; search for individuals who've been there and done that! Look for repetitive records of high achievement.

8. Always search for individuals who have been in the same organization for at least several years and have been promoted.

9. When hiring a manager for a department of ten, make certain the individual has experience managing at least ten individuals.

10. When searching for a direct report, make certain to call references. Speak with

people who have managed, worked alongside, and reported to the candidate. The objective here is to assess performance, productivity, and cultural fit. Did this person consistently meet/exceed expectations? Is this person a high achiever? Is this person accountable? Is this person a team builder? Is this person humble, hardworking, professional, and respectful? Is this person a winner?

11. When you have at least one or two top candidates, have a few others interview him/her, including subject-matter experts (vertical head) and other superstars in the organization with the same title (e.g., production specialist, production manager, etc.). This will provide a good opportunity to get the opinion of other leaders who know your culture and expectations of the organization.

12. Always recruit and hire talented people who will make you shine; you want team members who will make you proud.

Never settle!

This is a very important accountability issue. Your success depends on it. Don't hire underqualified team members! Searching for top talent is one of the most important responsibilities of a leader of excellence. Take it very seriously.

You are the CEO of your own position! Prove your accountability and commitment to excellence; be assertive, own it, and make hiring top talent a priority. It all starts with you!

With the right people on your bus, you can focus on pleasing your customers and achieving your strategic goals.

Communicating Objectives of Excellence

Here is an interesting phenomenon you may have experienced. Some colleagues are surprised or shocked when confronted regarding their poor and unacceptable performance. In essence, your team members are surprised to learn that they are not meeting expectations!

How can this possibly be?

Let's examine your responsibilities first:

1. Do you clearly and repeatedly communicate your functional and behavioral expectations to your team members? Are you abundantly clear about what you expect from the different positions on your team?

2. Are you very clear about the behaviors you expect to observe daily? For example, do you explain it is important to be respectful, professional, on time, hardworking, and customer service-oriented? Do you explain it is important to respond quickly to email, requests, and calls?

3. Do you clearly communicate with your

111

team members when expectations are or are not met?

How are you doing on holding up your end of the bargain? You want to recognize your team members for meeting expectations, but you also want to be clear when team members fail to meet expectations. As with hiring top talent, coaching, developing, and providing constructive feedback to your colleagues should be a continuous process—not an event. Leaders of excellence support and encourage team members, helping them as much as possible. But there are times when team members must face the brutal facts about their performance, especially when they do not meet expectations. Remember, this is not personal; it's about commitment to your customers and focus on quality and achieving excellence. Please treat your team members as grown-ups; they deserve to be in the know. You owe your team members complete honesty, candor, and transparency. If they don't receive constructive feedback, they can't strive for excellence.

Organizations employ workers from multiple generations, from millennials to baby boomers to those from Generation X and Y. Each generation of colleagues brings various attributes, wishes,

habits, perspectives, and demands. That's fantastic, as it allows for a diverse and fruitful community. However, please recognize that the organization itself must have one culture with one set of values; all colleagues, regardless of their history and background, must acculturate if they want to persist and succeed. Celebrate the diversity, but never compromise high expectations; standards for performance must remain constant at all times for every position.

An IEC Case Study

IEC acquired a set of several campuses on the East Coast in 2014, and the IEC leadership team quickly discovered that merging two cultures can be a very difficult and cumbersome process. No matter the best intentions of the two parties, the reality is there is an "acquirer" and an "acquiree." Inevitably, the acquiree feels like the forgotten member. In this case, there was also a significant geographical distance the company had to overcome (IEC headquarters is on the West Coast) as well as basic program and cultural differences. This is all very normal for a company merger, but that doesn't make it any less difficult, especially for the "acquiree."

The IEC leadership team knew that communication was key to successful integration. The company determined to send an "IEC cultural ambassador" to run a campus, to work with the new colleagues in order to help them understand and operate successfully within their new parent company's culture, and to hold "IEC culture workshops" in order to help the new colleagues assimilate to the very powerful, unique, and fast-moving culture of IEC.

By supporting one of the new campuses, the colleagues on the East Coast knew that the cultural ambassador was going through the same pain and challenges they were and could identify with them. The ambassador could also represent those challenges to the CEO and executive team, so IEC leadership could better understand the challenges faced by the newcomers. They spoke the same language.

The integration was a success! Over time, the new locations became acclimated to IEC's operating style and are now a set of highly energized, passionate, capable, and stable locations!

It is so critical to communicate frequently and keep everyone informed! There is no such thing as too much communication. Thinking, assuming, and wondering will lead to frustration, as it will hinder a leader's ability to be effective. So breakthrough leaders always ask, communicate, and share. They encourage team members to speak up and speak out. The only way leaders and teams can improve is to freely communicate their thoughts, insights, and observations. Leaders are only as good as their colleagues.

Equally as important is the timing of communication. When colleagues, employers, employees,

and customers call or email, leaders of excellence respond quickly. You may not always have the correct answer, but you must always respond and inform the other party of the process and next steps. Ideally, a response should occur within one hour (that's TRUE breakthrough customer service), but no inquiry or request should go without a response for longer than twenty-four hours. This includes weekends! Remember, leaders of excellence make things happen, and this requires timely and effective communication!

What Is Timely Communication?

Let's look at an example to illustrate the point.

A supervisor is under pressure to get an annual year-end inventory completed. He is working with Mike, who is being very evasive and unresponsive in his communication with the supervisor.

Supervisor: "Mike, were you able to get the inventory completed? Did we receive all of the backlogged items we were expecting? This is year-end, and we have to have it done today. We're out of time."

Mike: "No, it's not done. I emailed one of the vendors three weeks ago and they haven't responded yet."

Supervisor: "Did you send a follow-up email? Did you try calling them? Did you ask one of your team members to stop by their office to check in with them?"

Mike: "No. They should have answered my email. I

guess we'll just have to note that item as a shortage on inventory."

At first glance, it appears that Mike is "on it" because he has an answer for everything. He has emailed the vendor. He blames the vendor for not responding. After all, isn't that the vendor's job? It becomes clear that the job just isn't going to get done.

But let's examine this exchange in a bit more depth. What else could Mike have done?

- If the email didn't get a response, send another one. And another one. And another one.
- Call the vendor every single day. Leave a voicemail message each time.
- Stop by the vendor's office (if local) and request the information.
- Escalate to the vendor's next-level supervisor.

- Tell his own supervisor of the issue, so his supervisor could help address it.
- Any number of other scenarios in which Mike OWNED the completion of the inventory.

The bottom line is that Mike did not act as the CEO of his position! He sent ONE email and expected someone else to own it. But it was *his* job to get it done.

What do you think Mike's answer should have been?

Right! Mike's answer should be: "You bet the inventory is done! One of the vendors was slow on getting back to me, so I called and emailed every day. I texted him and his staff. I stopped by his office on Saturday and was able to get the information I needed. Inventory is done. Next!"

A leader of excellence is relentless in following through, following up, and finishing, even if it takes emails, calls, or personal visits. Leaders get it done. They don't make excuses; they take ownership. They are accountable!

Be Sure to Prioritize

Every single day, we are faced with the questions of what we should focus on, what we should handle, and what we should achieve. These questions of priorities are amplified when there are only a few people in your area—even more so if you're the only one!

Let's explore some guidelines leaders can focus on to determine priorities and be CEOs of their position in a culture of excellence.

Assess the impact to the organization. For example, if you have to decide between working on an important policy on product integrity versus a dress code policy for your department, pick the policy on product integrity. Why? Because product integrity is critical; it applies to all of your customers and affects the quality of your office, site, department, and the entire organization! Dress codes are important, of course, but not nearly as important as product or service integrity.

By prioritizing large issues over smaller issues, you create more impact; always take care of larger issues because these involve more people. For example, improving a sales and finance department for a

large site with more staff will have a greater impact on outcomes than working on a smaller issue, site, or department. Ideally, you want to focus on both but, if you cannot, pick the larger issue.

Have you heard of the 80/20 rule? Simply put, there are typically large issues in a department (20%) that, if properly addressed, will solve 80% of the problem(s) in that area.

While there are many methods of identifying and prioritizing issues, we might suggest displaying departmental issues on a Pareto chart. The Pareto chart allows you to identify the 20% that will provide a larger overall impact for your set of issues, regardless of the size of the site, department, or organization. Then attack the heavy hitters.

In our Figure A example, the top three heavy hitters are housing, transportation, and food. Solve the heavy hitter(s) and you solve the greatest impacting issues.

Figure A: Pareto Chart

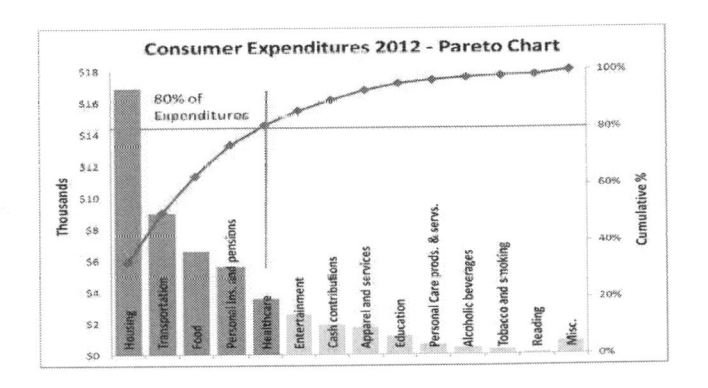

Available from: Bing Image Feed: http://www.bing.com/images/

Another important aspect of prioritizing is to select projects wisely. Always think big picture when investing your time and resources. Focus on what will create the greatest impact. At one point or another, you might have noticed several departments and numerous people working on a single project that makes up only a small percentage of your business. Every part of your business is important, no matter how small. But think about which efforts will make the greatest impact on the organization! Prioritize. These are the times when you have to outsource your trust and leverage talents at the site level.

Do not sweat the little stuff. And don't make something bigger than it is!

Only make decisions and focus on activities related to your organizational strategies and objectives. It makes no sense to worry about the overgrown trees in the employee parking lot if your customers are unhappy! And please don't try to convince others to worry about how those overgrown trees wither. Focus on your organization's strategies and objectives. Once you have achieved all objectives at expected levels, then allocate time to the overgrown trees.

The challenges you face are likely more complicated than the aforementioned scenario. But no matter the level, no matter the issue, no matter how complicated the problem seems, these basic principles work. If you're still unsure about how to prioritize, brainstorm with other leaders in your organization.

Remember, it is critical that leaders of excellence be wise and prudent with their time, energy, and priorities.

Focusing on Planning, Then Executing

We often get bogged down with hundreds of thoughts and activities, many of which may not actually matter. To combat this tendency, leaders must cultivate a results-focused culture.

The ideal approach to produce peak performance is to create thorough, thoughtful, comprehensive plans which are as detailed as possible. This makes execution more attainable and streamlined.

Of course, having a plan is important. An organization of excellence—a leader of excellence—must have a plan to guide the organization—the team—where they need to go. In essence, they must have a road map toward goal achievement—a road map toward success! For example, if we want to take our family on a vacation to Disneyland and we start our trip in New Jersey, we need a plan. We need to map our route! If not, we may very well start our trip in New Jersey, only to wind up in Canada! An effective organization must have a plan. Leaders of excellence have plans.

Once the plan is in place, leaders of excellence execute that plan! Leaders of excellence execute and produce expected results. Planning is done to ensure appropriate execution. Of course, we should

always look for a well thought-out plan with details and contingencies, but it is the ability of the leader to execute that makes all the difference. Many organizations plan, and plan, and plan, and . . . plan . . . but the successful organizations understand that planning is but the initial step. The value of execution cannot be understated.

You may be working in a large organization. One of the benefits of large organizations is that you learn how to scale, standardize, and develop processes and plans. An unfortunate result, though, is you may lose that spirit of entrepreneurship that allows you to innovate and execute. Strive for a healthy balance between large organization planning and small organization execution. As a leader of excellence and as the CEO of your position, you are accountable not for producing the best plan but for attaining the best results that meet and exceed expectations. Therefore, next time you are invited to another call and another committee meeting, remember your objective is to execute and produce results. So during those meetings, keep your eye on the ultimate prize: *results.*

Be aggressive, do not accept "can't" as an answer; have a sense of urgency in all you do and execute ruthlessly to produce expected results.

Driving BHAGS

We have to give Jim Collins credit for this one! In his book *Built to Last*, Collins introduced the Big Hairy Audacious Goal (BHAG). Collins tells us that the BHAG (pronounced bee-hag) is a 'clear and compelling goal' (Collins & Porras, 1994/2002, p.94) for the organization that galvanizes the spirit of the organization. According to Collins, like the moon mission, "a true BHAG is clear and compelling and serves as a unifying focal point of effort, often creating immense team spirit. It has a clear finish line, so the organization can know when it has achieved the goal; people like to shoot for finish lines. A BHAG engages people; it reaches out and grabs them in the gut. It is tangible, energizing, and highly focused. People "get it" right away, and it takes little or no explanation."

And so it is with the organization of excellence. We operate under the principle of the BHAG. We live it and breathe it!

What does BHAG have to do with a culture of excellence?

A culture of excellence is built on potential, not on a budget! Merely achieving budget is failure

to a leader of excellence—that signifies mediocre performance.

Many organizations build a budget and then play the "budget game" on how much they can get away with. "Under-promise and over-deliver" is a common mantra in many organizations. In an organization of excellence, however, the budget only serves as a minimum baseline. The target—the BIG HAIRY AUDACIOUS GOAL—in an organization of excellence is to drive the potential of the colleagues in the organization! There is no limit in an organization of excellence. Leaders of excellence only look at the budget as a set of numbers to completely demolish! Leaders of excellence add higher goals to a budget and then push to excel beyond those audacious goals!

Leaders of excellence never settle for "hitting the budget." Leaders of excellence laugh at the budget as we pass it by!

Years ago, during a strategic planning meeting, two members of an organization presented the "SuperPlan" to the CEO and his executive team. The SuperPlan was more than just a PowerPoint presentation with a set of numbers on a slide reviewing how the team would "hit budget." Not even close. The SuperPlan was a promise that these

members would so far exceed their budget that there would be virtually no relationship between the budget and the actual outcomes. The BHAG was so outlandish, so far-fetched, that no one believed it. Except the CEO, that is. The CEO made the promise to the team that they would have everything they needed to achieve their goals. He told them that he believed in them. Sure enough, that team did achieve their SuperPlan goals that year! In fact, they over-promised and over-delivered by an extraordinary amount. And in doing so, the team acted as a catalyst for the entire organization to drive for higher results and take chances.

Don't Allow Bureaucracy
to Get in the Way

Bureaucracy is a big problem for leaders of excellence. Even if your organization has various positions, titles, levels, and so forth, an organization of excellence must act and behave as a flat organization. Don't lose those features of entrepreneurship that allow you to get things done—done well and on time.

If supplies or products are in the storage room, your team should put them on the shelves for the customers to see! Who are you waiting for?

If a customer seems lost in your lobby, stop and help him or her.

If a department needs help, go help them!

It doesn't matter if you occupy the most powerful position in the company. Don't become a prisoner or a victim of your titles and positions! Get things done. Be empowered to meet expectations. No stories, no excuses, no fluff.

Trusting Your Superstars

If you are an executive or a member of a corporate staff, it is important to note that you have many superstars in your offices, in your sites, at your facilities, at your stores. They are just as good as you are! Being part of an executive team or corporate staff or having a higher title does not necessarily make you better! Trust your team members at your locations and empower them to make decisions and get the work done.

In most organizations, a very high percentage of your resources are in the field for the right reason—because that's where your customers are. Recognize that benefit and learn to use these resources intelligently.

Collaborate and work as a team. This concept of acting as one is difficult for many people to digest, but it is a critical paradigm to work toward. It is important to remember that all colleagues make up one organization. There is no "us and them"; it is just "us." To the outside world; to customers, to vendors, to employers, the organization of excellence appears as one organization. Our customers don't know (or care) what department a colleague might be in; therefore, any unfavorable

inaction and misbehavior is a reflection on the entire organization. Don't let ego, pride, or petty jealousy get in the way of building the strongest team, department, and organization. This is only possible when you empower your superstars to do their best work and then trust them to do it.

Furthermore, it doesn't matter what department you are in! Work is divided by departments to achieve order, ensure maximize efficiency, and create discipline. Therefore, regardless of what title you have and what department you are in, you must do all that is necessary within acceptable operations as well as regulatory frameworks to support your colleagues at every level. In essence, leaders of excellence are accountable for making their colleagues successful and their customers satisfied. In the culture of excellence, employees are one, and they must act accordingly.

At IEC, we are structured into what we identify as four different areas:

1. Admissions, which builds the value of education
2. Financial services, which provides finance options for access to education

3. Education, which delivers the value of education
4. Career services, which delivers the promise to help our students build a future they can be proud of

At IEC we view our admissions and financial aid areas as "one team" in spite of the "separation of duties" between the two teams. Although they have different functions, their ability to work together is vital to serve the customer (our students). Both teams are equally accountable for common results. Their mantra became *One team one mission*. Results improved dramatically and were evident in overall customer satisfaction and organizational outcomes.

Always Focusing on Solutions

From the time we are young children, we are socialized to see what's wrong with the world around us and to identify the person(s) who caused the problem. Identifying problems in organizations is terribly important. But finding solutions and solving problems doesn't stop there. What is much more important and significantly more difficult is finding thoughtful solutions to problems.

How do leaders of excellence facilitate this process? Simple! They use a solutions-focused approach. You may not be accustomed to gathering quantitative evidence, identifying and understanding the problem, and then developing and executing robust and creative solutions to produce expected results, but this is the most effective approach to finding and executing solutions. This is an essential skill for leaders of excellence. Having problems is not necessarily a bad thing—it's the nature of life on this planet and a normal part of every professional's job—but not having viable solutions creates negativity, dogma, and stagnation. One significant attribute that separates ordinary employees from CEOs of their position is the ability to solve difficult problems and exceed expectations.

Leaders will always face challenges both large and small regardless of their role or level in the organization. Organizations will always face challenges as well. But these challenges create opportunities for team development, professional growth, and personal mastery. Leaders must face the brutal facts and be deliberate in regard to their attitudes, behaviors, and actions. Most importantly, leaders of excellence look within and make changes to themselves and their performance before asking their colleagues to change. Leadership titles do NOT exempt a person from living organizational values; in fact, your title makes you a role model for others, responsible to do more and be more. In other words, you have to be the change you want to see in the team members around you.

Keeping Your Focus on Customer Service

One of the most powerful tools all organizations can access is right in their hands: access to the customer. Organizations of excellence ask their customers what satisfies them! Ask the customer how you can provide excellence and then go about providing it! A customer survey is an extraordinary tool that will allow you to do just that. Surveys help us (and our customers) identify what our customer needs and wants, and if we listen to the customer, we have our very own road to success! We are in essence asking them to tell us how to be great! So, let's be great!

Think about the 80/20 rule. If you gather data from the customer and put the information into the Figure A Pareto (http://www.bing.com/images/) analysis, there you have it! Start by satisfying the larger items so you can positively impact the majority of your customers and then work down the line to create greatness by going the extra mile. Work all the way down until you solve the smallest issues possible.

Customer service is arguably one of the most misunderstood terms. Providing customers with

breakthrough customer service doesn't mean you have to give them everything they want! In most businesses, there are multiple expectations for several different customers, both internal and external.

All customers must be treated with urgency, respect, dignity, kindness, courtesy, professionalism, passion, and care. The same behavior holds true with colleagues, employers, and outside organizations. Remember that your customers can always choose to go to another business for their needs. What will set you apart is all that you do to make your customers feel needed, wanted, and special. We have to always, always meet and preferably exceed customer expectations. Plan to treat your customers with excellent customer service at all times.

A culture of excellence strives to support leaders of excellence in all possible ways. Just as we ask customers what they need and then go about satisfying those needs, so must we approach our superstar staff. We must know what they need in order to be successful! These are our CEO superstars! We must give them the tools they need!

Supporting teams in the field and on the production line is vital, as is customer facing.

We must provide all internal customers

with customer service excellence. This means that we must exceed the expectations of each and every customer every day. Probably the easiest example is responding to emails, texts, and phone messages in a timely manner. This means within minutes when possible, hours when not. You might have read through threads of emails showing many managers and team members not responding to key questions and requests from customers for days; that is unacceptable. And forwarding an email to a colleague for further action does not exempt us from our obligation to respond. These are the most basic tenets of customer service—you understand the point!

So let us ask you! Are you exceeding the expectations of your customers, your team members, and your colleagues in other departments, sites and locations?

Seek First to Understand

Habit five of Stephen Covey's *The 7 Habits of Highly Effective People* advises, "Seek First to Understand, then to be Understood" (Covey, 2004, p247.). Simply put, focus on hearing rather than on being heard. How often are you thinking about what you'll say in a conversation rather than listening to what the other person is saying? Listen to understand! What is the customer or team member trying to tell us? What is their point of view? According to Covey, "Communication is the most important skill in life. You spend years learning how to read and write and years learning how to speak. But what about listening? What training have you had that enables you to listen so you really, deeply understand another human being from that individual's own frame of reference?" (Covey, 2004 p.249).

Furthermore, Covey suggests that, "The key is to genuinely seek the welfare of the individual, to listen with empathy, to let the person get to the problem and the solution at his own pace and time. Layer upon layer—it's like peeling an onion until you get to the soft inner core." (Covey, 1989/2004 p. 263)

How much better will your colleague feel

. . . how much better will your spouse, significant other, children . . . even friends feel when you actively listen to understand? Give them the gift of your time . . . the gift of your genuine *intent to understand*. Many problems in the world could be solved with this small but very powerful concept.

For example—how does it feel when you enter someone's office, or you are at a retail establishment, and the person you expect to serve you doesn't truly listen to what you need? What if they continued looking at their computer and don't even turn to face you? What if they continue talking to the other person behind the counter rather than asking you . . . and paying attention to . . . what *you* need? Although these seem like very small things, the message they present is enormous. What is your response when someone approaches you? Do you stop what you are doing and listen?

Leaders of excellence listen with the intent to understand! Don't listen merely to formulate your own response. After all, don't you want to know the truth? If you are a lifelong student, you'll have the courage to listen and learn.

Leaders of excellence are lifelong learners!

Always Seeking to Learn

As leaders of excellence, when we visit different stores, locations, plants, facilities, and so forth, we should always seek to learn a great deal from people at "ground level." Treat these visits as opportunities to get a wider view of your organization's reach. It is important that we let our teams know that we will not give up until we all create and sustain a fantastic organization and become a premier provider of goods, products, or services in our respective businesses.

Consistent with our quest to achieve greatness in all we do, we all have to know a great deal about all that is going on around us. Therefore, we can ask ourselves, "How much do we know about what we do individually and collectively on-site, regionally, and/or divisionally? Whether you are a CEO, a vice-president, a divisional leader, a site supervisor, a production worker, a clerical worker—it doesn't matter! In a well-functioning organization where each colleague is the CEO of their position, every colleague matters.

We need to be familiar with the measurable expectations of all that we do, and we must be familiar with the roles and responsibilities of our positions.

Furthermore, in an organization that promotes communication and shared understanding, employees should be informed and know about other departments' performances and achievements.

It is so very important to let our teams know that we also want to learn from *them*. In many cases (perhaps even in most cases), team members will be experts in what they do. We *should* learn from them!

Visiting locations also lets leaders of excellence assess the talent in the field. We get to see colleagues in action rather than on a conference call or on a report somewhere. Visiting locations lets us see the magic as it happens! It lets us in on their world! The real world—not a cubicle at a headquarters office!

When we visit locations, we can ask our field experts what they do, how they do it, when they do it, and with whom they do it. No one in the organization is the expert of everything. We all must learn and experience together. As one unit.

When we visit campuses, we can learn a few things by asking the right questions. If we truly want to learn as well as to assess the talent in the field, we can seek to understand the knowledge and commitment of the colleagues doing the work.

Some key questions to ask your team might be:

1. Do you "really" know what the expectations are for you and your department?
2. What are your roles and responsibilities?
3. How do you know when you are successful?
4. Do you know when your department is successful?
5. Do you know when your site is successful?
6. Do you know what success looks like for your region?
7. Do you know the numerical requirements of your role? Your department? Your region? What should it be?
8. How many employees do you have on your site? In your office?
9. Do you know what your colleagues in other departments "really" do?
10. Do you fully understand the relationship and interdependencies between all departments?
11. Do you know the expectations of your colleagues in other departments?
12. What do you know about your organization?

13. Do you know the vision and mission of your organization?
14. What is your role in making your department, your site, your office, your division, your organization successful?
15. What is your responsibility in making sure your customers are successful?
16. What does quality mean to you? What does quality mean to your department and to your role?
17. What does superior customer service mean to you, to your department, and to your office?
18. What does "greatness" mean to you, to your department, and to your office? Your company?
19. What does top performance mean to you, to your department, and to your office?

If your organization wants to achieve excellence, to meet and exceed business goals, and to be first in class in your community, all employees must have a shared understanding of individual and collective responsibilities. It is the responsibility of leaders of

excellence to ask themselves the tough questions and to seek answers to those questions—to learn.

The aforementioned discussion and associated questions are for every single member of the organization to address, especially you as a leader of excellence. It is perfectly okay to not have answers to one or more of the above questions, but it is not okay to ignore the questions altogether. Leaders have a responsibility to find answers to these questions. Go to your colleagues and ask and seek necessary answers! Take an active role in being a significant part of the solution in building your business. Be the CEO of your position. Take charge. Create your destiny. When every member of the organization takes such initiative, it's inevitable that you'll achieve your objective of building a world-class organization!

Holding Regular One-on-One Steering Meetings

Though you may attend all kinds of meetings during the course of your weekly duties in regard to operations, because of the size and focus there is little time to go deep with any one particular coworker.

Consider establishing one-on-one meetings to influence, mentor, and steer influential colleagues on your team. It doesn't matter what level or position this colleague holds; choose people of influence or those who would benefit from your influence.

One-on-one meetings can be very powerful when you and your colleague sit down in private, face-to-face, and just talk. Ask your colleagues how they're doing. Ask how their family is. Ask how things are going at work. Be authentic. Be genuine. Open the floor for discussion. Be sure to actively listen to their concerns, their issues, and their feelings so you can help steer, direct, or influence them when necessary. Always be thinking of how you can support the colleague's success.

In one-on-one meetings, you establish relationships with your colleagues that allow for trust, honesty, and rapport. They get the sense that you

honestly care. They feel they have a direct line to you. How powerful is that?

You can influence even the most difficult situations by mentoring your colleagues. But mentoring colleagues means you need to take the time to meet with them, to invest in them. These must be high-priority meetings, not the kind you just cancel because there is "too much going on right now."

One-on-one meetings are a prime way of influencing colleagues' adaptability to organizational culture. These meetings don't always have to be with direct reports—you can meet with anyone on your team: directors, associate directors, department leads, supervisors, lead employees, line employees—the position doesn't matter. It is the person . . . the colleague . . . the customer . . . that matters!

As you direct, influence, and mentor a colleague in the direction they should go, you may find that many "communication problems" you had with this person previously fade over time. With deeper relationships comes greater communication.

Asking Yourself the Tough Questions

As leaders of excellence, it is vital that we don't fool ourselves. "You can fool some of the people some of the time, but you can't fool all of the people all of the time." Every heard of that saying? Let's just break it down into something meaningful. Let's cut right to the chase. At the end of the day, what good does it do to try to fool anyone, much less ourselves? Why not deal in truth? Why not deal with the "brutal facts," even if they are about ourselves or our teams? Leadership requires character. Character is built through honest assessment.

Helpful questions might include the following:

1. Do I have the right talent on my team?
2. What have I done to make sure I have the best players on my team?
3. How many team members have I developed to perform at expected levels?
4. Have results in my area improved this week, this month, this quarter, and this year?
5. How would I rate my own productivity and performance as compared to expectations,

as compared to the best version of ME, and as compared to the best version of my business?

6. If I am meeting or exceeding expectations, what am I doing to ensure I continue to overachieve? If I am NOT meeting expectations, what significant actions am I taking to change the unsuccessful path I am on?

7. With all that I have done, what have been my measurable achievements in the past week, month, quarter, and year?

Remember, when you decide to excel: waiting, hoping, and praying, although therapeutic, won't help! You have to act with vigor, tenacity, grit, and conviction. Also understand that excellence and greatness aren't just pie-in-the-sky dreams; they are achievable for leaders of excellence every single day.

Positive Messaging

To our executive readers: organizations spend a lot of time and money on building their brand! But nothing builds your brand more effectively than your behaviors and actions as executives in the organization! As vertical heads and top operations executives, what you say and how you say it, what you do and how you do it, how you behave and how you treat others define you individually and collectively. Who you are and what you do define you as an organization because your team members emulate your behaviors—and then it all cascades to the front line. So what your customers experience is a reflection of who and what you are as executives. Indirectly and directly, you touch everyone in this organization.

The objective of staff and the executive team is to support an organization that has very high expectations; one that is always focused, disciplined, ambitious, accountable, and compassionate.

How do you achieve your objectives and develop a brand that would truly be the envy of your industry?

Although some of the following comments might seem a bit elementary, it's the basics that

count the most. Many organizations avoid and ignore these basic but critical issues, but these are the very topics that separate good from great organizations. As an organization grows, it is vital that its values remain constant. From the top to the bottom of the organization, employees must be focused on achieving objectives while remaining true to core values.

1. Do not share confidential information with your team members, colleagues in other departments, and/or friends outside of your organization. If in doubt, ask your superior what is confidential.

2. Do not share your dissatisfaction or unhappiness about something or someone that is bothering you with colleagues in your department, other organizational colleagues, or colleagues outside of your organization. Instead, speak with your superior or confront the person who is causing the problem. Leaders speak up and speak out. Regardless, venting to others, although innocent, projects a negative image of YOU and your leadership team.

3. Do not listen to rumors, and stop them

when you hear them. This should go without saying, but never spread rumors to others inside or outside of your organization. When you engage in such discourse, it reflects poorly on you as an individual. Worse, it reflects poorly on your organization, all the way up to your executive team. We do not want our internal or external colleagues to think our executives lack organizational tact, maturity, and sophistication.

4. Do not share negative feelings, emotions, or information on social media, either directly or indirectly. Remember, you are a leader, and what you say negatively influences people's perception of you and your organization. Also know that internal colleagues, industry vendors, and external colleagues view what you write on social media, so if you don't have any positive news, feelings, behaviors, or actions to share about your team or organization, refrain from posting about them. Again, leaders confront issues head on. If you have a problem, speak with your manager or the person responsible for the conflict.

5. Be disciplined! Discipline separates the organization of excellence from other organizations. Focus on your vision and strategies at all times. Leaders of excellence understand that discipline achieves expected results and supports your organization's strategies and annual objectives. Everything you do should focus on your annual objectives in support of your strategies. Your discipline and focus will then cascade to other levels of the organization. Exhibit and manifest behaviors associated with disciplined individuals and organizations.

Be sensitive to site priorities and expectations. It's really that simple.

The objective as members of staff is to support, guide, and partner with your colleagues at the "boots on the ground" levels to meet and exceed expectations in line with your strategies and annual objectives. Be sensitive to the following:

- Key customer dates
- The how and not always the what

- Calls and training sessions based on what is good for your colleagues
- Owning the outcomes
- The fact that site success is your success
- Being an action leader

Key customer dates. Don't have conference calls with local sites on key customer dates, as they will be busy serving customers. For example, when you are setting up a trip to visit a field location, double-check your calendar. Compare it with colleagues' calendars so you aren't all addressing the same issue from different locations or in different venues. Double-check to ensure your work is fruitful and meaningful. Then, when you perform the activity, get right down to doing the work. Help, train, show, and demonstrate how work gets done. Your top staff members will be those who help colleagues achieve expectations.

Focus on the "how" and not always the "what." The how might be the methodology of your approach. Is it compliant? Is it effective? Is your communication thorough? Respectful? Does it include those who need to know? How will information be communicated to others? How will I execute this quickly and efficiently?

Then, focus on the what. What procedures need to be followed? What processes need to take place? What information will be critical to those involved? What hours will the team need to work? Always confirm that your colleagues fully understand expectations and what needs to happen. The foundation must be confirmed. It's the *how* part that separates colleagues in the organization from one another.

Organize and plan calls and training sessions. These should be based on what is good for your colleagues at the site level, not what is good for you. Remember, your responsibility is to serve your colleagues and help them achieve expectations.

Own the outcomes. Own outcomes at the same level of accountability as your colleagues at the site level so you can partner with them in finding solutions and executing plans to meet expectations. Your staff members who "own" expectations are respected the most because they are known to care just as much.

Site success is your success. Therefore, when your colleagues at the store level, the site level, or the

department level are successful, you'll be success-ful. Plan your entire strategy and actions around this concept.

Be an action leader. Don't be a broker or consul-tant. Colleagues at the store level, site level, and the department level will appreciate advice, but they love those who can partner with them and get the work done to achieve expected results!

Remember, waiting, hoping, and praying will not enhance your team's ability! You have to take swift and definitive action to improve your team's strength. Do not be fearful of the attrition of poor or average performing team members, but do fear the attrition of your superstars who carry your de-partment, your stores, and your organization.

Catching People in the Act of Doing Something Right

If you are in a position of support or oversight for a number of employees, locations, stores, regions, and so forth, maintain respect and dignity as you visit different colleagues and locations. Don't be overly critical, trying to find out "what is wrong" with that location. In fact, focus on what is RIGHT with that location! Of course, you always provide direct, honest, and authentic feedback, but make sure your tone is supportive. Encourage and praise your employees for things they're doing right. That positive reinforcement goes a long way.

Let's look at an example to illustrate the point. Supervisor #1 and Supervisor #2 are giving feedback to Susan regarding some challenges facing her production team.

Supervisor #1: "Susan, your production team is doing it all wrong. I thought we told you the process was changed two weeks ago! Why do I have to come here to tell you that you're doing it wrong? Don't you listen on our conference calls?"

Supervisor #2: "Thank you for spending time with us today, Susan. We are very impressed with several components of your operation! The way

you reduced the number of steps in the process from ten to seven really helps increase efficiency! There are a couple of areas that need to be updated, though, so let's talk about those. We must not have communicated the changes properly. What else can we do to help you?"

Which would you be more likely to accept, appreciate, and make adjustments for? Which makes you feel more supported?

It's certainly okay to provide feedback on what is wrong. But it's essential to provide feedback on what is right! Catching people in the act of doing something right doesn't mean you have to couple it with something they are doing wrong. It is even better when you catch people in the act of doing something right and then you let them know. Imagine how motivating that is for your colleagues!

Keeping an Eye on the Financials

Leaders of excellence actively manage their financial budget.

Not all of us are born with a calculator-type brain. Not all of us enjoy running the numbers. But leaders of excellence learn to use historic report data and results in order to make meaningful changes in operations. For example, if your location is growing but you spend more money than you bring in then the funds aren't being used properly. Or perhaps you spend according to budget, but you don't grow according to budget. In that case, the funds still aren't being used properly. Leaders must be able to manage funds and track finances so expenses and revenue are in line with one another to meet expectations. If your outcomes are not in line with expectations, you need to make a change to your expenses. If working with financials is difficult then take charge! Find experts in your organization who can help you master the art of managing finances!

Watching the bucks means more than saving money. Being judicious with expenditures also sends a message of value to those around you. Colleagues look to leaders of excellence, watching their behavior closely; they'll notice if you are

modeling the values you espouse as CEO of your position.

Often, being fiscally responsible simply involves a little extra time, effort, and good thinking.

Consider the following IEC example as a case study.

An IEC campus leader noted that the chairs in an office were bought eight or nine years ago and were starting to fall apart. The leader's immediate reaction was to replace them. However, upon visiting his students' classrooms, he noticed that the chairs used by students, our customers, needed upgrading. The campus leader put his own office chairs on hold in order to better serve the customer, even though that particular campus was significantly below the expense budget.

Leaders of excellence should cut expenses when necessary and be prudent with their spending, but they can also build by making the right investments in the right areas. Don't shy away from discussing finances with your team; set the tone and play a significant role in only spending where necessary, which includes not spending on unnecessary luxuries.

In this example, the campus staff and customers saw that the leader was following through

with what he said he believed in—taking care of the team and the customers first. Staff began to feel more excited about new chairs and basic supplies. They felt heard; their boss was listening.

Being the CEO of your position; making the right choices; and keeping the team focused on how they can improve, execute, and achieve objectives is primary. Therefore, reducing any distractions—like the team not having the tools to succeed—is management's responsibility. Leading by example and doing what is right are values that make an immediate impact on morale and performance.

Leaders of excellence are resourceful, they ensure the efficient use of materials, and they prioritize spending in areas that enhance the customer experience.

Driving Results through
Strategic Focus

In a culture of excellence, team members know what is important and what to focus on. Leaders of excellence understand that what we focus on will get the attention it needs.

Leaders of excellence understand the Hawthorne effect.

The Hawthorne effect is a psychological phenomenon that produces an improvement in human behavior or performance as a result of increased attention from superiors, clients, or colleagues (Daniel & Rouse, 2018).

The Hawthorne effect was first seen in the 1920s at Western Electric Company's Hawthorne Works, from which the term is derived. The Hawthorne studies were designed to find ways to increase worker productivity. Increasing the amount of light in the workplace had a measurable positive effect on employee productivity. However, the researchers also found that when they lowered the lighting levels, productivity still increased. In fact, for a limited period after any change in the illumination level, the workers' average output increased. The researchers concluded that the specific

conditions tested for had nothing to do with the productivity increases (Daniel & Rouse, 2018).

What does this mean to us? The simple act of being observed made productivity increase. As simple as that! Of course, in different organizations this concept can take place differently, but the important thing to remember is that when we focus on things, they change. When we pay attention to our colleagues, to processes, to issues, they change. It is then up to us to decide HOW we can handle it as leaders of excellence to make sure these changes work toward our organizational goals.

Organizations of excellence understand the fact that what they focus on changes. As can be observed in the Hawthorne effect (Daniel & Rouse, 2018), when we focus on the important things, they change by the mere fact that we are focusing on them. You don't have to be condescending, mean, or negative. You can be respectful, understanding, and direct. The leader's job is to focus on things that are important to the organization.

What you focus on is what you change.

Running an organization requires focus on many, many areas. It requires a balance of several indices, all of which are important. At IEC, we know that as one area becomes unbalanced, we

must focus on it—we make it public, we track it. And the outcome increases! It's all about putting focus, expectations, and accountability on the areas that need it.

As in the case of setting our own BHAGs, once we make our target goals public, our teams know that we have to focus specifically on them in order to achieve them. We cannot allow ourselves to be distracted from those goals! This is key to organizational success. Leaders of excellence understand this concept, and they don't waste time on minor distractions.

Focus on it and you will achieve it!

And so you have it! What we focus on changes.

Wrapping Up

Hopefully our time spent together has been meaningful for you. It certainly has for us! You now have a "quiver" of "leadership excellence arrows" with which to operate. Do other organizations operate with their own culture, their own quiver of arrows? Of course they do! But is it as well defined? Perhaps not. Our message to you is that it is vital to establish a "leadership excellence precedence" in your organization—or even just for yourself—in order to be productive, successful, and happy in whatever you do as your vocation.

At the beginning of the book, Dr. Fateri indicated that he came upon IEC during his search for purpose. So it is with James York, coauthor, as well as many of the colleagues within the organization. We have found something we love—somewhere we fit. It involves extraordinary self-awareness, extraordinary commitment. Extraordinary effort. But for us, all of this has meaning. Our own purpose has been fulfilled.

And so it can be with you! Just find (or create!) the right organization—the thinking organization that commits its ideals on paper; an organization that involves colleagues in the development of a very special, very powerful, very meaningful experience. An organization that understands the importance of honesty, respect, and dignity.

At IEC, we have a saying. "Culture Eats Strategy for Lunch." This statement is typically attributed to behaviorist Peter Drucker (1982); however, we can all learn the importance of this lesson. If we don't have a culture we can believe in, a culture that drives powerful principles and concepts, then no matter how much we talk and talk and talk about our "strategy," it simply won't happen without a distinctive and well-defined foundation of culture.

You might be wondering which principle in the book is most important. The truth is that while we have certainly reviewed many concepts and principles in our time together (and each one can arguably be the most important one), the litmus test is how you determine to act, to lead, and to look at and accept the brutal facts. Your organization will undoubtedly be a bit different than IEC. Of course! That is as it should be. But the principles

and concepts we talk about are universal in nature. They apply across the board, no matter what organization you belong to or what you do within that organization.

Consider these concepts and principles as an umbrella—a set of constructs under which you operate. They become the "way you do business." You can operate with dignity, respect, honesty, kindness, and the other concepts in the book and be effective, efficient, impactful, and successful!

We wish you well!

Epilogue

Organizational culture is the single most important determinant of organizational success over a long period of time. In addition, organizational culture is the most significant factor in setting one organization apart from and above others. There are many articles and interviews that feature leaders of successful organizations discussing the stellar performances of extraordinary organizations, and more often than not they mention hard work, unique business theses, innovative product ideas, luck, and other similar factors as reasons for the organizations' success. These may be true, but they're not at the heart of organizational success—they're merely symptoms of that success. The fire that ignites hard work, innovation, passion, vigor, competitiveness, and accountability is *organizational culture*. All values and attributes of top-performing organizations are emerging properties of organizational culture.

In this book, we've shared with you many

thoughts, insights, observations, practices, and experiences that are all emerging properties of the culture we've deliberately built at International Education Corporation (IEC) to produce peak performance. This culture was developed to help the organization sustain viability during periods of turbulence, uncertainty, and trouble. Every organization has a culture. Some organizations are cognizant of their values, and they work hard to uphold them to promote greatness, while other organizations are completely unaware of who they are. Organizational culture develops whether it is deliberate or not. Organizations that sustain greatness over long periods of time have values that are shared by all team members. This is the secret to our success at IEC. Members of the IEC community all share the same values, and this has helped the organization sustain greatness through good times and bad.

It is hard to describe culture in motion, as the feelings and emotions are better felt than described. However, we've done our best to explain the great values that have allowed IEC and many other organizations to survive and prosper. The values that make up an organization's culture also empower individual team members to feel needed, to know they are important, and to believe that they

matter. People want to work for an organization that values their contribution, an organization that allows them to make a meaningful difference, an organization that recognizes excellence. Everyone wants to work for an organization he or she can be proud of, so leveraging that desire helps develop amazing culture. However, on the flip side, not fueling a person's pride at work will inevitably build a culture anchored in cynicism, dogma, stagnation, and skepticism.

Leaders of excellence spend ample time focusing on values that develop stellar culture because they know products, ideas, strategies, plans, and highly paid executives don't create greatness: *culture* produces greatness. This is the lesson we've learned at IEC. This is the lesson all leaders learn when they experience breakthroughs in organizations; culture creates greatness.

While the concepts, examples, and explanations of values in the preceding chapters are specific to our experience at IEC, these ideas will have the same impact on any organization, whether it is a small private company or a large nonprofit public organization. With proper leadership, organizational culture can be created in any organization so as to produce peak performance and ensure productivity.

It is important to note that the concepts explained in this book also apply to individuals at a personal level. Each person has the capacity to be fully accountable, to have vigor, intensity, passion, and to be the CEO of his or her position and life. Individuals do not have to wait for someone else to guide them. When applied professionally and personally, the attributes, skill sets, values, and concepts discussed in this book will have a powerful impact on a person's career and personal life.

Our ambition in writing this book was to create a platform for all organizations and individuals to take a personal role in creating their own destinies. We hoped to demonstrate it is possible for anyone to become the architect of their own future. Most importantly, we wanted to encourage every reader to become an active participant in shaping their own life. If I can do it—if we can do it—anyone can do it. But you must believe. You must take personal responsibility. You must push through all obstacles, barriers, and negativity to test your capacity and to become the best version of yourself.

Theorists have varied definitions of organizational culture and different opinions regarding the role excellence plays in organizational culture. But for the most part, theorists take a very academic

approach to defining and making attributions to cultural excellence. Academicians, organizational anthropologists, and business theorists have created sophisticated and thoughtful models depicting excellence in organizational culture. Organizations that have a clearly articulated mission, vision, and values statement are expected to achieve excellence in organizational culture.

Our approach to the subject has been more unorthodox by comparison. Although we share a strong academic background, we deliberately took a nonacademic practitioner-focused approach in describing a culture of excellence because we wanted to demonstrate how ordinary people create extraordinary cultures. We wanted to show you how employees with passion, ambition, vigor, trust, accountability, humility, imagination, respect, and love can create a culture of excellence by sharing the same values. We wrote this book for ordinary people and for practitioners because we wanted this book to be useful. We hope this book will do more than just collect dust on a shelf alongside hundreds of other books on leadership and organizational culture. We hope you'll use it on your journey to excellence. To your success!

References

Bing Image Feed. Pareto Chart. https://binged.it/2yo6KlZ

Collins, J. *Good to Great,* New York: HarperCollins Publisher, 2001

Collins, James C., and Porras, Jerry I. *Built to Last*, New York: HarperCollins Publishers, 1994/1997/2002.

Covey, Stephen R. *The 7 Habits of Highly Effective People.* New York:

Fireside Book by Simon & Schuster, 1989/2004.

Daniel, Dianne, and Rouse, Margaret. *Hawthorne Effect.* Retrieved May 26, 2018. http://whatis.techtarget.com/definition/Hawthorne-effect

Drucker, Peter F. *The Practice of Management.* New York: HarperCollins Publishers, 1982.

Merriam-Webster, s.v. "culture," accessed April 10, 2018, https://www.merriam-webster.com/dictionary/culture.

Appendix A

We the People of JEC

JEC has a magical culture. We have created a culture which most practitioners read about in text books and case studies. An organisation's culture goes to the very heart of its identity and the very essence of its existence. I never felt so strongly about the strength of an organisation's culture to take a deliberate approach to protect it and leverage it for the viability of our future as one of the best career education companies in the country. But I feel very strongly about our culture at JEC and its contribution to whom we are and who we must remain to produce and sustain top results in the future.

Although words cannot authentically capture and describe the true essence of our culture, the following are the collective attributes, values, and behaviors we exhibit at JEC. None of these behaviors are independent of one another and in fact they are inter-related, co-dependent, and it is their direct collective connectivity that creates our unique identity and our extraordinary culture. I ask that you share this document with your colleagues, discuss it regularly and make it a critical part of your work life every day.

- We lead through Recognition, Gratitude, Appreciation, Praise and Inspiration
- We have heart
- We love to serve
- We manage and lead by example
- We regularly measure and monitor all that we do to gauge performance and excellence
- We make thoughtful but quick decisions and we take action
- We are flexible, agile and nimble but we exhibit structure and discipline in all that we do
- We are very passionate about student success
- We embrace teamwork and strongly encourage open communication
- We integrate regulatory compliance in all that we do and never settle for less
- We have an appetite for growth with quality and integrity
- We are always hungry for more
- We will never be perfect and know we can always improve
- We learn and grow from our mistakes
- We always embrace greatness
- We make grass-roots investments that lead to student and employee success
- We have a sense of urgency
- We take personal accountability and look within for solutions
- We attract, hire, and develop the best talent
- We seek support and assistance when needed
- We promote from within
- We empower "all" of our people to take ownership and serve
- We praise in public and coach in private
- We are close to our business and we know the numbers
- We have enterprise-wide transparency

- We are professional
- We are respectful
- We are "grown-ups"
- We are 24/7
- We take pride in our work
- We operate under "One Standard of 'Excellence'" in all that we do within all departments
- We always focus on our core competencies with students being at the heart of our enterprise
- We take deliberate steps to celebrate achievements regularly
- We are super competitive
- We have caring, supportive, and nurturing environments
- We have a positive attitude
- We are high energy
- We are deliberate in our actions, always focused on results
- We focus on fundamentals
- We have fun as a team and enjoy what we do
- We focus on all levels of our educational model to provide a top quality student experience
- We demonstrate strong communication and common goals between departments; no silos
- We exhibit determination in all that we do; we never give up
- We are mindful of the big picture, which keeps us focused at all times
- Our team at the corporate office is aligned to serve and support the campuses
- We follow up and follow through on our commitments, priorities and responsibilities
- We face and accept the brutal facts and take action to address them effectively

We are JEC